MULTIMEDIA
MADNESS

SAMS
PUBLISHING

201 West 103rd Street, Indianapolis, IN 46290
A Division of Prentice Hall Computer Publishing

MULTIMEDIA
MADNESS

Ron Wodaski

This book is dedicated to my family. Without their support, this wouldn't be half the book it is.

Publisher
Richard K. Swadley

Associate Publisher
Jordan Gold

Acquisitions Manager
Stacy Hiquet

Acquisitions Editor
Gregory Croy

Development Editor
Dean Miller

Software Develpment Editor
Wayne Blankenbeckler

Production Editor
Fran Hatton

Copy Editor
Kristi Hart

Editorial Coordinator
Bill Whitmer

Editorial Assistants
Sharon Cox
Lynette Quinn

Technical Editor
Michael Jones

Cover Designer
Dan Armstrong

Book Designer
Michele Laseau

**Director of Production
and Manufacturing**
Jeff Valler

Imprint Manager
Kelli Widdifield

Production Analyst
Mary Beth Wakefield

**Proofreading/Indexing
Coordinator**
Joelynn Gifford

Graphics Image Specialists
Dennis Sheehan
Sue VandeWalle

Production
Nick Anderson
Ayrika Bryant
Rich Evers
Mitzi Foster Gianakos
Stephanie McComb
Sean Medlock
Juli Pavey
Angela Pozdol
Ryan Rader
Michelle Self
Dennis Wesner

Indexers
Michael Hughes
Joy Dean Lee
John Sleeva
Craig Small
Suzanne Snyder
Johnna VanHoose

Overview

Contents

Appendixes

About the Author

Ron Wodaski lives on the quiet shores of Puget Sound in the Evergreen state, where he somehow manages to keep up with the latest in things multimedia. He started out as a journalist, but caught the computer bug when he bought one of the original Osborne portables as a word processor.

He has had a variety of roles in the computer industry. He was a consultant for many years, writing programs in a variety of languages starting with dBASE and BASIC. Somewhere along the line, he graduated to C/C++ and then retired to Visual Basic and ToolBook. He has worn many hats in the computer industry—programmer, consultant, testing, project management, and product design—but his favorite is that of gadfly and critic.

He currently writes books on a variety of multimedia topics, creates a monthly multimedia column for NautilusCD, pens the occasional science fiction story, and writes documentation when he feels like it. When all else fails, you'll find him in a kayak somewhere in Puget Sound with the loons, gulls, and harbor seals.

Other books you may find of interest, all from Sams Publishing:

PC Video Madness	A complete guide to working with digital video. Covers all aspects, including using and selecting a camera, capturing and compressing video to your hard disk, and using digital video in a wide range of applications, authoring programs, and programming languages.
Virtual Reality Madness	A madcap look at the world of virtual reality. The focus is on cool virtual things you can do right now, with software you can buy right off the shelf. Includes complete software for creating landscapes and virtual environments on your very own PC.
C Programming Proverbs and Quick Reference	An irreverent examination of the nature of C programming, with an emphasis on seldom-covered topics such as architectures of convenience, testing, and team development.

Acknowledgments

I owe the biggest debt of gratitude to my wife, Donna, whose support was essential to completing both editions of this book. She is an excellent writer in her own right and contributed almost all of the effort that went into the Shopper's Guide.

I would also like to thank Steve Luper of *Nautilus* for his tireless efforts to make the CD-ROM a reality. Steve is hanging out on the bleeding edge of multimedia—if you like multimedia, Nautilus should be on your list of Things to Do. Grateful tips of the hat go also to the folks at Prentice Hall, particularly Dean Miller and Fran Hatton, whose development and editing, respectively, have added so much to this book. A book is really a collaborative effort, and without these two helping out, I wouldn't stand a chance.

A special thank you goes to my editor, Greg Croy, who went to bat in so many different ways to help make Multimedia Madness a reality.

I would also like to thank all of those on CompuServe who, wittingly or otherwise, contributed ideas, thoughts, and digressions that later found their way into this book. If you aren't already a member of CompuServe, you're missing out on one of the world's best idea exchanges. I volunteer as a section leader of section 7, *Hands-on Multimedia,* in the Multimedia forum. I welcome you to join in on our discussions of all things multimedia.

Introduction

Multimedia has changed in some dramatic ways since the first edition of this book was released. The book has had to change along with it. Even though it's only been a year, I have overhauled this book from stem to stern, from animation to video. Every chapter has been rewritten practically from the ground up. Here's the breakdown on what's new:

➤ New sound editors have appeared, and I've got 'em covered for you.

➤ Fractal Design Painter has a new version, and I have included detailed coverage of the new features.

➤ Adobe has finally shipped Photoshop for Windows, and it is now an Author's Choice. It replaces the current title holder, PhotoSyler.

➤ Presentation software has been evolving to include multimedia. Several new products involve a complete rethinking of how to do presentations, and you'll find them covered here. Expanded coverage includes Compel, Presenter, and Charisma.

➤ Sound card technology has advanced; the latest information is here.

➤ Double-spin CD-ROM drives have come way down in price, and I'll tell you where the best deals are.

➤ Graphics cards are also advancing; there are some significant changes you should know about.

➤ Digital video has seen major changes over the last year. I have included a lot of details about video editing software (Premiere and Media Merge), as well as information about new hardware products for video capture. I also have included detailed results of my testing of various capture cards and compression codecs.

➤ Many, many more manufacturers are selling multimedia upgrade kits. I have included information on a number of new choices.

➤ I have updated my "ultimate affordable PC" to take new technology and falling prices into account.

➤ Many new multimedia games are out; you'll find them listed here.

➤ Microsoft has introduced a variety of very solid multimedia products, including Encarta, Dinosaurs, Musical Instruments, and even Multimedia Golf. I provide complete descriptions and reviews.

➤ I have greatly expanded coverage of multimedia programming. I have expanded and updated sections on Visual Basic and ToolBook, and added coverage of Multimedia Viewer 2.0.

➤ 3D Studio is in a new version—Release 3—and I have updated coverage to include new features. The best new feature is the rendering speed and quality, both of which have increased.

➤ MIDI options have evolved, and the best news may well be the Hello Music! system from Yamaha. It offers general MIDI, superb sounds, an attractive price, and it is easy to add if you already have a sound card and just want great MIDI sounds.

➤ The Shopper's Guides, hardware and software, have been updated bigtime. Many additional products are covered, and most products have been updated to reflect new features.

Multimedia Extravaganza

This book isn't designed to be read from one end to the other, although you can do that if you want. You can start on any topic, anywhere you want. This book is intended to excite you about and involve you with multimedia. It includes two CD-ROM discs, and I strongly suggest you look at Chapter One, "This Book Is Multimedia," for information about installing them. If you don't own a CD-ROM drive, find someone who does. There is too much good material on the CD-ROM to ignore. The disk and CD-ROM are as important as the pages you hold in your hand.

Once you see the material on the CD-ROM, you will have a hard time resisting the impulse to get a CD-ROM drive for yourself!

Many aspects of multimedia are new, but many are familiar, too. Although sitting down with a paint program such as Fractal Design Painter is a wonderful experience that requires learning new skills, multimedia also grows out of what you already do with your computer.

For example, consider Word for Windows. Hardly the place for multimedia, you say? What if you could record notes about the document by speaking into a microphone, and listen to your notes by clicking icons in the document? That's multimedia!

The best way to use this book is to start with your own computer system. If you have a sound card, explore the chapter on sounds. If you have an interest in computer art, peruse the chapter on images. If you don't own any multimedia hardware, start anywhere that interests you—each chapter stands on its own. You can find out which apsects of multimedia appeal to you, and move from there.

Dive right in; the computing's fine. I tried to make the book as much like multimedia as I could, bowing only to the limitations of the print medium. I created a multimedia presentation that converts Chapter 2, "Sound Advice," into a multimedia extravaganza. You can find it on the CD.

That's multimedia for you—impossible to put on a floppy disk. If you can read this book without wanting to buy a CD-ROM drive, write and let me know why, OK?

What This Book Is About

This book is about what you can do today with multimedia using your computer at work or at home. It's also about multimedia's possibilities, new products on the cutting edge, and new ways of working with computers. This book covers the hottest hardware available, the software that redefines how you interact with a computer, and the tools that enable programmers and nonprogrammers to write multimedia programs.

A CD-ROM disk can store more than 600 megabytes of information. It takes time to explore everything on the CD-ROM provided with the book. The best part of the CD-ROM disk is that it includes a special edition of the CD magazine *NautilusCD*. You also will find software demos, working versions of programs, clip art, clip sounds, and many other multimedia goodies on the disk. One look at (or listen to) these examples should convince you of the possibilities in multimedia computing.

That's one of the "problems" with multimedia—its value remains unknown until you try it. For a historical parallel, the movie *Avalon* showed what happened when televisions were first sold. People didn't want to buy TVs because no one knew what they could do.

Until you try multimedia for yourself, until you try to solve a problem with it, or until you get down and have some fun with it, you have no idea how powerful multimedia is. The acceptance of multimedia has been slow because people want to see what multimedia can do. But prices are falling, your corner computer store now stocks CD-ROM drives, and CD-ROM software titles are multiplying faster than rabbits.

The real sign that multimedia has arrived is not in the multimedia titles or the sudden popularity of sound cards, but the number of ordinary software products available on CD-ROM.

CorelDRAW! has hundreds of wonderful illustrations and fonts available only on CD-ROM. Microsoft shipped the beta version of Windows NT on CD-ROM (a less-than-subtle hint to buy a CD-ROM drive). Putting CD-ROM drives into the hands of software developers starts them writing software for CD-ROMs.

That's one of the nice things about multimedia—when you strip away the pizazz and concentrate on the things you must do, multimedia enables you to do them much better. At its worst, multimedia is just too much data. At its best, it can be as refreshing to your imagination as a walk in the woods is to your state of mind.

What This Book Is Not About

I am not a salesman trying to sell you multimedia products. I'm more of an evangelist trying to sell you the multimedia concept. I'm excited about some of the products described in this book because they either do new things wonderfully or old things in wonderful new ways.

If a product was hard to install, difficult to use, or poorly designed, you will know about the problem. Sometimes a mediocre product is so affordable, it's still a good value for some users. I've tried to point out such products because they are an inexpensive way to get involved with multimedia. Remember, inevitable tradeoffs come with low prices. These tradeoffs include slower performance, fewer features, and (often) no upgrade path; let the buyer beware.

All hardware tests were conducted on a 486/66 with 12M of memory and a 1 gigabyte Micropolis 2112A IDE hard drive. Lighter software, such as games and "edutainment" products, were tested on a variety of platforms, from a 386/33 to my 486/66.

Choosing Outstanding Products

While writing this book, a new product arrived on my doorstep almost daily. On some days, there was a stack of boxes taller than I! It was difficult to consider every product in detail. Inevitably, some products were too hard to use, some did not install properly, and so on. These products were left by the wayside.

Many workmanlike products mentioned in the book and the Shopper's Guide meet typical needs, are great for specific tasks, or represent great values. However, certain products stood out. These products are powerful, well designed, a good value, and in some cases, easy to use.

Each chapter features one or more Author's Choice products—hardware or software—that I found exceptional in its category. The icon in the margin makes these choices easy to spot. In all cases, these are literal author's choices. They are the products I use, day in and day out, on my own machine.

Evolving Multimedia

Multimedia is growing and changing rapidly. This is as true now as it was for the first edition of this book. Even as I write this, there are serious discussions about standards and formats in the press, at conferences, and at international meetings. Prices continue to drop. More manufacturers and software companies are getting involved. This book is not, and could never be, the last word on multimedia, but I promise you this: there is more than enough information in this book to make the world of multimedia interesting and approachable.

As multimedia evolves, I will continue to issue updated editions of this book. I am interested in hearing from you about your experiences in multimedia. To contact me, you can join me in Section 7 of the Multimedia forum (GO MULTIM), where you can send me electronic mail. My CompuServe user ID is 75530,3711.

I will include in future editions the best stories and multimedia adventures you send to me. If you develop really interesting multimedia applications or presentations, they might make it on the next edition of the CD-ROM—but only if you tell me about them. Some of the material on the CDs that come with this book are, in fact, from folks on CompuServe.

Conventions Used in This Book

One way to make a book easier to follow is to establish a set of typeface conventions throughout the book. For this book, I use the following typeface conventions.

italics	used to introduce a new term.
monospace	used for code listings (both Visual Basic and C).

Visual clues also can be useful. There are several special icons in this book:

 An item of interest

 A special tip

 A common problem to avoid

PART **I**

Getting Started in Multimedia

This Book Is Multimedia[1]

[1] Yes, my habit of adding stuff in footnotes, first "noted" in my book Virtual Reality Madness, continues. You'll find humor, you'll find helpful hints, and you'll find background information down here at the bottom of the page. You have been warned!

T o get the most from this book, you'll need to treat it as multimedia. Neither the text alone, nor the CD-ROMs[2] alone, give you everything you're looking for. The *multi* in multimedia is something you should take seriously.

So let me emphasize something right here: Install the software now! For complete instructions, see the "Installing the CD-ROM" section in this chapter.

There are two CD-ROM discs packaged with this book. That's more than a gigabyte of storage space—1.3 gigs, to be (nearly) exact. Those two CD-ROMs have more than a thousand times the storage space of a 5.25" floppy disk—a floppy disk, by comparison, would be little more than a taste of what's on the CDs. If such enormous quantities of data can't convince you of the need for a CD-ROM drive (particularly in a multimedia computer), the quality and diversity of that data should.[3]

The CD-ROMs serve two different purposes. One was developed in conjunction with *NautilusCD*, a CD-ROM-based magazine. That CD is a special issue of *NautilusCD* produced for this book. Most of these files stay on the CD-ROM; a few must be installed to your hard disk. You'll find its magazine-like interface easy to use, while the multimedia and hotlinks give you access to many, many surprises. You'll find an assortment of *NautilusCD* stuff, as well as a multimedia version of Chatper 2 of this book, stock photos and sounds, shareware, and other goodies.

The *other* CD-ROM contains a wide variety of files, too:

➤ Working models and demos of multimedia programs, including Mutlimedia Toolbook, HSC Interactive, Compel, Curtain Call, Q/Media, Tempra Pro, Distant Suns, and Vista Pro 3.

---

[2]Yes, that's right: there are two CD-ROM discs included with this book. Even with 650 megabytes of storage space, one CD just wasn't enough to hold all the goodies we were able to locate. I found some of them, but my trusty sidekick Wayne Blankenbeckler, who works at Sams, is the real hero in locating much of the cool stuff—especially demo software and shareware—that you'll find on the CDs. If you find any cool shareware or demo software, send him a note on CompuServe at 74660,2216 telling him about it.

[3]Since the first edition of this book, the price of quality CD-ROM drives has continued to plummet. If you do not already own a CD-ROM drive, I've made arrangements with several manufacturers to provide you with some great deals—you'll find them at the back of the book.

I get no cut of the action on these sales; I'm simply trying to make it easy for you to get a CD-ROM drive. Just to make sure that the products being offered are reasonable performers, I have tested them the way they *should* be tested: in the real world. The testing consisted of giving the drive to my brother-in-law, who got his first computer just a few weeks before I started work on the second edition of this book. If he could install it and use it without problems, I allowed the drive to be mentioned here in the book. Simple, but effective.

➤ Working models and demos of graphics programs, including Fractal Design Painter (one of my favorites!), Intellidraw, and Typestry.

➤ Video and animation demo software, including Photomorph and Digital Morph

➤ Music and sound software demos, including Master Tacks Pro 4, Encore, Music Time, Power Chords, and Composer Quest.

➤ Stock photo samples from a variety of sources, including Digital Zone, Photos on Disc, Hot Clips, and MediaRights.

➤ Images and graphic art, including samples from Art Beats, relief maps, textures, and Business Backgrounds for Windows.

➤ More than 100 megabytes of sound samples, including the Hollywood Sound Library (yes, these are the actual sounds used in film production), Wave Library, MIDI Collection, and others.

➤ Font samples from the Font Company, Raynbow Software, Publisher's Paradise, and Safari Fonts.

➤ Shareware programs, including Paintshop Pro 2.0, Whoop It Up!, WaveS Sound Editor, Makin' Waves, WinJammer Pro, WinSong, Font Monster, Printers Apprentice, and others.

➤ I have also included WinCIM, the official Windows CompuServe access program. It includes free CompuServe membership and $15 worth of free connect time for new users.

I have included WinCIM because CompuServe is the best place to keep up to date with what's happening in the fast-changing world of multimedia. You can visit me in section 7 of the Multimedia forum (GO MULTIM).

In addition to everything listed here, we will continue to add goodies to the CD-ROM discs until the last minute. You'll need to pop the discs into your CD-ROM drive to see exactly what's been included.

Installing the Software

If you are going to get the most out of this book, you should install the software that comes with it right now, before you dive into the book—especially the software for the special edition of *NautilusCD*. It will show you what can be done with multimedia technology right now, today, on a regular basis. To save yourself time later on, go ahead and install the software now, using the directions in Appendix A, "A Guide to NautilusCD," and Appendix B, "The Demo Treasure Chest CD-ROM."

If you just don't have the room to install the CD-ROM access software, you can run some of the CD-ROM software directly. Use File Manager (or the equivalent) to view the directories on the CD-ROM discs. Double-click on EXE files to run various programs on the CD-ROM. I don't recommend this, however; a number of features on the CD-ROM require that you install the drivers for Video for Windows or other files in order to work at all.[4]

What Is Multimedia?

There are two schools of thought about multimedia. Some people say multimedia is nothing but hot air. ("Why would anyone want to invest in multimedia?" they say. "There's nothing to it!") Others say no one should be without multimedia. ("Multimedia is the greatest thing to happen to computers since color monitors!") When I started to experiment with multimedia, I was a skeptic. I thought I would wind up spending a ton of money on multimedia hardware, and all for just a few pretty pictures and some fancier beeps and clicks. That's not what happened at all! What I found was *amazing*.[5] The pictures, the sounds, the fun, and the powerful business presentations you can create with multimedia are wonderful. However, the most important thing about multimedia has to do with what a computer isn't, but could be. Let's look at some history to see what I mean.

Multimedia Is the Next Logical Step

The first personal computers didn't have graphics. Remember the MDA[6]—80 columns and 25 rows of text? If you compare the development of computers to

---

[4]That's Windows for you—and it's both an advantage and a disadvantage. As described in greater detail in the chapter about Windows multimedia, Windows offers a programmer independence from the low-life details of hardware. The price you pay for this privilege is that you can no longer put everything a program needs in one tidy little file. That's the price of progress.

[5]I wanted to use an adjective that doesn't sound like it was borrowed from a commercial for a laundry detergent, but I couldn't find one that conveyed the proper sense of wonder I felt about multimedia.

[6]That's the Monochrome Display Adapter, for those of you who were not using computers back in the early '80s.

changes in the broadcasting industry, the MDA was the computer equivalent of a crystal radio set. It wasn't fancy, but it worked. Then along came color and higher resolutions: CGA, EGA, and VGA. These were the equivalent of hi-fi sound—good clarity and crisp definition.

The emergence of multimedia is similar to what happened when stereo replaced mono. To some people, the difference between mono and stereo wasn't worth it—the equipment cost too much, the sounds weren't distinguishable, and the technology was too fragile. However, I challenge you to find a recent musical recording that isn't in stereo. If they are out there, they're buried under a ton of stereo recordings.

Stereo replaced mono because stereo was distinctly more lifelike and natural. Mono was nice while it lasted, but once stereo came along, everyone realized how unnatural mono really was. Multimedia does the same for computing: it makes you realize how unnatural it is to spend the whole day computing without sounds, without animations, without music and video and fireworks and e-mail[7] that talks.

That's the thing about multimedia: once you try it and become accustomed to it, you won't want to go back.

In the first edition of this book, a 5 1/4" disk accompanied the CD-ROM. It provided little more than a light snack; the CD-ROMs in this edition are the full-course meal. The number of installed CD-ROM drives has soared over the last year, and the lack of a floppy disk is a direct result. Look closely at these discs—you'll get hooked on multimedia. Computers are not only productivity tools, they're also communication tools. And just as we use body language, speech, and other signals to communicate, a multimedia computer does a better job of communicating than a "standard" computer.

For example, how would you go about proofreading a spreadsheet if you could do it any way you wanted? You probably would have someone read back the numbers to you, so you could verify them. That way, you don't have to concentrate on two things at once. Why not have the computer read back the numbers for you? That's multimedia at work.

---

[7]Short for electronic mail—yes, you can even send multimedia stuff over a network, or over phone lines these days.

Sensuous Computing

Multimedia is not a fun word, but multimedia on a computer is fun. We need a fun way to refer to multimedia. How about sensuous computing? That term should cause enough controversy to get multimedia off the ground![8]

Look around you. Everything in the world is a multisensory marvel of sights, sounds, and smells. People are designed to work in that kind of environment. People need many different sensations to comprehend and feel good about the world. As users become more involved with computers, the multimedia experience is the only sensible way to work with a computer.

Is the academic term "multimedia" any way to describe something this powerful, this significant, this much fun? Of course not. What should it be called? The term multimedia assumes that computers as we know them now are "normal," and that a multimedia computer is something special and out of the ordinary. The first thing we have to do is reverse that assumption. The way computers exist now is half-baked and preliminary, a mere shadow of the future. A computer is another way to represent the imagination. What we have now is *monomedia*.

In the future real computers will talk and listen, entertain and communicate. Multimedia is a logical step in that direction. It puts marvelous sights, incredible sounds, and clever programs in your hands. The best part is that multimedia is available today, and prices have fallen to the point where it doesn't take a lot of money to set up multimedia.[9] You can find advertisements for sound cards and CD-ROM drives for less than $300 for both—that's less than it once took to buy a small hard drive for your computer.

What Can I Do with Multimedia?

One important thing you can do with multimedia is relax. When I put multimedia on my computer, my stress level decreased quickly and significantly. Even little things, such as trying to move outside the margins of a document, became

---

[8]Sadly, no one has taken up my call to change the name Multimedia to Sensuous Computing. Sigh—it's really tough to start a trend.

[9]Since the first edition of this book, prices have continued to fall. There is no reason to expect that process to stop.

easier to live with—instead of that stupid, annoying beep, I could choose what sound I would hear.[10] I can make it as outrageous, or as sympathetic, as I want.

Multimedia has more sophisticated purposes also; I've put together a list that touches the high points.

With multimedia, you can:

➤ Browse through an encyclopedia and check out animations on everything from the circulatory system to an atomic nucleus during fission.

➤ Explore the intimate details of a musical selection, moving from discussions of the historical period, to explanations of the themes, to pictures of the composer, to a game that tests your knowledge of the music—well, you get the idea.

➤ Build a business presentation that includes sound effects, music, still pictures, animation, video, and text.

➤ Install software from CD-ROMs.[11]

➤ Explore your creative musical interests, even recording and editing music on your PC.

➤ Add sounds to files or tasks.

➤ Hold up a part for a complex machine in front of a video camera, and have the video appear on someone else's computer far, far away while you explain how to install the part.

➤ Look up a familiar quotation in seconds and listen to it spoken by the original speaker (stored for you on CD-ROM).

➤ Create interactive computer presentations at a low cost.

➤ Explore the topography of the Atlantic Ocean for a geology paper due tomorrow at 9:00 a.m.

➤ Create 3-D effects in a dozen different ways.

➤ Create animated birthday cards for your friends who have computers.

---

[10]For example, on my wife's computer, Windows starts with the sound of a large, sweet-sounding bell tolling in the distance. It ends with the sound of our dog, Sparky, barking. You'll learn a lot about Sparky, and his adventures, later in the book.

[11]No more having to stuff 10 or 12 floppy disks into your machine—just one CD-ROM is all it takes. And think of how much space is saved on your hard disk, and how many cool extras come on the typical CD!

➤ Call up a map of the country you're visiting next week, and with the click of the mouse, look up sights to see.

➤ Capture a video image from your wedding videotape to use as a bitmap on your Windows desktop.

➤ Watch Neil walk on the moon as he speaks those famous words.

➤ Play a game that uses interactive video.

➤ Give your child a multisensory gift: a children's dictionary with sounds, images, and animation.

➤ Record your thoughts about a letter and insert the recording right into the document for later review.

➤ Watch old Betty Boop cartoons.

➤ Send a video to your best friend of your dog doing tricks.

➤ Create illustrated top ten lists that would make David Letterman blush.

➤ Explore medical terminology, using pictures and animations to help out with the hard parts.

➤ Look up the history of the word "set" (all 150 or so pages) in the Oxford English Dictionary on CD-ROM.

➤ Make a sale using a lifelike animation on your color portable.

➤ Learn a new language by interacting with the written and spoken words.

There's no end to what you can do with multimedia.

Categories of Multimedia

Multimedia can be divided into three categories: fun material, powerful material, and creative material. The fun material is obvious—games, incredible animation sequences, and realistic sounds, just to name a few. The powerful material is well-designed software that enables computers to do things they've never done before. It ranges from clever software like Multimedia Beethoven, en-cyclopedias on CD-ROM, reference works, literature, and even magazines with sounds and sights (like *Nautilus).* The creative material is software that enables you to create your own multimedia programs, presentations, and tools. Of course, lots of software is fun *and* powerful *and* creative, like Multimedia Beethoven or Battle Chess (well, two out of three—fun and creative—ain't bad).

While writing this book, I received dozens and dozens of different multimedia products for evaluation. Even the worst products—hard to install, slow, or poorly designed—were much better than not having any multimedia. Check out the Shopper's Guide in this book. There is something for every budget.

If you don't have any multimedia equipment yet, the first addition you should make is a sound card. If you don't have Windows 3.1 or a 386 computer,[12] you have no reason to put off the upgrade any longer—prices are lower than they've ever been. You can put together a complete multimedia PC for less than $1,800.[13] If you already own any part of it—a 386 or better, Windows 3.1, or any multimedia hardware—the cost of full multimedia is less.

What is full multimedia?

a 386 computer (DX, 33 MHz or better)
at least an 80M hard drive (120M is better)
at least 4M of memory (8M is better)
a sound card (8 bits is acceptable, but 16 is much better)
a CD-ROM drive (at least 150K per second transfer rate, but 300K per second is better)

Low-Budget Multimedia Sound

Even if you don't own any multimedia hardware, you can use some of the multimedia capabilities built into Windows 3.1. A short program included on the floppy disk turns your PC speaker into a multimedia device.[14]

> If you have already installed a sound card, don't install the speaker driver. The sound card provides better sound than the PC speaker.

---

[12]However, I strongly recommend that you consider getting a 486 for multimedia—it won't cost much more.

[13]This is down from $2,000 in the last edition of the book—and the equipment you can get for that $1,800 is better stuff than $2,000 used to buy.

[14]Sort of multimedia, that is. That PC speaker is tiny, and may sound pretty thin.

If you've already installed the files from the floppy disk, use the following instructions to turn your speaker into a multimedia device:

1. Locate the icon for the Main program group and double-click to open it. Double-click the Control Panel icon.

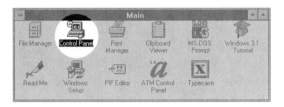

Figure 1.1. *The Control Panel icon.*

2. This opens up the Control Panel for Windows. Double-click the Drivers icon.

Figure 1.2. *The Drivers icon.*

3. The dialog box displays all the drivers installed on your system. A sample list of drivers is shown; your actual drivers listed might differ from what is listed in the figure. To use the speaker driver, be sure the MCI driver for Sound appears. It is normally installed when you install Windows 3.1. Click the add button.

4. Another dialog box opens. Notice that "Unlisted or Updated Driver" is highlighted. Click OK.

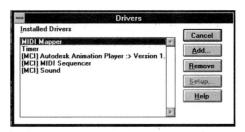

Figure 1.3. *The Drivers dialog box.*

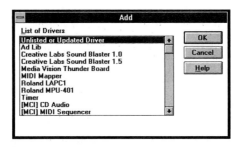

Figure 1.4. *Adding a driver.*

5. A dialog box appears and asks you where the driver is that you want to install. Because you've already installed the driver from the floppy disk,[15] the driver is located in the \MMM!\SPEAKER directory. If you installed to drive C:, type in the following:

Figure 1.5. *Installing a new driver.*

---

[15]You did install it, right? If not, go back to the section "Installing the Floppy Disk," and do it now!

13

6. Because only one driver was installed to that directory, only one driver is listed. Click the OK button to accept the choice.

Figure 1.6. *With only one driver in the directory, your choices are limited!*

7. If you already installed the speaker driver on your system, a dialog box asks whether you want to use the currently installed driver or the new driver. Unless you know the current driver is more recent than the replacement driver, click the New button.

Figure 1.7. *Overriding your old speaker driver.*

8. Now you are asked to perform a setup for the speaker driver. The following dialog box appears:

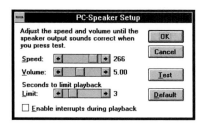

Figure 1.8. *The setup dialog box.*

You can adjust the sliders for Speed, Volume, and Limit, or you can click the Default button. If you click Default, the driver determines the optimum settings for your PC. (The Speed parameter must be changed for various CPU speeds so the sounds play correctly. Only change the default if you have a problem.) Press the Test button to determine if the settings are correct, then click OK.

9. With the sound driver installed, Windows asks whether you want to restart because drivers are loaded when Windows loads, and they cannot be changed while Windows is running. Click the Restart Now button.

Figure 1.9. *Restart Windows to load your new driver.*

To verify your computer is now officially semi-multimedia-ready, when Windows restarts, run the Windows File Manager. The File Manager icon (see Figure 1.10) is located in the Main Windows program group. Make the \MMM!\SPEAKER directory the current directory (see Figure 1.11).

Figure 1.10. *The File Manager icon.*

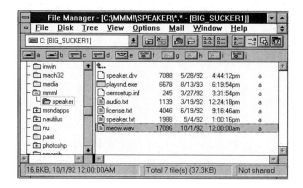

Figure 1.11. *The File Manager in use, with \MMM!\SPEAKER as the current directory.*

The only kind of sound file you can play using the speaker driver is a wave file. These files have the extension ".wav". Other sound files are incompatible with Windows or require special hardware beyond a simple speaker. In addition, you will not be able to play sounds through the speaker with any device that uses MCI (Media Control Interface) capabilities. Sadly, this includes the Media Player, an application that otherwise is extremely useful for playing multimedia files.

Why is the speaker driver limited like this? It's a matter of hardware—the speaker doesn't have any, other than a speaker cone. That means the CPU has to do all the work. The contortions required to make a speaker play wave sounds are CPU intensive—very un-Windows-like behavior. Windows (and MCI) normally chop up processing time into little pieces. The speaker driver needs the CPU all to itself, and therefore Windows can't work effectively with it. Fortunately, there are some Windows functions that will interact relatively happily with the speaker driver.

I have included a little Visual Basic program that will play wave files for you if you are using the speaker driver. You can make this little program your default program for .wav files. It will work with any sound driver you have installed, but it has some special features to make it work well with the speaker driver. Follow these steps to associate .wav files with this program:

1. In the program manager, click once on a file with the .wav extension to highlight it. Conveniently, there's a little wave file in the \MMM!\SPEAKER directory, meow.wav.

2. Click on the File menu, then on the Associate selection (see Figure 1.12). This opens the dialog box shown in Figure 1.13. Click on the Browse button to open the dialog box shown in Figure 1.14, and highlight the file \MMM!\SPEAKER\PLAYSND.EXE. Click the OK button.

If you are not using the speaker driver, you can use a different .wav player, SOUNDPLY.EXE. PLAYSND.EXE plays sounds that are not interruptible, to make sure that the speaker driver can play them acceptably. SOUNDPLY.EXE can be interrupted by pressing the Escape key, but will not work if you are using the speaker driver.

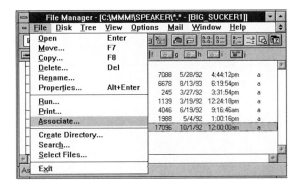

Figure 1.12. The File menu in the File Manager, showing the Associate selection.

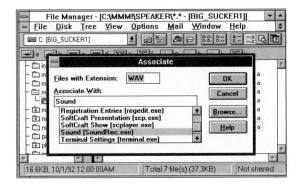

Figure 1.13. Associating wave files with the playsnd.exe program.

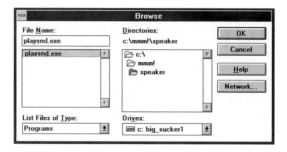

Figure 1.14. *Locating the file playsnd.exe.*

3. This returns you to the Associate dialog box, but the "Associate with"
text box now contains the full path to the playsnd.exe file, as shown in
Figure 1.15. Click the OK button to complete the association.

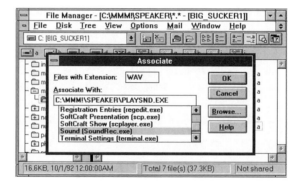

Figure 1.15. *The playsnd application will now be the default program for .wav files.*

Now, anytime you double-click on a file with the .wav extension, the sound
will play through your speaker. Try it now with the file meow.wav.[16] You should
hear a cat meowing.

---

[16]If you do not want to make playsnd.exe the default program for .wav files, you can simply use
drag and drop in File Manager to test your speaker driver. Click and hold on the filename
meow.wav, and then drag it to the filename playsnd.exe, and release the mouse button. If
everything is fine, you will hear the sound of a cat meowing through your speaker.

Sound Advice

T his chapter is about using sound in multimedia. It covers many of the kinds of sounds that Windows can use, as well as some interesting ways of using sound on your computer. I have also included some background on digital sound that will help you make sense of the software that's available.

In Chapter 1, you had the opportunity to install a sound driver for your PC speaker. This enables you to play sounds, but you may have noticed that the sound quality isn't very good. The PC speaker is simple and small. Depending on the type of speaker installed in your PC, the sound ranges from miserable to tolerable. Don't be discouraged if your computer's speaker sounds scratchy, thin, or both. The difference between your PC speaker and a sound card is similar to the difference between two coffee cans connected by a string and a telephone. Although playing with the PC speaker is fun, the speaker provides only a taste of what's possible.

Most of the material in this chapter requires a sound card rather than just a PC speaker driver.[1]

Types of Sound Files

There are two different kinds of sound files: those that store waveform information, and those that don't. Windows 3.1 supports one of each type. The Windows waveform format is called WAV (pronounced "wave"), and the nonwaveform format is called MIDI (pronounced "mid-ee"). MIDI stands for *Musical Instrument Digital Interface*.

Waveform Sound Files

A waveform file stores the data needed to reconstruct the waveform that produces a given sound.[2] When sounds are recorded digitally, the process is referred to as *sampling*. You can think of it as breaking the sound into tiny pieces and storing each piece as a small, digital sample of the sound. Waveform files have the extension .WAV.

---

[1]In other words, if you don't have a sound card yet, you're missing some cool stuff. A sound card opens the door to multimedia.

[2]Sound is made up of waves in the air. There are big waves and little waves, long waves and short waves. Each different kind of wave causes a different kind of sound. A .WAV file simply stores a digital representation of those waves.

Because of the volume of information stored, waveform files are often large.[3] When you play back a waveform file, however, you hear similar sounds no matter which equipment you use. The only difference is the quality of the sound. A computer with better speakers or a better sound card (or both) will do a better job at playing the sound, but that's the only difference from one computer to the next.

The PC speaker driver can deal only with waveform files with the extension .WAV. There are other formats of waveform files, but you can't play them in Windows unless you convert them to .WAV files. For example, Creative Labs Sound Blaster comes with software that plays .VOC files. Other formats include .SND and .MOD.

The Makin' Waves program on the floppy disk converts a variety of sound files to wave (.WAV) format. It's a simple program that does the job well. See Appendix A, "A Guide to NautilusCD," for more information.

Non-Waveform Sound Files

Non-waveform files (that is, MIDI files) store instructions instead of waveform data. For example, such a file might store things like notes and their durations. If you have a sound card that can play MIDI files, that sound card has many, many synthesized instruments on it, and the notes are played using one or more of those instruments. In other words, your sound card re-creates the music as if it were reading sheet music. MIDI files are normally used to store musical information only.[4] MIDI files have the extension .MID.

NOTE | Because MIDI (non-waveform) files contain instructions rather than actual sound data, the PC speaker is helpless when it comes to playing them.

There is an important implication that follows from the nature of MIDI files. Suppose you have a MIDI file that contains instructions for playing the song "Row, Row, Row Your Boat." These instructions are a lot like sheet music. They only tell

---

[3]Of course, large is a relative term—video files can be 100 or more times larger than audio files of the same duration.

[4]You also can store sound effects—sort of—but ignore that fact for now. I'll cover it later. I promise.

what notes to play, how long to play each note, and maybe how loud each note should be. That means that even if the MIDI file was created to be played as piano music, it would be easy to play the file as guitar music. This is true because the MIDI file doesn't store actual sounds, just the musical data. When you play back the file, you can choose which instrument is used.[5]

The actual format of a MIDI file is discussed later in this chapter. For now, it is enough to know you can't play MIDI files through your PC speaker; to generate the sounds, you need a *synthesizer*[6]—either a sound card that supports MIDI or a card that communicates with an external synthesizer. If you are musically inclined, MIDI offers many powerful and interesting possibilities that are discussed in Chapter 10, "Eenie-Meenie-MIDI: Keyboards." In particular, the MIDI format can be used to create original music for multimedia presentations. The results can be stunning with a high-quality synthesizer.

The Windows Sound Applications

Windows comes with two applications that play sounds: Sound Recorder and Media Player. The Control Panel also opens some doors to playing with sounds, and I have also supplied some additional applications (shareware and some of my own) that play sounds. In this section, you learn how to use various applications to have fun with sound.

Sound Recorder

With Sound Recorder, you can both play and record sounds. To do any recording you need a sound card with microphone or line-level inputs.[7] Most sound

---

[5]You will probably have to use some software to do this, of course—most MIDI files actually contain some indication of a default instrument or instruments to be used for playback. There are several different ways to choose different instruments at playback time—see Chapter 10 for the details.

[6]A synthesizer is anything that can respond to MIDI data and create sounds. Some synthesizers are extremely artificial sounding, whereas others can mimic natural instruments very effectively.

[7]"Line level" simply refers to the kind of signals you get from such things as tape recorders and CD players.

cards have one or both of these. If you don't own a sound card, check out Chapter 6, "Pumping Iron: Hardware," and the Shopper's Guide for more information. I strongly recommend some kind of sound card if you intend to work or play with multimedia.

> A microphone input should be used only for microphones! Think of a microphone as having a very tiny output level—it has to be boosted quite a bit to sound right. Line inputs, on the other hand— such as from a tape deck or FM receiver—have a comparatively high input level. Trying to input one of these through a microphone input could damage your sound card. In the language of sound professionals, line level is much "hotter" than a microphone input.

Sound Recorder is automatically installed in your Accessories group when you load Windows 3.1. You start the program by clicking its icon (Figure 2.1) in the Accessories group.

Figure 2.1. *The Sound Recorder icon.*

At this point, the only active button is record—it has a picture of a little microphone (Figure 2.2).

Figure 2.2. *Sound Recorder's record button.*

When you load a file into the Sound Recorder,[8] the play button also becomes active. The sound waveform is displayed in the waveform window (Figure 2.3). To play the sound, click the play button. If you have speakers or headphones connected to your sound card, you will hear the sound.

---

[8]To load a file, use the File|Open menu selection.

Waveform

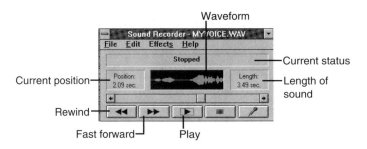

Current position

Current status

Length of sound

Rewind

Fast forward

Play

Figure 2.3. *Loading a waveform into the Sound Recorder.*

Recording Your Own Sounds

Recording with the Sound Recorder is easy. First, make sure you have some kind of sound source connected to your sound card, such as a microphone. Click the microphone icon in the lower-right corner of the dialog box.[9] After a brief pause, the Sound Recorder activates, and you can start recording. Try it! When you want to stop recording, click the button with the little square on it (second from the right, next to the microphone button, in Figure 2.3).

That "brief pause" varies in length, and you have to guess when Sound Recorder starts taping. Watch for the time numbers to start changing—that's your best clue that recording has started. If you aren't careful, you might lose the beginning of your recording.

You usually can record for about 60 seconds with the Sound Recorder. Depending on the amount of available memory, you might not be able to record for a full 60 seconds. Keep in mind that .WAV files quickly eat up disk space. I used a MultiSound card from Turtle Beach to record some mono sound at 22.5 KHz (16-bit resolution). A 10.4-second recording created a 459,054-byte sound file.

---

[9]That microphone icon might make you think that you can only record from a microphone. Wrong! You can record any sound that comes into your sound card, whether it be a voice talking into a microphone, your cassette deck connected to the sound card at the back of your computer, or even the TV audio connected to your sound card. Any sound source you can connect to your sound card can be recorded.

The Sound Recorder samples your voice at the rate of 11 KHz—most cards support that rate.[10] It's not exactly high fidelity (remember that CDs record at 44.1 KHz), but it's more than adequate for the range of frequencies found in the human voice. It may sometimes be an acceptable data rate for some simple music and sound effects.

If you have recorded a sound, be sure to save it as a file using the **F**ile|**S**ave As menu selection. Later in this chapter, you learn to embed that sound in an application. If you don't have a microphone, don't worry—you can embed any sound file you happen to have laying around.

Buying a Microphone

To get good recording results, you don't *necessarily* have to spend a lot of money on a microphone. If you're recording voices, you can sometimes get better results using an inexpensive mike. There are several reasons for this:

➤ If you have an inexpensive sound card, you don't need to spend a lot for a microphone. You can usually get good results by spending about 20–30 percent of the amount you spent on your sound card for a microphone. For inexpensive microphones, visit your local Radio Shack. For higher quality microphones, such as the kind used by radio and television professionals, you'll need to locate a local distributor who sells to the broadcast industry. Try looking under "sound systems" in the yellow pages.

➤ The human voice has a limited range of frequencies. An expensive microphone can record a wide range of frequencies that extends above and below those of the human voice. An inexpensive microphone can record only a limited range of frequencies, but those frequencies usually include the frequencies most common in the human voice. In addition, many inexpensive microphones in effect boost the frequencies common in voice recordings, which helps mask background noise.

➤ The performance of a microphone doesn't change as drastically with price as you might expect. You can get decent quality for $50–$100 and very good quality for $300, but you may have to spend more than $1000 to get really great quality. Unless you have special requirements, you can usually find a good general-purpose (voice and music) microphone for about $150–200.

---

[10]To change the recording parameters, choose File|New and select a rate that your sound card supports.

Even if you plan to record music, an inexpensive microphone might still be your best choice. However, this depends on many factors—the quality of your speakers, the type of sound card you're using, and how well the card reproduces sounds. Check the specifications for your sound card, and if possible, conduct some listening tests. If you are working with an 8-bit sound card, a microphone for $30 or less will give you the best results (in most cases, of course—there are some pretty lousy microphones available in that price range, too). If you have a mid-range 16-bit sound card such as the Pro Audio Spectrum or Sound Blaster 16, you can probably find the right microphone for about $50–$75. If you have a high-end 16-bit sound card such as the MultiSound from Turtle Beach, buy the best microphone you can afford. Such cards, which record at CD quality (low noise floor, 16 bits, and 44.1 KHz sampling), really benefit from the latest technology.

The same advice works for any other recording equipment you buy, such as mixers and tape machines. For any equipment that finds its way into a position between the sound source and your hard disk, don't spend any more—or less— than you need to match your current level of quality.

If you are recording by yourself, you might find it easier to record to tape before recording digitally—even though the quality of a record- ing from a tape isn't the same as recording directly. The keystrokes for recording in various software programs are sometimes not as easy as operating a tape recorder.

Media Player

Media Player is another Windows sound-capable application. Although Media Player has more options if you have both a sound card and a CD-ROM drive in- stalled, you can run the program with or without a sound card. The application can play .WAV and .MID files as well as music on a CD-ROM. It also can play other kinds of files, such as animation and video files. To run Media Player, you must have at least one multimedia device driver installed. Examples of device drivers include .WAV file support (other than the PC speaker), MIDI support, animations, digital video, and so on.

The Media Player is a simple, intuitive application. It looks a lot like a CD or cassette player as shown in Figure 2.4.

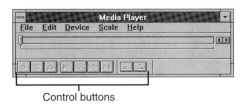

Control buttons

Figure 2.4. *The Media Player dialog box.*

This simple interface is used to control all multimedia devices. When you first start Media Player, the controls are dimmed. Your first step is to select the kind of multimedia device you want to use from the **D**evice menu (Figure 2.5).

Figure 2.5. *The Device menu.*

The devices you see depend on what drivers you have installed on your system. Because my machine is in a constant state of flux, with drivers being added and removed almost daily, I sometimes wind up with duplicates (as you can see in Figure 2.5).

There are two different types of devices—those that use files, and those that do not. CD Audio, for example, doesn't use files. If you select it as a device, the Media Player checks the device to see if there is a music CD in it and tells you how many tracks the CD has. If you select Sound as a device, you need to select a file to open before you can do anything with the device.

Suppose you do select Sound as the active device. After opening a file, Media Player automatically activates the buttons that are appropriate for a sound file, as shown in the top example of Figure 2.6.

As you can see, all the buttons are active except for Stop and Pause. Because nothing is playing, that makes sense. If you were to start playback by clicking the Play button, the Play button would become inactive, and the Stop button would become active.

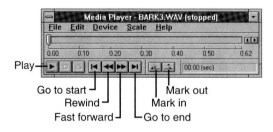

Figure 2.6. *Loading a waveform into Media Player.*

The lower half of Figure 2.6 illustrates an important new addition to the latest version of Media Player—the capability of using marks to select a portion of a file. If you use the Mark In and Mark Out buttons to mark the beginning and ending parts of a selection, you can then paste that portion of a file into another document with OLE (Object Linking and Embedding). OLE is explained in detail at the end of this chapter.

Control Panel Sound Controls

The Windows Control Panel offers some unique possibilities for working and playing with sounds. There are three features in the Control Panel worth mentioning:

➤ drivers

➤ sounds

➤ MIDI Mapper

> You will not see MIDI Mapper unless you have installed a driver that supports and plays .MID files.

When you add multimedia hardware to your computer, the manufacturer of the hardware provides device drivers that you have to install with the Drivers applet. The Sounds applet enables you to associate .WAV files with Windows system events (see the next section, "Playing with WAV Files"). These two tools are pretty easy to use. The MIDI Mapper, however, is a complex, sophisticated tool. Unless you are already knowledgeable about MIDI, stay clear of it for now.

Not to fear, however, because you get a tour of the MIDI Mapper in the section, "Playing with MIDI Files," later in this chapter.

Playing with .WAV Files

It's easy to play with .WAV files in Windows. Once you have a sound driver installed, any application that supports .WAV files can play them automatically! For example, as you learned earlier in this chapter, you can use Sound Recorder to play .WAV files. But it's not very exciting if you have to play the sounds this way. You can easily set up Windows so it plays sounds when certain *system events* occur.[11] These events are common events that occur whenever you run a Windows program, and they are listed in the next section, "System Sounds."

System Sounds

Windows has default system sounds that play every time certain system events occur. For example, the most common system event is the Exclamation; it sounds every time you try to move past the margins in a word processor. The default Windows sound for this event is CHORD.WAV, but you can use any .WAV file for this event. To see your current sound settings, open the Windows Control Panel and double-click the icon labeled Sound. You see a window that looks like Figure 2.7.

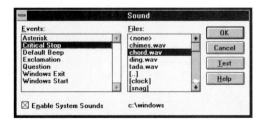

Figure 2.7. The Sound selection dialog box.

---

[11]There are all kinds of system events. The basic events are pretty obvious: starting Windows, exiting Windows, the default beep that occurs when you make a mistake. You can also get software that enables you to associate sounds with many additional system events, such as maximizing and minimizing windows.

On the left is a list of system events. On the right is a list of .WAV files. You can associate any wave file with any system event; it is then called a *system sound*. You are not limited to the wave files in the Windows directory; you can use files from anywhere on your hard disk(s).

Each system sound is generated under certain conditions. Application programmers decide when and under which conditions to generate the various system events. There are no hard-and-fast rules that would enable you to know exactly when to expect an event—you have to learn through trial and error with your favorite programs.

The best I can do is to provide a description of each of the system events; there is no way to predict when a given piece of software will generate each kind of event. Once you associate a sound with the event, however, you'll be able to listen and find out—kind of the back way around to the answer, if you ask me.

Asterisk—This usually occurs when a program alerts the user to something; it doesn't have to be an error. It can be anything the programmer who wrote the software thought it should be.

Critical Stop—Programmers generally save this event for serious problem situations, such as a program that cannot continue because of a serious error.

Default Beep—You hear this sound when the program generates a generic warning or when a desired sound could not be found. For example, you hear the default beep when you click outside a dialog box that must be closed manually before you can continue.

Exclamation—When the program needs to present information that requires no choices, you often see an Exclamation, such as an OK button.

Question—This event is usually generated in conjunction with a dialog box; the box has a large question mark in it.

Windows Start—The sound is played when you start up Windows.

Windows Exit—The sound is played when you exit from Windows.

Visual Basic Programmer Alert

If you're programming in Visual Basic for Windows, you can generate these types of message boxes with the `MsgBox` command:

➤ Asterisk

➤ Critical Stop

➤ Question

➤ Exclamation

Each of these generates the appropriate sound when displayed.

I have included lots of interesting wave files on the CD-ROMs; you can substitute these files for the default sounds included with Windows 3.1. Be sure to copy the sounds to your hard disk *first* so Windows can find them!

If you do not have a sound card, but are using the PC Speaker driver, you will be able to play and hear system sounds.

Playing with System Sounds

If you have a sound card, use the shareware program called *Whoop It Up!* (included on the floppy disk) and play around with the included MIDI and .WAV files. *Whoop It Up!* enables you to add sounds to dozens of additional Windows events as well as add sounds to events in Windows applications. You also can use MIDI files if you have a sound board with a built-in synthesizer installed.

You won't need to disable your system sounds if you just play with *Whoop It Up!* If you plan to use it as your main program for associating sounds with events, you should set your system sounds to <none> in the Control Panel. When you start *Whoop It Up!,* you see an information screen.[12] Click the I Agree button and you see the main *Whoop It Up!* screen, shown in Figure 2.8.

---

[12]*Whoop It Up!,* like many of the programs on the disks that come with this book, is shareware. The version on the disks is not as complete as the version you will get if you register the program. To register, look in the same directory where you find the program—there will be information there, usually in a read file, that explains how to register the software. In most cases, you will be asked to pay a small fee to register. This fee will get you the latest, full-featured version of the software and usually additional documentation (either printed or on disk) as well.

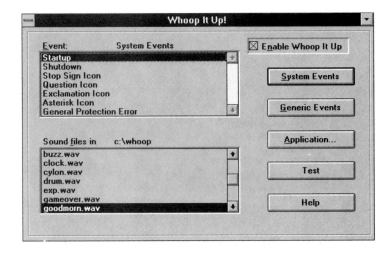

Figure 2.8. *The main screen of Whoop It Up!*

The list box at top left lists Windows events described in the previous section, "System Sounds." The list box at bottom left lists directories and any sound files (.WAV and .MID) in the current directory. On the right are five buttons that enable you to listen to sounds, attach sounds to events, and more. For example, to test play a file, select one of the .WAV or .MID files from the sound files list box. Then press the Test button at the right of the *Whoop It Up!* window. If you select a .MID file and your sound card supports MIDI, you hear music. Depending on your sound card, the quality of the music varies.

 Remember, .MID files won't play if you don't have a sound card with a built-in synthesizer. The speaker driver can play only .WAV sound files.

If you didn't hear music when you tried to play a .MID file, two things might have happened:

➤ You heard no sounds at all.

➤ You heard odd sounds.

If you heard no sounds, you might have to use the MIDI Mapper to ensure sounds are being routed properly. Most likely, the sounds are going to MIDI channels that are not supported by your sound card. See the Section, "Troubleshooting MIDI File Playing," later in this chapter.

If you heard odd sounds, it's likely that your sound card uses different instruments from the one that was used to record the MIDI file. You can use the MIDI Mapper to fix this problem in most cases.

Playing with MIDI Files

MIDI enables electronic musical instruments and computers to communicate with each other. The most common MIDI instruments are various kinds of keyboards, but there are many other kinds, such as MIDI guitars and breath controllers (a device you blow into that sends MIDI signals).

Many MIDI instruments don't look like instruments. Several companies (such as Roland, Korg, Kawai, Ensoniq, E-mu, and Yamaha) that sell keyboards also sell the synthesizer portion of the keyboard separately. These are called rack-mount synthesizers because they include a face plate you can use to mount the synthesizer on racks. These synthesizers are black boxes with LCD screens, and buttons and sliders that you use to program them. They have all the musical capabilities of their keyboard siblings, but they don't have keys; they are "played" by sending MIDI data to them.

To play a MIDI file (with the extension .MID), you need a card in your machine that supports MIDI. MIDI files do not contain information about sounds; they contain information about notes. You need something to generate sounds from the note information. Most sound cards support MIDI. For example, the two most popular sound cards (Pro Audio Spectrum and Sound Blaster) have built-in synthesizers. These synthesizers receive MIDI information and play the appropriate sounds. You also can buy a card that has a more sophisticated synthesizer, such as the Roland SCC-1 or Turtle Beach's MultiSound. For more information about synthesizing music, see the sidebar, *What Is a Synthesizer?*

What Is a Synthesizer?

A synthesizer creates sounds. However, synthesizers vary quite a bit in the way they produce sounds.

In the beginning, synthesizers made simple, uncomplicated sounds. They could make just one sound at a time—if you wanted a layered or more complex sound, you had to play two synthesizers at the same time. Then someone somewhere got the brilliant idea: Hey, these are electronic devices. Why not have one synthesizer tell another synthesizer what to do? All that was needed was some sort of electrical connection between them, and some method of communicating over that connection.

MIDI was the method that evolved to handle that communication. However, it left open how a given synthesizer created its sounds, or even what sounds it created.

Unlike a traditional musical instrument, a MIDI instrument has no strings to pluck or strum. There is no reed to vibrate, no resonant chamber to blow across. When you press a key on a MIDI keyboard, you are actually generating a voltage. The voltage indicates what note you want to play.

To generate the selected sound, the synthesizer uses one or more techniques. I can't really get into the details of sound generation (there are whole books written on the subject), but I'll give you an overview of what happens.

Today's synthesizers create sounds in two main ways:

➤ by creating sounds from scratch

➤ by playing sounds that are stored internally (either samples of actual instruments or made-up sounds)

In addition, some synthesizers use a combination of these two techniques. Such synthesizers take a sound that is stored internally and then do interesting things to it electronically to make it sound different.

Every instrument has a characteristic waveform. To create a sound from scratch, a synthesizer uses various techniques to shape a waveform, matching it as closely as it can to the desired sound. As you might expect, the more money you spend, the better the match.

Synthesizers that play stored sounds have an easier job: they can just play back the stored sound. The more memory the synthesizer has, the better the job it can do because more memory equals more room to store higher-quality sound samples. In many cases, you can alter or edit the stored sound in lots of interesting ways.

To create or modify sounds, you (and the synthesizer) have to work with the basic parts of a waveform:

Delay—Silent time between when the key is struck and the sound begins. Real instruments do not have a delay, but synthetic ones can.

Attack—The rising initial part of the sound. A pan flute has a slow attack, whereas a plucked guitar string has a quick attack.

Hold—The amount of time over which the level reached in the attack stays high.

Decay—The drop in volume of the attack portion of the sound, following the hold (if any).

Sustain—The continuing sound after the attack portion has completed. A plucked guitar string, for example, has a quick, loud attack, followed by a long but relatively quieter sustain.

Release—The behavior of the sound when the key is released. A sound may stop immediately upon release or it may continue for quite a long time.

By altering these parts of the waveform, a synthesizer can produce a wide variety of sounds.

The only thing most synthesizers have in common is that the manuals that explain the synthesis method (as well as the sound-editing techniques) are too brief to be of use to the new user. As use for synthesizers spreads into the business arena (you can create some incredible sound effects and music with quality synthesizers), I expect this to change.

MIDI Instruments

It's getting harder to tell the difference between a computer and an instrument because many of today's "instruments" are powerful computers with keyboards attached.

MIDI enables many different electronic instruments (and computers) to communicate with each other. For example, you can use one keyboard to tell another keyboard what to play. You can use a computer to record the keystrokes from a keyboard, then play them back using a sound card or a rack-mount synthesizer to generate the sounds. There are many variations on these techniques, but they all rely on a .MID file containing the instructions synthesizers use to play the music.

Because the instrument generates the sounds, there is a great deal of leeway in using .MID files. For example, you can set your keyboard synthesizer to produce an organ sound, and you can record yourself playing Bach's "Toccata and Fugue in D minor." If you play the piece back through another keyboard set to reproduce the sounds of bells, you hear the piece played on bells.

MIDI Sequencing

When you press the piano-like keys of a MIDI instrument, you are generating note ON and OFF messages (note ON is sent when you press the key, and note OFF is sent when you release the key). Other information, including the MIDI channel and how hard you press the key, is sent with these messages to a sequencer, which saves this data. Later, the sequencer can send the data back to any MIDI instrument to re-create the music.

> I have a Korg M1 sitting behind me, and it has a sequencer in it that I hardly ever use. It is capable of recording into memory what I play on the keyboard and then playing it back. More powerfully, I can add additional instrument sounds to the base track that I put into the sequencer. This layering enables me to compose complex music all by myself.

The early sequencers were hardware sequencers, and you can still find them around. Some modern keyboards include a built-in sequencer.

Although a hardware sequencer is convenient for musicians who travel (you don't have to lug a computer around with you), it's not user-friendly. Most keyboards have small screens for displaying information, and buttons often do "double duty" for regular use and sequencer use. Putting the sequencer onto a computer is the obvious answer, both for the studio musician and the business executive creating a multimedia presentation.

There are a number of good sequencer programs that run in the Windows environment, including Cakewalk Professional, Cadenza, and Master Tracks Pro 4. With these sequencers, you see the music in a format similar to a scroll in a player piano (Figure 2.9).

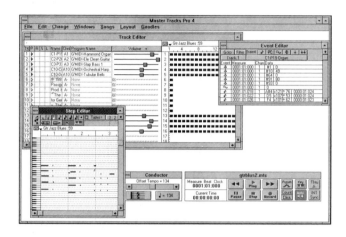

Figure 2.9. *A Master Tracks Pro 4 window.*

With most sequencers, you can now also view the music as traditional notes, as shown in a Cakewalk screen in Figure 2.10.[13]

In programs such as Finale and Encore, you work completely in note format, in a music *score* (Figure 2.11).

Depending on what you are doing, each method has its benefits. Consult Chapter 10 and the Shopper's Guide for complete information on the various sequencer packages.

The General MIDI Standard

Many of the keyboards and other MIDI instruments on the market have a selection of sounds and programs unique to the manufacturer. This variety has caused a great deal of confusion. However, the emerging standard, called General MIDI,

---

[13]The differences between sequencing programs have become fewer and fewer over time. For example, just a year ago the ability to view actual notes in a sequencer was rare—now it is common.

specifies which instruments are on which channels, as shown in the next section, "Instrument Sounds."

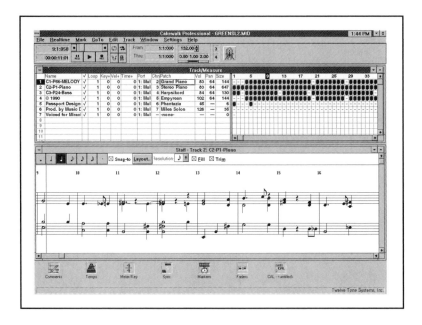

Figure 2.10. *A Cakewalk window.*

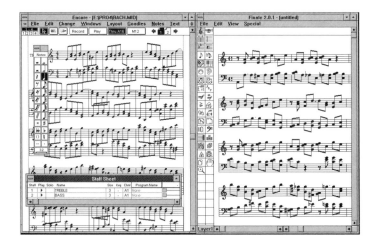

Figure 2.11. *Encore and Finale windows.*

Instrument Sounds

Table 2.1 shows the instrument sounds available with General MIDI along with their assigned program numbers. The sounds are generally grouped together by type of instrument or sound. The program numbers begin with 0 and end with 127; that's 128 sounds, the highest number that can be stored in seven bits. The eighth bit in the byte is reserved by the MIDI standard.

Table 2.1. General MIDI sounds.

Program Number	Description
0	Acoustic Grand Piano
1	Bright Acoustic Piano
2	Electric Grand Piano
3	Honky-Tonk Piano
4	Rhodes Piano
5	Chorused Piano
6	Harpsichord
7	Clavinet Chromatic
8	Celesta
9	Glockenspiel
10	Music Box
11	Vibraphone
12	Marimba
13	Xylophone
14	Tubular Bells
15	Dulcimer
16	Hammond Organ
17	Percussive Organ

continues

Table 2.1. continued

Program Number	Description
18	Rock Organ
19	Church Organ
20	Reed Organ
21	Accordion
22	Harmonica
23	Tango Accordion
24	Acoustic Guitar (Nylon)
25	Acoustic Guitar (Steel)
26	Electric Guitar (Jazz)
27	Electric Guitar (Clean)
28	Electric Guitar (Muted)
29	Overdriven Guitar
30	Distortion Guitar
31	Guitar Harmonics
32	Acoustic Bass
33	Electric Bass (Finger)
34	Electric Bass (Pick)
35	Fretless Bass
36	Slap Bass 1
37	Slap Bass 2
38	Synthesizer Bass 1
39	Synthesizer Bass 2
40	Violin
41	Viola

Program Number	Description
42	Cello
43	Contrabass
44	Tremolo Strings
45	Pizzicato Strings
46	Orchestral Harp
47	Timpani
48	String Ensemble 1
49	String Ensemble 2
50	Synthesizer Strings 1
51	Synthesizer Strings 2
52	Choir Aahs
53	Voice Oohs
54	Synthesizer Voice
55	Orchestra Hit
56	Trumpet
57	Trombone
58	Tuba
59	Muted Trumpet
60	French Horn
61	Brass Section
62	Synthesizer Brass 1
63	Synthesizer Brass 2
64	Soprano Sax
65	Alto Sax
66	Tenor Sax

continues

Table 2.1. continued

Program Number	Description
67	Baritone Sax
68	Oboe
69	English Horn
70	Bassoon
71	Clarinet
72	Piccolo
73	Flute
74	Recorder
75	Pan Flute
76	Bottle Blow
77	Shakuhachi
78	Whistle
79	Ocarina
80	Synthesizer Lead 1 (Square)
81	Synthesizer Lead 2 (Sawtooth)
82	Synthesizer Lead 3 (Calliope lead)
83	Synthesizer Lead 4 (Chiff lead)
84	Synthesizer Lead 5 (Sharang)
85	Synthesizer Lead 6 (Voice)
86	Synthesizer Lead 7 (Fifths)
87	Synthesizer Lead 8 (Brass + lead)
88	Synthesizer Pad 1 (New Age)
89	Synthesizer Pad 2 (Warm)
90	Synthesizer Pad 3 (Polysynth)

Program Number	Description
91	Synthesizer Pad 4 (Choir)
92	Synthesizer Pad 5 (Bowed)
93	Synthesizer Pad 6 (Metallic)
94	Synthesizer Pad 7 (Halo)
95	Synthesizer Pad 8 (Sweep)
96	Sound FX 1 (Rain)
97	Sound FX 2 (Soundtrack)
98	Sound FX 3 (Crystal)
99	Sound FX 4 (Atmosphere)
100	Sound FX 5 (Brightness)
101	Sound FX 6 (Goblins)
102	Sound FX 7 (Echoes)
103	Sound FX 8 (Sci-Fi)
104	Sitar
105	Banjo
106	Shamisen
107	Koto
108	Kalimba
109	Bagpipe
110	Fiddle
111	Shanai
112	Tinkle Bell
113	Agogo
114	Steel Drums
115	Woodblock

continues

Table 2.1. continued

Program Number	Description
116	Taiko Drum
117	Melodic Drum
118	Synthesizer Drum
119	Reverse Cymbal
120	Guitar fret noise
121	Breath noise
122	Seashore
123	Bird Tweet
124	Telephone
125	Helicopter
126	Applause
127	Gunshot

There are 16 channels available in the MIDI standard to play these sounds. You can play one sound per channel. Not all cards or MIDI devices support all 16 channels, however.

Drum Sounds

Channel 10 is different from the other MIDI channels when working in General MIDI.[14] Sound data sent to Channel 10 is used to play drum sounds.

---

[14]General MIDI is set up to use Channel 10 for drums, but the MIDI standard itself does not require Channel 10 to be reserved this way. Before MIDI became common on computers, each synthesizer designer could decide what instruments show up where. This was fine for performing musicians, who worked with a limited number of synthesizers. However, when MIDI moved to computers, this became a problem. If instrument 114 was an Oboe on one synth, and Steel Drums on another, how could you ever exchange MIDI files? General MIDI solved this problem by creating a standard set of instruments for computer-based MIDI.

The General MIDI standard calls for 46 drum sounds. Each drum sound is associated with a single note; the sounds are triggered by sending note-on messages to sound cards using Channel 10. Only the note numbers from 35 to 81 are included in Table 2.2. If you ever try to play a non-General MIDI song file that uses Channel 10, you probably will hear some rather chaotic sounds. Channel 10 uses normal note-on/note-off messages to play the drum sounds, and, as you can see in Table 2.2, there is a different drum sound on each note.

Table 2.2. General MIDI drum sounds.

Note Number	Description
35	Acoustic Bass Drum
36	Bass Drum 1
37	Side Stick
38	Acoustic Snare
39	Hand Clasp
40	Electric Snare
41	Low Floor Tom
42	Closed High Hat
43	Hi Floor Tom
44	Pedal High Hat
45	Low Tom
46	Open High Hat
47	Low-Mid Tom
48	High-Mid Tom
49	Crash Cymbal 1
50	High Tom
51	Ride Cymbal 1
52	Chinese Cymbal

continues

Table 2.2. continued

Note Number	Description
53	Ride Bell
54	Tambourine
55	Splash Cymbal
56	Cowbell
57	Crash Cymbal 2
58	Vibraslap
59	Ride Cymbal 2
60	High Bongo
61	Low Bongo
62	Mute High Conga
63	Open High Conga
64	Low Conga
65	High Timbale
66	Low Timbale
67	High Agogo
68	Low Agogo
69	Cabasa
70	Maracas
71	Short Whistle
72	Long Whistle
73	Short Guiro
74	Long Guiro
75	Claves
76	High Wood Block

Note Number	Description
77	Low Wood Block
78	Mute Cuica
79	Open Cuica
80	Mute Triangle
81	Open Triangle

Variations on a Theme

This combination of instrument sounds and drum sounds covers the most common instruments fairly well, but there still is a place for synthesizers that do not support the General MIDI standard. For example, the MultiSound card from Turtle Beach has a Proteus/1XR synthesizer on board. The card comes with a set of presets (built-in sounds) that support General MIDI. However, it also includes the standard sounds for the Proteus/1XR synthesizer. Most people agree that the Proteus selections sound better than the General MIDI sounds. To get the most out of this card, use the Proteus, and therefore nonstandard, sounds. However, because the card also supports General MIDI, you have the best of both worlds. The MultiSound also supports a hardware standard, MPU-401, which gives it even more flexibility.

The MultiSound card can play General MIDI selections, but if you want to create original music, you might want to choose the nonstandard configuration to get richer sounds. If you have only one synthesizer in your system, General MIDI makes the most sense—there is a wide variety of sounds, and most of the available software now supports the standard as well, or is moving in that direction.

Multimedia and General MIDI

MIDI instrument manufacturers who want to sell to the multimedia market are offering equipment that supports the General MIDI standard. Some, such as the MultiSound card from Turtle Beach, offer more than the General MIDI set of sounds. Windows 3.1 supports General MIDI, and that alone has been enough to make it a successful standard.

You don't have to know how MIDI works to use it—most of the time. However, a word to the wise: although you can play a .MID file using any MIDI instrument and produce some incredible sounds with high-end synthesizers, the General MIDI standard is loose enough that you sometimes have to clean up the inevitable loose ends. If you can't bear the suspense, check out Chapter 5, "Windows Multimedia," for information on working with the Windows MIDI Mapper.

Troubleshooting MIDI File Playing

If you have a sound card installed and have trouble playing MIDI files, there are several key things to check. The following list covers the most common MIDI problems and offers some suggestions for solving them:

➤ Ensure that you have installed a device driver for playing .MID files. Look for your hardware by name in the Drivers section of the Control Panel. Names of MIDI devices vary, but look for words such as sequencer, FM, synthesizer, Voyetra, and MIDI.

➤ Does your sound card support MIDI files? If it does, the documentation either mentions MIDI specifically, or it talks about a synthesizer on the card. You also might look for any files with the extension .MID in the sound card program directory to verify card capabilities, or try playing MIDI files from DOS.[15]

➤ The MIDI Mapper directs MIDI signals in the Windows environment. You can open the MIDI Mapper in the Control Panel. Make sure the current Setup describes hardware you have in your system. Hint: When you choose a setup, if a dialog box tells you the device is not installed on your system, either you have selected the wrong setup, or you haven't installed a device driver for MIDI, or something went wrong during installation. Try installing again.[16]

---

[15]You'll need to consult the documentation that came with your card to see how to play MIDI files in DOS.

[16]Sometimes, the problem lies with the file that the MIDI Mapper uses for information, MIDIMAP.CFG. If you do not see any setup information in the MIDI Mapper that pertains to your MIDI hardware, look for a copy of the MIDIMAP.CFG file with the programs that were installed for your hardware. For example, if you have a Pro Audio Spectrum 16 from Media Vision, you can find this file in the directory \PAS.

➤ Instead of playing MIDI signals through the synthesizer on the sound card, you may have chosen a setup that directs MIDI signals from the Out port on your sound card. For sound to play in this configuration, you must have an external synthesizer properly connected to the Out port. If that is not the case, select a setup that *does not* include the words "MIDI Out" or similar wording.

Digital Sound

At one time, the technology required to record or create digital sounds was found only in the largest recording studios. Today, you can record digital sound with a PC, a sound card, and a microphone.[17] This makes it easy to put digitized sound in your multimedia projects. To understand the advantages and disadvantages of digital sound, it is worthwhile to take a look at what sound is.

Technically speaking, sound consists of waves—troughs and peaks of energy—as shown in Figure 2.12. Your ears convert this energy into the incredible range of sounds you hear. The simplest sound wave is called a sine wave (Figure 2.12).

In a sine wave, the peaks and troughs line up exactly, and the distance between peaks is always the same. These characteristics define a sine wave: a picture of a pure tone. You don't find too many pure tones in nature, however. What you do find are waves such as the one shown in Figure 2.13.

The difference is not hard to notice. A natural sound is more complex than a sine wave because natural sounds are formed by the interaction of many different sounds. For example, when you pluck the string of a guitar, you get not one sound but many—the string vibrates not only along its full length but also in smaller segments. These additional sounds are called harmonics. Every instrument has a unique pattern of harmonics that gives it a characteristic sound.

In addition to harmonics, the characteristics of a sound can change over time—sometimes quite rapidly. In the case of a plucked guitar string, for example, the initial sound of the pluck changes quickly into the more-or-less steady string

---

[17]This is not to suggest that you will necessarily get the same level of quality on your computer that a large studio can achieve. Basic sound cards, in particular, introduce a certain amount of noise and inaccuracy into the recording process. If you really want CD-quality sound, you'll need at least a high-end card like the MultiSound from Turtle Beach.

vibration. The nature of the pluck also affects the sound. The string can be plucked with a finger, a fingernail, the thumb, a finger pick, or a thin or thick triangular pick.

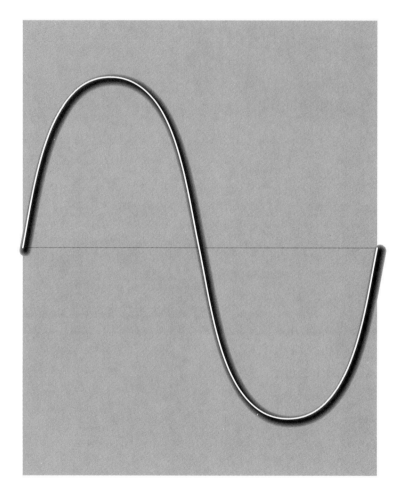

Figure 2.12. *A pure sound wave, called a sine wave.*

The bottom line is that natural sounds are extremely complex.

A sound wave tells you a lot about a sound (see Figure 2.14). For example, the higher the peaks, the louder the sound. The greater the distance between peaks, the lower the pitch of the sound. The technical term for loudness is amplitude; the technical term for distance between peaks is frequency.

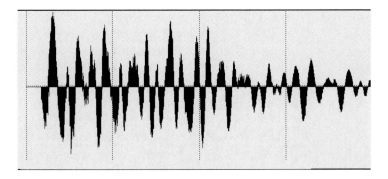

Figure 2.13. *A typical sound wave.*

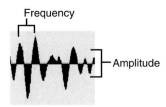

Figure 2.14. *The frequency and amplitude of a sound wave.*

The distance between peaks is measured by the time that passes before the next peak arrives (usually expressed in terms of cycles per second). The technical term for this expression is *Hertz* (abbreviated "Hz").[18] For example, a standard A pitch (often used for tuning purposes) is 440 Hz. A tuning fork set to A 440 vibrates back and forth 440 times per second.

Digital Recording

Before digital sound recording came along, sounds were recorded in ways that mimicked the wave nature of natural sounds, a process called *analog recording.* For example, when music was sold on records (remember LPs?), the recording consisted of little peaks and troughs cut into the vinyl surface. With a microscope,

---

[18]Now that I'm using footnotes, I can tell you where the word "Hertz" comes from. In the first edition, my editors thought I was getting too technical by delving into such fine points. However, I assume there are at least one or two readers who are interested in these things. After all, what's the sense in having an unabridged dictionary if one can't get some use out of it? The term "Hertz" is named after Heinrich Rudolph Hertz, the fellow who first investigated the phenomenon of waves caused by oscillations of an electric circuit.

you can see that the physical surface of the record looks like a typical sound wave (see Figure 2.13). Because sound is inherently analog, it can never be represented perfectly by a digital recording method. This is an important concept to keep in mind. Instead of trying to match the analog signal, a digital recorder samples the incoming sound at predetermined intervals. For example, Figure 2.15 shows a tiny portion of a sound wave.

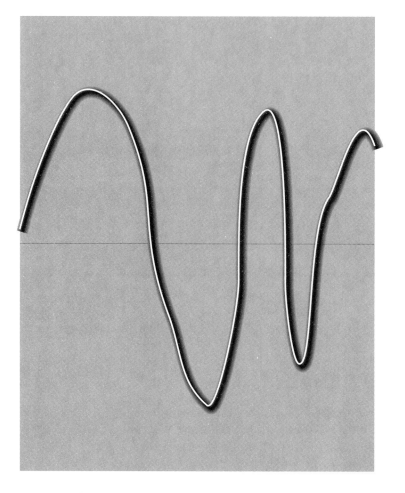

Figure 2.15. *An analog sound wave.*

If you sample this wave 11,000 times per second, you get a waveform that has steps in it—one step for each sample (Figure 2.16).

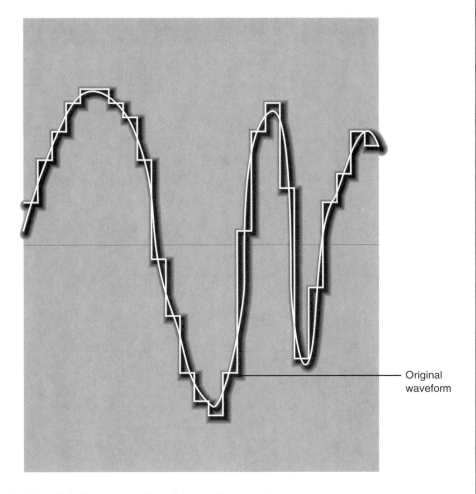

Original
waveform

Figure 2.16. *A digital representation of the analog sound wave.*

The horizontal direction measures time, and the vertical direction measures amplitude. Notice that the sample does not capture every nuance of the sound wave; it is limited to the value present at each sample point. Only the individual steps of the waveform are stored digitally—one value for each sample point. The time value is determined by the sample rate, and the amplitude value is determined by the vertical height of the wave.

This process generates a lot of data. If you record at 11,000 Hz, using a typical (8-bit) sound card, the process uses 11,000 such 8-bit samples (1 byte) every second. That's 11,000 bytes per second.

> **Bits and Pieces**
>
> The term used to describe the accuracy of a device is *resolution*. The term comes from the word "resolve." For example, if a device can resolve small details, you say it has a high resolution. In a digital device, high resolution is achieved by taking more samples, storing more information about each sample, or both.
>
> To take more samples, you must increase the sampling frequency. To store more information about each sample, you must use a larger container for each sample. Because the unit of digital storage is the bit, using more bits per sample enables you to store more information.
>
> A single bit has two states: on and off. By convention, the numbers 0 (off) and 1 (on) are used to represent these two states. This is called *binary representation.*
>
> In a PC, eight bits are commonly associated into a *byte.* By using various combinations of 1s and 0s, you can represent 256 different values using a single byte. If you use 16 bits (2 bytes—in Windows, it's called a *word*) to store the information, the resolution increases from 256 possible values to 65,536!

Playing Back Digital Sound

When analog sound is digitally recorded, the waveform is converted into a series of samples, each representing a tiny piece of data. For example, the stepped waveform in Figure 2.17 would be reduced to a string of bytes that would look nothing like sound at all:

```
09 13 27 4D 33 2A ...
```

When the time comes to play the recorded sound, you must reconstruct the original analog waveform from the digital information. To do this, your device constructs a waveform that smoothly connects the digital points (Figure 2.18).

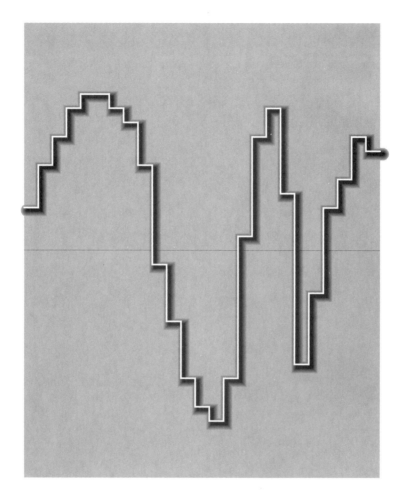

Figure 2.17. *A stepped waveform.*

Because the digital information is only an approximation of the analog information (analog is inherently continuous; digital is inherently stepped), the reconstructed wave is not an exact copy of the original. Figure 2.19 shows the difference.

To get greater accuracy between the two waveforms, increase the sample rate (more samples per second) or increase the number of possible values of amplitude (use more bits to store the data). Increasing the sample rate usually means doubling it. Some typical sample rates are 11, 22.05, and 44.1 kilohertz (*kilohertz* equals thousands of cycles per second and is abbreviated "KHz"). If you isolate a tiny portion of your sound sample, increasing the sample rate creates a more realistic representation of the sound.

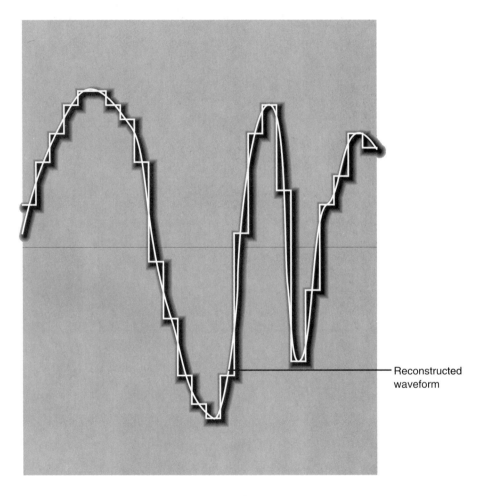

Reconstructed
waveform

Figure 2.18. *Your device constructs a waveform from the steps.*

Figure 2.20 shows a few thousandths of a second from the beginning of a piano sound. The sample was recorded at 44.1 KHz, with 16 bits of resolution. Figure 2.21 shows the same piano sound, recorded at 11 KHz, with 8 bits of resolution.

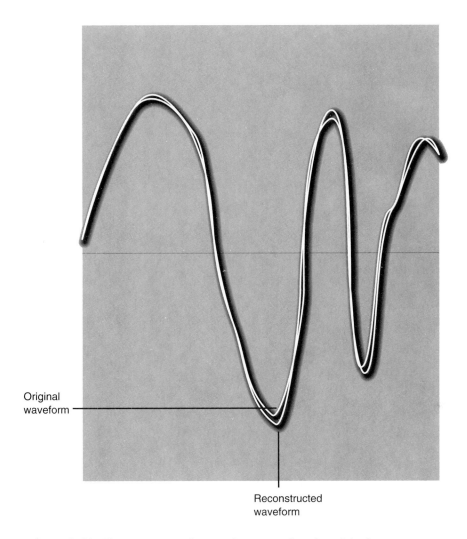

Original
waveform

Reconstructed
waveform

Figure 2.19. *The reconstructed wave almost matches the original.*

There are numerous differences between the waveforms, including changes to the peaks of waves, changes in the slope of the waveform, and a loss of high frequencies.

As the sample rate increases, you can resolve smaller details of the sound. High sample rates enable you to distinguish smaller distances between wave peaks. Because this distance determines the pitch (frequency) of a sound, higher sample rates enable you to accurately record higher-pitched sounds.

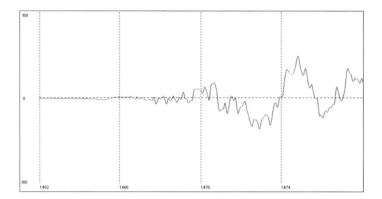

Figure 2.20. *A piano sound recorded at 44.1 KHz.*

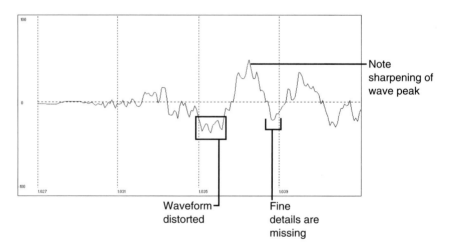

Figure 2.21. *A piano sound recorded at 11 KHz.*

Frequency Limits

There is a fundamental rule for digital recording (sampling): the sampling rate must be two times the highest frequency you want to record. The highest frequency you can record at a given sample rate is called the *Nyquist frequency,* named after the founder of this principle.

A simple illustration should demonstrate why you need to use such a high sampling frequency.

Figure 2.22 shows the waveform of a recording of a sine wave at 44.1 KHz, using 16 bits of resolution.

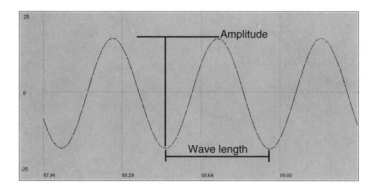

Figure 2.22. *A 44.1-KHz recording of a sine wave.*

The waveform is perfectly formed—all of the peaks and troughs are equal from wave to wave, and the outline of each wave is perfectly formed.

Now take a look at the same sound recorded at a lower sampling frequency—22.05 KHz, with 16-bit resolution (Figure 2.23).

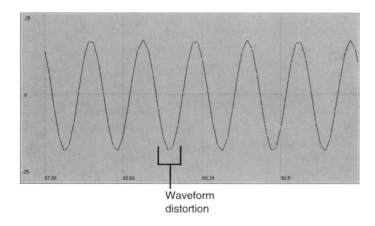

Figure 2.23. *A 22.05-KHz recording of a sine wave.*

The lower sampling frequency has marred the smoothness of the waveforms. The exact nature of the changes varies from wave to wave, so the resulting sound is not as smooth or as full. In effect, the reduced sample rate has created false variations in the waveform.

Ignore the apparent changes in scale of these illustrations; the differences result from the difficulty of selecting exactly the same section of the waveform. The same frequency was used for each sound. The time scale varies a little from one illustration to the next.

If I reduce the sampling frequency one more time, to 11 KHz, the waveforms become much more distorted (Figure 2.24).

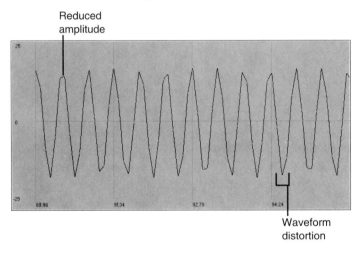

Figure 2.24. An 11-KHz recording of a sine wave.

The peaks and troughs have almost completely lost the smooth, rolling hills look of the original waveform. Some of the wave tips are nearly sheared off, and others are too pointed. Also, some peaks are not as high or low as they should be.

Whatever the sampling rate, false waveforms occur if there are any frequencies above the Nyquist limit. Even ultrasonic (beyond the range of human hearing) sound can cause false waveforms.

The solution is to remove any frequencies higher than one-half the sampling frequency before recording the sound. This kind of filtering is called *low-pass filtering*. The filter passes lower frequencies and blocks the higher ones. Only sounds that can be recorded accurately will make it through the filter.[19]

---

[19]When you are choosing software to use for editing sounds, such filtering should be on your checklist. When you change the sample rate of a sound, you want to make sure that all frequencies higher than one-half the sample rate are removed. This maintains the highest level of quality when you reduce the sample rate digitally.

Voice Versus Music Recording

The human voice does not have a wide range of pitches. Expressed as cycles per second, human speech ranges from about 100 Hz to 6 KHz. If you look at a frequency analysis of speech (Figure 2.25), you can see that most of the frequencies are in the lowest part of this range.

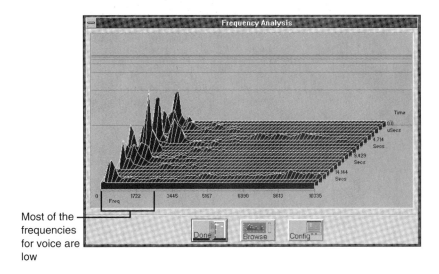

Most of the frequencies for voice are low

Figure 2.25. *A frequency analysis of human speech.*

Figure 2.25, a screen shot from the program Wave for Windows, is a plot of an entire sound file. Frequencies increase from left to right, and time increases from top to bottom. This sound file is a recording of my voice; most frequencies are quite low. There are some peaks in the range from 6–8 KHz; I checked them, and they are *sibilance* (the breathy noise you make on "s" sounds). Even if I remove these higher-frequency sounds entirely, the voice still sounds fairly natural. If all you want to record is speech, you only have to record frequencies up to about 6 or 8 KHz. The telephone takes advantage of this fact. A telephone line can't transmit sounds with a frequency of more than about 7 KHz. This enables the phone companies to save some money by using a less technically sophisticated system.[20]

---

[20]One side effect of this limitation is that modems can transmit only so much data over a phone line. The range of frequencies available is called the bandwidth—a narrow bandwidth, such as that used on phone lines, limits the amount of information you can send. Higher bandwidth technologies, such as fiber-optic networks, are changing things substantially.

Music adds a much wider range of pitches, including the entire spectrum of sounds you can hear. Human hearing ranges from 20 Hz to about 20 KHz. As you age, the range of frequencies you can hear narrows. Only the young or those with exceptional hearing can hear sounds with frequencies all the way up to 20,000 Hz.

For the reasons listed earlier in the section, "Frequency Limits," the sample rate has to be at least two times faster than the highest sound frequency you want to record. Because human speech extends to about 6 KHz, you need a sampling rate of at least 12 KHz to record speech with acceptable fidelity. The nearest "standard" recording rate is 11 KHz. Since human hearing ranges up to about 20KHz, you need a sampling rate of at least 40 KHz to record the full range of sounds that humans can hear. It's no coincidence this is close to the sampling frequency used on all CDs (44.1 KHz).

All this discussion is far from academic. Increasing the sample rate has its costs, mostly in terms of memory requirements. There are two kinds of costs: bit costs and total memory costs. You can have high fidelity by switching from 8 bits to 16 bits of resolution, or by simply recording more data. See the section, "Recording on Your Hard Disk," in this chapter to find out the effect that increasing the sample rate has on data storage requirements.

How Sound Cards Create Sound

If you have a Sound Blaster or a similar introductory sound card, the sounds you hear are created by a method called *FM synthesis*. FM stands for frequency modulation, the same technique used for some radio broadcasts. Your sound card modulates (or changes) the frequencies to emulate the sounds of various instruments. This is not a high-fidelity method of sound creation. If you have such a card, you may have noticed that most sounds are similar to one another; they only *suggest* the sound of the instrument they "reproduce."

Other sound cards, such as the SCC-1 from Roland or the MultiSound from Turtle Beach, contain recorded samples of real instruments, stored in memory chips on the card. Such cards reproduce sounds much more accurately, but they cost more than the FM-synthesis cards.

8-Bit Cards Versus 16-Bit Cards

There are two kinds of sound cards available for multimedia: 8-bit and 16-bit. Using 8 bits, you can store a total of 256 (2 to the 8th power) values. Using 16 bits, you can store a total of 65,536 (2 to the 16th power) values. Doubling the number of bits does much more than double the number of values.[21] An 8-bit card breaks a waveform into 256 separate steps, whereas a 16-bit card divides the same waveform into more than 65,000 steps. You get more fidelity from a 16-bit card, although 8-bit cards provide reasonable fidelity for some purposes, such as speech.

As the sample rate increases, the total amount of information increases. For example, at 11 KHz (a common sampling rate to use with 8-bit cards), there are 11,000 bytes of 8-bit data each second. At 44.1 KHz (a common 16-bit sampling rate), there are 88,200 bytes of 8-bit data each second. At that rate, a one-minute sample contains 5,292,000 bytes of data—that's more than 5M per minute. Stereo recording doubles that, and more than 10M per minute quickly uses up a hard disk! The average CD can hold as much as 680M of data, more than an hour of recording time in stereo.

Be aware of this trade-off between sound fidelity and memory requirements for digital sound. If you're on a budget, lean toward the 8-bit cards. They save you some money, but you can also use them with a smaller, less expensive hard drive. If you decide to go with a 16-bit card, keep in mind the additional costs for memory and hard-disk space. As prices for disk and memory storage continue to fall, this trade-off becomes less important.

Recording on Your Hard Disk

Depending on the speed of your computer and hard disk, you might not be able to record at the highest sound resolutions. Table 2.3 is a rough guide for what you can record on various hardware setups.

Table 2.3. Maximum recording speeds for today's CPUs.

CPU	Mode	Max Recording Speed
286	mono	44 KHz
286	stereo	22 KHz
386SX	mono	44 KHz
386SX	stereo	32 KHz (a nonstandard recording speed)

continues

---

[21]What it does, mathematically speaking, is double the exponent from 8 to 16—that's why there is such a huge difference.

Table 2.3. continued

CPU	Mode	Max Recording Speed
386	mono	44 KHz
386	stereo	44 KHz
486	mono	44 KHz
486	stereo	44 KHz

The numbers in Table 2.3 are only estimates—a fast or slow hard disk can make a difference too. If you plan to record at CD sample rates (44.1 KHz, 16 bits), you'll almost certainly want a large, fast hard disk.

The sound card you use can also play a role. The MultiSound, for example, uses a DSP[22] to off-load some of the sound processing tasks from the CPU. Thus, it has lower overhead than a cheaper sound card during recording. With the MultiSound, you can expect better performance during more demanding, high-data-rate recording.

Consider the rates at which data must be written to disk for various sample resolutions (Table 2.4). As you can see, the space requirements for CD-quality recording are pretty high—more than 10 megabytes per minute. My first hard disk was only 5 megabytes.

Table 2.4. Rates of recording.

Record Speed	Resolution	Mode	Data Write Rate/Minute
11 KHz	8 bit	mono	661K
11 KHz	8 bit	stereo	1.3M
11 KHz	16 bit	mono	1.3M
11 KHz	16 bit	stereo	2.6M
22 KHz	8 bit	mono	1.3M

---

[22]Digital Sound Processor.

Record Speed	Resolution	Mode	Data Write Rate/Minute
22 KHz	8 bit	stereo	2.6M
22 KHz	16 bit	mono	2.6M
22 KHz	16 bit	stereo	5.3M
44.1 KHz	8 bit	mono	2.6M
44.1 KHz	8 bit	stereo	5.3M
44.1 KHz	16 bit	mono	5.3M
44.1 KHz	16 bit	stereo	10.5M

Disk Compression Programs

If you use a disk compression program (such as Stacker, or the disk compression included in DOS 6.0), keep in mind that it slows down actual access to your hard disk by 10 to 15 percent. Depending on the speed of your hard disk, this overhead can be the critical factor when you record at higher resolutions and sample rates. If you can't record all the data, you lose information, and you'll hear stuttering in the recording. I also strongly recommend you don't use software disk compression for another reason.

Compression programs look for repeating data. If a pattern is found in the data, the pattern is saved once; as a result, the program uses less disk space. There is some overhead to keep track of how to put the file back together. Digital audio data is complex, and it has few repeating patterns—the data is essentially random in most cases. Depending on the compression method used, the act of "compressing" a digital audio file can result in an increase in the file size. This occurs when the overhead for putting the file back together exceeds the gain from compression.

Fragmented Files

You can make the hard drive you have now a more efficient recording medium. The way files are stored physically on the disk also can affect recording speed, especially at higher resolutions. When DOS stores a file, it puts it in the first available free space on the disk. As you add and delete files, the free spaces tend to break up into smaller and smaller chunks. If the free space is not big enough to hold the complete file, DOS looks for another chunk of free space and continues writing the file there.

This process is called *hard disk fragmentation*. It is bad for recording because DOS spends time finding free space for each segment of the sound file. If the next free space is somewhere across the disk, the travel time of the hard-disk head could cause a loss of data. If you are recording to a fragmented disk, DOS has to search for free space frequently—a little here, a little there. This search reduces the average seek time to a point where recording can become problematic.

There are several utility programs for defragmenting your hard disk. I recommend that you use one before you do any high-resolution recording, particularly stereo recording. These products include Disk Optimizer (Softlogic Solutions), SpeedDisk (Norton Utilities/Symantec), and Compress (PC Tools/Central Point). As a side benefit, defragmenting also speeds up disk access in general.

Creating Sounds

The issues involved in creating sounds (called synthesis) involve some of the same problems that must be overcome when recording sounds digitally. A sound wave is very complex and varies in subtle ways from one instrument to another. Creating such complex waveforms from scratch is a difficult challenge.

Because sound waves are so complex, engineers usually try to find ways to create complex waves from simpler building blocks. Early attempts at this resulted in very artificial sounds.

Then along came *additive synthesis*. Using this process, you can create sounds that are noticeably similar to familiar instruments, although sometimes lacking the subtlety of real instruments. Additive synthesis works by starting with a basic waveform and then adding other waves (frequently harmonics) to it to make it more complex. The process is extremely complex, and it has become economical only with the advent of today's high-powered microprocessors.

Other forms of synthesis are under development and hold promise for the future. *Physical modeling* involves careful study of an instrument to develop a mathematical model of the ways that it makes sounds. Notes can then be generated using the model. If the model is good enough, sounds based on the various techniques used to play the instrument can be generated.

For example, a violin can be bowed in many ways (not to mention plucked!). Re-creating the various sounds that result is a tremendous challenge.

For the time being, the best sound fidelity is achieved by sampling real instruments and then playing back the samples. Synthesis is often used to vary or color such sampled sounds rather than to create sounds from scratch. The majority of keyboard "synthesizers" sold today are actually filled with samples, not sound generators.

Sound-Editing Applications

There are a number of applications you can use to record sound files, but the one I like best is Sound Forge. I have also included some sound editing shareware on the disks, and Wave for Windows from Turtle Beach is also a very useful editing program.[23]

Sound Forge

Sound Forge is a brand new program, one that just came out as I was writing the second edition of this book. It is a program that I like very much, because it solved a long-standing problem that I had.

You might think that there aren't very many different ways to edit sound files, but that's not true. For the last several years, I had been using sound-editing software that had lots of nice features but wasn't very satisfying or easy to use. I was never quite sure what the problem was, but I knew it was there.

When Sound Forge first found its way to my desk, I didn't use it right away. I was extremely busy writing another book, *Virtual Reality Madness*. The company that sells Sound Forge kept calling me and asking me what I thought of their baby. I kept telling them that I was sorry, but I hadn't had a chance to use it yet. This went on for more than a month. Finally, just to stop the phone calls, I installed Sound Forge to give it a test run. I was immediately impressed, and I'll tell you exactly why I was impressed.

---

[23]In the first edition of this book, Wave for Windows was the Author's Choice for sound-editing software. Times, however, have changed—Sound Forge, which actually has a smaller feature set than Wave for Windows, has taken over. Wave's larger feature set is offset by a quirky interface. Of course, if Turtle Beach enhances the interface, they can always climb back to the top of the heap.

Figure 2.26 shows a typical Sound Forge screen. A stereo file is open, and there are separate tracks for the left and right channels. This is actually quite typical; nothing revolutionary so far.

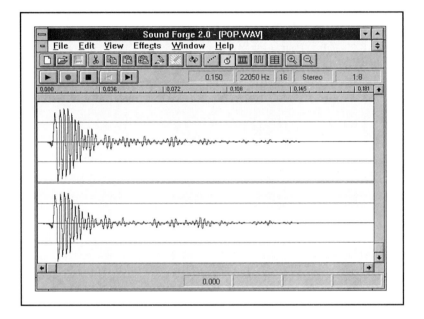

Figure 2.26. *A typical Sound Forge window with a stereo file open.*

It's not until you start to use Sound Forge that you realize how well designed it is. You see, the problem I had been having was that the interface—the buttons, menus, and such—of sound-editing programs had been frustrating me. Sound Forge is extremely well laid out, and it is a pleasure to use.

For example, most sound editors enable you to select just a portion of the sound file by dragging the mouse. Sound Forge is no exception as you can see in Figure 2.27. The selected section is shown in black.

How about selecting just one of the stereo channels? No problem with Sound Forge—simply click and drag in the top quarter of the sound track (see Figure 2.28). This might not seem like a big deal, but when you are editing sound files, such nice little touches make your job a lot easier.

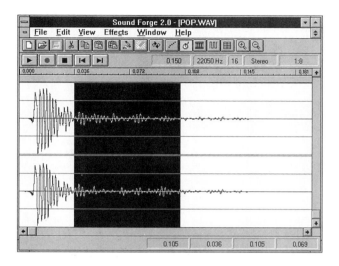

Figure 2.27. Selecting a portion of a sound file with Sound Forge.

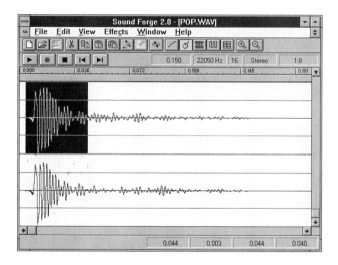

Figure 2.28. Selecting a portion of one stereo channel.

Sound Forge has one important feature in common with other sound editors: the ability to zoom in and show the actual fine detail of a waveform. In Figure 2.29, for example, the entire window shows just 0.022 seconds of the sound file.

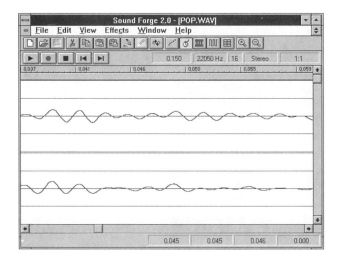

Figure 2.29. *A 0.022-second section of a sound file.*

One feature that I wish Sound Forge had is the ability to edit the sound wave as if you were drawing it with a pencil. Sometimes that is an excellent way to remove a pop or other glitch in the file. But Sound Forge does have some other cool features. One of my favorites is the use of graphs to do such things as fades and pans as shown in Figure 2.30.

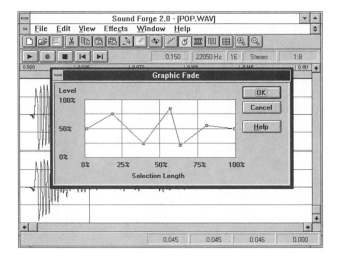

Figure 2.30. *Using a graph to structure a fade effect.*

In the example shown, I have created five nodes at various points along the timeline and then increased or decreased the relative sound level. Sound Forge then connects the dots, gradually fading or increasing the sound level from node to node. When, you may ask, might one need such a device? I used it to good effect while creating videos for the *Virtual Reality Madness* book.

I had a video that was a combination of four different segments showing Multnomah Falls, a famous waterfall in Oregon along Interstate 84. In some shots, the waterfall was quite close, so the sound needed to be loud. In other cases, the waterfall was shown in the distance, so the sound needed to be quieter. In still other segments, the camera zoomed in, and the sound level needed to change during the segment. To create the soundtrack for the combined video, I started with the clearest, cleanest audio I had recorded during filming. I loaded the video file into VidEdit and noted the exact timing for the changes I needed—fade in for three seconds, steady for two seconds, louder at nine seconds, and so on.

I then loaded the audio track into Sound Forge and used the Graphic Fade to set the sound levels. The result is included on one of the CD-ROM disks. The file name is MFALLS_P.AVI. Judge for yourself how effective this technique was.[24]

Sound Forge has many other nice features in its interface. For example, you can zoom just the selected area, and you can easily access such features as changing the sampling rate. Figure 2.31 shows a drop-down menu for changing the sample rate.

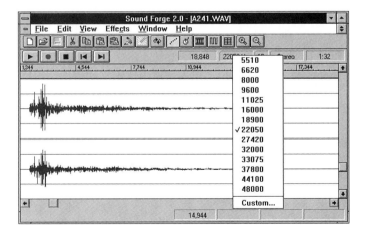

Figure 2.31. *Adjusting the sample rate using a drop-down menu.*

---

[24]I also added a music track to the audio. Sound Forge doesn't do mixing (can't have everything, I guess), so I used Wave for Windows to do the mixing.

Overall, Sound Forge is very strong on ease of use, and it has most of the features you'll need. It doesn't yet have a full feature set, however, and if you plan to do high-end editing, you'll probably also want to have Wave for Windows available for situations that Sound Forge can't handle.

Shareware Sound Editing

You do not have to spend money to explore sound editing, however. I have included a demo of a shareware program on the CD-ROMs that can get you started right away.[25] The program is called WaveS and was originally created as part of a contest for programmers developing software for the Pro Audio Spectrum sound card.

Figure 2.32 shows a typical WaveS screen. The open sound file happens to be a mono file, so there is only one track shown. WaveS can handle stereo files just fine.

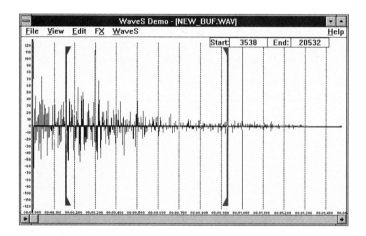

Figure 2.32. *A typical WaveS screen.*

WaveS has some nice features, and it is fun to play with if you do not already own a sound-editing program. However, it has a few quirks in the operation of the program that made it awkward to use. For example, look again at Figure 2.32.

---

[25]Of course, if you like the shareware program, you'll need to register it and pay the registration fee.

The selection markers are two vertical bars, not a region shown in black. I found this less exact, and somewhat confusing, as a method for selecting a portion of a sound file to work with.

However, the good news is that WaveS gives you a large number of fun sound effects that you can play with, as shown in Figure 2.33. You can change the sound level, reverse the sound, compensate for problem frequencies using equalization, add echo, and so on.

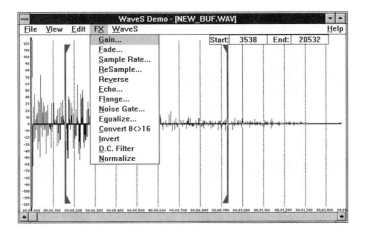

Figure 2.33. *The FX (effects) menu of WaveS.*

You can also select different ways of looking at the same sound file. Figure 2.32 showed the default method, the actual waveform. You can also look at the *average* waveform as shown in Figure 2.34. As you can see, this can improve the view you have of the sound file while editing.

You can also use WaveS to analyze the frequencies present in the sound file as shown in Figure 2.35. Most of the frequencies in this sample are at the low end of the sound spectrum.[26]

---

[26]You may not be used to referring to a range of sound frequencies as a spectrum—we usually think more of light as having a spectrum. However, anything made of different frequencies has a spectrum.

One very useful feature of WaveS is that you can create sound waves from scratch as shown in Figure 2.36. Table 2.5 describes the different kinds of waveforms you can create.

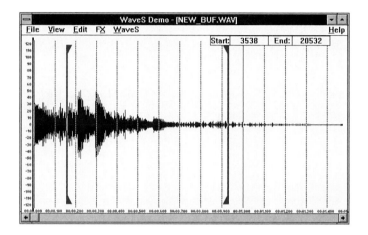

Figure 2.34. *Viewing the average waveform.*

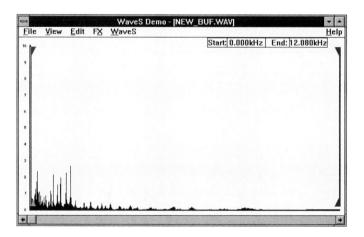

Figure 2.35. *A frequency analysis of a wave file.*

Table 2.5. The basic waveforms.

Waveform	Shape	Description
Sine		A pure tone, with smoothly changing waveforms.
Triangle		Sharply peaked waveform.
Square		Highly angular, square-shaped waveform.
Sweep		High-frequency, weaving pattern.
Noise		Random frequencies and amplitude.

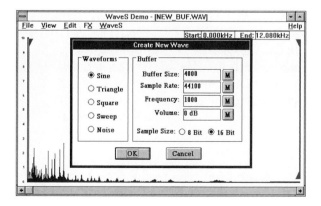

Figure 2.36. *Creating new wave data.*

Each waveform has a characteristic sound, and I have provided sample sounds on the disks, or you can use WaveS to create your own.

Wave for Windows

Wave for Windows is currently the most ambitious sound-editing program for Windows. It can utilize all the capabilities of whatever sound card you have, and you can modify sounds with the program's powerful editing tools. For example, you can make a sound louder or softer, silence or remove portions of the sound, perform a frequency analysis and display the results in a 3-D graph, mix and cross-fade sounds, import sound files, reverse or invert the file, and much more. You can apply these editing functions to the whole file or a selected portion.

However, even though Wave for Windows gets an Author's Choice, I feel it necessary to add a warning. The interface for Wave lacks the smoothness of the Sound Forge interface. As a result, I find that I use Sound Forge for everyday activities, and I only run Wave when I need some feature that Sound Forge lacks.[27]

Wave for Windows uses the hard disk like a tape recorder uses a tape. On a tape recorder, only the portion of the tape in front of the head is involved in playback or editing. With Wave, only a portion of the file is actually loaded into memory. For large files, it isn't even possible to load the entire file into memory. A 16-bit, 44.1 KHz, stereo recording uses more than 10M per minute. Not every computer has 10M of RAM to spare for every minute of audio. By loading only a chunk of the file, Wave can manipulate files of any size—an important requirement if you are using large files in a business presentation, for example. Even if you have a 10-minute stereo recording you want to use as a "bed" under an entire presentation, you can fade in and out and cross-fade voice-overs without worrying about running out of memory.

Figure 2.37 shows the opening screen for Wave for Windows. The bottom two-thirds of the window displays the sound waveform, whereas the top portion displays icons and information windows. A number of the waveform editing and analysis functions are found on the **T**ools menu, but the most commonly used functions are icons, such as the Play and Record icons. The Play icon plays the sound—a single click plays the currently displayed portion of the sound, and a double click plays the entire sound.

---

[27]I am curious to know which will happen first—will Sound Forge add features to rival those of Wave, or will Wave improve it's interface to rival Sound Forge? If you are in the market for sound-editing software, make sure you check the current state of affairs before choosing one program over the other.

Playback icon   Recording icon

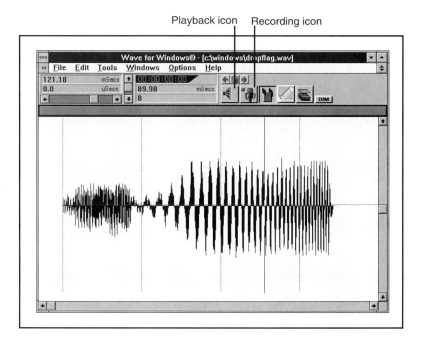

Figure 2.37. *The opening screen of Wave for Windows.*

To record a sound, click the Record icon. The default viewing mode is Display mode, but at higher magnifications you can edit the sound directly in Edit mode. The icon that looks like a stack of papers cycles backward through the most recent views of the file (as many as eight). If you click the Record icon, the dialog box in Figure 2.38 opens. Wave for Windows gives you complete control over the recording process, letting you select sample rates, bit resolution, stereo or mono recording, and more.

To record, you use the buttons in the middle of the dialog box. They operate like the buttons of a tape recorder. You also have access to many other controls in the Record dialog, including the ability to set the sampling rate, channels, and bit resolution. The level meters at the right of the dialog box enable you to monitor input levels—if the clipping indicators light up, stop recording and start over.[28]

---

[28]Clipping describes what happens when the incoming signal is too high, or "hot." If the level is too hot, it will overload your equipment. This is especially bad with digital recording—this means that all of the sounds that are too hot will have the same digital value, which is whatever number represents the highest value available. This is where the term "clipping" comes from. The lost data is "clipped" right off the top.

When you are finished recording a sound, click the Done button. The wave-form for the sound is displayed in the main Wave window (Figure 2.39).

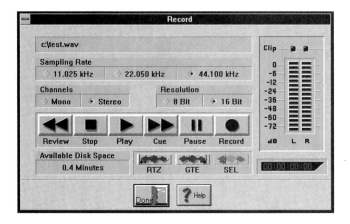

Figure 2.38. *The Record dialog box in Wave for Windows.*

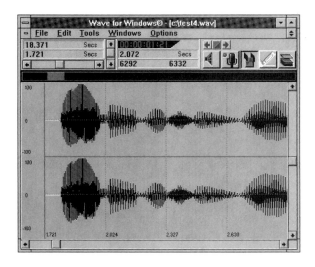

Figure 2.39. *A sample waveform opened in Wave for Windows.*

This wave is an overview of the sound. To select a smaller or larger view of the waveform, drag the mouse along the dark bar above the waveform window.

To select an area of the waveform as shown in Figure 2.40, click and drag the mouse anywhere along the waveform. The selected portion of the sound appears in a contrasting color.

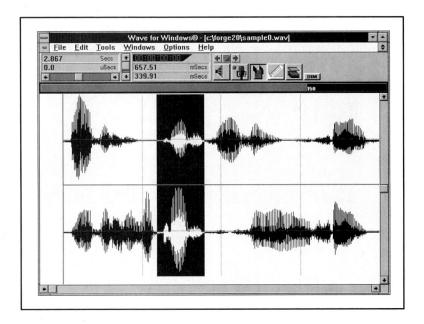

Figure 2.40. *Selecting a small portion of the sound file.*

A closer view of the selected portion of the sound reveals more of the details in its wave structure (Figure 2.41).[29] This shows about one-third of a second from the sound file; the time values are located at the bottom of the waveform window.

If you continue to zoom in, you can see the finest detail in the sound. At this stage, you can also directly edit the sound by using the cursor like a pencil. Figure 2.42 shows a very tiny fraction of a second from the sound file.

When a portion of the sound is selected, you still have the option to apply edits to the complete file. For example, when you choose Equalize from the **T**ools menu, the dialog box in Figure 2.43 appears.

---

[29]Unlike Sound Forge, which enables you to zoom the selected portion of the sound, I had to mess around quite a bit with the mouse to get the selected portion of the sound to fill the window in Wave for Windows.

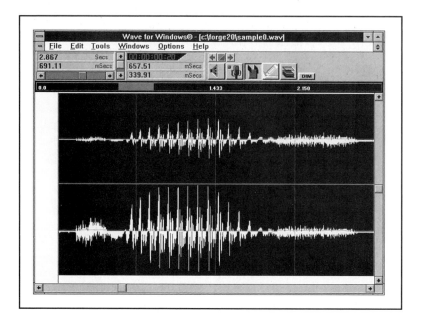

Figure 2.41. *Selecting an even smaller portion of the sound file.*

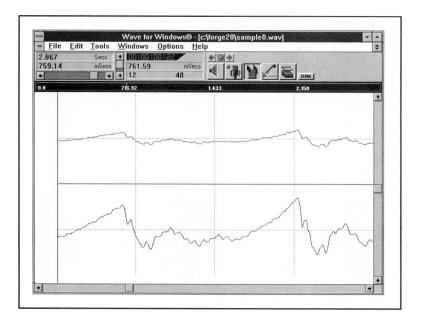

Figure 2.42. *Viewing a very small portion of a sound file.*

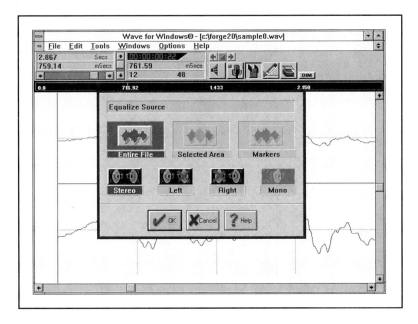

Figure 2.43. *The Equalize Source dialog box contains edit options.*

You can apply the edit to the entire file, the selected area, or, if you've applied any markers to the file, the portion of sound between the markers. You can apply the edit to the stereo signal or to the left or right channels individually.[30]

Clicking the OK button takes you directly to the Equalization dialog box shown in Figure 2.44.

Equalization is a process that enables you to adjust the amplitude of various frequencies in the waveform. For example, if someone speaks too close to the microphone, the sound might have too much bass. Using the equalization tool, you can reduce the amplitude (loudness) of the low frequencies and leave everything else intact. In Figure 2.44, two equalization effects are being applied.[31] The two octaves around the frequency 574 Hz are being boosted by 3 decibels, and

---

[30]This addresses at least partially the ability of Sound Forge to select a single stereo channel directly. However, I personally prefer the method used by Sound Forge over Wave's "after the fact" method.

[31]You can do up to four at one time.

the half-octave around the frequency 3870 Hz is being reduced by 6 decibels.[32] Equalization is a very sophisticated operation and requires a fairly deep knowledge of what kinds of sounds occur at what frequencies.

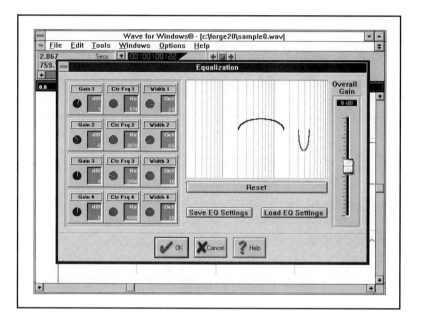

Figure 2.44. *The Equalization dialog box.*

Voice Recognition

Since the first edition of this book was printed, several companies have introduced new software products capable of limited voice recognition. The most common use of such products involves speaking into a microphone to make your computer do stuff. In almost all cases when the software recognizes some key word or phrase, it sends a sequence of keystrokes to an application.

---

[32]The decibel is used to measure sound levels. A change of +3 decibels doubles the apparent loudness of a sound, and a change of –3 decibels halves it. The decibel scale is logarithmic, which means that small numeric changes result in large apparent changes. For those who are interested, a decibel is defined as "equal to 20 times the common logarithm of the ratio of the pressure produced by the sound wave to a reference pressure, usually 0.0002 microbar."

InCube Demo Software

One of the more interesting software programs is InCube. The main window is shown in Figure 2.45.

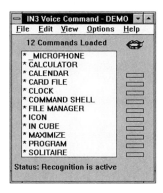

Figure 2.45. *The main window of InCube, a voice recognition program.*

In operation, InCube is simplicity itself. You speak into the microphone, and when InCube recognizes a key word or phrase, the associated action occurs. The rectangular boxes at the right of the window compose a level meter, and they blink in response to sounds. If only one or two boxes light up, the sound level is too low, and you should move closer to the microphone. If you haven't already installed the demo version of InCube from the floppy disk, you may want to do that now and follow along. You need a sound card and a microphone to run the demo.

To run the InCube demo, double-click the file name (IN3DEMO.EXE).[33] This displays the main window of InCube. Unlike the version shown in Figure 2.45, you won't see any asterisks to the left of the key words. An asterisk indicates that the key word is available for use. Before that can happen, you have to train InCube to your voice.

Click the Edit|Build Template menu selection. This displays the Build Templates dialog box. The first time you run the demo, you should see the Create and All radio buttons selected as shown in Figure 2.46. Make sure your microphone is turned on and correctly connected to your sound card. To start building a template, click the Begin button.

---

[33]The installation program decompresses the ZIP file that comes on the floppy disk.

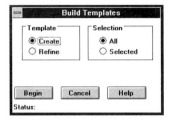

Figure 2.46. The Build Templates dialog box.

InCube prompts you with the words you should say as shown in Figure 2.47.[34] Just do what InCube says, and you'll be ready to test drive it in no time.

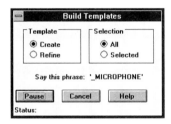

Figure 2.47. InCube prompts you to speak into the microphone.

Several things can go wrong, but InCube warns you if anything goes awry. For example, Figure 2.48 shows one kind of error message you might encounter: "Timeout: Check Mic/Audio." If you wait too long without speaking or if your microphone isn't connected properly, InCube will tell you it can't hear anything.

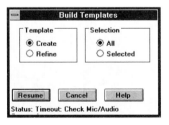

Figure 2.48. An error message from InCube.

---

[34]In the real version, of course, you can set up whatever words you need for your own purposes.

If you are too far from the microphone or if the input level of the microphone isn't set correctly, InCube displays the message shown in Figure 2.49: "Audio Input Level Is Too Low." To correct the problem, you should speak with your mouth about six inches from the microphone or check the input level using whatever utility shipped with your sound card.

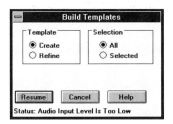

Figure 2.49. *InCube showing a problem with sound levels.*

Once you have said the requested word or phrase one time, InCube asks you to say it again as shown in Figure 2.50.

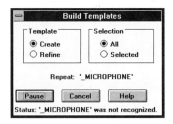

Figure 2.50. *InCube prompts you to repeat the key word.*

If you change your manner of speaking from the first time to the second time, InCube may complain as shown in Figure 2.51.

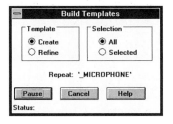

Figure 2.51. *InCube didn't like the way you said the word.*

85

Whenever InCube encounters a problem during training, you can click the Pause button to stop and remedy the situation. Then you can click Resume when you have corrected the problem. If you are following along with the demo now, you should simply continue speaking words as prompted by InCube. After you speak each word twice, InCube prompts you to speak each word one more time. After you have spoken all of the words, InCube will tell you (verbally) when it is ready, and then you can test it by speaking any of the available words. If InCube is working properly, an action results from each word and phrase that you say. For example, if you say "calculator" into the microphone, the Calculator application starts up. If it is already running, it becomes active.

If you purchase the retail version of InCube, you can create your own commands using the dialog box shown in Figure 2.52. You give each command a name; the name is the word or phrase you'll speak to cause InCube to carry out the command. The Keystrokes box can include other things in addition to keystrokes, such as the window class name (Figure 2.52). You can use the Window Class button to select a window, and InCube will determine what the class is for you.

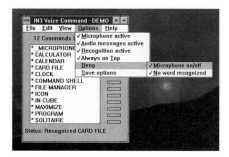

Figure 2.52. *Creating new commands.*

The View By Commands dialog box in Figure 2.53 enables you to view the current commands and the keystrokes that carry them out. The ICON command, for example, corresponds to the keystrokes {Alt}{Space}N, which activates the control menu of a window and minimizes it.

InCube offers a variety of options as shown in Figure 2.54. You can toggle the microphone on and off, and you can also turn off audio messages (after the first 14 seconds, the audio messages become quite oppressive). You can also make the InCube window stay on top of all other windows. This is handy because InCube displays a status message when it finds a match for the spoken key word. If the InCube window is on top, you can easily verify what's going on. For example, at the bottom of the InCube window in Figure 2.54, you can see the comment "Status: Recognized CARD FILE."

Figure 2.53. *Viewing commands with InCube.*

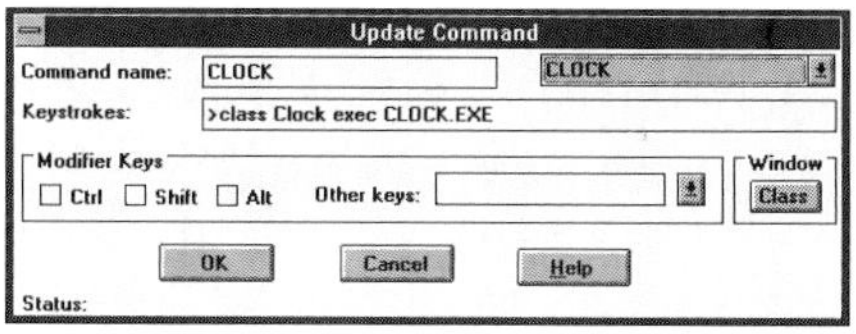

Figure 2.54. *InCube options.*

Comments About InCube

I really liked InCube. I have used several different voice recognition packages, and InCube was friendlier than many of them. It also worked very well, with some minor distractions.

But first, the good news. InCube recognized my speaking of a key word or phrase nearly 100 percent of the time. And it was able to do so even under adverse conditions. It could deal with the sound of typing (and I type very loudly!), and it could deal with my being a bit far from the microphone (up to two feet, instead of the ideal six inches).

It did have one problem, though. If I said a phrase that was close to one of the memorized phrases, InCube tended to treat it as the real phrase. For example, one of the phrases in the demo version is "Card file," which opens the Windows Card File application. I found that if I said "card smile," InCube would be fooled.

It would not be hard to watch yourself and avoid similar phrases for your commands. Because most of us do not talk a whole lot right in front of our computers, it is also unlikely that you will accidentally trigger a command. If you take a phone call or talk to a co-worker, you can easily toggle InCube on and off. I didn't feel that this problem was anything major, but it does show right where the limits of the technology are.

I highly recommend InCube as an alternative input method. It is especially useful for those situations where you are using the mouse and don't want to have to go to the keyboard for one little thing. It is also great fun—I like telling my computer what to do!

OLE and Sounds

OLE (Object Linking and Embedding) is a great feature of Windows 3.1. With OLE, you can make pictures and sounds into objects and then embed them in a file. Linking and embedding are similar concepts, but they work in different ways.

If you *link* an object, there is one copy of the object. The document with the link has only a reference to the linked object, not the object itself. If some other program makes a change to the object, the change is reflected in your program. If you *embed* an object, you place the data for the object into your document. You can use another program to edit, play, or display the data, but once you close the document, no other program can modify the object. The best way to explain this process is to show an example.

Creating an Object

In your Accessories group, there's an icon labeled Object Packager. This inelegantly named application is quite powerful—you can use it to package sound files and place them into spreadsheets, documents, and other files. Currently, this program does not work with all applications; you have to experiment to discover the files and applications it does work with. You should have the best success with applications that support Windows 3.1.

> **Very Important Note:** Many Windows 3.1 applications support OLE on their own; you do not need to use Object Packager to embed objects in such applications. You can simply Edit|Copy in the source document, and Edit|Paste in the destination.

> In addition, Microsoft has introduced a new version of OLE that has begun appearing in some software. It is even more powerful, but it will be some time before it becomes common.

Let's take a sound and embed it in an application file. If you recorded a sound earlier, you can use that file. If you didn't, you can use any wave file. For example, you can embed the sound in a Windows Write document. Open the Windows Write program by clicking its icon in the Accessories group. Open an existing file or create a new one by typing some text. Position the cursor where you want to embed the sound file.

Here's the procedure for embedding the sound file:

1. Go to the Accessories group and double-click the Object Packager icon (Figure 2.55).

Figure 2.55. *The Object Packager icon.*

The Object Packager screen is divided into two parts (Figure 2.56). The left part is called the Appearance window, and the right part is called the Content window.

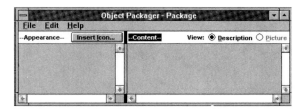

Figure 2.56. *The Object Packager screen.*

2. Select Import from the **F**ile menu. In the Import dialog box, select a .WAV file. If you didn't create a .WAV file earlier, pick any .WAV file you have handy. There are several in the Windows directory, as well as the .WAV files that came with *Whoop It Up!* The icon of the application used to create the imported file is now displayed in the Appearance window; in your case, this is the Sound Recorder icon. The name of the file appears in the Content window as shown in Figure 2.57.

Figure 2.57. *Importing a file with the Object Packager.*

3. Now select Copy Package from the **E**dit menu of the Object Packager
(Figure 2.58). This copies the object to the Windows clipboard.

Figure 2.58. *Selecting Copy Package from the Edit menu.*

4. Return to the document you created in Windows Write.

> The application you are placing the object into must be a client
> application, that is, "an application that is capable of accepting
> embedded objects." I lifted that circular definition from the Object
> Packager help file. What it is really saying is that not all applications
> accept embedded objects, and it is up to you to be careful.

5. Select **P**aste from the **E**dit menu of Windows Write. The package appears
as an icon in the document (Figure 2.59).

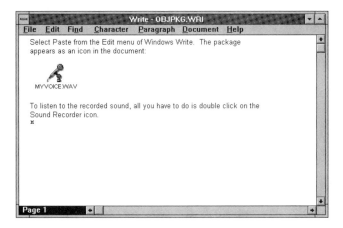

Figure 2.59. *The object has been embedded in a document.*

6. To listen to the recorded sound, double-click the Sound Recorder icon. You also can select Activate Contents from the **E**dit menu if the object is highlighted. To edit the object, select Package Object from the **E**dit menu; from the cascading menu, select Edit Package (Figure 2.60).

This takes you back to the Object Packager. Double-click the name of the file in the Contents window; this calls up the Sound Editor. You can modify the sound, but you cannot choose a different file to embed. You can only change files by using the Object Packager; you must import a different file.

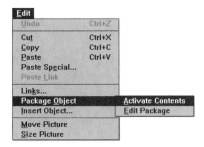

Figure 2.60. *Selecting Activate Contents plays the embedded sound.*

The Object Packager has other features. For example, you can use the button, Insert icon, to change the icon that appears in your document. You also can embed DOS commands. The Help files for Object Packager are well written, and you shouldn't have any difficulty putting sounds or other objects into your documents. When you exit Object Packager, the changes you made are saved in the embedded object.

An Editorial Comment

When I was working on this example, my son was sitting in the office and looking through a book of clip art. When I double-clicked the icon to play the recording of my voice, he was surprised and looked up. It occurred to me that the mental link between a document on the screen and a paper document might someday be gone forever. Looking at a Windows Write file with its sound icon, I realized there is nothing like it in the world of paper documents. I suddenly knew that someday, somewhere, someone will push the idea of document so far that we'll lose the connection entirely. There is always a place for paper, but I think something entirely new is in the making, and you are witnessing the beginning of that process.

Fun Sounds on the CD-ROM

A wide variety of sounds is included on the CD-ROM. Check them out; there are many .WAV and .MID files in various directories. Just run the Nautilus software to begin exploring the discs, or see Appendix B, "A Guide to the CD-ROM," for information.

I also have provided a number of shareware programs on the floppy disk that you can use to manipulate or edit sound files. These programs include WinJammer, for editing and playing back MIDI files; WaveEdit, for editing wave files; a demo of the InCube voice recognition software; the WaveS shareware demo; and Makin' Waves, for converting a variety of sound formats to .WAV files.

Sights to Behold

R emember the old saying, "A picture is worth a thousand words"? The phrase is just as true for computers.[1]

Imagine that you are writing a memo intended to persuade the boss to implement your new idea for widget production. If she's not familiar with how widgets are made, convincing her will be tough—unless you can include a picture of the new widget-builder right in your memo.

Although you might not think of images alone as multimedia, digital images have become an important part of multimedia as a result of the explosion of inexpensive sophisticated image-related hardware and software.

One of the biggest reasons for this change is the low cost of high-resolution video cards. You can purchase a video card with 1024x768 resolution and 256 colors for a little more than $100. Several years ago, I bought a (now discontinued) NEC Multisync Graphics Engine card with a Texas Instruments graphics coprocessor for almost $900. At the time, it was hot and fast technology. Now, it can barely keep up with low-end video cards. If you spend a little more—a few hundred dollars—you can buy a video card with hardware acceleration of Windows graphics. Such low prices mean just one thing: the days of high resolution are here to stay. You can run most multimedia programs at the lower resolutions, but the advantages of higher resolutions make a strong case for an upgrade.

Another major improvement in image technology for personal computers is the growing popularity (and shrinking price) of cards that support large numbers of colors. VGA started out with 16 colors, and the (affordable) high end once consisted of 256-color cards. Now you can purchase cards that support as many as 16.7 million colors, although not always at the higher resolutions, for less than $200.

---

[1]Of course, the ancients had neither video, movies, or animation, so they were unable to estimate the value of *motion* pictures. If I were so bold as to wax philosophical, I would point out that pictures gain their value from being closer to real experience than words, and that moving pictures come closer still to experience. For example, consider the value of being able to hold up a part from a complex machine to a video camera, and showing someone at a distant site how to insert the part—instead of having to describe the process. In such cases, moving pictures may well nigh be priceless because no amount of verbiage can explain something so complex. Perhaps we need merely revise the medium of exchange to find the value of motion pictures. Let's see, at 30 frames per second for video, a thousand pictures is a thousand frames is about 33 seconds of video.

These cards often are called 24-bit cards. To create 256 colors, you need one byte (8 bits).[2] Thus a 256-color card is also called an 8-bit card. You can also use 16 bits (two bytes) to display colors, and many cards do. Sixteen bits is the middle road for color—lots of bits for lots of colors, but not so many as to slow things down or drive up prices. You can get about 65,000 colors with a 16-bit card.[3] There is a general trend toward 24-bit (three bytes) cards, and a number of inexpensive 24-bit cards are hitting the market.

The least expensive 24-bit cards typically support only 24 bits in the low resolutions, like 640x480. It takes a great deal of memory to support 16.7 million colors at 1024x768,[4] and cards that can display 24-bit color at that resolution are often still fairly expensive (prices start around a thousand dollars, but that number is falling). The big issue with 24-bit cards is performance. It takes real horsepower to shove all those bits around, and horsepower—in the form of high-powered silicon on the graphics card—costs money.

With these facts firmly in mind, we can turn to the process of working with images on your computer. There are three basic steps involved in using images on a computer:

1. Acquiring an image

2. Modifying the image

3. Incorporating the image into a document, presentation, or program

Acquiring an Image

There are many ways to acquire an image. Some of them are easy, and some are more challenging:

➤ clip art

➤ scanned images

---

[2] One byte, consisting as it does of 8 bits, can hold 2 to the 8th power different values—256. Each bit doubles the range of possible values.

[3] To be exact, that's 2 to the 16th power colors, or 65,536.

[4] With 24 bits, the number of colors is exactly 2 to the 24th power, or 16,777,216.

➤ free images

➤ do-it-yourself images

Clip Art

There are many sources of clip art, with the quality ranging from useless to good. Some clip art is oriented toward the desktop publishing industry and is not particularly suitable for multimedia. This kind of clip art often is only available in black and white. Although the amount of color clip art is growing, the images are available in file formats, such as EPS (encapsulated PostScript), best suited for desktop publishing.[5] This is changing as multimedia art becomes a stronger market.

Check out some of the images on the *Multimedia Madness* CD-ROMs. Appendix B, "The Demo Treasure Chest CD-ROM," provides the details on contents. You can use the high-resolution images in your own multimedia creations. Figures 3.1 and 3.2 show two sample images from the CDs.[6]

I used Adobe Photoshop, an image editing program, to modify these two images. I then imported them into Toolbook, a multimedia authoring package, to create the sample application shown in Figure 3.3.

---

[5]The most common form of image file used in desktop publishing is the encapsulated postscript file, often simply called an EPS file. You can use such an image in multimedia, but most of the time you will need some method for converting the file to one of the formats commonly used in multimedia such as .pcx, .tif, or .bmp.

[6]Both of these images were originally found on regular issues of Nautilus CD, a monthly magazine that is published on CD-ROM. The folks at Nautilus (especially Steve Luper, a really great guy) prepared one of the CDs you'll find accompanying this book. Please note that these images are only for personal use; they cannot be used commercially without permission.

Figure 3.1. *A sample image of rocks under water from the CD.*

Figure 3.2. *A sample image of a boat from the CD.*

The picture of the boat was cropped, but was otherwise unchanged. The image of wet rocks was lightened considerably to make it a useful background.

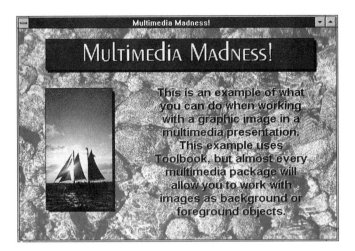

Figure 3.3. *A sample application using images from the CD.*

Scanned Images

Scanned images come in two varieties: those you scan and those someone else scans. These always are pixel-based images, available in file formats like .TIF, .PCX, and .BMP (bitmaps). The quality can be quite good if care is taken during the scan and if at least 256 colors are used. For best results, scan with the maximum number of colors and then convert to 256 colors.[7] Scanner software doesn't necessarily make the best choice of which 256 colors to use for a palette.[8] Software such

---

[7]For example, I have used a Hewlett Packard IIc scanner for several years, and I always scan color documents using 24-bit color. I then use Adobe Photoshop or Aldus PhotoStyler to convert to 8-bit color most of the time. Normally, you want to use whatever software you have that gives you the best quality color reduction. Each software package has its own way of making the decision about how to combine colors, and you should find the one that give you the best results for your tastes and needs.

[8]Palettes are something you only have to deal with when you use 256-color (8-bit) video displays. The current palette consists of 256 colors, but those colors can be any from a selection of more than 16 million colors. Thus, if one image uses palette A, to display another image with palette B, the current palette colors must change. After the change, image B will look right, but image A is now being shown with palette B—not pretty. Palettes are nice only if you display one image at a time. This is the primary limitation when working with 8-bit video—and it explains why I am a big fan of 16- and 24-bit video, where palettes are never used, and you can display as many images at one time as you desire.

as Aldus PhotoStyler or Adobe Photoshop gives you control over the final palette. Choosing the wrong colors can ruin an otherwise good image.[9]

If you scan your own materials, don't settle for anything less than a flatbed scanner if at all possible. Hand scanners are cute and useful in a pinch, but they don't cut it when you have many images, large images, or a critical image. It takes time and careful effort to get a good, hand-held scan. Unless you have a steady hand, you might have difficulty getting the results you want. The cost differential is pretty high, however—you can purchase a good color hand scanner for less than $500, whereas a good flatbed scanner is more than $1,000.

I define a "good" scanner as one that does the following:

➤ Scans at least 400 dots per inch (dpi)

➤ Supports 24-bit color (giving you up to 16.7 million colors)

➤ Scans at least a full 8.5 x 11 inch page in one pass

➤ Is supported by popular paint programs[10]

Many flatbed scanners have optional sheet feeders that enable you to scan multiple images without putting each sheet into the scanner. Sheet feeders are great when you have to scan large amounts of text, but when scanning images you normally will scan one page at a time. Each image usually requires some tweaking to be just right, so automating scans of images isn't usually profitable.

I use a Hewlett Packard ScanJet IIc. It scans as many as 400 dots per inch (dpi) in formats ranging from black-and-white to 24-bit color. It has done a great job for me, and I recommend it highly. I love the scanning software included with the unit, as well as the quality of the scans. Most of the time, I click the auto-exposure button and then scan to disk. Microtek also makes a highly regarded scanner. I haven't used it personally, but the reports are good. It comes with an excellent software package for editing scanned images.

There are other good scanners, and you can find more information about them in Chapter 12. A good flatbed scanner is an investment; expect to spend more than a $1,000 for a competent unit.

---

[9]There are two common problems from poor color reduction. One: excessive and obvious dithering, which loses detail in the image and makes it look grainy. Two: incorrect color substitution, which is even worse because the colors shift during the reduction.

[10]The best form of support is the TWAIN protocol. If your scanner supports TWAIN, most popular packages will be able to use your scanner.

Scanning raises the issue of copyright. If you scan images yourself, you are legally limited to images that are not copyrighted. Such images include anything in the public domain (images with expired copyrights and images never copyrighted), anything you create yourself, or anything you pay to have created. There is not much decent, non-copyrighted material available; most good images are owned by someone. There is a growing body of shareware images; some are included on the CD-ROMs.

The price of copyrighted scanned images can be steep because the copyright owner receives a fee. In general, you get what you pay for. The inexpensive images are often of poor quality, the expensive images are great, and there are all kinds of images in the middle. Currently, the best images are intended for commercial use; magazines, for example, pay steep fees for the images they use. There is some slow movement toward making these kinds of images available for more general use. This lowers costs. If more people use (pay for) an image, the per-use cost decreases as vendors compete for a share of the market.

Free Images

Free images come from a variety of sources, and the quality of the images ranges from worth-what-you-paid-for-it to exceptional. Many software products with a CD-ROM disk include an amazing amount of free images. Two multimedia titles from Asymetrix, Multimedia Make Your Point and MediaBlitz, include several disks—one for the actual software, and two or three full of compressed images, sounds, and animations. In addition, many products now come with a CD-ROM disc packed with images. In most cases, there are no serious restrictions on how you can use sample files. As a result, you can use them in everything from screen savers to business presentations.[11]

CompuServe is another source of multimedia images. A number of forums have images you can download and use. Some of the files are distributed as free images; others come with restrictions. Forums to check out include MULTIMEDIA, GRAPHICS (includes a number of related forums), and PHOTOFORUM. To move to a particular forum on CompuServe, type GO, then the name of the forum.

---

[11]In one case—the CD-ROM that comes with 3D Studio—there are some restrictions, but only on some of the files. Some of the examples that are included on the CD-ROM were supplied by real companies in the real world, and are only intended as examples of what can be done with 3D Studio. Those particular images may not be copied or reused; they are only there as a source of ideas and techniques.

Do-It-Yourself Images

Do-it-yourself images are the hardest to create, of course. If you are an artist, you may do quite well. If you're not, the latest drawing packages make it easier than ever for amateurs to produce high-quality artwork. Later in this chapter, I'll show you how to create an original image using Fractal Design Painter, a powerful and versatile drawing package.[12]

There are many image-editing packages available for creating original digital artwork, but these packages are used more frequently to modify or customize existing images such as clip art and scanned images. My favorite bitmap-editing program is Adobe Photoshop. It doesn't do absolutely everything, so I do recommend having a second image editor handy if you are really serious about your image editing. For most uses, however, Photoshop is all you will need. Photoshop is in a league of its own when it comes to editing photo-realistic images; that's why it's one of the Author's Choice packages for this chapter.[13]

I don't rely on a single image-editing program, however. Both PhotoStyler and CorelDRAW! are still on my hard disk. CorelDRAW! traditionally has been a program oriented toward desktop publishing. However, the latest version (4.0) can import most of the common bitmapped image formats—TIF, TGA, BMP, PCX. This feature makes it an excellent choice for anyone familiar with vector drawing packages. (There are two kinds of drawing packages: vector and raster. See the section "File Formats" for a discussion of vector versus raster.) Another useful image-editing program is Publisher's Paintbrush from Z-Soft.

The Electronic Snapshot: Photo CD

The introduction of Kodak's Photo CD has had an interesting effect on the image market. While Photo CD was intended primarily as a consumer product, it has many professional uses as well. Photo CD is just what it sounds like: it puts your conventional photographs on a CD and displays them either on a computer

---

[12]Many of these "drawing" packages can also be used to edit images that are scanned or purchased. You can perform simple changes—lighten an image, add a portion of a second image, etc. You also can do some amazingly sophisticated things using these packages, both for original art and modifying existing art.

[13]In the first edition of this book, the Author's Choice was Aldus PhotoStyler. While PhotoStyler is a great package, Photoshop is even better. Photoshop is more complete, and somewhat easier to use and understand, so it gets the nod this time around.

monitor or on your TV.[14] Either way, you will need a special CD-ROM player to display the pictures. While the cost of players is high—more than $600 is common—the fact the CD-ROM drives in computers can read Photo CD discs has been an important factor. There has been a decided movement toward support for Photo CD in new CD-ROM drive designs.

Once your photos have been placed on a CD at any photo finisher that supports Photo CD, you can use the images in a variety of ways. The important thing is that you now have the images in digital form. For a variety of reasons, the technical nature of Photo CD insures high-quality images in a minimum of space. Kodak offers several software packages for viewing and editing Photo CD images, and most major players in the image editing game now support import of Photo CD images. If you have a CD-ROM drive that supports Photo CD, you can easily and cheaply convert your photographs into digital form for use in multimedia work or play.

The bottom line is that Photo CD is much cheaper than having your images professionally scanned, yet the results can be used in all sort of publishing and multimedia applications. If you cannot afford a scanner, Photo CD offers a reasonable alternative.

Fractal Design Painter

Far and away the most interesting program for creating and editing images is Fractal Design Painter 2.0 from Fractal Design Corporation. It is definitely not just another paint program.

There have been dozens of paint programs available over the years, and they all have a similar interface: circles, squares, lines, colors, and fills. Fractal Design Painter enters a different dimension. The first time I used it, nothing worked the way I expected it to work. My first mistake was to expect the usual kinds of art-program elements, such as lines and circles. I was staring at a screen of brush

---

[14]You must, of course, have a CD player that can handle Photo CD disks. Most, but not all, CD-ROM drives made since the beginning of 1993 support Photo CD to some degree. Some drives support multiple session Photo CD; such drives can read all images on a CD even if they were not all put there in a single session. Others, and some older drives, support single-session Photo CD; such drives will only read the first Photo CD images put onto the CD. A session consists of all photos burned onto the CD in a single, continuous stream.

profiles, paper textures, and variables such as Hard Grainy Cover and Wet Variant. Clearly, I was in a strange new world.[15]

I finally turned to the manual, which is quite brief but to the point. As I turned each page, I felt tingles of excitement. I realized that this program is different. Usually, different is spelled d-e-a-t-h. The days are gone forever when a program can strike out in a new direction, right? Wrong. The people at Fractal Design Corporation have come up with a new way to create and edit digital images.

Fractal Design Painter doesn't do everything that conventional paint programs do, but it is easy to augment it with a traditional paint package. Fractal Design Painter is too important to dismiss just because it's missing a few conventional painting features!

Because Fractal Design Painter is so different, it's worth a moment to look at the way that the program presents itself. In fact, we'll be taking a fairly detailed and extensive tour of Painter. Figure 3.4 shows the opening screen of the program. A working model of Painter is provided on one of the CD-ROM discs. If you install the working model to your hard disk, you can follow along with the examples.

There are three smaller windows within the Painter window:

Toolbox—Allows you to select the active tool. Traditional drawing tools are on the left; *frisket*[16] tools are on the right.

Brush Palette—Allows you to select from among the various brushes—pencils, pens, crayons, chalk—there is a very large variety of brush types.

Color Palette—Used for selecting the current color. The palette is multipaged—you can keep related colors on a page, and flip to other pages as required.

---

[15]From my comments, you might assume that Fractal Design Painter is hard to use or hard to learn. Not so. I was merely stunned by how different it was from a traditional paint package. Actually, Fractal Design Painter is a lot like real-world drawing and painting—you'll work with pencils and brushes and erasers that behave amazingly like their counterparts. The key to getting up to speed with Fractal Design Painter is understanding how it implements each real-world object.

[16]A frisket is a sophisticated tool for masking. You can have one or many friskets active at one time, allowing you to have tight control over the image as you draw, paint, or manipulate the image.

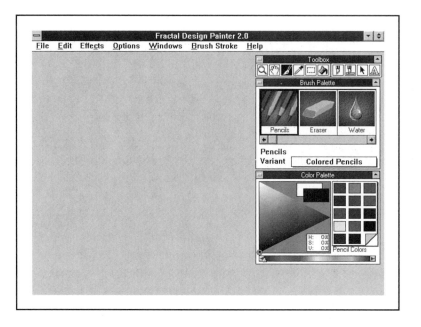

Figure 3.4. *The opening window of Fractal Design Painter*

When you open a document, it appears in a window of it's own; you can have more than one image document open at a time. Figure 3.5 shows an image from the CD-ROM that accompanies my book *Virtual Reality Madness,* opened in Fractal Design Painter.[17] The image is supplied on the CD-ROM. If you are following along at home, use the File/Open menu selection to load the file. During this section, you will learn how to manipulate an existing image to create various special effects.

Although Painter has many interesting drawing tools, it also has some excellent effects that you can apply to existing images. Figure 3.6 shows the effects menu—not that there are sub-menus for virtually all of the effects.

---

[17]This image is of a city that doesn't exist. It was created in 3D Studio, from one of the sample files supplied on the CD-ROM that comes with 3D Studio. It is one of many images created with various 3D and virtual reality programs, and included on the *Virtual Reality Madness* CD.

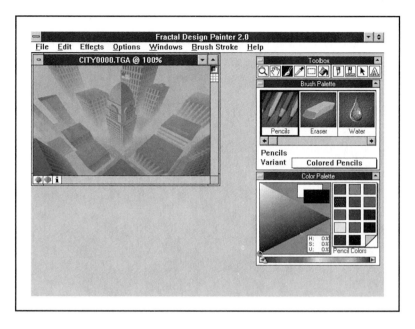

Figure 3.5. *Each document is opened in its own window.*

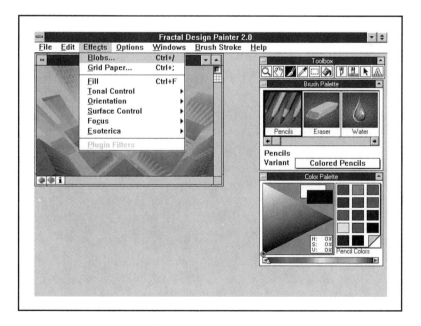

Figure 3.6. *The Effects menu selections.*

One of the more interesting effects is available under the Surface Control selection: surface texture. Figure 3.7 shows the dialog box for applying a surface texture.

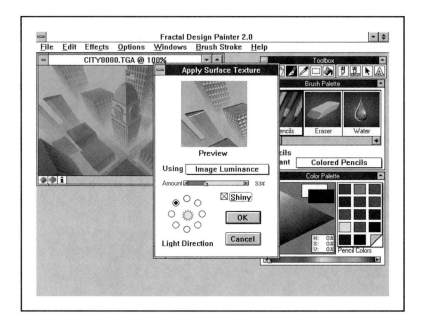

Figure 3.7. *The Apply Surface Texture dialog box.*

In this example, the brightness (image luminance) of the image itself is being used to create texture. The amount of texture applied is determined by the slider at the middle of the dialog box. In this case, the amount is 33%. The Shiny checkbox has been clicked, telling Painter to apply bright highlights to the texture. The light direction chosen is from the upper left, as shown by the graphic at the lower left of the dialog box. The upper portion of the dialog box shows a preview of the effect.[18]

Figure 3.8 shows the effect of adding surface texture based on the image luminance.

---

[18]I didn't like the shininess in this case. In later figures, you may note that the highlights are not shiny.

Figure 3.8. *Surface texture based on image luminance.*

There are a number of other options for controlling surface texture, as shown in Figure 3.9. We'll look at some of these options later.

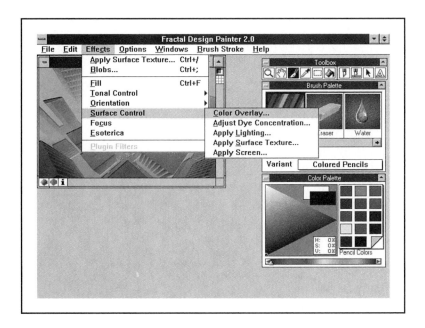

Figure 3.9. *The other surface control options.*

At this point, I thought the image looked a little dull.[19] The Effects/Tonal Control sub-menu offers a wide variety of options for modifying the image (see Figure 3.10).

---

[19]In technical terms, the image lacks good contrast.

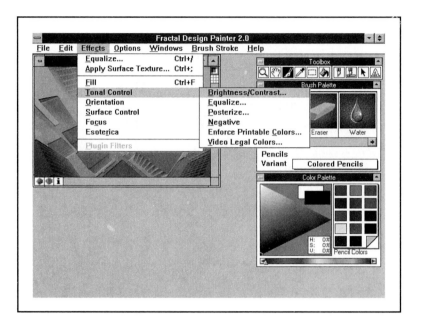

Figure 3.10. *Options for modifying image tone.*

A quick way to get good contrast is to equalize the shades in the image. Figure 3.11 shows the Equalize dialog box. The box at the top shows a histogram of the shades in use. Note that there is one shade, toward the white end (on the right), that predominates. Note also that there are no really black blacks, and even fewer really white whites. To equalize the image, Painter will spread out the shades toward both ends, and spread out the peak shown in Figure 3.11.

The result of our work so far is shown in Figure 3.12.

Let's apply a second surface texture—paper grain. One of the really neat features of Painter is that it lets you select from a large library of paper grains. There are many traditional papers that you can use for basic work, and a large number of unique, interesting papers that can be used for special effects. Figure 3.13 shows the default paper grain being applied to the image. Note the realistic appearance of the paper grain in the preview.

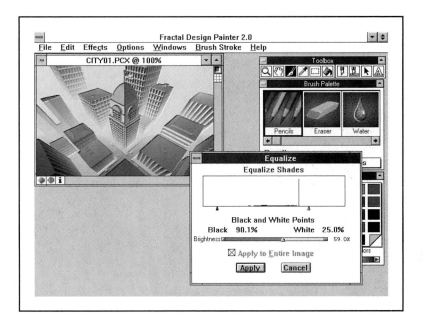

Figure 3.11. *The Equalize dialog box.*

Figure 3.12. *The shades in the image have been equalized.*

The result of adding paper texture is shown in Figure 3.14.

We now have an image that would be at home in any multimedia presentation. Figure 3.15 shows the figure in use for the monthly reports of the city of Metropolis.

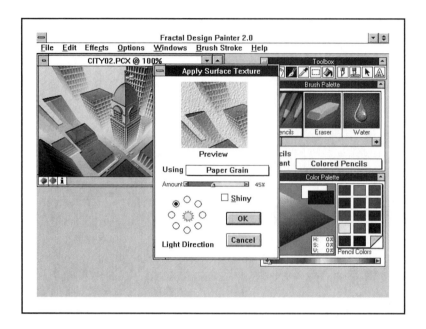

Figure 3.13. *Applying paper grain as a surface texture.*

Figure 3.14. *Paper texture added to the image.*

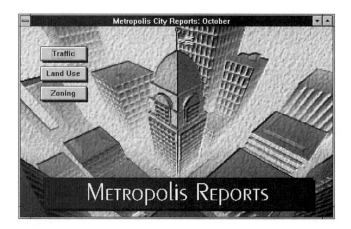

Figure 3.15. *The image of Figure 3.14 used as a background.*

We could continue to modify the image in Painter. Figure 3.16 shows the image with a soft pastel look, created using Painter's cloning abilities. With cloning, you can apply a painting method to an image automatically, or one stroke at a time. In this case, the pastel look has completely replaced the textures, and provided a dreamy, foggy appearance.

Figure 3.16. *A pastel look for the city image.*

Softening, dimming, lightening, and related techniques can be used to make any image into an unobtrusive background. Figure 3.17 shows the softened version of the image used in the Metropolis report program.

111

Figure 3.17. *The image of Figure 3.16 used as a background.*

Painter provides a large set of tools to use to create interesting variations of an image. Figure 3.18 shows a version of the image with noise added, with a high degree of contrast. Figure 3.19 shows the same image, but with softening added through cloning techniques.

Figure 3.18. *Noise and contrast added to the image.*

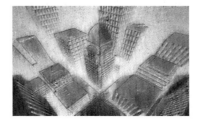

Figure 3.19. *The image of Figure 3.18 softened with auto cloning.*

So far, you have been learning about various effects that can be applied to an entire image. This is a great way to get started with Painter, but there is much more available to work with than just effects. You can also create original art with Painter. Creating art involves using the brushes. Brushes include all kinds of things, from pens and pencils to water color brushes and charcoal (see Figure 3.20).

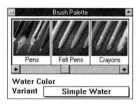

Figure 3.20. *A few of the brushes available in Painter.*

In Fractal Design Painter, each brush has variants; some have a few, and some have many. The variants usually correspond to real-world drawing or painting tools. For example, if you choose Brushes[20] instead of Pencils, you can choose a hairy brush, a Japanese brush, or another variant. The Eraser has variants ranging from Micro to Fat. The Brush Palette has a list of Methods you can use for each variant.

All this sounds complicated, and it is until you get used to it. The methods give you complete control over your brush, enabling you to simulate almost any painting tool (or create your own from scratch). While you are learning to use Fractal Design Painter, you can use the default variants and methods.

Buildup is just one of the basic methods. When you use the *Buildup Method,* you literally build up colors, one on top of another. When you put a color on top of another color, the colors get darker as a result of the layering.

If you use the *Cover Method,* colors simply cover each other; the color on top is the only one visible. Color values stay constant. There are also methods for the edges of strokes. Flat edges have fixed edges; boundaries between colors or between colors and paper are hard and sharply defined. Soft edges have smooth, gradual boundaries. Hard edges are neither as sharp as flat edges nor as smooth as soft edges; they lie somewhere between these two extremes. There are other

---

[20]Yes, it is confusing to call all painting tools brushes, and then to have a brush called Brushes, but there it is.

factors involved in methods. For example, a brush sensitive to paper texture is called Grainy. You also can specify Wet or Dry methods.

You can combine these methods in a variety of ways. For example, Soft Buildup mimics the behavior of felt tip pens. Grainy Soft Buildup behaves like a pencil. Grainy Wet Buildup mimics a watercolor brush—the pigment pools at the edges of the stroke and the brush "loses" pigment as the stroke lengthens.

If you think Fractal Design Painter works much like traditional drawing and painting, you are right. Even after using it for hours, it's hard to put the program away. The program is amazing.

Fractal Design Painter also comes with additional libraries of brushes, and you can create your own. You do not have to stick with traditional brush types— you can invent "impossible" kinds of brushes by varying the characteristics of the brush. For example, Figure 3.21 shows a window where you can specify the size of the brush.

Figure 3.21. *The Brush Size dialog box.*

The large circle shows the overall size of the brush, and the shapes to the left are profiles of various kinds of brush tips. Each tip has a unique process of putting colors on paper. By clicking your mouse anywhere in the Size slider, you can change the size of the brush. The slider marked "±Size" can be used with a pressure-sensitive stylus for expression in your brush stroke. The inner black circle indicates the size of the brush under minimum pressure, and the outer circle indicates the size of the brush under maximum pressure.[21]

---

[21]Conveniently, Painter allows you to set the pressure scaling every time you start the program. This allows you to take your natural stroke into account on any given day—a little more one day, a little less another day.

Because the brush is the basic tool you will work with in Painter, there are many levels of control over its behavior. In addition to the size and methods described above, there are three dialog boxes that control brush behavior. You can use these dialogs to establish exactly the characteristics you want in a brush.

Figure 3.22 shows the Brush Behavior dialog box. There are nine sliders that control various parameters. For example, by increasing the Dab Location Variability, you can create a brush with an irregular stroke. The controls for Brush Paint Reservoir control how long a stroke you can make before "running out of paint."

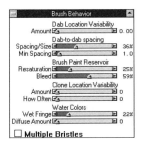

Figure 3.22. *The Brush Behavior dialog box.*

Figure 3.23 shows the Expression Palette dialog box. This dialog is used to determine which brush movements control which brush characteristics. For example, the pressure you use on the stylus normally controls the size of the brush, but you could just as well use the horizontal velocity of the brush to determine size changes. You can even change such things as color and penetration with pressure, direction, velocity, etc.

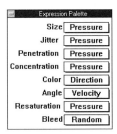

Figure 3.23. *The Expression Palette dialog box.*

You can also go for a custom look for your brush, as shown in Figure 3.24. The sponge, for example, is commonly used as a brush in water color, while the erase cloud allows you to softly alter existing "pigment."

Figure 3.24. *The Brush Looks dialog box.*

Pressure-Sensitive Stylus for Drawing

When I called the folks at Fractal Design Painter to ask for a copy of the program, they suggested that I get a digitizing tablet with a pressure-sensitive drawing stylus to use with the program. I got one, I used it, and I fell in love with the device. I use it instead of my mouse for everything in Windows. The model I work with is from Calcomp: the Drawing Board II with a cordless, pressure-sensitive stylus. A pressure-sensitive stylus looks like any common pen—it has a point and a little clip so you can put it in your pocket. It also has a small button you click like a mouse button. If you press the pen down hard enough, the point clicks, too.

The stylus comes with a digitizing tablet—a flat, plastic-coated board with some electronics inside to communicate with the stylus. The tablet connects to the PC's serial port. Tablets range in size from six by nine inches to the size of a table. For most uses, the little tablets do the job and they don't take up too much desk real estate. Architects, draftsmen, and cartographers use the larger tablets to create drawings. I used a 12 inch square tablet, which I find ideal for artwork. That's large for the average desk, and the smaller sizes work well, too, if you are low on available space.

When I press the stylus on the tablet, a small transmitter in the stylus sends a signal to the tablet. This enables the tablet to determine the location of the stylus. As I move the stylus on the tablet, the Windows cursor moves on the screen. Pressing down on the stylus is the same as clicking the left mouse button. If you click a little button near the tip, it is the same as a double-click. You also can double-click with the tip of the stylus, but the little button is much easier.

At first it was awkward to use the stylus, but I noticed it didn't tire my hand like using the mouse does. I hold the stylus the way I hold a pen or pencil, which is less stressful than clutching a mouse. I recommend the stylus for the lack of finger fatigue. Once I got the hang of it, I began using the stylus with Fractal Design Painter. The tip of the stylus is pressure sensitive—it can detect whether I am pressing down on the tablet softly or really bearing down. A special Windows driver passes this information on to Fractal Design Painter, and the program varies the width of my strokes depending on the instantaneous pressure. Pressure sensitivity works only with programs that specifically support it.

A tablet and pressure-sensitive stylus cost considerably more than a mouse (see Chapter 12 of the Shopper's Guide), but if you work regularly with a mouse, you should consider a stylus as an investment in the health of your hands. There is a tendency to clutch the mouse even when you aren't moving it. The stylus is just like a pen, and you tend to put it down when you don't need it. When I have to work at a computer with a mouse, I notice the mouse-clutching problem almost immediately. I also no longer have a problem with tendonitis in my right hand.

If you plan to use Fractal Design Painter, a pressure-sensitive stylus takes you to a completely different level of fun and power. You can buy several different kinds of styluses. Some come with a cord, and others are cordless; some are pressure sensitive, and others aren't.

There are a number of other windows available in Painter, such as the Toolbox (Figure 3.25). There aren't a whole lot of tools in the toolbox—just the basic icons you may be familiar with from simpler paint programs.[22] You can change zoom,

---

[22]On the Macintosh, that is—these icons may be more familiar to you if you have some background with Mac paint programs.

move the image within a window, activate the current brush, select colors or portions of the image, do fills, etc.

Figure 3.25. *The Fractal Design Painter Toolbox.*

Fractal Design Painter also gives you access to colors through a palette (Figure 3.26).

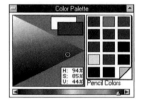

Figure 3.26. *The Color Palette.*

You can select any color (or hue) with the color bar at the bottom, and then select various levels of saturation and value with the color triangle above it. You also can select from default colors in the boxes at the right.

One of the nicest features of Fractal Design Painter is the ability to select a paper texture. There is a complete paper palette, shown in Figure 3.27. Painter comes with a number of paper texture libraries, ranging from watercolor to canvas to rice paper to the completely bizarre for those occasions when nothing short of madness will do.

Figure 3.27. *A variety of paper styles are available.*

There are two ways to use paper texture. If you select a texture in the paper palette, all brush operations use that texture; the effect is instantaneous. You also can apply the texture to an existing drawing. If a brush is sensitive to texture, you see the bumps and hills as you paint. If the brush has a high penetration factor, the color "soaks" through the texture to the bottom. Figure 3.28 shows a variety of brushes on a paper texture. Charcoal and chalk show the texture clearly, while most of the other brushes—felt pen, air brush, water color brush—show hardly any texture at all.

Figure 3.28. *Various brushes showing and hiding paper texture.*

With light pressure, the charcoal sticks only to the peaks of the paper; you can make out the underlying texture in the figure. The effect varies according to the amount of pressure you apply. You get a swath of charcoal equivalent to the hand pressure on the paper fibers.

Fractal Design Painter is full of interesting and powerful dialog boxes. For example, even when all you want to do is a fill, you have many interesting options. Figure 3.29 shows the Fill Palette dialog box. It shows three of the many options available for filling—contiguous filling, filling just the selection, or filling an area marked by a frisket.[23]

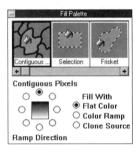

Figure 3.29. *The Fill Palette dialog box.*

Let's take a look at how easy it is to create artwork in Painter. Figure 3.30 shows a painting of a rhubarb plant dating from the 1700's. For this example (and to make my life a little easier), I placed the image under the transparent sheet of the CalComp Drawing Board II, and traced it in Painter. Before tracing, I created a small calligraphy pen.[24]

Figure 3.31 shows the result after just a few minutes of sketching. There were two phases in the drawing process. The first phase involved focusing on the original artwork on the drawing tablet. The second phase involved minor touch-up work focusing on the computer screen.

To add a little spice to the drawing, I added a color background as shown in Figure 3.32. It's not quite as nice in black and white[25].

---

[23]A frisket is similar to a selection area, but much more powerful.

[24]To create the pen, I first selected pens, and then chose the variant Calligraphy pen. The size was much too large for a pen and ink drawing, so I simply shrunk it to a workable size.

[25]This was accomplished using friskets. I used Painter's very powerful Magic Wand to make a frisket of just the black portions of the drawing, and then placed the background outside the frisket.

Figure 3.30. *A classical illustration of a rhubarb plant.*

Rhubarbarum

Figure 3.31. *A drawing created in Fractal Design Painter.*

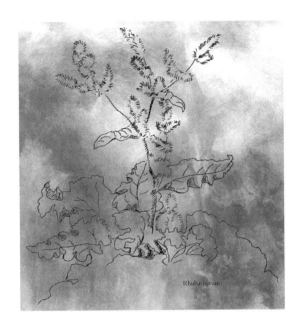

Figure 3.32. *A background added to the drawing.*

I wasn't quite satisfied with the results. I thought that the drawing itself was nice, but the background took something away. However, I liked the background, so I decided to see if I could use Painter to make the drawing portion of the image stand out better against the background. My first thought was to darken the leaves a bit. Figure 3.33 shows the selection area of just the leaf, copied and then pasted into a new window. This wasn't necessary, but I wanted to use another image editor, Photoshop. We'll explore Photoshop in detail later in this chapter, but it was ideal for this operation, so I switched to using it. Consider this a sneak preview.

Figure 3.33. *Pasting the selection into a new window.*

Figure 3.34 shows the Variations dialog in Photoshop. It allows you to alter the color or tone of an image while viewing all of the possibilities at one time. It is enormously clever, and extremely useful. I clicked several times on the Darker image and the More Green image to generate the result shown in Figure 3.35. My intent was to darken, and make more green, the background colors showing through the leaf. This would make the leaf darker and more realistic, while re-taining a sense of transparency by showing the background texture "through" the leaf.

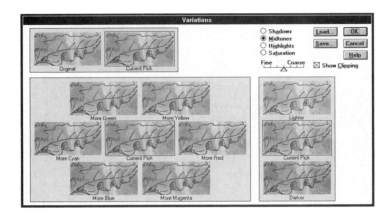

Figure 3.34. *The Variations dialog in Photoshop.*

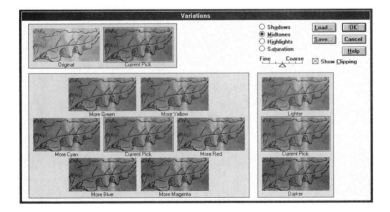

Figure 3.35. *A darker, greener, selection.*

Figure 3.36 shows the actual darkened selection. Compare it to Figure 3.33.

Figure 3.36. *The darkened selection.*

The darkened selection could now be pasted back into the original image, as shown in Figure 3.37.

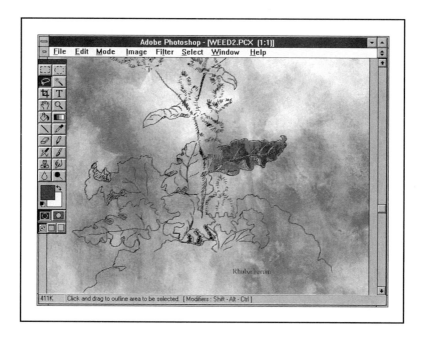

Figure 3.37. *A darkened leaf.*

Figure 3.38 shows a second leaf darkened. This process would then be applied to all of the other leaves to create an interesting and subtle illustration. To learn more about Photoshop, see the next section of this chapter.

Figure 3.38. *Another darkened leaf.*

Adobe Photoshop

When Adobe released a Windows edition of their long-time Mac program Photoshop, a collective sigh went up from all of us PC fanatics who worked with images. Photoshop is the cream of the crop when it comes to image editing. The program doesn't have every single feature you could want, but it has a huge number of useful features, and most of them are both accessible and well designed.

The opening window of Photoshop is shown in Figure 3.39. For such a powerful program, Photoshop has a pretty simply interface. There's a menu at the top, and a toolbox at the left.

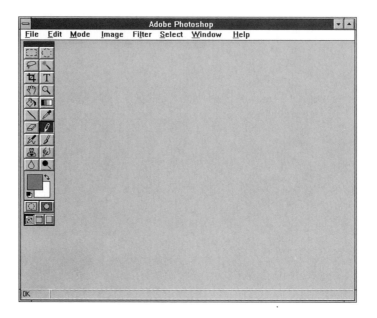

Figure 3.39. *The opening window of Photoshop.*

 Don't be fooled by the simple appearance of Photoshop. Every tool, every menu selection, has hidden depths than can be most useful when you are editing an image and need something to be just exactly right.

Just for fun, after I captured the opening screen of Photoshop, I loaded the bitmap file into Photoshop (see Figure 3.40). Each image is opened in a window, and you can have multiple image windows open at one time.

Photoshop is a deep and powerful program. Rather than try to give you a superficial view of all of the various tools, I'm going to show you what it's like to actually work with Photoshop. I've created a little project—putting my dog Sparky on the moon. There are three base images that will be used to create the final image: the file s1.bmp was captured from a videotape of Sparky playing fetch in our driveway;[26] the file fulerth8.bmp is a shot of the earth from space (from NASA), and the file flag8.bmp shows an astronaut on the moon, and is also from NASA.

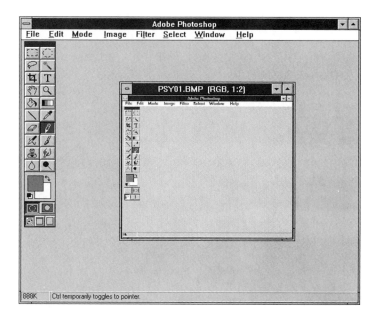

Figure 3.40. *Photoshop with an image of itself opened.*

The goal of this exercise is to put Sparky into the moon image, with the earth in his mouth—just as though he were playing fetch with the astronaut. We will begin with the image of Sparky. The first task is to isolate just Sparky's image, eliminating the background.

Photoshop has a tool called a magic wand—the icon for it even looks like a magic wand. Its purpose is to select areas of similar color. To tell the magic wand how similar a color must be to be included in a selection, you double-click the magic wand tool to display the dialog box shown in Figure 3.41.

The higher the Tolerance number, the larger the selection area will be. I chose a setting of 96 to start with, and then clicked OK. I then clicked on Sparky, and let the magic wand attempt to find the pixels similar to the one I clicked. Figure 3.42 shows the result. The dotted line marks the extent of the selection.

---

[26]The image was captured with the VideoLogic Captivator, and is of excellent quality. The ability of the Captivator to capture still video images outclasses all other cards in its class.

Figure 3.41. *The Magic Wand Options.*

Figure 3.42. *The selection area created with the Magic Wand.*

As you can see, the selection is a bit too much in some areas—it has selected some portions of the background in the area underneath Sparky's tail. Note also that the lighter areas—Sparky's feet and the tip of his tail—are not part of the selection. With Photoshop, it's easy to add to and subtract from the selection. However, what I actually did was change the Tolerance setting to 80, and reselect. This solved the extra selection area near the tail. I then used the Shift+Magic Wand to add the white portions of Sparky to the selection. The result is shown in Figure 3.43. Note that the paws and tail tip are now part of the selection, and that there is less slop around the edges of the tail and shadow.

Figure 3.43. *A slightly different selection area.*

When I went back to change the Tolerance to 80, I also clicked the Anti-alias checkbox in the Magic Wand Options. This has the effect of softening the edge of the selection.[27] It is very important to watch the edges of material pasted into existing images—differences in color, texture, and value can cause serious visual problems at the edges of objects if you are not careful.

Figure 3.44 shows the result of pasting the selection into a new image document. Note that the edges are slightly blended into the background. Note also that there is a small fringe around Sparky, and that we have copied his shadow as well as his image. All of these will be dealt with later in this demonstration.

Note also that Sparky's mouth is incomplete—to say the least! The missing portions do not need to be dealt with now. When I put the earth/ball in Sparky's mouth, I can touch up the rough edges.

---

[27]Later, in the PhotoStyler demonstration, you'll see a different way of dealing with edge problems.

Figure 3.44. *Pasting Sparky into a blank image.*

The next problem to deal with is the size of Sparky's image. It's about the same size as the entire man-on-the-moon image. Figure 3.45 shows the dialog box for changing image size. The width of the image is 626 pixels; I changed it to 200 pixels—about one-third. Because the Proportion checkbox is marked, the Height of the image will be automatically adjusted to keep the same overall proportions in the image.[28]

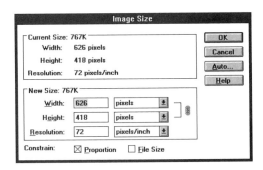

Figure 3.45. *Changing image size.*

---

[28]You can also change the proportions to alter the appearance of the image. Just click the Proportion box to turn it off, and then enter the desired Width and Height values.

Figure 3.46 shows the reduced image. Despite the fact that we have drastically shrunk the image, the quality of the image is quite good. Photoshop does a great job at changing image size without losing the overall appearance of the image.

Figure 3.46. *The reduced image.*

Let's consider the lighting in the image of Sparky and the image of the man-on-the-moon. In Sparky's case, the light is coming from the right. In the man-on-the-moon's case, it's coming from the left. This is easy to deal with—simply do a Horizontal Flip of Sparky's image (see Figure 3.47).

Figure 3.47. *Sparky's image has been flipped horizontally.*

Now we are ready to put Sparky's image into the moon image. To reselect just Sparky (we have no use for the white background), use the Magic Wand tool with a Tolerance setting of 1. Click on the white background to select it, and then use the Select/Invert menu choice to invert the selection. Edit/Copy to copy Sparky to the clipboard, and then Edit/Paste him into the moon image (see Figure 3.48).

Figure 3.48. *Sparky has arrived on the moon.*

Things aren't quite right, however. For one thing, Sparky's image is darker than the moon image—he stands out as obviously not a native. In addition, there is a bit of a white line around him—that's the anti-aliasing coming back to bite us. Sparky's shadow also isn't right—it doesn't match the other shadows. Figure 3.49 shows a close-up of the problems—we have more work to do.

Figure 3.49. *A close-up of the problem areas.*

The moon image appears coarser than Sparky's image. We can change Sparky's image to match using the Posterize command. The Posterize dialog box is shown in Figure 3.50.

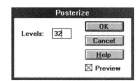

Figure 3.50. *Posterizing Sparky.*

Posterizing reduces the number of colors in an image—in this case, from 256 to 32. Among other things, this makes an image appear grainier or coarser. Figure 3.51 shows the result.

Figure 3.51. *Sparky is now more grainy, and matches better.*

But the match is still imperfect. Even after posterizing, Sparky's image still has more gradual shading than the moon image. Increasing the contrast of Sparky's image will reduce the gradual shading. The result is shown in Figure 3.52.

FLAG8B.BMP (RGB, 1:1)

Figure 3.52. *Increasing the contrast of Sparky's image.*

We still have that light fringe around Sparky. The Select/Defringe menu choice can be used here. Figure 3.53 shows the Defringe dialog—you need merely specify the number of edge pixels to remove (1 or 2 usually does the trick; more than that, and the image edge begins to look stretched). Figure 3.54 shows the results.

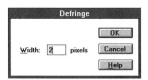

Figure 3.53. *Defringe dialog box.*

The shadow area under Sparky is now a problem (see Figure 3.55). It is much too light.

Figure 3.54. *Sparky's fringe is gone.*

Figure 3.55. *The shadow under Sparky is too light.*

The Brightness/Contrast controls are perfect for darkening the shadow. I set Brightness at -60 to significantly darken the shadow, and the result is shown in Figure 3.56.

Now that Sparky fits into the picture, we need the earth ball to put into his mouth. Figure 3.57 shows the image of the full earth. I used the circle selection tool to select just the planet portion of the image.

Figure 3.56. *Sparky's shadow matches the other shadows now.*

Figure 3.57. *The full earth image.*

I then pasted the image into a new document, and shrunk it to be just a little bigger than Sparky's head (see Figure 3.58). This is an extreme reduction, so much detail is lost. Note that the selection area omits a portion of the planet image at the upper left—this is where Sparky's mouth will cover part of the planet.

Figure 3.58. *The shrunken planet.*

To complete the demonstration, I used Edit/Copy to copy the earth image to the clipboard, and Edit/Paste to place it into the moon/Sparky image. Figure 3.59 shows the result.

Figure 3.59. *Sparky with the ball in his mouth.*

The ball stands out too much, so I selected the right-most portion and used the Brightness/Contrast controls to darken it (creating a shadow effect). Figure 3.60 shows the result.

Figure 3.60. *A shadow has been added to the ball.*

Sparky is now a full-fledged moon dog!

This exercise shows only a small fragment of the full power of Photoshop. Later in this chapter, in the section Image Effects, I have included some examples of how Photoshop can be used to create fascinating special effects.

Aldus PhotoStyler

PhotoStyler was the author's choice in the first edition of *Multimedia Madness*. It's a few bytes short of the absolute nirvana of Photoshop, but I still keep it on my hard disk because there are some things it does well. It lacks a few features found in Photoshop, but it packs enough of a wallop to be spotlighted in this chapter. For a fair comparison, I will use PhotoStyler to repeat the effect created with Photoshop: putting my dog Sparky on the moon.[29]

---

[29]Almost all of the capabilities in this example are also present in Photoshop, by the way.

Keep in mind that PhotoStyler is not cheap; it carries a price tag commensurate with its power. However, if you want any real control over your images and you must work quickly and efficiently, you have no choice but to go with one of the high-end, high-cost packages—Photoshop or PhotoStyler. It's futile to save a few hundred dollars on a cheaper package and then spend hour after hour trying[30] to make it do what you want. Sometimes you can succeed with a lot of time and effort, but many times you can't do what you want to do.

PhotoStyler is at its best when editing photo-realistic images, such as a scanned photograph. You also can use it to create original images, but the level of difficulty is higher than for Fractal Design Painter. It takes a steady hand and a great deal of patience to create an image from scratch.

PhotoStyler's strengths are its selection tools and image manipulation capabilities. It comes with a variety of selection tools. The obvious ones are there, such as squares, rectangles, circles, ellipses, and odd-shaped areas. PhotoStyler's neatest selection tool, however, is the Magic Wand tool. Its icon is even shaped like a magic wand (Figure 3.61). Its operation is similar to that of Photoshop.

 Figure 3.61. *The Magic Wand icon.*

To use the Magic Wand tool, click the cursor on a pixel and let the wand do its thing. It will look for, and select, pixels of similar color and/or brightness. You can control the range of contiguous colors or grays it will select. For example, double-clicking on the icon brings up a dialog box that lets you select the range of similarity. The default is 64, but you can enter anything from 1 (only the same color) to 256 (every color). The tool examines each nearby pixel to see if it falls into the desired range. If the pixel does, it is included in the selection, and PhotoStyler now compares the pixels near the newly included pixel. If not, the tool moves on to the next nearby pixel. The process continues until there are no more contiguous pixels in the desired range.

With the wand tool, click the background of an image and wait until PhotoStyler determines which pixels are close enough in value to the one you clicked. For a typical image size on a 386/33 computer, this takes about 10 seconds. For faster computers, this time is less. PhotoStyler enables you to add or

---

[30]and failing...

subtract from a selection, and you can use the Magic Wand or any other selection tool to do so. It's easiest to show an example. Figure 3.62 shows a videotape image of my dog Sparky I captured with Truevision's Bravado board.

Figure 3.62. *A video scan of my dog Sparky.*

It's not hard to see that this is a video capture; you can see the video scan lines.[31] If they are not evident in the full-scale picture, they sure are when you enlarge the picture six times (Figure 3.63).

To reduce this effect somewhat, I applied a Gaussian blur to the image (Figure 3.64). A Gaussian blur uses randomization to blur, instead of just "smooshing" things around. It introduces random noise into the picture. This noise effectively hides small details such as scan lines while leaving the larger details clear.

Enlarging the figure shows that scan-line effects are now eliminated (Figure 3.65).

---

[31]They are the horizontal lines in the image. Different video capture boards will do a better or worse job of controlling the scan line effect. A brand new board at the time the second edition was being written, the Captivator from VideoLogic, does an outstanding job of eliminating the scan line effect in a captured video image.

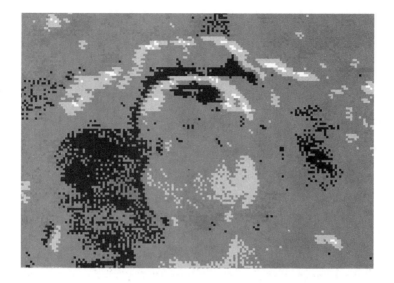

Figure 3.63. *Sparky is made up of scan lines.*

In addition, you can adjust the amount of Gaussian blur. I used a setting of 15 for this example; each image has its own best setting, and you can undo and redo until you get the right balance. Higher settings remove more detail; lower settings preserve more detail.

As you can see, the image background is rather blah; it has to go. I couldn't use the Magic Wand to select all the background area; the colors and values vary too much. I used the free selection tool to carefully mark the outline of Sparky's image. The icon is the traditional lasso (Figure 3.66).

To select Sparky's image, I adjusted the view to 2:1 to see more detail, then clicked various points on the boundary between Sparky and the background. When selecting an outline, you can afford to be picky—you can click hundreds of times to create a precise outline. The resulting selection area isn't perfect because the original was a video image; video is not a high-resolution imaging method. (Because video images move, you can accept a relatively low resolution and still get a reasonably clear picture of what you see. A still image, on the other hand, gives no motion clues and looks less sharp.)

Figure 3.64. *Sparky after a Gaussian blur.*

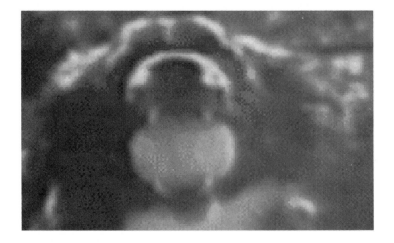

Figure 3.65. *Sparky, sans scan lines.*

 Figure 3.66. *The free selection tool icon.*

PhotoStyler indicates the selection area with a moving marquee (Figure 3.67).

Figure 3.67. *The marquee indicates the selection.*

This results in a selection area that includes only Sparky. Using the Edit menu, you can copy the image to the clipboard for temporary storage. I created a new image by pasting from the clipboard (a nifty capability shared by both PhotoStyler and Photoshop). The background color was set to white, so the new image looks like Figure 3.68.

I can reselect Sparky's image by clicking the Magic Wand tool on the white background. Of course, this selects the background, not Sparky, but PhotoStyler includes an Invert Selection button which quickly changes the selection from the background to Sparky. I can now insert Sparky's image on a different background— something more interesting. How about putting Sparky on the moon again? Go to the File menu and open another file. PhotoStyler lets you open as many files as will fit in available memory.

Fortunately, I just happened to have a picture of a man on the moon. (See Figure 3.69.)

143

Figure 3.68. *Sparky's captured image.*

The next step is to paste Sparky's image into the moon image. In this case, Sparky's image was as large as the entire moon image. PhotoStyler enables you to resample images; I reduced Sparky's image to about 35 percent of its original size. When I pasted Sparky's image into the moon image, it appeared at the top-left corner, surrounded by the selection marquee. Using a selection tool, I moved Sparky around in the moon image (Figure 3.70).

Figure 3.69. *Man on the moon.*

Figure 3.70. *Putting Sparky on the moon.*

Because the original image did not include the bottom portion of Sparky's rear legs, it seemed most appropriate to put him at the bottom of the moon image. The first thing I noticed was that Sparky's image is somewhat lighter (it has less contrast) than the background image. Something needs to be done to make the two images as close in brightness level as possible. PhotoStyler provides the perfect tool—Brightness & Contrast adjustment. Figure 3.71 shows the Brightness & Contrast dialog box.

Figure 3.71. *The Brightness & Contrast dialog box.*

The Brightness & Contrast dialog box contains slider controls for both brightness and contrast. Look closely at the right side of the dialog box. There is a box called Channel with four radio buttons. If the top button is selected, you are adjusting the brightness and contrast of all three color channels at once: red, green, and blue.

You also can elect to adjust the brightness and contrast of one channel at a time. For example, if the red component is too bright, you can reduce the brightness of the red in the image. For my purposes, it was sufficient to adjust all three colors at once. To make Sparky appear more like the background image, I wanted to increase the contrast of his image (Figure 3.72).

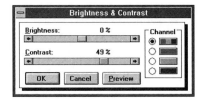

Figure 3.72. *Adjusting the contrast to 49 percent.*

When I clicked the close button, only Sparky's image darkened (Figure 3.73). Adjustments you make while a selection area is active only apply to the selection.

Figure 3.73. *Adding contrast to Sparky.*

Now there's another problem: Sparky's image stands out too harshly against the background—it's obviously not part of the original image. You can create a soft edge between the selection area and the background. This edge ranges from one to five pixels (Figure 3.74).

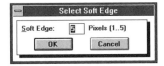

Figure 3.74. *The Select Soft Edge dialog box.*

Notice how the soft edge selection (Figure 3.75) has a different shape than the original selection (Figure 3.73).

The pixels at the boundary of the background and the selection have been altered so the image blends into the background. Some of the background pixels are now included in the selection, and some pixels from the selection are now part of the background. Everything looks fine, so it's time to "drop" Sparky onto the background by clearing the selection (there's a button for it on the Selection palette). (See Figure 3.76.)[32]

Figure 3.75. *Sparky sticks out a bit.*

---

[32]PhotoStyler and Photoshop handle this business of blending an image into an existing image differently, but the general result is similar.

Figure 3.76. *Sparky isn't highlighted anymore.*

Hmmm... He doesn't blend in all that well, does he? Although the soft edge command does blend the selection with the background, it is not a miracle tool—there are some highlights on the Sparky image that are too bright to blend in; these little white pixels stand out.[33] If you examine Sparky in detail, you see the exact nature of the problem (Figure 3.77).

The solution is the Blur tool. Its icon is shown in Figure 3.78.

If you double-click the Blur icon, you see a dialog box that presents the options for using the Blur tool (Figure 3.79).

You can blur all the pixels you touch or only the pixels that are lighter or darker than a color you choose. You can choose whether the blur is heavy, light, or medium. You also can select the shape of the Blur tool—round, square, or oblong, large or small. This gives you complete control over the process. Figure 3.80 shows the result of some careful blurring.

---

[33]This is one area where the Photoshop tools are more effective. If you recall, we were able to eliminate the edge pixels easily in Photoshop using the Defringe command.

Figure 3.77. *Sparky doesn't exactly blend in.*

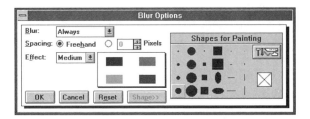

Figure 3.78. *The Blur tool icon.*

Figure 3.79. *The Blur Options dialog box.*

The bright pixels that stood out are now safely blended. Now display the entire image at its actual size, as shown in Figure 3.81.

Figure 3.80. *Blurring Sparky into the background.*

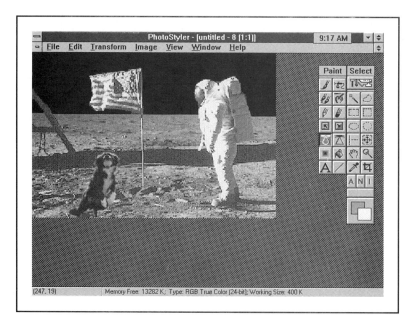

Figure 3.81. *Sparky, post-blending.*

Sparky is starting to look like a native moon dog, but there is still one problem—everything but Sparky casts a shadow. The solution is called the Clone tool. I used some of the existing shadows as a source for Sparky's shadow. The Clone icon is shown in Figure 3.82.[34]

 Figure 3.82. *The Clone icon.*

To use the Clone tool, hold down the Shift key and click the region you want to clone. You can adjust the size of the brush like you did for blurring. I "painted in" the cloned texture in the area where I wanted Sparky's shadow. With careful positioning, I cloned the slightly darker top edge characteristic of the shadow of the Lunar Module (Figure 3.83).

For comparison, look at the following screen capture. Notice the differences between the original image of Sparky and the final image of Sparky the Moon Dog (Figure 3.84).

Figure 3.83. *Giving Sparky a shadow.*

---

[34]The Clone tool is an extremely good reason to keep PhotoStyler around even if you have Photoshop as well.

Figure 3.84. *The final version of Sparky on the moon.*

This example shows only the beginning of the power of PhotoStyler. You can create separations, do blended fills, use any available system font, blur and sharpen selections, apply 2D and 3D special effects, adjust contrast, brightness, color balance—the list goes on. This is a package well worth your consideration.

Image Effects

Over the last year or so, there have been some significant advances in the use of computers for image manipulation. It has become relatively easy to create special image effects without needing to perform complex operations.

Fractal Design Painter is an example of total control over this process—Painter gives you a tremendous amount of raw power. With Painter, you can customize effects to an endless degree.

There are now products that will perform a subset of these operations automatically—Aldus Gallery Effects is a fine example of such a product. Image editing software, like Photoshop, is also beginning to offer interesting effect possibilities.

Aldus Gallery Effects

Aldus Gallery Effects allows you to create special effects in your images very easily. Even though it is easy to use, the results are actually quite spectacular. For example look at Figures 3.85 and 3.86, which show examples of the effects available. Figure 3.85 shows the effects in Volume 1 of Gallery Effects, and Figure 3.86 shows the effects in Volume 2.

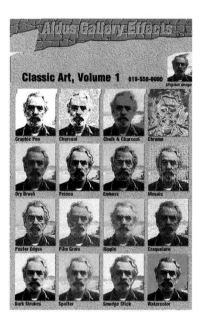

Figure 3.85. *Examples from Volume 1, Gallery Effects.*

Gallery Effects is easy to use. Figure 3.87 shows an original image—a man holding tulips. This image is taken from a scanned photograph.

Figure 3.88 shows the dialog box that is used to define the parameters of the effect. In this example, the effect is watercolor. There are three controls available for tailoring the effect:

Brush Detail—Controls the level of fine detail in the brush strokes.

Shadow Intensity—Controls how dark the shadows will be when the effect is applied.

Texture—Controls the level of brush texture in the final image.

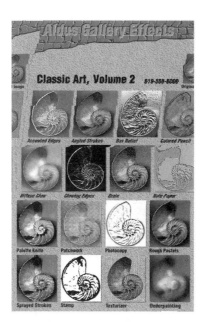

Figure 3.86. *Examples from Volume 2, Gallery Effects.*

Figure 3.87. *An original image, without effects.*

Figure 3.89 shows the results of applying the Watercolor effect.

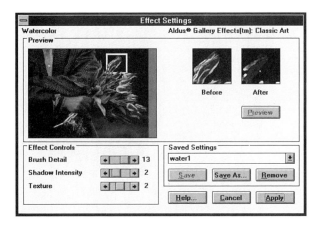

Figure 3.88. *A Gallery Effects dialog box.*

Figure 3.89. *The modified image with the Watercolor effect.*

I was very impressed with the capabilities of Aldus Gallery Effects. The quality of the resulting images was very high, and the variety of images (and their variations) was impressive. Figures 3.90 through 3.92 are, in effect, a gallery of Gallery Effects.[35]

---

[35]Puns absolutely intended.

Figure 3.90. *A carousel horse with a Chrome effect.*

Figure 3.91. *The watercolor effect on a face. The watercolor effect is especially good for adding interest to recognizable but plain images.*

Figure 3.92. *The colored pencil effect applied to an animal image.*

Photoshop Effects

Without question, Gallery Effects is a fun and easy way to add interest and excitement to your images. However, programs like Photoshop are actually quite capable of creating interesting effects on their own as well.

To illustrate, I will take a simple image of myself, and modify it in a variety of ways using only Photoshop. The base image, shown in Figure 3.93, is pretty bad looking—not only am I having a "bad hair day," but beard stubble is clearly evident. Only a fool such as myself would ever think of using such an image, unretouched, in a publication.

Fortunately, if this were the only image at hand, there are some useful and some bizarre things that can be done to enhance it in Photoshop. For example, I could use the Pointilize filter to transform the image into a painting in the style of Seurat, as shown in Figure 3.94. It's not very impressive in black and white, but in color the face shows clearly, but the blemishes (such as beard stubble) are gone.

Figure 3.93. *A useless, unretouched photo of the author on a bad day.*

Figure 3.94. *A pointilized version of the image.*

The Find Edges filter, shown in Figure 3.95, is another interesting approach to take. This reduces the image to its edges, which suggests some kind of Peter Max possibilities.[36]

Figure 3.95. *An image created with only the edges.*

You can also combine filters to create an image—even if some of the intermediate steps look like garbage. For example, to arrive at Figure 3.96, I first applied the Mosaic filter, which reduces the image to small single-color squares. I then applied the Find Edges filter.

This image is not very useful (at least in my opinion!), but if it is overlaid onto the original image using a dissolved paste, the results suggest a RoboCop-like author (see Figure 3.97). To achieve this effect, I used the Edit/Paste Controls menu choice to display a dialog that allows me to choose how much of each image will appear after pasting. I used about 70% of the underlying image, and 30% of the pasted image. After pasting, I used the Facets filter to soften the effect just a little bit, arriving at the result in Figure 3.97.

---

[36]Are you old enough to remember Peter Max? He was an artist popular in the '60s. His style used outlines and colors to suggest fantasy landscapes.

159

Figure 3.96. *A double-filtered variation of the author.*

Figure 3.97. *The combined image shows a little from both of its parents.*

You can take this process as far as you like. The pair of images in Figure 3.98 were manipulated in so many different ways that I lost track, but I thought they made an interesting, if bizarre, self-portrait.

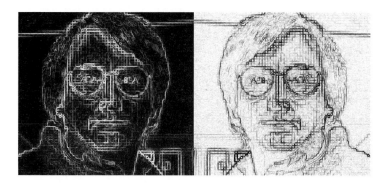

Figure 3.98. *A bizarre self-portrait of the author.*

Video Mode Advice

As you probably guessed from this chapter's spotlight sections, I'm a big fan of spending the money to do things right. When it comes to selecting (and paying for) the video mode you will use with Windows—especially for image editing—I have some strong opinions.

A Little Advice

Here's my philosophy: If you are going to buy something, determine which product will do everything you need at the lowest price. If you can find fifty-dollar software that does the job, buy it. If you need to spend $500 on software to get the job done right, buy that.

In other words, don't spend any more than you have to.

Don't settle for software, or hardware, that does less than what you need it to do. Beyond that, budget is a concern. Buying less than what you *need*, however, is a recipe for regret.

The minimum video mode for running Windows (let alone multimedia) is 800x600, a superVGA mode. This is a physical minimum. Any lower resolution makes your screen so crowded it's hard to enjoy the benefits of Windows. However, the additional cost of even higher resolutions is so minimal that you should strongly consider them.

You're not exactly crippled if you are working at 640x480, of course; everything still runs fine. Many programs, however—authoring, image manipulation, and similar programs—are easier to use at higher resolutions. Most importantly, you can display a larger portion of your current work file, giving you a more global point of view. This is an important advantage for many programs.

I have a laptop computer that runs Windows only in VGA (640x480) mode; it's a real pain. It's great to be so mobile, but I see only 15 lines of text! The window caption, rulers, status lines, etc. take up far too much room. On my regular machine,[37] I see 45 lines of text. I did buy a portable computer that enables me to use the higher resolutions when I'm not on the road. I can connect an external monitor to the portable and select either 800x600 or 1024x768 video (interlaced, unfortunately), so I'm compromised only while I'm on the road.

If you are not already familiar with the subject of interlaced monitors, allow me to explain:

In normal, non-interlaced mode, the image is "painted" onto the screen one line at a time, from top to bottom. This happens many times per second, so the image is relatively steady-looking. As long as the image is refreshed more often than you can detect by eye, your brain is fooled into seeing a steady image.

But it takes time to scan each line in the image. The more lines, the more time it takes. Interlacing offers a way to cut the number of lines scanned on each pass in half. On the first pass, all of the odd lines are scanned, leaving the even lines as they are. On the next pass, the even lines are scanned, and the odd lines are left alone. The problem with this technique is that it cuts the rate at which the screen is being refreshed in half, creating an obvious and annoying flicker.

I always have found interlaced displays just about impossible to use for more than an hour or so. If you have to, you can do it, but the flicker can easily create eyestrain and give you a headache.

---

[37] My regular machine normally runs at 1024x768, with 16-bit color. In a pinch, I can switch to 1280x1024 and 256 colors.

Ron's Rule Never run Windows at anything less than 800x600 resolution unless you are forced to by circumstances out of your control, such as wars, floods, and portable computers.

If there is any way to get yourself up to 1024x768 resolution (non-interlaced), do it. You won't regret it, and you don't have to spend very much. Street prices on 1024x768 boards are falling faster than the prices of any other peripherals. Monitor prices aren't falling as fast, but you can get a decent monitor at a reasonable price—about $400, and maybe a little less by the time you read this. I don't recommend buying the very cheapest monitors because the image quality is sometimes not adequate for regular use.

If you can afford it, buy one of the larger monitors (17 inches or larger). They cost a bundle, but they are much easier on the eyes. I initially settled for a 15-inch monitor (a Sony 1304). It worked well for me, although I did have to squint at times. Still, it was a good compromise; maybe being farsighted has something to do with it.

It wasn't until I picked up a Nanao 550i 17-inch monitor that I understood what the fuss over large monitors is all about. Not only does the monitor have a rock-steady, crisp image, but it also is much more pleasant to have somewhat larger text, icons, and images. If budget is a concern, you can get OK results with 1024x768 on a 15-inch monitor. If you will be using the monitor for long stretches, however, and you can afford it, you will find that the larger (and higher quality) monitors give you a net increase in your productivity. The reason is simple—you won't find yourself straining to see what's on-screen, and you can work for longer periods without strain. For complete information on recommended cards and monitors, see the Shopper's Guide later in the book.

Higher resolutions are important for Multimedia. If you haven't worked at the higher resolutions yet, you won't understand how important they are until you use one for a few days; after you do, you'll never go back without a fight. If you already have a high-resolution setup, you know what I'm talking about. Here are some of the advantages of the higher resolution setups.

Doing "Things" with All That Real Estate

The first thing you can do is take advantage of programs like Norton Desktop for Windows. For example, you can put many icons right on the desktop instead of leaving them buried in program groups. Icons on the desktop are ready for a double-click at a moment's notice.

This is Windows the way Windows was meant to be.

But wait—how many icons can you put on the desktop, anyway? Well, it depends. If you are running Windows at VGA resolution (heaven forbid), you can put maybe half a dozen icons on the desktop before it starts to become crowded. On my laptop, I keep five icons on the desktop; on my main machine, I keep about 30. From my perspective, both setups seem to use about the same amount of real estate. Because my main machine has a 500M hard drive and many programs to keep track of, the extra real estate makes program access manageable.

I can group the icons on my main machine according to how I work—desktop publishing, writing, fonts, image processing, and so on. If I use a program in two different areas, I have room to repeat the icon. This allows me to move quickly and easily from program to program.

More importantly, I have enough room so that I can run programs at less than full screen, and I still have the necessary icons immediately available. On the VGA screen, every application needs all the room available. (They need even more, realistically, but you can't use what isn't there.)

But the biggest advantage of acres and acres of screen real estate is that it gives you new ways of working under Windows. The power promised by overlapping windows does not become apparent until you work at the higher resolutions.

Image Editing at Lower Resolutions Is Not Possible

Even at the highest resolutions (1280x1024 and up), image editing is a challenge. You can never have enough room to edit a large, high-resolution image. Think about it: 300 dpi is a lot of pixels! Trying to edit one of these images at a low resolution is a nightmare.

Let's compare high- and low-resolution image editing. Figure 3.99 shows an image being edited at actual size in PhotoStyler (1024x768, 65,000 colors).

Figure 3.99. *High-resolution image editing.*

Figure 3.100. *Low-resolution image editing.*

Figure 3.100 shows the same size image on a VGA screen (640x480, 65,000 colors).

On the larger screen, almost the entire image can be viewed at one time. On the smaller screen, only a small portion of the image can be viewed—you would have to scroll around to look at various parts of the image.

Multitasking Demands Screen Real Estate

Ever since Windows was introduced, multitasking—the ability to run several program simultaneously—has been one of most talked-about features. Unless you have enough screen real estate available to manage all the windows involved in a multitasking session, however, you can get lost quickly.

For example, to create a multimedia presentation, you often use a number of programs. A typical session might include all of the following:

➤ scanner software

➤ image-editing software

➤ a secondary image editor for special effects

➤ a database program for tracking schedules and files

➤ a word processor or editor for composing text and keeping notes

➤ a presentation program

➤ a sound editor

➤ an image viewer

That's just a partial list. There are also little utilities floating around, such as screen-capture programs and calendar programs. If you don't have enough real estate available to sensibly arrange all those programs, how are you going to keep track of what you are doing and where you've put everything? If you don't have enough room, it might never occur to you to try some things that would be easy with enough screen space.

Ron's Rule   You can never have too much screen real estate.

Speaking of multitasking, this a good place to point out how I manage to keep track of the huge number of illustrations in each of the chapters in this book. Figure 3.101 shows a sample window of the program ImagePals from U-Lead

Systems. You can spot a number of the illustrations from this chapter—most of them are from the section on Fractal Design Painter.

Figure 3.101. *A typical ImagePals window.*

ImagePals made it easy to keep track of figures. It also is very handy for batch conversions. My screen capture program saves screens as bitmaps (.BMP files), and my publisher wants .PCX files. With ImagePals, I could convert all of the figures for a chapter at one time, which saved me an enormous amount of time. ImagePals will also print large numbers of images, which was invaluable for adding text to the images, and seeing how the color images would look in black and white.

WYSIWYG and Higher Resolutions

Many products such as word processors claim to offer WYSIWYG (What You See Is What You Get). Until you see such products on a high-resolution monitor, however, you haven't really seen what you're getting. For example, I installed Adobe Type Manager on my laptop with the VGA screen. I hardly noticed a difference! The pixels are still so big that the characters still suffer from the *jaggies*—no amount of smoothing can get rid of the jagged edges. On the other hand, when I put Type Manager on the main machine at 1024x768, the difference was stunning. My wife now can lay out a flyer for a garage sale knowing that her printout will match the screen representation.

The Eyes Have It

A good monitor at high resolution is much easier on the eyes. I used a Sony 1304 monitor for two years, and I now use a Nanao 550i. With both monitors, I can stare at the screen all day. There are a number of other excellent cards and monitors, and all of them are well worth the cost. However: the larger Nanao is easier on the eyes, because everything is larger—icons, text, images, etc.

A low-resolution screen is inherently harder on the eyes because of the inevitable jaggies. I used to get headaches from working at the computer; I thought I would have to find another way to write until I invested in a top-quality monitor. If for no other reason than comfort, get a high-resolution setup!

Price/Performance Ratio

The price of a good high-resolution video display board has fallen to the point where it is difficult to justify not buying one. Even products that tack on video support as an afterthought, such as cards that output to VCRs, are including support for 1024x768.

High-resolution video brings you peace, prosperity, and the *real* Windows product you've always wanted. I wouldn't settle for anything less than 1024x768, with Windows acceleration built into the video card, and a monitor that's rock-steady with brilliant colors and sharp definition. You should be able to purchase that kind of setup for less than $600.

Don't settle for anything less than a 256-color board. If you plan to view or create video, nothing less than 16-bit color will do the job really well. Of course, you can now buy 24-bit (16.7 million colors) video boards for less than $200. A good example is Diamond's Speedstar 24x, which I installed recently in the kids' machine; it works great and the installation for Windows is easy.

File Formats

There are many file formats for images, each with its own reason for being. You don't have to know much about what is in the file formats unless you plan to write programs that read and write them. When the time comes to choose formats, or when you have to deal with a new format, it is useful to have some background information about the formats. The most common file formats include the following.

PCX

This format has been around for a long time, but it is becoming less common. Many changes have been made to keep the PCX format up to date—including adding more colors and higher resolutions—but more modern formats are replacing it anyway. Although support for this format is common, it should not be taken for granted when you use a given software package. It is not one of the formats supported by default in Windows, and some Windows software does not support it.

TIFF (Tagged Image File Format)

This format has been around for some time, but the latest versions of the specification make it a capable format. This file format is common in the desktop publishing world, and almost all software packages support it. The most recent versions of the TIFF format allow for image compression; it's a handy format for large files when you have to move them between computers. Some software will not read compressed TIFF files, however.

BMP (Bitmap)

This format burst into use with Windows 3.0. It is an uncompressed format, so file sizes can be quite large. As a result, it is seldom the format of choice for large or high-resolution images. However, there is widespread support for it in the Windows world, and you should be prepared to deal with it anyway. Some programs work only with this format and the other Windows-specific file formats—DIB and WMF.

DIB (Device Independent Bitmap)

This is another format popularized by Windows. Files saved in this format can be displayed on a variety of devices. The file format is similar to BMP. I can open DIB files with PhotoStyler even though there is no menu choice for the format. I just set the file type to BMP. This format is used mostly by programmers who have to worry about displaying images on a variety of devices.

GIF (Graphics Interchange Format)

This compressed format was developed for use on CompuServe. Most of the images you can download from CompuServe are in this format. Software packages' support for the format is increasing, and there are several shareware viewers/converters available. One of the most popular is Graphics Workshop, which I have included on the floppy disk. See Appendix A, "A Guide to NautilusCD," for more details.

EPS (Encapsulated PostScript File)

This format had its origins in the desktop publishing world, but its use has become common for a certain type of image. It stores an image using PostScript code. It is not always easy—or even practical—to convert from other formats to EPS, but you can convert EPS files to other formats. Because almost all programs are incapable of displaying an image from an EPS file (it is intended to be sent to a printer that supports PostScript), EPS files often contain a low-resolution TIFF image for viewing purposes. See the section on vector versus raster images.

WMF (Windows Metafile Format)

This format, also associated with Windows, isn't commonly used. Support for the format outside of Windows is limited, but it is handy because many Windows programs support it—even if they don't broadcast such support. It is a vector format, but as the word *metafile* suggests, it can combine both vector and raster images.

TGA (Targa)

This was the first popular format for high-resolution (24-bit) images. The name comes from the original Targa board, the first true color video board. Most video capture boards support this format, as do most high-end paint programs.

CGM (Computer Graphics Metafile)

This is another file format that was designed as a "standard." Like many other alleged standards, this one splintered into so many sub-standards (pun intended) that it was never really a standard. As the word *metafile* suggests, it can combine both vector and raster data.

HPGL (Hewlett Packard Graphics Language)

This file format is used for output to plotters, although some other hardware devices support it as an emulation. The format is less common than it once was, although certain fields, such as CAD (computer aided design) use it frequently.

JPEG (Joint Photographic Experts Group)

This is a recent format designed for maximal image compression. JPEG uses a new kind of compression called *lossy compression* (not to be confused with "lousy compression"). *Lossy* refers to a compression scheme that actually loses some of the data needed to reconstruct the image. The idea is that the human eye won't miss the lost information. See the sidebar on compression techniques for more information.

Raster versus Vector Images

Omnes Imagia in bis partes divisa est.

This paraphrase of Caesar's famous opening line in his book on the Gallic War can be translated roughly as "All images are divided into two classes." Although the Latin is bogus, the concept is not. There are two kinds of images in use on computers—vector and raster.

Raster images, used with paint programs, are composed of pixels, and each pixel has qualities (such as color and lightness) associated with it. The bigger the image, the more pixels it has, and the larger the file size. Vector images are not composed of pixels. These images include instructions used to reconstruct the objects that make up the complete image. For example, a circle might be described in terms of its center, radius, and the line weight used to draw it.

Each kind of image file has its uses. The primary difference between them has to do with pixels. If you try to enlarge an image made of pixels (raster images), you just turn the pixels into larger blocks. This enlarges rough edges, and at large sizes, the jagged edges are unacceptable. A vector image, on the other hand, does not use pixels; you can enlarge the image to any size you need and get smooth lines. Sometimes you need pixels—trying to break down a photograph into objects would be an exercise in frustration; you could wind up with one object per pixel!

A raster format is best for photographic-style images, whereas a vector image works best with many drawings. Skilled operators can blur the distinctions between the formats by pushing them to their limits. (When I say *drawings* I do not include paintings—images you would create with a pixel-based paint program. Paintings are closer to photographic images than drawings.) Consider some examples. The image of my office in Figure 3.102 is a raster image.[38]

Figure 3.102. *A raster drawing.*

The image in Figure 3.103 was created with CorelDRAW!, a vector-based drawing package; CorelDRAW! was used to illustrate the concept of a sound wave in Chapter 2. The various parts of the drawing are objects, and each object has a description in the file.

---

[38]In the earliest editions of this book, the caption for this image said it was my office. This led to a great deal of confusion, because, as you can see from my earlier self portrait, that's not me in the image at all!

The EPS format is commonly used for this task; it uses the PostScript programming language to describe the various objects in a file. Although most PostScript code is generated by programs to send to PostScript printers, you can write PostScript code. Here's some code that will draw a one-inch square on a page and print it.

Figure 3.103. *A vector drawing.*

PostScript command	Explanation
144 144 moveto	Establish initial position
72 0 rlineto	Draw first side
0 72 rlineto	Draw second side
-72 0 rlineto	Draw third side
closepath	Fourth side
stroke	The lines are strokes, not filled
showpage	Print it

The word vector is used to describe some formats because of the mathematical meaning of the word: a direction and a length. To draw a rectangle, I used four vectors—one for each side, each perpendicular to the previous one.

The choice between these image formats depends on the kind of image you have and how you plan to use it. For example, if you include a scanned photo in a newsletter, you have to go with a raster format. If you are designing a company logo, a vector format works better because you can scale the image to any size without the problems inherent with pixels. You can use a small version of the logo on letterhead, and a large version as the banner on the newsletter. If you plan to combine raster and vector images, you can either use a program that accepts both as imports (PageMaker and some animation programs) or use a format that can incorporate both kinds of images (such as EPS or CGM files).

As software evolves, it is becoming less important to choose the format in advance. For example, CorelDRAW! versions 3.0 and 4.0 support export to a wide variety of file formats, both vector and raster. In general, the more photographic the image, the more likely it is that you need to use a raster format.

Image Compression-Techniques and Issues

High-resolution images use large amounts of memory and hard disk space. For example, a full color image of a single 8 1/2- by 11-inch page can occupy more than 20M! Although commercial studios can afford the huge hard disks to store this kind of data, most users need some form of compression to make practical use of high-resolution images.

There are two different kinds of compression available. One method looks for repeating patterns in the source file. Instead of storing all the source data, it stores the patterns plus instructions for combining them to re-create the original file. Using this technique, the restored file is identical to the source file.

The other kind of compression is called *lossy compression*. As the name implies, some data is lost during compression. Instead of looking for repeating patterns, lossy compression methods perform a sophisticated mathematical analysis on the source data. These methods vary, but they are all complicated, full of references to cosines, DCT (discrete cosine transform), forward DCTs, Q-factors, and quantization matrices. Instead of trying to convey what each of those terms mean, I'll try to explain lossy compression in English.

There are many ways to store image data. The most common method used on PCs involves RGB—the proportions of red, green, and blue that make up the image. Using 8 bits (1 byte) to store the color information enables you to store as many as 256 colors for each pixel. Using fewer than 256 colors results in a low-quality image. Expanding the number of bits to 16 or 24 gives you 32,768 or 16.7 million colors, respectively. These images are much more photo-realistic, particularly at higher resolutions.

Thus, the better the image, the more data you have to deal with, and the amount of data grows rapidly as image quality increases. It is not unusual to see file sizes of 24M for large, 24-bit color images. Even the best compression techniques begin to falter with this much data. Looking at an image as a combination of red, green, and blue is not efficient.

However, there are other ways of looking at color. For example, you can separate a color into its hue, saturation, and brightness. Any such description is a mathematical model for a color, and each model has advantages and disadvantages.

Lossy compression techniques do have one salvation: many offer a way to control the amount of loss. You can specify a factor that controls how severely the compression affects picture quality. If you can accept some image degradation, compression ratios of 40:1 and more are possible.

The most commonly supported lossy compression method is called the *Joint Photographic Experts Group (JPEG)*. In addition to converting from RGB to make compression simpler, JPEG arranges the colors in the image to determine which are more commonly used. By specifying a Q factor, you can determine how many of the less frequently used colors are dropped (converted to more commonly used colors). This gives you some control over the degree of image loss involved in the compression. This explanation is over-simplified, but it gives you some idea how lossy compression can be varied.

JPEG breaks the image down into small blocks and compresses each block before moving on to the next. This allows for compression-on-the-fly, but it introduces some problems too. Block boundaries can become over-emphasized, distorting an image at high compression ratios. JPEG also has a harder time handling colors that involve high

frequencies (blue). This means that bluish colors have fewer variations. Because this limitation matches the eye's reduced capability to
distinguish blue color variations, this isn't usually a problem.

Lossy compression has tremendous advantages when compared to
conventional compression techniques. If nothing else, the ability to
reach compression ratios of 10:1, 20:1, and beyond without seriously
distorting an image dramatically overshadows the paltry 2:1 and 3:1
compression ratios used on text files.

Because lossy compression involves sophisticated data handling, it
takes time to perform the calculations. Several manufacturers offer
hardware that has built-in image compression, but its use is limited
to special situations. The benefits of hardware compression are
significant—as much as 20 times faster than software compression.
However, unless hardware compression/decompression becomes part
of most PCs, software has to do the job.

Lossy compression has its problems. Compressing a restored file a
second time (for example, after additional editing) results in further
loss of data, and additional image degradation. Certain applications,
such as medical imaging, cannot tolerate any loss at all.

Creating Images

If you are like most people, the idea of creating your own original images is a
scary one. However, it would be a mistake to completely ignore the possibilities
of creating original art with PCs. Most of the packages available today do not
require drawing skills; they require average hand-eye coordination. If you want
to draw a circle, for example, you don't draw it freehand—there is a Circle tool in
almost every product on the market.

When one of my clients needs an image—for an ad campaign, a product bro-
chure, or a package—they think I am supposed to come up with the image. However, that's not the best way to do it. I always feel the client should be the one to
create the image. My job is to be a good mechanic, and turn the client's ideas
into a good-looking image. A good image isn't just a clever design. It needs to

reflect the ideas and the personality of the person or company it represents. Sometimes, cleverness is the wrong approach. For example, the right image might be a simple, geometric design.

If you like the idea of creating your own artwork, but feel out of your area of expertise, here are some tips to get you started:

➤ *Keep it simple.* A few well-placed objects are much easier to control than many. If you are not an experienced designer, avoid complex or multi-layered images. Stay within boundaries you know you can handle.

➤ *Use a vector-based program.* It is easier to create a professional-looking image with this type of a program. Creating an image with a raster program is actually quite challenging—even though the most common paint programs create raster images. The basic painting metaphor is attractive, but it's also a hindrance—paint programs require good draftsmanship for many operations.

Vector programs, on the other hand, are both forgiving and more rigid in their approach. They are forgiving because you create distinct objects rather than forever changing pixels. Long after you first create an object, you can select it, edit it, and see the results of your change. This object orientation is a little harder to get used to than the simple painting metaphor, but the advantages for the non-artist are worth the effort.

➤ *Think in terms of balance.* For example, don't overload one side of the image with objects or colors.

➤ *Use diagonals.* Giving your image a strong diagonal emphasis can be an easy, effective way to organize the elements of the image. Diagonal lines are inherently more interesting than horizontal and vertical lines. Just as important, don't overdo the same diagonal—use varying angles and an occasional straight line for variety.

➤ *Develop your eye.* No matter what you think of your own design sense, you can develop it further. Stop and look at what you have done so far. Does it please you? Is there anything that seems out of place or not quite right? What could you do to improve it?

➤ *Solve individual problems.* Good design involves a series of challenges and resolutions. For example, you look at your image and say to yourself, "There's too much green." It isn't always obvious what you might do to fix the problem. Study it for a bit, mull over the different possibilities, and then give one or more of your ideas a try. Then step back, look it over, and decide if there are any more problems to solve.

➤ *Know when to stop fiddling.* Let's face it—an image is never perfect. You can always look at it from a different perspective. When your eye only finds picky details, you've got a winner.

➤ *Don't take criticism too seriously.* Art is a subjective medium. There is room for many opinions. Separate the facts—a poorly scanned logo, an orange background that clashes with blue letters—from opinions: "That's silly," or "Who told you that you could do that?" If someone else has to approve the artwork, you might have to incorporate some things that offend your taste. When that happens, you're dealing with something all creative types have to live with; take it as a sign of your success.

Multimedia images aren't different from any other kind of images. There are other mediums that use sequences of images, including slide shows, overheads, and storyboards. The basic rule for sequencing images is to keep in mind what the juxtaposition of images means to the observer.

For example, if your presentation uses two *head shots,*[39] consider the relationship of the images. Are both people looking in the same direction? Are they looking at each other or out into space? Even if the two images are displayed in sequence, and only one image is seen at a time, the observer relates them to each other because of their proximity in time.

The most important idea to remember is to trust your own sense of what's right. There is no substitute for intuition when it comes to creating original images.

Buying Images

There are an increasing number of useful images appearing on the market. As I mentioned earlier, there are many sources for basic clip art. Most of the available art is in vector formats (primarily EPS files), which you can modify with programs such as CorelDRAW!, Freehand, or Illustrator. Most images are black-and-white or gray-scaled, but more color images are now available.

Most of the available vector images were created with desktop publishing in mind, and they might not have the "oomph" you need for a multimedia presentation. Raster images work well as both backgrounds and accents. Photo-realistic

---

[39] Head shots are photos of people, including head only or head and shoulders.

images, in particular, can be impressive. See the Shopper's Guide for more information.

Amazing Images on the Disc

There are many images on the CD-ROM discs that accompany this book. Most of them are in GIF format; if you have to use them in other formats, the shareware program Graphics Workshop is included on the floppy disk. You can use it to convert to various file formats.

All images exist as 8-bit (256 colors) files. I have also included several 24-bit (16.7 million colors) files; they are in TIFF format. They duplicate some of the 8-bit images. If you have a 16- or 24-bit video display, compare them to see the differences. If you have a 256-color card, most software that supports 24-bit color dithers the image to make it a 256-color image on your screen.

I have included images in a variety of categories, including:

➤ beautiful scenes

➤ NASA space images

➤ nature

➤ structures

For complete information about the images on the disks, please see the Appendixes.

Putting It All Together

I
n this chapter, I emphasize the *multi* in *multimedia*—combining sights and sounds into complete presentations. Sights and sounds are the two basic el ements of any multimedia or interactive presentation. Sights include text and images, both of which come in a variety of formats such as animations, word-processing files, spreadsheets, video and still clips, and more. Sounds also come from a wide variety of sources, including .WAV and .MID files and CD audio. The art of combining these widely disparate parts is the essence of multimedia presentations.

There are many tools you can use to create multimedia presentations using programming. I discuss this in Chapter 8, "Manning the Pump: Multimedia Programming." In addition, there are other tools for creating these sight and sound extravaganzas—*authoring tools,* which are covered here in this chapter. I have also provided an example application created with ToolBook, a multimedia programming tool, to show you what you can expect at the high end. If you really want control over your multimedia presentation, ToolBook offers a lot of power—it's hard to decide whether ToolBook is a programming tool, or a high-end authoring tool.

The following products are covered in this chapter:

Action!—An inexpensive but powerful package for creating presentations with lots of cool moving pieces. Multimedia interface is easy to use, but lacks support for overlay video or detailed interactive media control.

Compel—A very nicely designed first effort from Asymetrix. A little slow, but this package has a lot to like. Integrates multimedia from the ground up—it even checks to see whether you have the hardware installed that a presentation requires, and adapts well if you don't.

Charisma—A new version just released by Micrographix. This is a major redesign of the product to include multimedia support. I was only able to play with an early beta version, but this is a package to watch.

Softcraft Presenter—A modestly multimedia-capable presentation package. The interface is convenient, but multimedia support is only average. Good, however, if you are looking to transition into more multimedia, rather than lots of multimedia. Key cool feature: automatic palettes. This alone makes it worth a serious look for any image-intensive presentation. Also worth a look is Presenter's "intelligent clip art"—a scripting language for graphics that you can use to animate graphics.

Media Blitz—Does one thing, but does it well. Media Blitz enables you to arrange media objects using a timeline metaphor. You can then use OLE to integrate the combined objects into any application that supports OLE.

HSC Interactive—An icon-based package for creating interactive presentations. It's the little brother to Icon Author. It has some weaknesses, but is very good for full-screen presentations with complex multimedia sequences. The icon part of the interface is great, but other aspects of the program are sometimes more primitive and awkward than I liked.

Multimedia ToolBook—A real power-house multimedia development tool; can be used for presentation[1] or for serious application development. Takes a while to really get the hang of ToolBook, but Multimedia support is very well thought out. You can do simple stuff quickly and easily, but plan on studying the extensive script language if you want detailed control. See also Chapter 8 for programming details.

Icon Author—A high-end and expensive authoring tool. Uses an icon metaphor for arranging the elements of your presentation. Primarily designed for fancy, interactive kiosk-style presentations. Supports many high-end hardware devices, such as laser discs, that the average package does not. If polish, panache, and hot hardware are part of your requirements, Icon Author is a good choice. Heavy reliance on icons, however, makes it awkward for very large projects.

Combining Sounds and Images

There are many packages available for combining sounds and images, ranging from new releases of old standards (like Harvard Graphics for Windows) to programs designed specifically for high-powered, interactive multimedia (like Icon Author). It seems as if another multimedia program is announced every week.

Because multimedia is still in its early stages, a wide range of products is available; the market has yet to decide on areas such as the most convenient way to develop a multimedia presentation, the acceptable level of quality for color, resolution, and sound, and many other details. In contrast, the database, word processing, and spreadsheet markets have settled down considerably. Over time, the same thing will happen to the multimedia market. Until that happens, however, you'll need a map and compass to find your way through the thicket of available software.

---

[1]If you opt to use ToolBook for your presentations, you can have a very, very high degree of customization that will take your presentations to a new level of sophistication.

Dividing the Offerings

There are several ways to divide up the available offerings. Here's an overview of the different categories of authoring software. Later in this chapter, you can find specific information about some of these packages.

Low-Cost Packages

There are budget packages that enable you to combine sounds and images, but you have to do it on the software's terms. Just because an inexpensive package is labeled as multimedia, don't assume that it is high-quality multimedia. The technology for handling 256-color and 24-bit color images or for handling Wave files is not necessarily built into multimedia software. You should check these "no name" and generic products carefully—if they look too good to be true, they probably are. Such software typically sells for $150 or less; most shareware packages are in this range.

Old Software with New Capabilities

The next level of software consists of older packages that now have support for multimedia. Many presentation packages, for example, have scurried to support multimedia; Harvard Graphics for Windows was one of the first to do so, and Freelance wasn't far behind. The level of support in this category varies from merely adding pictures to full-fledged multimedia capabilities. In some cases, the multimedia support is thoughtfully planned and it works well. In other cases, beware of the traps. See the software section of the Shopper's Guide for specific information.

In some cases, the software has been completely redesigned to support and integrate multimedia; Charisma is an example. Many companies hate to do this, because it means the user has to learn a whole new way of interacting with the software. However, if you spend a little time with these packages, the ones that were built around multimedia really stand out from the ones that simply added it to what they already did.

The most outstanding example of the "build it from the ground up" approach is Compel. Multimedia options are always right at your fingertips, and sounds and videos play without problems or hesitations. In fact, the only knock I have against Compel is that it's a bit on the slow side,[2] but future versions should address that.

Professional Packages

The next level is the bottom rung of the professional software ladder. These packages usually have a price under $500. Most of these packages are designed for you to assemble a multimedia presentation. Examples include HSC InterActive and Multimedia ToolBook. Ease of use, suitability to task, and quality and consistency of product vary.

Next come the high-end, professional authoring packages; these can cost several thousand dollars. They are primarily intended for the development of commercial multimedia or interactive presentations. These packages can be used in kiosks at trade shows or tourist attractions, or for fancy, high-tech business presentations. Software titles at this level include Icon Author and Authorware.

Is It Multimedia or Is It Margarine?

It seems like everyone wants to jump on the multimedia bandwagon. Some companies think that putting their software on CD-ROM qualifies for the multimedia moniker, but it doesn't. This tendency to label anything and everything as multimedia will probably pass. Until it does, however, it will continue to annoy thoughtful people who hate to see things purposely mislabeled. The roots of this problem are the broad reach of the word multimedia and the tendency to try to make a few dollars wherever the opportunity exists. Loosely speaking, many of these packages are multimedia of one sort or another. If it is going to be called multimedia, though, it should be multimedia. See the section later in this chapter, "When Is It Really Multimedia?" for my thoughts on how to tell the difference.

Multimedia Word for Windows

For example, when I heard there was going to be a multimedia version of Word for Windows, I was very excited. I use the program for almost all my writing (including this book, for example), so immediately I was looking forward to the

---

[2]The key to using Compel is to have the hardware it needs to run well—say 8 to 12 megabytes of memory on a fast 486.

possibilities—direct support for sound, perhaps, or even a whole new look to the product.[3]

When the product arrived, I looked at the packaging to see whether any new features were included that met my expectations. At first, I was disappointed. I noticed only one new feature—a marriage of Word for Windows with Microsoft Bookshelf, an established multimedia product.[4] Bookshelf has been around for years. I found myself thinking that this event should have been celebrated as a marriage of a multimedia product to a monomedia product—similar to the political marriages in Europe a few hundred years ago in which one powerful family hoped to expand its influence by marrying into another powerful family.

Word for Windows married well when it teamed up with Bookshelf. I recommend the combined product to anyone who has to do research while they write. And, as it turns out, it really is multimedia. The package, however, didn't hype what I consider to be a perfect example of integrating multimedia into an existing package sensibly.

Voice Annotations

I installed this new version of Word for Windows, thinking I could at least make good use of the on-line resources in Bookshelf. I wanted to insert a picture in this section of the book so I pulled down the **I**nsert menu (Figure 4.1). There, at the bottom of the menu, was what I had hoped for—integrated sound.

Integrated sound is pretty simple to use. If you click the **V**oice Annotation menu selection, it loads Sound Recorder, which appears over your document (Figure 4.2).

You can record a sound by clicking the microphone icon. Choose Update from the Sound Recorder's **F**ile menu, then exit. Voilà—a voice annotation in your document (Figure 4.3).

To play the sound, double-click the microphone icon in the Annotations window. Otherwise, voice annotations behave like regular annotations.

---

[3]Although I wonder how Microsoft's programmers could interpret such a subjective concept.

[4]If you aren't familiar with Bookshelf, it is a combination of Thesaurus, Dictionary, Almanac, and other reference sources. It includes sounds, animations, and images that easily qualify it as a multimedia product.

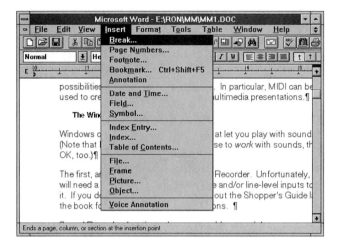

Figure 4.1. *Voice Annotation is available in the multimedia version of Word for Windows.*

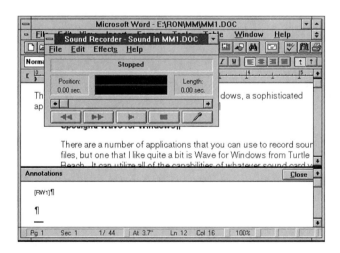

Figure 4.2. *The Sound Recorder dialog box.*

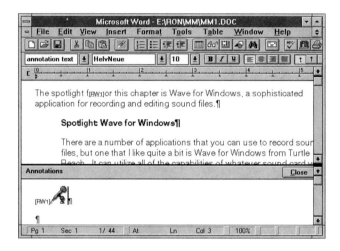

Figure 4.3. *An annotation is added to the document.*

When Is It Really Multimedia?

Now that multimedia is (finally) becoming popular, every company wants to call its product a multimedia product. Here are my criteria for determining when a product is multimedia-capable.

Direct Playing of Sounds

You should be able to play sounds by clicking an icon, or the sounds should play automatically when the appropriate part of the program is reached.[5]

Support for a Variety of Image Formats

These days, the better packages support a zillion different image file formats. You really do need support for a wide variety of formats. If you want to work in Windows, be sure the product has support for bitmap files (*.BMP). If you plan to download files from CompuServe, direct support for .GIF files makes life much easier. Sure, you can get a program to convert the files, but if you do more than a few files it gets frustrating.

---

[5]Is OLE good enough to qualify for multimedia? Most of the time, the answer is no. If the implementation is very well done (see Media Blitz elsewhere in this chapter for an example), I'll give it a thumbs up.

If you plan to use images from a variety of sources, make sure you have support for TIFF files (*.TIF), too. If you plan to interface to vector-based drawing programs (Illustrator, CorelDRAW!, Freehand, and so on), be sure encapsulated PostScript files (*.EPS) are supported. If you have another program you use to create images, make sure its format is supported as well. Bottom line: the more formats a program supports, the better. Having to stop and load a conversion program is a hassle in the world of multimedia.

Integration of Multimedia Elements

This is a subjective call; there are no hard rules for good integration of multimedia. To me, a program integrates multimedia well when the sounds and images don't jump out at you—they fit tightly into the operation of the software. If image and sound support feels "tacked on," you might want to steer clear. Odds are, you'll try one day to do something only to find out it's not there. One key thing to look for: support of MCI command strings. This enables you to enter simple text to make multimedia things happen. For example, to open a video file in a window, you might say `open c:\windows\myfile.avi style popup alias vid`.

Size

The whole point of multimedia is that today's CD-ROMs, huge hard disks, and high-resolution/high-speed video cards make it possible to store and access enormous amounts of data. If a program stops short in the size department, it isn't really multimedia. Even games are now available on CD-ROMs. If the software can't handle large files or it comes on one floppy disk, look twice to see whether it's real multimedia software.

Novelty

Yes, novelty. What good is multimedia software if it doesn't strike out in new directions and take advantage of new technology? Take live video in a window—this is a whole new way to use your computer; the software should do things you've never thought of before. If all you get is a talking head in that window, that's a weak use of the medium. If sound and text are integrated with the video, or if you get interactive control, that's real multimedia in action.

Not Ready for Prime Time?

There's one more thing to consider with multimedia (or alleged multimedia) software: is it ready for prime time yet? Among the many software packages that have passed through my hands in the last few months, several were good products but they weren't quite finished. This lack of polish can make the software frustrating to use. This is a pet peeve of mine—software that's released before it's ready.

In my experience, there is nothing malicious about the release of unfinished software—often, the manufacturer did not think through the ways that customers would use the software. I suggest you protect your investment in the product and tell the vendor what's missing. If I think the software has good points, I take the time to fax or call tech support and explain what I think is wrong or missing. For example, the first release of Compel had a few bugs. Compel was so well designed, it would have been a shame to let a few bugs ruin the product. I spent the time to let Asymetrix know what was wrong, and they fixed the problems in an interim release, 1.0a.[6]

If the vendors are trying to produce a good product, they listen and improve the product. This was certainly the case with Asymetrix; they listened to what I had to say and made the changes that were needed. This is usually what happens, and in this case, everybody wins.[7]

It takes a lot of effort to create a software product (especially for Windows and multimedia), and in the case of a small startup company, it's usually a labor of love. New software gets created because someone is passionate about an idea or concept. No vendor wants to fail; most would love to know what you think. Rarely have I met a vendor who didn't care about improving the product. Unlike other software, multimedia software is still in the baby stage—what you and I think about a product still means something.[8]

---

[6]If that's not the version you have, call Asymetrix for an update.

[7]If it doesn't happen, I like to hear about it—send me a message on CompuServe, in the MULTI-MEDIA forum, section 7.

[8]On the other hand, maybe I'm a little over optimistic here. I've been on development teams, and there are times when the sheer bureaucracy of a company will get in the way of producing a good product. Thankfully, most such companies suffer in the sales department, but a lot of dollars get wasted when this happens.

Softcraft Presenter

Presenter is one of those programs whose true nature only becomes clear after you've used it for a while and poked around into the menus and dialog boxes. Put another way: there is much more here than meets the eye.

A lot of these features don't have a whole lot to do with multimedia, unfortunately. The version of Presenter I used (Version 2.0) was the first version to integrate multimedia, and some key features that I like to use are missing. Presenter is an example of an existing product which has had multimedia grafted on, rather than a product that has multimedia in its blood.

For example, you can associate sounds with objects in a slide, and when the object becomes visible, the sound will play. You cannot, however, add a button and have it play a sound when the user clicks on it. This makes Presenter specifically a presentation program from a multimedia standpoint. Although you can cruise through a presentation interactively (clicking to go from slide to slide, or to reveal bullets), you cannot interact very much with multimedia objects.

I didn't think that Presenter was as easy to learn, or as well organized, as Compel. However, the more I used it, the more I got a good feel for the way things were organized. Once you get the general drift of the program, it gets progressively easier to learn.

Figure 4.4 shows the opening look of Presenter. There is a set of text-labeled buttons at the top, a toolbox of drawing methods on the left, and a second toolbox (with color and other tools) on the right. When you start, you are the proud owner of a one-slide presentation, complete with background and title text block. Not fancy, but very workmanlike.

Most of the time, you would then switch to the Outline mode and begin entering slide titles and bullets. Figure 4.5 shows the appearance of outline mode after entering some slides and bullets. The keyboarding is simple—after you type a slide title, press return to drop down to bullet level. After the last bullet, press the backspace key to return to the title level. I found it very easy to create slides this way. You can use the rightmost listbox at the top of the window to change the default new slide type. However, in outline mode, you are limited to word charts.

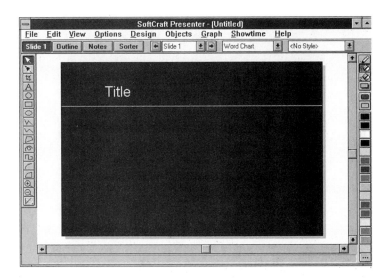

Figure 4.4. *The Softcraft Presenter startup window.*

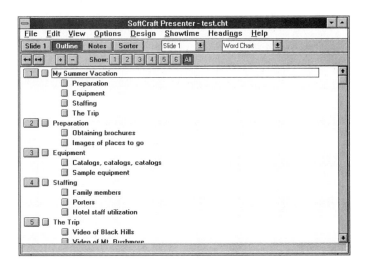

Figure 4.5. *Working in outline mode.*

There is also a slide sorter mode (Figure 4.6). As you can see (if you have good eyes), each slide and bullet was conveniently created just by entering the basic information in the outline mode.

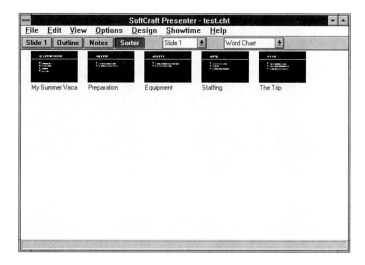

Figure 4.6. *Working in sort mode.*

Setting up links between slides is easy. Simply select a bullet or other object, and click the Showtime menu (see Figure 4.7). Click New|Modify Slide Jump to open the dialog box shown in Figure 4.8.

Figure 4.7. *The Showtime menu—the key to cool features.*

On the left are the various kinds of jumps you can use. You can jump to slides by number, or to relative positions such as next and previous. One important option is "Return to Last Jump." This enables you to return to where you came from without having to know which slide it was. Thus, if one slide can be jumped to from many other slides, you don't have to keep track of where you came from.

If you prefer to jump to slides by title, there is a list on the right-hand side of the dialog box.

Figure 4.8. *Editing slide jumps.*

Presenter comes with a more-than-adequate supply of drawing tools; you can design your presentation right in Presenter most of the time. When you are ready to view the show, click Showtime|Slide Show[9] to open the dialog shown in Figure 4.9. This dialog gives you control over many aspects of the slide show. This is where you choose whether the slides will advance manually or automatically, and the default type of slide transition.[10]

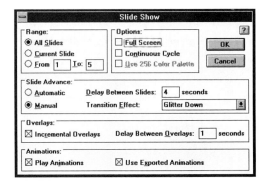

Figure 4.9. *Setting slide show options.*

Pay particular attention to the section labeled "Overlays." If you do not turn on overlays, some animations will not play correctly. If you do turn on overlays, all of your sounds and animations will play automatically as the slide or overlay

---

[9]Or press F2 if it's only the current slide you wish to view.

[10]You can specify transitions for each slide if you wish, as well as many other properties.

layer appears. You also can turn off animations by un-checking the "Play animations" check box.

If you prefer to set the exact nature and timing of events in a slide, you can
select the Showtime|Slide show transitions menu selection to display or change
the settings for the current slide (Figure 4.10).

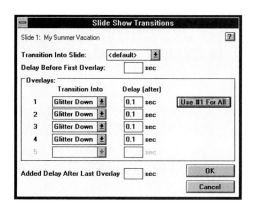

Figure 4.10. *Setting slide options individually.*

There are two kinds of timing issues for a slide. The slide itself can have a
transition and a duration; each of the bullets (called an overlay) also can have a
transition and a duration. I found this odd and confusing at first, but it may simply be a result of not doing presentations for a living. The process works well—in
Figure 4.10, I set a one-tenth second delay between each bullet/overlay item and
set the effect as Glitter Down. The glitter effect is quite nice, but impossible to
describe.[11]

Using multimedia elements is straightforward. To add videos or bitmaps, use
the File|Import Picture menu selection. This lists all of the files in a wide variety
of formats, including bitmaps, animation's, videos, and movies. You can resize
bitmaps as you place them. You could also resize a video as you place it, but I
don't recommend it—videos play more slowly if they are not at their normal size.
Figure 4.11 shows a video placed into a slide. The video will play as soon as you
enter the slide.

---

[11]And I couldn't do a screen capture, either; I can't interrupt the effect while it's happening. Sigh.
Every technology has its limits.

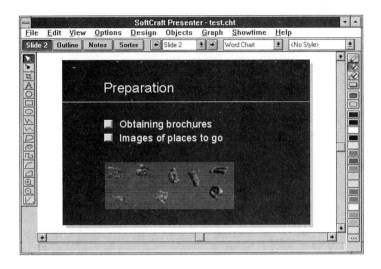

Figure 4.11. *A video in a slide.*

To have videos play when they are clicked (or any other multimedia data type, for that matter), use OLE. Open the file in Media Player, and copy it to the clipboard. You can then paste it into the presentation. You can use the Edit|Configure option while in Media Player to configure the exact appearance of the linked object. Figure 4.12 shows a second video object added to the slide as an OLE object.

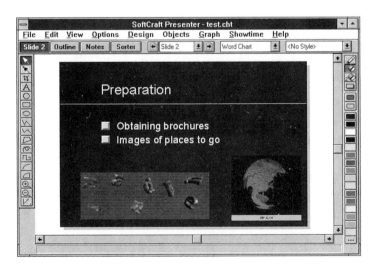

Figure 4.12. *A video added as an OLE object.*

Bitmaps can be placed and resized if necessary. Figure 4.13 shows a slide with two bitmaps. Presenter supports a wide variety of formats, like a good multimedia program should.

Figure 4.13. *An example of a slide with bitmaps.*

Presenter supports all color modes from 8-bit (256 colors) to 24-bit (16.7 million or true color). If you will be working or viewing in 8-bit color, Presenter has some nice features worth knowing about. If you do not specify otherwise, a single palette will be created automatically for your presentation. If you have a large number of images, you may find that this is not optimal—trying to create a single palette for many different images involves heavy compromise. You can either specify your own palette (it must be the palette of one object in the presentation which you designate), or you can use palette fades (to white or black) between slides—the latter approach enables Presenter to create multiple palettes, which will give you much better results on 256-color displays. If your presentation will be viewed on 8-bit displays, I strongly recommend using Palette fades between slides. It will solve many of your palette problems. In fact, this one feature alone may make it worth your while to look into Presenter.

One final note: like Compel, Presenter does not care what size the presentation is played back at. You can play it in a window, you can play it full screen and you can play it at any resolution. Presenter will take care of scaling the slide elements—fonts, bitmaps, and so on—so they appear correct. Figure 4.14 shows the same slide as in Figure 4.13, but at full screen. Note that all aspects of its appearance remain the same. The only changes are improvements—the bitmaps are now displayed in a larger format, and more details are visible.

Figure 4.14. *Playing a presentation at full screen.*

One word of caution, however. Animations and videos aren't scalable the way bitmaps are. You need to be sure to play at full screen and to have the video or animation play at its natural size to avoid scaling delays, or playing out of position.

Softcraft Presenter offers another interesting feature called "intelligent clip art." This enables you to add scripts to objects. The most common use is to animate chart objects. Most of the time, the script will be constructed for you as you manipulate the object. For example, you can make one object self-scaling with respect to another object. You could create a triangle that will resize itself when a circle is stretched or moved.

To do this, simply create a triangle with the polygon line tool. The script for the object looks like this:

```
line b5 {
  slide = 1;
  pointlist =
      [
        <<680, 1996>>,
        <<1323, 1301>>,
```

```
           <<1853, 1996>>
        ];
    closed = 1;
}
```

To attach the triangle to the circle, you click and drag one of the resizing handles of the triangle over the corresponding resizing handle of the circle, all the while holding down the *a* key. This modifies the script automatically:

```
line b5 {
  slide = 1;
  pointlist =
      [
        <<680, 1996>>,
        <<x(between(<<680, 1996>>, b6.topright, 54)),
          y(between(<<680, 1996>>, b6.topright, 100))>>: 0,
        <<x(between(<<680, 1996>>, b6.topright, 100)),
          y(between(<<680, 1996>>, b6.topright, 0))>>: 0
      ];
  closed = 1;
}
```

However, the anchor point of the triangle remains absolute, at the point <<680, 1996>>. To make the triangle respond to the circle, you can use any text editor to globally replace <<680, 1996>> with b6.bottomleft:

```
line b5 {
  slide = 1;
  pointlist =
      [
        b6.bottomleft,
        <<x(between(b6.bottomleft, b6.topright, 54)),
          y(between(b6.bottomleft, b6.topright, 100))>>: 0,
        <<x(between(b6.bottomleft, b6.topright, 100)),
          y(between(b6.bottomleft, b6.topright, 0))>>: 0
      ];
  closed = 1;
}
```

Now, wherever the circle leads, the triangle will follow—both objects now have the same extents.

This is just a simple example of what you can do with this technology in Presenter. Perhaps the most exciting possibilities lie in the area of MCI commands; Softcraft plans to add this capability—and it should be in the product by the time you read this. The list of capabilities in the language used for "intelligent art" is huge; you can do just about anything you can think of. It is an interesting feature, though obviously not for the beginner.

Charisma

Charisma has *real* charisma. If looks were everything in a software package, Charisma would be the package of choice. The interface to this package is extremely good looking. I received an early pre-beta copy of Version 4.0 of the software, and I was very impressed. The version I used wasn't sufficiently complete for me to give you a solid recommendation one way or the other, but I would strongly suggest you look at it closely when the time comes to buy. This product is sleek, sexy, and feature rich. If the final mix comes together, it may well turn out to be an Author's Choice in a future edition.

Let's take a quick tour of Charisma. Keep in mind that the exact details of the product may differ from what you see here when Version 4.0 is released.

As soon as you run the product, you encounter the "good look" I referred to (see Figure 4.15). The first thing you see is not the main window; you are interviewed by a pretty little dialog box. It wants to know what you would like to do. At first I thought it a bit much and assumed that the experienced user would be able to turn this feature off. But as I used the product, I realized that it made sense to enter the product this way—if you open an existing project, you follow one logical path. If you are starting a new one, you follow another, which I will show in detail here. For once, I actually liked the hand-holding.[12]

Figure 4.15. *Getting started with Charisma.*

The next dialog is likewise handsome (see Figure 4.16). This dialog enables you to choose the background for your presentation. The preview window is large enough for you to see the details of the background, and you always have the option of not loading one.

---

[12]I almost always prefer to find my own way.

Figure 4.16. *Selecting a background (or master style).*

The next step is to add a slide; here, also Charisma makes no assumptions. And that is why I like this approach: because it makes no assumptions for me. I can pick and choose, easily and comfortably, the elements of my presentation. Figure 4.17 shows the dialog for adding a slide. The template descriptions are shown on the left, and a large preview window on the right gives you precise details about the slide templates.

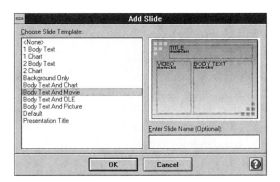

Figure 4.17. *Selecting a template for a new slide.*

I know this is a horribly subjective thing to say, but I just felt that Charisma was so helpful and polite. I've heard of user friendly, or intuitive software; this is the first time it ever occurred to me that there could even be a category called polite software.

I chose the "Body text and movie" slide template; this led me to the main Charisma window (see Figure 4.18). There is a toolbox at the left, a toolbar at the top,[13] and several additional buttons at the bottom of the window.

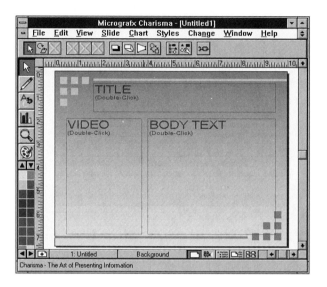

Figure 4.18. *The Charisma window.*

The three areas of the slide are clearly marked; no confusion there. To put copy in an area, all you need to do is double-click; the appropriate action occurs automatically. For a video, you'll see the Multimedia Manager (Figure 4.19). There are several ways to use the manager in addition to the file view you see here. You can also add multimedia objects to a catalog and simply pick the objects from the catalog. The Multimedia Manager is the multimedia heart of Charisma. Any time you add a multimedia event, button, or file, you do it with the Multimedia Manager.

---

[13]As you can see, several of the buttons are blank (marked by a large "X"). These functions were not yet active in my pre-release copy of the software.

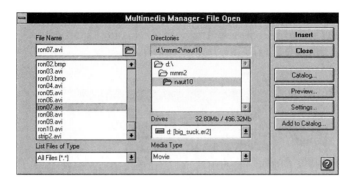

Figure 4.19. *The Multimedia Manager.*

If you click the Settings button, you see a controller appropriate to the current multimedia object type. The settings for a video are shown in Figure 4.20.

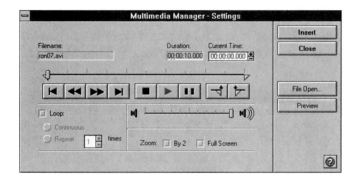

Figure 4.20. *Settings for a video object.*

The set of options is as complete as you will find. There is less text and more reliance on graphics here, but all of the controls are large and clearly marked. Clicking the Insert button places the video in the video area of the slide. By default, the video is centered vertically and horizontally, but you can change those manually if you need to. Figure 4.21 shows the video in place in the slide.

Figure 4.21. *Adding a video to a slide.*

You can easily add your own multimedia events. Just select an object and click the Slide|Hyperlink menu. If you choose to add a multimedia event or playback, you'll see a dialog that enables you to associate any multimedia file with an object. Clicking the Set button opens the Multimedia Manager, where you can select from the current catalog, pick a file from the disk, or add a new file to the catalog.

Charisma also adds support for right clicks. Figure 4.22 shows the popup menu that appears whenever you click the right mouse button. The exact contents of this menu may change in the final released product.

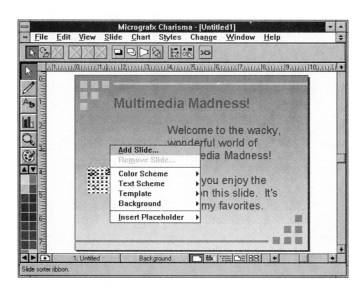

Figure 4.22. *The right-click menu.*

Overall, Charisma shows great promise. If you are interested in Multimedia presentations,[14] this package deserves a close examination before you buy. Charisma and Compel, for now, are the two most progressive and multimedia-intensive presentation products on the market. And yes—Charisma does include a slide outline mode.

Budget Authoring

The creation of multimedia presentations doesn't have to be expensive. There are several software packages available that give you a surprising amount of control at an attractive price. Two good examples, MediaBlitz and Multimedia Make Your Point, are produced by Asymetrix, the company that produces the high-end authoring package Multimedia ToolBook.

You can use MediaBlitz to include sound, images, animation, and other multimedia source files in multimedia presentations. The key element that makes MediaBlitz so easy to use is a visual score that you can use to arrange the elements of the presentation. I discuss this product in more detail in a later section of this chapter.

Multimedia Make Your Point helps you create multimedia presentations that are similar to slide-based presentations. Instead of simple slides, however, you can include multimedia elements with a slide. For example, you can play a sound before, during, or after displaying a bulleted item, or play a sound while the slide is displayed. You also can include animations and digitized video.

Several multimedia upgrade kits include a software package called Action! (The exclamation point is theirs, not mine.) For example, the multimedia upgrade kits both from Creative Labs (the makers of Sound Blaster) and Media Vision (home of the Pro Audio Spectrum) include Action! (They include Version 1.0, however, which is not the latest release.)

MediaBlitz

At one time, I worked as a free-lance radio journalist. Although radio deals strictly in sound, it's now common to layer multiple sounds in tracks on a tape recorder.

---

[14]And if you have read this far, presumably you must be, right?

These tracks run parallel to each other, and you can put any sound anywhere on any track. For example, I might have a track with nothing but street noise serving as a background. On another track, I might put my own voice telling a story about a bus strike. Combined, these tracks give the impression of being out in the street. On a third track, I might add the sounds of buses coming and going, opening and closing their huge folding doors. When all these tracks are played together, it creates a feeling of "being there."

MediaBlitz uses the concept of tracks, but instead of putting only sounds together, you can put a different multimedia device—and consequently, another medium—on each "track" (Figure 4.23).

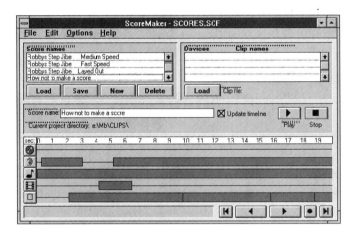

Figure 4.23. *Each medium has its own track.*

Although MediaBlitz isn't the only program to use the track metaphor (Macromind's Action! also uses it), the simplicity of the interface lends itself to the task at hand-organizing and orchestrating media clips for inclusion in presentations. In this regard, MediaBlitz has a limited focus. It is not, for example, useful for presentations that rely on text. It is intended as a tool for working with CD audio, Wave audio, animations, and MIDI files.

To create more complex interactive presentations, you can use MediaBlitz as an add-on to ToolBook or other programs. Version 3.0 of MediaBlitz even comes with a special .VBX file that makes it extremely easy to add a MediaBlitz score to your Visual Basic programs. You can use ToolBook to control the overall flow of a presentation or interactive session and then play MediaBlitz clips and scores at appropriate times.

MediaBlitz actually consists of three programs:

ClipMaker—This program enables you to create libraries of clips. Clips can consist of Wave audio, MIDI files, animations (FLC, FLI, MMM, AVM), or CD audio. The primary purpose of ClipMaker is to select exact portions of existing files for later inclusion in scores using ScoreMaker.
ScoreMaker—This is the heart of MediaBlitz. Using ScoreMaker, you can create complex multimedia scores with clips collected and modified in ClipMaker. You can determine when sounds, animations, and pictures appear, and you can position images and animations.
ScorePlayer—This program plays scores created with ScoreMaker.

Creating a Presentation

As you have done with other products, you learn how MediaBlitz can be used to create a multimedia *blitz*. Blitz is the right word for a product that focuses on the flashier aspects of presentations.

There are three steps involved in using MediaBlitz:

1. Create one or more clips.

2. Combine clips into a score.

3. Play the score with ScorePlayer.

Consider how these pieces work together. You can begin by creating some clips using ClipMaker.

Creating Clips

The opening screen of ClipMaker looks like Figure 4.24.

This is only one of the ways ClipMaker can appear, however. Depending on what kind of clip you are creating, ClipMaker displays whatever controls are appropriate for that type of clip. In this case, it is set up for creating a Wave audio clip.

➤ The top third of the window contains a list of devices and the clips for each device that are currently available. There are also some buttons for saving, loading, creating new clips, and so on.

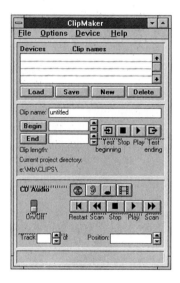

Figure 4.24. *The opening screen of ClipMaker.*

➤ The middle third contains controls for editing a clip. You learn more about these controls in a moment.

➤ The bottom third contains controls for playing or displaying a clip—rewind, play, and so on. Only the bottom third of the window changes, depending on which type of clip you've loaded.

You can create a wave audio clip using one of the audio files MOUSEOUT.WAV, located on the CD-ROM. It is located in the directory for the ToolBook demo I created. In case you want to follow along at home, see Appendix B for more details. The full wave file contains a speech from one page of the demo. The complete text reads as follows:

Sounds will keep playing until they are done. Images will disap
pear as soon as your mouse leaves the area of the hotword.

This example involves creating a clip that has just the first sentence of this two-sentence wave file. MediaBlitz works well in this area.

First, click the Load button—that's the Load button in the bottom third of the window, not the Load button in the top third. This brings up a typical file load dialog box. Once you've loaded the file, the only indication that it's loaded is the filename and size in the bottom part of the window (Figure 4.25).

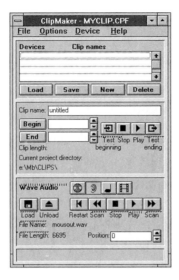

Figure 4.25. *Loading a file into ClipMaker.*

You can now click the Play button to play the file. You can rewind, skip ahead, and so on to position to any point in the wave file. To mark the beginning and ending points of the desired clip, you can use the Begin and End buttons in the middle part of the window. I rewound the clip to the beginning and clicked the Begin button—creating a beginning point of zero. I then played the Wave file and pressed stop right after the last word I wanted to keep. I also took a moment to enter a name for the clip, SNDPLAY (Figure 4.26).

Figure 4.26. *Adjusting the end point of a wave file.*

Unfortunately, the end point was not correct. When I played back the file using these settings, I heard

"Sounds will keep playing until they are done."

I used the up and down arrows (to the right of the End box) to move the ending point back (see Figure 4.26 again). I repeatedly used the Play button (in the middle third of the box) to check to see whether I had the right ending point. The correct setting for the end of the clip turned out to be 1975.

You can edit animation and MIDI clips in the same way. You also can edit CD audio clips. (When I say CD audio clip, I mean the CDs you play on your stereo, not CD-ROM disks.) The only difference in creating a CD clip is that the bottom third of the window contains controls appropriate for a CD; the middle third, where you set the beginning and ending points, stays the same.

To save the clip, click the Save button (top third of the window); it is saved with the name you gave the clip. You can also save multiple clips in a clip file (Figure 4.27).

Figure 4.27. You can save several clips in one clip file.

I added these additional clips to illustrate how to use clips to create a score in ScoreMaker.

Creating a Score

The opening screen of ScoreMaker looks like the screen in Figure 4.28.

➤ The top-left area lists the available scores. You can store multiple scores in a score file; there is room to list several.

➤ The top-right area lists the clips in the currently loaded clip file. Both the device name and the clip name are shown.

➤ The middle of the ScoreMaker window contains the name of the current score (used when you are creating a new score) and buttons to play and stop the current score.

➤ The bottom portion is the timeline. There is one line for each type of device (from top to bottom, they are CD, Wave audio, Sequencer, Animation Clip, and Bitmap).

➤ There is a status bar at the bottom and a set of controls for moving around on the timeline.

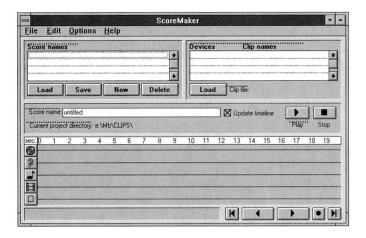

Figure 4.28. *The opening screen of ScoreMaker.*

To create a new score, the first thing you do is load a clip file (Figure 4.29).

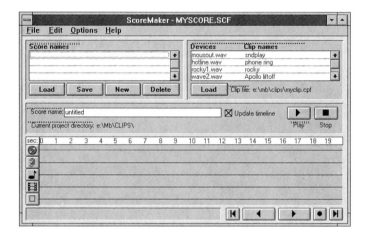

Figure 4.29. *Loading a clip file into ScoreMaker.*

To put a clip into the score and on the timeline, double-click the clip name. A bar appears in the timeline, starting at zero time (Figure 4.30). The bar is as long as the clip and uses the seconds markers above the timeline.

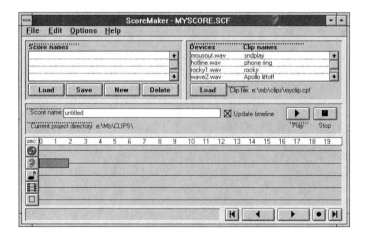

Figure 4.30. *Adding a sound clip to the Timeline.*

You can select any clip with ScoreMaker; the selected clip is shown in a lighter color than the other clips (Figure 4.31).

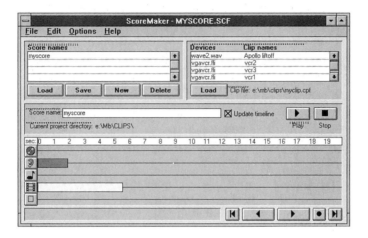

Figure 4.31. *The video clip is lighter than the sound clip.*

You can click and drag the current clip along the timeline, placing it exactly where you want (Figure 4.32).

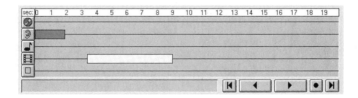

Figure 4.32. *You can move a clip to another point on the timeline.*

You can add as many clips as you want, positioning each one at the appropriate point on the timeline (Figure 4.33). If you position the same kinds of clips on the same timeline, MediaBlitz does not complain.

However, because MCI is used to play the clips, you should take MCI behavior into account. If, as in the preceding example, Wave files overlap, each Wave file starts playing at the indicated position, This stops the previous Wave file from playing. You also can add files to the score; you are not limited to the clips you put into the clip file. This is not a limitation of MediaBlitz; it is standard MCI behavior.

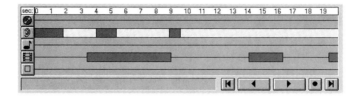

Figure 4.33. *Each track can have several clips.*

Playing the Score

When you have created a score, you can use ScorePlayer to play it. The screen for ScorePlayer is shown in Figure 4.34.

Figure 4.34. *The ScorePlayer screen.*

A list of the score names contained in a score file is displayed at the top, and the list of scores to play is shown at the bottom. There is a button to initiate playing of the scores. In this case, you have only one score to play.

Although MediaBlitz's ScorePlayer is great on its own, you also can include scores into ToolBook presentations. This is no surprise because both programs come from the same company—Asymetrix. However, MediaBlitz was written in ToolBook.

Version 3.0 of MediaBlitz was released just as we were going to press with the second edition of this book. It adds some significant new features, including:

➤ Any application that uses OLE can incorporate a MediaBlitz score

➤ Complete support for Visual Basic is provided in the form of a .VBX file that gives you access to all the features of Score Player right in Visual Basic

➤ C/C++ programmers can access Score Player features directly via the DLLs provided with Version 2.0

➤ You can create scores and play them as screen savers. A separate screen saver is available for playing MediaBlitz scores

➤ A packaging utility collects all parts of a score in one place for easy portability

➤ A wide range of transition effects has been added for bitmap transitions

I was very pleased with Version 3.0 of MediaBlitz. It gives you a simple way to create non-interactive multimedia shows. Recommended.

Presentation Software

I would guess that most of the multimedia that is happening right now in the business world is happening in the presentation arena. Presentations are the life-blood of the corporation. Ideas, new products, and organizational concepts are all communicated most effectively in presentations.

Presentations with slides and projectors have been fading for several years, ever since the introduction of products like Harvard Graphics. The computer has become a standard presentation tool. Hookups to large-screen TVs, LCD screens for use with overhead projectors and other advances have made some pretty fancy presentations possible. Now, with the additional of multimedia, the average user can do some amazingly hot stuff.

When it comes to multimedia presentation software, there are two ways you can go. You can stick with your familiar presentation package as it adds multimedia, or you can go with a new package that is built around multimedia. Personally, I'd go with the new; that's why Compel is the Author's Choice for this category. Because an Author's Choice is a product I use myself, this tells you that when I need to create a presentation, I turn first to Compel. It does lack a few important traditional presentation features, but I feel that the strong support for multimedia enables me, overall, to create a better presentation.

If you do need to stick with your present presentation package, you may wait a while for certain multimedia features, or you may need to hunt around to find them. At some point, almost any package is going to require an overhaul to really support and integrate multimedia. I think it makes sense to bite the bullet and act now—Compel is young and easy to learn. You can grow with it as it matures and say you were there at the beginning.

Compel

I had to really think hard about giving Compel an Author's Choice. I have a kind of love-hate relationship with the product. On the one hand, the interface is so well-designed for multimedia development that I get excited using Compel. On the other hand, it is slow, and there were a few troublesome bugs in the first release.

But the interface is so good, the multimedia access so convenient, that I feel, well, compelled to give Asymetrix a pat on the back. Compel is what a multimedia presentation package should be. Let's keep things in perspective: this is a first release and has nowhere to go but up—additional features, more control over the details of multimedia presentation, and faster performance. Compel is like that great vacation spot you've found before anyone else even knows it's there. You won't find the usual chain restaurants, there's no mall to shop at, but you can relax and do what you want to do, when you want to do it.

Why do I feel so strongly about Compel? In preparation for writing this chapter, I had to actually use all of these products (and a few that didn't measure up and thus aren't included here) to create presentations. I sweated with some, groaned with others, and even enjoyed using a few others. The last one I used was Compel, and when I fired it up and found everything so accessible and well-organized, it felt like home. And then, when feature after feature offered me the kind of control I really want for my multimedia presentations, I was hooked.

But that's enough sales pitch; let's take a look at Compel. Figure 4.35 shows a typical starting screen for Compel.

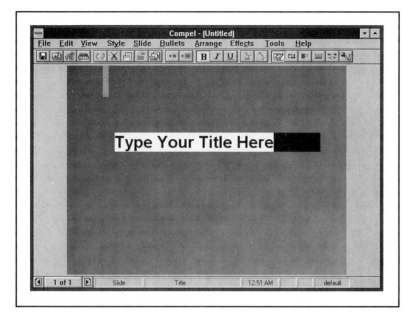

Figure 4.35. *A typical Compel startup screen.*

As with most presentation packages, the background is a default template.[15] The text for the title is selected and ready for you to type in your own title. After you do so, you can add bullets by clicking on one of the buttons in the toolbar. In just seconds, you have a completed slide (Figure 4.36).

Right next to the new bullet button, you'll find the New Button button. Any object can have multimedia properties, but, well, buttons are kind of traditional. This also gives me a chance to point out a nice feature of Compel. Most software doesn't use the right mouse button; Compel does. Right-clicking on objects opens a little dialog box that is kind of like a little application. Figure 4.37 shows the dialog box that pops up when you right-click a button.[16]

---

[15]You can, of course, define any template as the default.

[16]The dialog box is different for various kinds of objects.

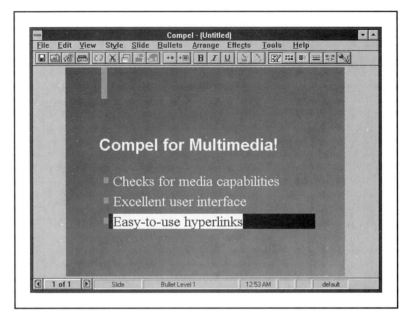

Figure 4.36. *A completed slide.*

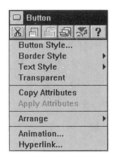

Figure 4.37. *A right-click dialog box.*

This little dialog gives you instant access to just about everything that has anything to do with buttons. I like this concept quite a bit, but it's a different way of working. Putting it just a right-click away means you don't have to use it if you don't want to. What it does is eliminate hunting all through the menus for a feature you need; it's just right in there in a handy-dandy dialog box.

Let's explore to show what I mean. Clicking Button Style displays the dialog box shown in Figure 4.38.

Figure 4.38. *Setting the button style.*

From this dialog, you can set the text of the button, define it as one of seven different types of buttons, and access related information, such as the character attributes (and, as I've begun to expect from Compel, that dialog is very well organized, too).

OK; now we have a button; let's do some multimedia. Click the button to select it, then click the Effects|Media Link menu selection to display the dialog shown in Figure 4.39. The list box on the left displays triggers—things that can cause a media event to start or stop. The right list box in Figure 4.39 displays the different media actions Compel supports—it's a very complete list.

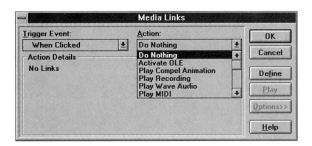

Figure 4.39. *Adding a media link.*

For example, Figure 4.40 shows the dialog for playing digital video. The dialog shown acts like a control center—you can access various details of the operation from this dialog. For example, you can create a viewer for the video by clicking on the Create Viewer button.[17] A list of previously loaded digital video clips (if you loaded any) is shown at the lower left. To add one or more new clips, click the New button.

---

[17]A single viewer can be used by any number of media events.

Figure 4.40. *Editing a media link.*

The real fun hides behind the Edit button. Click the Edit button to display the dialog shown in Figure 4.41. This dialog enables you to set a starting point for the clip, and ending point, and it contains convenient buttons for playing just the beginning or ending segments so you can check them for accuracy. You can control the clip exactly, and easily, using these controls. In Figure 4.41, the video itself is playing at lower right.

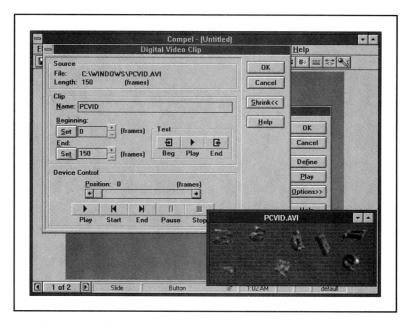

Figure 4.41. *Editing a digital video clip.*

This control is typical of the multimedia controls in Compel. They give you detailed, exact control over the media clips you use in your presentation. I give Compel high marks for its completeness in this area.

However, there's more. Return with me now to the dialog shown in Figure 4.40, only this time, I have clicked on the Options button to display additional features (Figure 4.42). For example, you can play the video once, continuously, or repeat it a specified number of times. You can scale the video to the size of the viewer you created for it, or you can simply center the video on the viewer. Other useful options are also available.

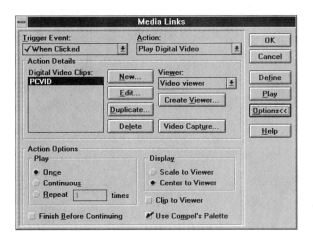

Figure 4.42. *Editing a media link.*

The result of adding the video is shown in Figure 4.43. When you actually play the presentation, it can occupy the full screen (Figure 4.44). Another nice thing about Compel is that, no matter what size screen you play it on, Compel neatly scales all of the elements of the presentation. This means that you can show the presentation at any screen resolution without worrying about the size of the text objects, whether the presentation will look OK, and so on. There is an exception: video. Video clips are played at their actual size when you center them in a viewer. If you want the video to resize to fit, scale the video to the viewer (see Figure 4.42).

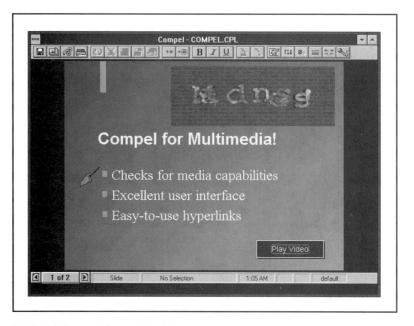

Figure 4.43. *Adding a video to the slide.*

Figure 4.44. *Playing a presentation full screen.*

Overall, Compel may lack some of the fancier presentation tools. But when it comes to multimedia, you can't beat it.

Action!

In the last edition of this book, I used and reported on Action! Version 1.0.[18] This time around, I'll be looking at Version 2.5. The changes are substantial and important. They aren't enough to give Action! an Author's Choice,[19] but the product has improved quite a bit.

Version 1.0 of Action! had two problems: it was slow, and the feature set was somewhat limited. It did some cool things, but there were too few of them. In Version 2.5, Action has been speeded up a little, and there is now an extensive set of tools and effects. Action! gets its highest marks for completeness and loses a few points for being somewhat disorganized. It also does not integrate multimedia as effectively as, say, Compel.

Action! takes its own approach to creating a presentation. Many packages are based on a series of slides, but Action! is based on scenes. The slide itself is a backdrop against which all kinds of actions take place. Figure 4.45 shows the opening screen of Action! There is a toolbar at the left and a play controller at top right. These and several other Action! windows can be moved around if they get in your way.[20]

To get started, you need to load a template. Action! comes with more than a dozen template families. Each family contains individual slide templates suitable for all kinds of standard presentation tasks—charting, intro slides, text slides, tables, and so on. You can preview each template in a little window. It's not enough to see the details of slides you aren't familiar with, but big enough to identify slides you already know.

---

[18]What is it with exclamation points in product names? Is it just me, or is this weird?

[19]It was good enough to get an Editor's Choice in PC Magazine, but I disagree for reasons I make clear shortly.

[20]However: Action! uses an MDI interface, which means you cannot move the windows outside of the Action! window itself.

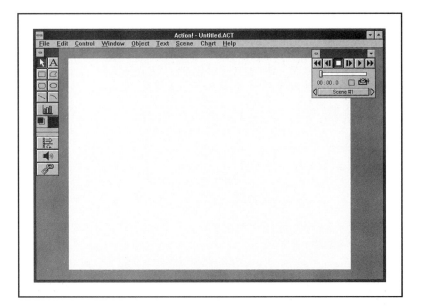

Figure 4.45. *The Action! screen.*

The selected template is loaded into the current scene; each scene can have a different template. Figure 4.46 shows a template loaded into a scene. I have clicked on several of the elements in the template to select them. Note that the elements are surrounded by a solid white line. This indicates that the elements are part of the template. You cannot edit template elements directly. You must click the Promote to Scene menu selection if you want to change something that is in a template.[21]

There are two kinds of editing. Double-clicking on an object opens the Edit Object dialog, shown in Figure 4.47. Many of the features of Action! are located right here. The list box near the top of the dialog box includes a list of events and object characteristics. The appearance of the rest of the dialog box depends on which event or characteristic you select. The Hold event in Figure 4.47 is used to control an effect that occurs during the hold phase of an object. In this example. there will be a sparkle effect around the text object. You can specify the kind of effect, its duration, and the color of the effect. If you were editing the Enter event, you would be able to specify the Transition effect, any motion you want for the object, and the duration of both.

---

[21]In Compel, you can edit template elements directly.

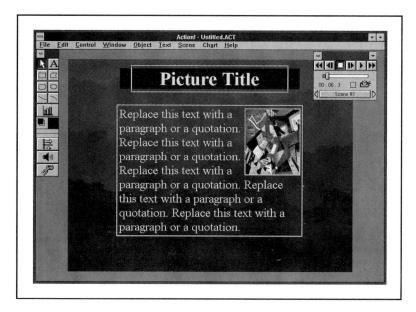

Figure 4.46. *A template loaded into a scene.*

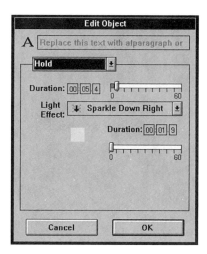

Figure 4.47. *Editing an object.*

Action! gives you the ability to control nine items for an object.

Enter—Effect when the object enters the scene.

Hold—Effect while the object is in the scene and after the entry completes.

Exit—Effect when the object leaves the scene.

Duration—How long the object is in the scene.

Content—Varies, depending on the kind of content. Used to define and describe the contents of the object.

Color—The color of the object.

Ink and Shadow—Determines the transparency of the object and whether it has a shadow.

Sound—Controls sounds associated with the object.

Link—Link to other objects and scenes. Used for jumping to other scenes, or to pause or start operations.

This is only one aspect of controlling objects. It's useful for setting specific properties and characteristics, but there are better ways of handling certain properties. The two most useful are the Timeline and the Content List.

Figure 4.48 shows the Content List. It shows the contents of your presentation in outline format. You can edit textual content entries directly, and you can call up the trusty old Edit Object dialog by double-clicking an object's entry in the Content List. You also can click and drag to move objects from one scene to the next.

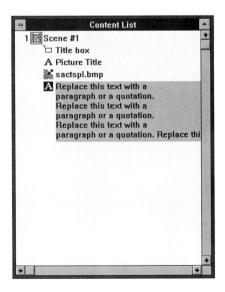

Figure 4.48. *The Content List.*

226

The Timeline, however, is the key to using Action! effectively. I edited the elements that were promoted into the scene earlier as shown in Figure 4.49. Editing is easiest in what is called *compressed view*. To change to compressed view, click the check box at the center of the Play controller. This locks and displays all objects so you can edit them. If you do not use compressed view, all objects will be in whatever location—including off screen—that is appropriate for the current time. For example, if you are currently two seconds into the current scene and an object doesn't enter the scene until four seconds later, it won't be on the screen.[22] Figure 4.50 shows such a situation—the text is being hidden from the top down, as is the bitmap. The title text is flying out to the left, and the title bar is flying out to the right.

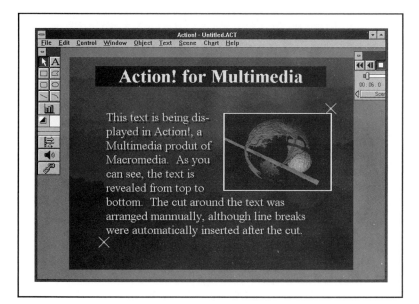

Figure 4.49. *The edited scene in action.*

---

[22]The play controller shows the current time to the nearest tenth of a second, and the Timeline window has a position indicator that indicates the current time.

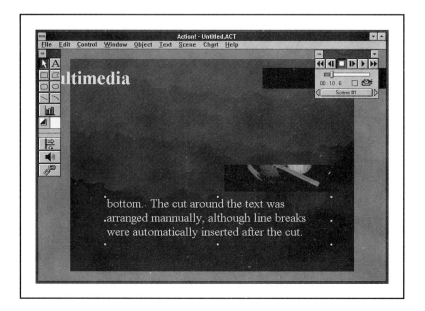

Figure 4.50. *A scene with partially hidden objects.*

Figure 4.51 shows a timeline for the one-scene project. Note that there is one horizontal line for each object in the scene. From top to bottom, these are the title, the black box behind the title, a bitmap, the text at center screen, and a rectangle behind the bitmap. You can grab and move objects in timeline view, and adjust the duration of Enter, Hold, and Exit events. Most importantly, the Timeline view gives you a very convenient way to get a conceptual view of the overall scene and the relationship of the various elements over time.

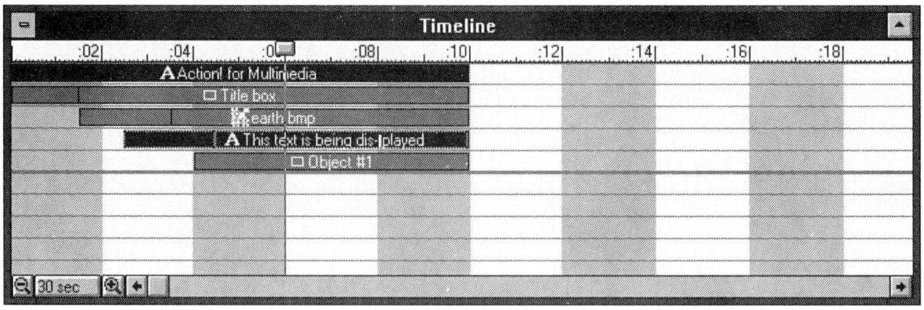

Figure 4.51. *The Timeline window.*

There are three buttons at the base of the toolbox that are worth mentioning. From top to bottom, they are the Action, Sound, and Link buttons. Click the Action button and then an object; this opens the dialog shown in Figure 4.52.

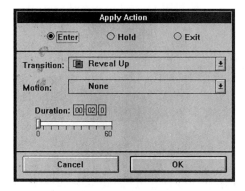

Figure 4.52. *The Apply Action dialog box.*

You can add Transitions or motion to an object in this manner. The Action button makes it easy to add these effects.

The Sound button is a tacit acknowledgment that sounds are one of the most common media elements added to presentations. To add a sound, click the Sound button, then click an object to open the Import dialog box.[23] Once you have selected the sound, you'll see the dialog in Figure 4.53. This enables you to establish the start time, duration, delay, looping, and other characteristics of a sound.

The Link button is used to give objects the ability to move around in the presentation. Basically, this enables you to turn almost any object into a button. Figure 4.54 shows the Link dialog, with a list of the events and actions you can link with.[24]

---

[23]Not shown in a figure, but it's basically a File Open dialog with a button added for previewing sounds.

[24]So shoot me—I ended a sentence with a preposition.

Figure 4.53. *Editing a sound.*

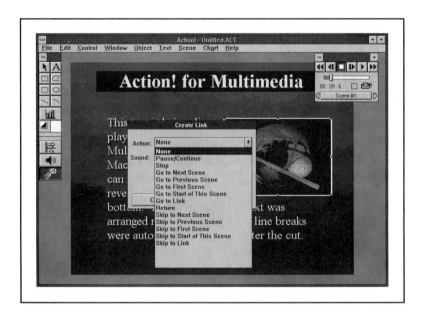

Figure 4.54. *Creating a link.*

In the first edition of this book, I wasn't all that positive about Action! as a multimedia presentation tool. That has changed. Action! now has a very full and useful feature set. In addition, it gives you multiple ways of getting at the multimedia objects in your presentation. It's not as well organized as Compel, but the built-in animation can give your presentations an active look. You can create some very good-looking presentations with very little effort. For example, I scanned in the cover of my book *Virtual Reality Madness* for a project I was working on, and

I loaded it into the example presentation for this chapter—and the result was very professional looking (Figure 4.55).

Figure 4.55. *Another page from the presentation.*

The only problem I had with Action! was in the use of video files. Some files did not play properly in 16-bit color video display mode. They played slowly. Otherwise, this feature-rich package is well worth a close look. However, as you can see in Figure 4.56, Action! does provide detailed control of video clips you use. It's not quite as well organized or clear as the dialog in Compel, but it gets the job done.

Figure 4.56. *Digital Video Editor.*

HSC InterActive

InterActive is a very accessible authoring program. Basically, you select icons, then assign properties to the icons. Presto—instant multimedia.

Well, it's not actually that easy. Good multimedia has a lot of information in it, and organizing and keeping track of the information still takes some brain power. However, InterActive takes some of the sweat out of the process. Many conventional presentation programs (like Power Point or Aldus Persuasion) use outlines to help you keep track of the order of the items. InterActive uses icons arranged in a flow chart to take you to the next logical organizational step.

This product makes multimedia accessible. It is thoughtfully designed—it provides a good deal of structure, but the structure is enabling rather than limiting. InterActive is based on a much more expensive authoring package, Icon Author from AimTech. It keeps much of the user interface, but it does not include the multimedia database features of Icon Author.

The Icon-Driven Interface

InterActive is icon-driven.[25] To create a presentation, you drag icons around and drop them on a form. Then you set various properties for the icons, such as conditional expressions, images to display, sounds to play, and so on. You use something called a Content Editor to make such changes.

To some degree, InterActive reminds me of certain aspects of Visual Basic (which you learn about in Chapter 8, "Manning the Pump: Multimedia Programming"). Even more than the physical similarities, the conceptual similarities give InterActive an advantage—if time is critical, and the task is not too technical. Scripting languages like Asymetrix ToolBook are powerful, and you can do all kinds of things in your own way. If you do not have the time for that, however, or if you don't want to learn a scripting language, InterActive provides a simpler interface to work with. The usual penalty applies: scripting gives you power to customize, so you will have to follow along in the paths that Interactive gives you. They are useful paths, but frustratingly narrow at times.

As with any product that is conceptually different, it takes a little time to get used to how InterActive works. I don't think you will regret the investment—

---

[25]It is also a subset of what you get with Icon Author, a product reviewed later in this chapter.

that is, unless you plan to distribute your application. The current version of InterActive cannot work with relative pathnames for MCI commands; you have to know everything from the drive to the exact directory ahead of time. Frustrating. I have complained loud and long about this difficulty. As this edition was going to press, HSC was beta testing a new install routine that will deal with many issues related to distributing your Interactive applications.[26]

Using InterActive, HSC has created a multimedia demo that is included on the CD-ROM.

Working with InterActive

Consider the basic structure of an InterActive presentation. When you open a new file in InterActive, you see a screen with a Start icon in a window (Figure 4.57).

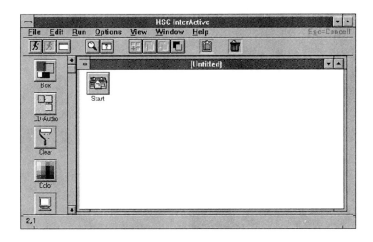

Figure 4.57. *Opening a new file with InterActive.*

There are a few other features in this screen shot that are worth looking at. Near the top of the InterActive window is a toolbar; the most commonly used functions can be accessed here. On the left side of the window are the icons I've

---

[26]For the latest information, the best source is HSC itself on their CompuServe forum. To get there, type GO MULTIVEN. You'll find a section there just for HSC.

been talking about. Only a few icons are visible; there are many more. The visible icons can be used to

➤ Draw a box on the screen, outlined or filled.

➤ Play CD audio from any point to any point.

➤ Clear an area.

➤ Color an area.

➤ Display a bitmap or animation.

Not visible along the left of the window is an icon called Menu; it is a combination icon that causes many icons to appear. If you click the menu icon and drag it to the Start icon, the screen in Figure 4.58 appears.

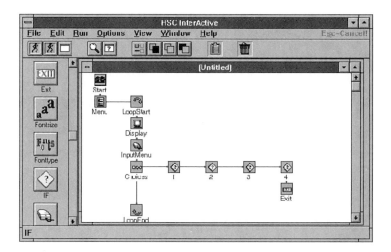

Figure 4.58. *Clicking the menu icon generates a display of several icons.*

This provides an easy way to create structure for a presentation. The icons that were inserted form a simple logic chain that sorts though any choice made by the user. There is a Loop Start icon to mark the beginning of the loop, followed by a display icon (it causes a bitmap or an animation to be displayed) and an input menu. When program flow reaches the input menu icon, the user is asked to choose one of several options. The choice is passed to the Choices icon, which then branches to one of the numbered icons.

The generic icons you created won't do what you want, however; you need a way to specify what each icon does. InterActive uses a Content Editor for this. Double-clicking an icon brings up its Content Editor (Figure 4.59).

Figure 4.59. *The Content Editor dialog box.*

Each icon has its own kind of Content Editor. This is the heart of InterActive. Instead of having to write programs with a script language, you are guided to the next step via the editors. InterActive also comes with a program called IconAnimate. Using this program, you can develop linear presentations—that is, presentations that are not interactive and that do not branch. Figure 4.60 shows an icon animation that puts a spaceman in orbit around an image of the Earth.

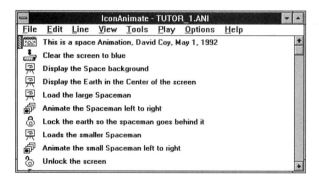

Figure 4.60. *The IconAnimate window.*

Each line in the animation, if double-clicked, can be edited to control that aspect of the animation. For example, to control the method and speed of the movement of the spaceman in front of the Earth, double-click the icon labeled "Animate the Spaceman left to right." This displays the dialog box shown in Figure 4.61.

235

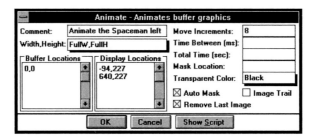

Figure 4.61. *The Animate dialog box.*

As you can see, you can control the speed, duration, and other factors. You can then incorporate your animation in an InterActive presentation.

The Bottom Line

Overall, InterActive does a lot of neat multimedia stuff, but it has some dinosaur habits that need to be addressed. One of the two multimedia presentations I created for the CD-ROM was built using InterActive. I like the icon approach for creating fluid presentations, but the weak spots—hard-coded pathnames and poor text support—need to be addressed in future versions before this can become a leading product.

If you have large amounts of text in your presentation, InterActive is not the best way to go—you can write only one line of text per icon. You must enter the text in a Content Editor, then you have to position it without seeing the text. If you must have large chunks of text, it's better to use a paint program to assemble the text in a graphic you can import.

I will continue to use InterActive because it has a good interface, but I look forward to improvements with anticipation. If you have serious multimedia needs and like the icon-based approach, look into Interactive's big brother, Icon Author. Icon Author fills in some of the holes in Interactive's feature set, but it does suffer from a few interface problems of its own. Icon Author is reviewed in full later in this chapter.

Multimedia ToolBook

Ah, ToolBook. In terms of power, it has plenty—but be prepared to pay the price of power. You'll need to spend some time learning the ins and outs of this programming tool.

However, the price of power with ToolBook is a little steeper than it has to be. ToolBook's capabilities are not covered as clearly and completely as they need to be in the documentation. This means you will need a supplemental source of information. There are two places you can turn: books about ToolBook programming,[27] and Asymetrix technical support staff.

Fortunately, the technical support crew at Asymetrix does a great job at answering questions.[28] I don't mean to scare you away from ToolBook with all of this talk; I just want you to go in with your head up knowing what to expect.

ToolBook is based on objects and *event handlers,*[29] which give you sophisticated control over what occurs in your application. A handler is nothing more than a script that tells ToolBook what to do when the event occurs. Events include elements such as EnterPage, MouseUp, and so on. ToolBook needs better control over the creation and editing of these handlers. Visual Basic, particularly in Version 2.0, gives you more effective ways of working with event handlers.

ToolBook handlers are associated with objects. Almost everything is an object—buttons, bitmaps, hotwords in text, boxes, pages, and so on. To put a handler into an object, you select the object with the mouse and use the menu to access the object's script.[30] There are some sample scripts in Chapter 8, and in the next section, "A Sample ToolBook Application."

---

[27]Asymetrix has a list of current books on their own BBS, and there is a list in the MULTIMEDIA forum, section 7, as well that I try to keep up to date. My own book, PC Video Madness, includes a good introduction to multimedia programming with ToolBook, including a complete list of the multimedia functions.

[28]Probably the most convenient place to access this support is on CompuServe, in the MULTIVEN forum where Asymetrix has a section of their own. I've been very impressed with the Asymetrix folks on CompuServe—hardly a day goes by without some cool code example passing by in answer to a question. You can learn a lot just by hanging out. Say hi to Greg and Chris and the rest of the gang.

[29]When an event occurs, such as a mouse click, the event bubbles around in ToolBook until it finds a handler attached to some object, such as a button or a page.

[30]You can also access the script by holding down the Control key and double-clicking on an object.

Unlike most authoring tools, ToolBook is a complete programming environment and is designed from the ground up to be used in multimedia software development and for creating presentations. Multimedia ToolBook is powerful because it is a script-based product. Unlike HSC InterActive, ToolBook involves programming. This is an advantage when you want tight control over what happens on-screen. It does increase development time, however.

ToolBook has an interesting development interface. You can write scripts that apply to an entire *book,* as Asymetrix calls a complete program. You also can write code that applies to a particular page or to an object on a page, and you can link the elements of your application or presentation to move easily between pages. It is the ability to create actual applications, rather than mere presentations, that sets ToolBook apart from most other multimedia authoring systems. For example, the commercial applications Multimedia Beethoven and Composer Quest were both created with ToolBook.

A Sample ToolBook Application

Here's a look into one of the sample applications that comes with ToolBook: SPACE.TBK.

This screen is typical of the kind of screens you can create in ToolBook; it is one of many in the application. In ToolBook lingo, it is called a page (Figure 4.62).

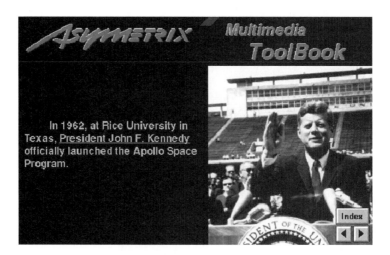

Figure 4.62. *A sample ToolBook page.*

There is more here than meets the eye, as you see in a moment.

Author Mode

By pressing F3, you can switch from Reader mode to Author mode. This enables you to work directly with the elements of the application. As a reader, clicking a button makes the button take some action. As an author, you can program the button to take actions. These actions can be anything ToolBook can do, including

➤ Going to another page

➤ Popping up a window

➤ Playing a sound, animation, or other multimedia file

➤ Launching a Windows application

➤ Branching to another part of the program

There are three buttons at the lower-right corner of the previous figure (4.62), but they are not a part of the page; they are a part of the background. The title at the top is also part of the background. Only the image of Kennedy and the text are part of the current page. This multi-layered approach is a key feature of ToolBook.

Layering is designed to reduce programming effort. By programming the buttons once as part of the background, you can then use them on any number of pages. If you try to click any of the buttons, you cannot select them while viewing the page. If you select Background from the menu, you see the screen in Figure 4.63.

Only the elements that are part of the background are now visible. Now you can select any of the buttons by clicking it. If you do, you can use the **O**bject menu to inspect the button properties using the dialog box in Figure 4.64.

This dialog box can be used to give the button a name, a label, a border style, and other properties. The buttons on the right give access to a button script and linking capabilities.

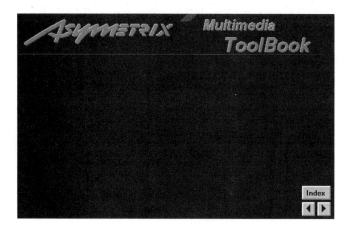

Figure 4.63. *Selecting Background generates this screen.*

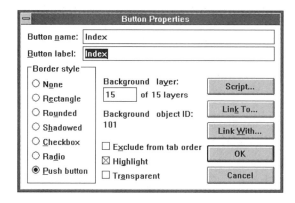

Figure 4.64. *The Button Properties dialog box.*

Scripts

You can place scripts at any level of a ToolBook application—the background, a page, or a specific object. Here is an example of a script at the page level that is called whenever a button is released:

```
to handle buttonUp
  system s_rplaying, s_devices, s_wOpen
  if object of target is in "hotword,paintObject"
    if "waveaudio" is in s_devices
      if s_rplaying is true
```

```
      get tbkMCI("stop 2w","")
      break buttonUp
    end
    if s_wOpen
      get tbkMCI("play 2w from 0", uniqueName of self)
      set s_rplaying to true
    else
      request "The wave file for this script could not be opened." &&
              "It may have been deleted."
    end
  else
    request "No wave audio device is present."
  end
  end
end
```

This piece of code illustrates several principles of script programming in ToolBook. The most important is that scripts are event-based. This code is a handler that is called to handle all button-up events on the page where it is found. The handler checks to see whether a Wave audio clip is playing, and if it is, stops playback. The handler then plays the current Wave audio clip. In addition, the handler does some error checking to make sure that the sound is present, or that it can be played. If you are a beginning programmer, you may find it more convenient to put buttonUp handlers in the objects themselves, instead of the page. This keeps your scripts to a more manageable size.

Let's look at one of those lines of ToolBook code more closely. Consider the line

```
if "waveaudio" is in s_devices
```

This is a very English-like sentence, and it is typical of ToolBook. `waveaudio` is a simple text string, and `s_devices` is a variable. The line will evaluate to `True` if the text is found in the variable.[31]

Figure 4.65 shows another page from the application.

This page has many more buttons. Notice that most buttons refer to various multimedia devices, such as video, CD audio, and Wave audio. Multimedia ToolBook includes full support for any multimedia device. This page also shows an example of a large text window with a scroll bar for reading text not currently visible. ToolBook includes a wide range of Windows elements that you can use when designing an application.

---

[31]Elsewhere in the application, the set of available multimedia devices was placed into the variable.

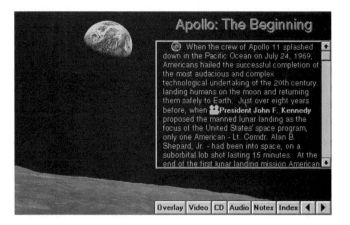

Figure 4.65. *A page with a scrollable-text window.*

ToolBook includes so much that you are more likely to be snowed under (at least at first) than to find yourself unable to do something.

Linking Events

Figure 4.66 shows another page from the application. Notice the text at the left of the image.

Figure 4.66. *Another page from the application.*

This is a common task in multimedia presentations—the user (or *reader* in ToolBook lingo) clicks an object or area, and some action takes place. In Author mode, you can click the spaceman's face plate. Grab handles appear at the corners of the active area and along the sides (Figure 4.67). You can use these handles to adjust the size of the object.[32]

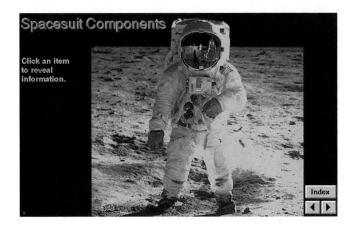

Figure 4.67. *You can use the handles to adjust the size of an object.*

You can pull down the **O**bject menu (Figure 4.68) and select Graphic Properties.

This brings up a dialog box that contains, among other things, a Script button (Figure 4.69). This box is typical of the dialog boxes associated with objects. With it, you can change the object's properties, such as its script.

Clicking the Script button displays the script behind the face plate (Figure 4.70).

This script causes the text to be displayed when the face plate area is clicked.

---

[32]This object is in reality a simple rectangle that has been made transparent. This enables the user to click on various areas of the bitmap and cause different handlers to be called—the button click goes to whatever object is under the mouse cursor.

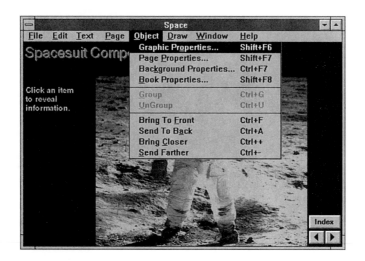

Figure 4.68. *The Object menu.*

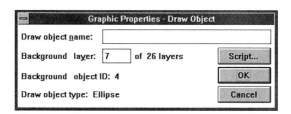

Figure 4.69. *The Graphic Properties dialog box.*

Figure 4.70. *The face plate scripts.*

Multimedia Devices

You have now looked at code in an object script and in a page script. Here is a bit of code from a background script:

```
—This function checks for the presence of
—the devices used by this book,
—initializes the ones that are present, and returns a list
—of successfully initialized devices.
to get initMediaDevices

  get tbkMCI("close all","")
  set retValue to null
  get tbkMCI("sysinfo all quantity","")
  if it <> null
    step i from 1 to it
      set item i of devList to tbkMCI("sysInfo all name" && i,"")
    end
    set sysErrorNumber to 0
```

When this code is finished, a comma-separated list of installed multimedia hardware will be in the variable devList.

This is just the beginning of the portion of the script that handles initialization of multimedia devices. This code first closes all devices, then determines the total number of devices available (sysinfo all quantity). It then steps through each device, obtaining information about each device and storing it for later reference.

Later in this same script, the various multimedia devices are initialized. Here is the portion of the script that initializes CD audio:

```
—Initialize cd-audio
set sysErrorNumber to 0
if "cdaudio" is in devList
  do
    get tbkMCI("open cdaudio shareable wait","")
    get tbkMCI("status cdaudio mode","")
    if (it is null or it is "not ready") or tbkMCI("status" && \
      "cdaudio media present","") is false
        request "The CD audio device is not present or is not \
        ready." with "Retry" or "Cancel"
        if it is "cancel"
          set cond to true
        else
          set cond to false
        end
    else
      get tbkMCI("set cdaudio audio all on","")
      push "cdaudio" onto retValue
      set cond to true
    end
  until cond
end
```

This code builds on the previous example. It checks to see whether CD audio is in the list of available devices (`devList`); if so, the code opens it (`open cdaudio shareable wait`). It checks the current mode and then determines whether there is a disk in the drive. It also checks for any possible errors. As you can see, you can have as detailed a level of control as you desire.

The Bottom Line

This is just a sampling of the power of ToolBook; Chapter 8 goes into greater detail about programming with ToolBook. How useful is ToolBook? Well, I have seen it used to create complete prototypes of major Windows applications. I can't name names because of a nondisclosure agreement I signed, but one of the major database packages was ported to Windows only after a comprehensive prototype was developed using ToolBook.

In many cases, the ToolBook prototype turns out to be the final product. It's hard to beat the flexibility of ToolBook when it comes to serious multimedia development. If it's power you need, ToolBook should do it. I have quoted sample scripts extensively to give you some idea of the level of programming skills you need to get the most out of ToolBook. Although you also can use ToolBook for basic multimedia tasks, you should see whether one of the simpler packages, like InterActive, might be easier to use.

Databases and Multimedia

Ever since Windows first came out, there has been a lack of solid database software for it. This is beginning to change. Several excellent products are now hitting the market. Filemaker, a popular Macintosh database product, is now available for Windows. Approach, a new database program, has been well received. There are several other Windows databases that have been around for a while, such as SuperBase, but these really didn't catch on. In the near future, look for many of these standard database products to be updated to handle multimedia.

Some database products are multimedia in the sense that you can store images in the database. None of the mainstream database products, however, are true multimedia products using the criteria I mentioned earlier. There are some products that are specifically designed as multimedia database products, but they are not useful as general-purpose databases.

Because multimedia files are often very large, only database products designed with such large files in mind can be used to store multimedia files. In addition, sound and image files are binary data; only a few databases are prepared to accept binary data.

What is binary data? The simple answer isn't very helpful: binary data is anything that isn't text. Text data is anything that uses numbers, letters, and special characters. The computer uses a subset of all possible byte values to represent text data. In particular, the values from 0–31 are not used. Binary data can use any byte value at all. If a database is not expecting non-text characters, their presence will almost certainly cause severe problems.

The term *BLOB* (Binary Large Object) is now a popular term for binary data. A BLOB can be anything at all, so the term isn't very specific. A database that says it supports BLOBs isn't telling you much because there are so many varieties of binary file formats—dozens of image formats, many sound file formats, animation files, and so on. If the database says it supports BLOBs, take a closer look to see exactly what it can work with. In some cases, it might be easy to store something, but impossible to make use of it after you do.

Because multimedia involves such large data files, it seems inevitable that databases will take a larger role in multimedia. This will involve much more than just tacking on multimedia support. In the not-too-distant future, database software will need to be able to seamlessly display, play, or locate multimedia data the way they handle simple text today.

Icon Author

At first glance, Icon Author looks a lot like HSC Interactive (see Figure 4.71). You might even think that you are looking at the same product. There are the icons at the left of the window, and the toolbar beneath the menu, and that little Start icon at the upper left of the window. Compare to Figure 4.22 to see what I mean.

However, there are differences, and the deeper you dig into Icon Author the bigger they are. And Icon Author is *deep*. Here are some differences that I see as key ones:

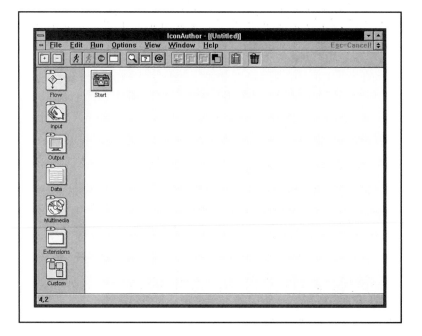

Figure 4.71. *The Icon Author main window.*

➤ Icon Author includes support for a wide variety of specialized video and audio hardware, such as laser disc players that can be controlled remotely, and high-end overlay video hardware. But you have to ask the question: with the recent advances like Video for Windows, the Intel Smart Video Recorder, and others—is this kind of hardware still needed? You bet. If you want the best, you have to go with this kind of hardware. If you're betting the farm—corporate boardroom presentations, a classy set of kiosks at trendy locations—and want the best look, Icon Author supports the kind of hardware you are going to need.[33]

➤ Text support is better—you can read in a file if you want to, rather than the one-line text entries that are allowed in Interactive. Thus, Icon Author is a more broad-based tool than Interactive. Interactive hits its

---

[33]But change is in the wind. Slowly but surely, high-end hardware is being supported with standard Windows multimedia drivers. A recent example: the DVA/4000 and Media Space from VideoLogic. As this happens, it gets easier and easier to access the high-end hardware from the easier, more accessible software packages.

limits with interactive presentations, while Icon Author can be used in much more complex ways, and to convey much more complex and larger quantities of information.

➤ Layout controls are also better. I don't personally like the way that the controls work, but there are definitely more and better controls than in Interactive.

➤ Support tools and utilities are both more complete and more numerous. Animation, hot spots—you'll get more and better control over the details of your application.

With that in mind, let's take a look at Icon Author. Figure 4.72 shows a project with a menu icon added. To add the icon, you just grab it with the mouse in the icon list at the left and drag it over the Start icon. It is actually a compound icon, and all the icons you see in Figure 4.72 appear when you release the mouse button.

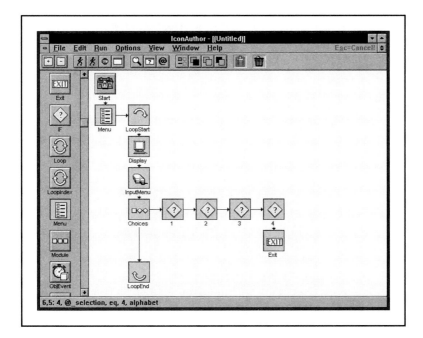

Figure 4.72. *Adding a menu icon.*

This structure is the heart of flow control in Icon Author. The LoopStart and LoopEnd icons define the beginning and ending points of the loop, which will continue to execute until the Exit branch is encountered. The Display icon defines an image that will serve as a background, and the InputMenu icon defines hot spots the user can click on. The Choices icon directs the user's input to the four numbered icons. The numbered icons are actually If conditions—if the response is the number under the icon, that branch of the loop will be followed. The branches are empty right now, of course, but that is easy to change.

Let's flesh out this menu skeleton. Like Interactive, Icon Author uses Content Editors to change values in icons. Different icons have different values for you to change. The display icon's Content Editor (see Figure 4.73) has four entries: the file type, the filename, location coordinates, and parameters for any special effects.

Figure 4.73. *The Display Content Editor.*

The special effects entry (SquareIris,Out,Medium) is not something you're going to have to memorize. There is an editor for effects as shown in Figure 4.74. You simply select an effect, a modifier,[34] and a speed.

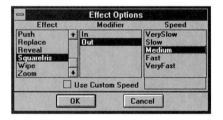

Figure 4.74. *Selecting a special effect for a Display icon.*

---

[34]The list of modifiers changes depending on the effect.

Setting up the input menu is a little different. The object here is to draw little squares that will serve as hot spots that the user can click on.[35] This means that the underlying graphic must contain graphic elements that are clearly menu selections. Figure 4.75 shows one of the graphics that comes with Icon Author as an example. You will, of course, need a separate graphic for each input menu, and a Display Icon to display it.

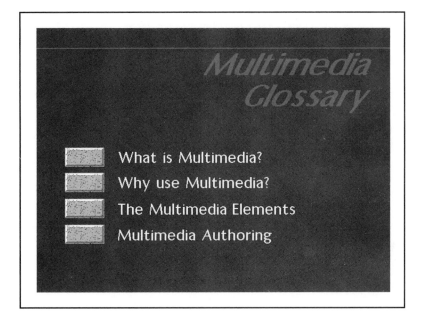

Figure 4.75. *A sample menu graphic.*

Of course, you can display any graphic at any time with a display icon. It's not limited to menu duty.

The Content Editor for the If icons enables you to check the value of variables. Icon Author may not have a procedural language, but it does have variables.[36] Figure 4.76 shows an If Content Editor with its default values—and they are just fine for this situation. The key thing to note is the variable name in the entry for Condition 1: @_selection. This is a *system variable*. System variables are ones that Icon Author manages for you—you can just check to see what the value

---

[35]If the user clicks away from the hot spots, they will hear a little buzz.

[36]There are, of course, icons for setting the value of variables.

is. The @_selection variable tells you which hot spot got clicked. If hot spot 1 gets clicked, the If icon will compare @_selection to Condition 2 (a value of 1), and get a result of True. Program control then flows to any icons that come after the If icon. You also can change the labels on the If icons from numbers to more descriptive text.

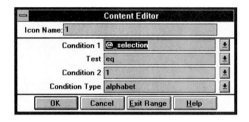

Figure 4.76. *An If icon's Content Editor.*

You can nest menus. Figure 4.77 shows a second level of menu icons added under what used to be the #1 If icon.

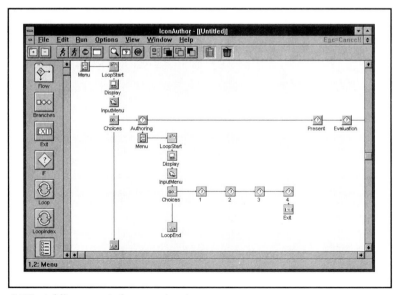

Figure 4.77. *Adding a nested menu structure.*

This is good, of course, but it raises an issue. By the time you have added all of the menu icons—and all of the other icons you need—things get really crowded. I found it hard to keep track of where everything was after a while. I would suggest working out the flow of your application before you sit down and start programming, so you'll have a general plan to refer to. This makes it easier to keep track of what is where.

You can add more choices to the menu by simply adding additional If icons. To determine what each branch does, you simply add the appropriate icons under the If icon. Figure 4.78 shows a whole bunch of icons. In this example, they are actually quite simple—they do things like draw boxes, underline text, and show my name. There are icons for selecting the current font, setting the font size, drawing circles, pausing before going back through the loop, and so on.

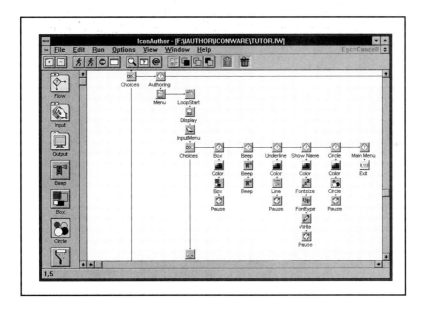

Figure 4.78. *Adding icons to the menu branches.*

When it comes to multimedia, it's really very easy to do. There is an MCI icon, and its Content Editor is shown in Figure 4.79. You use MCI commands, and you can even receive information back from MCI (just put a variable name in the MCI Result box). In the example, the MCI command plays a video file: `play c:\windows\pcvid.avi`. Note also that any error information is also placed into variables for easy reference in the application. You can test for an error and display an error message.

Figure 4.79. *A multimedia Content Editor.*

In addition to the individual MCI icon, which enables you to create any command sequences you desire (from the simple to the complex), there are several standardized icon groups you can use for playing MIDI or Wave files, or CD audio. All you have to do is supply the filename in the Content editor, and you've got a complete multimedia control structure. Figure 4.80 shows an example for playing a Wave file.

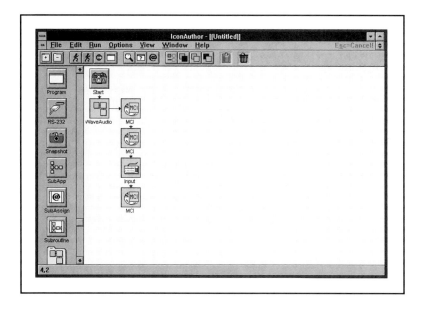

Figure 4.80. *Icons for playing a wave file.*

These icons execute the following MCI commands:

```
open filename alias audio
play audio
```

```
<input icon>
close audio
```

The Input icon between the `play` and `close` commands waits for a mouse click—any mouse click stops playback by allowing program flow to proceed to the `close` command.[37]

The simplicity of this structure is a testament to the standardization that MCI has brought to multimedia. Any hardware you use that comes with an MCI driver will be this easy to control—video and MIDI are as easy as Wave files.[38]

In addition, Icon Author includes numerous icons that deal specifically with the specialized, high-end hardware that is also supported by Icon Author (whether or not it has MCI drivers). For example, there is an icon for moving to a specific frame number in a video played from laser disc.

Icon Author definitely has the power you need to create sophisticated presentations. It is definitely the product to use if you need the kind of hardware support it offers. However, I think that the future of multimedia development will have to rely more on a mixed approach: graphical tools plus programming. Relying so much on icons can actually get in the way of developing your application. A little code is a good thing. Sometimes, it's the only efficient way to get the job done.

However, there is one area where Icon Author offers much more than other multimedia development environments. Icon Author is tailored for the business that absolutely, positively, needs to succeed with their multimedia applications. If a lot of money is riding on the outcome, if you really, really have to get it done right the first time—and especially if both multimedia and programming are new to you—then Icon Author may be your best bet. The purchase price includes four days of training at Aimtech's facilities. This hand-holding is valuable, and the less experience you or your company has in multimedia and/or programming, the more valuable it will be.

---

[37]The input icon has nothing to do with MCI. It's just another Icon Author icon.

[38]Well, almost—you might need another icon or two for video, and video offers many more MCI options so you may *want* to use more icons to make it do exactly what you want it to do.

Windows Multimedia

The Evolution of Windows Multimedia

The Windows flavor of multimedia is not the same as DOS or Macintosh multimedia. The differences are not great, but they are significant.

Windows does, of course, have elements in common with both the Macintosh and DOS. For example, Windows and the Macintosh treat multimedia as an integral part of the environment, and Windows shares the PC with DOS every time it runs.

The differences between Windows and DOS are the most significant. In DOS, the individual programmer designs and codes all elements of the user interface, including menus, buttons, and so on. In Windows (and on the Macintosh) these elements are predefined; a programmer need only turn to the services made available to him or her.

Here's another important difference: almost all Windows programs look superficially the same, but DOS programs are free to use a variety of different looks. Windows 3.0 did some tinkering with the interface, but the Windows environment remained essentially unchanged. The basic elements—windows with borders, buttons, dialog boxes, and so on—stayed pretty much the same.

DOS screens, on the other hand, vary quite a bit. Programmers are free to experiment, and they have—there is quite a variety of interfaces out there. Some interfaces use windows, some don't. Those that use windows handle them differently, with different ways to zoom, maximize, minimize, and so on. There simply are no standards in the pure DOS world.

As far as the Mac interface is concerned, it has many of the same elements Windows does, but it is the subtle differences that make *the* difference.

According to Apple, Windows is very similar to the Macintosh, but that is overstated in my opinion.[1] I find the Mac interface to have quite a different feel. In Windows, for example, it's easy to resize a window, but on the Mac I fumble

---

[1]Comparing these two operating systems is like saying a car and a pickup truck are nearly identical because they both have four wheels, use a steering wheel, and have brakes and an accelerator pedal. As anyone who has driven both knows, they are very different in handling and other characteristics. A pickup truck usually has a stiffer suspension, has different gear ratios in the transmission and rear end, and seats only two or three persons. You can, if you want to, buy a truck with a softer suspension and other car-like characteristics, but you can also buy Mac-like interfaces for Windows.

with the resizing controls every time. In other ways, the Windows interface is clunky—the Mac's Finder, for example, is a more elegant way to handle multi-tasking.

Although Windows strongly encourages similarity of program interfaces, it does not *require* it (at least not so far). For example, consider the opening screen for the Windows program Fractal Design Painter (Figure 5.1). Originally a Macintosh program, it uses a more or less Mac-like Windows interface, right down to the little horizontal lines on it sub-windows.

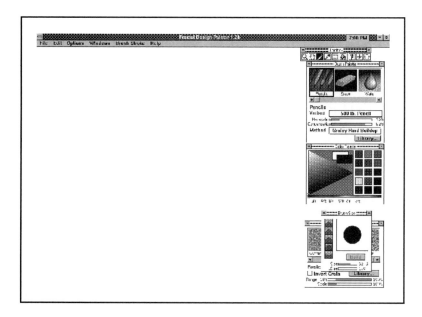

Figure 5.1. *The opening screen of Fractal Design Painter.*

The most significant differences between the Windows and Macintosh platforms, however, are found under the surface of the screen.

A history lesson is in order.

The Granddaddy of Multimedia

The Macintosh started out as a multimedia machine. When you turn on even the most basic (or ancient) of Macintoshes, you hear a little chime sound. This tells you that all is well with the machine. If all is *not* well, there is a problem with the machine, and it makes a different sound.

It is the *existence* of these sounds that is significant. The Macintosh comes with the ability to make sound—real sound, not the weak imitation sounds the PC speaker is capable of. A PC speaker beeps; a Mac plays a chord every time it is turned on.

I started working with PCs in the early '80s. It wasn't until several years ago that a Macintosh found its way to my desk. It came with a feature I found intriguing: sound. I could select which sounds to play when certain events occurred—ejection of a disk, a program error, startup of the machine, and so on. I could even play music. My favorite was the old, "Th-th-th-that's all folks!" from the Warner Brothers cartoons. The built-in sound capability sets the Macintosh apart from the hardware on which Windows runs.[2] On a PC, you have to add sound capability yourself. This made DOS and Windows the poor relations of the multimedia world. It took Windows 3.1 architecture to create standardization that made multimedia hardware manufacturers pay attention to PCs.

Windows Standards

How (and why) did Windows impose these standards, you ask? Allow me a brief digression.

In DOS, most programmers bypass the operating system and directly tell the hardware what to do. This was essential in the early days of the IBM XT computer because the hardware services provided by DOS were just too slow to be useful. Writing to the hardware was always faster, so programmers stuck to that method even when the machines became faster.

Windows, however, attempts to impose some order on communication with the hardware. Windows uses hardware drivers, and you can access the hardware through the drivers only. For example, a driver controls your video display. The

---

[2] However, I have an interesting story to tell. I had the opportunity to work with a Mac Quadra on a multimedia project recently. I found that, in some ways, support for multimedia on the Mac was ahead of the PC. At the same time, I discovered that there are ways in which the Mac is still backward. For example, if you decide to put sound on your PC, you have a wide choice of sound cards at a wide range of prices and capabilities. The Mac comes with built-in sound—but it's 8-bit sound, which is not adequate for some uses. However, because of this built-in support, there is not a lot of hardware available for putting 16-bit, high-quality sound into a Mac! The support for sound on the Mac was good enough to give us all a thrill, but at the same time that support put a damper on advancing the standards.

driver sits between all programs and the screen. If a program wants to display something on the screen, it tells Windows what it wants, Windows passes the information to the driver, and the driver handles the job of making the hardware do the actual work. This isolates the hardware from the programs that run on it. There are many advantages to this approach; one of the most important is that it lessens the ability of any one program to crash the entire system. Another advantage is that a programmer doesn't need to know anything about the hardware. He or she can simply tell Windows what to do, and Windows can worry about the hardware.

From the Windows side, all drivers of a given type are supposed to look similar so that any software program can call the driver in a standard way. For example, within Windows, if you want to display a bitmap in a window, there are just a few basic ways of doing that. On the hardware side, the drivers can be as different as they have to be to do the job. One driver might copy the bitmap into hardware buffers in case it must be redisplayed later, while another may not even care what happens later. As Windows has evolved, the degree of rigidity imposed on drivers has grown. Future versions of Windows promise to isolate the hardware as completely as possible.

This isolation is bad news for programmers who must write standardized drivers, but it's good news for users because working with sounds and images—multimedia—is easier. Although it's slower to do things this way, the ever-increasing power of today's machines makes that a moot point.

That is why Windows and the success of multimedia are intimately related. In the DOS world, it takes a lot of effort to program for the various pieces of hardware that are out there. Under Windows, standardization at the driver interface makes that aspect of software programming simpler. When a driver for a certain piece of hardware is written and available, everyone can simply use it.

At least, that's the theory. It's not always that simple. It's not always possible to isolate the user from the hardware. This is especially true of new technology, and there's a great deal of new technology involved with multimedia. For example, when I was working with NTSC (National Television Standards Committee) video cards, I found that various cards had drivers that were very different; I could never assume I knew what to expect from one card to the next. Sound cards also have significant differences that make it all the way through to the Windows side of the drivers. For example, some allow you to set interrupts, and some don't. This will change over time, as it did with video drivers.

There is an important advantage to the way Windows works with drivers. If a manufacturer writes a Windows driver for a hardware product, all Windows applications gain access to that hardware product. In DOS, the manufacturers have to write a driver for each software product they want to support.

The Market for Multimedia

Windows multimedia is still evolving. If, as I suspect, multimedia becomes the standard way to use computers, you have the opportunity to watch this evolution from the very beginning. I first became involved with personal computers more than a decade ago, and I have been repeatedly fascinated by the new ways computers are used as technology evolves.

At the same time, the standardization enforced by Windows has made multimedia hardware a relatively safe purchase—I don't expect any dramatic changes at the hardware level that can't be handled by drivers. There will be changes, but not to the point of quickly obsoleting what's available today. The prices of today's high-end equipment are falling, and these pieces will be the introductory- and mid-level hardware of the future.

The greatest immediate changes are likely to occur because of the rapidly increasing volume of hardware sales. As companies sell more units (and deal with the intense pressures of rapid growth) they can afford to spend more money on research and development; they also can lower unit costs. Perhaps more importantly, companies will have to compete on the basis of the service they provide their customers, not just on hardware sales.

For example, I had some trouble with several of the consumer-level products sent to me for review purposes. That's not unusual; inexpensive equipment sometimes has compatibility problems because it hasn't been tested as extensively as a high-end product. It is reasonable, however, to expect that a call to technical support should resolve the problem. In general, I found that the fast-growing companies were unable to devote enough resources to service and support—they apparently couldn't train new staff quickly enough to keep up with the demand. You should be aware of this trade-off when you invest in low-cost multimedia hardware. Whenever you can, get a no-questions-asked, money-back guarantee.[3]

---

[3] Since the first edition of this book, this has begun to change. The companies that were experiencing the fastest growth—like Creative Labs and Media Vision—have been investing in larger customer support operations.

Where Do You Go from Here?

There is a continuum of multimedia capabilities in the computer world, and it is always expanding. The first personal computers (and many computers in use today) were *monomedia* computers. Although the computers operated as a visual medium, it was a boring level of vision—text only. Graphics eventually made their way onto PCs, but the process was gradual and lacked standardization at first. Eventually, we arrived where we are today, with a wide variety of media available on and in our computers.

The early text-based computers sit at one end of the multimedia continuum. Slightly more advanced are DOS computers with video cards capable of simple graphics. The next spot is occupied by machines with basic sound cards. These cards are capable of synthesizing sounds (although they sound artificial) and they reproduce natural sounds, but with low fidelity. Usually, these sound cards have 8-bit resolution.

Even more advanced are sophisticated sound cards capable of more lifelike synthesis and digital recording with 16-bit resolution. Then you can add CD-ROM drives, which can store multimedia programs and large amounts of data. There is a tendency to put big databases or large research materials that use CD-ROM drives under the multimedia umbrella, but I don't think this is appropriate.

Ron's Rule A CD-ROM drive is not inherently multimedia. It's just one way to store the huge masses of data that make multimedia possible.

The most recent addition to the multimedia continuum is NTSC video (the kind of video you record on a VCR or view on a TV monitor). This is the cutting edge of multimedia and involves such things as digital video recording, Microsoft's AVI (Audio Video Interleaved) file format, and outputting VGA signals to videotape and monitors.

It's impossible to say where multimedia is going because the direction depends both on the inventiveness of industry and the whims of the marketplace. Many of us would like to see multimedia move toward virtual reality, but that may be wishful thinking. My idea of virtual reality stretches to such fictions as are found in William Gibson's book, *Neuromancer,* in which anyone can plug themselves into the worldwide information networks. In reality, researchers are having a difficult time creating a decent yet inexpensive set of goggles to project virtual reality to the eye, and the issue of tactile sensing remains difficult and expensive. It's not as easy for a computer to sense textures, for example, as it is for you and me. In fact, it's a really big deal when a computer can tell the difference between two surfaces.

Nonetheless, the idea of a seamless link between sensual reality and computational reality is exciting, particularly if the trends in personal computing can be extended to the heights of virtual reality.

The Windows Approach

Right now, it's time to get back down to earth. Windows is a long way from virtual reality,[4] but it's also a long way from text-based DOS programs. It's hard to know if the original designers of windowed environments had multimedia in mind when they designed their products, but the design has held up well. Still, there are some ways in which multimedia is pushing the limits of what computers and operating systems can handle. The main issues are file sizes, speed of access to data, and hardware capabilities. Let's consider how Windows handles each of these issues.

Multimedia File Sizes

There is one fact you can count on when discussing multimedia: the files are going to be large. Each multimedia format seems to stretch the limits a little further. For example, AVI files (the digital video format introduced by Microsoft) eat up from 5 to 20M per minute.[5] Multimedia's success relies on finding ways to deal with such huge files.

CD-ROM drives are the first important method available for storing such large files. You can't record onto a CD-ROM cheaply (yet), but CD-ROMs are a great way to store lots and lots of data—cheaply. The disks are much less expensive than any other medium when it comes to large files. Even the drives have become less expensive—there are CD-ROM drives available for under $200, and I recently saw a complete multimedia upgrade kit advertised for less than $350.

---

[4] On the other hand, those 3D buttons are, technically speaking, virtual buttons.

[5] It could be worse, too. AVI files almost always use some form of data compression. Without compression, a full-screen, full-color video file would take 1.5 gigabytes per minute!

Such inexpensive drives are not the fastest available, but they do work. Even better, prices are continuing to fall.

Hard drives are getting cheaper, too—a good thing, because a simple program can eat up 10–20M of disk space. Some software distributed on CD-ROM copies the program files to your hard disk, and that can eat up 5M or more in a hurry.

Today's machines come with hard drives in the 200–350M range, signaling that storage capacity on even the average machine is increasing rapidly. This is a key element to making multimedia more than a fad. Unless multimedia is affordable, it won't catch on.

Windows has taken advantage of these changes; I wouldn't be surprised one of these days to see a new file system available to make it more competitive with the Macintosh.[6] One of the big advantages of multimedia on the Mac is that you can name a file in an entire sentence if you want to. When it is possible to put tens of thousands of files on one hard disk, the time for the eight-character filename and the three-character extension is long past.

Speed of Access

When you manufacture a hard drive with more capacity, you also create a faster hard drive. After all, the physical size of the hard drive isn't increased to give it more capacity; the density of data is increased. Because you can now access more data in the same space, access times become shorter. For example, if you double the number of bits that can be stored on a square inch of hard disk surface without making any changes to the hardware (except adding the capability to read that many bits), you automatically reduce the access time because the distance between bits is shorter.

In addition to higher data densities, the hardware found in disk drives is also changing. The result is that high-capacity hard drives are actually much smaller than their ancestors were. However, no matter how fast you make a hard drive, memory on chips is inherently faster. If only we could use memory instead of hard disks, we could access data almost instantly. There is a combination of memory and hard disk that makes the best of both worlds. You probably already use it: it's called a *cache*.

---

[6] Windows NT should make alternate file systems a reality.

Disk Caches

A *cache* is a chunk of memory used to store data from the hard disk. If that data is needed, it is read from the cache instead of the hard disk. This process is called a *cache hit,* and it saves a lot of time. The savings is small for any one hit, but if there are many hits, the savings add up. For example, I have a Fujitsu 500M drive in one of my computers. It has an average access time of 12 milliseconds. If I use a cache with it, the average access time drops to about 7 milliseconds—nearly twice as fast.

The Fujitsu drive is also a marvel of miniaturization—those 500M are packed into a half-height, 3 1/2-inch case.[7] I bought a second one for a new computer, and I have been satisfied with my purchase. However, keep your eyes open for better hard disk price-to-performance ratios—prices are currently falling fast.[8]

Windows and DOS have more or less kept pace with these changes. Both come with a caching program (smartdrv.exe), but both have to catch up to the Macintosh and OS/2 by adding support for more sophisticated file systems.

CD-ROM Access Times

Access times are also a consideration for CD-ROM drives; there is a wide range in their access times. You get what you pay for in this department—the more you pay for a drive, the faster the access times. However, don't expect anything near what a hard drive can accomplish. CD-ROMs have access times ranging from 250 milliseconds to 750 milliseconds and more. Although they are slower than hard drives, CD-ROMs make up for it by storing more than 600M on a disk that can be manufactured for less than $2 per copy in large quantities.

Another consideration with CD-ROM drives is *transfer rate,* the rate at which the unit can transfer data to the computer. The minimum transfer rate for multimedia is 150K per second. Better drives double that figure to 300K per second. If you are in the market for a CD-ROM drive, I strongly suggest getting a drive that has a 300K-per-second transfer rate—the so-called double-spin drives.

---

[7] Just recently, I added a 1.05 gigabyte Micropolis hard drive—it's also a half-height, 3 1/2-inch format.

[8] When I wrote the first edition of this book, that drive was about $1400. Now, it's down below $900.

Hardware Capabilities

The focus of hardware development is the CPU (Central Processing Unit). When anyone discusses hardware advances, it's almost always in terms of the CPU chip, whether it's the movement from the 8088 chip to the 80486 chip or the arrival of the new Pentium chip.

The more advanced CPUs have made all the other hardware advances possible. In the beginning there was the lowly 8088. It could address 1M of memory, but engineers decided that no one needed that much memory; they reserved 640K for programs and saved the rest for internal use by the hardware and BIOS.

Even more important was another limitation well-known to programmers—all memory was divided into segments of 64K. In many ways, this is as serious a limitation as the 640K barrier. Having a segment of 64K means that anything that happens inside one segment happens quickly, and anything that has to cross segments happens more slowly. It takes more code to cross a segment boundary—comparable to adding an area code to a long-distance phone number.

The processors after the 8088 should have eliminated this limitation, but the need for backward compatibility keeps it around. Windows is trying to do away with things like the 64K segment limit, but only time will tell if it really will happen.

The 80486 added all kinds of goodies to the basic architecture, such as an internal 8K cache, tightly packed transistors (the closer they are together, the faster electronic signals can move between them), a 32-bit internal bus, and an integrated coprocessor. The Pentium increases performance with even fancier technology, most of which hasn't made it into the day-to-day lingo of the computer world. Things like pipelining and pre-fetch queues will soon be all the rage, I am sure! These hardware advances are well out in front of the software advances, however. The next version of Windows is expected to take advantage (finally) of some of the advanced capabilities lurking in the hardware.

Multimedia Tools in Windows

Windows includes several tools for working with multimedia that are automatically installed with Windows. Most are lurking in the Accessories Group, although a few can be found in the Control Panel. The multimedia-related programs and control panel elements include:

➤ Media Player (application)

➤ Sound Recorder (application)

➤ Object Packager (application)

➤ Sounds (control panel applet)

➤ Drivers (control panel applet)

➤ MIDI Mapper (control panel applet)

You can find specific information about working with these applications in Chapter 2, "Sound Advice." The next section focuses on one program that hasn't been discussed so far: the MIDI Mapper.

MIDI Mapper

The MIDI Mapper is often described as difficult to use. That, however, is an unfair assessment. The mechanics of the MIDI Mapper actually are very straightforward—it's the innards of MIDI that can be difficult. We'll look at MIDI and the MIDI Mapper together, which should clarify how to use this occasionally essential application. If you already understand MIDI, the MIDI Mapper should be a snap.

The MIDI Mapper starts with a small dialog box (Figure 5.2):

Figure 5.2. *MIDI Mapper's opening dialog box.*

The box at the top contains three radio buttons. These are the keys to understanding how the Mapper works:

➤ **S**etups

➤ **P**atch Maps

➤ **K**ey Maps

Setups

With the **S**etups button highlighted, clicking the N**a**me list box reveals a list of possible setups. Each setup relates to a specific MIDI card. There are more setups available than your sound card or MIDI card supports; these setups are installed with Windows. Other setups might be installed when you install the drivers for your sound card; if you change sound cards, you might find some old setups in the list box.

The dialog box in Figure 5.3 appears if you try to edit the setup for LAPC1 (a MIDI card from Roland).

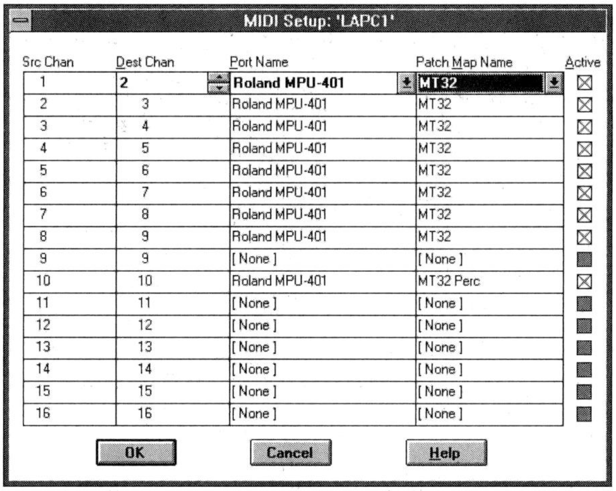

Src Chan	Dest Chan	Port Name	Patch Map Name	Active
1	2	Roland MPU-401	MT32	☒
2	3	Roland MPU-401	MT32	☒
3	4	Roland MPU-401	MT32	☒
4	5	Roland MPU-401	MT32	☒
5	6	Roland MPU-401	MT32	☒
6	7	Roland MPU-401	MT32	☒
7	8	Roland MPU-401	MT32	☒
8	9	Roland MPU-401	MT32	☒
9	9	[None]	[None]	■
10	10	Roland MPU-401	MT32 Perc	☒
11	11	[None]	[None]	■
12	12	[None]	[None]	■
13	13	[None]	[None]	■
14	14	[None]	[None]	■
15	15	[None]	[None]	■
16	16	[None]	[None]	■

Figure 5.3. *A MIDI Setup dialog box.*

The column at the far left lists the source channels. There are 16 available channels in a MIDI setup (although you can buy cards that give you 32, 64, or even 128 channels, those cards are normally used by professional musicians).

The second column lists the destination channel. If MIDI data specifies a channel in the Source Channel column, the program remaps the data to the corresponding channel in the Destination Channel column. For example, in Figure 5.3, channels 1 through 8 are mapped to channels 2 through 9.

The third column specifies a port name; this must come from the list of available ports. If you have one card, you have only one port to choose from (barring installation of a multi-port card). To access the list of ports, click a channel and use the Down Arrow to access the list of available ports.

Patch Maps

The far right column in Figure 5.3 is titled Patch **M**ap Name. A *patch* is MIDI jargon and refers to a specific instrument, such as a piano or a guitar. A patch map is similar to a setup, but whereas a setup maps channels, a patch map maps keys. Look at the patch map in Figure 5.4.

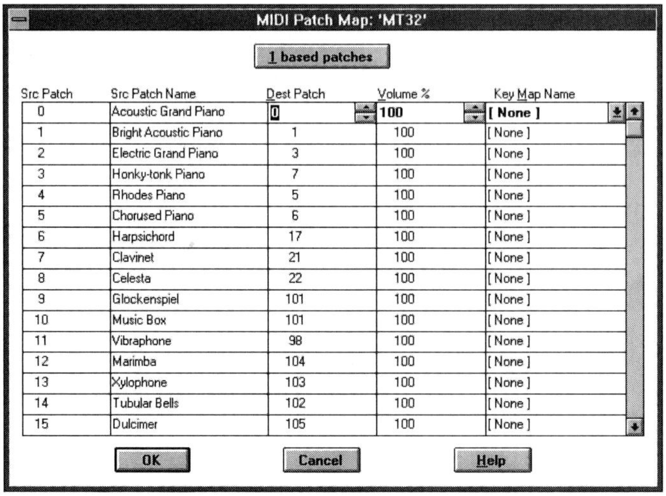

Src Patch	Src Patch Name	Dest Patch	Volume %	Key Map Name
0	Acoustic Grand Piano	0	100	[None]
1	Bright Acoustic Piano	1	100	[None]
2	Electric Grand Piano	3	100	[None]
3	Honky-tonk Piano	7	100	[None]
4	Rhodes Piano	5	100	[None]
5	Chorused Piano	6	100	[None]
6	Harpsichord	17	100	[None]
7	Clavinet	21	100	[None]
8	Celesta	22	100	[None]
9	Glockenspiel	101	100	[None]
10	Music Box	101	100	[None]
11	Vibraphone	98	100	[None]
12	Marimba	104	100	[None]
13	Xylophone	103	100	[None]
14	Tubular Bells	102	100	[None]
15	Dulcimer	105	100	[None]

MIDI Patch Map: 'MT32'

1 based patches

OK   Cancel   Help

Figure 5.4. *A MIDI Patch Map dialog box.*

As you might expect, the first column on the left lists source patches; the next column contains names. The computer ignores the names; they are there for the users. The third column lists the destination patches.

For example, look at the third line down. The source patch is number 2 (Electric Grand Piano). The destination patch is number 3—that means if the MIDI data in a sequence calls for patch number 2, the program maps the data to patch number 3. As long as the instrument that receives the data has an Electric Grand Piano patch on number 3, the sounds are produced accurately.

The fourth column lists a volume percentage; this can be used to map volumes if they differ between source and destination.

The fifth column is titled a Key Map Name. Key maps can be used to map a keypress to a different key.

Key Maps

There are two reasons for mapping keys. One involves instrument ranges. You might want to map a key to raise or lower the pitch of an instrument by an octave. For example, when using my Korg M1 keyboard, certain instruments are in the wrong ranges; I can use the MIDI Mapper to adjust them by an octave.

The other reason for remapping keys involves percussion patches. Unlike normal instruments, most drums have different instruments associated with each key. A key map enables you to match different drum sets to one another. For example, Figure 5.5 shows a percussion patch map. This is the simplest of the mappers I have discussed—source key on the left, name in the middle, and destination key on the right.

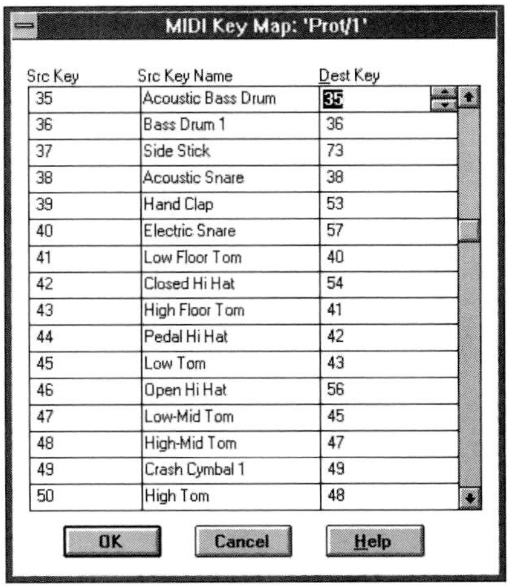

Figure 5.5. *A MIDI Key Map dialog box.*

Mapping is a basic concept—one number goes into the mapper, and another number comes out. The concept becomes complicated when you try to apply mapping to a real-world situation because there are so many channels, patches, and keys to keep track of. Nonetheless, mapping does work. In most cases, manufacturers provide the necessary maps to handle their equipment. However, you may have to create your own maps for MIDI equipment that doesn't support General MIDI.

Microsoft's Multimedia Contributions

In this chapter, I don't choose or recommend a specific product. Instead, I focus on the company that developed Windows—Microsoft. By adding multimedia support to Windows 3.1, Microsoft is responsible for a sudden surge of interest in multimedia.

Microsoft is an interesting company. Unlike most other major hardware or software vendors, Microsoft generally has had a continuous pattern of growth. In addition, Microsoft has set standards in a wide variety of areas. Also, Microsoft consistently issues software that requires the latest hardware to run reasonably well. That's a polite way of saying that their new releases tend to run slowly until the hardware catches up. Not every company is willing to take such a stand. Most companies try to be backward compatible—new software offerings have to run on even the oldest, slowest equipment.

Microsoft, however, always has been pushing forward, and I think that is the primary reason for the phenomenal success the company has enjoyed. The company's philosophy makes business sense. If you revise your product (and do a good job revising it), you can sell it again to the same customer. Most of the industry has caught on to this idea, but Microsoft has been doing it all along. IBM was the first master of this technique, but they did it in a market they could control more effectively: high-ticket mainframes.

Microsoft also offers value. I have yet to be seriously disappointed with a Microsoft product, which is not to say that Microsoft does everything right the first time; sometimes it takes a while.

I Remember Windows 1.0!

I remember when the first version of Windows, 1.0, came out. The version was years late, and it was not adequate for serious work.

When Microsoft released version 2.0, the company showed a willingness to learn from experience. Much of the awkwardness of version 1.0 was gone, and the whole interface was more useful. But the second version of Windows begged for serious hardware. Windows 3.0 wasn't much different—it put even larger demands on the hardware. And with version 3.1, Windows grew to about 15M for a typical installation. And woe to the user who didn't have at least 4M of memory to run Windows![9]

The features of Windows 3.1 put multimedia squarely on the PC for the first time. There had been some DOS-based products, but the inclusion of multimedia within Windows itself put things in a whole new light. In effect, Microsoft put multimedia capability onto a million (and more) computers within a matter of months. All you needed to be multimedia-ready was Windows 3.1.

Although I don't always agree with Microsoft, I tip my hat to the company that made multimedia a Serious Thing on IBM-compatible PCs.

Video for Windows

Microsoft's latest contribution to the multimedia world is Video for Windows. This is Microsoft's answer to Quick Time on the Macintosh, and it sets a standard for incorporating digital video under Windows. I explore the details of Video for Windows in Chapter 11, "Lights, Camera, Action: Video for Windows." In this section I want to take a moment to examine the process of setting standards for a new member in the multimedia family—*digital video*.

Video is a data-intensive medium. As you probably know from surveying standard video cards, higher resolutions rapidly chew up memory (and dollars). NTSC video (the kind you are used to seeing on video tapes and TV) is no exception to this rule. Video "moves" at the rate of 30 frames per second. Each frame is an individual image with its own storage requirements. As a result, video data rates are even more intensive than audio data rates.

When I wrote the first edition of this book, the hardware for real-time compression of video was extremely expensive. The cost for such hardware was in the $2,000 to $3,000 range, pricing most PC users out of the hardware-compression market. How times have changed—my favorite hardware-assisted, real-time compression card, the Intel Smart Video Recorder, can be had for less than $500. If you are willing to compromise a bit, you can compress after you capture, and such cards sell for hundreds of dollars less.

Before Video for Windows came along, there were some attempts to standardize digital video for the PC, involving both hardware and software-only solutions.

---

[9] Of course, 8M or 12M is much better these days.

However, until Microsoft introduced the AVI file format used by Video for Windows, no one was able to set any kind of standard that the industry could rally around.

There will be some griping about the AVI standard. Some people will object to Microsoft setting the standard. Some will say the standard should be controlled more tightly, whereas others will say that the standard needs to be loosened up. Some people will argue that AVI is not professional enough, and still others will say it is too hard for consumers to use.

Everyone is right and everyone is wrong. In fact, the AVI standard has proven to be quite capable—many companies have introduced hardware or software that is based on the standard in some way. Hundreds of millions of dollars have been spent to design, manufacture, and market these products. This money was spent, and these products became available, for only one reason: Microsoft created a standard. Almost instantly, technology that had been flailing about had a focus and spread quickly into use. Once a standard gets set—and once everyone believes that the standard will work—everyone can move forward. I fully expect Microsoft to advance the AVI standard much like they advanced Windows from version to version, but the basics are already in place. Progress is being made.

The Windows Multimedia API

This section takes a look at multimedia authoring and programming. If you aren't interested in programming, you can skip to the next chapter; I'll be covering only programming-specific topics for the rest of this chapter.

Many authoring programs and development tools enable you to access some of the innards of Windows used by C programmers. The set of functions programmers use to write Windows programs is known collectively as an *API (Application Program Interface)*. Although there are hundreds of functions in the Windows API, you can gain a lot of power using only a handful of them.

There are two ways that software grants access to the API. One method enables you to call the functions directly; this method is preferred by programmers when they want complete control. Visual Basic is an example of this method.

The other method hides the function calls, presenting the user with dialog boxes or script commands. The user can pass information in the boxes and commands to the multimedia part of the API, called the *Media Control Interface (MCI)*.

Programs that use this method include HSC InterActive and Multimedia Toolbook.[10] If you want to access multimedia with such tools, you need to learn how to work with MCI.

Either of these methods gives you a great deal of control over Windows multimedia. The method you choose depends on what programming tools you work with. This section of the chapter first looks at a few API functions that you can use to gain quick access to multimedia. I then discuss the Command String Interface, which gives you more detailed control over multimedia devices; then, a brief look at the Command Message Interface, which is most often used by C programmers.

sndPlaySound

The `sndPlaySound` function enables you to play sound files (*.WAV) with minimal fuss. Here is the C-language declaration of the function from the Windows API:

```
BOOL sndPlaySound(, wFlags)
```

The return value is `TRUE` if the function successfully played the sound; otherwise, the function returns `FALSE`.

To use this function in the authoring package or development environment of your choice, you have to create a declaration that conforms to the rules of your software package. For example, to declare this function in Visual Basic, add the following line to the declarations section of a module:

```
Declare Function sndPlaySound Lib "mmsystem" (ByVal SoundName
➡As String, ByVal wFlags As Integer) As Integer
```

This statement translates the C-oriented data types of the original statement into information Visual Basic can understand and work with. Look at each parameter of the function so you can see the capabilities of this function.

The first parameter of the C and Visual Basic declarations is a string, and it can specify either a filename or a variable containing the waveform data. You must specify the correct flags in `wFlags` if you plan to use a memory variable for the sound data. The second parameter is a `WORD` in the C version; in Visual Basic this is treated as an Integer. Table 5.1 lists the flags that can be used.

---

[10] You can use the Windows API directly with Toolbook, however. It's just not as easy as it is with Visual Basic.

Table 5.1. Flags for sndPlaySound.

Flag	Definition
SND_SYNC	Tells the function to play the sound synchronously. In other words, the function will not return until the sound has played completely.
SND_ASYNC	Tells the function to play the sound asynchronously— the function returns immediately after the sound starts playing. You can stop asynchronous playing with a special call to sndPlaySound (using NULL instead of a string for the first argument).
SND_NODEFAULT	Normally, if sndPlaySound can't find the sound you told it to play, it plays the sound defined as the default sound in WIN.INI. This flag tells the function to play nothing if your sound is not found.
SND_MEMORY	Tells sndPlaySound the sound name points to a variable in memory, not a filename.
SND_LOOP	Causes the sound to repeat until you stop it with a special call to sndPlaySound (using NULL for lpszSoundName). Only asynchronous sounds can be looped.
SND_NOSTOP	If you use this flag when you play a sound, you cannot stop the sound; if you try to play a second sound before the first sound is finished, the second sound isn't played.

mciExecute

Whereas sndPlaySound is limited to playing sounds, mciExecute offers access to much more of the multimedia world. You can use the function to play animations, play and record sounds, and more. mciExecute uses something called the *Command String Interface*. The full set of commands are explained below (you can also find information about mciExecute in Chapter 4, "Putting It All Together"). The following line is the C declaration for mciExecute:

```
BOOL mciExecute(lpstrCommand)
```

The next line is the Visual Basic declaration of the same function:

```
Declare Function mciExecute Lib "mmsystem" (ByVal MCI_Command
➥As String) As Integer
```

This function is straightforward. It takes only one parameter: the string to execute. The return value is TRUE if successful, and FALSE if not. mciExecute has one significant limitation—it only establishes communication in one direction. You can tell an MCI device what to do (for example, play a track on a CD), but you can't receive any information (such as the current track number). To establish two-way communication, use the function mciSendString.

mciSendString

This function gives you complete access to the Command String Interface. You can tell devices what to do, and you can obtain information about devices. Not all packages that grant access to MCI enable you to access mciSendString. For example, with HSC's InterActive (the icon-based authoring system), you can specify the command to send to an MCI device, and it calls mciSendString for you. Visual Basic, on the other hand, lets you call mciSendString directly. (See Chapter 4, "Putting It All Together," for a demonstration that uses a Visual Basic program provided on the floppy disk.)

The following is the C declaration for mciSendString:

```
DWORD mciSendString(lpstrCommand, lpstrReturnString,
                    wReturnLength, hCallback)
To use this function in Visual Basic, write the following declaration:
Declare Function mciSendString Lib "mmsystem" (ByVal MCI_
➥Command As String, ByVal ReturnString As String, ByVal
➥ReturnLength As Integer, ByVal Handle As Integer) As Long
```

Unlike sndPlaySound and mciExecute, mciSendString has four parameters. You only have to pay attention to three of them; you do not have to work with the Callback capability. Callback involves more sophisticated use of the Windows API and is beyond the scope of this book.

The first parameter of mciSendString is the same as the only parameter used by mciExecute: the command string to execute. The second parameter of mciSendString specifies a return string. If there is any information being passed back by MCI, the information is placed in this string. The third parameter is the length of the string you pass for the return information. The fourth parameter is a handle to a window to call back if you include "notify" in the command string.

mciGetErrorString

There is one other useful function: mciGetErrorString. If mciSendString returns an error, you can get the error message by passing the error code to mciGetErrorString. The following line is the C declaration:

```
WORD mciGetErrorString(dwError, lpstrBuffer, wLength)
```

To use this function in Visual Basic, use the following declaration:

```
Declare Function mciGetErrorString Lib "mmsystem" (ByVal MCI
➡Error As Long, ByVal ErrorString As String, ByVal ReturnLength
➡As Integer) As Integer
```

The first parameter is a long integer (DWORD in C) that contains the error code. The second parameter is a string into which the error message is placed, and the third parameter is the length of the string (to prevent overwriting adjacent memory).

Command String Interfaces

The Command String Interface is the heart of MCI control. Using these strings, you can construct commands to send with mciExecute, mciSendString, or, if your application supports the capability, to send directly to the MCI devices.

The syntax of these commands is structured but fairly English-like, so the commands are not difficult to use. The commands are layered as follows:

➤ *System Commands* are not sent to devices; they are handled directly by MCI. Examples include sound and sysinfo.

➤ *Required Commands* are MCI commands that all devices are required to support. Examples include open, close, and capability.

➤ *Device-Specific Commands* apply to specific devices. For example, there are different commands for WaveAudio and AVIVideo because one deals only with sound, and the other deals with sound and pictures.

➤ *Optional Commands* apply to specific devices, but a device is not required to support them (most do). MCI provides special commands, like capa- bility, that enable you to find out if a device supports any given command in this category.

➤ *Vendor-Specific Commands* are supported by a specific vendor for a specific piece of hardware. Software that uses these commands normally works only on the specified hardware.

There are two kinds of MCI devices—simple and compound. Simple devices do not use files; CD-ROM players are an example. Compound devices use files; WaveAudio and AVIVideo are examples.

Command Strings

Many applications, including Visual Basic, InterActive, and Toolbook, use the Command Strings Interface to control multimedia devices. Tables 5.2, 5.3 and 5.4 list some of the commands available for the more common devices. For more complete information, consult the documentation that comes with the Multimedia Development Kit from Microsoft. As new devices are added, they are supported with a set of commands appropriate to the device. For example, even though AVI is still in beta as I write this, it already has a full complement of commands.

To find out what devices you have installed in your system, open your SYSTEM.INI file and check the [mci] section. Or, you can load Media Player and note which devices show up in the Device menu.

The basic format for a command string is

```
<command> <device name> <arguments>
```

For example, to play particular tracks on an open CD audio device, you could say:

```
play CDAudio from 3 to 5
```

The command is play, the device is CDAudio, and the arguments are from 3 to 5. In the command tables (5.2–5.4), you should put the device name between the command and any arguments shown.

MCI System Commands

System commands, listed in Table 5.2, are not sent to a device. They are interpreted directly by MCI.

Table 5.2. MCI system commands.

Command	Arguments	Description
sound		The device name must be a sound from the [sounds] section of WIN.INI.
sysinfo	quantity	The sysinfo command is used to get information from MCI. Quantity as an argument returns the number of devices listed in SYSTEM.INI. The device name must be a standard MCI device.
sysinfo	quantity open	Returns the number of devices of the type specified in the device name that are open.

Required Commands (All Devices)

The commands listed in Table 5.3 must be supported by all multimedia devices.

Table 5.3. Required MCI commands.

Command	Arguments	Description
capability	can eject	Returns true if the device can eject media.
capability	can play	Returns true if the device can play.
capability	can record	Returns true if the device can record.
capability	can save	Returns true if the device can save data.
capability	device type	Returns a device type.
capability	has audio	Returns true if the device plays audio.
capability	has video	Returns true if the device plays video.
capability	uses files	Returns true if the device uses files.
close		Closes a device or a device element (such as a file).

Command	Arguments	Description
info	product	Returns a null-terminated description of the hardware associated with a device.
open	alias <alias>	Opens a device and assigns an alias name. The device can be referenced by the alias.
open	shareable	Opens a device in shareable mode. To share, all subsequent opens must include the shareable argument also.
open	type	Opens a device by specifying the type of device.
status	mode	Returns the current mode of the device. Modes include not ready, paused, playing, and stopped. Some devices support open, parked, recording, and seeking.
status	ready	Returns true if the device is ready.

Device Types

The names and number of valid devices will change as new technologies and devices are developed. Valid device types, at the time of writing, are

> animation
> dat
> other
> scanner
> vcr
> waveaudio
> cdaudio
> digitalvideo
> overlay
> sequencer
> videodisc

Basic Commands

The basic commands, listed in Table 5.4, are optional, but they are supported by many different devices. One of the more common uses of the Command String Interface is playing video files. Digital video has quite a few extensions to the basic command set, and these are covered in detail in Chapter 11, "Lights, Camera, Action: Video for Windows."

Table 5.4. Basic MCI commands.

Command	Arguments	Description
load	<filename>	Loads a file from disk.
pause		Stops playing.
play		Plays the selection.
play	from <x> to <y>	Plays the selection from the x position to the y position.
record		Starts recording data.
record	insert	Inserts new data starting at the current position.
record	from <x> to <y>	Specifies the starting and stopping positions for the recording.
record	overwrite	New data overwrites existing data starting at the current position.
resume		Resumes playing or recording on a paused device.
save	<filename>	Saves the device element.
seek	to <position>	Seeks to the specified position.
seek	to start	Seeks to the beginning of the media or element.

Command	Arguments	Description
seek	to end	Seeks to the end of the media or element.
set	audio all off/on	Turns on or off audio output.
set	audio left off/on	Turns on or off left channel audio output.
set	audio right off/on	Turns on or off right channel audio output.
set	door closed	Loads media and closes door if available.
set	door open	Opens door and ejects media if possible.
set	video off/on	Turns video output on or off.
status	current track	Returns current track number.
status	length	Returns the total length of the media.
status	length track <#>	Returns the length of the specified track.
status	number of tracks	Returns the number of tracks on the media.
status	position	Returns the current position.
status	position track <#>	Returns the position of the start of the specified track.
status	start position	Returns the starting position of the media or element.
status	time format	Returns the time format.
stop		Stops the device.

Command Message Interface

The Command Message Interface is not as easy to use as the Command String Interface. Instead of strings, this interface relies on Windows messages. Windows programs communicate with each other and with Windows using messages. A message is nothing more than a number, so it is not as friendly as a string.

The Command Message Interface uses the function `mciSendCommand` to send commands to MCI. This function is used by programmers because it gives them control of multimedia at a lower level than the Command String Interface does. In other words, there is less code overhead, which gives the programmer more control over what happens.

This kind of control comes at a price. You have to learn more material and keep track of more information while you program. This is true at every level of the programming world—the more control you have, the harder it is to program. If you want more speed, this is the way to do it.

Let's take a look at how the command message interface works. The following source code uses `mciSendCommand` to query all multimedia devices in the system to see if they are open.[11] If successful, it returns the value it obtained from MCI. Otherwise, it returns zero.

```
int PASCAL NEAR get_number_of_devices(void)
{
  MCI_SYSINFO_PARMS sysinfo;
  DWORD dwDevices;

  /*  Set things up so that MCI puts the number
      open devices directly into dwDevices.
  */
  sysinfo.lpstrReturn = (LPSTR)(LPDWORD)&dwDevices;
  sysinfo.dwRetSize = sizeof(DWORD);

  if (mciSendCommand(MCI_ALL_DEVICE_ID,
      MCI_SYSINFO,
      MCI_SYSINFO_OPEN ¦
      MCI_SYSINFO_QUANITY,
      (DWORD)(LPMCI_SYSINFO_PARMS)&sysinfo) != 0)
    return 0;
else
    return (int)dwDevices;
}
```

---

[11] This example is taken from my book, *PC Video Madness*. If you plan to work with digital video at any level—programming, authoring, or just for your own enjoyment, *PC Video Madness* has important information you can probably use.

Look more closely at what is going on in this example. The first things to notice are the variable declarations at the top of the function:

```
MCI_SYSINFO_PARAMS sysinfo;
DWORD dwDevices;
```

The variable sysinfo uses a data type that is declared as a structure in mmsystem.h:

```
/* Parameter block for MCI_SYSINFO command message. */
typedef struct tagMCI_SYSINFO_PARMS{
  DWORD dwCallback;
  LPSTR lpstReturn;
  DWORD dwRetSize;
  DWORD dwNumber;
  UINT dwDeviceType;
  UINT wReserved0;
} MCI_SYSINFO_PARMS
typedef MCI_SYSINFO_PARMS FAR * LPMCI_SYSINFO_PARMS
```

This structure contains variables that are used to send and receive information. The address of the structure is one of the arguments to mciSendCommand, as you can see from the declaration of mciSendCommand:

```
DWORD WINAPI mciSendCommand (UNIT uDeviceID, UINT uMessage, DWORD
dwParam1,
DWORD dwParam2);
```

The parameters for mciSendCommand are described in Table 5.5.

Table 5.5. Parameters for mciSendCommand.

Parameter	Description
uDeviceID	This is the device ID of the device that is to receive the command. There are two special cases: use NULL when you are opening a device, and use MCI_ALL_DEVICE_ID when you want to address all devices.
uMessage	This is the message you are sending. Typical messages include MCI_OPEN and MCI_CLOSE.

continues

Table 5.5. continued

Parameter	Description
dwParam1	Specifies flags. Flags are used to signal that certain actions or results are required. For example, you could use the flag MCI_WAIT with an MCI_OPEN message to specify that you want MCI to complete the open before returning control. The equivalent with a command string would be open digital video wait.
dwParam2	Specifies a pointer to a parameter block for the command. The parameter block is a structure that contains elements relevant to the message. In the example above, the system information parameter block is used. The block used varies for different messages.

Before calling mciSendCommand in the example, you need to assign some values to particular members of the sysinfo structure:

```
sysinfo.lpstrReturn = (LPSTR)(LPDWORD)&dwDevices;
sysinfo.dwRetSize = sizeof(DWORD);
```

When these values have been set, it's time to call mciSendCommand:

```
if (mciSendCommand(MCI_ALL_DEVICE_ID,
    MCI_SYSINFO,
    MCI_SYSINFO_OPEN ¦
    MCI_SYSINFO_QUANITY,
    (DWORD)(LPMCI_SYSINFO_PARMS)&sysinfo) != 0)
```

The device ID is set to MCI_ALL_DEVICE_ID because we are addressing all devices in this case. The message is set to MCI_SYSINFO. There are two flags used: MCI_SYSINFO_OPEN and MCI_SYSINFO_QUANTITY. This combination of flags results in getting the number of devices open, instead of a list of names of devices. The results will be placed in the sysinfo structure.

This is just a small sample of using command messages, but it is typical. For more information on using command messages, consult the Windows Software Development Kit from Microsoft, or join the WINSDK forum on CompuServe.

II PART

Pumping Up the Volume

6

Pumping Iron: Hardware

The cost of multimedia hardware has been falling for several years, and it has plummeted since the first edition of this book was printed. This is putting exciting new hardware into the hands of consumers. The results haven't always been what you would expect. That's because there are two kinds of multimedia hardware: convenient and inexpensive.[1] This isn't universally true, but it is true often enough.

There are two trends bringing prices down. The first is a traditional one: economies of scale. As more people buy a product, the unit cost goes down. This occurs because the cost of the factory and related equipment is spread over a larger number of units.

The second trend lowers prices too, but it also introduces some problems. This is subtle, but important to be aware of.

When a product is first introduced, you can usually bet that it was designed and engineered by some of the best people in the field. New technology requires new thinking, and new thinking requires exceptional talent and a lot of time and determination. For example, the very best video capture boards—the well-engineered ones—are still somewhat expensive. They deal with the subtleties of the problem: interactions with other equipment in the computer, timing issues, analog-to-digital conversion, and so on.

As new technology matures, the information needed to design it and manufacture it spreads. At first, however, something is missing. This missing factor is information about subtleties. It's like building an atomic bomb: many of us learned the basics in high school or college science courses. An atomic bomb consists of a few subcritical-mass chunks of plutonium and a conventional explosive to drive them together. Once together, they achieve critical mass and go "Boom!"

Were you aware that it took many years of intensive research and experimentation to figure out how to design that conventional explosive so it would push those plutonium chunks together in just the right way?[2] That's an example of an important subtlety.

Until the subtleties surrounding a new multimedia hardware product are generally understood, less expensive models will not be as reliable as you really want them to be. I have gone on at such length about this issue because it is so

---

[1] Of course, there are still some of the old dinosaurs around: inconvenient and expensive.

[2] The technique now has a name—shaped charges. These days, they can blow things up exactly right.

critical to the success of multimedia. If you get impatient or ignore the growth pains of the industry, you can easily get discouraged. But, once a new technology really spreads through the industry, more and more of the subtleties are understood by more and more people, and the general level of quality at the low-price end goes up steadily. For example (speaking of video capture cards), the Intel Smart Video Recorder, VideoLogic Captivator, and the Video Spigot all demonstrate that sophisticated, reliable technology is arriving at the low-price end (well, under $500 anyway).[3]

The digitizing of new kinds of information—that's what multimedia really is—isn't easy or trivial. However, as you have discovered, once you can digitize things such as images, sounds, and video, you can do things with them that no one ever could before. That's the real promise of multimedia.

In the first edition of this book, I said: "At various places in this chapter, you're going to find out about hardware that is troublesome to install or that has compatibility problems. Within the next year, as product designs stabilize and as the subtleties become better known, that will go away. For example, sound cards have been notorious for troublesome installation. It is not uncommon to have to pull a board back out, change some jumpers or switch settings, and try again."

This has changed. At that time, Media Vision had just begun shipping sound cards with an installation program that figures out what you already have in your computer and then sets the sound card to fit right in. I have now had a chance to try this technology, and it works well. Fewer and fewer boards require you to change jumpers right on the board—you can now usually do it in software.[4]

We are now somewhere in the midst of the true beginning of multimedia. There has been an awful lot of research and development, and now we are beginning to reap the benefits.

This section gives you the inside story on many aspects of multimedia hardware, including:

---

[3] When I began writing the first edition of this book (August 1992), it took about $3,000 to get the hardware for real-time compression of video. The Smart Video Recorder is selling for under $500 now.

[4] In fact, this is a useful way to evaluate a multimedia product. If you have to physically change jumpers on the board, there's a good chance that you are holding older technology in your hands. Unless you see a clear reason to buy such hardware (like a darn good price), look elsewhere. Provided, of course, that there is an "elsewhere"—it seems like every new technology (video capture was no exception) requires that you change jumpers.

➤ Sound cards

➤ CD-ROM drives

➤ PC graphic display video cards

➤ Video capture and overlay cards

➤ MIDI hardware

➤ Multimedia upgrades and PCs

You can find more information about these products in the hardware chapter of the Shopper's Guide. At the end of this chapter, I attempt to define the "Ultimate Affordable Multimedia PC."[5]

Sound Cards

You can find good sound cards at good prices, but remember, you get what you pay for. The major problem with sound cards isn't price, it's the way sound on PCs evolved.

On the Macintosh, sound has been part of the machine from the beginning; sophisticated sound support is a built-in feature of the Macintosh at the hardware level.[6] All the PC had was a dinky little speaker and some primitive ways to drive it. As a result, when you wanted to add sound to the PC, there were no standards to dictate how you should do it. Even worse, sound evolved around games, and the rules, standards, and conventions that spontaneously arose did so for reasons that musicians and multimedia authors find frustrating today. For example, most sound cards use FM synthesis.[7] Although this method is fine for producing inexpensive, amusing sounds for games, it's not a good way to make

---

[5] Warning: with the advent of digital video, you'll find that the ultimate affordable PC is a bit more demanding than it used to be.

[6] Although this can be limiting in its own way. For example, the built-in support is limited to 8-bit resolution (see Chapter 2, "Sound Advice," for a discussion of bits and resolution). This has hindered the widespread introduction of 16-bit audio on Macs. When you have a decent solution available automatically, there's less incentive to invest in an upgrade. When you have nothing (that's about where I rate the PC speaker in terms of multimedia capabilities), you're more motivated to upgrade.

[7] See Chapter 2, "Sound Advice," for information about sound generation.

music. FM synthesis can only approximate the sound of real instruments.[8] It cannot capture the nuances of their sounds. In fact, all FM sounds have a characteristic digital "color" that is not suitable for making music.

The early developers of sound cards also made assumptions about how the cards would fit into the PC architecture. But PCs have evolved, and more and more devices must share limited resources within that architecture. At the same time, many software products rely on those early assumptions about things such as addresses and interrupts. Today, nearly every sound board must be configurable in terms of port addresses, interrupts, memory it maps to, use of direct memory access (DMA) channels, and so on. Unless the manufacturer spends time and money developing automated methods for detecting what peripherals your computer is using, you have to know how to handle these settings yourself.[9] Once you do get your equipment configured, however, you're home free—you can simply use your multimedia PC.

The sections that follow provide a report on various sound cards, either from my experiences or from other sources, such as the technical-support staff at the various companies, conversations with other users, and wisdom gleaned from magazines and messages on CompuServe.[10] Two excellent products—the Roland SCC-1 and Turtle Beach's MultiSound—both get an Author's Choice award. The SCC-1 provides very good MIDI sound—it's an excellent upgrade to put next to your existing sound card. The MultiSound does both MIDI and .WAV files to perfection.[11]

---

[8] I'm being kind here. The high-end of synthesis uses *wave table lookup,* which stores actual digital samples of sounds. FM synthesis is to wave table lookup as a tricycle is to an Indy car.

[9] In most cases, no matter how good a job the software does, you may have to find out yourself what port addresses are in use on your machine. It's a very good idea, in this multimedia age, to keep a record of at least the port addresses in use by the various cards in your machine. If you have a database product, build yourself a simple database that tracks the following information: card name, interrupt number, port address, and memory buffer address (if any). This will help you enormously if you wind up having to resolve a conflict with new hardware.

[10] I've said it before, and I'll say it again: to explore multimedia without being a member of CompuServe is asking for trouble. There is so much useful knowledge shared on the CompuServe multimedia forums—it's an investment that will save you huge amounts of time and money. Besides, you can send me messages there.

[11] Perfection is a pretty high standard, and the MultiSound is the only sound card for your PC that hits this standard.

Roland SCC-1

The Roland SCC-1 is a small, unassuming card that puts a great selection of MIDI sounds into your PC. The SCC-1 is something of an anomaly in today's multimedia market, yet for the right person it is an excellent choice. The SCC-1 is not like the Sound Blasters and Pro Audio Spectrums. It doesn't deal with .WAV files but rather focuses all its power and attention on the synthesis of sounds. The card does MIDI with dash and polish, and the sounds it produces are probably the best, dollar for dollar, in today's market.

I installed the SCC-1 in our kids' computer, along with a few other products from Roland (the PC-200 MIDI keyboard controller and a pair of Roland MA-12C speakers) to create a musical workstation.[12] The combination was dazzling. I already had a Sound Blaster with its proprietary CD-ROM drive installed on the computer. I did not want to give up the CD-ROM, so I was counting on the two cards coexisting—fortunately, they got along well. However, I don't use the synthesis section of the Sound Blaster any longer—the SCC-1 goes far beyond FM synthesis.

The SCC-1 stores digital samples on the card, so it creates sounds that are very realistic and pleasant to listen to. The piano, for example, sounds like a piano— a nice surprise to someone who loves the sound of a good piano. It is notoriously difficult to synthesize a good piano sound—musicians pay thousands of dollars for good piano synthesizers. Naturally, the SCC-1 doesn't compete with such high-priced equipment, but the sound is accurate enough to please. Most of the other 127 sounds in the General MIDI spec are also as good; you can create a decent ensemble by playing several instruments at the same time.[13]

If the sounds of the SCC-1 are its strength, the documentation is its weakness. The documentation appears to have been written originally in Japanese, and the translation is poor. You can, fortunately, make sense of the most important parts. Surprisingly, the documentation is probably more of a hindrance to advanced users than to beginners. If you are a beginner with MIDI, the only possible stumbling block would be during the installation, but installation is so simple that it's not likely to be a hassle.

---

[12] I liked the speakers and the keyboard both so much that I bought them for myself. The speakers are especially good—very rugged, and great sound. If you're going to have a great card like the SCC-1 or the MultiSound, good speakers are a must.

[13] And, if you use the SCC-1 with games, you'll find out what you've been missing.

Because the SCC-1 supports Roland's MPU-401 interface (the de facto PC MIDI standard for MIDI cards), you can use it right out of the box with most sequencing software. It also supports General MIDI, so you can get it up and running under Windows right away. The more advanced MIDI user, on the other hand, has to decode the obscure manual to get the SCC-1 to work beyond General MIDI. If you know other electronically oriented musicians, you can pool your experiences—there are quite a few SCC-1s out there.

A quick note to help with installation: the SCC-1 documentation never tells you how to get the product working with Windows. It's actually very easy: just use the Drivers icon in the Control Panel to install the MPU-401 driver that comes with Windows.

The SCC-1 represents a good value for the money; see the Shopper's Guide for details on price and availability. It is ideal if you already have a sound card and want to beef up your MIDI capabilities substantially.

Turtle Beach's MultiSound

If the SCC-1 shines with its sounds, the MultiSound does it one step better. It offers very good MIDI sounds and adds a flawless Wave device. Many sound cards brag about CD-quality; the MultiSound is the only one that really delivers.

The MultiSound is worth every penny. It is a few pennies more than regular sound cards—you can find 16-bit sound cards for around $250, and the MultiSound sells for about twice that. However, if sound quality is at or near the top of your list, the MultiSound is the only choice. The sounds—MIDI and Wave— are *absolutely* clean. You can reliably access any instrument on the card and get a pure, clean sound. You can record from a CD to your hard disk and not be able to hear the slightest difference between the original and the recording.[14] The

---

[14] There are a number of sound cards that, on paper, are capable of the recording with 16 bits of resolution at 44.1 KHz, the rate at which CDs are recorded. However, if you use a cheap microphone to record a CD, it will still sound cheap—the CD merely preserves the quality of the input. Sound cards behave the same way—16-bit resolution and 44.1 KHz don't mean anything unless the sound card itself is noise-free and accurate. The term for this kind of response is "flat," and the response of the MultiSound is almost exactly flat. Most other cards have response curves that deviate substantially from flat. Flat, of course, means that if you graph the response, it will be flat all the way from the low sounds of bass to the high sounds of a cymbal crash.

MultiSound was designed for two specific markets: professionals who make business presentations, and musicians. It does a good job in both areas, but it is also a wonderful addition to any multimedia computer.

Unlike the SCC-1, the MultiSound can handle digital audio as well as MIDI. The MIDI section is capably represented by a commercial synthesizer, the Proteus/1 XR from E-mu. The Proteus packs 4 megabytes of samples onto the card, including many original and interesting sounds not part of the General MIDI standard. All of the sounds are vivid, exciting, and realistic. Some are stunning in their sonic realism.

As for Wave files, the card can record and play back at CD quality: 16 bits, 44.1 KHz. Although some of the less expensive cards also record at these specifications, the remarkably noise-free MultiSound does a better job—even a good recording can be spoiled by noise in the electronics, or by noise picked up from other components in the computer.

The MultiSound is the perfect choice if

➤ You create business presentations that use digital audio.

➤ You love making your own music.

➤ You are a perfectionist and want the best sound available.

If you order a MultiSound, be aware that some items you might expect to be parts of the basic package are options—a manual for the Proteus/1 XR capabilities and MIDI cables, for example. Turtle Beach does not charge high prices for these options. Turtle Beach says most people who buy the unit don't order the options, so if you want them, be aware that you have to spend another $50 or so to get them. See the Shopper's Guide for more details.

Synthesizers and the MultiSound

Although the MultiSound qualifies as a professional product, it also appeals to another audience: closet musicians. If you dream of pounding a keyboard at Carnegie Hall but you're doomed to a life of lead-fingered oblivion, this card can turn even average keyboarding into a sonic delight with the quality of its sounds.

It's difficult to describe sounds with text. Turtle Beach has a CD available that demonstrates the capabilities of the MultiSound. See the Shopper's Guide for details.

The MultiSound is different from inexpensive sound cards because the cheaper cards use FM synthesis; you can only do so much using frequency changes to modulate a sound wave. The MultiSound, like the SCC-1, stores digital sounds right on the card. However, the MultiSound uses 4M of memory to store its sounds. As I mentioned in Chapter 2, more memory equals better quality sounds.

The MultiSound uses a set of *presets* that are popular among electronic musicians.[15] They come from the Proteus/1 XR, a synthesizer made by E-mu. The presets contain exceptionally clear, clean sounds. In addition, you get software that you can use to edit the presets to your own tastes.

The presets are based on a set of 384 sounds stored in the 4M of memory on the card. A software front-end is supplied (it mimics the front panel of a physical Proteus/1XR; see Figure 6.1) so you can create your own presets. It operates exactly like a real Proteus/1XR. You can save your presets to your hard disk and even make them the default if you want. You'll need to order the Proteus manual to do this.

Figure 6.1. *The software front-end supplied with MultiSound.*

The MultiSound comes with a second set of standard presets: General MIDI. Unlike the Proteus presets, which are stored right on the card, you must load the General MIDI presets onto the card from the hard disk, which is easy to do. Once they are loaded, you can make the General MIDI presets the default.

---

[15] A preset is a set of sounds stored in a synthesizer. They are called presets because they are set up before you use the machine and will be there whenever you turn it on. The MultiSound enables you to create your own presets if you so desire.

Although the General MIDI sounds are great, the Proteus sounds are out of this world—some of the best you will hear. The General MIDI sounds are built from the same base sounds as the Proteus/1 XR sounds, but they are not as full and realistic as the Proteus sounds.

The Bottom Line

Both the SCC-1 and the MultiSound are solid choices for good sound cards; they are head and shoulders above the competition. This is as true now as it was when I wrote the first edition of this book. The SCC-1 represents an excellent value (if you already have, or don't need .WAV file support). Although it's more expensive, the MultiSound is worth every penny. However, if you plan to work only with General MIDI, back up and check out the SCC-1.

Pro Audio Spectrum

Made by Media Vision, the Pro Audio Spectrum (PAS) series is my choice for a good card at a lower price over either the SCC-1 or the MultiSound. The Media Vision cards support MIDI (with an optional cable) and .WAV files. They use FM synthesis to create sounds, so the MIDI isn't great, but it is acceptable, especially for games and playing around.

These cards represent a good value, but only if you buy a card for the right reasons. Media Vision, for example, has been providing better customer support than its competition, although there are a few gaps. Media Vision's installation software is usually very good.[16] The software bundles are good values, and the performance of the cards tends to be better than the competition.

All PAS cards (as they are commonly known) incorporate FM-based synthesizers. Although these sounds are good for games, they're only adequate for music-making.

The PAS cards are one step ahead of the Sound Blaster. With PAS cards, you do not have to peel open your computer to change elements such as interrupts and DMA channels—you can make these changes with software. The industry must move in this direction, and I applaud Media Vision for doing it.

---

[16] Media Vision pioneered the use of software configuration among low-priced sound cards.

Another point in the PAS series' favor is that it incorporates a standard SCSI controller.[17] This means you can choose almost any standard SCSI CD-ROM drive, and there are many to choose from.[18]

Overall, the Pro Audio Spectrum cards represent a good value. They are not perfect, but you get good materials for your money. Even though I use the MultiSound as my sound card, I have a Pro Audio Spectrum in one of our machines. This is the second such card we've tried, and both worked well no matter what other hardware was in the machine. This speaks well of the engineering at Media Vision—I can't say the same thing about Sound Blasters. These little things increase my confidence in a company's products.

Media Vision Audioport

Media Vision produces another sound device—the Audioport. It's not a card; it's a small box about the size of a slim pack of cigarettes that connects to your parallel port. (It's a nice size for laptop computers.) Because of its size, the Audioport also has a small speaker that's better than a PC speaker but not good enough for daily use. The unit has jacks for headphones or external amplified speakers, which improve the sound quality. You can also plug in a microphone for recording.

When I tested the Audioport, I was using Norton Desktop for Windows on my portable, and Media Vision told me that I wasn't the only one who experienced problems with the Audioport driver under Norton. If I started Windows without the Audioport sitting on the parallel port, Windows seems to forget that drivers are installed. Because this is a portable, there are many times when I don't use the Audioport; this is rather frustrating.

---

[17] The hardware is based on the Trantor SCSI card, so you can count on support for driver upgrades.

[18] Media Vision maintains a list of CD-ROM drives compatible with its hardware on CompuServe. To find it, GO MULTIVEN and look for the Media Vision section. They also upload new drivers for easy download. Creative Labs, at the time of this writing, was not present on CompuServe.

Otherwise, this is a fun product, particularly for laptops. If you regularly use a laptop to make business presentations, the Audioport and some small, self-amplified speakers could make a big difference. Keep in mind that the Audioport uses 8-bit sound, and it has a simpler FM synthesis module than its brethren, the Pro Audio Spectrum cards. However, the Audioport is also cheaper. If you're on a budget or you want to provide sound capability for the kids' computer, the Audioport is a useful choice.

Thunderboard

The Thunderboard (also from Media Vision) is a card with roughly the same capabilities as the Audioport. The major difference is the Thunderboard provides two watts of amplified output, compared to the Audioport's one-half watt. The Thunderboard also includes a joystick port. Media Vision also offers a board called Thunder and Lightning which combines the features of the Thunderboard with a 24-bit SuperVGA card. I did not get a chance to try one myself, but it appears to be a good value. I haven't heard any negative reactions on CompuServe or elsewhere, which is a good sign.

Sound Blaster Family

Although the Adlib was the first successful sound card, the Sound Blaster has become the most popular. It is available in several models, ranging from 8–16 bits, and some have advanced features. All models use FM synthesis to create MIDI sounds. The more expensive models use more sophisticated FM synthesis chips, but the sound improvement is not dramatic. You can augment the top-end model with a daughter card that adds wave-table synthesis (the Wave Blaster).

I have mixed feelings about the Sound Blaster. I used the Sound Blaster Pro for this review; when the card performed well, it performed quite well. When it didn't perform well, I had serious problems with it.

Let me tell you the story.

Creative Labs sent me a multimedia upgrade kit consisting of a Sound Blaster Pro, a MIDI kit (MIDI cables and sequencer software), and a CD-ROM drive. The hardware installation instructions were clear, although I did have to figure out how to set the jumpers on the card—a time-consuming process because I had to pull all the cards out of my machine and balance the interrupts. I also had to give up one serial port to fit the Sound Blaster into my machine. Of course, I probably have more things plugged into my machine than most folks—a scanner, tape backup, three (now two) serial ports, a bus mouse, a digitizing tablet, and so on. Nonetheless, I eventually succeeded in installing the hardware.

> If you decide to use nonstandard interrupts and DMA channels for the Sound Blaster, remember that the original Sound Blaster was hard-wired to specific settings. Some software developers assumed they could use those settings to communicate with the Sound Blaster. When the Sound Blaster added configurable settings, not all software was updated to use this option. In other words, if you use nonstandard settings, some software might not run properly—or at all.

Software installation was not difficult, but when I added the Sound Blaster drivers under Windows, I had a nasty surprise—the FM synthesizer freaked out on me. It played for a few seconds, and then all heck broke out—hums, clicks, whooshes, and all sorts of other strange sounds came out of the speakers. At one point, I could hear the hard-drive access sounds through my speakers.

At first, I assumed the board was bad; I called Creative Labs' technical support. They were clearly overloaded with tech support calls. This wasn't a surprise. I had seen on CompuServe in various forums a number of messages from Sound Blaster owners asking for help. Creative Labs finally agreed to send me a new board. When the new board arrived, I had the same problem but only in the original computer; this board worked fine in another computer. It's hard to say whether Creative Labs or the computer manufacturer is at fault on this one. I can tell you that I did not have these problems with the Pro Audio Spectrum 16. I also can tell you that the Sound Blaster has been flawless in the kids' computer.

The Sound Blaster, especially in the Multimedia Upgrade Kit bundle from Creative Labs, can be problematic, but it still represents a good value. If all you want is a sound card, compare prices with the cards from Media Vision. If you want the most inexpensive multimedia bundle, the Sound Blaster makes more sense than many others.

Windows Sound System: Business Audio

Microsoft rarely goes into the hardware side of the business, so their entry into the sound card market was something of a surprise. Unlike many of the other cards reviewed here, the Sound System is not intended to compete in the fun and games market.[19] In the user manual, Microsoft states that this product is intended for business use. While this is true, technically speaking, let us not forget that the Windows Sound System was one of the first sound cards to ship with voice recognition software. So perhaps I should take back what I said about this card not being aimed at the fun market. As I said in the first edition (and my thinking hasn't changed), "I just got finished playing with the voice recognition program, and it is *fun.*"

The Sound System comes with headphones and a microphone, and it is easy to set up and use. You also can connect external speakers.

Voice Recognition

The voice recognition support is surprisingly well thought out. It is very simple to use. The software determines what application you are running and presents a list of predefined macros that cover the common tasks: File|Open, OK for dialog boxes, and so on (see Figure 6.2).

Clicking the button labeled Train... opens the dialog box shown in Figure 6.3.

When you click the Start button, the program prompts you to speak the word or phrase that'll be used to activate the macro. You say the words three times, when prompted. The program decides whether you said them clearly enough (that is, it tries to detect high levels of background noise that might cause problems), and, if it is satisfied, it stores the training session.

In this example, if you are in Word for Windows and say "open," the Open dialog box appears automatically. I don't know what co-workers will think about you talking to your machine, but it's a lot of fun to tell your computer what to do, and the program works amazingly well.

---

[19] The MultiSound is also not the best choice for games—it will not work with games that demand Sound Blaster compatibility. The MultiSound uses a different architecture to improve performance, and this is not compatible with some games.

The software does not actually recognize the words you speak (for that kind of technology, you'll have to wait—well, if you have the money, you can get it now, but I'm talking *lots* of money). The voice-recognition software merely uses clever techniques to recognize the characteristic features of each wave form. It stores these in a database. When you speak, it compares the features of the spoken words with the database, and, if it finds a match, it activates the macro.

Clever as the method is, it's not perfect. You should put the microphone in the same place each time, and you should try to speak with a consistent set of inflections and the same loudness each time. Any moderately loud background noises confuse the program entirely.

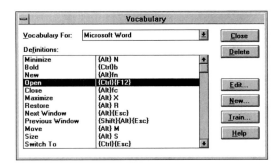

Figure 6.2. *The software presents a list of predefined macros that perform common tasks.*

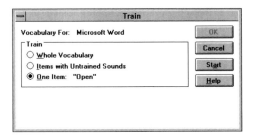

Figure 6.3. *The Train dialog box.*

Supported Applications

The following applications are supported by the voice-recognition software, and you can train it for others:

Aldus PageMaker
Lotus 1-2-3 for Windows
Micrografix Designer
Microsoft Excel
Microsoft File Manager
Microsoft Mail
Microsoft Money
Microsoft PowerPoint
Microsoft Program Manager
Microsoft Project for Windows
Microsoft Word for Windows 2.0
Microsoft Works for Windows
Microsoft Write
Norton Desktop
WordPerfect for Windows

For users of either of the two spreadsheet products, the Sound System comes with a truly nifty feature: a proofreader, which plays back the contents of a spreadsheet (or a selected range) so you can verify the figures. It has a small vocabulary of common spreadsheet terms (170), including numbers, signs, days of the week, units of time, currency types, and terms such as "debit" and "credit." You can adjust playback speed, add terms to the dictionary, or create new dictionaries. You can proof in either row or column order.

You do not need to own a Window Sound System to get Voice Recognition. Since the first edition, other companies have begun to ship voice-recognition software with their sound cards (such as Creative Labs). You should also check out the InCube software demo on the CD.[20]

---

[20] I also provide some details about InCube in Chapter 2, "Sound Advice."

Audio Controls

The card comes with other interesting software too, such as a music box program that you can use to play audio CDs. You can even program the CD to play songs in any order (Figure 6.4).

Figure 6.4. *Programming the CD.*

The controls for the music box are intuitive. For example, the volume control contains controls for left/right and loudness. Even the level indicators are thoughtfully implemented: green means a low level, yellow means a high but acceptable level, and red means the level is too high.

The Sound System also includes a neat sound management utility called Sound Finder (Figure 6.5).

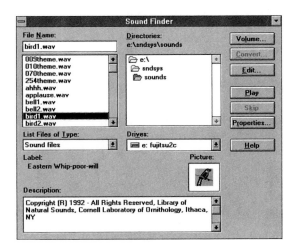

Figure 6.5. *The Sound Finder sound management utility.*

You can use the utility to associate icons with the sounds. When you embed the sound in an application (which is as easy as dragging the icon to the destination, such as a document in a word processing program), the icon is displayed, and you can play the sound by double-clicking the icon.

Sound System comes with a good set of sounds. If you click the Play button in Sound Finder, you can listen to a sound. If you click the Edit button, the Quick Recorder is invoked (Figure 6.6).

Figure 6.6. *The Quick Recorder.*

You can record, play, and stop sound files with the Quick Recorder. You can also set it to full menus to reveal a more powerful editing environment (Figure 6.7).

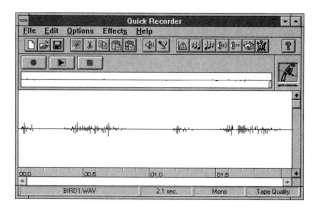

Figure 6.7. *Quick Recorder set to full menus.*

There is now a full complement of tools in the tool bar below the menu, the sound wave form is displayed, and more information about the sound file is displayed in the status bar.

The Bottom Line

I found the Windows Sound System innovative and practical. It provides a useful business solution, and as long as you don't expect to use it with game software, I can recommend it. I'll let you explain to your friends why you are talking to your computer—or why it talks back to you.

The Sound Card Future

There are many other sound cards available, and new models are constantly being introduced. Currently, there is a flood of new cards. The advent of Windows 3.1, with its support for sound, has given a big push to the market. Downward pressure on prices is likely to continue well into 1994, and it will be a tough job to keep up with all the models that will be introduced. The quest for inexpensive good sound, however, is likely to remain elusive until there is a low-cost substitute for FM synthesis.

Speakers

No matter how good the sound is that you get from your sound card, you won't hear it without decent speakers. You could go to your local audio store and pick up a pair of speakers for as little as $20, but I don't think you'll be satisfied with the sound.

The electronic components in the better sound cards, such as the SCC-1 and the MultiSound, are capable of generating sounds that challenge the capabilities of even $3,000 audiophile stereo systems. That doesn't mean, however, that you have to go out and spend that much money to enjoy your sound card.

You should, however, buy speakers that are appropriate for your sound card. I have tried several different units, and you can find the details of my search in the Shopper's Guide.

If you are using a conventional sound card with FM synthesis, you should not have to spend a lot of money on speakers. Any of the self-amplified speakers in the $100–$200 price range should do a great job. A 16-bit card that you use for music recording might justify speakers priced up to $300.

If you plan to use speakers for business presentations, you should add another consideration besides sound quality: sturdiness. You are likely to find yourself moving such speakers around a lot. I found the Roland MA-12C speakers to be very durable and solidly built, and the sound is quite good.

If you are a music buff and will be using a high-end sound card, you should invest in a kind of speaker called a *studio monitor*. Monitors usually have better-than-average fidelity and can handle a larger range of sounds—lower lows and higher highs.

There is no real limit at the high end, as any audiophile can attest. For example, the organ sound in my Korg M1 keyboard has very powerful bass, just like a real pipe organ. The only speakers I own that can reproduce it with true low-frequency fidelity are the ones in my home stereo system, which consists of a 200-watt subwoofer and two satellites. All three speakers have an exceptional capacity for accurate sound reproduction—I never would have known how good the M1 sounds without having connected it to these speakers.

CD-ROM Drives

A CD-ROM drive is more than just a critical part of a multimedia PC. I'd rather have a CD-ROM drive than a sound card any day. I really like many of the available CD software titles. As a writer, I naturally have a soft spot for any decent reference work. The sheer amount of data you can pack onto a CD-ROM boggles the mind. Of course, I also like it when a game vendor stuffs oodles of sounds and images on a CD to create a hot game title.

The time has finally arrived when many software vendors either include CD-ROM disks with their products or make their product available on a CD-ROM. This usually translates into hundreds of sample files, bigger and better help files, clip art, clip sounds, and so on—materials that make a software product either easier to learn and use, or more powerful and useful. Recent examples include Autodesk's 3-D Animation Studio and Animator Pro, Media Blitz and Compel from Asymetrix, CorelDRAW!, and Microsoft's Word for Windows, just to name a few. This trend was evident when I wrote the first edition, and it is rapidly becoming a torrent.

Here's something I said in the first edition: "This is the moment in multimedia history when the line between 'A CD-ROM drive is a neat thing to have' and 'A CD-ROM drive enhances your computer' is being set down." Well, that was true then, but things have changed even more. A CD-ROM drive is rapidly becoming an essential part of a computer.

Because a CD-ROM is not inherently multimedia (after all, you could use one just for accessing large amounts of data), you can get a drive in one of two ways: bundled with a sound card or as a drive alone.

CD-ROM Bundles

When a drive is bundled with a sound card, it usually comes as a complete multimedia upgrade kit. Such kits, if advertised as a "Multimedia PC Upgrade Kit," must pass the requirements of the Multimedia PC Marketing Council. Most manufacturers of multimedia upgrade kits are licensed by the Council; see "The MPC Standard" section later in this chapter for more information. Many of these manufacturers do not manufacture their own CD-ROM drives; they include drives from other manufacturers in their upgrade kits. The drive included might change over time, so check into the specific products when you buy.

There are now three kinds of bundles:

➤ Low-cost

➤ Moderate cost/mid-level performance

➤ High-performance

A year ago, there were only two possibilities—the first and the last. There was no middle road. Before I explain, let me define my terms.

Low-end drives are those that barely meet the standards for a CD-ROM in a multimedia PC—150K/sec data transfer rate being the most commonly mentioned. Some low-cost drives do not even meet the MPC standards. When I wrote the first edition of this book, the cost of high-end drives was high enough that there was a real need for low-cost drives, even if their performance was marginal.

Moderate-cost, mid-level performance drives are a new phenomenon. A year ago, these were the high-end drives whose key features were: double-speed (300K/sec) and multi-session support.[21]

---

[21] Multi-session refers to a drive's ability to read Photo CD discs which have multiple photo sessions recorded on them.

High-performance drives have gone up a notch. They still cost at least $500–$600, and they still offer better performance. However, the difference is no longer as dramatic.

Unless your budget is very tight, I strongly recommend purchasing one of the mid-level drives. The difference between them and the low-end drives is large. For one thing, they transfer data twice as fast—300K/sec versus 150K/sec. This is the most noticeable difference. The ability to view multi-session Photo CDs may or may not interest you personally, but it will be handy if you ever make use of them.

You can purchase such drives for less than $300, and that price is likely to fall somewhat over time. Many such drives now come in multimedia upgrade kits. For example, Creative Labs offers a 300K/sec drive combined with a 16-bit version of the Sound Blaster, whereas Media Vision offers the Fusion Double CD 16 kit which includes a Pro Audio Spectrum 16, speakers, a NEC 55 internal drive, and an excellent selection of CD-ROM products. Such upgrade kits now range from $600–$800. A year ago, all such kits were more than $1,000.

If you must have the very best performance, you can spend more money for a more sophisticated setup. More expensive CD-ROM drives, such as the high-end drives from NEC, Toshiba, and Texel, still transfer data at 300K/sec, but they reduce the average seek time to 200 ms or thereabouts. Mid-level drives usually have seek times of around 300 ms, and low-end drives can have times of .5–1 seconds.

If you buy a bundled drive, you are limited by the capabilities of the sound card, so you should consider your purchase carefully. The principal advantages of the bundles are the convenience of everything in one package and the certainty that the various pieces have been tested together.[22] With the increasing number of mid-level systems, you are more likely than ever to find upgrade kits that do not sacrifice features for price.

Pieces and Parts

If you elect to purchase a CD-ROM and the other components of your multimedia system separately, you can choose the best component in each category. You must do your homework, however, to ensure that all the pieces fit together. If

---

[22] Well, one would hope so, and when you are buying from the well-known companies, this is always true.

you plan to buy the top equipment, you should not have a problem; the engineering in such units is usually advanced and compatible.[23] If you are putting together a budget system, you should be doubly careful to ensure that you either buy components that do not conflict with one another or get a money-back guarantee. Don't assume that low-cost components will work together.

Another critical point is this: If you plan to buy a low-cost CD-ROM drive, make sure it meets minimum multimedia standards. There are a number of drives on the market (usually the cheapest) that do not meet minimum standards. Most multimedia software requires certain levels of performance in order to play videos, make music, play wave files, and move other data where it is needed. The single most important statistic is the transfer rate; the drive must be able to transfer at least 150K/sec while using no more than 40 percent of the CPU's available capacity. The second most important statistic is average access time. Faster is better. The average seek time is required to be one second or less for multimedia purposes, but times under 600 ms should be your goal for even the cheapest drives.

In some ways, building your own multimedia system is similar to putting together a component stereo system, with one added task: making sure that all the system components work together properly. If you put together a home stereo system, you don't have to worry about whether the CD player can communicate with the amplifier; you just connect them with the cables provided. Inside a computer, however, all the devices share the same data bus, interrupts, memory access, and so on. Unless each device is highly configurable, you might find there's no way for them to work together. As the market matures, this area should standardize.

What Should You Buy?

Which drive should you buy? It's hard to say; a number of good units are now out there at good prices. I have used several different drives for testing purposes. I've had very good luck with drives from Toshiba, NEC, and Texel. All of these were 300K/sec drives with average access times of 280 ms or better. You can find such drives right around $400. If you want to save some money, look at the drives

---

[23] Watch out for newly introduced hardware, however. New hardware may still have a few bugs. If you do opt for new technology, stay in touch with the manufacturer for updates to the firmware in your drive. If you experience problems, it is likely a result of bugs in the firmware. (Firmware is the code in a ROM chip in the drive that controls basic functions of the drive.)

and upgrade kits from Creative Labs and Media Vision. Creative Labs is now shipping a very inexpensive double-speed drive (made by Matsushita) that offers 300K/sec data transfer and 300 ms access times. It even comes with a simple but practical SCSI card for $299 (street price). It's called the Omni CD. I put one in my brother-in-law's computer, and it's working fine.

Whatever you buy, I strongly recommend that you insist on the following features unless you must watch pennies closely:

➤ Double-speed drive

➤ Average seek time of 300 ms or less

➤ Multi-session Photo CD support

Lastly, make sure that either the drive can connect to an existing SCSI port or a SCSI port on your sound card, or that the drive comes with a reliable SCSI card. You should be able to find the whole shebang for about $300–$350, and that price will go down over time.

Graphics Display Cards

I've been using a high-resolution graphics card for so long (more than two years at 1024 × 768 and up) that I'm always surprised when I see someone running Windows at a lower resolution.

The prices for such cards have decreased since the time I bought mine. My first hot graphics card was a NEC MultiSync Graphics Engine card, with 1M of memory, a Texas Instruments graphics coprocessor, and 256 colors at 1024 × 768. In September 1990, I paid almost $900 for it. Today, I can order a card with similar performance and capabilities, but with 16.7 million colors at 640 × 480, for less than $200. One example that I have tried myself is the Speedstar 24x from Diamond. It doesn't have a graphics coprocessor, but it's optimized for Windows graphics and does at least as well as my old card. In fact, I liked the performance and colors of this card better than Diamond's more expensive Stealth VRAM card, which does not do 24-bit graphics and costs about a third more.[24]

---

[24] A word of caution, however. As of mid-1993, some folks were experiencing some problems with the drives for these cards. In particular, the Windows drives for the Stealth card were showing some problems in conjunction with Video for Windows. Please verify that Diamond has supplied updated drivers if and when you buy.

New graphics cards are appearing weekly, so it's not possible to cover the field adequately here—by the time you read this, the high-end cards will be a little faster, the low-end cards will be a little less expensive, and many new cards will have found their way to market. What I will do is give you the information you need to make a good buying decision for multimedia use.

Today's Market

The market for video cards has gone completely haywire. There are no standards, unless you count the fact that there are a finite number of high-resolution chip sets being soldered into what seems like an infinite number of brand-name cards. New models are introduced at a whim, and fortunes are made and lost as new advances overtake the old.

This is a wonderful time to buy a card because prices have fallen to ridiculously low levels. It's hard to make a serious mistake when buying a card because virtually every card has some form of speed enhancement. Also, most quality cards on the market have 1024 × 768 resolution, and non-interlaced monitors sell for several hundred dollars.[25]

Speed Thrills

This brings you to the main point about video displays and Windows: there is no substitute for speed. At high resolutions, Windows moves so many pixels that unless your card provides some way to off-load the work from your CPU, you have slow graphics and slower operations.

When I hooked up my laptop to an external monitor, I learned how effective the new chip sets are. I use a Texas Instruments Win 4000 25/DX with 1M of video memory. This memory is useless when I use the LCD screen, but it is supposed to come into play when I hook up an external monitor, delivering up to 1024 × 768 × 16 resolution. When such high resolutions—and it's a fast display too—come installed in an economy laptop, video speed has arrived for real.

---

[25] On the other hand, you get what you pay for with monitors. If you will be sitting in front of that monitor for more than an hour a day, spend more to get something that will be easy on your eyes. I have a Nanao F550i, and it is wonderful. We also have a SuperMatch 17-inch monitor from SuperMac that has great color.

256 Versus 16.7 Million

When I bought my NEC MultiSync card, the possibilities of 256 colors, particularly at 1024 × 768 resolution, excited me. Even though I heard stories about 24-bit color and its 16.7 million colors, I was happy with my card. What could be better than what I already had? I thought that 256 colors looked completely photo-realistic. For three reasons, I withstood the urge to get a 24-bit board for two years:

➤ I had shelled out almost a thousand dollars for my 256-color board.

➤ It was going to cost twice that to get 24-bit color.

➤ The 256 colors looked good.

While writing the first edition of this book, I thought I should at least look at 24-bit color. A representative from Diamond mentioned they made an inexpensive 24-bit board. Diamond sent me the Speedstar 24X and I installed it. I viewed a 24-bit file in PhotoStyler in 256 colors so I could compare the two images. I turned down the resolution on my computer to 640 × 480 so I could use all 24 bits of color. When the image came up in 16.7 million colors, I immediately saw the difference. Although I don't think it's necessary to have 16.7 million colors, you would have trouble editing graphics files in any other mode. The Speedstar 24X only does 24-bit color at 640 × 480, so economy 24-bit color does come with some restrictions.

For everyday Windows activities, I like 1024 × 768 resolution too much to give it up. However, I do like the option of 24-bit color when I need it or want it. If you want to go into desktop publishing professionally, buy a card that can process 24-bit colors at the higher resolution. However, the Speedstar 24x is fine for occasional use.

Spectrum/24

If you want 24-bit color at 1024 × 768 or even higher resolutions, I strongly recommend the Spectrum/24 card from SuperMac. I received one recently for review, and this is one great card. The installation is easy, the colors are bright and accurate, and this card is fast. Really fast. I'll put it this way—the Spectrum/24 handles 24-bit video at 1024 × 768 faster than the high-end card that it replaces handles 256-color video at that resolution. That's *fast*.

I can't overstate how pleased I have been with this card. It's a bit pricey, but the high end usually is. Matrox makes a line of similar cards, but I have not had

Author's Choice

the chance to try one, so I can't recommend their products—I prefer to recommend only stuff I've actually used. However, recent magazine articles about their products have been positive.

What Should You Buy?

I've already made my recommendation for the high end. At the low- to mid-levels, you could do well with any of a variety of cards. It's just not possible to recommend one video card over another in a book; by next week, some other product might have stolen my heart (and an ever decreasing piece of my wallet). Currently, I like the Speedstar 24x from Diamond because it represents such a solid value, but ask me again next week. I've been using the Ultra Pro local bus video card from ATI on one machine. Although it's more expensive than the Speedstar, it's a very fast card, with very solid color. It can do 24-bit video at up to 800 × 600, and 16-bit video at 1024 × 748.[26] Folks on CompuServe have recommended and panned certain cards. I haven't tried them myself, but I have heard good things about the Appian Renegade, and various problems were reported with the Orchid P9000 and STB Power Graph X-24.

In general, if you are looking for the best combination of price and performance, the following features should be high on your shopping list:

➤ Ability to do 24-bit graphics (at least at 640 × 480).

➤ Ability to do 16-bit graphics at your most common resolution (800 × 600 or 1024 × 768).

➤ Speed.

➤ More speed.

You might wonder why I am pushing so hard to avoid 8-bit graphics. It's more than just the extra colors. It's the way 8-bit color works that will become more and more of a problem. Eight-bit color uses palettes. That is, each image consists not of colors but of numbers that point to colors in a palette. You can only have one palette open at a time. If you load an image that uses a different palette, any currently displayed images will not look right—because the image consists of references to slots in a palette, the references no longer point to the correct colors. This can be very frustrating. Most software does its best to work with 8-bit

---

[26] Requires the 2M VRAM version of the card.

color, but more and more software can also handle 16- and 24-bit color. And if you work with Video for Windows (and it's getting hard not to because more software products use video), the advantages of 16- and 24-bit color will be even more obvious. I can't say it loudly enough:[27]

Ron's Rule If you buy a new video card, make sure it does not use 8-bit color at your everyday Windows video resolution.

Local bus video also deserves a close look. The 32-bit local bus connection gives video a very real boost. You can get a 66-MHz version of this local bus setup for under $3,000.[28] If you're willing to settle for less pure speed, you can get 16-bit color and a local bus for under $2,000.

MIDI Cards

MIDI is probably the most misunderstood aspect of multimedia. Most of the users I know who actually grasp its potential are musicians. It's unfortunate that more users don't understand MIDI, because the type and quality of music possible with MIDI offers many advantages.

Unlike .WAV files, MIDI files don't take up much room. The wave-form information isn't stored in files; it's stored in the MIDI card or instrument that plays the music. A MIDI file only contains information about notes—such as what note to play, when to turn it on, and when to turn it off. If you have any inclinations toward music, consider quality MIDI cards and instruments. I guarantee that the music you generate will be different and impressive. Even if you're not musically inclined, there is a growing body of MIDI files with sounds to suit every need and every taste. There are hundreds of MIDI files available on CompuServe alone, and most are free.

The most common way to work with MIDI on a computer is to use a sequencer such as Cakewalk or Master Tracks Pro.[29] Unlike a traditional note-oriented piece of sheet music, both of these programs rely on a special form of notation that

---

[27] Besides, if we all stop using 8-bit graphics, programmers will have a much easier time of it. Internally, Windows specifies colors in the 24-bit format (RGB). Dealing with palettes is a big hassle for programmers.

[28] And this includes a generous 340M hard drive and plenty of memory.

[29] Or one of the shareware sequencers included on the CD, such as WinJammer (see Chapter 10, "Eenie-Meenie-MIDI: Keyboards").

makes it easy to work with MIDI data. Most sequencers operate in this mode, and some (like both Cakewalk and Master Tracks Pro) enable you to see one or more tracks in regular musical notation. You might prefer to work with a program that specializes in notation, like Encore or Finale. If you need more background information about MIDI, check out Chapter 2, "Sound Advice." You can find more information about sequencers in Chapter 10, "Eenie-Meenie MIDI: Keyboards."

> With the newer versions of many sequencers, you can play digital audio (that's .WAV) files during the MIDI playback by embedding MCI commands. If you plan to mix digital audio and MIDI sounds, make sure your software supports this. I like the way that Master Tracks Pro has incorporated this feature.

Sound Cards and MIDI

Most low-end sound cards have MIDI capabilities. Many game sounds use the MIDI capabilities of these cards for sound effects and mood music. The key to getting any real MIDI functionality out of one of these cards, however, is getting the MIDI signals out of the card and into a real MIDI instrument. Remember, the low-end sound cards generate sounds by FM synthesis; this is not the way to generate cool sounds. To produce great sounds, you need either sophisticated signal processing, or digitally encoded sounds from real instruments, or both.

You might need to purchase an optional kit to get the MIDI signals out of the card and into your MIDI instrument. Kits cost usually $50 or less, and they often consist of little more than a cable with standard connectors for MIDI.

> If you plan to use MIDI to make music, make sure you can live with the quality of sound your card generates. Alternatively, make sure that your sound card can communicate with whatever external MIDI device you have now or might buy later.

Once you hear a decent synthesizer, you will no more want to go back and listen to a low-end sound card with FM synthesis than you will want to go back to a CGA monitor. (I say CGA rather than monochrome because in my opinion the "quality" of a CGA monitor is even worse than monochrome.)

You can separate sound cards into the functions they perform:

➤ Digital playing and recording

➤ Sound synthesis

➤ MIDI communications

Digital Playing and Recording

Not all cards do digital recording, which gives a card the ability to play and record Wave files. Cards come in 8- and 16-bit varieties. Eight-bit cards are "for fun only." Sixteen-bit cards come in two flavors: inexpensive but somewhat noisy, and expensive but clean, clear, and beautiful. Your sound card must support digital recording if you are going to use it with any of the new voice-recognition software. You generally get better results with better sound cards. For example, I wouldn't expect to get similar results from a $90 8-bit card and a $500 16-bit card.[30]

Sound Synthesis

There are inexpensive FM synthesizers, but they have characteristic beepy sounds. Higher-end synthesizers are available on some cards—the Roland SCC-1 and Turtle Beach MultiSound come immediately to mind. High-end cards usually use some form of look-up table where sound samples are stored. The less expensive MIDI cards, like Turtle Beach's Maui card, store the samples in compressed form to keep prices low. All sound cards use MIDI to communicate with the synthesizer. This means that anything that can generate MIDI signals can communicate with the card's synthesizer too, if the card has MIDI cables.

MIDI Communications

If the sound card supports MIDI, it uses MIDI internally to communicate with its own synthesizer and externally (if so equipped) to communicate with any MIDI

---

[30] I wonder if this will ever lead to the expression "8-bit" to mean something cheap, much as "two-bit" once did. Of course, that two bits was a 25-cent piece, and an 8-bit audio card costs a lot more than that.

instrument. In other words, you can route MIDI signals to MIDI instruments and have the instruments play the sounds instead of, or in addition to, the sound card's synthesizer. You can use the software that comes with your card to determine whether the MIDI signals go to your sound card, external device, or both.

Mixing MIDI with Digital Audio

If you already own a low-end sound card and you can accept its digital audio, you might want to try either the Roland SCC-1 or the Turtle Beach Maui cards to add quality MIDI sounds. For example, if you own a Pro Audio Spectrum 16 and you're tired of FM synthesis, adding an SCC-1 gives you excellent synthesis. If you use the Pro Audio Spectrum 16 to connect your CD-ROM, your setup is even more cost-effective. I use that setup in one of our machines, and it works great. If you want to move immediately to high-quality audio and advanced MIDI synthesis, the MultiSound is an excellent choice.

MIDI for MIDI's Sake

If you like music and want to play, then you might not need digital audio capabilities at all. If that is the case, you have two ways you can go. You can use a synthesizer card (like the SCC-1 or Maui) as your sound card; it should be compatible with the MPU-401 standard or come with a Windows driver. You also could put a simple MIDI-only card (one without a synthesizer) into your machine and connect it to an external MIDI device such as a keyboard synthesizer. Your best choice for such a MIDI card is one from Music Quest. See the Shopper's Guide for more information.

Keyboards, Controllers, and Synthesizers

You can divide MIDI instruments into several categories. A keyboard is an obvious category; it sits right out there in the open. It has white keys and black keys, and if you press them, sounds come out, right? Nope—the sound part is wrong. The keyboard does nothing more than generate MIDI signals—note ON, note OFF, and so on. The synthesizer is only there for convenience. You can purchase a keyboard without a synthesizer, and a synthesizer without a keyboard.

If a keyboard unit does not contain its own synthesizer, it is called a controller. This type of keyboard is used to control other MIDI instruments, but it doesn't produce its own sounds. If a keyboard unit contains a synthesizer, it is really two different components in a single case—just like buying a stereo amplifier with a built-in FM receiver. The MIDI signals generated by the keyboard are routed to the synthesizer to make sounds just as they would be if the synthesizer were a separate unit. The synthesizer has no idea where the MIDI signals come from. As a result, it responds the same to the keyboard as it would to a sequencer program.

You can buy a synthesizer without a keyboard, much like you can buy a keyboard without a synthesizer. The front panel usually has buttons and an LCD screen for input, and cables are attached at the rear. You control these synthesizers with MIDI software on your PC, a keyboard controller, or other MIDI instruments.

Here are some more or less formal definitions of the three concepts:

Keyboard—The piano-like keys and the case that holds them. It may or may not also include a synthesizer.

Controller—A keyboard that is used to control other devices. Usually, but not always, the other devices are synthesizers.

Synthesizer—A device that generates sounds electronically. May reside inside a keyboard case, or in a small rack-mount case of its own.

All three devices can be interconnected with 5-pin DIN cables. These are standard cables carried by most music and electronics stores. Devices that include a synthesizer usually include MIDI In and MIDI Out, and may also include a MIDI Through port. A controller usually only contains a MIDI Out port.

MIDI Road Map: In, Out, and Thru

A discussion of MIDI hardware isn't complete without a brief explanation of the concepts of In, Out, and Thru. A MIDI device must support at least one of these methods of communication. A pure keyboard controller, for example, has no need to receive any data; it usually has only an Out connection.

The MultiSound, on the other hand, has a synthesizer; it needs an In. You might have other instruments in a MIDI daisy chain, so the MultiSound also has a Thru port. The Thru port takes everything received from the In port and sends it down the line. You can link approximately five instruments this way; if you need more, you need special MIDI equipment. The Out port sends the MIDI data generated or used by the device. For example, if you have a computer sending MIDI data for a rhythm section to a keyboard you are playing, that incoming data is sent to the Thru port, and the lead line you play is sent to the Out port.

MIDI to the Max

The acquisition of leading-edge MIDI technology is an art form practiced by more people than I expected. It is not uncommon for someone to spend two, three, or even five thousand dollars on the latest synthesizer. This urge for the best equipment does have some positive fallout: there is a strong market in used goods. Because everyone wants the hot new hardware and software, you can often find used equipment at bargain prices.

The place to start when configuring a MIDI PC is with the MIDI card. You have two basic choices: putting in a MIDI card that also has a synthesizer on it, or putting in a card that handles only MIDI communication.

If you want a synthesizer in your PC, there are the two choices mentioned earlier in the book: the SCC-1 from Roland and the MultiSound from Turtle Beach. These two are the best of their class. There are other such cards at more economical prices; the Turtle Beach Maui is worth a look.

The SCC-1 is MIDI only; there is no Wave support—keep that in mind if you buy it. The synthesized sounds are first class all the way. The MultiSound is a superb synthesizer, and it also supports Wave audio. The MultiSound has a low-noise, 16-bit recording capability for Wave files; you can record at CD-quality levels with it. If you need Wave or MIDI sound for business use, this is the card to buy. If you are a perfectionist or a serious hobbyist, this is also the card to buy.

Both cards support MIDI In and MIDI Out; the MultiSound also supports MIDI Thru.

If you plan to use an external synthesizer, look seriously at the MIDI cards from Music Quest. They are very popular and reliable.

If you want ruggedness and convenience in your speakers, I recommend the Roland MA-12C. With three inputs and a case that looks strong enough to practice elephant tricks on, these speakers are ideal for hard use. The speakers are bright-sounding and responsive, both pluses when working with the wide frequency response of digital sound. The low-end is weak, which is not surprising when you consider the size of the speakers. Built-in bass and treble adjustments enable you to compensate for these characteristics.

If sound is your primary concern when purchasing speakers, the Altec Lansing ACS300 is the way to go. It is a three-part speaker system that includes two clamshell satellites and a subwoofer. You can move the subwoofer out of the way and adjust the satellites to suit your needs. The sound quality is excellent. These speakers were my favorite a year ago, and nothing has come along to replace them in my estimation.

Now you have to add a keyboard or controller. If cost is an issue, the Roland PC-200 is an excellent choice as a controller. It provides a good feel at a low price, and it includes velocity sensitivity, meaning that if you play more softly, the music is softer. If you want more than a simple controller, there are two directions you can pursue. You can buy a piano-like controller, or you can buy a synthesizer with a good keyboard. If you like the feel of a piano, forget the extra synthesizer and buy a good keyboard controller. If you want more sounds to choose from, try a synthesizer. There are plenty of good synthesizers; the key issues are the quality of sound and keyboard feel. Basic consumer units sell for less than $750, whereas more sophisticated—but still amateur—synthesizers sell for as much as $2,000. Professional synthesizers are in the stratosphere with prices of $3,000 and up.

I checked the MIDI forum on CompuServe for suggestions on good high-end controllers; several users told me their favorite "piano feel" keyboard controllers (with apologies if I missed any):

➤ Roland A-80

➤ Yamaha KX-88

➤ Rhodes MK-80

➤ Roland FP-8

➤ Fatar Studio 88

Computer plus card plus controller plus speakers equals the basic system. Using the components listed, you can create and hear exciting sounds. You can spend anywhere from a few hundred dollars for everything up to as much as you care to spend.

Going Further

If you want to expand your MIDI setup further, you can try an external synthesizer (that is, without a keyboard) such as the Roland Sound Canvas or the Yamaha TG-100. Both support General MIDI, and both are stand-alone units; you can't use them unless you have some kind of MIDI interface in your computer. You can install a MIDI interface in a variety of ways. You can buy a MIDI-only card (such as the cards from Music Quest), or you can use a MIDI/synth card such as Roland's SCC-1.

The nice thing about the Sound Canvas and the TG-100 is that they enable you to expand and improve the range of sounds you can generate, without having to perform further surgery on your computer. This approach is fundamental to MIDI—one port connects to all of your MIDI hardware.

The Sound Canvas is not a rack-mount model; it sits flat on the desk. The controls are located on the top of the unit, and they include a large (for synthesizers) LCD screen, as well as buttons for raising and lowering the reverb and chorus, and changing instruments (among other things). The Canvas also has a set of eight slider controls that speed up common types of data entry.

The TG-100 is a half-width rack unit; all the controls are squeezed onto the front of the machine. As a result, it is not as friendly to use as the Sound Canvas, but it is very compact—particularly if you use it in a rack, as many musicians would.

For studio work, the Sound Canvas comes out ahead because its controls are more accessible and friendly. For traveling or making presentations, the TG-100 is much more convenient.

As far as sounds go, the Sound Canvas wins hands down. There are about five or six sounds that I like better on the TG-100, but that's not enough to make a difference.

The Sound Canvas delivers clear, clean sounds that are very realistic (except the synthetic ones, of course). There are a few sounds that are below par, but overall its sounds are solid. In fact, it goes beyond what I believe is necessary for the average presentation. Its impact is even greater if you use speakers that are up to the task.

The TG-100 delivers good sounds, certainly good enough for a business presentation. While not as clear and crisp as the Sound Canvas, the only major flaw is a certain "digital flavor" to the sounds. Many of the sounds have a hint of their digital origin—for example, an over-sharp attack on the cello sounds or a slight ringing in the piano sounds.

I would not expect anyone but an audiophile to quibble about these aspects of the sound, however. Until I connected both the Sound Canvas and the TG-100 to the same keyboard and compared the units by playing a sound first on one and then on the other, I was very pleased with the TG-100. Considering the price differential, I have no problem recommending the TG-100. It represents a good value. But if you have the money, or require very solid sound reproduction (short of the ultimate, but the ultimate has a way of costing tons more money), I'd recommend the Sound Canvas.

MIDI for Business

I've asked around, and it appears that MIDI is rarely used in business presentations; that's a shame. However, it's also an opportunity for you.

Most users who include music and sound in their projects are using Wave audio. They either buy clips from various services or they record their own sounds. Few business users record their own sounds; most must use the same sounds as everyone else.

If everyone else is dunking for apples in the same bucket, why not try a different bucket?

There are many sources for MIDI. Almost every musician, amateur or professional, works with MIDI. There is a large MIDI network as well. There are hundreds of MIDI files on CompuServe. The users who put those files on CompuServe are also available to create, modify, or otherwise deliver MIDI-based music. There are also commercial libraries of MIDI sounds.

All of this gives you a variety of ways to work with MIDI files. You can modify and tweak existing files, hire musicians to create MIDI-based music, or even create your own with a keyboard or a sequencer.

Why hasn't MIDI taken the business world by storm? In a word, standards. Or, more precisely, in a phrase, a lack of standards.

Almost every manufacturer has a different way of implementing the specific sounds on its synthesizers. MIDI uses numbers to tell a device which sound to play. If keyboard A is told to play sound 5, you might hear a grand piano. If keyboard B is told to play sound 5, you might hear a glockenspiel. This is great if you are a creative musician looking for variety of sounds. This is not so great if you want to play your presentation on different hardware at different times.

Don't worry. The General MIDI standard solves these problems (see Chapter 2, "Sound Advice"). More synthesizers support the standard every month. If you want to get creative, you can use most synthesizers to modify the preset General MIDI sounds or replace them with other sounds; you get the best of both worlds.

There is no guarantee that this will lead to a Golden Age of MIDI. I wish it would, though. The kinds of sounds you can create with MIDI span the full range of musical expression; listen to a demo of the MultiSound to see what I mean. Everything from rock to soul to fusion to reggae to classical to chamber to symphony to My Personal Funk can be laid down successfully with MIDI. You can even do special effects with MIDI. Check out the list of General MIDI sounds in Chapter 2.

Digital Video Cards

Digital video is the latest hot fad in the computer world. I shouldn't say that, though; I'm a big fan of video myself. Video is an extremely effective way to communicate. One of the first things they teach you at Writer's School is "Show, don't tell." They teach that because it's what works. If you show someone how something works, they will really understand it. If you just tell them that it exists, you haven't communicated very much.

Video is all about showing, not telling. Suppose you have a new product you'd like to sell, but it's really complicated to explain. It might be a new manufacturing process, for example. What if you could just take a video camera along, make a video showing the important stuff, and then distribute that video to anyone with a computer? That would be a much more effective technique of letting the world in on your secret.

Digital video starts as an analog signal coming out of a video camera or VCR. In the United States, the signal is called an NTSC signal, which is named for the National Television Standards Committee.[31] It's the type of signal you watch on a television.

---

[31] That's some way to make whoever is on that committee famous. As if knowing what committee set the standard is going to help anything.

Digital video is a video signal that has been captured by a computer, digitized, and stored on a hard disk or some other typical computer medium (like CDs). It is not the same thing as the video monitor you use with your computer, and it is most certainly not the same thing as NTSC video. Let's define some terms:

Computer video—This is the video you've seen on your computer monitor for however many years you've used computers.[32]

Digital video—This is video that has been digitized and stored on a computer disk.

NTSC video—This is the video of TVs, VCRs, camcorders, and related devices.

Digital video cards are the closest thing to black magic in the entire multimedia kingdom. Over the last year, for both editions of this book and for *PC Video Madness*, I slaved over hot computers trying to get various video cards to work. In some cases I gave up, even after calls to technical support. In other cases, I was thrilled with the results.

The Truth About Video

In the first edition of this book, I said, "The truth about video is very simple. To paraphrase a line I saw on the Multimedia Forum on CompuServe, recordable video is either easy or inexpensive."

This is not as true as it used to be. You can find a few good solutions at the low end (under $500 for video). There are no optimal solutions in the low-end price range, but there are several useful alternatives.

If you have a few thousand dollars to spend, you can have great video, and you can have it now. If you have $400–$1,000, you can have good video, and you can have it now. If you have less than $400, prepare yourself for four possibilities:

Touchy video—This depends on how well your NTSC video card cooperates with your computer and the other cards in it. I'm not talking about areas such as interrupt conflicts. I'm talking about the apparent inability of some video cards to coexist happily with all other kinds of equipment.

---

[32] If you've been around computers for a long time, you may recall when it was called a terminal and had a keyboard attached to it, and the computer was somewhere in another state.

Symptoms include wiggly screen display, missing video signals, ghosting, and other unpredictable phenomena.

Missing data syndrome—When converting VGA to NTSC, you can run into a different set of programs. NTSC video uses fewer scan lines than computer video. A line one pixel high cannot decide if it should show up on the TV monitor unless there is special circuitry available to deal with the problem. The technology is called anti-flicker, and it is highly desirable when you want to output to NTSC either on tape or a TV monitor.

On-again, off-again display—This is the worst situation, and it occurs when your machine and the cards in it throw a fit, forcing the video signal into another dimension. The only hope is to reboot and cross your fingers.

Missing video syndrome—This occurs when the video card has some kind of problem with your computer or the other hardware installed in it. You spend an hour installing the hardware and running the diagnostics, get bloody knuckles from pulling cards in and out of your machine, and wonder how dangerous static discharges really are. No video of any kind shows up on your monitor no matter what you do.

The art of NTSC video input and output is a costly one to master. You can either pay cash for a high-end board, or you can pay with your time after purchasing a low-end board. However, you could get lucky. Several weeks of experimentation clearly shows that the same board could be troublesome in one computer and fine in the next. I did not get the opportunity to experiment with different boards from the same manufacturer in one computer, but I wouldn't be surprised if that made a difference, too.

What I did do was install almost a dozen video capture and overlay cards (see Chapter 11, "Lights, Camera, Action: Video for Windows," for endless discussions about the varieties of video on the PC) onto a 486/66 DX2 PC with a Micronics motherboard.[33] The result is very simple to report: the more expensive the board (i.e., the more engineering that went into its design), the better it performed. Let the buyer beware when it comes to NTSC video.

---

[33] I have had very good success with the Micronics motherboard. They appear to have done a great job with the design. I am forever putting new and different equipment into that poor board, and it not only holds up physically to the abuse, but virtually every piece of hardware I have thrown at it has worked. The ones that didn't work failed for reasons having nothing to do with the Micronics board.

Outputting VGA to VCRs

Sending computer graphics to a TV or video recorder is probably the most common reason for combining NTSC and computer video. The hardware that does this is called an *encoder*. It's difficult and expensive to do this right. I already mentioned the biggest problem—flicker. Flicker results when thin horizontal lines on the computer monitor are displayed on the NTSC video device. Because NTSC video has fewer scan lines, thin lines show up intermittently. Many of the less expensive units do not do anything to reduce flicker. Look for flicker reduction when you purchase a board. The Bravado, along with its optional encoder, is a good solution, as are the VideoVGA and VGA Producer Pro. All other systems should be regarded as suspect until you try them.

Ron's Rule Do not attempt to output computer screens to video unless you use some form of anti-flicker technology. Otherwise, the resulting output insults all in attendance, which could prove embarrassing. This establishes the minimum qualification for TV display.

Combining NTSC and Computer Video

The next step up involves mixing VGA video with NTSC video. You have to spend almost $1,000 to get good results. Even then, expect to have to do a fair amount of tuning to get good images. For example, with a product like VideoVGA from Truevision, I can use live video as the desktop for Windows operations—not on my computer screen but on a TV monitor. You can do this by selecting a color or brightness level to use as a "key" color or luminance. The key drops out of the computer image, and it can be replaced by the video image.

The VideoVGA was a solid performer when I used it for basic tasks, but it exhibited some ghosting problems when I tried to use it with S-Video (SVHS) input signals. It is only capable of sending VGA screens (640 × 480) to a TV or VCR. This is typical for this type of card. Because the mechanics of converting higher resolutions are so complex, you can't expect reliable performance unless the unit is designed specifically for Super VGA resolutions.

There are two boards that seem to be at the top right now—the VideoVGA, and the Magni VGA Producer Pro. Both boards have a reputation for good engineering, steady images, and well-designed software. The Bravado/encoder combination adds a new twist: you can include video in a window in the output to NTSC video. If you are not impressed by that idea, think about it for a minute.

Video Capture

Capturing single video frames is not that hard. The portions of the computer system used for such captures are capable of handling the amount of data involved. A single-frame capture in 24-bit color takes up a little less than a megabyte of space.[34] That means that, in most situations, the capture can happen in memory. Because only one frame is captured, the computer can use all the time it needs—there are no more frames to capture.

On the other hand, trying to capture video frames in real time poses *major* challenges. There are 30 video frames each second. An 8-bit full-screen image (640 × 480) contains 307,200 pixels; if you save with 24 bits per pixel, that's 921,600 bytes—nearly 1M. That's only one frame![35]

At that rate, a minute of video would take up 1,658,880,000 bytes—about 1.5 gigabytes. It's not exactly practical to have that much hard disk space available for recording.[36]

There are a number ways to deal with the sobering reality of large video-data files. Chapter 10, "Eenie, Meenie, MIDI: Keyboards" goes into all the gory details, but I'll cover some of the more hardware-oriented issues here.

There are some obvious things you can do to reduce the data rate. The two most obvious are, well, obvious. You can use a smaller image size, and you can use fewer colors.[37] You can also use data compression, faster hardware, and larger hard disks.

In Chapter 2, "Sound Advice," I talked about various compression techniques. I hinted that the place where compression becomes critical is in real-time video capture. Now you know why!

---

[34] This assumes capture at 640 × 480. Some video cards, such as the Super VideoWindows, actually capture at larger sizes and thus have even larger files to write.

[35] Heck, it's easy to impress with numbers when you are working with video. Video is very deceptive—that little TV in your living room (OK, maybe yours isn't so little) is handling an amazing amount of data. Analog technology does have it's advantages.

[36] He says, with a certain amount of understatement.

[37] But this is deceptive. Believe it or not, if you add up all the variables involved, it's actually sometimes more efficient to deal with 24-bit color than 8-bit color. Palettes have something to do with this, but the fact that NTSC video doesn't use the RGB color model has much more to do with it. The time it takes to convert from NTSC's native YUV format to RGB and then to palettes can slow things down.

Hardware Compression

You might also recall I mentioned that putting compression algorithms in firmware was as much as 20 times faster than software compression. Last year, I said, "These techniques are ideal for video capture; there's just one problem: the hardware costs about 20 times more than the software solution. Hardware compression boards are in the $2,000–$3,000 range." My, how times have changed. Would you believe that you can now get hardware-assisted compression for under $500?

Intel more or less stunned the digital video field when it introduced the Smart Video Recorder in the late spring of 1993. This board uses Intel's i750 chip to compress video in real time, during capture, using Intel's Indeo compression scheme. This represents a major breakthrough. No longer must one capture first, and then sit through the slow process of compression afterward. Now the steps for digital video have been reduced to this:

Step 1: Capture the video.

It could not possibly get any easier—there are no additional steps. At worst, if you blow it and record a bit of video you don't want, you can delete that portion of the clip and then save in VidEdit using the No Change compression option.[38]

For some situations, the Smart Video Recorder is not enough. If you need full-screen, full-motion video, turn to boards like the Media Space/DVA-4000 from Video Logic, or check out the compression add-on for the Bravado. See the Shopper's Guide for details.

What You Can Do Today

With today's hardware and software, you can inexpensively capture single-frame video images and medium-resolution, real-time images. If you have the hot new hardware, you can capture high-resolution, real-time images. However, you need the fastest machines, hardware compression, and a top-of-the-line video-capture board.

If you have fast hardware—a 486/66 DX2, say, with 8–12M of memory and a very fast (8–12-ms seek time) hard drive, and an Intel Smart Video Recorder (ISVR), you can capture video at up to 320 × 240 at 15 frames per second (fps). The ISVR

---

[38] And you really, really should use that No Change compression option if the video is already compressed. Double compression can lead to all kinds of performance problems when you play back the file, especially if you try to play it from a CD-ROM disc.

can also do 160 × 120 at 30 fps. Other boards are also capable of 160 × 120 at 30 fps, such as the Captivator from VideoLogic and the Video Spigot from Creative Labs. None of these boards do overlay; the Bravado and Media Space/DVA-4000 are the cream of the overlay crop.[39]

Killer Hardware

Last year, the heading for this section was intended as a joke. I said, "The current state of technology doesn't offer any killer video-capture hardware, at least not at prices the majority of users can afford." The times they are a changin'—killer video capture is here.

Unfortunately, there are some real dogs, too. I tested several video cards; some were killers, some barked louder than your neighbor's dog. The ones worth commenting on are:

➤ Intel Smart Video Recorder

➤ VideoLogic Captivator

➤ Creative Labs Video Spigot

➤ Media Space/DVA-4000 from VideoLogic

➤ Bravado from Truevision

➤ Super VideoWindows from New Media Graphics

➤ Video Blaster from Creative Labs

Intel Smart Video Recorder

I have already sung the praises of this board. It compresses in real time; what more could you ask for? Nonetheless, the ISVR (as it is affectionately known) isn't perfect. However, it is the capture card of choice for most situations.[40]

If you merely want to capture video and then use it without editing (or with only minimal editing), the ISVR is just about perfect. For example, if you plan to add talking heads or product demonstrations to your presentations using video, the ISVR is your card. You can capture and compress in one step, which is a great savings of your time.

---

[39] See Chapter 11, "Lights, Camera, Action: Video for Windows," for more information about overlay boards.

[40] Until, of course, something better comes along from Intel or someone else.

However, you won't always want to compress while you capture. If you plan on even modest editing—even something as simple as combining two video clips—you should not capture and compress at the same time. If you compress a clip twice, not only will the image quality degrade (sometimes to the point where the result is not usable), but you may encounter serious performance problems as well.

Ron's Rule Never compress a video clip twice. If you are making changes, compress after you make *all* of the changes.

You do not have to compress when you capture with the ISVR—it also captures raw video, which you can edit and compress later. Although it can't capture at the same high data rates when the video is not compressed, it is still at or near the top of my list on all performance criteria.

My Smart Video Recorder is installed in my main machine, and I use it for the bulk of my video capture.

Captivator

A VideoLogic Captivator is installed in our other machine. The Captivator excels at still video captures, and it's not too shabby when it comes to motion capture, either. However, I mostly use it for still capture. If you do still capture most of the time but you still need a capable motion capture board, the Captivator is the answer.

See Chapter 11, "Lights, Camera, Action: Video for Windows," for examples of what the Captivator can do. It very conveniently has both the best still-image capture and excellent motion capture capabilities.

When I tried still captures with other video capture cards, I found all kinds of problems. Some are obvious, like a too-blurry image. You should expect a certain amount of blur from a video capture because a video camera is just not a high-resolution device. However, most boards blur the image even further.

A single video frame is made of two fields, each with half of the horizontal scan lines in it. To create a single frame image, a capture card must do a very good job of preserving the alignment of the two fields. Some boards are so bad at this that they capture only one field or the other. The Captivator does a superb job of aligning the two fields.

Other areas where the Captivator does a great job include color accuracy, sharpness, contrast, and preservation of fine textural details in the image.

Video Spigot

The Video Spigot is really a very fine video card, and you won't be disappointed if you get one. It is just below the Captivator in both image and performance, and it misses an Author's Choice by the tiniest of margins. I used a Video Spigot as my backup capture card until the Captivator was introduced.

The Spigot captures up to 30 fps at 160×120, and it also does a good job at 240×180. You need very, very fast equipment to handle 320×240 at any reasonable frame rate, however—that, of course, is where the Smart Video Recorder excels. The ISVR captures high frame rates with special hardware (the i750), whereas the Spigot does it with good old-fashioned clever design.

Media Space/DVA-4000

Media Space/DVA-4000 is big-guns video. It involves video compression technology from C-Cubed. This technology has been around for a while now, and it is reasonably mature. That is, it works reliably and predictably. VideoLogic has introduced Video for Windows support for the Media Space, which gives you the best of both worlds.

However, this technology, unlike Indeo, does not operate with software playback. You need the same hardware for playback that is used for recording. The advantage is that you can have 640×480, full-screen, full-motion (30 fps) video. To put this technology into perspective, it costs several thousand dollars to outfit a computer with this hardware. However, if you want the best, this is it. For example, if you are installing a system in a corporate boardroom, it makes sense to use the best technology—you only need a few systems: at least one for development, and another for delivery. The Media Space would also be wickedly good in a kiosk system.

The Media Space relies on overlay technology, so you need a VGA or SuperVGA card in your system as well. VideoLogic can tell you which VGA cards they support when you make a purchase—the list has been growing. The image quality is very, very good.

Bravado

The Bravado board from Truevision is in the middle between the Spigot/Captivator/ISVR group and the Media Space, both in price and features. The Bravado is an overlay and capture card, so it is very versatile. You can add an encoder module for outputting to tape, and you can add hardware compression for very high performance like the Media Space. In this, it is more versatile than the Media Space.

The Bravado has built-in VGA capabilities, so you do not need a separate VGA card. The Bravado's SuperVGA support is OK, but it does not compete with the very fast video cards out there. However, if you want the variety and quality of video support that the Bravado offers, this is an acceptable compromise. In many cases, overlay boards are unable to work cooperatively with the high-end boards anyway.

I do not recommend the 8-bit version of the Bravado, which only gives me 16 colors at 1024×768. I can't do any image processing to my captured images with so few colors. The Bravado 16 is the only way to go.

I give the Bravado board especially high marks for engineering. I initially had some reservations about the software supplied with the Bravado, but the most recent versions have cleared up all the issues I had. In particular, the Bravado comes with an MCI driver that enables you to control overlay features in any software, programming language, or authoring system that supports MCI calls. This includes almost everything these days—heck, you could do still-image capture from Word for Windows should you desire to do so.

The Bravado is a good choice, but it's somewhat expensive. However, in the right situation, it's really the only board to buy. If your needs require video overlay, still-image capture, motion-video capture, real-time compression with hardware-assisted playback, and VGA output to tape, as well as SuperVGA Windows resolutions, then the Bravado is perfect. No other video board combines all of its features.

Super VideoWindows

Next came the Super VideoWindows card from New Media Graphics. It combines both overlay and video capture, both still and motion with Video for Windows. If you need to do overlay and capture but are on a budget, this is the card to choose. Image quality is good, and installation is reasonably easy to do.

As with all overlay boards, it connects to an existing VGA board.[41] And, as with all overlay boards, the results are mixed. Think about what is going on. On

---

[41] New Media Graphics also sells a VGA daughter card for use with the Super VideoWindows. If you are conservative—and there is reason to be—then you might want to try that option.

the one hand, you have a very high-frequency, precisely aligned video display signal (also known as VGA). On the other hand, you have an NTSC video signal, which is completely different in nature—it is interlaced (it has those two fields), has a different frequency, and, horror of horrors, it is analog to boot. Thus, it can only be merged with the VGA signal after the VGA signal has been turned into an analog signal. What I'm trying to say here is that this is a very touchy thing to balance, and that you simply cannot expect to have juicy, ultra-fast, high-end SuperVGA with your video overlay. Not at these prices, anyway.

With all that in mind, the Super VideoWindows board works well. It is not as polished as the board from Truevision, but the Super VideoWindows board comes with examples of how to use the board with Visual Basic and Toolbook. And it costs a lot less than the Bravado. If you are on a budget, the Super VideoWindows is a good choice if you need the specific features it offers.

Video Blaster

The first video board I tested (for the first edition of this book) was the Video Blaster from Creative Labs. It is a very low-cost overlay-plus-capture card, and, despite some definite flaws, it represents a real bargain if you need video on a budget or just want a card to play around with.

The Video Blaster suffers from the usual problems of an overlay card, only more so. As its low price might suggest, the engineering is not up to the level of the other overlay cards I have covered here. Compatibility with existing VGA cards is not as common as I would like to see, but Creative Labs can fill you in on the VGA cards that the Video Blaster can coexist with. In general, the faster or more feature-laden the video card, the less likely that the Video Blaster can coexist with it. I also found that the Video Blaster tends to have problems in fast 486 hardware—some folks had to return their Video Blaster after trying it in a fast 486. You may well find out that the VB will not operate properly in your setup. You can try a different video card (that's what I did to finally get it to work in a 396/33 I had on hand), but if your computer hardware is having trouble with it, there is no easy solution.

I checked CompuServe for other Video Blaster users, and the results were mixed. Some people had no problems whatsoever with the Video Blaster, whereas others had a variety of problems ranging from "It won't work at all" to "The images are jumpy." If budget is your concern, just make sure you can return the hardware if it doesn't work properly for you. If it does work, the image quality and performance are what you might expect—pretty average. I had some trouble with color drift during capture, and the clarity of the images was only so-so.

The Bottom Line

All of these boards are compatible with the AVI standards. Some, which I have noted, require special hardware for playback. There is one other limitation you should be aware of. Overlay boards that use the Chips & Technology chip set limit the amount of memory you can have in your system.[42] These boards map video-capture memory into the first 16M of system memory, and thus you cannot have more than 14M of memory in your system.[43]

If video capture—especially motion-video capture—is your goal, I strongly recommend that you steer away from an overlay board and focus on one of the capture-only cards. If you really need overlay, be prepared to make some sacrifices in Windows video performance.

The bottom line is that video is now here to stay. The hardware for video is here at a good price. What does the future hold? I expect to see more and more video display cards add some form of hardware support for Video for Windows playback, particularly with the major codecs like Indeo and Cinepak. Both Intel and SuperMac are working closely with various video card companies to help them add this support.

I also expect to see more advanced codecs like JPEG, motion JPEG, and MPEG make their appearance soon. Right now, a few expensive cards offer these high-tech compression solutions, but several companies were working on products at press time that will lower the price barrier on these technologies. They are very sophisticated technologies, and the cost will come down slowly at first. In fact, it looks like these technologies will appear first in consumer game products, such as CD-I and 3DO.[44]

If you want to get a look at the current state of the art, there are plenty of AVI files on both CDs. Look for files with the .AVI extension. If you do not know how to play video files, or if you have not yet installed the Video for Windows runtime, see Chapter 11, "Lights, Camera, Action: Video for Windows," for full details.

---

[42] That includes the Bravado, the Super VideoWindows, and the Video Blaster.

[43] The reason for this is built into the ISA bus. Any card on the ISA bus can address memory only in the lower 16M of memory. The width of the bus simply does not permit more than that. Some EISA systems enable you to play around with memory, which gives you more flexibility in working with these cards.

[44] CD-I has been around for a while, and quite a few titles are available. 3DO is new as of the fall of 1993. Both technologies require a proprietary player that displays output on a TV monitor.

Multimedia Upgrade Kits

A multimedia upgrade kit is the fastest way to put true multimedia on your computer. The standard kit contains a sound card, a CD-ROM player, the necessary cables, and often a variety of software packages, including games, encyclopedias, almanacs, and so on.

This section provides information about the more popular kits. For detailed information, consult the Shopper's Guide.

The two major players in the multimedia upgrade kit arena are Creative Labs and Media Vision. These companies are also the ones who are the major players in the sound card market. When you buy a sound card, it may well be from Creative Labs or Media Vision even if it has another company's name on it.

Neither of these companies is in the CD-ROM business, so they are bundling other drives with their sound cards. In general, Media Vision has chosen higher quality units than Creative Labs, but their prices are a little higher too. As with many things multimedia, you get what you pay for, by and large. However, we are rapidly approaching the point where mid-level CD-ROM drives—and sound cards, for that matter—are becoming commodities. This means that, for a given price, you get pretty much the same set of features. The differences are more in terms of support and upgrade policies rather than features.

If you are interested specifically in the high end, consider the upgrade kit from Turtle Beach. It includes the MultiSound—unquestionably the premiere audio card—a high-performance Texel CD-ROM drive, and a SCSI card for the CD-ROM drive. This gives you high-end performance in all aspects of your multimedia system.

The introduction of inexpensive double-spin CD-ROM drives is changing the face and price of multimedia upgrade kits. By the time you read this, further changes may have occurred. Check the offerings currently available when you make your purchase. See the section "CD-ROM Drives," earlier in this chapter, for some important guidelines on CD-ROM drives.

Media Vision

Media Vision recently completely redesigned their multimedia upgrade line of products. All of them still offer a version of the 16-bit Pro Audio Spectrum card. The emphasis has switched from inexpensive CD-ROM drives to double-spin CD-ROM drives. Both internal and external CD-ROM drives are available.

I have used both internal and external CD-ROMs, and there really isn't any performance difference between the two types. In fact, the very same CD-ROM drives are used in both situations. The external units add a power supply and some electronics as well as a case, which is why they cost more than internal drives. I use my external unit with both my desktop PC and my portable.

Media Vision's upgrade kits span the full range of sound and CD-ROM drive options. The mid-level kit is installed on one of our machines; it's called the Fusion Double CD 16. It includes a NEC 55 CD-ROM drive, a PAS 16 sound card, and Labtec speakers, and it comes with several CD-ROM products—The 7th Guest, Compton's Encyclopedia, and Arthur's Teach Trouble. The installation is exceptionally trouble-free, and it has been flawless in use.

Media Vision also offers multimedia upgrade kits that feature high-end NEC CD-ROM drives.

Creative Labs

Creative Labs has also completely revamped their upgrade line. Just as Media Vision now does, Creative Labs features the new generation of mid-level CD-ROM drives. You can get three different combinations—low-end CD-ROM and 8-bit audio, or mid-level CD-ROM with low-end audio, or mid-level in both departments.

For example, the Discover CD16 upgrade kit offers the basic 16-bit Sound Blaster plus a low-end CD-ROM drive. Be careful here: this kit doesn't meet my minimum specs—no double spin, and no multi-session support. Its primary plus is a low price.

However, consider the DigitalEdge CD upgrade kit. It comes with Creative Labs' best sound card and CD-ROM drive—the Sound Blaster 16ASP and a double-speed, multi-session CD-ROM drive. It's still an economical system because it uses a mid-level (350 ms access time) CD-ROM drive. The software bundle is good:

➤ Aldus PhotoStyler (special edition, which means limited version)

➤ Microsoft Bookshelf

➤ Microsoft Works for Windows

➤ Macromedia Action! and Authorware Star

➤ VoiceAssist speech recognition

Creative Labs also offers Edutainment systems, which bundle a lot of cool software—games, reference works, children's software, and others.

Several of the Creative Labs kits use a proprietary interface between the sound card and the CD-ROM, so you have no choice but to use both products together. The price of these products is often very attractive, but if you like to mix and match, look elsewhere.

The full range of Creative Labs products is covered in the Shopper's Guide.

Mail-Order Multimedia

Here's another statement from the first edition of this book: "I haven't seen any original multimedia upgrade kits offered by the mail-order vendors." Wow—there has been a huge change in this area! Many mail order vendors not only offer their own multimedia upgrade kits now, but many mail order system vendors offer all kinds of multimedia options. Of course, the mail order companies also offer all of the usual upgrade kits from Creative Labs, Media Vision, and others.

Unlike the name brands, mail order kits are more of a shot in the dark. In general, if the kit is offered without identifying the company that makes the various components, I recommend steering clear. On the other hand, if the manufacturer and model numbers are clearly identified and you know the value of each component, look for a good price. The biggest danger with off-brand upgrade kits is that they might contain one or more sub-standard components. If you see a good price and can verify quality, you may well get a great value. Pay particular attention to return policies.

The key issue with any kit is simple: how well do the parts work together? See the sections, "Multimedia Upgrade Kit Vendors" and "Multimedia PC Vendors," for a list of companies that have officially licensed the MPC logo from the Multimedia Marketing Council. Although the Council cannot police such licensees, if a company went to the trouble of licensing (license fees run to six figures), they probably at least mean well.

Do-It-Yourself Multimedia

You can also roll your own multimedia PC. For maximum guaranteed performance, you can put the CD-ROM drive of your choice in your machine and link it with the SCSI board of your choice. If you plan to purchase a high-end sound card such as the MultiSound, or a MIDI-only card such as the SCC-1 from Roland, this is probably the best way to go.[45] The MultiSound has a provision for internal connection to CD-ROM audio, but it does not have an on-board SCSI port.[46] The SCC-1 is not designed for digital audio, and it should coexist peacefully with almost any CD-ROM drive or digital audio card. I have used it successfully with both the Sound Blaster and Pro Audio Spectrum cards.

The Multimedia PC

What makes a PC a multimedia PC? The Multimedia PC Marketing Council has defined two levels of MPC (Multimedia PC) compliance. Level 1 requires the specifications listed in Table 6.1, and Level 2 requires the specifications listed in Table 6.2.

---

[45] However, Turtle Beach does offer a multimedia package, including the MultiSound, a high-performance Texel CD-ROM drive, and a SCSI card.

[46] This was done to keep the card as noise-free as possible.

Table 6.1. MPC Compliance Level 1 Configurations.

Minimum Full System Configuration, Level 1	
Component	*Description*
CPU	386SX or compatible microprocessor
RAM	2M of RAM
Magnetic storage	Floppy drive, hard drive
Optical storage	CD-ROM with CD-DA outputs
Audio	DAC, ADC, music synthesizer, on-board analog audio mixing
Video	VGA graphics adapter
Input	101-key keyboard (or functional equivalent), two-button mouse
I/O	Serial port, parallel port, MIDI l/O port, joystick port

Minimum Upgrade Kit Configuration, Level 1	
Component	*Description*
Optical storage	CD-ROM with CD-DA outputs
Audio	DAC, ADC, music synthesizer, on-board analog audio mixing
I/O	Serial port, parallel port, MIDI l/O port, joystick port

Table 6.2. MPC Compliance Level 2 Configurations.

Minimum Full System Configuration, Level 2	
Component	*Description*
CPU	486SX/25
RAM	4M of RAM
Magnetic storage	Floppy drive, 160M hard drive
Optical storage	CD-ROM with CD-DA outputs. Transfer rate of 300K/sec. Seek time of 400 ms or better CPU usage no more than 60 percent at 300K/sec Must support CD Audio, CD XA, multi-session, and Subchannel Q standards
Audio	Sample size: 8 and 16 bit. Sample rate: 11, 22, and 44 KHz. Input mixing and MIDI In/Out/ Through required. CPU usage 10 percent or less
Video	640 × 480 with 16-bit color or better
Input	101-key keyboard (or functional equivalent), two-button mouse
I/O	Serial port, parallel port, MIDI l/O port, joystick port

Minimum Upgrade Kit Configuration, Level 2	
Component	*Description*
Optical Storage	CD-ROM with CD-DA outputs. Transfer rate of 300K/sec. Seek time of 400 ms or better. CPU usage no more than 60 percent at 300K/sec Must support CD Audio, CD XA, multi-session, and Subchannel Q standards
Audio	Sample size: 8 and 16 bit. Sample rate: 11, 22, and 44 KHz. Input mixing and MIDI In/Out/ Through required. CPU usage 10 percent or less

I want to emphasize that these are minimum requirements as defined by the Multimedia PC Marketing Council. I recommend that you go a little further than Level 2 in the power department when it comes to the Ultimate Affordable Multimedia PC. How far? See the next section, "Ron's Ultimate Affordable Multimedia PC," for details.

Ron's Ultimate Affordable Multimedia PC

My recommendation for a useful, affordable, and still powerful multimedia machine would be a 486 DX platform, 8M of RAM, at least a 200M hard drive, and a 1024 × 768 resolution, 16-bit color video setup (card and monitor). Is that affordable? I've seen ads in *PC Magazine* for a 486/33DX with 8M of RAM, a 212M hard disk, and a 1024 × 768 × 64K card and monitor for just $1,795. The 486/33 is a good deal because you can upgrade later to a 66-MHz machine (internal to CPU only) by adding an Intel Overdrive chip.[47] Options include a local bus, larger hard disk, and a 17-inch monitor.

As for the multimedia part, how about a Media Vision Fusion upgrade kit (double-spin CD-ROM, 16-bit sound card, and MIDI—all the basics) for $600? That's a total of $2,400, and you have a great PC and multimedia good enough to author with.[48] Speakers, headphones, and a microphone are not included in this price, however; spend as much or as little on those as you like. You can get away with spending less than $50 for all three, or you can spend thousands.

Of course, if you plan to develop multimedia presentations with any seriousness, buy the fastest machine you can find (I chose a 486/66 myself, but Pentium is worth consideration). You also might want to get a high-performance CD-ROM drive, and a 1-gigabyte or larger hard drive. If you plan to do video capture, a large, fast hard drive is essential.

You can get by with less, but if you are at all serious about multimedia, the more powerful platform will reward you repeatedly with quicker access times, speedy graphic displays, and room to breathe under Windows.

---

[47] However, beware of options that allow you to upgrade to a Pentium chip. To perform at its best, the Pentium really requires a specialized motherboard design. Few, if any, conventional 486 motherboards are capable of supporting the Pentium with the special additional features it needs to really zoom along.

[48] If you are willing to settle for the Level 2 standards, you can go multimedia for less than $2,000.

The MPC Standards

Each of the components specified as part of the minimum standards has some standards of its own that are worth knowing about. In the spirit of completeness, I provide in this section a breakdown of the following components and the requirements for each:

➤ Optical storage

➤ Audio

➤ Video

➤ User input

➤ I/O

➤ General specifications

The component descriptions based on the Multimedia PC Marketing Council's published standards.

These standards are pretty technical. If technical specifications are not your cup of tea, feel free to skip to Chapter 7, "Priming the Pump: Software."

Optical Storage

Level 1 requires a CD-ROM drive with sustained 150K/sec transfer rate. In addition, the drive must meet the following requirements:

➤ Average seek time of 1 second or less

➤ 10,000 hours MTBF

➤ Mode 1 capability (mode 2 and form 1 & 2 optional)

➤ MSCDEX 2.2 driver that implements the extended audio APIs

➤ Subchannel Q (subchannels P and R–W optional—if R–W subchannel support is provided, additional APIs must be implemented in MSCDEX driver. Specifications for these additional APIs are available from Microsoft.)

The drive must be capable of maintaining a sustained transfer rate of 150 K/sec, without consuming more than 40 percent of the CPU bandwidth in the process. This requirement is for read block sizes no less than 16K and lead time of no more than is required to load the CD-ROM buffer with 1 read block of data.

I recommend the drive have on-board buffers of 64K and implement read-ahead buffering (read-ahead buffering is described in a specification available from Microsoft).

Drives that meet level 2 specifications have to aim a little higher. They must be capable of a 300k/second transfer rate, but they can use up to 60% of the CPU bandwidth to do that. They must also support the multisession and CD XA standards. Seek time must be 400ms or better. I highly recommend drives that meet or exceed the level 2 spec—you'll be much happier with the performance.

Audio

Requires a CD-ROM drive with CD-DA (Red Book) outputs and a front panel volume control. As an option, CD-ROM XA audio may be provided.

Requires an 8-bit (16-bit recommended) Digital-to-Analog Converter (DAC) with:

➤ Linear PCM sampling

➤ DMA or FIFO buffered transfer capability with interrupt on buffer empty; 22.05 and 11.025 KHz sample rate mandatory

➤ 44.1 KHz sampling rate desirable

➤ Optional stereo channel

➤ No more than 10 percent of the CPU bandwidth required to output 11.025 or 22.05 KHz; no more than 15 percent for 44.1 KHz.

Requires 8-bit (16 bit recommended) Analog-to-Digital Converter (ADC) with:

➤ Linear PCM sampling

➤ 11.025 KHz mandatory (22.01 KHz, or 44.1 KHz sampling rate optional)

➤ DMA or FIFO buffered transfer capability with interrupt on buffer full

➤ Microphone input

Requires Internal synthesizer hardware with multi-voice, multi-timbral capabilities, six simultaneous melody notes plus two simultaneous percussive notes.

Requires Internal mixing capabilities to combine input from three (recommended four) sources and present the output as a stereo, line-level audio signal at the back panel. The four sources are:

➤ CD Red Book

➤ Synthesizer

➤ DAC (waveform)

➤ Auxiliary input source (recommended but not required)

Each input must have at least a 3-bit volume control (8 steps) with a logarithmic taper. (4-bit or greater volume control is strongly recommended.) If all sources are sourced with -1 OdB (consumer line level: 1 milliwatt into 600 ohms=OdB) without attenuation, the mixer will not clip and will output between 0 dB and +3 dB. Individual audio source and master digital volume control registers and extra line-level audio sources are highly recommended. (Guidelines for synthesizer implementation available on request.)

The Level 2 spec requires support for 44kHz sampling, as well as both 8- and 16-bit resolution. The CPU usage must be 10%, not 15%, for 44kHz sampling. In addition, the MIDI section must support In, Out, and Thru cabling.

Video

Requires a VGA-compatible display adapter, and a color VGA-compatible monitor. A basic Multimedia PC uses mode 12h (640x480, 16 colors). An enhanced configuration, referred to as VGA+, is recommended with 640x480, 256 colors.

The recommended performance goal for VGA+ adapters is to be able to blit 1, 4, and 8 bit-per-pixel DIBs (device independent bitmaps) at 350K pixels/second given 100 percent of the CPU, and at 140K pixels/second given 40 percent of the CPU. This recommendation applies to run-length encoded images and non-encoded images. The recommended performance is needed to fully support high-performance applications such as synchronized audio-visual presentations.

The Level 2 spec sensibly specifies at least 16-bit color support at 640x480. You are better off going to 16-bit color at a higher resolution as well.

User Input

Requires a standard 101-key, IBM-style keyboard with standard DIN connector, or a keyboard which delivers identical functionality utilizing key-combinations.

Requires a two-button mouse with bus or serial connector, with at least one additional communication port remaining free.

I/O

Requires a standard 9-pin or 25-pin asynchronous serial port, programmable up to 9600 baud, and a switchable interrupt channel.

Requires a standard 25-pin, bi-directional parallel port with interrupt capability.

Requires one MIDI port with In, Out, and Thru, and must have interrupt support for input and FIFO transfer.

Requires an IBM-style analog or digital joystick port.

General Specifications

In addition to these hardware requirements, the Multimedia PC Marketing Council specifies that system software must conform to the multimedia functions in Windows. The specifications for these functions (collectively known as the Windows API) are provided in the Microsoft Windows Software Development Kit *Programmer's Reference*, Volumes 1 and 2.

IBM Ultimedia

There are many ways to look at multimedia. One way is to call it something else entirely. That's what IBM has done: IBM's PS/2 multimedia product line goes by the name of Ultimedia.[49]

IBM's Ultimedia products are designed to work together. They are also designed for IBM's PS/2 line of computers. If there is one (very large) multimedia universe, this is just a different galaxy of products—the concepts involved should be familiar if you've read the rest of this book.

IBM's involvement with multimedia goes pretty far back—back to where it wasn't really being thought of as "multimedia." Back to before the first IBM personal computer.

---

[49]IBM also has an aggressively priced ISA-bus line of multimedia PCs. See the Shopper's Guide for details.

The first fully multimedia-capable personal computer model was the PS/2 Ultimedia Model M57 SLC. The company also introduced a wide range of products you could put in your PS/2 for multimedia, including updates to several existing products, and the introduction of three new ones:

TouchSelect—an add-on touch screen for existing monitors.

PS/2 TV—a fully integrated, low-cost video solution.

Action Media II—an adapter to capture and play back real-time digital video and audio.

IBM also established a special program to assist developers of multimedia products.

IBM's support of multimedia, even under a different name, marks a key point in multimedia's movement toward the broadest possible implementation. When a company as large and well-established as IBM hitches itself to the bandwagon, something is really starting to happen.

Big Blue and Apple

One of the most interesting IBM-related multimedia developments, however, is one that surprised just about everyone when it happened—the joint venture between Apple and IBM, Kaleida.

Kaleida was formed to develop a wide range of multimedia software technologies. It is a reaction to a simple fact: putting multimedia into current personal computers isn't always the best way to go.

For example, putting TV on a computer screen is relatively easy, but storing that information on the hard disk is anything but easy. A single minute of full-motion, full-frame video takes up about 1.5 gigabytes of storage space.

Most manufacturers are looking at alternative technologies, hoping that their idea for better ways to handle digital multimedia will be the "Next Great Thing," perhaps replacing or at least supplementing personal computers. Most of these new ideas start with some way to handle the vast amounts of data involved in multimedia.

That's Kaleida's purpose—not only to monitor where the hardware is going, but to anticipate it, seek it out, and develop applications that make the most of hardware advances. These advances might involve personal computers, and they might not.

It's not easy to guess where Kaleida might go. What is most interesting is that it exists at all—one more road sign that says, in large letters: *Multimedia!*

The Platform for Ultimedia

As a platform designed specifically for multimedia, Ultimedia establishes a fairly high minimum standard of support for multimedia:

➤ 386/20 SLC processor

➤ CD-ROM XA drive

➤ 160M SCSI hard disk

➤ 4M of memory

➤ SCSI controller card

➤ 2.88M, 3 1/2-inch floppy drive

➤ XGA graphics

➤ CD-quality audio subsystem

➤ Enhanced speakers

➤ Microphone

➤ Multimedia controls on the front panel (volume control, jacks for microphone and headphones)

➤ OS/2 2.01 (with Multimedia Presentation Manager/2 Extensions) as the operating system, with support for DOS and Microsoft Windows

The hardware line also includes digital and audio extension capability. Ultimedia DV adds built-in, hardware-assisted digital video support for real-time video capture and playback. Ultimedia AV links in the wide spectrum of video-disc-based products developed over the last several years.

Ultimedia Computers

All Ultimedia hardware builds on the standards listed above. At press time, the currently available models were the ones listed in Table 6.3.

Table 6.3. Ultimedia Computers and Their Components.

Model	Components
Ultimedia	386SLC 20-MHz processor
M57 SLC	8K internal cache; Upgradable to 486SLC2 processor; 160M SCSI hard drive (17-ms average access time); 8M of memory, expandable to 16M; 16-bit Micro channel architecture; Three available slots; Parallel and serial ports; 16-bit XGA adapter, 1024 × 768 × 256 colors or 640 × 480 × 65,536 colors
Ultimedia	486SLC2 50/25-MHz processor
M57 486SLC2	16K internal cache; 212M SCSI hard drive (12-ms average access time); 8M of memory, expandable to 16M; 16-bit Micro channel architecture; Four available slots; One parallel and two serial ports; Microphone; 16-bit XGA-2 non-interlaced adapter, 1M of memory, 1024 × 768 × 256 colors or 640 × 480 × 65,536 colors
Ultimedia	486SLC2 50/25-MHz processor
DV M57 486SLC2	16K internal cache; 212M SCSI hard drive (12-ms average access time); 8M of memory, expandable to 16M; 16-bit Micro channel architecture; Action Media II/A digital video adapter; Three available slots; One parallel and two serial ports; Microphone;

	16-bit XGA-2 non-interlaced adapter, 1M of memory, 1024 × 768 × 256 colors or 640 × 480 × 65,536 colors
Ultimedia M77 486SX	486SX 33-MHz processor
	8K internal cache; 212M SCSI hard drive (12-ms average access time); 8M of memory, expandable to 32M; 32-bit Micro channel architecture; Three available slots; One parallel and two serial ports; Microphone; 16-bit XGA-2 non-interlaced adapter, 1M of memory, 1024 × 768 × 256 colors or 640 × 480 × 65,536 colors
Ultimedia M77 486DX2	486DX2 66/33-MHz processor
	8K internal cache; 212M SCSI hard drive (12-ms average access time); 8M of memory, expandable to 32M; 32-bit Micro channel architecture; Three available slots; One parallel and two serial ports; Microphone; 16-bit XGA-2 non-interlaced adapter, 1M of memory, 1024 × 768 × 256 colors or 640 × 480 × 65,536 colors

Ultimedia Video

In addition to the computers listed in Table 6.3, IBM offers a video capture board developed in conjunction with Intel—the Action Media II. These boards enable you to capture as many as 30 frames per second of full-motion video from a variety of sources, including mass storage (disk drives), digital networks, and analog video (VCRs, videodisc players, camcorders, and broadcast TV). The boards offer a Capture Option to access analog video devices.

The key to operating the Action Media II cards is hardware-assisted compression. Compression technology is critical to the use of video on PCs. By using hardware to accelerate the compression process, the Action Media II cards enable you to display smooth video on the PC screen. Hardware-assisted compression is so fast that it can be done in real time. Each frame is compressed as it is received. Using software-only compression, you must take time after the capture to compress the video data.

Video signal input can be either NTSC or PAL, and S-VHS and RGB encoding is supported. Audio input is supported for line, CD, or microphones. Audio output is stereo, with a signal-to-noise ratio of 60 dB, and 50-dB channel separation from 15 Hz to 15 KHz.

You can do video capture in real time at up to 512×480 resolution, and you can capture still images at up to 612×576 resolution in either 8- or 24-bit formats. When viewing, the real-time video image can be up to 256×240 pixels. You can scale the image up or down to fill more or less of the screen.

In addition to capturing video data, you can use the boards to overlay video images onto the computer screen. In other words, you easily can combine standard and video graphics on a display screen.

There are two models of these cards—the Action Media II Display Adapter (2M), and the Action Media II Display Adapter/A (2M). The /A model is used with the AVK programming interface and requires additional system memory (6M instead of 4M). You can connect one monitor to both the XGA and Action Media II outputs, or you can connect one monitor to each output.

The Capture Option is a daughter card that you can add to either Action Media II display adapter. It adds support for real-time compression of incoming analog video signals. The daughter card and the main display adapter are both needed for doing video captures.

Neither card can be used if you have either of the following PS/2 options installed:

> 8514/A display adapter
> PS/2 M-Motion Video Adapter/A
> PS/2 Image Adapter/A (there are exceptions; contact IBM for details)

Both cards have the following external interfaces:

> Analog RGB video output and sync to a VGA or XGA color monitor
> Two-channel (stereo) audio output
> Auxiliary Video Extension input
> RGB input

Capture bus for attaching the Capture Option daughter card

Analog S-VHS auxiliary output (suitable for input to TV or VCR) for digital video only

SCSI connector on the Action Media II card for attaching a CD-ROM drive; CD-ROM data only available to applications running on the adapter

Ultimedia TV

You also can add a television to your PS/2 computer. This is ideal for many kinds of applications—video-based training, watching the World Series at work (if they ever have day games again), and so on. On the serious side, you easily can monitor a financial news network while you work on a proposal due later that afternoon.

PS/2 TV is a box that sits outside of your computer. It's not small, unfortunately, at 10 by 13 inches, and a little over 2 inches high. It weighs 8 pounds. It supports 181 channels, including cable television.

The unit supports both full-screen and picture-in-picture (PIP) modes of display. Access to these modes is by mouse or keyboard.

Multimedia Upgrade Kit Vendors

Several vendors have obtained licenses from the Multimedia PC Marketing Council to manufacture multimedia upgrade kits.

Vendors who are shipping kits as of November 1993:

ACS Computer PTE LTD
CompuAdd Corporation
Creative Labs, Inc.
Exxis Technologies
Media Resources
Media Vision
MediaSonic
NEC Technologies, Inc
Olivetti Adv. Tech. Center
Procom Technology
Tandy Corporation

Turtle Beach Systems
Aztech Systems
NCR

Multimedia PC Vendors

You can always buy a PC configured for multimedia. For example, Tandy offers multimedia PCs in its Radio Shack stores, and the following vendors have either announced or are shipping multimedia PCs at the time this book was written:

ACMA Computers
ACR Systems, Inc.
Advanced Logic Research
ATronics International
Axik Computer, Inc.
Blue Star Marketing, Inc.
Brysis Data, Inc.
Clover Computer Systems
CompuAdd Corporation
EPS Technologies
Epson Direct
Fujitsu America, Inc.
International Instrumentation
MegaMedia Comp. Corp.
Mind Computer Products
National MicroComputers
NEC Technologies, Inc.
Olivetti Adv. Tech. Center
Philips Consumer Electronics
Siemens Nixdorf
Tandy Corporation
Technology Integrated Products
Unitek Technology
Zenith Data Systems

Although many of the computers sold as multimedia contain all of the necessary ingredients, the quality of the ingredients varies dramatically. Before you buy, get a list of the multimedia components in the machine. If you know who makes the sound card, the CD-ROM, the speakers, etc., you can make a much more informed decision. Here are some key things to watch for:

➤ Slow CD-ROM drives

➤ Off-brand sound cards

➤ Cheap speakers

➤ Cheap microphones

Most mail-order computer sellers and resellers are offering all kinds of off-brand and house-brand multimedia PCs. Unfortunately, the majority of systems being sold—at least the base systems—have mediocre multimedia components. It is a very definite "buyer beware" market. Not all the news is bad. I have heard very positive things in particular about Tristar from various CompuServe members. Tristar offers a wide variety of multimedia upgrades. However, you'll have to ask for them. As with many vendors, the base line of multimedia machines does not include components that I recommend.

Time did not permit me to personally review multimedia PCs, so I can't vouch for any of these systems. If you have any experience with them and want to share that experience with other readers, see the Introduction to this book for information about how to get involved on the CompuServe Multimedia Forum. That forum has ongoing discussion where you can learn about the experiences of others, and share your own as well. As the field of multimedia expands, that will be the only way to get the real story.

Priming the Pump: Software

A ll the hardware in the world doesn't do you any good without software. With all the emphasis on hardware development, the importance of software often is overlooked.[1]

In the old days, when there were plenty of different hardware vendors to pick from, both mini and micro—Z80, IBM, UNIX, Digital, Data General, and some long-gone PC compatibles like Eagle and the Victor 5000—the following truism was almost always the first statement out of a computer consultant's mouth:[2]

Select the software that meets your needs, and then pick the hardware platform that runs the software.

There are a lot of vendors in the personal computer market, but almost all of them use the same operating system—MS-DOS. MS-DOS is basically the same on any machine, which makes PCs interchangeable as far as the software is concerned. Even Macs can be set up to run MS-DOS software.[3] Still, the basic idea of the old saw remains a truism: without adequate software, the hardware is meaningless. Hardware is a canvas to paint on—a sophisticated canvas, of course, but still only a canvas to paint on with software.

You can now buy whatever hardware you need for multimedia—video capture cards, CD-ROM drives, sound cards, and so on. However, not every software package uses the multimedia capabilities available in the hardware to their best advantage. On the other hand, in the best of multimedia software, the multimedia portion takes on a life of its own.

Since the first edition of this book, several really hot multimedia programs have hit the streets. These programs represent major efforts to create integrated, full-featured multimedia software. Microsoft has done an outstanding job at placing multimedia software at the front of the pack. In this chapter, you'll get a hands-on look at a variety of multimedia software. If it seems as though there are an awful lot of packages from Microsoft, there's a good reason for it. Microsoft introduced some very classy multimedia products in 1993 and has some great products planned for 1994.

---

[1]Overlook it at your risk, however!

[2]Yes, I remember "the old days." It's incredible to think how far personal computers have come in not much more than a decade.

[3]Although a Mac running MS-DOS isn't a real match for a PC. This is called emulation, and it's never as fast as the real thing.

Encarta

By far the most remarkable multimedia software product introduced in 1993 is Encarta, a multimedia encyclopedia from Microsoft. I try not to be overly impressed with new software, but Encarta has real depth. Rather than try to impress you with mere words, I'll take you on a detailed tour of Encarta. After you've seen Encarta, you'll get to see another Windows multimedia encyclopedia, *Compton's Interactive Encyclopedia*. The comparison demonstrates how powerful and useful Encarta is. Compton's isn't a bad product; it's simply hard to compare anything to Encarta.

When you install Encarta, it'll be clear that Microsoft puts a strong multimedia effort into the product. Figure 7.1 shows a window from the Encarta setup program. Note that, during the installation, the software tests every aspect of system performance, including the hard disk, audio support, MIDI support, CD-ROM drive, memory, and more. If any problems are encountered in any portion of your multimedia setup, you receive exact information about dealing with the problem.

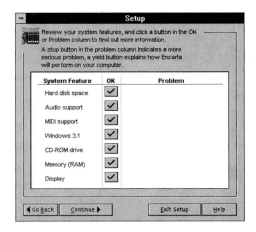

Figure 7.1. Encarta tests multimedia system capabilities during installation.

After the system test, Encarta presents you with two options for installation (see Figure 7.2). The recommended option enables Encarta to run faster, but it takes up more room on your hard disk. The other option doesn't use as much hard disk space, but it runs slower. The fast option uses almost 8M of storage, whereas the slower option uses only 2.5M.

Figure 7.3 shows the Encarta opening screen. The most interesting feature is the zebra image at the lower center of the window. If you do not open the encyclopedia immediately, random pictures appear in this spot. You can click on the picture, and Encarta will take you to the encyclopedia page corresponding to the image.

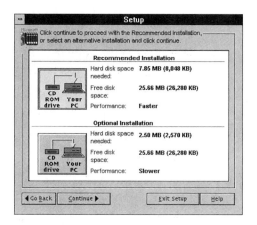

Figure 7.2. *Choosing the Encarta install options.*

There are many ways to use Encarta. The Category browser, shown in Figure 7.4, is great for cruising through the encyclopedia. To start, pick an area of interest using the buttons in the left portion of the window. This displays categories specific to your area of interest. When you select a category, you get a list of topics that you can view. For example, if you select History as the area of interest and United States History as the category, a list of specific topics is displayed in a subsidiary window as shown in Figure 7.4.

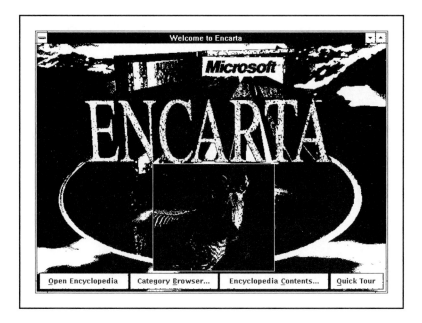

Figure 7.3. *The opening screen of Encarta.*

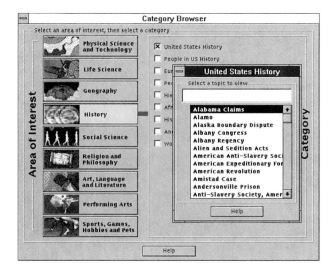

Figure 7.4. *Using the Encarta Category Browser.*

The encyclopedia itself is both attractive and informative as shown in Figure 7.5.

The encyclopedia offers the following features:

Button bar—The button bar at the top of the Encarta window gives you quick access to various features. The button you'll use most frequently is the Find button, which is described in detail later in this subsection. The Gallery gives you instant access to multimedia stuff, and the Atlas and Timeline are different ways of exploring information.

Category display—The category display, located in the upper left portion of the window, tells you the category the current article belongs in. You can change categories using the buttons below the picture. In Figure 7.5, the category is Language.

Media display—The lower left portion of the window contains the current media element for the displayed article. This is usually a picture or a still from an animation.

Article text—The right side of the window contains the current article. In Figure 7.5, the article describes the letter "A."

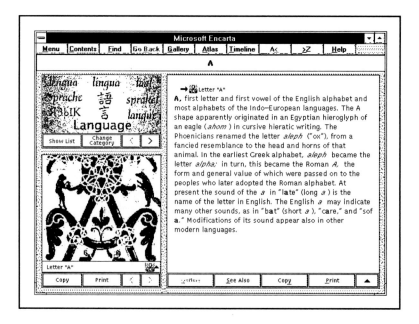

Figure 7.5. *A typical entry in the Encarta encyclopedia.*

The key to Encarta's usefulness is the different ways you can access the information it contains. New and youthful users will appreciate the simple but practical "Wizard" method of hunting for data. Figure 7.6 shows a typical Research Wizard window.[4]

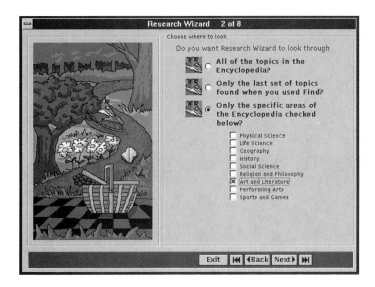

Figure 7.6. *The Encarta Research Wizard.*

Research Wizards help you find data by breaking the process into pieces. As you'll see shortly, the questions that the Wizard (presumably as sly as the fox in the illustration in the left portion of the Wizard window) asks are based on the contents of the Find window. For example, note that in Figure 7.6 the list of "specific areas" corresponds to the areas of interest in the Category Browser (Figure 7.4). For this example, I have clicked on "Art and Literature."

Figure 7.7 shows the next window presented by the Research Wizard.[5] I have entered "dog" so that the Wizard will search for topics that contain the word dog.

---

[4]Research Wizards are an optional method of seeking data. If you know what you want, there is a shortcut method, which is described later in this section.

[5]Note that the fox, who was peeking out of a tree in the last figure, is now sitting in the middle of the road eating a piece of pie. Mmm, mmm, good—research sure is satisfying!

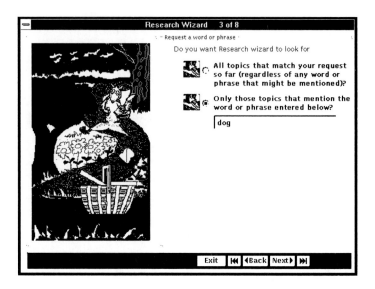

Figure 7.7. *Specifying initial search criteria.*

The next step involves further refining the search. Figure 7.8 shows the next window, where I have entered the word "cat." The Wizard enables me to specify how I want the words dog and cat to be related. I can search for articles that use either word, both words, or both words near each other.

You can continue working with the Research Wizard until you have narrowed your search adequately. You can define a time period in which to search (I used 1900 to 1990 for this example), or you can specify cities (using additional Wizard screens not shown here). When you have set the search criteria, click on the Find! button. It's on the last Wizard screen. It serves the same function as the Find! button at the bottom of the Find dialog box. Encarta finds all the articles that meet your criteria. The Topics Found window, shown in Figure 7.9, lists all of the articles.

To see the article, click on its name in the Topics Found window. Figure 7.10 shows the portion of the article containing the search criteria: a date between 1900 and 1990 (1928 to be exact), and the words "dog" and "cat." Note that Encarta found the words even though they are used in the plural.

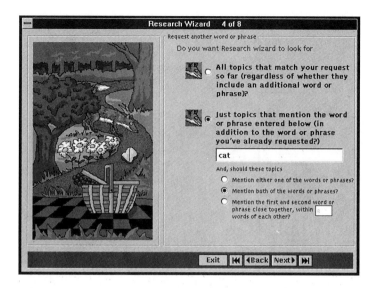

Figure 7.8. Specifying additional search criteria.

Figure 7.9. The Topics Found window.

If the Research Wizard seems cumbersome, you can simply click on the **F**ind button on the button bar and enter search text in the resulting Find window (Figure 7.11).

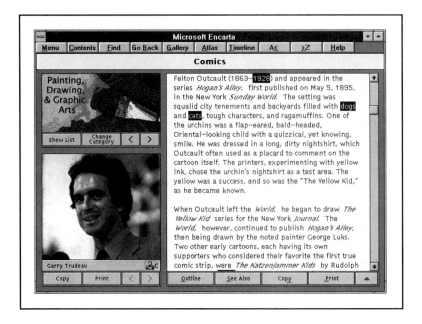

Figure 7.10. *The article found with the assistance of the Research Wizard.*

Figure 7.11. *The Find Window.*

You can specify more than just a simple text string for a search. Clicking the Hints button displays the Hints dialog box shown in Figure 7.12. By following the examples provided, you can construct a variety of useful searches.

If you want to specify a more complex search, click the More Choices button in the Find window. This displays the expanded Find window shown in Figure 7.13.

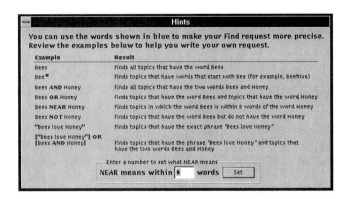

Figure 7.12. *Specifying more complex search criteria.*

Figure 7.13. *The expanded Find window.*

The expanded Find window enables you to specify areas of interest: media types (called *gallery* types) including Picture, Animation, Audio, and Map; biographies; date ranges; and place names. When the search is ready, click the Find! button to display the Topics Found window. To read an article, click the article name.

Encarta offers several useful features for finding additional information and for keeping track of what you have found. You can open a See Also window that lists related articles, and you can create bookmarks or open a text editor to make notes. You can copy text and images to your word processor if you are preparing reports. For the ultimate test of encyclopedia software, two of our kids used various encyclopedias during the school year to create reports. Not only did our kids (ages 11 and 13) find Encarta to be their favorite research program, the reports they prepared using Encarta got the best grades. These kinds of results contribute to my high regard for Encarta. Face it—the best interface in the world doesn't help if the content isn't good.

Encarta was released right before Microsoft introduced Video for Windows, so there are no video clips in the original edition. Microsoft will ship an update each year, so look for video in the next edition of Encarta. The animations are very helpful, however. Figure 7.14 shows one example. It is an animation that clearly demonstrates how the eye focuses on a moving object. The animation is accompanied by a thorough, professional narration.

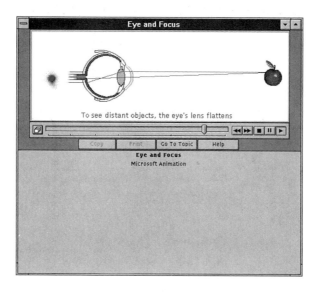

Figure 7.14. *A sample Encarta animation.*

Three additional Encarta features are worth mentioning: the Atlas, the Timeline, and a game called Mind Maze. Figure 7.15 is a sample window from the Atlas showing British Columbia, Canada. The Atlas does not allow you to go to a related article, so it is the weakest portion of Encarta. There is so much data on the Encarta disc that it would require a second disc to provide a complete Atlas.[6] However, the Atlas does have one really neat feature: you can get a pronunciation of most place names. That's handy for such places as Nanaimo, in British Columbia.[7]

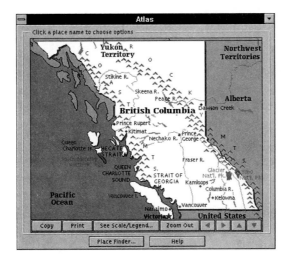

Figure 7.15. *The Encarta Atlas.*

The Timeline, shown in Figure 7.16, enables you to see the relationships between historical events. This ability to put events in perspective is an invaluable teaching tool. To get more information about an event, just click on it.[8]

Figure 7.17 shows the opening screen of Mind Maze.

---

[6]Very few companies have marketed CD-ROM products that have more than a single CD. Would the market pay for multi-disc software? There's only one way to find out, and Encarta would be an ideal way to test the possibilities.

[7]For those who are curious, it's pronounced "na-nigh-mo."

[8]My favorite factoid: ice cream dates back to 2000 B.C. in China.

Figure 7.16. The Encarta Timeline.

Figure 7.17. Encarta's Mind Maze.

This interactive game challenges you to find your way through a maze by answering questions. You can select the degree of difficulty. For example, at the easiest level, you'll face questions such as:

```
Click the word or phrase that best identifies an independent agency
of the US government, headquartered in Washington DC:
```

1. American Law Institute

2. United States Air Force Academy

3. Smithsonian Institution

4. Brooklyn Institute of Arts and Sciences

You can read an article about each choice, but as time goes by the number of points you get for a correct answer goes down. At the highest level of difficulty, the questions are not nearly as obvious:

```
Click the word or phrase that best identifies Hindu-Buddhist temple
near Mageland on the island of Java in Indonesia:
```

1. Perret, Auguste

2. Lutyens, Sir Edwin Landseer

3. Bibiena

4. Borobudur

If you score lots of points, you are rewarded at various levels with certificates, duly signed by the Dean of Students, William H. Gates (see Figure 7.18).

Mind Maze is a lot of fun and an excellent way to expand your knowledge of the world around you.

Overall, I have almost nothing but praise for Encarta. As far as I can see, it is the Best in Class among CD-ROM-based encyclopedias. If you have been looking for an encyclopedia for the kids, or for yourself, Encarta is the best of the best. I recommend it highly.

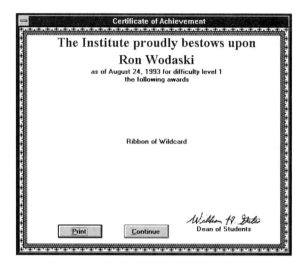

Figure 7.18. *A Mind Maze Certificate of Achievement.*

Compton's Interactive Encyclopedia

Encarta is a tough act to follow, and I have given the job to Compton's Interactive Encyclopedia. Compton's is commonly found in CD-ROM upgrade kits along with the drives, speakers, sound cards, etc. For example, when I received Media Vision's Fusion Double CD 16 upgrade kit, Compton's came along at no extra cost.[9]

Because you may find yourself looking at Compton's as part of an upgrade package, I thought you might like to see how it handles. So, enough jawing— come on and take a test drive!

When you start it up, Compton's presents the window shown in Figure 7.19. The work area/article display area is to the left, and buttons for instant access to features are at the far right.

---

[9]This is an excellent multimedia upgrade kit if you are looking to add all the basic ingredients at one shot. It includes a double-spin CD-ROM drive, good software, a 16-bit sound card, and speakers. The price is good too. Best of all, it installed without a hitch and worked great.

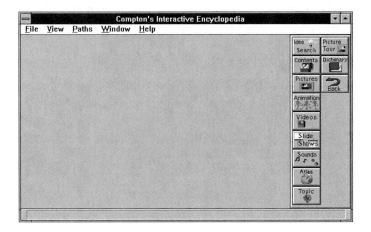

Figure 7.19. *The Compton's Interactive Encyclopedia.*

For example, clicking on the Contents button brings up a complete list of contents as shown in Figure 7.20.

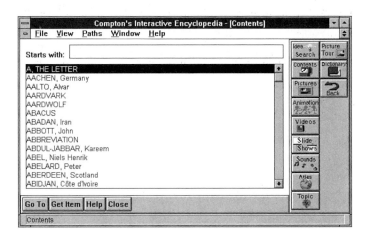

Figure 7.20. *The Contents page.*

The search capabilities of Compton's are basic and straightforward. When you click the Idea Search button, the window shown in Figure 7.21 appears. You enter a text string in the Search for entry field, click the Search button at the bottom of the window, and the search engine looks for an article, picture, or fact index matching it.

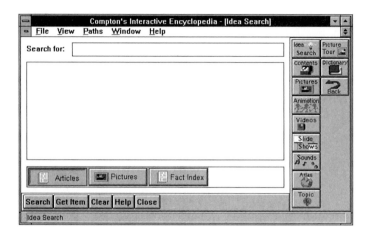

Figure 7.21. *Searching with Compton's.*

You can use the Topic Tree also to explore for information. It enables you to click on successively more detailed topics until you find the one you want to view. Figure 7.22 shows the Topic Tree in use. I started with a major topic, History and Civilization. It is in the left-most window. Lowercase text indicates that additional subtopics are available. I just kept clicking until I found an interesting topic (AFGHAN WARS). Intermediate topics I encountered along the way included Civilization, Warfare, and Wars and Battles. For some subjects, this is a useful way to find appropriate information. However, it is best used for exploring areas of interest rather than as a research tool.

Like Encarta, Compton's comes with an Atlas. Also like Encarta, it enables you to explore everything from large-scale features of the world down to smaller-scale features about the size of states and provinces. Compton's also includes many animations, but they are not as well done as those found in Encarta. For example, Figure 7.23 shows a Compton's animation frame.

The animation contains useful information, but it is best viewed in step mode as a series of slides rather than as an animation. For example, the text shown in this figure appears in only one frame of the animation. To read it, you must use single-step mode.

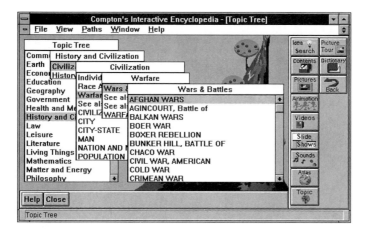

Figure 7.22. *The Compton's Topic Tree.*

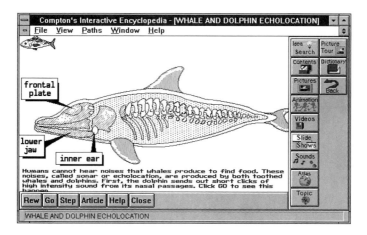

Figure 7.23. *A Compton's animation frame.*

Figure 7.24 shows a typical Compton's article. Note the use of icons in the left margin to indicate an image (the camera) and a cross-reference (the pages with an arrow).

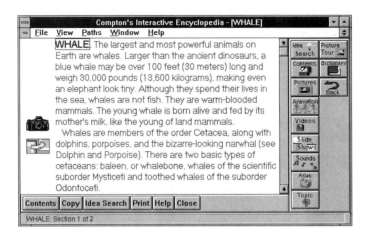

Figure 7.24. *An example of a Compton's article.*

The pictures that accompany articles (an example is shown in Figure 7.25) are useful but not of the same caliber as the ones provided by Encarta.

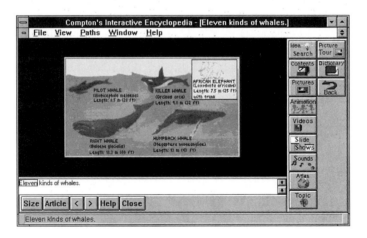

Figure 7.25. *An example of a Compton's picture.*

Overall, I (and our kids) found Compton's to be a useful, practical encyclopedia. If you acquire it as part of an upgrade pack, you'll get some real use out of it. If you are in the market to buy only an encyclopedia, try Encarta first.

Dinosaurs

Encarta is cool software, but Microsoft has come up with a software product with an even higher cool factor: Dinosaurs. At almost every level, Dinosaurs is an exemplary piece of software. The artwork is superb, the research is solid and comprehensive, the material is clearly presented, cross-referencing and hypertext/hypermedia links are extremely powerful, and the sound effects are just plain great. In addition, as any kid will tell you, Dinosaurs are absolutely fascinating creatures. Figure 7.26 shows the opening screen of Dinosaurs.

Figure 7.26. *The opening window of Dinosaurs.*

The Stone-Age buttons at the bottom of the window provide access to the various features of Dinosaurs. They are similar to the standard features in the two encyclopedias presented earlier in this chapter:

Atlas—The Atlas button displays a world map. Clicking on a continent displays a map of the continent containing images of the various dinosaurs that lived on the continent. For example, Figure 7.27 shows the Atlas page for North America. Clicking on an image takes you to a window containing detailed information.

Timeline—The Timeline button displays on a single page the entire time when dinosaurs lived on the earth as shown in Figure 7.28. You can select various periods, such as Cambrian, Jurassic, and Miocene. Clicking on a time period displays the dinosaurs alive at that time.

Families—The Families button displays images of dinosaurs grouped by family as shown in Figure 7.29. Clicking on an image displays more detailed information.

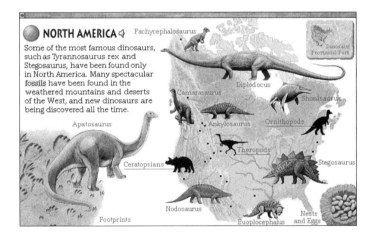

Figure 7.27. *The Atlas page for North America.*

From each type of page, you keep clicking buttons until you arrive at a specific dinosaur. Figure 7.30 shows the page for the Pterodactylus.

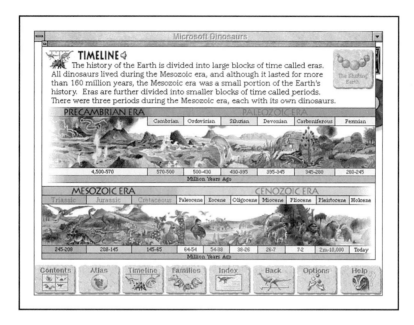

Figure 7.28. *The main Timeline page.*

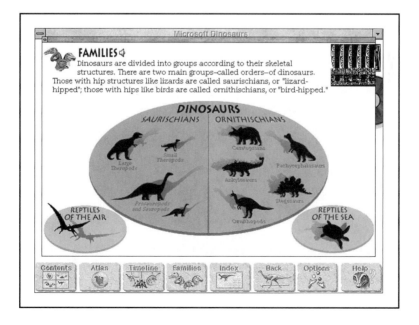

Figure 7.29. *The main Families page.*

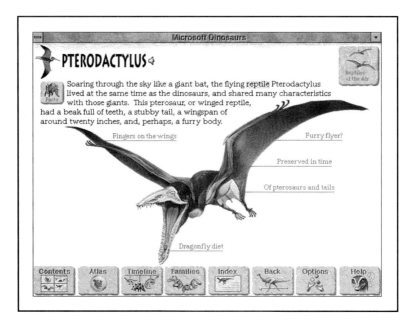

Figure 7.30. *The page for Pterodactylus.*

From the basic page about a particular dinosaur, you can also access other related pages. The text on the lines pointing to the Pterodactyl each bring up a page containing detailed information. For example, if you click on "Furry flyer?" you will see the page shown in Figure 7.31.

Figure 7.31. *The page for Furry Flyer.*

The fascinating thing about Dinosaurs as multimedia software is the fluid way you can move from subject to subject, dinosaur to dinosaur, learning lots of neat stuff along the way. The interface is cleverly designed to enable you to roam wherever your ideas take you, without doubling back on your tracks. As you roam, there are lots of cool dinosaur sounds to add interest.

In addition to the meat of the program (and there's plenty of that), Dinosaurs offers several interesting features. For example, there are dinosaur movies (actually Video for Windows files)—Figure 7.32 shows four frames from a movie about the demise of the dinosaurs. The images are well done, and the narration, music, and sound effects are all first rate.

Figure 7.32. *Four frames from a dinosaur movie.*

The Picture Gallery is also a wonderful feature. You can copy any of a large number of dinosaur images to the clipboard, or you can make an image into wallpaper for your desktop. Figure 7.33 shows a sample picture in the Picture Gallery opening screen.

You can also have fun with the Dinosaurs screen savers. There are two of them, and one is shown in Figure 7.34. The screen saver consists of dinosaur footprints that appear to walk across your screen and are accompanied by different kinds of thumping noises. The other screen saver displays dinosaur faces.

Figure 7.33. *The Dinosaurs Picture Gallery.*

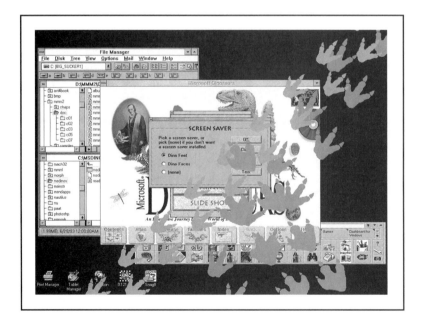

Figure 7.34. *A Dinosaurs screen saver.*

Overall, Dinosaurs is a fascinating and involving piece of software. I recommend it highly.

Multimedia Beethoven

Multimedia Beethoven is now several years old, but it holds up very well against current multimedia software. Although there are clever software packages, visually pleasing packages, and intellectually stimulating packages, few succeed so well as Beethoven in all three categories. In addition, Multimedia Beethoven has something extra—it has soul, a richness and depth that goes beyond the technical competence of the software.

Multimedia Beethoven is an interactive program built using Multimedia ToolBook, an authoring package with powerful and sophisticated programming capabilities. Many other multimedia products have been built with ToolBook, including the Nautilus software used to access the various items on the *Multimedia Madness* CD-ROM.

The Aesthetics of Multimedia

When I go to see a movie, I always pay close attention to the first few seconds of the film. If the director has paid careful attention to the film and crafted it with the care it deserves, the first few seconds often set the mood accurately and powerfully. I always get excited when I see an opening like that because the rest of the movie seldom disappoints me. A good example of a movie that sets the mood with a carefully balanced mixture of humor and pathos is *The Big Chill*.

Of course, it's also possible that the early good impression slanted my point of view toward a positive critique. The same thing is true of a multimedia presentation. For example, Multimedia Beethoven starts powerfully, making the best use of the available material. When you start the program, the opening screen is simple; (see Figure 7.35). However, the software developers set the program so Beethoven's Ninth Symphony starts playing immediately. The music is marvelous, and it gets things off to a good start. I have yet to see someone fail to smile as the music comes up. Few people are accustomed to the idea of fine music coming from a PC.

The opening screen is simple: a bust of Beethoven and a list of the five "chapters" in the program (Figure 7.35). While this window is displayed, you hear the strains of Beethoven's Ninth Symphony from the CD.

Figure 7.35. *The opening screen of Multimedia Beethoven.*

This section leads you on a tour of Multimedia Beethoven. It teaches you about the five chapters of Multimedia Beethoven to show the diversity and creativity of the program. With the first chapter, "A Pocket Guide," you can quickly listen to any part of the symphony by clicking a description of the part. In Figure 7.36, for example, I have clicked the Joy Theme (the text is marked in bold), and you can see the timing of that selection in the Time monitor in the bottom-right portion of the screen.

The chapter "Beethoven's World" is full of information about Beethoven's life and times (Figure 7.37). It provides an excellent context for the music and musical discussions, and it often relates historical events to the music. It also includes graphics relevant to the topics.

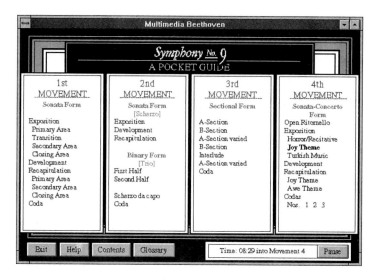

Figure 7.36. *The opening screen of the chapter "A Pocket Guide" (note the time monitor in the bottom-right portion of the screen).*

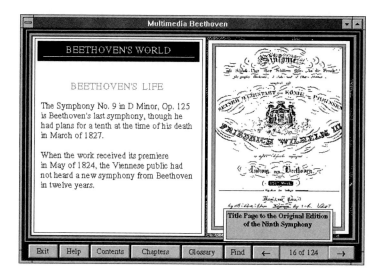

Figure 7.37. *A screen from the "Beethoven's World" chapter (note the reproduction of the title page from the original edition of Beethoven's Ninth Symphony).*

The chapter, "The Art of Listening," provides a sophisticated musical analysis of the Ninth Symphony. The opening screen lists the four movements of the symphony and topics that provide a context for the musical discussions. In many ways, this is the most visually and aurally exciting chapter of the program. There are screens that enable you to look at the music in intimate detail, such as the discussion of dotted rhythms in Figure 7.38.

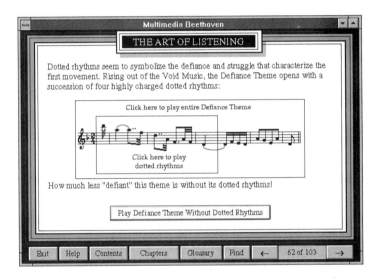

Figure 7.38. *A screen featuring an analysis of the first movement from the chapter, "The Art of Listening."*

You can click the notes to hear the Defiance theme played or you can click the button bar at the bottom to hear a variation of it without dotted rhythms. This kind of detail is typical of the listening chapter. As if all this were not enough, the chapter also provides a Close Reading of the symphony (Figure 7.39). A series of screens provides ongoing commentary on every second of the performance; you can listen to each bit of music, or you can sit back and let the music and the commentary roll past.

The chapter, "The Ninth Game," is a game that tests your knowledge of the symphony. To do well, you must listen to the symphony and read the other chapters carefully. For example, consider the multiple-choice question posed in Figure 7.40.

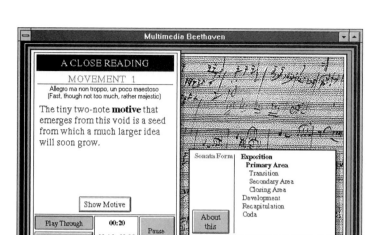

Figure 7.39. *A screen from the chapter, "A Close Reading," (note the commentary provided for this selection).*

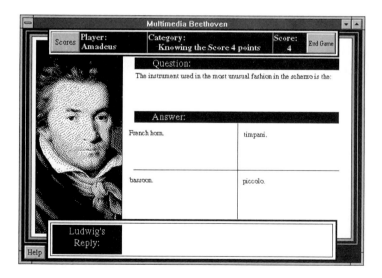

Figure 7.40. *Multimedia Beethoven's trivia game.*

If you answer a question correctly, the black-and-white image of Beethoven gets a colorful accent, including a gold tooth or sunglasses (Figure 7.41).

Figure 7.41. *An enhanced image of the composer is produced when a question is answered correctly.*

I offered a close look at this program for two reasons. First, it's such an excellent piece of software that I want to encourage you to go out and get it if you have any interest in music. Second, it illustrates the kind of thought, preparation, and effort that must go into a multimedia presentation of the highest quality.

Musical Instruments

Sound is a powerful medium, as Multimedia Beethoven demonstrates so capably. Another Microsoft multimedia application, Musical Instruments, provides an effective, interesting musical tour that covers more instruments than you ever imagined existed.

There is an enormous amount of detail and a large helping of musical examples to hold your interest. There are, as you might expect by now, different ways to get at the information on the CD-ROM. Figure 7.42 shows the Contents page of Musical Instruments.

The interface to Musical Instruments is, as you can see, similar to Dinosaurs, and the organization owes a certain debt to Encarta. Some of the other aspects of these two products also are present but hidden below the surface. For example, the coverage is exhaustive—under the letter H in the A–Z of Instruments, you'll find entries for Harp; Harp,Irish; Harp,Vera Cruz; Harpsichord; Hichiriki; Highland Bagpipe; Horn,English; Horn,French; Horn,Hand; Horn,Side-Blown; and Hurdy-Gurdy. If you choose Instruments of the World, you can check out the Central and South American instruments—Vera Cruz Harp, Claves, Bongos, Steel Drum, Panpipes, Kena, Cuica, Congas, Charango, Maracas, Timbales and more.

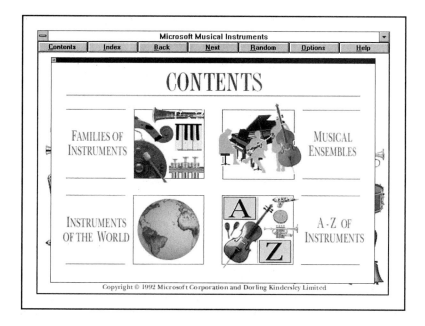

Figure 7.42. *The Contents page for Musical Instruments.*

As you might expect, there is sound at every turn—you can hear short and long selections for each instrument as well as the sounds of various ensembles and groups. Figure 7.43 shows a typical instrument page from Musical Instruments, the Irish Harp.

To hear a sample sound, click the Play icon. To see and/or hear more about an instrument, click on the text.[10] For example, Figure 7.44 shows detailed information about a harp's sound box. It demonstrates many of the typical sound features of Musical Instruments.

---

[10]Only text in red leads to additional information.

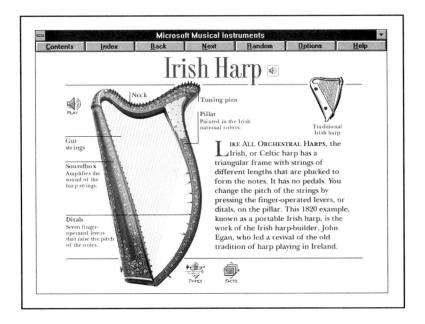

Figure 7.43. *The page for the Irish Harp.*

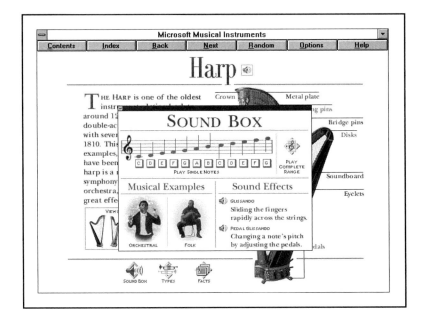

Figure 7.44. *Detailed information about an instrument.*

Three features are worth looking at here:

Sample sounds—The top portion of the window displays a scale, which can be used to play individual harp notes. You also can play the complete scale by clicking the icon to the right of the scale.

Musical examples—There are two musical examples available for the harp—an orchestral selection, and a folk selection. These are complete, high-quality selections.

Sound Effects—This section features two examples of harp-playing technique: glissando and pedal glissando.

Wherever you go in Musical Instruments, you find this level of detail. The sounds are consistently well done. For example, look at Figure 7.45. It shows a variety of musical ensembles. Clicking on any of the images displays specific information about the ensemble, including musical samples, details about instruments, and even some hot licks on a Les Paul guitar.

Figure 7.45. *Musical Instruments ensembles.*

Musical Instruments is a lot of fun—in fact, it's an ethnomusicologist's[11] dream come true. I highly recommend it.

Cinemania

So far I've covered Dinosaurs, famous classical musicians, encyclopedias, and musical instruments. What else could there be? The movies, that's what: Microsoft's Cinemania.

Cinemania provides a wide range of information about movies: stills, famous lines you can listen to, Academy Award nominations and winners, capsule reviews, and more. How about a capsule review of Cinemania itself: although you might think the movie database isn't as far ranging as it could be and you might not always agree with the reviews,[12] you will:

➤ Learn things you've never heard before about movies.

➤ Look up movie terms that were always baffling to you.[13]

➤ Scope out past winners of Academy Awards—or just cruise through the nominees.

➤ Review a series of films by a particular director or actor.

In other words, there are many different ways to use Cinemania. As with the other Microsoft multimedia titles, you can look up a single item of interest, or you can browse through the database using different techniques, associations, and hyperlinks.[14] Figure 7.46 shows the possible routes to the data that Cinemania offers.

You use the remote control to maneuver around in Cinemania. The labels on the remote's buttons change according to the current context. Most of Cinemania's screens also contain a button bar you can use to reach major

---

[11]That's someone who studies folk music very seriously.

[12]Come to think of it, when has there ever been a movie reviewer you could really rely on?

[13]For example, what is a gaffer, or, for that matter, a best boy? Gaffer: Chief electrician on the set, in charge of lights. Best boy: the Gaffer's assistant.

[14]A "hyper" anything is just a fancy way of describing links to data that may actually be in very different physical locations. For example, if you were reading a review of *The Maltese Falcon* and clicked on the name of Bogart, you could look through a list of his other movies to locate one you were interested in and then jump right to the review of that movie.

features of the program as illustrated in Figure 7.47. This figure presents a typical Cinemania screen, which displays a capsule review of *Dog Day Afternoon* by movie critic Leonard Maltin as well as the movie's director and cast. Any text that is underlined serves as a *hot link*. Clicking on hot-link text gives you more information. Note that the buttons on the remote control are completely different from the ones for the Table of Contents screen and that additional information about the movie (an "R" rating, running time, the fact that is has won awards, etc.) is displayed in the remote's "screen."

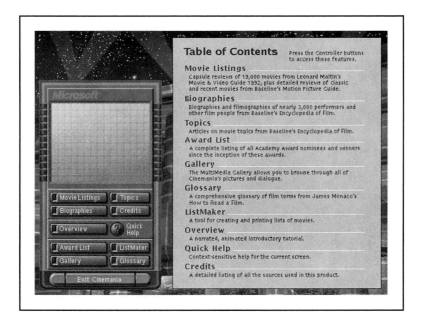

Figure 7.46. *The Cinemania Table of Contents.*

Cinemania also includes a MultiMedia Gallery as shown in Figure 7.48. You will find movie stills, sound clips of famous lines, and photos of the stars. The little icon to the left of each item tells you what kind of multimedia treat you will get. For example, the figure shows a gallery entry for *The Wizard of Oz* which consists of a movie still (movie camera) and a sound clip (microphone).

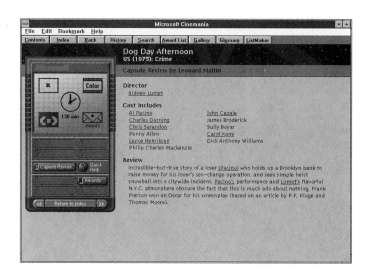

Figure 7.47. *A Cinemania capsule review.*

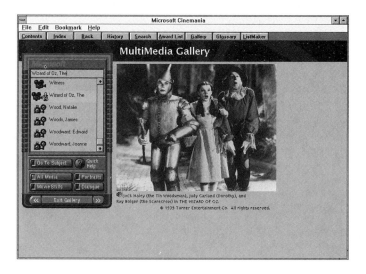

Figure 7.48. *A movie still from the MultiMedia Gallery.*

One of my favorite features was the Glossary, where I could finally learn about all the esoteric terms used in the movie industry. Figure 7.49 shows a few of the entries under "A."

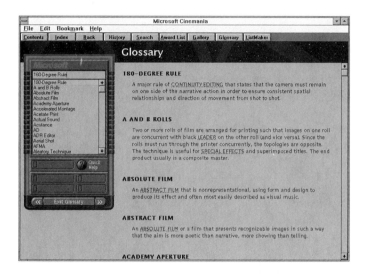

Figure 7.49. *The Cinemania Glossary.*

Overall, Cinemania is both entertaining and educational. At our house, it's always near the top of the stack of CDs next to the computer. Microsoft released the 1994 version of Cinemania just as we were going to press. It includes video clips from a number of movies. In addition, the information about movies and stars has been updated and expanded. Cinemania now represents an even better value for the movie lover.

Games

Multimedia really lends itself to games. Using a CD-ROM, game developers now have many times more storage space to work with.[15] Heck, some games (such as the Seventh Guest) now come on multiple CDs!

---

[15]A 3 1/2-inch floppy disk holds about 1.4M of data, whereas a CD holds more than 650M. That's about 464 1/4 floppies. How would you like to install 465 floppies next time you buy a game? I agree—a CD-ROM is better.

How this extra storage space is used varies from game to game. One of my favorite games is Battle Chess from Interplay Productions. It is a 3-D version of chess with a twist. When you capture a piece (or when one of yours is captured), an animated battle takes place. The battles are done with a sense of humor, the details are delightful, and the characters are drawn with wonderful detail. Figure 7.50, taken from the promotional literature that accompanies Battle Chess' CD-ROM version, gives you the general idea. The on-screen battles are not much different than the figure, although they take place right on the chessboard, not full screen.

Figure 7.50. *Chess anyone? Multimedia adds an extra dimension to Battle Chess.*

The original version of Battle Chess, limited by space on floppy disks, had interesting but limited animations. With the move to CD-ROM, there's plenty of room to store complex and interesting animations. The animations are also accompanied by realistic sounds. For example, you can hear a pike crashing to the floor and bouncing away and the screams of a dying pawn.

The Carmen Sandiego games have been among the best-selling games for some time. The original—Where in the World is Carmen Sandiego?—is now out on CD-ROM, and additional titles are also available. It's not a Windows software product, but it's such a great multimedia product I couldn't pass up a mention. Both my kids—11 and 13 years old—love it. It does best with young teenagers.

The authors make excellent use of the CD-ROM's capacity for huge amounts of data—they now include more material in more pleasing ways than was possible with the floppy version. For example, many of the images come from the collection of the National Geographic Society, and the music includes selections from the Smithsonian's collections. When played with a good MIDI card (I tested this program with the Roland SCC-1, but any MIDI card will work), the sounds are fantastic.

Sometimes games show up in unexpected places. When I received Multimedia Beethoven, for example, I was surprised to find a game called The Ninth Game. Composer Quest from Dr. T.'s Software is more or less a game too. As with Multimedia Beethoven, these games are an excellent incentive—they encourage you to use the rest of the software so you can do well at the game. Composer Quest also provides information as you play; a wrong answer results in clever hints.

Multimedia Is for Games Too

I work with computers all the time, and you might think I'd be glad to have a computer game at hand for an occasional break. *Au contraire, mon ami.* What better place for recreation than where I happen to be already? But, alas, I haven't found much to enjoy.

I thought perhaps there was something about computer games that made them less entertaining than regular games. They struck me as graphically interesting for about five minutes, and then I found them to be pretty boring. The big problem I had was that computer games were so artificial. But if you add some sound, some high-quality animation (thanks to all the storage space on a CD-ROM), and maybe some sound synthesis, then you've got my attention like never before. This harks back to the concept of monomedia that I mentioned in the introduction—real computers are multimedia computers, and anything less is only a cheap imitation.

Composer Quest

"It's not how you play the game—it's whether you win that matters." Face it—that's how most of us attack any game we encounter. We all like a challenge, but we like to win, too. A good game has to balance the challenge with the abilities of the game player. Otherwise, the game isn't fun. If it's too easy to win, boredom sets in quickly. If it's too hard to win, frustration ensues.

Then there are the games that are so much fun that winning and losing move from the foreground into the background. In my experience, it's a rare game that's so much fun to play you can ignore winning. Encarta's Mind Maze, for example, doesn't present much of a real challenge in the maze part. It's the questions that provide the thrill (or the frustration!).

Composer Quest, on the other hand, provides its real pleasure in the playing. As you can see from its opening window (Figure 7.51), you have only two choices: you learn or you play. This is mildly but harmlessly deceptive: either way, you learn.

Figure 7.51. *The Composer Quest opening window.*

Playing the game is easy: you listen to a musical selection and then set off in quest of the composer if you do not know who wrote the piece. Figure 7.52 shows the start of the process. Clicking on the large ear in the upper right portion of the window gets you started.

Figure 7.52. The beginning of the quest.

Figure 7.53 shows what happens next: you must set a date you think is appropriate for the selection. After you choose a year, click the Go! button to begin the quest.

When you "arrive" at the date you set, you will see some composers (see Figure 7.54). You may first be asked to select a style appropriate to the musical selection whose composer you are seeking. Clicking on a composer either wins the game if it's correct or gives you a hint if it isn't.

When you do choose a composer—even if it is not the one you seek—you are presented with lots of information about the composer. Figure 7.55 shows a typical composer window (featuring Louis Armstrong).

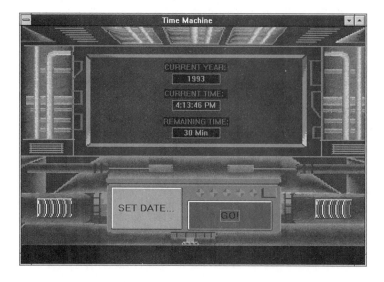

Figure 7.53. *Setting the date for the quest.*

Figure 7.54. *Choosing between the composers.*

Figure 7.55. *A typical composer window.*

Overall, Composer Quest contains tons of useful and interesting information. The game is more about gaining knowledge than anything else.

Living Books

When Media Vision sent me their Fusion Double CD 16, several CD-ROM products were included in the package. One of the products turned out to be a very pleasant surprise: Arthur's Teacher Trouble.

This is one in a series of children's books that Broderbund provides on CD-ROM. The interface to the books is familiar because it is based on books. The opening menu, for example, is simple as you can see in Figure 7.56. It looks like a book and provides two main choices: reading and playing.[16]

Figure 7.57 shows a typical page from a Living Book. Here, on the printed page, it looks just like any page from a children's book. There's some text and a background picture. Before you say "ho-hum" and move on, allow me to describe what the CD-ROM version is like.

---

[16]It seems that the need for a game in a CD-ROM product is overwhelming, doesn't it?

Figure 7.56. *The menu of Arthur's Teacher Trouble.*

Figure 7.57. *A typical page from a Living Book.*

As you enter a page, a female voice reads the narrative text slowly, clearly, and with appropriate feeling. Quotations are read in the voice of the character. Before, during, and after the reading, characters might move in sophisticated animations.

If you choose the "play" path through the book, you can have some fun with each page after the reading: The characters adopt simple movements, and appropriate background sounds play. When you click an object in the environment, an animation plays.

These animations are not mere afterthoughts. They can be very complex and involve many characters and objects in the scene. For example, if you click on the window of the door to the science lab in the scene shown in Figure 7.57, a finger traces out the word "help" from inside the lab. Then fingers scrape against the inside of the glass. Finally a head peaks out, and the character giggles and winks. Clicking on the doorknob generates a different animation as does clicking on the door itself.[17] By clicking on different persons and objects in this scene, you can see socks rolling up and down, views into the imaginations of the characters, monsters in the lockers, and so on.

Overall, Living Books are innovative and have superb production details. I recommend them highly for kids of all ages.

Information at Your Fingertips

CD-ROM drives excel at one thing: providing plenty of room for data storage—up to 680M of data and up to 72 minutes of sound. This makes them an ideal repository for large databases, and software vendors have been releasing more titles in this category. Some of these databases involve multimedia, and some don't.

For several years, obscure but large databases have shown up on CD-ROM. You may not even be aware they exist. For example, when I visit my local bookstore to ask about a book, the clerk turns to a computer system that has all the books currently in print (and many forthcoming titles) on a single CD-ROM. Each month, the store receives a new disk updated with all the changes. Although this hardly passes for multimedia—it's only text, after all—I'm in favor of anything that puts more CD-ROM drives in computers. Every CD-ROM drive sold increases the pressure on software companies to put out titles on the medium.

There are also quite a few info-titles available on CD-ROM at the consumer level featuring reference materials such as dictionaries, almanacs, and encyclopedias. Several of these are included in CD-ROM bonus packages with various

---

[17]Clicking on the door results in an explosion in the science lab.

multimedia upgrade kits. For example, I received Compton's encyclopedia with the upgrade kits from Media Vision and Creative Labs. Microsoft's Bookshelf is another commonly included package, and it contains an almanac, a concise encyclopedia, two quotations sources, and a dictionary, among other features. There is also a growing body of children's info-titles, such as the Macmillan Dictionary for Children. This area didn't blossom until multimedia increased in popularity because until that happened the prospective audience was just too small. With CD-ROM drives finding their way into more homes, the number of titles has increased sharply during the last year. This trend should accelerate in the coming year.

Multimedia Reference Disks

If ever there was a software category made for CD-ROMs, this is it. Putting an encyclopedia on a CD-ROM doesn't even push the limits of the medium—room is still left over for animations, sounds, and video clips. There are three things to consider when purchasing an encyclopedia:

➤ What is the quality of the material on the disk?

➤ How useful is the search software that gives you access to the information?

➤ How useful and complete is the multimedia support?

The answers to these questions can be very telling when it comes to making a choice. If at all possible, study the product at your local computer store. An encyclopedia is a major choice, and you are likely to be stuck with it for years, so it's worth the time it takes to select one that works for you. I found Encarta to be well ahead of the rest of the pack and would recommend it for just about anyone looking for an encyclopedia on CD. However, because encyclopedias are frequently included with upgrade kits, you may find yourself with an encyclopedia whether you want one or not.

For example, consider two packages: Compton's Multimedia Encyclopedia for Windows and Grollier's Multimedia Encyclopedia for DOS (a Windows version is also available). In both cases, the actual text of the encyclopedia is of good quality. There is a substantial difference, however, in the way each one accesses information. Grollier's features a simple search method. It's easy to use, intuitive, and it displays the information quickly. It is ideal for younger children (under 10) who are just beginning to learn how to use an encyclopedia. Compton's, on the other hand, has more ways to search for data and would work well with a teenager.

To test each program, I relied on the kids' homework assignments—at least once a week, someone needed to do some research. We attempted to find relevant material using both encyclopedias, and in almost every case we located the correct reference more quickly using Grollier's.[18]

Microsoft's current entry in the information market is called Bookshelf. (No, I have not forgotten about Encarta. Encarta is so far ahead of everything else out there in the information category that it deserves a category all its own.) Not merely an encyclopedia, Bookshelf contains a variety of reference sources, including a compact encyclopedia, two quotation resources (Bartlett's and Columbia), an almanac, and a dictionary. It is most useful as a quick reference or as an accessory for writers. A special version that includes a tightly integrated link to Word for Windows is available as well. This special version enables you to automatically include citations and footnotes—ideal for that college research paper. Whatever encyclopedia or reference product you choose, it will be a valuable addition to your software library.

Databasics

Multimedia databases are already a big hit with many companies, but not necessarily in flashy ways. The simplest multimedia databases combine two kinds of text—some of the text is stored conventionally as bytes, and some is stored as images of text.[19] In the lingo of the professionals, text stored as a graphics image is called *ink*. You can't load ink into your word processor, but you can view it as an image any time you want to just by recalling it from whatever document or database it is stored in.

For example, if you have an American Express card, your monthly bill consists of images and text. You get a billing summary, but you also get a picture of each of your transactions, including your signature. This makes it easy to verify

---

[18]If you have more than one encyclopedia, you'll find that each encyclopedia has its own focus as well. When you look up a given topic, one encyclopedia might provide a quick overview whereas another might provide plenty of details.

[19]When text is stored as bytes, you can edit the text. When it is stored as an image, it cannot be edited.

the transactions. The insurance industry is also big on this technology because it stores documents in original form, which is useful if there are questions, disputes, or litigation.

At the grass-roots level (that is, on a PC near you), you will find that most mainstream Windows database software now enables you to store any kind of image—an employee's ID photo, images of products in an inventory, pictures of attendees at a conference, and so on.

Lenel Systems International recently introduced several multimedia database products. Although many mainstream products are moving toward sound or image storage, Lenel's products are headed toward the ultimate goal: integrating all the programming, data storage, and playback into one product. Their databases offer a developer interface where you can roll your own products in many Windows programming environments, such as C/C++ or Visual Basic. They also offer a product called MediaOrganizer, which is a multimedia database application. Typically, this combination means power at the price of complexity.

Managing Multimedia Data

Many new issues are involved in managing multimedia data. Unlike traditional data—names, addresses, or single images—multimedia data usually has action associated with it.

Here's an example. Suppose I want to store a video clip in my database. It's a brief clip from a movie I have in my collection, and I want to create a catalog with short clips so it's easier to remember which is which.

Even if I can store the file data, I have a problem when I want to use that data: how do I display the clip? Does the database have to know how to do that, or can it just hand off the task to some other program? In either case, how does it work? Who's in charge? Is it even a good idea to store the clip data in a file? What do I do with the original clip—I now use twice as much disk space unless I delete the original. If I do delete the clip, the only way I can view it is with my database product.

What's a programmer to do?

> As you might guess, there are no easy answers. MCI, the Media Control Interface, offers the easiest way to deal with the action issues—playback, recording, placement, and so on. What it does not define is the hand-off between the database and MCI—as long as MCI gets usable data, it couldn't care less where it comes from.
>
> Here's my two cents on the issue: Multimedia databasing will not really work until the idea of a file name goes away. Multimedia data can be a .Wave file on your hard disk, a selection from a CD audio disk, or a two-minute clip on a video tape. Until database soft-ware makes it conceptually easy to deal with this variety, multimedia data will be a pain by requiring too much operator intervention.

Because some big corporations use multimedia data storage, you might expect some to trickle down to the personal computing arena, but like most trickle-down theories, this one doesn't wash. The kind of stuff involved in storing images of accident reports doesn't have much use on your average PC. These applications are boring, middle-of-the-road, and everyday kinds of things—dry, practical stuff.

This is not what is driving multimedia. As I describe in the beginning of the book, *fun* is driving multimedia into the computer market. It's exciting to hear sounds where once there was silence.[20]

It isn't the kind of concept that lends itself to being sold to a business mind-set, however. That's why everyone thinks of multimedia in terms of recreation and home computers.

If computers start talking, people will have to work in private offices instead of cubicles. Otherwise, the cacophony will grind business to a halt. The cost of such a conversion would be staggering. Wouldn't it be great, though—a private office where you can be intimate with your machine, perhaps have it toss off a lilting little laugh when the boss sends you E-mail about that problem with the Eckely account.

But I digress. The point is that multimedia makes a computer more immediate, more "alive." Not in the sense of artificial intelligence or anything such as

---

[20]Punctuated only by the high-pitched whine of an aging monitor transformer or the wheeze of an over-powered cooling fan. Who am I kidding—computers have had sound from the beginning. It's just been extremely ugly sound.

that. More alive the way a wall with a great picture is alive, or more alive the way a house feels when you've got huge ferns hanging from the ceiling. It is more alive because you have the ability to put more things that are human into it, and to get them back out.

That's where multimedia databases come in. As the data grows and as computers become more capable of storing numbing amounts of data, you will need a way to get to the information without working at it. I'm willing to bet the farm on this simple fact: The real benefits of multimedia won't arrive until database products can seamlessly manipulate all kinds of multimedia data. This will happen when it's inexpensive to store digitally an entire movie, an entire photo album, and so on.[21]

Unless this storage revolution happens, multimedia will not reach its full potential. Perhaps it won't happen. Perhaps it will never be cheap enough to convert movies to digital data. Perhaps the staggering storage requirements will be too much to manage. Perhaps there is an end to progress.

I doubt it, however. As long as there's some money in it, the big companies that are leading the way on multimedia are going to spend the research dollars that put bleeding-edge technology into our hot little hands.

When you consider the kinds of databases you and I use every day, the biggest problem involved in creating and maintaining multimedia databases is that the data involved is just plain different.

Until recently, much of the data stored in databases was either text or numbers. In either case, the data limits were well defined, and the information could be stored in files without much of a hassle.

However, 24-bit images, Wave audio, CD audio, video, and other data formats present new challenges in database design. Falling memory and disk prices are moving the industry to the point where it is almost economical to turn all kinds of data into digital information. If it's digital, it's a candidate for storage and retrieval in a database.

The methods for storing multimedia data and then gaining access are still evolving. For example, here's a quick look at Turtle Tools, which comes with the Sound Ideas sound effects library. Figure 7.58 shows the opening screen of the program.

---

[21]Of course, this is already starting to happen. You can put your entire family photo album on CD down at your local camera store. Well, the store might have to send it out, but you get the idea: the future is arriving as we speak.

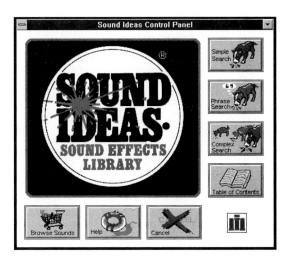

Figure 7.58. *The Turtle Tools sound effects library.*

I'm not wild about the product design, but it does offer five different ways to find sounds:

Simple search—You enter a string, and the database looks for that sound.

Phrase search—You enter a phrase, and the database looks for sound titles and/or descriptions that include the phrase.

Complex search—You can enter criteria of different types to try to find an appropriate sound.

Table of contents—A brute listing of the sounds, which you can then plod through at your leisure—not the best way to tackle a huge database unless you have time to spare. It's like going through the yellow pages without knowing the category you should be looking under.

Browse sounds—Cruise through the sounds and play them as you go to see what will work for you.

For example, if you choose Phrase search, you see the dialog box shown in Figure 7.59. For this example, I entered the phrase "door closing."

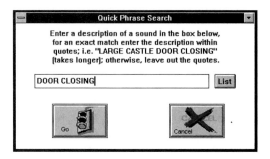

Figure 7.59. Searching for a phrase.

Figure 7.60 shows the result of the search—a sound whose title contains the word "door" and whose description contains the phrase "door closing." You can listen to various forms of the file by clicking the buttons at the right, or you can jot down the file name and use the Windows File Manager to copy it to your hard disk. This is one area where the product could be improved—it would be much easier if you could click a Copy button and then specify a destination directory.

Despite the interface limitations, I'm happy to use Sound Ideas. The quality of the sounds is very high, and it is a very useful collection.

Conventional products such as dBASE, Foxpro, Paradox, and the products that compete with them in the marketplace have had to either adapt to the new forms of data or see themselves replaced.

Consider the typical multimedia presentation. Right now, you must store each piece of the puzzle in a separate file. Products such as Media Blitz fill in the gap by tracking the separate files. In some ways, Media Blitz is a database product even though it does not physically store multimedia files in a database. Other products, such as Agility/VB from Apex Software, can store the kinds of digital data found in multimedia applications, but they are not usually thought of as multimedia products.

If multimedia is the newest and most volatile area of personal computing, multimedia databases are at the far edge of multimedia. Anything can happen.

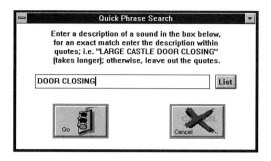

Figure 7.60. *A sound that matches the search criteria.*

Sounds and Pictures

This is where much of the fun is in multimedia. As you learned in Chapter 2, "Sound Advice," there are two distinct kinds of sound files—those that store wave-form data (Wave audio) and those that store note, or playback, data (MIDI). Interesting software is available for both kinds of sound files. Most of the really good sound software for recording and editing is already covered in Chapter 2.

As important as the recording and editing of sounds is, however, another area deserves equal concern: how well does mainstream software incorporate the use of sounds? As multimedia becomes more popular, there's a rush to incorporate sounds into various programs.

Some applications, such as Word for Windows, do a good job of integrating sound. The *Multimedia Madness* CD-ROM contains a demonstration of how Word incorporates sound. The integration is both simple and elegant—there is a menu choice for adding a sound, and it takes you directly to a sound recorder.[22] This enables you to record your comment and get right back to work. For a word processor, where all you need to do is create and listen to voice annotations, this approach is a perfect example of the old saying, "Less is more."

When it comes to things like animation or creating multimedia presentations, however, less is simply less. For example, the Animation Player that comes with Multimedia Explorer (about which I say more later) enables you to connect only

---

[22]You can specify the default program for sound recording by associating the program with the .WAV file extension in File Manager.

411

one sound file with an animation. Media Blitz uses the opposite approach; it enables you to add as many sounds (and animations and bitmaps) as you want to use.[23]

More and more mainstream software packages are finding ways to add sound. The mere presence of sound support, however, does not guarantee its usefulness. Keep a wary eye on the upgrade brochures to see if the ways you can use sound make sense for the way you work.

Possibly the hottest new use for sound will revolve around speech recognition. Since the first edition of *Multimedia Madness,* several new speech recognition packages have come along. This is only the beginning. Affordable technology is currently limited to voice commands, but the Holy Grail of speech recognition is known as continuous speech recognition—the ability of a computer to correctly translate your normal speech into written text. IBM has introduced a system that enables developers to integrate continuous speech recognition into their software. The catch is that some extremely high-end hardware is required to accomplish this. Nevertheless, technology is now at the point where you can make serious use of voice recognition in your everyday use of your computer.[24]

I can't say how comfortable people will be with talking to their computer (especially in a crowded office), but if it catches on, speech recognition is one of those technologies that could revolutionize the way we use computers. Products such as the Windows Sound System or InCube enable you to literally tell your computer what to do. As an added bonus, such packages sometimes also include speech generation capabilities, which enable your computer to read back spreadsheet data, for example. This is a technology to watch as well.

With images, the fun comes from several directions—scanning images, creating your own images, and editing existing images. Still images are only part of the picture, so to speak. Various forms of animation are available, including multimedia movies, Animator flicks, video capture, and AVI (Audio Video Interleaved, also known as Video for Windows).

---

[23]However, Windows has a limit for what and how many multimedia types it can handle at one time. For example, if you have 8-bit video, displaying more than one bitmap at a time requires that you force each bitmap to use the same palette or risk the dreaded "palette flash" when you change palettes to display a new image. For another example, you can only play one (sometimes two) wave files at one time.

[24]If you decide to experiment with voice recognition, probably the most important thing you can do is to get a so-called "noise canceling" microphone. Such a microphone is good at ignoring background noise.

This variety of formats is both a blessing and a curse. Fortunately, Windows supports formats with drivers so you can easily add a new format to your repertoire, but it's disconcerting to see a dozen drivers competing for attention when I run Media Player. I sure hope somebody set all that up correctly. Still, I must admit it's a lot of fun playing with all the different formats.

The growing use of images is limited by two factors:

➤ The large size of photo-realistic images.

➤ The effort required to create good photo-realistic images.

If you plan to purchase images, the market is skewed toward the high end right now. Until recently, the main market for photo-realistic images was the publishing industry—magazines, trade journals, newsletters, and so on. This is a relatively small market, so the cost per picture is quite high, running above $500 per image in many cases. That's far more than a business user or a hobbyist can afford. However, the quality of such images is almost always high. The images are attractive, and there are no blemishes or flaws in the scans. These files are often 24-bit color at high resolutions, and file sizes of 20M or 40M are common.

For most of us, that level of quality isn't necessary. However, we all still want images that look good—pleasing colors and compositions, crisp detail, and so forth. It will take a larger market than currently exists to provide the incentive for consistently better images. Nonetheless, products are beginning to appear and, although they can hardly be considered cheap, are much more affordable. One example appeared in a press release I received via E-mail recently from Digital Zone, a Seattle image company. They offer 50 images on a CD-ROM in Photo-CD format, all from professional photographers. The price for a disk is $599—about the cost of a single image in the regular market for images. This comes to about $12 per image. Image quality is high—you could use these images for magazine covers if you wanted to. You get unlimited use of the images, and you can modify them as you see fit. Digital Zone says they intend to release up to 250 such discs over the next five years.

The market for images is expanding rapidly, and so is the variety of images available. Over the next year, there will be a shoot-out over price and quality, and we'll all be winners because prices will go down and quality will go up as companies compete for our business.

There is one possible flaw in that scenario. It's called a scanner. If scanners get cheap enough, you can create your own images, and you won't have to rely on outside support. A market will always exist for the kinds of images the average computer user can't create—exquisite sunsets, beautiful models, and so on. There's a good chance that inexpensive scanners could make it possible to handle most imaging tasks on your own.

Scanning Software

I use a Hewlett Packard Scanjet IIc to do my scanning. It does such a great job that I want to show you how it works. Although this scanner model is several years old now, you can still purchase it—it has held up very well. The software front end to the scanner has a simple design, is easy to use, and is reasonably functional. It consists of a small control box and a large scanning area (Figure 7.61).

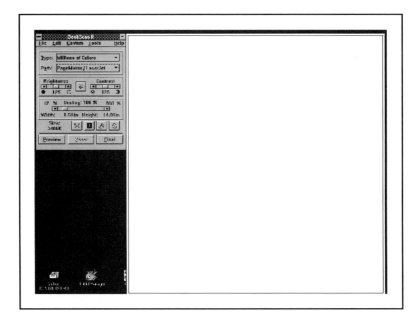

Figure 7.61. *Control box for Scanjet IIc.*

The scanning area is adjustable; I routinely make it as large as possible so I can get a good look at what I'm scanning. This compact design is easy to use, but it still gives me what I need. Look closely at the control box in Figure 7.62.

Figure 7.62. DeskScan II control box.

With the settings at the top of the control box, I can make two important choices before I scan: the Type of image (black-and-white, halftones, 256 colors, 16.7 million colors, and others) and the Path. The Path box is not what you might think; the term "Path" is more than a little misleading. Path usually refers to the image path—where the image ultimately is stored on the disk. In this case Path means (I'm reaching to grasp what Hewlett Packard engineers might have been thinking) the software+hardware path. For example, you can pick a path called PageMaker/Laserjet. Even this is misleading; the Path really indicates at which resolution you must save the image. For example, if the path is PageMaker/Laserjet, the images will be saved at 300 dpi—the resolution of the destination device. Is that clear? It wasn't to me, and I wish they had used a different name.

The next box, with Brightness and Contrast sliders, can be used to manually adjust image exposure. However, I seldom do this. The Yin/Yang symbol between the two sliders is a button that tells the software to calculate automatically the optimum exposure. To use it, preview the scan (the button at the bottom-left of the dialog box), click and drag to select a portion of the image to scan, and then click the button with the Yin/Yang symbol. (I refuse to call it the "Yin/Yang button." This is one of the most obscure "intuitive" icons I've ever seen—that is, there is no text to explain its use outside of the documentation.)

I find the exposures to be excellent. If I have an image with special needs, such as a face in shadow, I can select the face only, perform an auto exposure, and then select the part I want to scan. The automatic exposure applies to the entire image.

The Preview button does a quick, low-resolution scan of the entire scanning bed, whether you need it or not (Figure 7.63). Fortunately, the scan is so fast this is not really a problem.

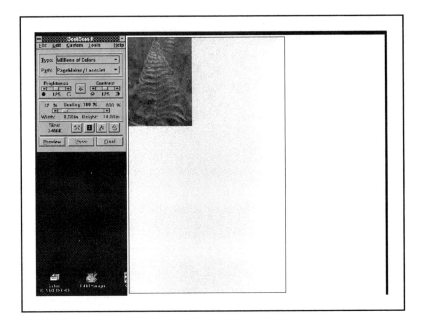

Figure 7.63. *Low-resolution scanning with the preview button.*

As soon as you have previewed the scan and set the exposure, you can either perform the final scan or zoom to see the portion of the image you selected (Figure 7.64).

The final results are excellent as shown by Figure 7.65, a gray-scale scan of a color photograph.

The photograph had a few blemishes (you can see some of them in the screen shots), which I later touched up using PhotoStyler.

If necessary, you can scale the image using the control box. This is handy for desktop publishing applications because scaling a raster image can introduce moiré effects—light and dark bands that are artifacts of the scaling process.

Figure 7.64. *Scan and zoom to see portions of the image.*

Figure 7.65. *The final result.*

Animation

Animation—if only it were as easy to create as it is to play. Animation consists of as many as 30 images *per second*. How long does it take you to create a single image using a paint program? Can you imagine how long it would take to create a minute of animation using a paint program?

The keys to creating animations are tools that simplify the transition from one frame to the next. There are two important ways that the better animation software packages help out:

➤ Tweening

➤ Tracing

To tween, you first create an object on one frame. You then place it at a different location on a second frame. This could be the next frame, or it could be a hundred frames later. The software then takes care of creating the frames in between. This animates the object between the two reference points you established. Because the software does most of the work, this is a very effective way to animate. You should look for this feature in any animation package you buy.

You use tracing when you are drawing each frame yourself. The software should include features that make tracing easy. You should not have to draw each image completely from scratch. The main features to look for that support tracing are

➤ Blue images

➤ Copy image forward

➤ Copy changes forward

The actual names for these techniques vary from one software package to the next.

Blue images aren't always blue; the term is a holdover from a traditional animation practice. A blue pencil was used to annotate a working drawing because the color blue did not show up when the image was copied.

This is how you use a blue image:

1. Draw one frame. For the purpose of this example, suppose you draw a frog sitting on a water lily, and the frog ultimately jumps off the lily pad.

2. Copy the image to the following frame as a blue image. The entire image appears on the screen as one color. It might be blue, or you may be able to define what color it is. The image is not editable, nor is it part of the image in the new frame. It is only there as a guide.

3. Trace over the blue image to create the new frame. Adjust the position of any elements of the drawing that move from the last frame to this frame. For example, the frog's body may lift slightly as the legs begin to flex for the jump.

4. When you finish tracing, delete the blue image and move to the next frame.

Instead of copying a blue image, you may also want to copy the entire frame and then make changes to it. If only a small part of the image is changing, this can speed up your work. You should also be able to copy an image to all frames to use as a background. The lily pad, for example, might work well in the background. You can use copy image forward for this.

Once you've copied the background to several frames, you can use copy changes forward to copy only the things that change to the next frame. Copying changes is useful when animating an object. Because the object does not change shape, you can copy it forward, move it, then copy it forward again. This is a substitute for tweening, by the way, in packages that do not support tweening.

The animation package Animator (from Autodesk) is part of a product called Multimedia Explorer. It's a DOS program, although Explorer comes with an animation player for Windows.

Animator is the little brother to Animator Pro, a full-featured animation package from Autodesk. Autodesk is the company that produces AutoCAD, the high-end, computer-aided design package. Autodesk has other AutoCAD-oriented software that has great multimedia potential. One program is 3-D Studio. You learn more about Animator Pro and 3-D Studio in Chapter 9, "Animation."

In this chapter, you learn about Explorer to give you an idea of how animation works and how you can use it with multimedia. Multimedia Explorer includes the following items:

➤ A program to play animations under Windows

➤ A program to create animations

➤ Hundreds of animation files

419

In the program group created for Explorer (Figure 7.66), there is an icon for the Animator, an icon for the Animation Player, and six icons for the sample animations.

Figure 7.66. Multimedia Explorer's Animation program group.

The Animation Player

The opening screen of the Animation Player is unassuming (Figure 7.67). The menu bar at the top of the window contains the controls for stepping backward (<) and forward (>), stopping (**S**top), and playing (>>). Because no animation file is loaded, these controls are dimmed.

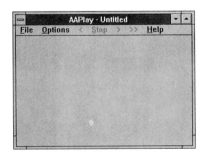

Figure 7.67. The opening screen of Animation Player.

Clicking the **O**ptions menu displays several choices (Figure 7.68).

Figure 7.68. *Animation Player's Option menu.*

These options include the ability to play the animation full-screen. With the options relating to colors, you can adjust the limited number of colors available with 256-color displays. In almost all cases, the default option selections produce good results. If problems arise, they usually result from conflicting palettes. The average multimedia computer has only 256 colors available at one time; this is called a *palette.* If the palette used by the animation is different from the screen palette, either the screen or the animation will have the wrong colors. Tools like Animator Pro or VidEdit (in Video for Windows) give you the ability to adjust palettes or to find common palettes for objects with similar but different palettes. (I've said it before and I'll say it again: 8-bit, 256-color displays are the bane of multimedia computing. If you are serious about multimedia, get a 16- or 24-bit display and consign palettes to where they belong: the past.)

If you load an animation, you can examine the choices on the **F**ile menu shown in Figure 7.69.

Figure 7.69. *The Animator's **F**ile menu.*

You can create animation scripts that enable you to play more than one animation in a sequence. This is similar in concept to Media Blitz scores, but it is limited to animations.

The Edit Script dialog box (Figure 7.70) has many components.

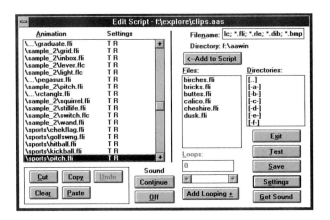

Figure 7.70. *The Edit Script dialog box.*

The large box at the top left lists the animations included in the current script. The buttons (**C**ut, Cop**y**, **U**ndo, Clea**r**, and **P**aste) below this box are used to make changes to the script. You also can add sound to the script with the Get Sound button. The remainder of the buttons are used to add animations to the script and to perform file operations. If you choose to associate a sound with an animation or script, you see the dialog box in Figure 7.71.

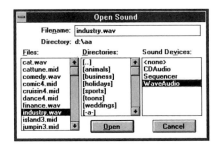

Figure 7.71. *The Open Sound dialog box.*

The two boxes on the left are standard: Files and Directories. The box on the right specifies the kind of sound file you want to use: CD, sequencer (MIDI), or Wave.

You also can customize the settings for an animation by choosing **F**ile|Anim Se**t**tings (Figure 7.72). The adjustable settings include speed, length, and duration of the animations, as well as when and how to play any associated sound.

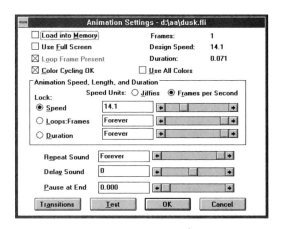

Figure 7.72. *Animation Settings.*

The real power of Multimedia Explorer, however, is the capability to create your own animations.

Creating Animations

The animation program included with Multimedia Explorer, Animator, is a slightly simplified version of Animator Pro. The Pro version has an interface similar to the standard version, but the professional version has some important additional capabilities.[25] (See Chapter 9, "Animation," for a closer look at Animator Pro.) Figure 7.73 shows a typical Animator screen.

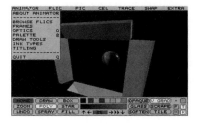

Figure 7.73. *Animator screen and options.*

---

[25]The most important difference is that the Pro version can work at larger animation sizes, such as 640 × 480.

Animator is a DOS program with a unique interface that took some getting used to.[26] The menu is located at the top of the screen. When the mouse passes over a menu choice, the menu drops down—no need to click. You get used to it after a while, especially if you have some experience on the Macintosh.[27]

The bottom of the screen shows one of many possible control panels. The various control panels enable you to select colors, lines, fills, drawing styles, and so on. They also include controls for stepping through the animation frames and *cels*. A cel is a single object in a frame. A frame can be built using one or more cels; only one cel is active at a time. For example, if you are animating a frog that is catching a fly, you might start by putting the frog on the background as shown in Figure 7.74.

Figure 7.74. *The frog alone against a black background.*

To animate the fly, you need to make it a cel. You begin by painting it into one frame as shown in the left half of Figure 7.75. In this case, I painted the fly into frame 2 (of 90 total frames).

To make the fly a cel, use the Cell|Get menu choice to copy it to the cel buffer. Select Time painting (click the "T" button on the Home panel) to enable tweening. Then move to the destination frame, number 20, and use Cell|Paste to paste the cel. Animator enables you to position the cel anywhere in the frame; I chose the spot shown in the right half of Figure 7.75. Animator then displays the Time Paste panel, which has a Render button. Click the Render button to render the frames from 2 to 20 with the fly in a different position in each frame.

It's much easier to do than it is to describe.

---

[26]The interface, although extremely different, is full-featured and worth the effort to learn.

[27]Of course, this is about the only similarity it has to the Mac interface.

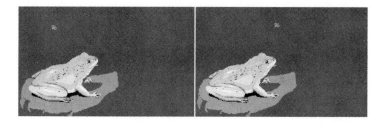

Figure 7.75. *Two steps in the animation of the fly.*

To give the fly's motion a somewhat realistic path, I added several additional tweens moving the fly in different directions at different speeds—just like a real fly. These take the fly to frame 60 where the frog's tongue is going to hit the fly and start dragging it toward the frog's mouth. I used a final tween to move the fly across that distance in three frames because a frog's tongue moves so quickly.[28]

That takes care of the fly's motion. I then needed to animate the frog's tongue, and tracing is the best way to do that.

Animator has a useful feature called *Clip Changes* that copies the changes you make in a frame to the cel buffer. You can then paste them into the next frame, add some more changes, clip the combined changes, paste those in the following frame, and so on. This makes it easier than you might think to create more sophisticated animations.

For example, look at the two frog images in Figure 7.76. They are two consecutive frames from the frog animation. The image on the left shows the fly somewhat further along in its course, and the frog's tongue has just begun to extend from the mouth. (Before creating the tongue, I used tweening to put 10 small circles in 10 frames to mark the path of the tongue starting with frame 51 so the tongue and the fly meet in frame 60.)

I painted the tongue in frame 51 (using Animator's paint tools) and then copied it to the cel buffer using the Trace|Clip Changes menu choice.

---

[28]Determining how many frames to use for a given animation is something you learn from experience. There are no hard-and-fast rules.

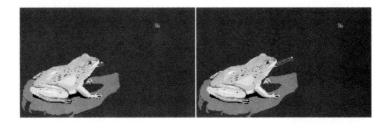

Figure 7.76. *The frog making its catch.*

I then switched to the next frame, pasted the cel, and moved the cel to where the tip of the tongue should be in the new frame. I then back-filled the missing portion of the tongue by painting as shown in the right half of Figure 7.76. I continued this simple process until the tip of the tongue arrived at the same position as the fly in frame 60. I used the same techniques to snap the tongue back to the frog's mouth, except I used only a few frames to make it move more quickly.

It takes a lot more effort to describe this than it did to do it; I completed the entire animation in less than five minutes. Once you become familiar with the techniques that an animation package uses, you can accomplish a lot with minimal effort.

There are many uses for animations, although they are also just plain fun. You may find, as I did, that creating animations is a relaxing way to enjoy your computer.[29] If you need a reason to purchase the software, a program like Animator enables you to create dazzling animations for business presentations with surprisingly little effort. On the other hand, if you want to put the time in, you can create sophisticated animations. You might want to consider Animator Pro, however, if you are that serious about animation.

I included the frog animation on the CD-ROM disk along with a simple Visual Basic program that enables you to play animations accompanied by a sound. It's called MADNESS.EXE, and I recommend playing the frog animation (FROG.FLI) using the sound file GOTIT.WAV.

The MADNESS program is easy to use; a sample screen is shown in Figure 7.77.

---

[29]"What did you do today, honey?" "Oh, I had some fun creating a frog tongue—and the fly turned out really great."

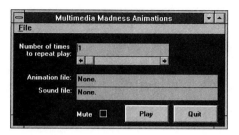

Figure 7.77. *A MADNESS screen.*

Run the program from the *Multimedia Madness* CD-ROM using the **File**|**Run** command in Windows—the file name is MADNESS.EXE. You can also copy the .EXE file to your hard disk. Make sure you have VBRUN200.DLL and CMDIALOG.VBX in your Windows system directory, or the program will not run (these are Visual Basic 2.0 runtime libraries).[30] Once the program is running, follow these steps:

1. Open an animation file using **File**|**Open Animation**.

2. Open a sound file using **File**|**Open Sound**.

3. Play the combination using **File**|**Play**.

That's all there is to it! You can play any animation and/or sound file. The program also includes a slide control to adjust the number of times the animation repeats (see Figure 7.77). Because the sound and animation are synchronized, you cannot stop the application until they have completed playing. If you have Visual Basic version 2.0 or later, you can open the source files to see how this synchronization is accomplished. Refer to Appendix B for information on locating CD-ROM files.

During playback, the current repeat number is shown at the top right, and the Madness icon smiles at you as shown in Figure 7.78.

The most significant limitation of Animator is that it is limited to MCGA resolution: 320 × 240 and 256 colors. You can't create animations at higher resolutions, and you can't use existing images unless you convert them to this size and resolution. However, Animator shares many features with its big brother, Animator Pro, which is profiled in detail in Chapter 9, "Animation."

---

[30]If these two files are not in your Windows system directory, copy them from the CD.

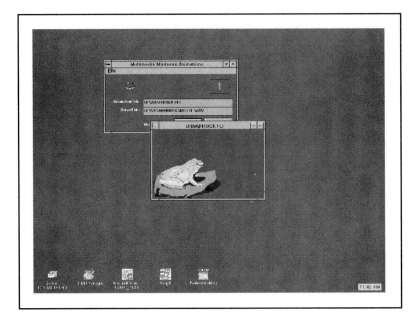

Figure 7.78. *The smile of the madness icon.*

This is only a taste of what you can do with animations. There are several animations on the CD-ROM (see Appendix B for details), and the capabilities of several other animation packages are described in detail in Chapter 9.

Manning the Pump: Multimedia Programming

F or those who like to program, multimedia programming offers far and away the most bang for the buck.[1] It's quite easy to program some pretty amazing multimedia extravaganzas—much easier than I expected it to be when I started out.

The reason for this is simple: Visual programming environments. When you can see what the results will look like as you program, it's much easier to create cool stuff. The bottom line on the better visual programming environments is that they provide a lot of power for a (relatively) small amount of effort. The first of these was ToolBook, and Visual Basic is the most popular. Other packages are moving in this direction, too; Multimedia Viewer 2.0 is a good example.

If you aren't interested in programming, feel free to explore the other chapters. This chapter provides a basic overview of the issues involved in programming for multimedia followed by several detailed looks at exactly how one programs using specific programming tools. Before I start, here's a little rule I use to evaluate programming tools for use with multimedia:

Ron's Rule A good multimedia programming tool offers

➤ An easy introduction for the casual user

➤ Access to the guts of Windows[2] for the serious user

➤ Intimate relations with Windows MCI[3] capabilities

➤ Powerful features (apart from Windows API and MCI) that enables a power user to create original work

Few packages score high on all those measures, but the best tools hit at least three out of four. Of the three packages I present in this chapter, each has at least one weakness:

---

[1]Which brings to mind an apocryphal (translation: of doubtful authorship or origin) story about playtime. Many years ago, I heard it said that psychologists had determined how to tell which toys children would play with most. Their technique consisted of measuring the effort required to use the toy against the benefit derived. In plain English, if you were in the market for a child's birthday gift, a toy with big results from little effort was your best bet. Of course, that phrase I used above—"the most bang for the buck"—makes it clear that most of us understood this idea a long time ago.

[2]I am referring, of course, to the Windows API—that set of functions which enables "real" Windows programmers to do whatever they dang well please.

[3]Media Control Interface.

Visual Basic 3.0—The interface to MCI falls short of where it really needs to be. The most important omission is *callbacks*.[4] Third-party tools offer a remedy.

Multimedia Viewer 2.0—Also does not offer the degree of intimacy with MCI I think necessary.

Multimedia ToolBook 1.53—Doesn't offer the same ease of access to the Windows API as the other two products.

Two words are used to describe the creation of multimedia software: programming and authoring.[5] Programming involves the writing of code, like this:[6]

```
/* GetIniSettings — Get initial bounce settings from WIN.INI
 * Params:  hWnd — Handle to window
 * Return:  None
 */
static void GetIniSettings()
{
    /* Load initialization settings from CONTROL.INI. */
    wMaxSpeed = GetPrivateProfileInt(szAppName,szSpeedName,
➥DEF_SPEED,szIniFile);
    DelayTime = GetPrivateProfileInt(szAppName,szDelayName,
➥DEF_INIT_BDELAY,szIniFile);
    ShortTime = GetPrivateProfileInt(szAppName,szSDelayName,
➥DEF_INIT_MDELAY,szIniFile);
    wMagnify  = GetPrivateProfileInt(szAppName,szMagnifyName,
➥DEF_INIT_MAGNIFY, szIniFile);
    ChangeFreq  = GetPrivateProfileInt(szAppName,szChangeName,
➥DEF_INIT_CLEVEL,szIniFile);
    GetPrivateProfileString(szAppName, szPlayFileName,
➥DEF_FNAME,szFileToPlay, STRLEN, szIniFile);
    bBlankScreen = GetPrivateProfileInt(szAppName, szBlankitName,
➥DEF_BLANKIT,szIniFile);
    bMuteAudio  = GetPrivateProfileInt(szAppName, szMuteName,
➥DEF_MUTE,szIniFile);
    bRepeatPlay  = GetPrivateProfileInt(szAppName, szRepeatName,
➥DEF_CONT,szIniFile);
    bPassword  = GetPrivateProfileInt(szAppName, szIsPassword,
➥FALSE, szIniFile);
```

---

[4]This is the ability to tell MCI about a function you want called when MCI is done with something. Another term used to describe this capability is *notification*—that is, MCI notifies you when it is done.

[5]Sometimes you'll hear the word "scripting" used. ToolBook uses this term, and it is generally regarded to be at a point somewhere between programming and authoring.

[6]This code is taken from the screen saver sample code provided with Microsoft C/C++ 7.0 and modified for use in a screen saver I wrote (supplied on one of the CD-ROM discs; look for VIDSAVER.SCR).

```
      /* Check the values we just loaded! */
      VerifyIniSettings();
}
```

This example is in C. It reads data stored in an .INI file, and puts the values it finds there into program variables. Most languages operate on the same basic principle: lines of code are used to make things happen. The C stuff above is pretty obscure—you would need to know C to really understand what's going on. Other languages are more English-like in their approach. For example, here is some code written in OpenScript, the programming language used by Multimedia ToolBook:

```
to handle ButtonUp
    system fPath
    system VideoText

    put SelectedText into VideoText
    put word 1 of VideoText into WhichVideo

    get tbkMCI("close vid","")
    get tbkMCIchk("open "&fPath&WhichVideo&" alias vid","",1)
    get tbkMCIchk("break vid on 27","",1)
    get tbkMCIchk("play vid","",1)
end
```

The two lines in bold are particularly easy to understand; they read just like English sentences. The complete handler[7] gets the name of a video file and puts it into the variable WhichVideo, and then uses Windows MCI command strings to open the video and play it.[8]

Some languages—Visual Basic, for example—combine code with other programming techniques. Authoring packages, on the other hand, rely primarily on some kind of graphical interface that enables you to specify what you want.

The line between authoring and programming is beginning to blur, however. Programming packages are adopting some of the techniques used in authoring packages, and vice versa. All three of the products described in this chapter, for example, combine code and graphical tools for developing multimedia software. Even C/C++ programmers can have the best of both worlds with products like Visual C/C++.

---

[7]ToolBook calls such things handlers rather than functions. Why? Because they handle events—in this example, a button-up event that occurs when you click on an object.

[8]This particular snippet of code comes from the Virtual Madness! application on the CD that accompanies my book *Virtual Reality Madness*.

In this chapter, I show you in specific examples how to program for multimedia. I have evaluated each of the products described here in terms of its ease of use and capabilities so that you can make an intelligent choice when the time comes to buy. Additionally, this chapter introduces you to the multimedia programming capabilities that are built into Windows—the Media Control Interface (MCI)—with a special focus on the Command String Interface.

It was really hard to come up with an Author's Choice product for this chapter—all three of these products really qualify. Used in the right way at the right time, all three products deliver capably. Table 8.1 shows each product's strengths and weaknesses in a little more detail. I've also thrown in HSC's Interactive to round out the comparison.

Table 8.1. Multimedia Programming Strengths and Weaknesses.

Product	Strengths	Weaknesses
Visual Basic 3.0	Powerful access to the Windows API	Multimedia support lacks callback capability
	Visual Programming interface	Takes a while to get the hang of things
	Event- and object-oriented programming	
	Supports timers	
	Extensible via .VBX files (visual controls)	
	Very strong third-party support via DLLs and .VBX files.	
	Runtime can involve numerous files	

continues

Table 8.1. continued

Product	Strengths	Weaknesses
Multimedia Viewer 2.0	Sophisticated, built-in support for text searching	Very unconventional approach to development
	Many common programming tasks aided by new Hot Spot editor	Nonprocedural interface sometimes cumbersome to use
	Can access DLLs directly and easily, including Windows API	Many repetitive tasks not yet automated in current version
	Provides easy access to hyper-linking capabilities	It can be difficult to keep track of all the pieces in a Viewer application.
	Provides only simple solution for text-intensive applications	
Multimedia ToolBook 1.53	Powerful OpenScript language	Power is matched by complexity; takes quite a while to master ToolBook's capabilities
	Visual development interface	Installed base is smaller than Visual Basic; less third party support
	Event- and object-oriented programming	
	Full multimedia support, including callback and notification	

Product	Strengths	Weaknesses
	Animation capabilities	
	Supports timers	
	Strong technical support department at Asymetrix	
Interactive	Simple, icon-based interface	Very limited support for text
	Limited support for some MCI features	Limited in support for runtime installations
	Includes animation software	

When should you use each of these products? Here are my recommendations:

Visual Basic—Visual Basic is effective when you need access to the Windows API. You don't need to mess around with things like global memory to use the API functions. This makes it relatively easy to address technical areas with the API. You can also use Visual Basic for "quickie" applications—where the simple support offered by the MCI .VBX control is all you need, or where a few simple calls to the MCI command strings will do the job.[9]

Viewer—Viewer's main strength is with projects containing a lot of text. For example, when I decided to create a multimedia version of Chapter 2 of this book, Viewer was the perfect choice. That chapter contains a lot of text as well as figures, sounds, and a few programs to run. Viewer's built-in text search capabilities make it a natural for text-intensive applications. If you need fancier capabilities in other areas, Viewer can work with other development tools—such as Visual Basic and Visual C/C++—to enable you to create custom solutions. Microsoft's Cinemania (see Chapter 7) was built with Viewer, Visual Basic, and C/C++.

---

[9]These terms are covered later in the chapter if you are not familiar with them.

ToolBook—ToolBook shines in two areas: support for MCI command strings, and visual design. If multimedia elements dominate your requirements list, then ToolBook is your best choice. At the very least, you can use ToolBook to prototype—but you may well discover that the prototype is really the final program. Products such as Multimedia Beethoven and Composer Quest (as well as the Nautilus CD magazine) attest to the capabilities of ToolBook.

The truth is that all three of these products are at the top of the list—but each one is at the top of a different list. So I'll cop out on choosing one of them as an Author's Choice—this author has chosen all three to use in particular situations, so all three get the designation.

There are other multimedia-oriented programming and authoring packages out there, but these are the three I use day in and day out to get the job done.

Multimedia with Visual Basic

In this section, you learn how to use Visual Basic (often called simply VB) to create a sound player/recorder.

Visual Basic, from Microsoft, revolutionized Windows programming in a very short time. Until the introduction of Visual Basic, Windows programming required either a sophisticated knowledge of C or C++, or learning to use a product such as Actor or Smalltalk. ToolBook was available before Visual Basic, but the earlier versions lacked the smooth integration of media support that ToolBook offers today. C/C++ programming is complex and requires a serious commitment to learning a lot about the internals of Windows. Both Actor and Smalltalk are easier to use than C but not to the degree that a beginning programmer would feel comfortable with them.

Visual Basic, on the other hand, is accessible even to novice programmers. It is a marvelously well-designed product. It takes a bit of getting used to—it's not like other programming tools that preceded it—but it's well worth the effort to learn.

It is truly a visual programming tool. You create applications mostly with your mouse by moving various items into place on a window (called a *form*). Once everything is in place, you usually have to write at least some code to tie it all together, but you can create sophisticated applications with surprisingly little code.

Proof of Visual Basic's ease of use can be found in the popularity of the product among all sorts of programmers. The power of Visual Basic is evidenced by the growing number of commercial and shareware packages arriving in the marketplace.

The Professional Toolkit

Here's some instant advice if you are thinking about buying Visual Basic: the Professional version of Visual Basic includes extra features you shouldn't be without. The Professional Toolkit, for example, includes a custom control that gives you quick access to most multimedia functionality. With just plain Visual Basic, you do not have this simple access, nor do you have a bunch of dandy custom features that come only with the professional version.

I'm not sure why it is called the Professional version because most features it includes make Visual Basic easier to use. Normally, professional programming tools add power by giving you access to the guts of the language or system. The Professional version includes that access, but it also makes Visual Basic easier to use. I recommend it to everyone.

Building a Multimedia Application with VB

I want to show you how easy it is to create a multimedia application using the MCI control in the Professional Toolkit. (MCI stands for Media Control Interface.) The tutorial in this chapter is based on Visual Basic Version 2.0; if you have Version 1.0, the screen will look different, but the multimedia capabilities are still there if you have the Professional Toolkit. Version 3.0 makes little change to Visual Basic's multimedia capabilities.

The MCI control comes with the Professional Toolkit. If you don't have the Professional Toolkit, you can't do this at home. Sorry!

In this example, you create a Visual Basic application for playing and recording sound files. If you don't have Visual Basic, you still can follow along to understand the step-by-step procedures.

Once you have Visual Basic up and running, you see an opening screen that looks like Figure 8.1.

Figure 8.1. *The opening screen for Visual Basic 2.0.*

On the left of the screen is a tall, narrow window—the toolbar. It contains icons that enable you to quickly access all kinds of standard Windows interface elements, such as text boxes, radio buttons, drop-down boxes, and so on. If you are not familiar with these terms, they represent features you see every time you use a Windows application.

Visual Basic gives you access to the heart and soul of Windows. It's easy— you click the toolbar to select something, drag on your form to indicate the size you want it to be, and then write a little code to link it to all the other elements on the form. Each of these "elements" is called a *control* in Visual Basic lingo. You learn how to do it in this sample application.

Adding Controls

The first thing to do is add the MCI custom control to the VB toolbox. The items in the toolbox are Windows elements, such as text boxes, buttons, and so on, that you can add to your application. With Visual Basic you can add new items—such as the MCI control—to the toolbox. Select **A**dd File from the **F**ile menu to open the dialog box in Figure 8.2.[10]

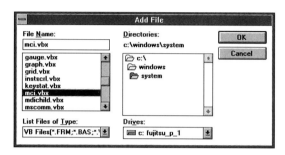

Figure 8.2. *The Add File dialog box.*

The filename for the MCI custom controls is MCI.VBX. Like all .VBX files, it is located in the Windows system directory. VBX files are nothing more than tools that you can add to the toolbox. (Advanced programmers can even create their own.) In Visual Basic each tool puts a *control* onto a form. Controls are objects on the form—text boxes, radio buttons, and so forth. Click OK to load the file.

Visual Basic adds the MCI custom control's icon to the toolbox at the bottom of the toolbox (Figure 8.3).

If there is no blank project open yet, you must start a new project by selecting **N**ew on the **F**ile menu.

Next, double-click the MCI icon you added to the toolbox. This puts an MCI control on the main form (Figure 8.4). The main form looks like any other window in Windows and is automatically created by Visual Basic whenever you start a new project.

---

[10]If you are already using Visual Basic, your toolbar may look different from the illustration. You may already have the MCI custom control available—if so, skip ahead.

Figure 8.3. *The toolbox and the MCI custom control icon.*

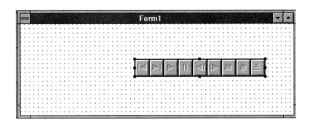

Figure 8.4. *The MCI control—the fourth icon from the left.*

The control has everything you need to operate a multimedia device: rewind, play, fast forward, pause, stop, and record. The icons on the buttons follow the conventions used on CD players, tape recorders, and VCRs.

Adding a Dialog Box

Next, add a Common Dialog control.[11] Common dialogs were introduced in Windows 3.1. This gives you a simple way to add support for features such as File

---

[11]It is so called because it is common to a variety of operations.

Open, File Save, Choose Color, and the like. To add the Common Dialog, double-click its icon in the toolbox (Figure 8.5).

Figure 8.5. *The Common Dialog icon.*

If this puts the Common Dialog control over the MCI control, move the Common Dialog control over to the side (Figure 8.6). Click the control and drag it to the desired location.

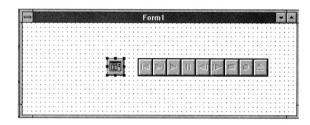

Figure 8.6. *The Common Dialog control moved over to the side of the toolbox.*

Next, you have to set a few properties for the Common Dialog control. Properties are associated with all Visual Basic controls. By setting properties for size, color, location, and font size, you can customize your application. Some properties are common to almost all controls; some controls have properties that apply only to them. Figure 8.7 shows properties available for the Common Dialog control.

Set the Properties as follows:

Property	*Setting*
DefaultExt	"WAV"
DialogTitle	"Select a Wave file"
Filter	"Wave files (*.wav)|*.WAV"
FilterIndex	1

The most convenient way to access the Common Dialog box (it is used to open and to save files) is with a menu. Select the Menu Design choice on the Window menu, and the dialog box in Figure 8.8 appears. You use this to create a File menu for the application.

441

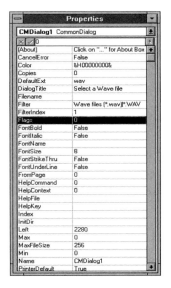

Figure 8.7. Properties for the Common Dialog control.

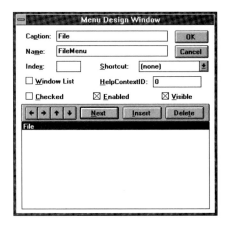

Figure 8.8. The Menu Design Window dialog box.

In the Caption text box, enter the text that appears on the menu bar—File, as shown in the previous figure. This is the menu caption that will appear on the application's menu bar. For the Name, enter FileMenu. The name is used to reference this menu item in Visual Basic code; do not put a space between File and Menu.

Now click the Next button. This takes you to the next menu item. In this case, where there is no next item, Visual Basic creates a blank one. Enter Open Sound File for the Caption and OpenCtl for the Name. Before continuing, click the right arrow button to indent this menu choice in the list. This makes the new menu choice a part of the File menu. When you do this, you see a dotted line to the left of the caption as shown in Figure 8.9. If you don't do this, the menu choice, Open Sound File, appears on the main menu bar rather than on the File menu.

Figure 8.9. *The dotted line shows that the Open sound file choice is part of the File menu.*

Click the Next button again. Add another Caption (Exit) and Name (ExitCtl) as shown in Figure 8.10.

Figure 8.10. *A new menu item.*

Click OK to close the Menu Design Window dialog. Click File, which now appears on the menu bar. Notice that the two menu items you entered appear on the File menu (Figure 8.11).

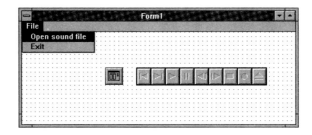

Figure 8.11. *These items were added to the File menu from the Menu Design Window.*

Adding the Visual Basic Instructions

You have to put some Visual Basic instructions behind these menu choices to make them effective. While the File menu choices are displayed, click Open sound file. This opens a code window as shown in Figure 8.12.

```
                          PLAYER.FRM
Object: OpenCtl            ±  Proc: Click              ±
Sub OpenCtl_Click ()
    Dim MCI_CLOSED As Integer
    ' This value for closed taken from VB docs:
    MCI_CLOSED = 524

    ' Use Common dialog to select file to open.
    CMDialog1.Action = 1

    ' See if the device is already open.
    If MMControl1.Mode <> MCI_CLOSED Then
        ' Device is open; close it.
        MMControl1.Command = "Close"
    End If

    ' Set the filename in the MCI control.
    MMControl1.FileName = CMDialog1.FileName

    ' Open the device.
    MMControl1.Command = "Open"
End Sub
```

Figure 8.12. *The code window of a sound file.*

Notice that there are two small boxes at the top of the code window. The one on the left specifies the object the code is associated with; it is the name of the menu choice you double-clicked—OpenCtl. The box on the right specifies the procedure this code goes with. It's labeled Click, which means this code executes when the menu choice is clicked. This is typical of Visual Basic coding.

Notice that Visual Basic adds the first and last lines of code automatically. The first line of code,

```
Sub OpenCtl Click()
```

informs Visual Basic where this code fits into the overall scheme of the application. Sub indicates that this is a subroutine, not a function. A function has one or more arguments, and a subroutine has none. OpenCtl combines the menu name—OpenCtl—with the procedure name—Click. In this tutorial, you can see how Visual Basic automatically provides code for you to build on.

Type the following code (an annotated version is shown in Figure 8.12) in the code window:

```
MCI_CLOSED = 524
CMDialog1.Action = 1
If MMControl1.Mode <> MCI CLOSED Then
     MMControl1.Command = "Close"
End If
MMControl1.FileName = CMDialog.FileName
MMControl1.Command = "Open"
```

If you are not yet familiar with Visual Basic and the code seems mysterious, well, that's how code is until you learn it. This code sets a variable to the value that indicates whether an MCI device is closed, calls the Common Dialog box to get a filename, checks to see if the device is already open (and closes it if it is), passes the filename to the MCI control, and then opens the device.

How does the code know which MCI device to open? Well, you have to tell it. Minimize the code window to get it out of the way, and then double-click anywhere on the main form. Double-clicking on a form opens the code window for the form itself rather than a control on the form (Figure 8.13). This time the object is the form (that's where you double-clicked), and the procedure is Load—that means the code is executed when the form loads. The Load procedure is (in Visual Basic terminology) an *event;* the code you enter is executed when the Load event occurs. The code is the *procedure*[12] for the Load event.[13]

---

[12]A procedure is nothing more than a group of lines of code that perform some task.

[13]There are many types of events in Visual Basic. Examples include MouseUp, MouseDown, KeyPress, Click, Resize, Unload, and DragDrop. Visual Basic is an event-driven programming language; when an event occurs, it triggers action or executes code.

445

Figure 8.13. *The code window for a form.*

If the current procedure is not Load, click the arrow to the right of the box and then select Load from the list that appears. By adding code to the form's Load event, you can assure that certain things happen as soon as the form displays onscreen.[14]

Between the lines Visual Basic provides, type the following lines in the Code Window.[15]

```
MMControl1.Notify = 0
MMControl1.Wait = 0
MMControl1.Shareable = 0
MMControl1.DeviceType = "WaveAudio"
```

When this code executes, it establishes a few settings. In the last line, it informs the MCI control that it should direct all activity to the WaveAudio device. The code also informs the MCI control that you want to play Wave files; this is how it knew that you wanted to play Wave files. An MCI control in Visual Basic can refer to only one type of multimedia device.

You have one more menu choice to provide code for: Exit. On the main form, click File, then click Exit (see Figure 8.14.). Enter the following code in the Code Window:

```
MMControl1.Command = "Close"
End
```

---

[14]Technically speaking, the FormLoad event occurs before the window displays. This means you should avoid putting any code that displays things in the FormLoad event—you might see those items before the window itself gets drawn properly.

[15]Refer to Figure 8.13 for some comments about the lines of code.

This code closes the WaveAudio device and ends execution of the program. It's important to close the device. If you don't close it, no other program can use it.

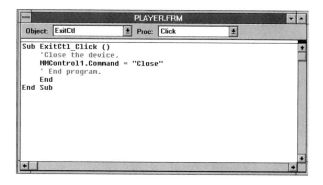

Figure 8.14. *The Exit menu choice.*

Running the Program

To run the program from within Visual Basic, press the F5 key. Click the File menu, and then click the Open sound file choice.

The Common Dialog appears, and you can use it to locate and select a .WAV file that you would like to play. (If you can't find anything, try the directory that Windows was installed in; it has a few sound files in it.) Click OK to close the Common Dialog box. Figure 8.15 shows what you see on your form.

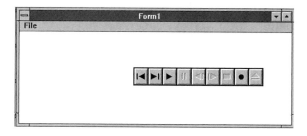

Figure 8.15. *The MCI control buttons.*

Notice that the MCI controls are no longer dimmed—the usable controls are now shown in black. The following chart lists the control buttons (from left to right) and their corresponding actions:

447

Control	Action
Previous	Move to previous item
Next	Move to next item
Play	Play from the current item
Pause	Pause playing
Back	Move backward
Step	Move one item forward
Stop	Stop playing
Record	Begin recording
Eject	Eject media

Not all buttons are supported by all devices, and some buttons only become active at certain times. The Pause button, for example, is not enabled until you start playing. You don't have to worry about this, though. The MCI control queries the device to determine what capabilities it has and adjusts the buttons based on what it learns.

To play the file you selected, just click the Play button.

 If you installed the speaker driver, you probably won't hear anything. The speaker driver is not supported by the MCI control.

Exit your application and return to the Visual Basic design mode by clicking File and then Exit. If you wish, save the application now using the File|Save menu selection. You can use the filename SOUND.FRM for the form, and SOUND.MAK for the make file.

Adding Record Capability

You can easily add recording capability to the application. Select Menu Design from the **W**indow menu, then insert a new menu choice after Open sound file called Save sound file. Use the Caption and Name shown in Figure 8.16.

When you finish, click the OK button to return to the main form. On the main form (not the Visual Basic menu), click File, then click the Save sound file menu item. This opens a Code Window (Figure 8.17). Type the following command between the lines Visual Basic already added for you:

```
MMControl1.Command = "Save"
```

Now when you run the application, you can click the Record button, add sound to the file you loaded, and then save it. This saves the new data using the same filename you loaded.

Figure 8.16. *Adding recording capability to the application.*

Figure 8.17. *A Code Window for the **SaveCtl** menu item.*

This concludes your look at a Visual Basic multimedia application. It took some time to explain, but now you can do it. The Professional Toolkit enables you to access the raw power of Windows directly.

There are times when you want more control over what's happening than a Visual Basic custom control gives you. You could, of course, write a program in C or C++, but that could take most of your adult life if you don't already know C or C++.

You can get more control right in Visual Basic. With Visual Basic, you can access many standard Windows API functions. This capability is at the heart of the sample application in the section "Visual Basic and the Command String Interface" later in this chapter.

449

Programming Overview

If you are going to program for multimedia under Windows, there are some basic things you need to know. The basic methods by which Windows handles multimedia are covered in Chapter 5, "Windows Multimedia." In this chapter, I cover the methods available for accessing multimedia functionality. These methods apply to almost any language you might use, but the details of implementation may vary. The way you call and declare a function in C, for example, differs from the way you call and declare it in Visual Basic. However, you can call many of the same multimedia functions in a variety of languages, authoring packages, and script-based products.

At the highest level (in programming terms, that means the easiest-to-access level), Windows provides a function for playing sounds: `sndPlaySound()`. It won't give you access to every multimedia capability, but it does give you an easy way to add sound to your applications.[16]

Using this function, you can create a surprisingly wide variety of effects. To play a sound, you tell `sndPlaySound` the name of the file the sound is in, and the function does everything else required. It opens the file, reads it into memory, sends it to the appropriate device, and then closes the file. You learn how to use it in the following section "Visual Basic and the Command String Interface."

The next level down toward the guts of the computer involves something called the Command String Interface. This enables you to access a variety of multimedia devices—from CD Audio to animations—using plain English text. You gain some additional control at this level. You can play only a portion of a sound, for example, or you can play other files besides .WAV files. You can even cue the CD player to a song and then play the selection through your speakers. This level is good for most high-level software, including Visual Basic, InterActive, and ToolBook. Beginning to intermediate C programmers are also likely to use this interface because it is easier to master.

Another step closer to the computer takes you to the Command Message Interface. At this level, you have more control. You are responsible for opening the file, for opening the device that you want to play it on, and so on. You have to keep track of many more details, but you also have a great deal of control. Most accomplished C programmers work at this level, although you can use the Command Message interface in many high-level packages as well.

---

[16]Another plus when working with `SndPlaySound`: it will play sounds if you have the speaker driver installed.

Finally, you come to the lowest level, the one that most of us will never program at: writing the actual drivers that control how Windows interfaces with multimedia hardware. At this level, you have ultimate control—and total responsibility! It's not for the weak of heart. C/C++ and assembly language prevail here.

C/C++

The two main competitors for the C programmer's Windows dollar are Microsoft and Borland. Each company sells a powerful C development environment for Windows. The Microsoft C compiler has one important advantage: it comes from Microsoft, the folks who developed Windows.

On the other hand, the Borland C compiler also has an important advantage: many programmers prefer the development tools that come with it to those that Microsoft provides. Of course, the introduction of Visual C/C++ may well change the status quo.

It is hard to go wrong with either product. Both compilers are powerful and both include development tools that make it easier than ever to program for Windows. Rather than try to show you how to program in C for Windows, I simply direct you to your local computer bookstore. You can find an astounding number of books about C/C++ programming because of the recent surge in interest in these languages. *C Programming Proverbs and Quick Reference* (by yours truly) contains seldom-seen advice on the actual practice of C programmers, including testing, debugging, program documentation, and related topics. It also provides a reference of all common C functions, operators, and so on.

Visual Basic and the Command String Interface

Now you are going to use a multimedia application developed in Visual Basic that bypasses the MCI control from the Professional Toolkit. You can do this with a powerful feature in Visual Basic: the capability to access the Windows API (Application Program Interface).

This gives Visual Basic much of the power of C, although this doesn't do anything about Visual Basic's overhead—in C, the computer does what you tell it to do; in Visual Basic, there are quite a few layers between you and the computer. This means that applications developed in Visual Basic run more slowly. As hardware speeds increase, this is supposed to become less of an issue. Unfortunately, software companies are always adding more functionality, which tends to slow things down—a vicious cycle.

The Windows API consists of the functions that make Windows tick internally. This includes everything from setting the focus to a given window to putting graphics on the screen. Microsoft did an interesting thing when they created the functions that make up the multimedia portion of the API. They created a "door" (if you'll pardon the play on "Windows") called the Command String Interface. You can use this door to do anything you want with multimedia.

mciExecute and mciSendString

The door consists of two functions. By passing simple, English-like sentences to mciExecute,[17] you can play CD audio, run animations, and so on. These sentences are called *command strings*. Unlike SndPlaySound, mciExecute gives you access to the full range of multimedia devices, although with certain limitations.

The second function, mciSendString, enables you to establish two-way communication with multimedia devices. It works with command strings just like mciExecute does, but it adds a few useful features that you learn about shortly.

Before you start, please recognize that you cannot use the full range of command strings with mciExecute. A number of these commands are used to query a device. Such commands return a string with information about the device they refer to. With mciExecute, this return string gets "lost." (You never see it anyway.) If you want to get at these return strings, you have to use mciSendString instead. This is not a serious problem, however, because most of what you want to do can be done using mciExecute.

(For a parameter-by-parameter examination of mciExecute and other related functions, refer to "The Windows Multimedia API" section in Chapter 5.)

A Sample Application

Even if you are not familiar with Visual Basic or with Windows programming, you still might find this section useful. The Command String Interface is used by

---

[17]The mci in the function name indicates Media Control Interface.

many multimedia applications. You can, for example, use the Command String Interface from within many authoring packages, such as HSC InterActive. Even Master Tracks Pro supports it in the latest release.

If you do not own Visual Basic, just follow along; much is revealed that you can use in other programs.

The project name is MMTEST.MAK; you can open it in Visual Basic if you want to examine the source code. It's pretty simple; the application takes the command strings you type on the form and passes them to either `mciExecute` or `mciSendString`.

Running the Application

The program window for MMTEST has the following elements:

➤ A text box in which you can type those wonderfully simple near-English command strings. In the example, you are querying the Waveaudio device to get its name.

➤ A button to click when you're ready to execute the command.

➤ A button to use when you want to exit.

➤ A text box to report if an error occurs.

➤ A text box to display any messages that are returned by `mciSendString`; in this case, the name of the Waveaudio device (Sound).

➤ Two radio buttons: one to use `mciExecute` and one to use `mciSendString`.

➤ One or two labels to explain what's going on.

To use the application, type a command and then press Execute. You can select either `mciExecute` or `mciSendString` as the function to call. If you select `mciExecute`, errors are reported in dialog boxes created by `mciExecute`.

The command strings are the key to using this application. For example, the following set of commands plays a music CD:

```
open cdaudio
play cdaudio
```

When you want to stop the music:

```
stop cdaudio
close cdaudio
```

On the other hand, if you put the CD that comes with this book in your CD-ROM drive, you can try the following. Adjust the drive letter for your drive, of course, and this only works if you have already installed the Video for Windows driver (see Chapter 1, "This Book Is Multimedia"):

```
open d:\windham\narell\narell.avi alias AVIFile
play AVIFile
close AVIFile
```

Declaring the Functions

To use the two MCI functions in a Visual Basic application, you have to declare them in the Declarations section of the form.

If you were programming in C, this is how you would declare the functions:

```
BOOL mciExecute(lpstrCommand)

DWORD micSendString(lpstrCommand, lpstrReturnString,
                    wReturnLength, hCallback)
```

This is relatively obscure, but then that's the nature of C as a language.[18] Here is how you declare the functions for Visual Basic:

```
Declare Function mciExecute Lib "mmsystem"
➡ (ByVal MCI_Command As String) As Integer

Declare Function mciSendString Lib "mmsystem"
➡(ByVal MCI_Command As String, ByVal ReturnString As String, ByVal
➡ ReturnLength As Integer, ByVal Handle As Integer) As Long
```

There is an additional function that you'll also find useful—mciGetErrorString, which gives you a text string that describes the nature of an MCI error. Here's the Visual Basic declaration:

```
Declare Function mciGetErrorString Lib "mmsystem"
➡(ByVal MCI_Error As Long, ByVal ErrorString As String,
➡ ByVal ReturnLength As Integer) As Integer
```

These Visual Basic examples have the distinct advantage of using mostly real, complete words for the declaration. This means you can access much of the power of windows without having to put up with obfuscation. (There are some things you can't do from Visual Basic, at least easily, but it is still a very accessible way to program in Windows.)

---

[18]C is built more for the guts of computers than for the human mind. C is popular because it gives a programmer access to very low-level machine stuff while still maintaining a (mostly) understandable human interface.

The Visual Basic Code

The following Visual Basic code sends MCI commands using these three functions—mciExecute, mciSendString, and mciGetErrorString. If you have Visual Basic Version 2.0 or greater, you can examine the code by double-clicking the Execute button of MMTEST while in Visual Basic's design mode.

```
Sub Command1_Click ()
   Dim MCI_String As String ' For passing command string.
   Dim ReturnString As String * 1024  'Buffer for return messages.
   Dim ErrorString As String * 1024   'Buffer for error messages.

   ' Get command to execute from text box.
   MCI_String = Text1.Text

   ' Determine which function to use (check a global variable).
   If mciMethod = MCI_EXECUTE Then
      ' Use mciExecute.
      result% = mciExecute(MCI_String)
      'See if the sound was played.
      If result% = 0 Then
         Text2.Text = "Error."
      Else
         Text2.Text = "OK!"
      End If
   Else
      ' Use mciSendString
      result2& = mciSendString(MCI_String, ReturnString, 1024, 0)
      ' See if an error occurred.
      If result2& = 0 Then
         Text2.Text = "OK!"
         ' Display returned message, if any, in a text box.
         Text3.Text = ReturnString
      Else
         ' Get error message using mciGetErrorString
         result% = mciGetErrorString(result2&, ErrorString, 1024)
         Text2.Text = "Error."
         ' Display error message in text box.
         Text3.Text = ErrorString$
      End If
   End If

End Sub
```

Let's take a look at what happens at a few key points in the code (namely, the lines in bold in the code above). The first thing you do is get the text of the MCI command from a text control and put it into a program variable:

```
' Get command to execute from text box.
MCI_String = Text1.Text
```

It's very, very easy to use `mciExecute` to execute the MCI command:

```
' Use mciExecute.
result% = mciExecute(MCI_String)
```

The `mciExecute` function returns a value, which you can check to determine if an error occurred.[19] The `mciSendString` function is slightly more complicated to use but very useful because it returns information in a string:

```
' Use mciSendString
result2& = mciSendString(MCI_String, ReturnString, 1024, 0)
```

There are four arguments used in `mciSendString`: the MCI command, a string that MCI can use to return information to you, the length of the variable `ReturnString`, and a zero. The fourth argument of `mciSendString` isn't usable in Visual Basic—it involves callbacks, and Visual Basic doesn't support callbacks. Because it isn't used, you supply a zero. If an error occurs, the return value of the function will be a number. To find out what the number means, pass it to `mciGetErrorString`:

```
' Get error message using mciGetErrorString
result% = mciGetErrorString(result2&, ErrorString, 1024)
```

The error message will be contained in the string variable `ErrorString`. The three arguments used by `mciGetErrorString` are: the error number returned by `mciSendString`, the string variable,[20] and the length of the string variable.

You can use `mciExecute` and `mciSendString` to send just about any valid MCI command string. For a detailed list of the string commands, refer to Chapter 5 and the section "The Windows Multimedia API." I cannot overemphasize the importance and power of the Command String Interface. Used with `mciSendString`, it gives you the power to access any multimedia device. Such access can include querying the device to discover its capabilities, determining the cause of errors, and controlling the device's operations.

Perhaps the most important aspect of the Command String Interface is that it gives you instant access to new multimedia technologies. If you purchase a video digitizing board (used to capture still and motion video images from TVs, VCRs,

---

[19]`mciExecute` displays an error message if an error occurs. For example, if the file you want to play isn't found, `mciExecute` displays a dialog box informing the user. `mciExecute` does not report the nature of the error to you, but it does tell you if an error occurred. In the code example, you check the return value to see if an error happened.

[20]Both `mciSendString` and `mciGetErrorString` use this technique for returning string information. Because you must specify the length of the string variable, you must use a fixed-length string! Note that two fixed-length strings are declared at the top of the function.

and camcorders), you can use the Command String Interface to control capture and playback from any software product that supports MCI. This means you can be up and running with a new technology in a matter of hours—an unprecedented level of access to the cutting edge of multimedia.

Multimedia Programming with ToolBook

I have had an interesting and varied relationship with ToolBook over the years. I first encountered ToolBook when it was brand new. The company I worked for at the time was using it to develop a prototype of a major software package. I was not part of that team; I was involved in testing, debugging, and C programming on a related project. One of the developers on the ToolBook project (who just happens to have become my wife in the meantime) showed me what she was doing with ToolBook.

My first reaction was puzzlement. I had never done any Windows programming, and ToolBook seemed very puzzling. ToolBook programming is based on objects, events, and handlers. Once I understood how these three things work together in a ToolBook program, I became fascinated with what I could accomplish using ToolBook. That was several years ago, and I'm still discovering new tricks.

ToolBook Basics

ToolBook has its own language for describing itself. A ToolBook program is called a *book,* and each window in the book is called a *page.*

Let's define those three items I mentioned above:

Object—An object can be many different things. Graphics, blocks of text, pages, buttons, lines, and even the book itself are all examples of objects. ToolBook has a palette that you click to select the current object type during development. You can select an object and then move it, change its color or contents, and write code that applies to the object.

Event—Events are simply things that happen. A mouse click, a mouse movement, changing to a new page—all of these are events. You can also define your own events and "send" them to objects.

457

Handler—A handler consists of code, and every handler handles some event. For example, you can write a handler in a button to handle a mouse click;[21] you can write a handler at the page level to handle the event of entering a new page. Handlers are placed in the *script* of an object.

To develop a ToolBook application, you put objects on each page of the book and then write handlers that respond to events associated with each object. Every event "bubbles up" to a higher level until it finds a handler. The lowest level consists of objects you create, like buttons and text fields. The highest level is the book itself. For example, you might put a ButtonUp handler in every button's script, or you could put one giant ButtonUp handler in your book script. The hierarchy of event handling starts with individual objects and proceeds upward to the book script:

```
ToolBook Hierarchy
Book script
      background #1
              bitmap graphic #1
              bitmap graphic #2
              text field #1
              text field #2
              button #1
              page #1
                      button #1
                      button #2
                      text field #1
                      bitmap graphic #1
                      bitmap graphic #2
              page #2
                      button #1
                      button #2
              page #3
                      button #1
                      text field #1
      background #2
              button #1
              button #2
```

---

[21]In truth, each mouse click is made up of two distinct events: MouseDown and MouseUp. Sometimes you need to make this distinction—for example, you might want to flash the button in a particular way when it is clicked. To do so, change the button at MouseDown, and change it back at MouseUp.

```
page #4
        button #1
        button #2
        group #1
                button #3
                button #4
                text field #1
        group #2
                button #5
                button #6
                text field #2
page #5
        button #1
        text field #1
        text field #2
```

For example, if you click button #2 on page #4, ToolBook will first look for a ButtonUp handler in button #2. If none is found, it will look for a ButtonUp handler in page #4, then in background #2, and finally in the book script. As a second example, if you click bitmap graphic #2 in background #1, ToolBook will first look for a ButtonUp handler in bitmap graphic #2, then in background #1, and finally in the book script. Groups add another layer to the pattern because you can also put a handler in a group's script. For example, if you click button #6 in group #2 of page #4, ToolBook will search for a ButtonUp handler in this order: button #6, group #2, page #4, background #2, the book script.

Just to add a little spice, you can add the "forward" command to a handler to send it up the chain even though you wrote a handler for it. For example, you might have a ButtonUp handler in the book script that plays a beep sound. After handling the ButtonUp events locally, you would forward them so the book script can make the beep sound happen.

Creating a ToolBook Application

That's enough background information; let's look at how you can create a multimedia application using Multimedia ToolBook. Figure 8.18 shows the appearance of the final application, which will play a video file. The application consists of a window where the video will appear and various buttons to control playback.

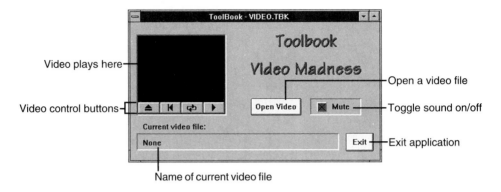

Video plays here

Video control buttons

Open a video file

Toggle sound on/off

Current video file:

Name of current video file

Exit application

Figure 8.18. *The ToolBook Video Madness application will look like this.*

Figure 8.19 shows the starting point for creating the application: a blank ToolBook window. ToolBook has two modes of operation: author and reader. Figure 8.19 shows the author mode, which has full menus. (Figure 8.18 shows the reader mode, with all menus removed.[22]) The author mode also includes a small box at lower left that you can use to move to the various pages in your application.

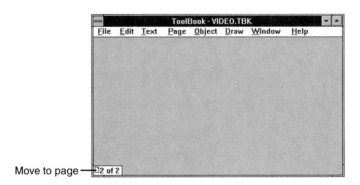

Move to page

Figure 8.19. *The ToolBook opening screen.*

To begin, add a simple rectangle to the page (Figure 8.20). You can use the Color Palette (not shown) to change the color of any object; I chose black for this object. This object was created using ToolBook's drawing tools.

---

[22]You can keep some of the menu choices around in reader mode, but they are not needed for this application.

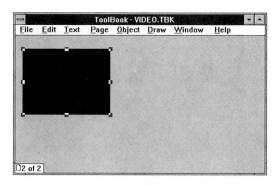

Figure 8.20. *Adding a rectangle to the application.*

Each object in a ToolBook application can have properties. Figure 8.21 shows the dialog for setting the properties of a graphic object. I have given the object a name—video—in the Draw Object Name field. You can use this name to refer to the object in your handlers.

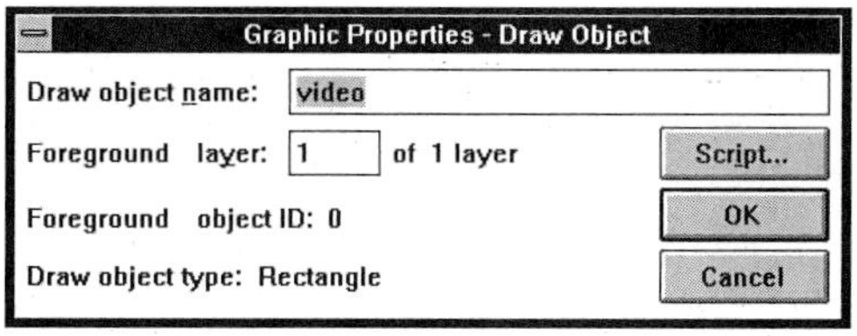

Figure 8.21. *Giving an object a name.*

Next I added[23] a number of miscellaneous objects to the application (Figure 8.22). These include some text and various line objects to create a 3-D look.

The word None at the bottom of the page is a text object; ToolBook calls these *fields*. Figure 8.23 shows the properties you can set for a field; there are a lot more than for a rectangle.

---

[23]To add a new object, you click in the tool palette, and then click and drag on the page to determine the size and shape of the new object.

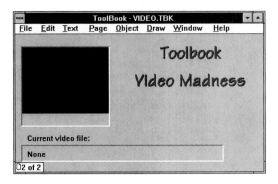

Figure 8.22. *Adding miscellaneous objects to the application.*

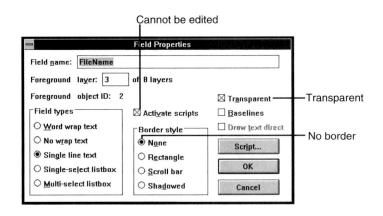

Figure 8.23. *Setting properties of a field.*

This object also gets a name, FileName.[24] There are two other things worth noting. One, the Activate Scripts checkbox is checked. This is usually done to permit a text field to be used just like a button, but in this case I did it to prevent the user from typing in the field when the program is run. Two, I made the field Transparent so that only the text itself will show up against the background.

So far, all you have done is add objects—you haven't written a single line of code yet. That's now going to change when you add the new button shown in Figure 8.24.

---

[24]Not all objects need names. Normally, you only name an object if you need to refer to it in a handler somewhere. Most objects don't need a name at all.

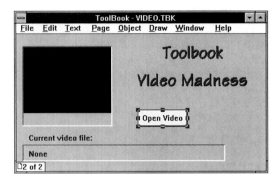

Figure 8.24. *Adding a button to open video files.*

Press Control+F6 to enter the button's text: Open Video. Then double-click the button while holding down the Control key to open its script. Enter the following lines of code:

```
to handle ButtonUp
    send GetFilename
    put my filename into text of field "FileName"

    — Close the alias in case it happens to be open.
    get tbkMCI("close vidFile","")

    get tbkMCIchk("open" && my filename && "alias vidFile style
➥popup","",1,1)
    — Place the video window within our rectangle
    get tbkMCIPositionWindow("vidFile", bounds of rectangle "video","")
    — Display the video window.
    get tbkMCI("window vidFile state show","")

    — Turn sound on or off, as required.
    if checked of button "MuteButton" is True
        get tbkMCIchk("setaudio vidFile off","","")
    else
        get tbkMCIchk("setaudio vidFile on","","")
    end if
end ButtonUp

to handle GetFilename
    system FileOpen

    get OpenDlg(".","*.avi", "Select a video file.", "Select Video
➥File")
    if it is null
        set FileOpen to False
        clear my filename
```

```
        break to system
    else
        set FileOpen to True
        set my filename to it
    end if
end
```

There is a lot happening in these two handlers. The first handler is executed when the MouseUp event occurs—that is, when you click the Open Video button. The second handler gets called by the first handler. Let's look at these two handlers closely.

The ButtonUp handler begins by generating an event with the send command:

```
send GetFilename
```

This event goes first to the current object (the Open Video button), and because there is a handler here, it will go no further.[25] The GetFilename handler is described below.

The GetFilename handler puts a filename in a local variable, filename. Note the use of the word my to indicate that the variable is local. The filename is placed into the text field you created on the page:

```
put my filename into text of field "FileName"
```

Just in case a video file is already open with the alias VidFile, you close it:

```
— Close the alias in case it happens to be open.
get tbkMCI("close vidFile","")
```

Note that the function tbkMCI is used to pass the command string to MCI.[26] Even if there is an error—that is, even if no video file is open with the alias VidFile, no error will be reported. This behavior is ideally suited to the task at hand.

---

[25]You can also send events to specific objects. For example, to send a ButtonUp event to a button, you would type send ButtonUp to <button name> substituting the actual name of the button.

[26]The second argument for tbkMCI is null in this example. You can use the second argument to specify an object that will receive notification when the command completes—this is how ToolBook supports callbacks. The following code shows how easy it is to handle notification:

```
to handle tbkMMNotify status, operation, device
    if status && operation && device = "successful play vidFile"
    get tbkMCI("close vidFile","")
    end if
end tbkMMNotify
```

Sometimes, of course, if an error occurs, you want to notify the user. For example, the following statement, which opens the video file, uses the function `tbkMCIchk` to pass the command string to MCI:

```
get tbkMCIchk("open" && my filename && "alias vidFile style
➥popup","",1,1)
```

There are four arguments used by this function: the MCI command string, the object to notify (null in this case), and two additional arguments. The third argument controls whether an error message should be displayed when an error occurs, and the final argument controls behavior after the error.

If you enter a null ("") for the first argument, no error message will display; `tbkMCIchk` will behave just like `tbkMCI`. Any non-null argument will cause the error message to be displayed by MCI. If you enter a null for the final argument, ToolBook will continue with the next line of code after the error. If you enter any non-null value, ToolBook will act as though the "break to system" command was encountered. This causes ToolBook to ignore the rest of the code in the handler.

These two functions, `tbkMCI` and `tbkMCIchk`, are your gateway to MCI in ToolBook. Use them instead of `mciExecute` and `mciSendString`. They give you access to ToolBook's own multimedia support, including callbacks.

Once the video file has been opened,[27] you need to position the playback window. This is a bit tedious using MCI command strings, but ToolBook offers an easy alternative: the `tbkMCIPositionWindow` function. The following bit of code positions the window and then displays it:

```
— Place the video window within our rectangle
get tbkMCIPositionWindow("vidFile", bounds of rectangle "video","")
— Display the video window.
get tbkMCI("window vidFile state show","")
```

`tbkMCIPositionWindow` takes three arguments. It is an extremely flexible function, depending on exactly what you pass as the arguments. The three arguments are:

Device—The filename or alias of the open device (in this case, `vidFile`).

Position—This argument can be one of the following:

---

[27]In this case, as a popup window; a popup has no caption or borders.

➤ The new position for the window, expressed as x,y coordinates.

➤ The new bounds for the window, expressed as x1,y1,x2,y2 coordinates, where x1,y1 defines the position of the top left corner, and x2,y2 defines the position of the bottom right corner.[28]

➤ The keywords `full screen` or `full page`, to specify that the new bounds for the window should be the full screen or the full client window of the current ToolBook instance.

Options—These can be either null, as in this example, or one or more of the following:

`pixels` specifies that the coordinates are given in pixels. If `pixels` is omitted, the coordinates are assumed to be in ToolBook page units.

`page units` confirms the default units to be used and changes nothing.

`absolute` overrides the default origin used to compute the position of the window. If you specify `absolute`, the position or rectangle will be relative to the screen; otherwise, the position or rectangle will be relative to the top-left corner of the current ToolBook client window.

`relative` confirms the default origin and changes nothing.

`client rectangle` (can be abbreviated `client rect`) specifies that the given bounds are for the desired client rectangle of the window rather than for the window frame. This is useful if you want to make the contents of an overlapped window match the bounds of an object on a ToolBook page.

If this function seems a little complicated, that's because of the power involved. Without this function, you would have to write literally hundreds of lines of code to control playback position.

The last lines of code in this handler determine if audio should be heard. You haven't added it yet, but there will soon be a checkbox button that will be used to determine if audio is on or off. When you open a file, you simply see if the button is checked or not, and then send the appropriate MCI control to turn audio on or off:

```
— Turn sound on or off, as required.
if checked of button "MuteButton" is True
    get tbkMCIchk("setaudio vidFile off","","")
```

---

[28]This is used in the example: `bounds of rectangle "video"`.

```
else
    get tbkMCIchk("setaudio vidFile on","","")
end if
```

In just these few lines of code, you have opened the file, positioned it at the exact boundaries of a ToolBook rectangle, and set audio on or off. As you can see, the key to MCI access are the two functions, `tbkMCI` and `tbkMCIchk`.

The second handler in this button is used to get a filename. It declares a system variable, `FileOpen`, which is used to determine if in fact a file is open by other objects and their handlers.

```
system FileOpen
```

To get a filename, use the `OpenDlg` function to open a dialog box with all of the usual file-open capabilities:

```
get OpenDlg(".","*.avi", "Select a video file.", "Select Video File")
```

The verb `get` puts the return value of the function in the ToolBook system variable `it`. You can check the value of `it` and act accordingly. If `it` is null,

```
if it is null
```

then set `FileOpen` to `False`, blank the variable that normally holds the filename, and break to the system:[29]

```
set FileOpen to False
clear my filename
break to system
```

If `it` has some value, set `FileOpen` to `True` and put the filename into the local variable `filename`.

```
else
    set FileOpen to True
    set my filename to it
end if
```

This may seem like a lot of activity in just one object script, but this is actually pretty typical of ToolBook code. It is usually short and to the point, with a lot happening in a few lines of code.

Now let's return to the ToolBook window. Figure 8.25 shows the addition of another button, labeled "Exit." This button can be used to terminate the application at runtime.

---

[29]That is, abort the handler and return to the system level. This means we will not go back to the handler that called us.

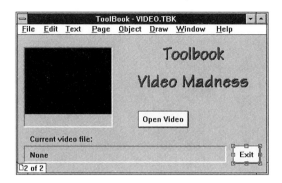

Figure 8.25. *Adding a new button.*

The code for the Exit button's script is very simple:

```
to handle ButtonUp
     send exit
end
```

Next you add four buttons below the video rectangle as shown in Figure 8.26. These buttons will be used to control playback of the video.

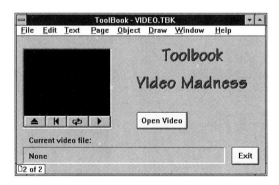

Figure 8.26. *Four buttons to control video playback.*

From left to right, these buttons will: close the file, rewind the file, initiate looping playback, and play the file.[30] Let's look at the code that accomplishes each of these tasks. First is the code for the close button:

---

[30]The images on these buttons are actually a special font provided with ToolBook that contains symbols rather than letters.

```
to handle buttonDown
    system FileOpen

    — Make sure file is open.
    if FileOpen is False
        break to system
    end if

    get tbkMCIchk("close vidFile","")
    send setcaption "Play" to button "play"
    put "None" into text of field "FileName"
    set FileOpen to False
end
```

This code is straightforward: if no file is open, the handler breaks to the system. Otherwise, a call to tbkMCIchk closes the file and a few housekeeping details are taken care of.

The rewind button is equally straightforward. It also checks to make sure a file is open and then uses the MCI command seek to move to the first frame of the video. It also creates an event with the send command, sending it to the play button.

```
to handle buttonDown
    system FileOpen

    — Make sure file is open.
    if FileOpen is False
        break
    end if

    get tbkMCI("seek vidFile to 1","")
    send setCaption "play" to button "play"
end
```

The loop button puts ToolBook's callback/notification capabilities to good use. When it calls tbkMCIchk, it uses self as the second argument. This identifies this button as the object that should receive notification when the MCI play command completes.

```
to handle buttonDown
    system FileOpen

    — Make sure file is open.
    if FileOpen is False
        break
    end if

    get tbkMCIchk("play vidFile",self, "", "")
    send setCaption "pause" to button "play"
end
```

469

When the play completes, a tbkMMNotify event is sent to the loop button. The following code, located in the buttons script along with the above buttonDown handler, handles the event:

```
to handle tbkMMNotify stat, mcimode, dev
    conditions
    when mcimode is "play" and stat contains "success"
        get tbkMCI("seek vidFile to start",self)
    when mcimode is "seek" and stat contains "success"
        get tbkMCI("play vidFile", self)
    end
end
```

As you can see, it watches for two specific situations: when a play command completes, it then seeks to the beginning of the file. Note that when it does so it again sets itself as the object to be notified. When the seek to start completes, another tbkMMNotify event is sent, and the file is played again. This process repeats over and over until you close the file.

The play button also has multiple handlers. One handler takes care of actually playing the file, and the second one is used to control the appearance of the play button. When nothing is playing, the play button displays a right-facing arrow; while a file is playing, the button displays a vertical pair of bars. The bars indicate that the play button is now a pause button.

```
to handle buttonDown
    system FileOpen

    — Make sure file is open.
    if FileOpen is False
        break
    end if

    get charToAnsi(char 1 of my caption)
    if it is 167 — pause
        get tbkMCIchk("pause vidFile","",1)
        get yieldApp()
        send setCaption "play"
    else
        get tbkMCIchk("play vidFile","",1)
        get yieldApp()
        send setCaption "pause"
    end
end

to handle setCaption what
    if what is "pause"
        set my caption to ansiToChar(167) — pause
```

```
        else
            set my caption to ansiToChar(173) — play
        end
end
```

The code in the Open Video button's script referred to a mute checkbox; now is the time to add it. Figure 8.27 shows the Mute button added.

Figure 8.27. *Adding a Mute button.*

I've played some tricks to make the Mute button look like it does; that's not how a standard ToolBook checkbox button looks. The 3-D graphic elements are actually just lines drawn on the page, and the checkbox itself was made transparent. However, as you can see in Figure 8.28, if you place the invisible checkbox on top of the graphic elements, it will be the object that receives mouse-click events.

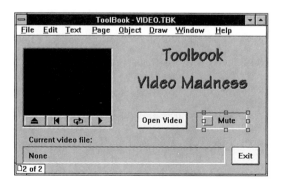

Figure 8.28. *The invisible Mute checkbox.*

Figure 8.29 shows the various pieces of the Mute "button" spread out. The checkbox itself can be identified by the box-shaped handles that mark its margin. Note that the × indicating that the box has been checked shows up even if the box is invisible. The dark square box to the left of the text "Mute" is red and has a name, MuteOn. When the button is clicked, the red box can be made to appear and disappear. Here is the code for the Mute button:

```
to handle ButtonUp
    if Checked of self is True
        get tbkMCIchk("setaudio vidFile off","","")
        show field "MuteOn"
    else
        get tbkMCIchk("setaudio vidFile on","","")
        hide field "MuteOn"
    end if
end
```

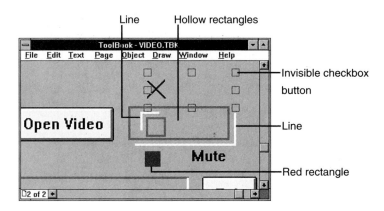

Figure 8.29. *The various pieces of the Mute button.*

If the button is checked, audio is turned off and the little red box named MuteOn is displayed. If the button is not checked, audio is turned on and the little red box is hidden. Figure 8.30 shows the application in action, with the Mute button checked and a video playing in the rectangle.

However, the application is not quite complete. You need to add a handler to the book script that will be executed when the book opens. This is called the enterBook handler, and it is common to add one to a ToolBook application. You typically use the enterBook handler to set up various parameters for the application. The following enterBook handler establishes the initial value of the FileOpen variable and sets the system variable sysChangesDb to False—that way, the application can be exited without the user being asked if he wants to save changes. Because your application makes changes to the contents of a test field, this is a necessary step.

Figure 8.30. *The application in action.*

In addition, the code hides the menu bar (it won't be needed) and sends the sizetopage event.[31] It then forwards the enterBook event—just in case ToolBook needs to do anything further. It's always a good idea to forward this event.

```
to handle enterBook
    system FileOpen

    set FileOpen to False
    set sysChangesDb to false

    hide menubar
    send sizetopage
    forward
end
```

This concludes the tour of Multimedia ToolBook. ToolBook is a very powerful tool for multimedia development. It can take a while to really get the hang of using it—there's a lot of power available, and the documentation is weak. However, if you persist, you will be rewarded with a powerful tool in your development arsenal.

---

[31]When you remove the menu bar, the size of the page and the size of the window no longer match. Sending this event forces the window to be resized to match the page size. As a side effect, the whole application is placed at the center of the screen.

Programming with Multimedia Viewer 2.0

Of the three programming tools I describe in detail in this chapter—Visual Basic, ToolBook, and Viewer—Viewer is by far the most enigmatic and difficult to describe. On the one hand, you can use Viewer to quickly create a multimedia application from a text file, adding sound, video, animation, images, and so on. On the other hand, Viewer is a bit quirky to use and can be frustrating at times. I find myself really enjoying working with Viewer, and then all of a sudden I run into something that I can't get to work, so I go back to the documentation, puzzle it out awhile, and then suddenly I realize how it is done. Then I'm happy again.

The reason for these bouts of frustration comes straight out of the very essence of Viewer. Viewer is, well, different.[32]

Different is not bad, however. For example, instead of developing your application in some kind of fancy graphical interface, you do it in a word processor—Word for Windows is "home base" for Viewer. Viewer is a compiler. You feed it your Word for Windows file, and out comes a multimedia application.

Because Viewer is so different, I provide a very detailed tutorial that shows a variety of things you can do with Viewer. I also explore the basics of working with Viewer because there aren't yet very many books out to help you get started with it.

Viewer Overview

Here's an overview of what you need to do to create a Viewer application:

1. Collect everything that will be part of the application, including the text, bitmaps, videos, animations, sounds, and so on in one place. This can be one directory or a series of directories.

2. Convert all materials to the formats Viewer uses. This means putting your text into Word for Windows, images into .BMP or .DIB files, and so on.

3. Format the text as you want it to appear in the final application. This includes such things as paragraph indent, bold/italic, fonts, font size, and so on.

---

[32]Unless you count the Windows Help system, from which Viewer was derived.

4. Divide the text into topics and add topic titles and keywords.[33]

5. Add multimedia elements (pictures, videos, animations, and so on).

6. Compile the application with the Viewer Project Editor.

Of course, you won't follow exactly these steps in exactly this order every time. You can easily go back and add more multimedia elements, revise text, and so on—after all, you are working in a word processor. You can work on any part of your file at any time.

This ability to move around anywhere in your file is part of the flexibility and the confusion of Viewer. It is up to you to keep yourself organized at all times. For example, Viewer won't give you a list of your context strings, so you'll need to track them down if you lose track. The secret: don't lose track!

Getting Started with Viewer

Once you have collected all the pieces you need for your application, open the text file in Word for Windows. If the document is not already a Word for Windows file, it won't look like much before you start. Figure 8.31 shows a typical bit of text, which just happens to be Chapter 2 of the book you hold in your hands.[34] As you can see, the layout isn't much to look at. The font is Courier and not very appealing.

The first step is to switch to outline view (the **V**iew|**O**utline menu selection does it) and arrange the material in outline form, as shown in Figure 8.32. This makes it easy to organize the material and to change it later if you so desire. You can use the formatting capabilities of Word for Windows to change the format of any level of the outline all at once, which makes it very easy to modify your overall design down the road.

You also need to format the text itself. This includes such things as deciding on a font for the text and laying out special features like tables, figure captions, and so on. Figure 8.33 shows a section of the text that contains a table with formatting finished.

---

[33]In Viewer, what you would normally call a keyword is referred to as a *context string*.

[34]Chapter 2 appears as a complete Viewer application on the Nautilus CD-ROM disc.

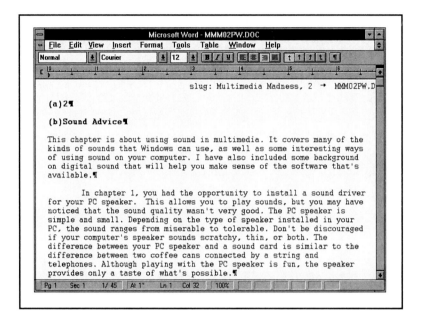

Figure 8.31. *Text opened in Word for Windows.*

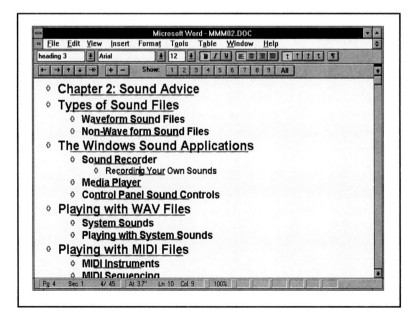

Figure 8.32. *Rearranging everything into an outline.*

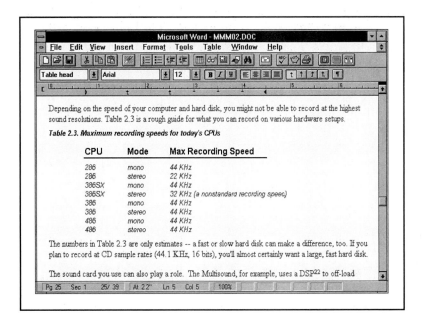

Depending on the speed of your computer and hard disk, you might not be able to record at the highest sound resolutions. Table 2.3 is a rough guide for what you can record on various hardware setups.

Table 2.3. Maximum recording speeds for today's CPUs

CPU	Mode	Max Recording Speed
286	mono	44 KHz
286	stereo	22 KHz
386SX	mono	44 KHz
386SX	stereo	32 KHz (a nonstandard recording speed)
386	mono	44 KHz
386	stereo	44 KHz
486	mono	44 KHz
486	stereo	44 KHz

The numbers in Table 2.3 are only estimates -- a fast or slow hard disk can make a difference, too. If you plan to record at CD sample rates (44.1 KHz, 16 bits), you'll almost certainly want a large, fast hard disk.

The sound card you use can also play a role. The Multisound, for example, uses a DSP[22] to off-load

Figure 8.33. *A formatted table in the text.*

Once everything is nice and pretty, you are ready to get started with the actual work of tailoring the text for use with Viewer. To begin, go to each outline heading in the text and add a hard page break before it by pressing Control+Enter.[35] Word for Windows adds a thin line where you place the page breaks as shown in Figure 8.34.

The text between each pair of page breaks is referred to as a *topic*. In the final application, all text in a topic appears as a unit.

This is about as far as you would want to go with only your word processor running. It's time to start using the Viewer Project Editor. To begin, save the file using the RTF format.[36] This is the format supported by Viewer. It's an all-text form of saving the file that preserves all the formatting information in the file. Normally, Word for Windows uses a binary format—that is, it uses a lot of computer shorthand to store formatting information. An RTF file, on the other hand,

---

[35]You cannot simply use Word for Windows' ability to add page breaks in styles; you have to add a real page break by hand or by macro. Viewer will also do this for you, but I prefer to go through the entire document by hand adding the page breaks because then I know I haven't missed any.

[36]Rich Text Format—that is, everything about the formatting is described in text.

uses only text to describe what's going on. For example, here's a section from the .RTF file for the Chapter 2 document:

```
\par \pard\plain \s31\qc\li216\ri216\sa240\sl-240\keepn \b\i\f4\fs20\lang1033
Figure 2.17. A stepped wave form.

\par \pard\plain \s3\li216\ri216\sb120\sa120 \f3\fs20\lang1033 There are
numerous differences between the wave forms, including changes to the peaks
of waves, changes in the slope of the wave form, and a loss of high frequen-
cies.

\par As the sample rate increases, you can resolve smaller details of the
sound. High sample rates enable you to distinguish smaller distances be-
tween wave peaks.
```

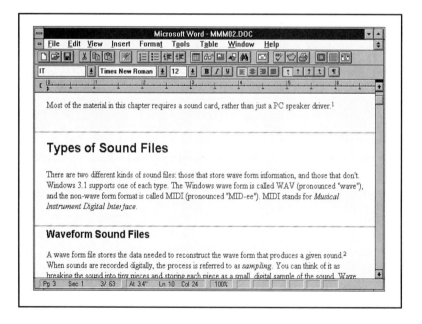

Figure 8.34. *Adding page breaks to each outline heading.*

Everything that follows a backslash (\) specifies formatting information. For example, \par means new paragraph, and \keepn means keep together with next paragraph. \li216 specifies a left indent of 216 units, and \ri216 does the same for the right margin.

I have some very good news: you can, and probably will, never have to look at the guts of an RTF file if you use Viewer.

The Viewer Project Editor

Figure 8.35 shows the Viewer Project Editor window. There is a menu at the top, a button bar, a text field for entering filenames, and a large work area with two strange-looking labels attached: RTF and Baggage.[37]

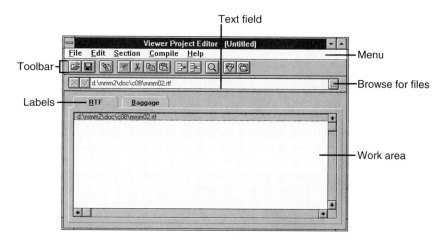

Figure 8.35. *The Viewer Project Editor.*

To add an RTF file to the project, you can enter the name into the text field, or you can use the button with three small dots at the right of the text field to browse for files. All RTF files you add show up in the work area when the RTF label is active. Baggage refers to everything else that goes into your project—bitmaps, sound files, and so on. To see your baggage, click the label.

Before using the Project Editor, you should click the Edit|Preferences menu selection to display the Preferences dialog box (Figure 8.36). You might need to enter the path to Word for Windows, and you can select the hot key to use for the Topic Editor, about which you will learn more later. I would suggest either Control+Shift+T, or Control+Shift+Alt+T.

---

[37]Have no fear; all will be revealed.

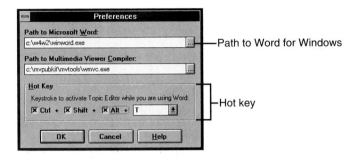

Figure 8.36. The Preferences dialog box.

Now a little diversion. Because Viewer wants to work with .RTF files and Word for Windows works with .DOC files, you have to take some extra steps to save your work as an .RTF file. Fortunately, Viewer comes with a macro that you can install in Word for Windows that makes saving as an .RTF file very, very easy. I strongly recommend you take the time to install this macro. Figure 8.37 shows the macro itself.

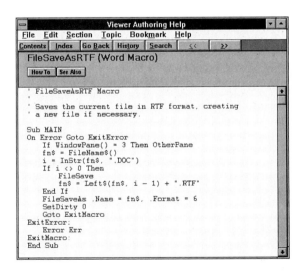

*Figure 8.37. The **FileSaveAsRTF** macro.*

You don't have to understand what the macro does, or how, to use it.[38] Pages 2–25 and 2–26 of the Viewer documentation tell you how, step by step. If you are adventurous, add a Save as RTF command to your file menu using Tools|Options|Menus.

To edit the .RTF file from the Project Editor, just double-click the filename in the work area. This will run Word for Windows.

> **Hint:** To make Word load faster, keep an instance of Word for Windows running as an icon at all times. You don't even have to have a file open because the Project Editor will open a new instance for each file you edit.

Once you have the .RTF document open in Word, it looks just the same as it did when it was a .DOC file—an .RTF file contains all of the formatting information. The Word document also still has those page breaks you added earlier between the topics.

The Viewer Topic Editor

Topics are the heart and soul of Viewer. Each topic is a single unit as far as Viewer is concerned. However, Viewer needs a little more information. Viewer uses *topic titles* to refer to your topics, and it uses *context strings* to move to a topic. To add titles and context strings, you use the Topic Editor. Place the cursor after a page break and before the first character in the first line of a topic. To access the Topic Editor, simply use the key combination you set in the Project Editor's preferences dialog. This displays the New Viewer Element dialog box shown in Figure 8.38.

Note that the second element is highlighted: `Context string (# footnote)`. Time for a heavy sigh: what is this stuff about a "# footnote?" I shall attempt to explain. Remember when I said that Viewer was different? Well, Viewer is *different*.

---

[38]It's actually a pretty simple macro. It just replaces the .DOC extension with the .RTF extension and then saves the document with "Format = 6". That's the .RTF format, of course.

Figure 8.38. *The New Viewer Element dialog box of the Topic Editor.*

Think of your text file as the contents of the multimedia program you want to create. You need some kind of container for the content, right? Well, there sort of isn't one. The text file itself contains the instructions about how to access the information in your Viewer program.

For example, you use a context string when you want to jump to a topic. Using some mumbo jumbo that I will show you shortly, you use the exact context string to tell Viewer: go to the topic with this context string. The information about the context string is stored in a footnote. That's right: in a footnote. This is nothing more than a bit of smoke and mirrors, but it works. On the one hand, the context string information is safely out of the way, in a footnote, where it won't get in the way of your text content. On the other hand, you can use the View|Footnote menu selection to display footnotes and see what's what. Weird, but it works great.[39]

Look back at Figure 8.38. The first seven entries all cause footnotes to be created, each with a different symbol. For example a topic title gets a "$" footnote, and a topic-entry command gets a "!" footnote. Each footnote contains whatever cryptic Viewer command is required. In the first version of Viewer, that was the bad news. However, Version 2.0 of Viewer takes a much more sensible approach. The Topic Editor constructs the cryptic Viewer command for you.

---

[39]When I am explaining Viewer to someone in person, this is the point where I begin to feel like a guy who has seen a vampire or a ghost, and I'm trying to explain it to someone who did *not* see it. I get the strangest looks. Perhaps one of those puzzled looks is on your face right now. As I said, all will be revealed. Do not despair!

To proceed with creating a context string, click the OK button. Figure 8.39 shows the result: the Viewer Topic Editor in all its glory. On the left is a list of the current Viewer Elements. On the right is a Context String. Because, in my case, I have positioned the cursor in the very first topic—the Introduction—I have cleverly used the context string Introduction. Click OK to close the Topic Editor.

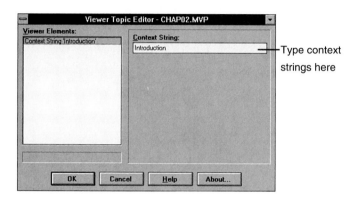

Type context strings here

Figure 8.39. *Editing a context string.*

Pretty heady stuff, I know. But let's not stop now: let's add a topic title. I prefer to keep things simple; life has a way of complicating things, so why invite problems? Open the Topic Editor again, without changing the position of the cursor, and this time choose Topic title ($ footnote). Click OK, which displays a slightly different Topic Editor window (Figure 8.40). This time, instead of Context String on the right, it says Title. Big deal—I entered Introduction again. This is something I do, always: my titles and my context strings are always the same. Mostly. Context strings have restrictions:

➤ They can be a maximum of 255 characters long.

➤ They consist only of letters A–Z, numbers, periods, and underscores.

➤ Each context string must be unique.

➤ Context strings are not case sensitive.

Titles have some rules, too:

➤ Only one title per topic is allowed.

➤ Titles can be a maximum of 127 characters long.

➤ Embedded spaces are okay.

483

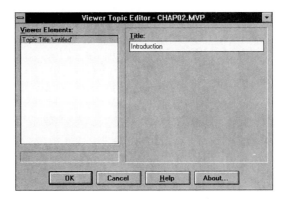

Figure 8.40. *Adding a topic title.*

Thus, if I use a space in a title, I will use either an underscore or a period in the context string. For example, one of the context strings in my Viewer project is `Voice_recognition`. The corresponding title is `Voice Recognition`. I used a title of `Table 2.1: General MIDI Sounds`, and the context string was `Table_2.1`.

Figure 8.41 shows the results of these actions back in Word for Windows. I opened the footnote window to show what's going on. Ignore the existing footnotes; I had not yet converted the footnotes to regular text.[40] I have added points to two of the footnotes. One is a context string, and the other is a topic title. Note also that the special footnote characters have been added at the beginning of the section—right after the page break and right before the first text.

Before you move on to the next batch of Viewer goodies, you should make sure that hidden text is displayed in your document.[41] To do this, use the Tools|Options menu selection to display the dialog box shown in Figure 8.42. Make sure that the checkbox for hidden text is checked as shown.

---

[40]Viewer does not display any of your text that happens to be in footnotes. It assumes that anything that's a footnote should stay hidden. Because I used footnotes extensively (why, we're in a footnote now, aren't we?), I had a lot of converting to do.

[41]Word for Windows uses hidden text to enable you to put notes in your document that can be hidden at print time, or any other time for that matter.

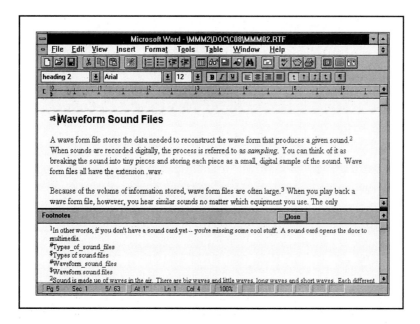

Figure 8.41. *The footnotes as they appear in Word.*

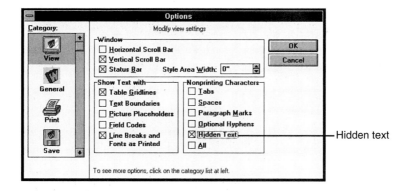

Figure 8.42. *Displaying hidden text.*

Creating a Table of Contents

The first topic in a Viewer application is usually a table of contents. Sadly, Viewer will not create one for you. You have to do it yourself. If you are using an outline, it's relatively easy to create a table of contents. Switch to outline view, collapse all text so that only the outline shows (as shown way back in Figure 8.32), and then use File|Print to print the outline. You'll get just the outline on the print-out. Use that to select the topics that you want to appear in the contents. You can show just the main topics or you can show every topic in your document— the choice is up to you. What you choose will probably vary with the nature and complexity of your text contents.

With the outline in front of you, move to the top of your document and type in the various topic titles as shown in Figure 8.43. You may want to indent, use larger and smaller fonts, and so on to show the relative importance of each topic to the reader.

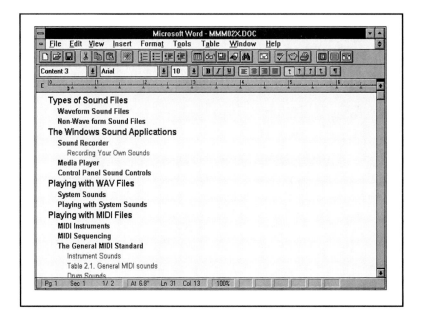

Figure 8.43. *Entering the table of contents manually.*

You should also add a topic title and context string, both saying "Contents." This enables you to refer to the contents just like any other topic. Look at Figure 8.44. Note that there are the usual two footnote markers ("#" and "$") before the text at the top of the window.

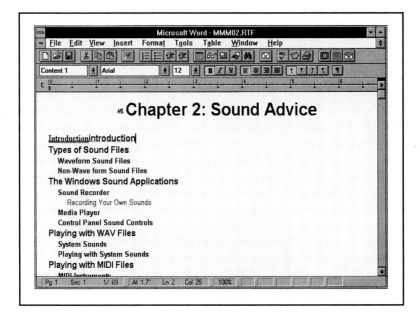

Figure 8.44. *Adding a table of contents.*

Look at the line that says `Introduction`. Note that the word *introduction* is repeated twice. The first instance has a double underline, and the second one has a thin, dotted line under it. This is more Viewer magic at work. First, I'll explain what this is, and then I'll show you how to do it in the privacy of your own desk.

The first instance of the word *introduction* is the word that will appear in the table of contents. The double underline means that Viewer will make it appear in green when the application is run. This is a text *hot spot*—that is, if the user clicks on the hot spot, something will happen. The second instance of *introduction* determines what will happen. It is hidden text.[42]

It is also a context string. This combination—double-underlined text followed by hidden text—is Viewer's way of creating a jump to a topic. This is perfect for a table of contents. The user sees a list of words highlighted in green. When he clicks on a word or phrase, Viewer takes him to the associated topic.

---

[42]Hidden text is indicated in Word by that little dotted underline. If you don't set hidden text to display, you won't be able to see all the cool stuff that Viewer's Topic Editor adds to your document, and you can't edit it, either.

To create a hot spot:

1. Select the text that will be the hot spot. The next entry in the table of contents is Types of Sound Files. I selected the entire phrase.

2. Press the hot-key combination that invokes the Topic Editor. This displays the dialog box shown in Figure 8.45. Click OK. This displays the dialog box shown in Figure 8.46.

3. Click Jump to 'jump_or_command'. Tab twice to move the cursor to the entry for Context String. Type in the context string of the destination. In this case, that is Types_of_sound_files. Click OK.

Figure 8.45. *Adding a text hot spot.*

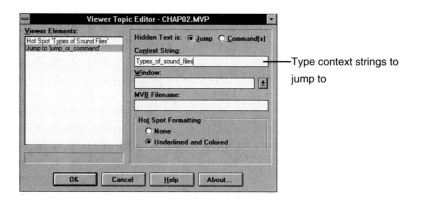

Figure 8.46. *Editing a text hot spot.*

You repeat this process for each entry in the contents. The result looks something like Figure 8.47, with each contents entry followed by hidden text specifying the topic to jump to.

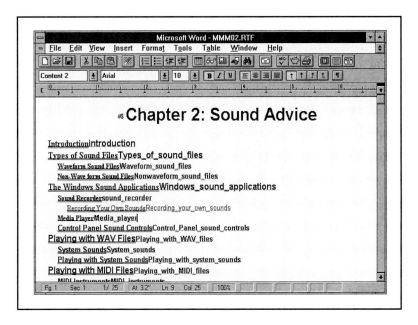

Figure 8.47. *Hot spots have been added to all contents entries.*

Using a Viewer Application

When the application is compiled, all you will see are the contents entries themselves, not the hidden text, as shown in Figure 8.48. Each entry shows up in green and with an underline.

Clicking on an entry in the table of contents jumps you to that topic. For example, if you click `Playing with System Sounds`, you jump to the text shown in Figure 8.49. Note that you haven't added any figures yet; the reference to Figure 2.8 is still just text.

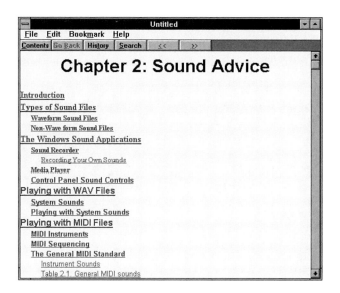

Figure 8.48. *The actual Viewer application.*

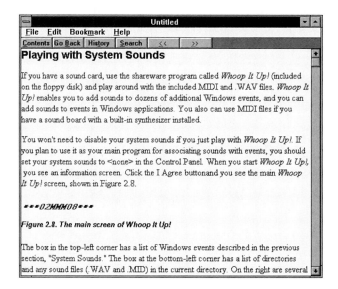

Figure 8.49. *Jumping to a topic.*

The good news is that, by simply adding topic titles, context strings, and a table of contents with hot spots, you can create a simple Viewer application. While you have the application up and running, let's take a look at some of the features that you get for free when you use Viewer. By free I mean you do not have to do any programming on your own to make anything happen—it's just there.[43]

For example, by simply clicking on the Search button that Viewer so kindly put into your application, your users can search for things that interest them. Figure 8.50 shows the search dialog, where I have entered the word *piano* as a search criteria.

Figure 8.50. *The built-in search capability of Viewer applications.*

Clicking the OK button executes the search. Figure 8.51 shows the results: a list of topic titles that contain the word *piano*. To view the contents of the topic, just highlight it and click the Go To button.

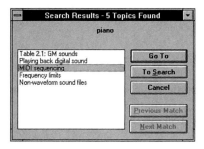

Figure 8.51. *A list of topic titles.*

Figure 8.52 shows the result: a topic with the search word highlighted.

---

[43]Wouldn't it be great if all programming languages gave you lots of stuff for free like this?

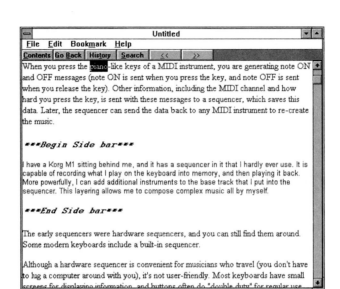

When you press the piano-like keys of a MIDI instrument, you are generating note ON and OFF messages (note ON is sent when you press the key, and note OFF is sent when you release the key). Other information, including the MIDI channel and how hard you press the key, is sent with these messages to a sequencer, which saves this data. Later, the sequencer can send the data back to any MIDI instrument to re-create the music.

Begin Side bar

I have a Korg M1 sitting behind me, and it has a sequencer in it that I hardly ever use. It is capable of recording what I play on the keyboard into memory, and then playing it back. More powerfully, I can add additional instruments to the base track that I put into the sequencer. This layering allows me to compose complex music all by myself.

End Side bar

The early sequencers were hardware sequencers, and you can still find them around. Some modern keyboards include a built-in sequencer.

Although a hardware sequencer is convenient for musicians who travel (you don't have to lug a computer around with you), it's not user-friendly. Most keyboards have small screens for displaying information, and buttons often do "double duty" for regular use.

Figure 8.52. *A topic with the search word highlighted.*

This concludes (mostly) your introduction to Viewer. Now, let's look at how to add some multimedia elements to the application.

Adding Multimedia Elements

Viewer can work with any kind of multimedia data: bitmaps, sounds, MIDI files, videos, animations, and so on. If you have hardware and a driver to support it, you can use the data type in Viewer. Viewer largely relies on MCI, the Media Control Interface, built into Windows 3.1 and later versions. This means that if you buy some hot new multimedia hardware, you can use it with Viewer as long as it has an MCI driver.[44]

Let's look at an example. One of the topics in Chapter 2 introduces the file types WAV and MIDI. I wanted to add the correct pronunciation for these abbreviations, so I recorded two little .WAV files, one pronouncing each word. The filenames are WAVE1.WAV and MIDI.WAV. The desired behavior is to have the correct file play when the user clicks on the words WAV and MIDI in the text.

---

[44]And, these days, what manufacturer in their right mind would introduce multimedia hardware without an MCI driver?

To begin, I selected the text MIDI and then pressed the hot key to invoke the Topic Editor. Figure 8.53 shows what the Topic Editor looks like in this situation. Note that I have clicked the Command(s) button at upper right, instead of Jump. This means that when the selected text is clicked, a command will be executed instead of a jump to a topic.

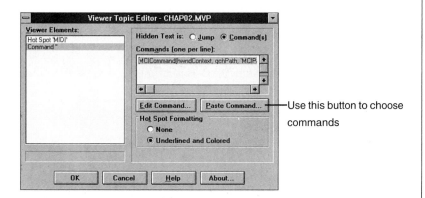

Use this button to choose commands

Figure 8.53. *Creating a hot-spot command.*

To choose a command, click the Paste Command button (Figure 8.54); you'll see a list of available commands. Scroll to the MCICommand, click it to highlight it, and then click OK.

Figure 8.54. *Selecting a command to paste.*

To edit the command, click the Edit Command button. This displays the dialog shown in Figure 8.55.

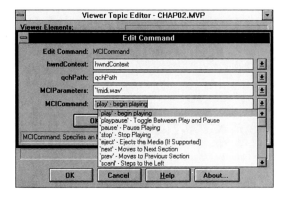

Figure 8.55. *Editing a command.*

In the bad old days before Viewer 2.0, there were no dialog boxes like this one. You had to remember the possible choices for a command and type them into your document as hidden text. The Topic Editor makes the process much easier. You merely select from the available choices in most cases. For example, consider the choices shown in Figure 8.55:

hwndContext—This is merely the current Viewer window. You shouldn't change it; this is a Viewer internal variable.

qchPath—This is another Viewer internal variable. It refers to the title's filename. Just leave this alone, too.

MCIParameters—These are standard MCI parameters, such as the name of the sound file for example.

MCI command—You can choose from the list of available commands; refer to Figure 8.55 for examples.

In most cases, all you need to supply are the filename and the command, then click OK. The file will be added to the baggage section of the project as shown in Figure 8.56.

Figure 8.57 shows the results in the .RTF file. The selected text is now double-underlined, and the hidden text that follows it was placed there by the Topic Editor.[45] For example, the hidden text for the MIDI hot spot looks like this:

```
!MCICommand(hwndContext, qchPath, '!midi.wav', 'play')
```

---

[45]To edit hidden text, select both the underlined text (the hot spot) and all of the hidden text related to it, and then press the hot-key combination for the Topic Editor.

Enter filename here

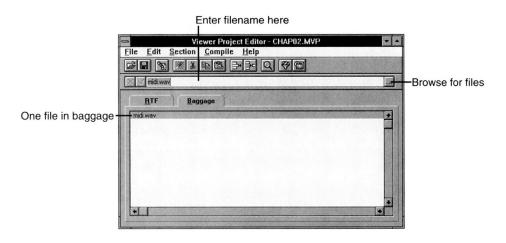

Browse for files

One file in baggage

Figure 8.56. *The file has been added to the project baggage.*

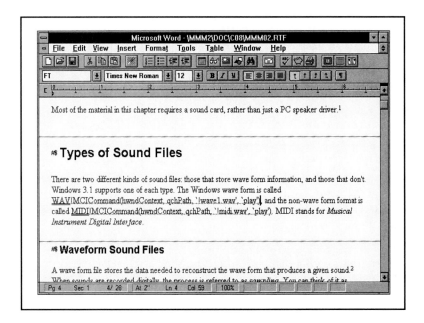

Figure 8.57. *The Topic Editor enters the hidden text automatically.*

You can also display bitmaps. To show a bitmap within the text window, simply position the cursor where you want the bitmap to display and press the hot-key combination for the Topic Editor. This displays the New Viewer Element dialog box; choose Picture (using ewX with MVBMP2) and click OK. This displays the Picture Options dialog shown in Figure 8.58.

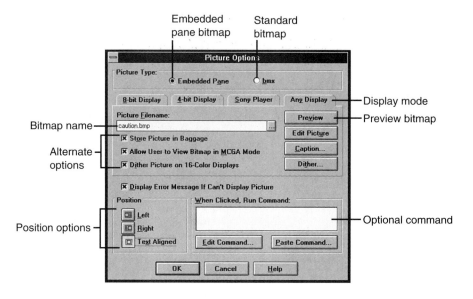

Figure 8.58. *Setting picture options.*

Viewer offers two kinds of picture options: Embedded Pane and bmx. In most cases, you'll want to use the Embedded Pane option. The bmx option is a carryover from the earlier version of Viewer. Embedded panes are much more flexible because they can work at various color resolutions. For example, in Figure 8.58 I have selected the Any Display option. This means that Viewer will automatically adjust the image to display as clearly as possible on different kinds of video cards. There are only two items you need to pay attention to in this dialog to display a bitmap: the Picture Filename (in this case caution.bmp) and the Position (in this case, Text Aligned). Left position puts the image at the far left, Right at the far right, and Text Aligned puts the image right with the text, just as if it were a single character of text.

Click OK to save the option, which displays the Topic Editor as shown in Figure 8.59. This shows the hidden text for displaying a bitmap:

```
{ewc MVBMP2, ViewerBmp2, [mcga dither]!caution.bmp
```

This simply includes the commands for displaying the bitmap caution.bmp with the mcga and dither options added so that the bitmap will display properly on any system.

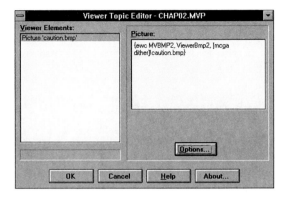

Figure 8.59. *Hidden text for a bitmap.*

In this particular case, the bitmap is going to be used to display a caution message. If you refer back to Figure 8.58, you will notice that there is an area at lower right with the label, "When clicked, run command:". Any command you enter in this area will be executed when you click on the bitmap. To select a command, click the Paste Command button. In this case, I want to display the caution message in a popup window. The command for this is PopupID. To edit the command, click the Edit Command button, which displays the dialog shown in Figure 8.60.

Figure 8.60. *Editing the **PopupID** command.*

There are just three possible entries:

TitleFile—This is again qchPath, the Viewer internal variable that refers to the current title.

Context—This is the context string that identifies the text that is to show up in the popup window. You can add the caution message just like any other topic, but it doesn't really need a topic title; topics with titles show up in a search, and I did not want this text to show up in a search. Figure 8.61 shows the new topic and its context string.

PopupName—This is blank. As you will learn shortly, you can create and define your own popups. In this case, by leaving it blank, Viewer will use the default popup window. This is fine for your caution message.

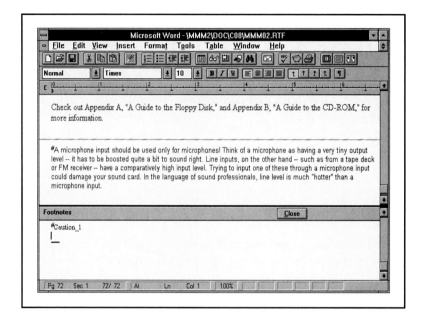

Figure 8.61. A new topic has been added.

Figure 8.62 shows the text inserted into the document to effect the display of the bitmap and the popup command when the bitmap is clicked. Note that this text is not hidden text; it is enclosed instead in curly braces.

When the title is compiled with the Project Editor and then run, the bitmap is displayed at the same place in the text as the command in Figure 8.62 (see Figure 8.63). The popup window is automatically positioned and filled with the topic text when you click the bitmap.

While describing how to add a bitmap and command, I alluded to the fact that you can define your own windows for your application. So far, all the windows you have seen are the ones that Viewer supplied by default. This is convenient because it enables you to build an application quickly and easily. However, sometime you will want to take control of the appearance of your application, and Viewer enables you to add additional windows and set the characteristics of all windows in the applications. To add, edit, or delete windows, use the

Options|Window Definitions menu selection in the Project Editor. This displays the Window Definitions dialog box as shown in Figure 8.64.

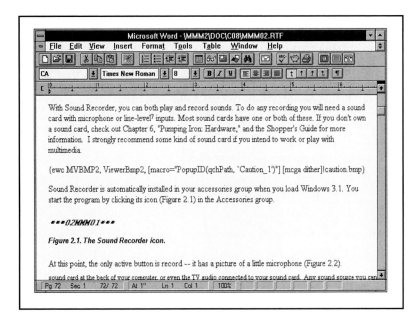

Figure 8.62. *The command to display the bitmap.*

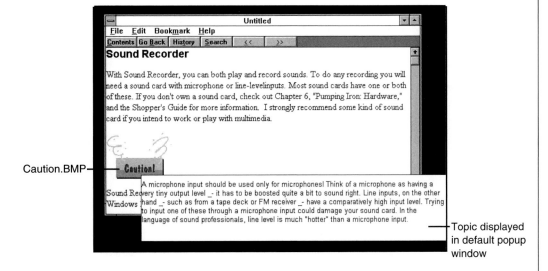

Caution.BMP

Topic displayed in default popup window

Figure 8.63. *The bitmap and the popup window.*

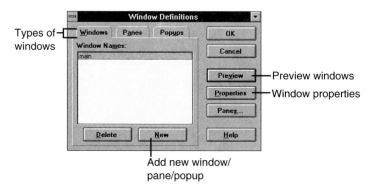

Types of windows → (Windows, Panes, Popups)

Preview windows

Window properties

Add new window/ pane/popup

Figure 8.64. *The Window Definitions dialog box.*

At this point, only one window is defined: main. Each window has properties you can set. The properties for a window vary with the type of window. For example, I created a new window for displaying bitmaps. Figure 8.65 shows the kinds of properties that you can set for a window.

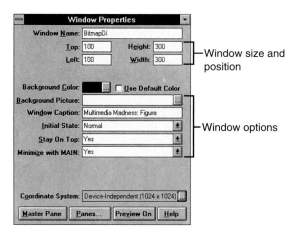

Window size and position

Window options

Figure 8.65. *Setting window properties.*

You can add a caption to a window, determine its initial state, make it a "stay on top" window, and so on. You also can define the location and size of the window; however, it is easier to set location and size in preview mode. Figure 8.66 shows the new bitmap window preview.

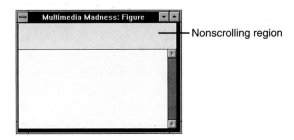

Figure 8.66. *A window preview.*

You can stretch or move the preview to change the characteristics of the window in the Window Properties dialog. In addition to adding new windows, you can add new panes to existing windows. Figure 8.67 shows two panes in a window: the master pane at the bottom and a pane with the name "Pane2" in the rest of the window. This gives you a great deal of flexibility. I added several windows, and several panes to each window, to create the look I desired for my application. (If you want to peek ahead, Figure 8.71 shows the final result.)

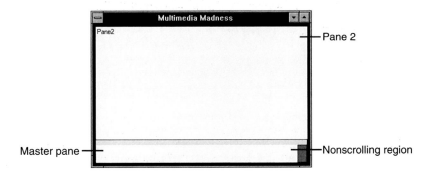

Figure 8.67. *Adding a pane to a window.*

By default, each topic in your application is a separate unit. That is, you can only jump to it using the techniques I have described so far. Sometimes this is fine, but, in most applications, you will want the user to be able to "turn the page" and go to the next unit of information. To do this, you must create topic groups. The topics that belong to a group act like a series of pages.

The easiest way to create groups is to work with the outline version of the application you created way back at the beginning. I printed out the topic outline and then used a pencil to mark the topic groups. You can have nested groups. For example, here are the first eight topics of my application for Chapter 2:

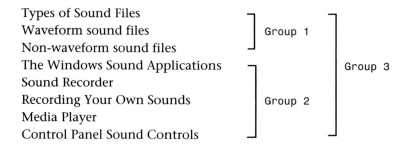

Types of Sound Files
Waveform sound files — Group 1
Non-waveform sound files
The Windows Sound Applications — Group 3
Sound Recorder
Recording Your Own Sounds — Group 2
Media Player
Control Panel Sound Controls

Each group gets a name. In the above example, Group 1 is called "Sound Types," Group 2 is called "Windows," and Group 3 is called "Getting Started." I went through the complete outline, marking groups in this fashion and then used my sheets of paper to enter the group names into the project editor (see Figure 8.68).[46] Note that each group has a short name with no spaces and a longer title that does have embedded spaces. You refer to the groups by name, but when Viewer displays the groups for the user, it uses the titles.

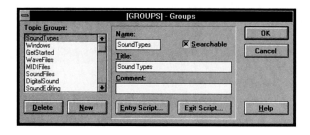

Figure 8.68. *Adding groups in the Project Editor.*

All that this does, however, is create the group names. To add topics to a group, you have to go to each topic and—you guessed—add another footnote at the beginning of the topic. For example, to add a topic to the MIDIFiles and SoundFiles groups, move to the beginning of the topic, and position the cursor after any currently existing footnote characters in the first line of the topic. Press the Topic Editor hot-key combination. From the list of New Viewer Elements, select Topic groups (+ footnote). This displays the Topic Editor.

In this example, I have added two groups to the topic; they are listed at lower right. Note that I have selected a group as a *browse sequence*, located at upper right. The Topic Browse Sequence is MIDIFiles (a topic group), and note also that there

---

[46]Use the Options|[GROUPS]-Groups menu selection.

is a Browse Sequence Number. I used numbers of 010, 020, 030, and so on to designate each "page" in the browse sequence. This will enable the reader to browse through related topics using Viewer's navigation buttons.

I mentioned that I created additional windows and panes for my title. Let's take a look at how to use these windows and panes. One of the panes I created is a small one at the upper left of the main window. When I added the pane, I reduced the width of the master pane as well.[47] I wanted to add an image of the cover of my book to this pane. Figure 8.69 shows a topic entry command[48] that I added to the table of contents. Because Viewer automatically loads the contents topic when the application starts, this has the effect of displaying the bitmap of the book's cover when the application starts.

Figure 8.69. *Editing a topic entry command.*

In this case, I have added a pane name—`'Win1P1'`—where a topic will be displayed. The topic is `'Book_image'`, and the only content of the topic is a Viewer command to display an embedded-pane image. Figure 8.70 shows the result.

I also added a window to display bitmaps. It contains a large pane at the top to contain the bitmap and a small pane at the bottom to contain the figure caption (see Figure 8.71).

It's very easy to display the bitmaps. I created a topic for each bitmap, which naturally has a context string corresponding to the figure number. For example, Figure 8.72 shows three places in the text where clicking on a text hot spot will cause a bitmap to display.

---

[47] All of this was done by clicking and dragging in the preview window from the Project Editor.

[48] A topic entry command is just another footnote. It causes a command to be executed when a topic is entered.

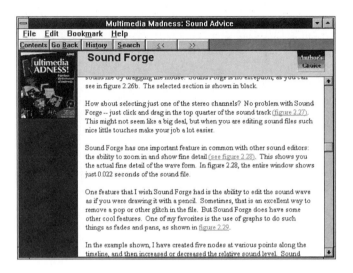

Figure 8.70. *The book image displayed in a pane.*

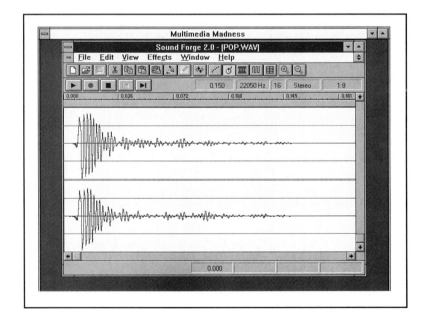

Figure 8.71. *The bitmap window.*

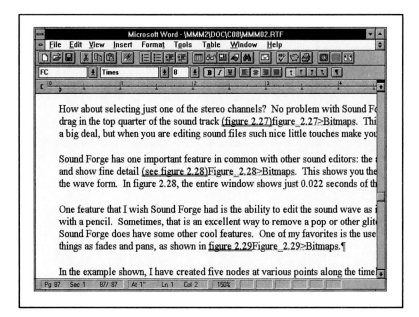

Figure 8.73. *Hot spots for displaying a bitmap.*

The text hot spot is, as usual, double-underlined. The command to display the topic containing the bitmap command is in hidden text, and so is the figure caption. For example, for Figure 2.28 of the application, the hidden text is:

```
Figure_2.28>Bitmaps
```

The context string for the topic is `Figure_2.28`. The `>Bitmaps` portion of the command is shorthand for "display the topic in the window `Bitmaps`." I didn't enter this by hand; the Topic Editor created the entry after I edited the command in a dialog box as usual.

Viewer Summary

There is a lot more to Viewer than I have been able to show you here; this was just a taste of the possibilities. Viewer contains many commands and options that enable you to control many aspects of the appearance and flow of your application. If you will be working with an application that contains lots of text, Viewer is your best bet for turning it into a multimedia extravaganza.

III

PART

Full-Blast Multimedia

Animation

As I mentioned in the introduction to this section, I have always found animation fascinating. Of all the things that computers can do, this is the one thing that strikes me as the most amazing. Some of my child-like sense of wonder still persists, so playing with the Author's Choice product for this chapter—3D Studio from Autodesk—literally gave me goose bumps. Now if 3D Studio just had sound drivers....

Well, in a way, it does. Once you have created the final rendering,[1] you can easily play it back in Windows as part of a multimedia presentation. 3D Studio is a DOS product, and considering how graphics-intensive it is, that's a good idea. The overhead of an environment like Windows would slow it down. 3D Studio does a lot, and I'd hate to wait any longer than I had to for all those nifty features.

What features, you ask? On to the Author's Choice![2]

Autodesk 3D Studio

Although animation is only a part of what you can do with 3D Studio, it does it so well that it would be a serious omission to leave it out of the discussion. Its CAD-like interface and deep, complex feature set might make it seem like an intimidating choice for everyday animation. The results, however, might convince you (as they did me) that it's worth whatever it takes to learn—if only to impress the heck out of everyone![3]

In fact, I found that there was a lot that I could do without getting things too complicated. 3D Studio comes with an extraordinarily large tutorial manual, for

---

[1]Last edition's comment: "You can create amazingly realistic animation with 3D Studio." Well, this year, release 3 of 3D Studio is out, and it is much better—and it was pretty darn hot to start with.

[2]I should confess right up front that 3D Studio is in a different class than the other Author's Choice products in this book. First of all, the price is very high—$2,995 retail. 3D Studio is a professional product, and there is nothing at the consumer level that even comes close. Software like Playmation, 3D Workshop, and Imagine 2.0 are interesting, but they are not 3D Studio. Even so, those packages cost as much as $500, so it apparently takes serious money to work in 3D.

[3]And I do mean impressive. With 3D Studio, you can create the kind of wild, 3D animations you see on TV or at the movies. The new release pretty much turns your PC into a graphics workstation, so if $2,995 sounds expensive, compare it to the five figures it's going to take to get yourself a graphics workstation from Sun or Silicon Graphics (including software, of course).

example. Each tutorial covers a different aspect of the program, enabling you to do a specific task in a tutorial before trying it on your own. It is by far the most comprehensive set of tutorials I have ever seen.

If you haven't seen 3D Studio before, it's actually a very simple program. You create a 3D scene using the same kinds of views that are used for mechanical or architectural drafting—Top, Front, Side, and Perspective. You can also use some ancillary tools—the 2D Shaper (a drawing tool), a 3D Lofter (a clever 2D to 3D converter), and a Materials Editor (a design environment for surfaces). Finally, for creating the animation, there is a sophisticated Keyframer. The Keyframer enables you to create paths for objects—just put the object into the starting frame, jump to a later frame, and move the object to its new position. The Keyframer calculates all of the intervening positions for you.[4]

By way of demonstration, this section walks you through a modified version of the second tutorial in the 3D Studio manual. Keep in mind that the tutorial in the manual is much more specific, offering detailed explanations of the concepts and tools involved in each step. I give the manual high ratings for making 3D Studio approachable for the average user.

The opening screen for 3D Studio (see Figure 9.1) is more or less the kind of screen required for any 3D program—it provides the four basic views I mentioned earlier.

If you took mechanical drawing or drafting courses in high school (or anywhere else along the line), you'll recognize this layout. Clockwise from the top left:

➤ A top view of the subject.

➤ A front view of the subject.

➤ An optional User view (usually set at an angle to display the 3D object to best advantage). 3D Studio enables you to adjust the User view in many ways;[5] you'll see some of them shortly.

➤ A left view of the subject.

---

[4]Of course, it does a lot more than just paths—it does morphing, object linking, deformations, and tons of other cool stuff.

[5]For example, you can show the view through a camera (yes, you can create cameras) in the User port.

511

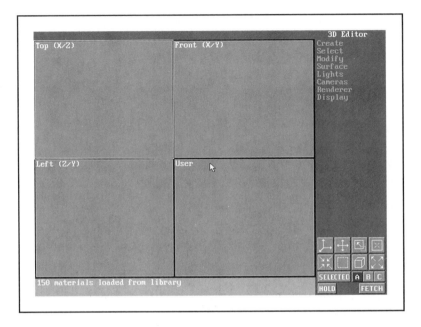

Figure 9.1. *The opening screen of 3D Studio.*

Figure 9.2, for example, shows a peek ahead at the four views of the object you'll be creating in this example: a simple table.

The views used in Figure 9.2 are called *wireframes*. Because it is much easier for the computer to display a wireframe instead of a fully rendered object, most work done in any 3D program uses wireframes.[6] Some 3D programs, such as Virtual Reality Studio, allow you to work in rendered 3D, but the rendering is extremely simplistic and uses only a 320 × 200 VGA screen.

Creating a Drawing

You can use a mouse to work with 3D Studio, but I prefer to use a digitizing tablet that includes a work surface and a stylus. Tablets come in all sizes, from 6 × 9 inches to 4 × 6 feet.[7] There are two kinds of styluses. One is shaped like a mouse

---

[6]How much faster? Well, it takes a second or two to display a very complex wireframe on my 486/66. It takes several minutes to render the scene at 640 × 480.

[7]The larger sizes are used to digitize large, existing materials like maps and architectural plans.

and has a cross hair; it is usually used for tracing. The other kind of stylus looks like a pen and comes in two flavors—cordless and standard. For drawing, the cordless pen stylus is ideal. I used a Calcomp Drawing Board II with a cordless stylus for this example, and it performed flawlessly. I found it much superior to a mouse for drawing tasks—the natural motion of the pen lends itself exceptionally well to drawing.[8]

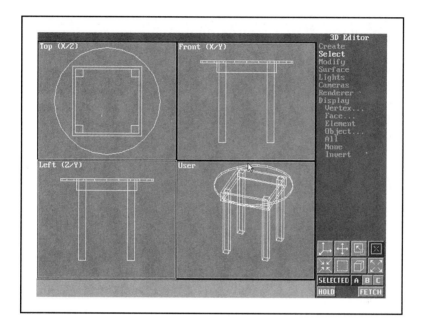

Figure 9.2. *Four views of a sample object.*

Back to 3D Studio: you can easily blow up any one of the views to nearly full screen for detailed work by clicking on the second icon from the right in the top row of icons in the icon panel (at bottom right; see Figure 9.3).

I added a grid to this view to make it easier to draw precisely.[9] To draw a circle the size needed for the table, for example, I can move the cursor to coordinates –200,200, click once, move to 200,–200, and click again (see Figure 9.4).

---

[8]I also use the pen and stylus for all my Windows work, and the stress on my hands is much less than with a mouse. The stylus is also ideal for working with many drawing programs, particularly Fractal Design Painter.

[9]The grid is made up of the little white dots.

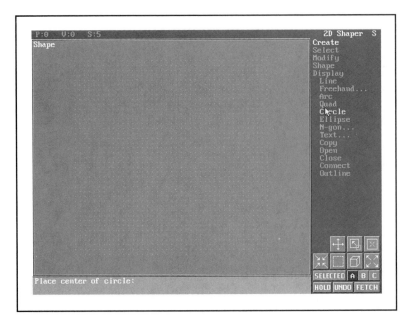

Figure 9.3. *One of 3D Studio's views enlarged to nearly full screen (note the icon panel in the lower-right portion of the screen).*

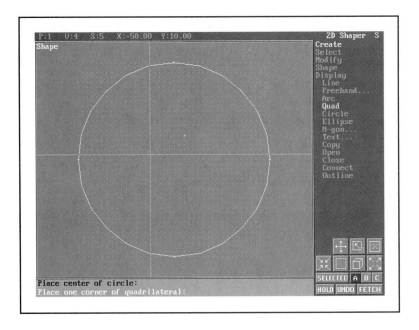

Figure 9.4. *An example of a circle drawn with the aid of a grid.*

This drawing, you may note, is strictly two-dimensional. It is being created in the 2D Shaper. The name of the current workspace is shown at the top right of the screen. The 2D Shaper is a little bit like vector drawing programs such as CorelDRAW! or Illustrator. In other words, you draw with shapes, not areas of color.

Once you have created a 2D image using the Shaper program, you can import your shape to the 3D Lofter. The Lofter gives you the tools to create 3D images from 2D shapes. *Lofting* is the process of extending a 2D shape into the third dimension. Figure 9.5 shows an example of a 3D Lofter screen. The Lofter gives you a wide variety of tools for creating 3D shapes. You can loft along complex paths, for example, and you can loft by rotating.

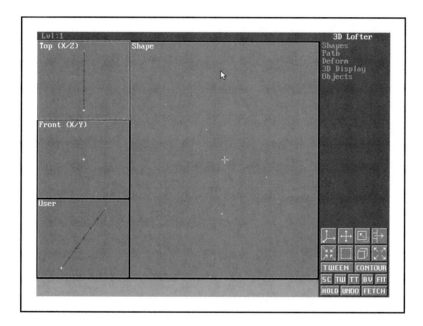

Figure 9.5. *The 3D Lofter program (note the lofting lines in the Top panel and the User panel).*

Once you have lofted the shape into three dimensions, you can move the lofted shape to the 3D Editor. The Editor has an amazing variety of tools. This is the real strength of 3D Studio as well as its biggest obstacle: the layers of menus take a long time to get familiar with. This means it takes a long time to become proficient with 3D Studio—but it also means that, if you get an idea, there's a way to make it happen. In the Editor, you can rotate or scale the object, deform it in creative ways, combine primitive shapes to create complex forms, apply surface materials and textures, and so on. At this stage, the object is called a *mesh* object (another way of referring to a wireframe object). Finally, you can import the object (or objects) into the Keyframer and animate it. And that's just the overview! Now let's take a stab at actually doing something.

3D Lofter

Now that the circle for the table top is completed in the 2D Shaper, you can move to the 3D Lofter program (see Figure 9.5).

Again, four views are provided but in a different arrangement.[10] The lines with hash marks are lofting lines. Any lofted shape is lofted according to the direction, type, and length of the lofting line.[11] The first task at this point is to retrieve the circle from the Shaper program. Use the Shapes|Get menu selection (see Figure 9.6).

Note that the cursor arrow in Figure 9.6 is positioned over one of the icons in the lower-right of the screen. This icon, shaped like a simple cube, rescales boxes to show the entire object or scene. I used it to display the complete circle in all of the boxes (note that loft lines in the Top panel and the User panel are shortened in this screen shot).

The list of words on the right side of the screen is a 3D Studio menu (see Figure 9.6). The top level of the menu consists of Shapes, Path, Deform, 3D Display, and Objects. The current selection at this level is Shapes (note the highlight). The next level of the menu pertains to the actions that you can perform with Shapes:

Put...
Pick
Move
Rotate
Scale
Compare

---

[10]You can select several different arrangements of the basic four boxes, and you can vary what is displayed in each box.

[11]There are other details you can control, such as the number of sections in the new object. If you plan to deform an object, give it extra sections so it will deform smoothly.

Center
Align...
Delete
Steps

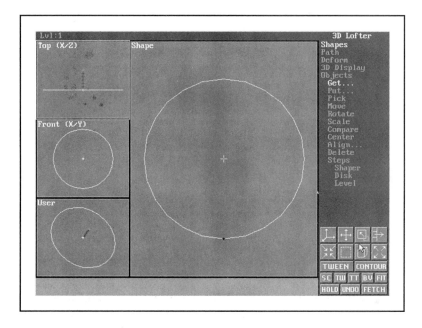

Figure 9.6. *The 3D Lofter program with a shape imported from the Shaper program.*

Items followed by ellipses (such as the current highlighted choice, Get...) contain further submenus; all other items act immediately when chosen. Prompts are displayed below the drawing area. The Get... submenu includes the following choices:

Shaper
Disk
Level

These are the three places you can Get a shape to use in the 3D Lofter. If you want to loft the circle to make it a disc use the Top view to change the length of the loft line (called a *path* in 3D Studio lingo). To shorten a line that is too long, click on the free end of the line and drag it with the mouse. (3D Studio enables you to limit movement to either vertical or horizontal directions if you want to make a perfect adjustment.)

517

To execute the loft, click Objects in the top menu level. This displays two possible choices: Make and Preview. The second choice, Preview, enables you to preview the 3D object to ensure that everything is set correctly. The first choice, Make, displays a dialog box with options for making the 3D object (see Figure 9.7).

Figure 9.7. *The Object Lofting Controls dialog box.*

The Object Lofting Controls dialog box is a typical example of 3D Studio dialog boxes. Although I had to go to the reference manual to find out what the choices in the dialog boxes could do for me, the manual is well organized, and this was not a chore. In fact, if two dialog boxes are similar, the reference manual repeats information in both places so that you don't have to zip all over the manual when you have a question. I like this way of doing things, and I wish more reference manuals were as considerate of my time. I won't go into the details of this dialog box here, but I will say that there is an option or a fill-in for just about anything you might want to do. This is a very powerful product.

The actual lofting is quick, and the result is just what you might expect: a disc (see Figure 9.8).

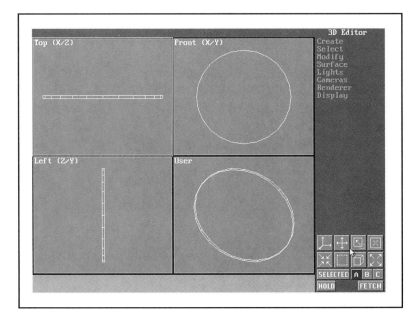

Figure 9.8. *A circle lofted in the 3D Lofter to form a disc.*

To complete the table, four legs and something to attach them to are needed. Go back to the 2D Shaper to create these shapes, and turn them into 3D shapes in the 3D Lofter. Now you can move to the 3D Editor to examine the results in three dimensions. Figure 9.9 shows the result of "attaching" the lofted legs to a table top.

The only difference in processing between the table top and the other parts is the amount of lofting—all other steps are identical.

While you are in the 3D Editor, you can take care of a simple detail. Note that the Top view actually shows a side view, and the Front view shows the Top view. Use the Modify|Object|Rotate command to set things right (see Figure 9.10).

A table is nice, but what about putting a gold goblet on it? You can create an outline for the goblet with the 2D Shaper (see Figure 9.11).

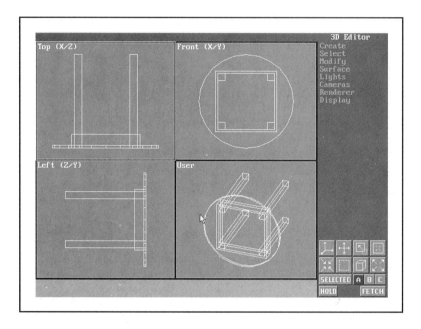

Figure 9.9. *A table top with four attached legs.*

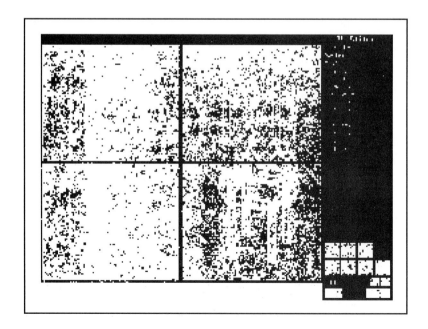

Figure 9.10. *A corrected 3D view of the table.*

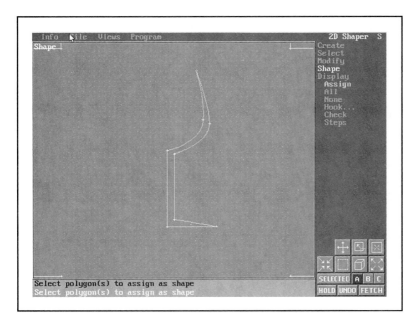

Figure 9.11. *An outline of a goblet created with the 2D Shaper.*

You can create this outline by drawing simple lines and adjusting the curvature. Use Path|SurfRev (short for Surface of Revolution) to create a 3D shape by rotating the 2D shape and selecting the details of the rotation (see Figure 9.12).

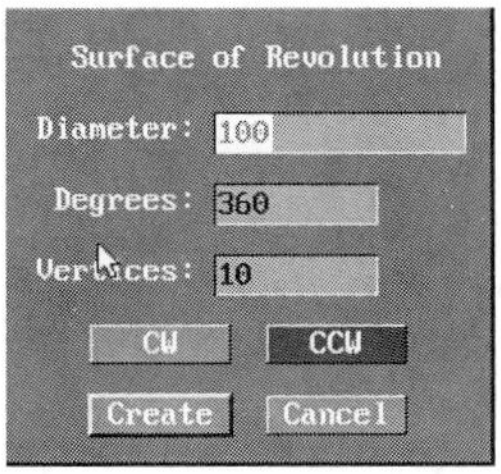

Figure 9.12. *The Surface of Revolution (SurfRev) dialog box.*

The most important variable to note in this dialog box is "Vertices." This number determines how many steps are used in the rotation. More steps equals greater realism and more time and memory for rendering; fewer steps equals less realism but faster processing. Using a fairly high number of steps (10) creates the rendition of the goblet shown in Figure 9.13.

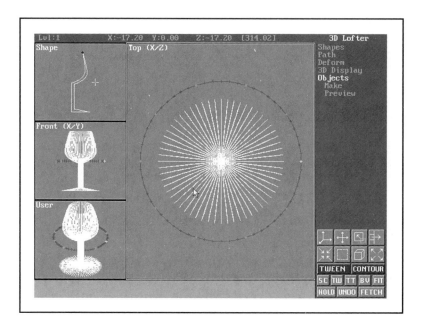

Figure 9.13. *An enhanced goblet created with SurfRev (surface of revolution) lofting.*

The four boxes in the 3D Lofter are defined as follows:

Shape	Contains the original imported shape (2D)
Front	A view from the front of the 3D object
User	An angled view of the 3D object
Top	Shows the object from the top

Note that the Top view shows that the object actually consists of a rotated series of 2D shapes. You can now use the 3D Editor to scale and move the goblet to a position "on" the table (see Figure 9.14).

Rendering an Image

Rendering is the process of taking the wireframe (also called mesh) objects and applying surface textures, lighting, and colors to create a realistic, three-dimensional image. Release 3 of 3D Studio is the first release of the product to support ray tracing.

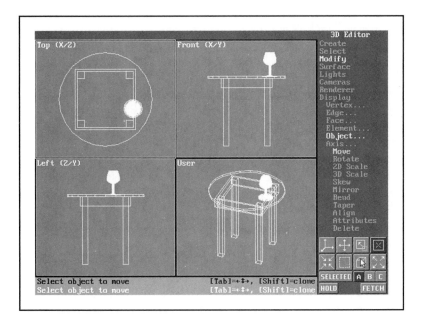

Figure 9.14. *Four views of the table with the placed goblet.*

Ray Tracing

The hottest thing in 3D right now is *ray tracing*. This is one of the most sophisticated techniques available for creating 3D images. It results in the most natural-looking results in the rendered image.

Ray tracing involves a huge number of calculations. It takes into account the positions of all objects in the scene as well as of sources of light and the position of the observer. The technique then uses fancy mathematics to trace the paths of light rays. It doesn't trace every light ray; the only ones that matter are the ones that arrive at the observer's point of view.

While using 3D Studio over a period of several weeks, I developed a great appreciation for ray tracing. For example, ray tracing allows objects with transparent maps to cast correct shadows. Shadow mapping "sees" the entire object at a very early stage of the rendering, while ray tracing is able to trace a light ray through each part of the object after the transparent portions of the surface are established. Coupled with other advanced features in the new version of 3D Studio, this package truly does put graphics workstation capabilities on the PC.

The first step in the process is to choose the materials to apply to the objects. 3D Studio comes with a large selection of materials, and you can also create your own. You can specify a variety of properties for a material using the Materials Editor. You then apply the materials (stock or custom) using the Surface|Material|Assign menu selection. When the scene is rendered, each object has the surface texture and colors associated with it in the Materials Editor. The Materials Editor screen is shown in Figure 9.15.[12]

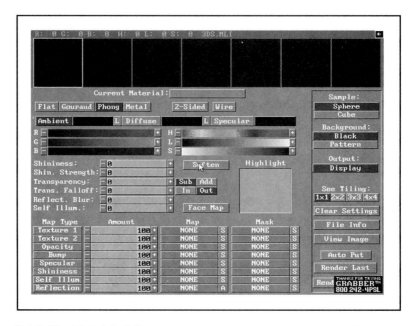

Figure 9.15. *The Materials Editor screen.*

---

[12]All 3D Studio screens are SuperVGA resolution. I used the Grabber screen capture program to capture some of the images in this chapter. You can always tell; there's a little black box that says Grabber. This is because I used the shareware version of the program—I discovered it too late to use the registered version. I did register, however—and I suggest you do the same when you find a shareware program that you use. I have looked for more than a year for a competent SuperVGA capture program and was very pleased to find Grabber—I recommend it highly.

Creating a Material

To use a gold material for the goblet,[13] you have two choices. You can use the stock gold material provided with 3D Studio, or you can create your own. Because this is a tutorial, I'll have you create your own. You create new materials by setting the various properties in the Materials Editor. To create Gold, you need to set the following properties:

Ambient	The color the material has in ambient (room) light
Diffuse	The color the object has under direct but diffuse illumination
Specular	The color of highlights (specular reflections)
Shininess	Controls the size of specular reflections—the shinier the material, the tighter and smaller the reflections.
Shininess Strength	Controls the brightness of the specular reflections.

The Shininess and Shininess Strength sliders interact. The small graph right of center screen in the Materials Editor shows the effect of these two controls.

Because gold is a very shiny color, use a value of 66 to control shininess and a value of 86 for shininess strength. You can also specify other properties for special purposes, such as self-illumination, transparency, or texture maps (you don't need any of that for gold, however). Click the Render button to display the settings on a sphere (see Figure 9.16).

Although you can't see the gold color in the black-and-white image, it is quite realistic. 3D Studio comes with a large library of common materials, so you won't have to reinvent the wheel. However, it is often fruitful to explore possibilities beyond the basic materials in the library. For example, there is a large list of buttons occupying the bottom third of the Materials Editor screen. The buttons at the left describe the effect of each setting. In each case, the Map is some kind of image that controls each effect. In general, white pixels have the maximum impact, and black pixels the least. Values in between cause mid-level effects. For example, when using the bump effect, black areas are valleys, and white areas are high spots. Gray values fall in the middle.

---

[13]Anything less would spoil the demo.

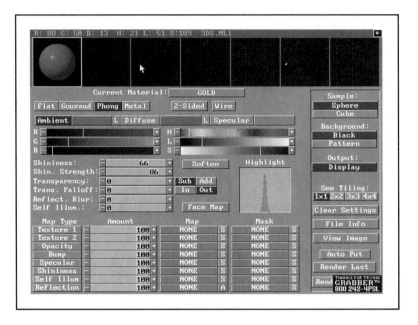

Figure 9.16. *The settings display of the Render button.*

Texture 1   This paints an image on the object. You can even use animations to create moving textures.[14]

Texture 2   You can apply a second texture. To allow the first texture to show through, define Texture 2 as a decal; one color then becomes transparent allowing Texture 1 to show through.

Opacity   You can create partially transparent objects—the image controls which portions of the image are transparent and which are solid.

Bump   Creates a surface texture.

Specular   Controls areas where specular highlights will form.

Shininess   Controls degree and position of shininess.

Self Illum   Controls degree and position of self-illumination.

---

[14]I use this for a variety of interesting effects, but my favorite is to put video files onto objects for cool digital video effects (there's an example later in the chapter).

Reflection   Controls degree and position of reflections. The letter A, if clicked, results in an automatic reflection map. Shinier material reflects more, and you can control the degree of blur in the reflection.

Adding a Camera

You can render from any of the four views—Top, Left, Front, and User—but it's more fun to create a *camera*. You can place a camera easily using the menu choice Camera|Create (see Figure 9.17).

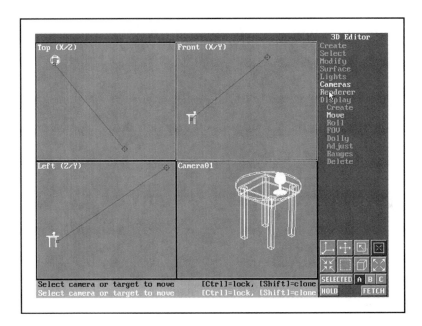

Figure 9.17. *Four views of the table and goblet.*

You may notice in Figure 9.17 that I switched the lower-right view from User view to Camera view. This enables you to view the scene through the Camera. You can change the focal length of the lens, move the camera in and out (called *dollying*), pan the camera from left to right, and so on. It's just like working with a real camera.

Adding lights

Before you render, add lights to the scene. Without lights, illumination would only be from *ambient* light. Ambient light is pretty boring—much like the illumination on an overcast day, the light seems to come faintly from everywhere. There are two kinds of lights that you can add: omni and spot.

An omni light is like sunlight—its rays are parallel and seem to come from an infinite distance. A spot light is, well, a spotlight—you can aim it, you can adjust the aperture, and so on. You can place a light by clicking in any view with the menu choice Lights|Create|Omni and Lights|Create|Spot. For this example, I created two omni lights to give general illumination to the scene and a spotlight to emphasize the goblet (see Figure 9.18).[15]

Rendering

Rendering a 3D scene is easy. The Renderer|Render menu choice displays lots of information about the rendering process (see Figure 9.19).

You can, of course, set all of those variables before you render. Figure 9.20 shows the final result.

Should you decide to make changes to your scene, you can work directly with the 3D objects in the 3D Editor. To shrink the goblet, for example, select it (it is a single object) and choose Modify|Object|Scale. It takes only a few seconds to make these changes.

I was pretty impressed by how easy it was to make this table and goblet, but I wondered what it would be like to create a more complex table. I spent about an hour creating a table with turned legs and an inlaid wood top (see Figure 9.21). (I threw in a glass globe just for fun.)

---

[15]Spotlights have some great features. For example, you can use a spotlight as a projector—to play an animation or merely to use a bitmap to simulate the light from a flashlight.

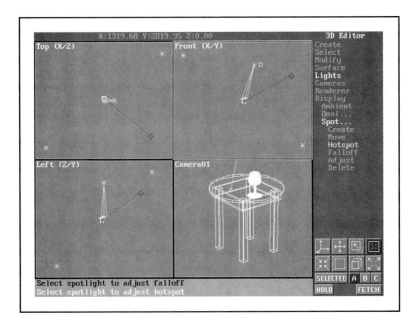

Figure 9.18. *Four views of the table and goblet accented with omni and spot lights.*

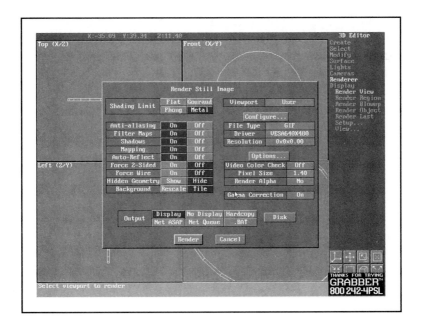

Figure 9.19. *The Render Still Image dialog box.*

529

Figure 9.20. The rendered table and goblet.

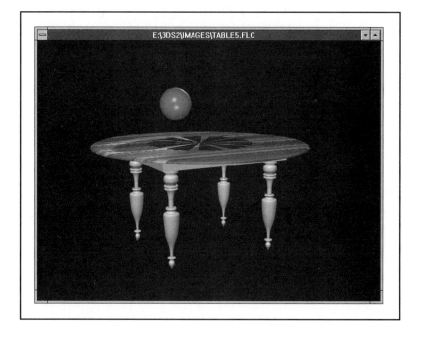

Figure 9.21. An example of an enhanced table created with 3D Studio.

If you are more of the outdoor type, a patio table might have more appeal (see Figure 9.22).

It's easy to animate a scene using the Keyframer. All you have to do is move to a given frame, reposition an object (you can do this with things like lights and cameras too), and the Keyframer automatically creates the in-between frames. You can even directly edit the path that an object will travel. The path has a dot for each frame making it easy to tell how fast an object is moving.

Figure 9.22. *An example of a patio table created with 3D Studio.*

Once you have set up the animation, you can play it using the mesh objects; generate a low-resolution gray-scale version; or render the animation in full 3D. There are lots of fully rendered animations on the CD included with this book for you to explore (they have extensions .FLI and .FLC). You must install the Autodesk animations MCI driver to play them, however.

3D Studio Animation

Let's look at the steps needed to create an animation. Figure 9.23 shows the 3D Shaper, where I have entered some text.[16] This text will be the title of a video production, and you'll fly it in against a video in the background.

The next step is to loft the text into a 3D object. I imported the text as a shape into the 3D Lofter and lofted it a short distance (see Figure 9.24).

---

[16]Release 3 of 3D Studio supports both bezier fonts (supplied with 3D Studio) and PostScript font files (.PFB).

531

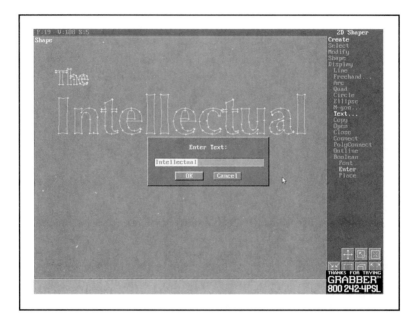

Figure 9.23. *Creating text in the 2D Shaper.*

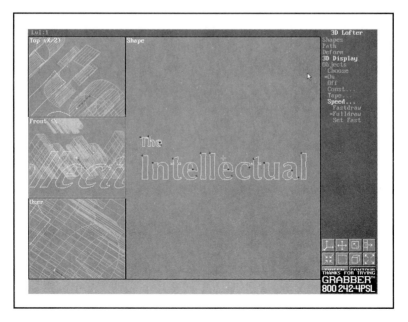

Figure 9.24. *Lofting the text in the 3D Lofter.*

You can then import the lofted shape into the 3D editor (see Figure 9.25).

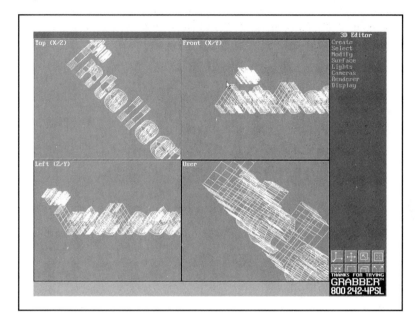

Figure 9.25. *Importing the lofted shape.*

To align the text with a Front view, use the Modify|Object|Align menu selection—pick a face that will be aligned to the view, and 3D Studio does the rest. Figure 9.26 shows the result.

Next, I created a box object. It will be used to play the video. Figure 9.27 shows the objects in the 3D Editor aligned as they will be in the final frame of the animation. To move an object, use the Object|Modify|Move menu selection.

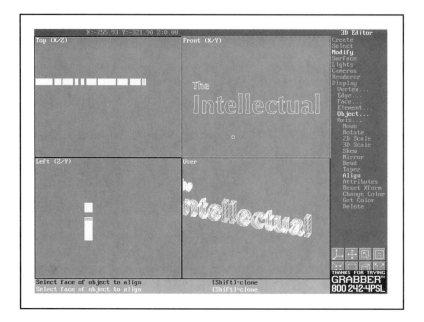

Figure 9.26. *The object has been properly aligned.*

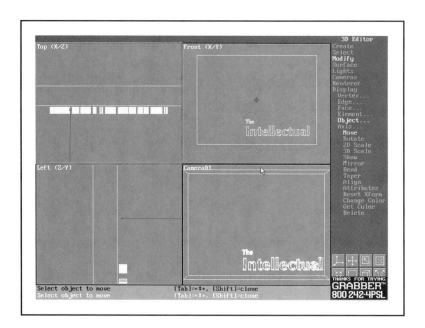

Figure 9.27. *Adding a box object and aligning objects.*

Video for Texture Maps

To play the video on the box object, you must first convert it to a .FLC file. You need Animator Pro[17] to do this. The process begins in VidEdit, the Video Editor that comes with the full package of Video for Windows (not the runtime). Load the video file you wish to use, and select the entire file (using the Mark In and Mark Out buttons). Then use the File|Extract menu selection to display the dialog box shown in Figure 9.28. Choose DIB Sequence as the file type in the list box at lower left. This enables you to export the video file as a series of numbered bitmap files. For the filename, use a name with four characters followed by the number of the first frame—DEMO0001.BMP, for example. Make sure you use the .BMP extension; the default .DIB extension will cause problems.

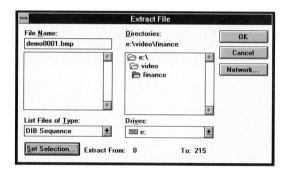

Figure 9.28. *Exporting a video file as numbered bitmaps.*

Once the bitmaps have been created, you need to convert them into a .FLC file. Some shareware programs will do this, but the best option (when it is available) is to use Animator Pro to create the .FLC file. Animator Pro has some very sophisticated palette controls that you can use to adjust palettes for multiple files.

Use the POCO|Numpics menu selection in Animator Pro to display the dialog box shown in Figure 9.29. Choose the second selection, Load Pics as Flic.

This displays the dialog box shown in Figure 9.30. Find the filename of the first bitmap in the series (RISK0001.BMP in this example), and click on it. Then click the Load button. If a flic is already loaded, you will have the option to Append, Insert, or Replace; choose Replace.

---

[17]You'll learn more about Animator Pro later in this chapter.

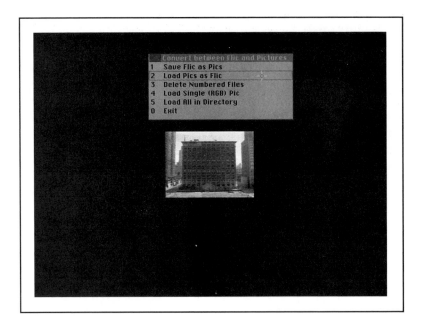

Figure 9.29. *Loading numbered bitmaps.*

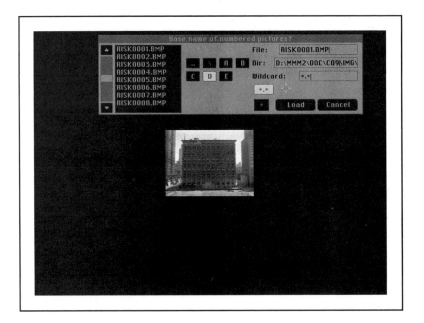

Figure 9.30. *Selecting the first file in the series.*

This displays yet another dialog box, shown in Figure 9.31. In most cases, you will want to choose option 4, `Load in 256-level color`. This preserves the colors of the video as much as possible. Each image will have its own palette giving you different colors for each frame. For example, in a recent video I converted this way, there were about 100 frames and a total of more than 20,000 colors.[18] Preserving the colors this way is especially important if the original video (and the bitmaps) used 24-bit color.

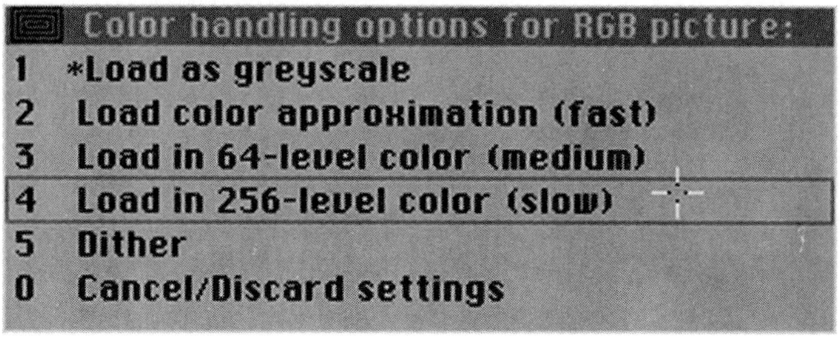

Figure 9.31. *Choosing load options.*

It may take a while to load all the bitmaps, and the palette will flash. The background will also change colors; ignore it—it's just something that goes with all the palette changes. When the bitmaps have been loaded, save as an .FLC file using the Flic|Files menu selection. Be sure to save the file in the \3DS\MAPS directory so it can be used as a texture map.

Using the Materials Editor

Now you can use the Materials Editor in 3D Studio to create a material that uses the .FLC file as a texture map. Figure 9.32 shows the file DEMOLISH.FLC being loaded as a texture map. To open the file dialog, just click the Map button to the right of the Texture 1 button.

To see what the map will look like, click the Cube button near the top of the right-hand column of buttons. Then click the Render Sample button at the bottom of the same column. Figure 9.33 shows three sample materials that use bitmaps. The three rendered samples are at the top of the screen. From left to right are the material using the DEMOLISH.FLC file, a material based on a video

---

[18]If you merely want to play the flic file, having a separate palette for each frame isn't a good idea—there will be messy flashes as the palette changes for each frame.

of a man putting his head in a lion's mouth, and a material based on a video I took of a spider. The current material is the spider material. Note that, in addition to the texture map, I have added an Opacity map and a Self-Illumination map. The Spider video has a black background. Because black areas are transparent in an Opacity map, the spider material is mostly transparent—only the spider would show up. The self-illumination button works similarly, with the light areas of the spider appearing to cast its own light. The end result, therefore, is a glowing spider that will appear to move over whatever surface is behind it—the background of the spider video will drop out because of the Opacity map.

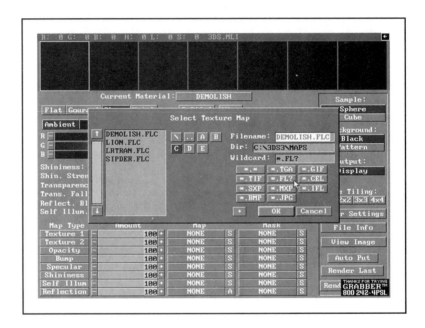

Figure 9.32. *Loading a texture map.*

The Keyframer

That's enough background; let's do the fun part. Look closely at Figure 9.34. It is a Keyframer screen, and I have added a few items to the scene. The Front view has been enlarged, and it shows three copies of the text object. The one at lower right is distorted. The additional objects are copies of the original. It's easy to make copies—just hold down the Shift key while you perform most operations, such as Move. The distorted shape was modified with the Modify|Object|Bend menu selection.

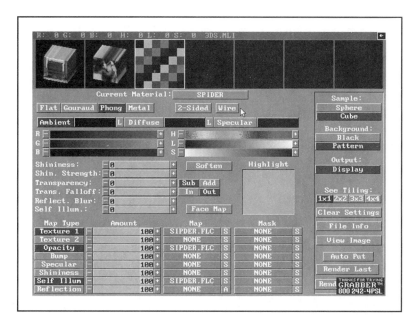

Figure 9.33. *Three sample materials with animated textures.*

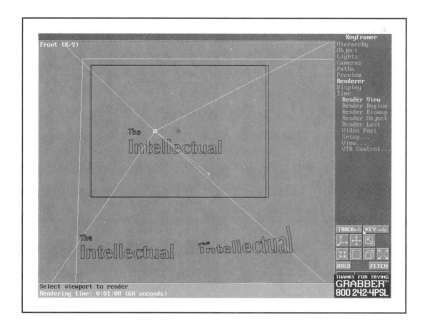

Figure 9.34. *Working in the Keyframer.*

This distorted object can be used to generate a morph. A morph is very easy to do.[19] Simply make a copy of an object, distort or change it in some way, and then move to the frame where you want the morph to conclude. Use the Modify|Object|Morph menu selection to select the source object and the morph object. Bingo—instant morph, as shown in Figure 9.35.

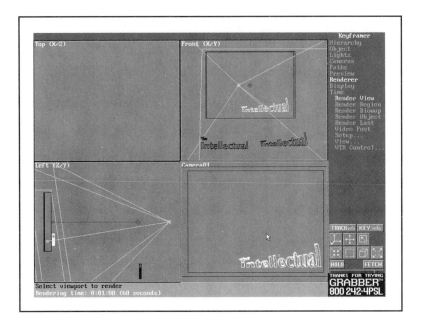

Figure 9.35. *A completed morph.*

Rendering an animation is very much like rendering a still image; the only difference is that you are rendering to either a .FLC file or a series of bitmaps. In this case, Because you are rendering with the intention of loading the frames back into VidEdit, rendering as a numbered series of bitmaps makes the most sense. You can load these into VidEdit using the File|Insert menu selection; choose DIB Sequence as the file type. Figure 9.36 shows a frame from the completed animation loaded into VidEdit.

---

[19]The main requirement is that the base object and the morph object must have the same number of faces and vertices.

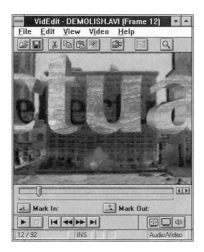

Figure 9.36. *A frame from the animation loaded into VidEdit.*

Note that the text object is in the process of flying into the scene, while the video is playing in the background, as if on a screen. The text object casts a shadow; I created a spotlight for that effect.[20]

Figure 9.37 shows a frame farther along in the animation. The text object has now come to rest against the background. It still casts a bit of a shadow to make it stand out against the background.

As the video continues to play, the morph comes into play as shown in Figure 9.38. The text bends down on the left and up on the right, and then it returns to normal. The complete video is included on the CD.

3D Studio Gallery

I had a lot of fun creating the examples using 3D Studio. I created many more examples than I could include here. The best ones are on the CD-ROMs where you can play them by double-clicking on the filename (they all have an .AVI extension and so will play automatically if you installed Video for Windows).

---

[20]I turned down the ambient light and turned up the spotlight to make sure there would be a shadow. I verified its intensity by rendering single frames.

Figure 9.37. *The text object has stopped moving in frame 45.*

Figure 9.38. *The midpoint of the morph in frame 72.*

Before moving on, let's look at a frame from a 3D Studio animation that shows various features and capabilities of the program. Figure 9.39 shows a frame from an animation that uses Opacity maps in the materials. The globe uses a material with a Bump map that is a map of the world. A variation on the bitmap is used as an Opacity map so that the seas are transparent. The variation has black for the oceans so that they are completely transparent.

Figure 9.39. *A frame showing a material with transparency.*

Animation for Business and Art

Well, that was fun, but now it's time to get down to business because a lot of animation is being used these days in the business world.[21] The days of the slide presentation are nearing their end, folks. Why show slides when you can show the action? There has been a flood of presentation products that support all kinds of multimedia elements, and many of them offer at least crude animation capabilities. For some uses, that might be enough, but for real animation you need real animation software. The best such products are fluid and powerful.

---

[21]Not that you couldn't use 3D Studio to create some really dramatic business presentations, but that price tag would be hard to justify for everything but the most critical applications.

This situation has unfortunately created a conflict in the animation software world, and, as with all things computer, conflicts involve tradeoffs. On the one hand, business users need animation software that is mostly accessible and yet powerful. On the other hand, designers need animation software that is mostly powerful yet accessible. If you are going to get involved with animation, you are going to have to make a choice.

Your choice affects the kind of animation you do and the results you can expect. Business animation, for example, usually involves moving a fixed image along a path. With this technique, you load an image, specify the path, and the program takes care of the movement at playback time.

The more creatively oriented programs enable you to work more closely to the frame-based model. You can do *morphs,* shorthand lingo for changing one object or image into another, and get tight control over palettes, a must when dealing with a variety of images. A 256-color palette is pretty limited, and any two images can use very different palettes. If you plan to display both images at the same time, you need to create a combined palette that can be used by either image.

Consider the following animation software products:[22]

Product	Category
Action!	Business
Animation Works Interactive	Business
Animator	Creative
Animator Pro	Creative
Deluxe Paint Animation	Creative
PC Animate Plus	Business

Animation Works Interactive is not so much an image creation program as it is a program that enables you to take images you already have and animate them. Its strength is that it enables you to work with these images as objects. This feature makes creating animations easier because you can focus on what to do with the objects instead of figuring out how to create each frame. For example, you can create complex paths for the various objects, and, at playback time, everything will go just where it should.

---

[22]Some are more animated than others. Action!, for example, is technically a presentation product, but it offers some of the most complete animation capabilities in its class.

Animator and Animator Pro are programs that enable you to work on an animation frame by frame. They both include tools that do some tweening for you. Tweening involves three steps: creating a start frame, creating a finish frame, and generating the in-between frames.

Animator is actually sold in a package called Autodesk Multimedia Explorer, which includes a Windows animation playback utility and a CD-ROM full of images and animation examples. It differs from Animator Pro in that it is limited to an MCGA screen (320 × 200 with 256 colors). This makes Animator an interesting choice, and it gives you many of the sophisticated tools of Animator Pro if you can live with the low-resolution screen size. Animator Pro carries a price of just under $800. Animator sells for less than $200.

Deluxe Paint Animation is very inexpensive, listing for less than $135. It includes sophisticated image-manipulation techniques such as anti-aliasing (smoothing jagged edges by blending the colors slightly). You can paint on multiple frames at once, and the program provides a simple method for moving images across multiple frames. You can create a custom brush consisting of the image and then paint a line across the background. The image will move along this line, one step forward in each frame (you can specify the number of steps).

PC Animate Plus is also inexpensive, coming in at less than $200 list. It offers a good set of tools and sophisticated movement control, but it suffers from some design flaws. For example, previews are done with box outlines of objects, making it very hard to check your work in progress. Its strength is that it has the capability to work with higher resolutions, like 1024 × 768 with 256 colors. You can also include sounds in your animations if you have a Sound Blaster.

Because Action! was discussed earlier within the context of authoring a multimedia presentation (see Chapter 4 for details), this chapter examines the following packages:

➤ Animator

➤ Animator Pro

➤ 3D Workshop

➤ Animation Works Interactive

First, however, a look at the basic techniques involved in animation might be useful.

Animation Techniques

Animation relies on a quirk of human vision—if you see a sequence of images depicting steps in a process, you see motion instead of the individual steps. The images, however, must move quickly enough to sustain the illusion. Although different media move at different rates, 24 to 30 frames per second is a typical requirement for smooth motion.

In almost all animation, there is a stationary background and a moving foreground. The reason for this division is simple: if only a small part of the image changes, there is less work to do from one frame to the next.

Traditional Animation

To make an animated cartoon, the first step involves creating the key frames in the sequence. This step is usually done by advanced artists. The assistants have the job of creating the art for the frames between the key frames. The artwork is done on transparent plastic so it can be easily overlaid on the background. To create the final animated sequence, the plastic sheets, known as *cels,* are laid on the background one at a time and photographed.

Computer Animation

Computer animation creates more possibilities. The computer, for example, can create the in-between images. Using the computer for animation puts the processing power of the CPU on your side, and it can enable you to use all kinds of special effects without necessarily having any technical knowledge of the mathematics or principles involved.

Tweening

Different software packages implement tweening in different ways. A package like Animator uses tweening in a slightly untraditional sense. An Animator *tween* creates intermediate shapes between frames, each of which contains one of the standard animator polygons. This is more like *morphing* (short for metamorphosing) than a traditional tweening. PC Animate Plus, on the other hand, uses tweening in the traditional sense: it actually creates frames between the key frames.

These variations on the traditional jargon are only annoying if you know the jargon in the first place or if you have to move from one product to another. They are an inevitable result of the difference between traditional techniques and the techniques made possible on computers.

Cels

The concept of cels can be confusing. It helps to consider the original meaning of the term in traditional animation: the single plastic image that is overlaid on the background. It is common to have multiple cels in a frame. In a given frame, for example, perhaps only the character's arm moves. In this case, there is a cel for the character's body and another cel for the moving arm.

Most animation packages support the cel concept in one way or another—sometimes it's nothing more than an extra clipboard for storing images; sometimes it's made up of multiple images. Figure 9.40 shows an example of a cel from Animator.

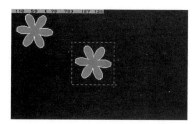

Figure 9.40. *An Animator cel.*

This cel was made by copying the image of the flower in the top-left corner of the cel buffer. The cel was then recalled and moved to the position you see on the current frame. To create an animation this way, paste the cel into each frame, moving it slightly each time. This is useful if you want to move an object along a complex path. If you want it to move in a straight line or a series of straight lines, use tweening.

Tracing

An easy way to create the next frame in a sequence is to trace the preceding cel (or, in some cases, the one that comes next). Not all software, however, supports this feature. Other packages rely on it heavily. This method is similar to traditional animation.

There are different ways of displaying the underlying image, including using another color (often blue) to represent what you are tracing and normal colors for the current frame.

Keyframing

This method refers to a different kind of keyframing than what is used in traditional animation, and it is only available in the high-end packages like 3D Studio or Topas Animator (from AT&T Graphics Software Labs). Refer to the section "The Keyframer" earlier in this chapter, It demonstrates keyframing in 3D Studio.

Morphing

Have you ever seen that commercial where a car turns into a tiger? Or the beer commercial where the couple's clothes (and hairstyles) change before your eyes? That action is known as *morphing* (short for metamorphosing). Not many low-end products have it, although it is included in both Animator products. 3D Studio, as you might expect, contains sophisticated morphing capabilities. Figure 9.41 shows a simple example of morphing from Animator (which calls the process *polymorphic tweening*). These are frames 1, 8, 15, 22, 27, and 32 from a 32-frame sequence.

Color Cycling

The colors in a 256-color palette are referred to by their color index. This is a number, from 0 to 255, that indicates which color in the palette to use. Although there are 64 (6 bits each) possible values for each of the red, green, and blue components of each color in the palette (giving you a choice of 262,144 colors), the palette can only contain a total of 256 colors. Each palette, however, can pick those 256 colors from all of the possible combinations of the 262,144 colors.

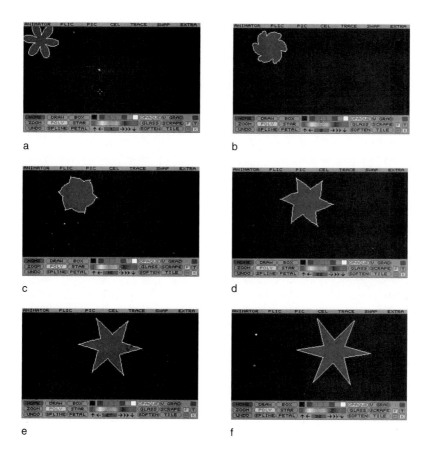

a
b
c
d
e
f

Figure 9.41. *An example of morphing (polymorphic tweening) in Animator.*

It is not possible, obviously, to display a color that is not in the palette. However, it is a simple task to rotate the palette. That is, you can move the color index table by one value. The color that was in index 10 can be moved to index 11, for example, for all colors.

The effect on the screen is subtle, especially if the palette consists of related colors—a given pixel's index does not change. If a pixel had color 11, it now shows the color that used to be in 10. This effect varies with screen content, but if the palette uses graduated colors in the index positions—from white through gray to black, for example—then the changing palette indices will simulate motion. Unfortunately, this is much easier to demonstrate than it is to explain.

Paths

If you don't need to morph an image as it moves, you can simply specify a moving path. Some products enable you to specify a distance parameter, which shrinks and enlarges the image as it is moved "farther" and "closer."

The methods for controlling the path and the number of steps vary from one product to another. Some, such as Animation Works Interactive, enable paths to interact with each other. For example, you could establish a path for a moving car and create a path relative to the car for an object "inside" it. The inside object then follows the complex path that corresponds to the car motion and its own motion.

Key Colors and Masking

A key color is a color that can be dropped out of an image, enabling some other image to "show through." A common example of this is the way that the weather map appears behind the meteorologist on the 11 o'clock news. This is an excellent way to create interesting background effects, but not all software products support it. Of the previously mentioned packages, only Action! does not support key colors.

Masking enables you to mark an area of a frame that will not be affected by the current effect. This can be handy if you need to move an object behind another object.

Onion Skin/Tracing

This technique enables you to create a new frame based on an existing frame. Only Action! and Deluxe Paint Animation lack this feature.

Wipes and Fades

This enables you to reveal a different frame using horizontal or vertical transition, or to smoothly fade one frame into another. Some products only fade or wipe to solid colors (Action! and PC Animate Plus), and others lack the feature entirely (Deluxe Paint Animation). These other products, however, offer a number of transition effects.

3D Effects

All of the products previously listed except Action! and Animation Works Interactive support spinning an object in the *z* (third) dimension (depth).

Animator

Animator is part of Autodesk's Multimedia Explorer package, and that gives it quite a bit of punch. This package ships with a CD that is crammed with complete animations and still backgrounds you can use with your own animations.

Animator inherits a lot of power from its big brother: Animator Pro. A few features are missing, of course (thus, the low price). The most important drawback, however, is that although Animator Pro can work with images at large sizes, high resolutions, and 24-bit color, Animator is limited to 256 colors and 320 × 200 pixels (also known as MCGA), and it requires a VGA board and monitor. If you can live within this range, Animator is one heck of a program. This program is an inexpensive way to get a lot of sample animations and a good way to learn the basics for upward migration to the Pro package.

You can, however, develop professional-looking animations with the basic package—several ship with Multimedia Explorer. Some of the best Animator animations use 256 gray shades enabling you to achieve excellent visual results. You could even reserve a few key colors for emphasis on your palette.

One of the most powerful tools included with Animator is a tool Autodesk calls a tweening tool. However, this is not a classic tween. It is more like a morph because it enables you to transform one shape into another. Although you are limited to changing one stock shape into another, it's not like you can transform anything into anything else (use 3D Studio for that). (Refer to the "Animation Techniques" section for an example of polymorphic tweening.)

Creating an Object

The opening screen for Animator is shown in Figure 9.42.

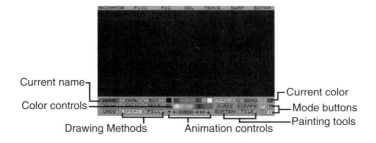

Current name

Color controls

Drawing Methods

Current color

Mode buttons

Painting tools

Animation controls

Figure 9.42. The opening screen of Animator.

In this figure, the menu is located at the top of the screen, and the home panel is displayed at the bottom of the screen. Depending on what you are doing, different panels are displayed at the bottom of the screen. The name of the current panel appears at the top-center or top-left portion of the panel.

One interesting feature of Animator is that you can select from a wide variety of drawing and painting tools. The drawing tools define the brush (line, box, star, and spray), and the painting tools define the method the brush uses (opaque, gradient, soft edge, and tiling). You can display up to six of each in the home panel. Clicking on any displayed tool with the right mouse button enables you to replace it with one of the other tools.

To create an object, select the drawing tool and the painting method. Left-click to start, and click again to complete. Once you create an object, you can copy it to the cel buffer using the Cel|Clip menu choice (see Figure 9.43).

Figure 9.43. A drop-down cel buffer menu.

The cel image is stored apart from the main screen, but you can look at it any time, and you can easily paste the cel into the current frame using the Cel|Paste menu choice (see Figure 9.44).

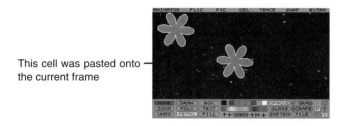

This cell was pasted onto
the current frame

Figure 9.44. An example of a pasted cel (the center image).

If you want to specify a screen region as the cel, use the Cel\Get menu choice. This menu item enables you to draw a box around the portion of the screen you want to use as the cel (see Figure 9.45).

The boxed area is
now defined as a
cel

Figure 9.45. Using the Cel\Get menu choice, the boxed area is now defined as the cel.

Animator enables you to work creatively with the cel. By defining different key colors, you can determine what portion of the cel is or is not transparent (see Figure 9.46).

Figure 9.46. An example of transparency using Animator.

In Figure 9.46, the flower petal fill color is transparent (that is, it was selected as the key color), enabling the current frame image to show through.

Animating Existing Images

Although the flower-petal image doesn't look all that impressive (it's a very simple two-color shape), Animator supports 256 colors and enables you to import realistic images (see Figure 9.47).

Figure 9.47. *An imported "realistic" image.*

Animator contains a swap buffer as well as a cel buffer. You can copy the current image to the swap buffer—the swap buffer is "behind" the current frame—and this enables you to create some nifty special effects. You can use a thick brush with the Scrape method, for example, to scrape away a black background and reveal the contents of the swap buffer (see Figure 9.48).

Figure 9.48. *An image altered using the Scrape method.*

Animator also gives you the power to work in creative ways with 256-color images. You can take the image of the woman's face and create a mirror-image face—a face that is identical on the left and right sides—by copying the right side of the face to the buffer and moving it left (see Figure 9.49).

Figure 9.49. *An example of a mirror-image alteration.*

After applying a mirror transformation and stretching the image to 100 percent, the completed image looks like Figure 9.50.

Figure 9.50. *The completed image after applying mirror transformation.*

3D Workshop

3D Workshop is an intriguing product that does some of the same things that 3D Studio does but at a lower cost. Before you get too excited, you should know that it is no competition for 3D Studio. It is, however, a very inexpensive way to explore 3D modeling and animation. Its opening screen is quite similar to 3D Studio's opening screen (see Figure 9.51).

Instead of the text menus that 3D Studio uses, 3D Workshop uses pull-down menus (actually, 3D Studio does feature a few pull-down menus, but they are mostly for file operations and related tasks). The scrollable area at the right side of the screen lists all objects in the scene. Animation playback controls are located at the bottom of the screen.

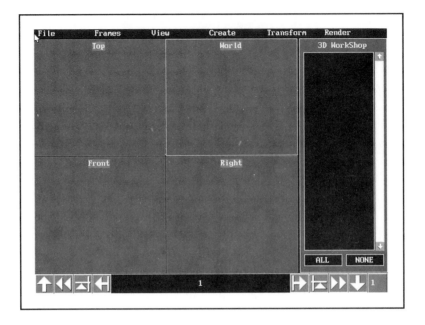

Figure 9.51. *The opening screen for 3D Workshop.*

Creating an Object

To create a new object, draw it on the Make Objects screen (see Figure 9.52).

In this example, I will create a surface-of-revolution object (3D Workshop calls it a *spin template*) that enables you to control several variables of the spin, including a less-than-360-degree spin (see Figure 9.53).

Like 3D Studio, 3D Workshop enables you to attach materials to surfaces, and you can view an object as a wireframe (see Figure 9.54).

You can also render the object (see Figure 9.55).

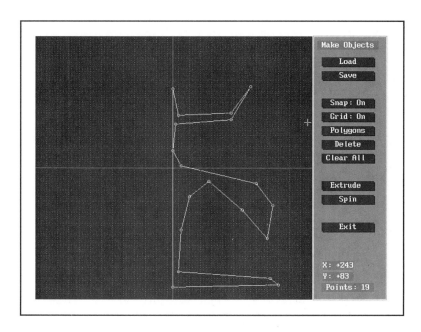

Figure 9.52. *The first stage of a new figure created with the Make Objects screen.*

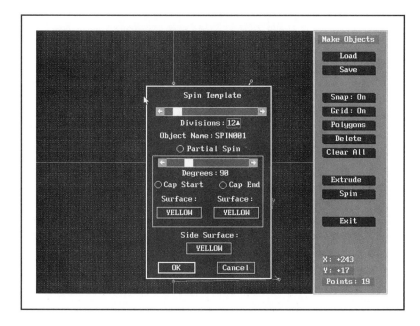

Figure 9.53. *The Spin Template dialog box.*

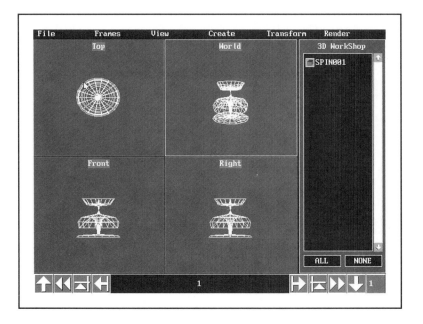

Figure 9.54. *Four views of a wireframe object.*

Figure 9.55. *An example of a rendered object.*

As you can see, the rendering quality is not up to the level of 3D Studio. Then again, the price is also not up to the level of 3D Studio.

Although I found that 3D Workshop was occasionally unable to do what I wanted it to do, I recommend it if you want to explore the concepts and capabilities of 3D animation. It offers many of the features of 3D Studio. Although the results are not what I would call professional, and the speed of the program is slower than 3D Studio, it undeniably gives you access to the world of 3D animation at a remarkably low price.

Professional Animation: Animator Pro

The heavyweight in the animation division is Animator Pro from Autodesk. It doesn't have the sheer power of a 3D modeling program like 3D Studio, but it does allow you to create just about any kind of animation. Unlike its little brother, Animator, Animator Pro can be used at high screen resolutions, including 640 × 480, 800 × 600, and 1024 × 768. In order to use the higher resolutions, you need a video board that either supports VEDA standards directly or includes a device driver that adds VEDA support.

The key features of Animator Pro include:

➤ The ability to create cels and to use a swap screen to quickly create cel-based animations with imported pictures

➤ Support for palette management. When you only have 256 colors to work with, the capability to merge palettes, create new palettes, and edit palettes can be invaluable

➤ Support for traditional traced animation with sophisticated tools for copying changes from one frame to the next and viewing the contents of adjoining frames

➤ Time-based drawing support. This feature enables you to create and import images that are automatically tweened when pasted

➤ A sophisticated programming language—POCO—that enables you to create your own special effects (or use third-party effects). The latest version of Animator Pro comes with a POCO routine that enables you to build animated presentations interactively

A new version of Animator Pro was released as this book was going to press. It includes only minor changes to the program. The best reasons to buy it (Version 1.3) are that it comes with a CD that contains a large selection of quality animation samples and that it reads and writes .bmp files directly.

Like 3D Studio, Animator Pro has excellent documentation. Although the program is superb for creative animation, there is an extensive (several hundred pages) tutorial covering just about anything you would ever want to do in a business animation. The tutorial manual also covers many aspects of sophisticated animation techniques.

If you want to create professional-looking animations with lots of razzle-dazzle, Animator Pro gives you the capabilities. However, like any really powerful program, Animator Pro takes some time to learn. Fortunately, the documentation is well organized and complete.

Creating an Image

The Animator Pro screen (see Figure 9.56) is similar to the Animator screen. Although the menu bar is still located across the top and the home panel is still at the bottom of the screen, there's a lot more screen real estate to work with. I worked at 640 × 480 with 256 colors for this example.

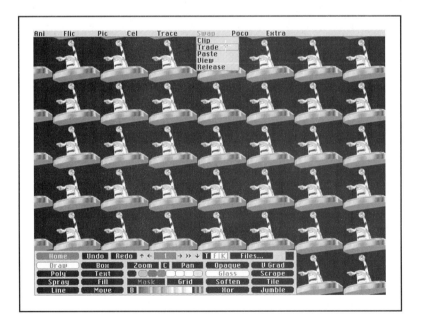

Figure 9.56. *The Animator Pro opening screen.*

Animator Pro comes with a large number of sample files—both animations and still pictures. I imported a picture of a faucet for this example (see Figure 9.57).

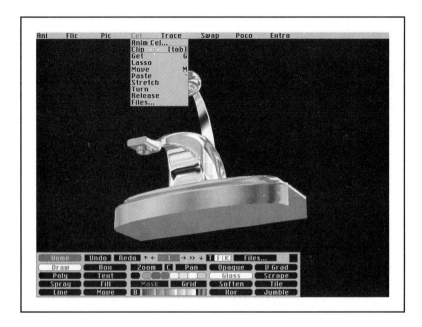

Figure 9.57. *An imported sample file from Animator Pro.*

As you can see in Figure 9.57, the Cel menu is open, and Clip is selected. Cel|Clip copies the current image and makes it the current Cel. *Cel* is an animation term that refers to a single item that is being animated. You can make the entire current image a cel, or you can select a portion of the image. I also selected Swap|Clip to put a copy of the image into the swap buffer.

In addition to its strong animation capabilities, Animator Pro is also a capable (if idiosyncratic) paint program. For example, there are a number of built-in special effects that are easy to access (see Figure 9.58).

For this example, I used Shrink x2 twice to make the image one-quarter of its original size (see Figure 9.59).

You can now select Tile as the painting method (this pastes an image repeatedly to fill a given space) and choose Apply Ink from the Pic menu to get a background consisting of many little faucet images (see Figure 9.60).

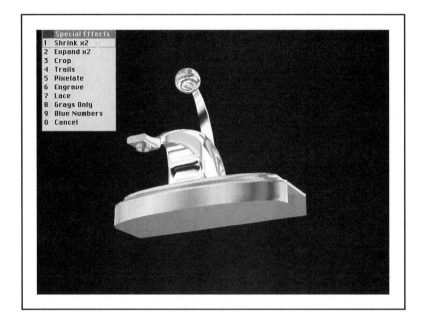

Figure 9.58. *Animator Pro's Special Effects menu.*

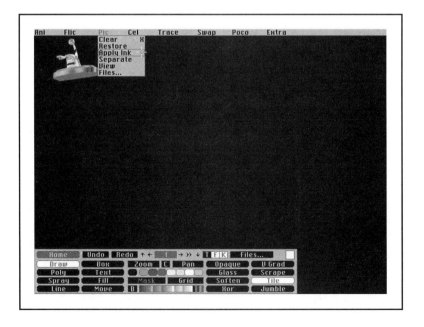

Figure 9.59. *An example usage of the Shrink x2 menu item.*

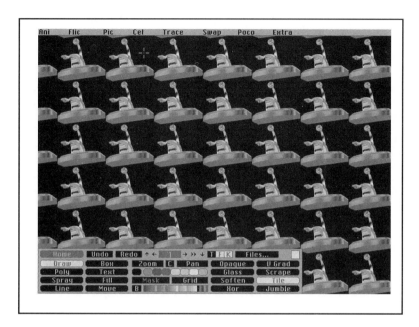

Figure 9.60. *A tiled-image background pattern.*

Because this pattern is too bright to be used as a background, use the Glass tool to darken it. The Glass tool applies 50 percent of the current color to the image. If you choose black as the current color and again Apply Ink, the image is darkened and becomes more appropriate for use as a background pattern (see Figure 9.61).

Manipulating Images

Animator Pro also contains a Swap menu that enables you to manipulate a swap buffer. If you recall, Swap|Clip was used earlier to put a copy of the current image into the swap buffer. If you want to place the original, full-size image on top of the background, select Swap|Trade to make the screen from the swap buffer visible. Select Cel|Clip to make the faucet the current cel and then select Swap|Trade again to return to the background.

Selecting Cel|Paste puts the current cel (the cel was created at the beginning of this process) into the image as the current selection (see Figure 9.62).

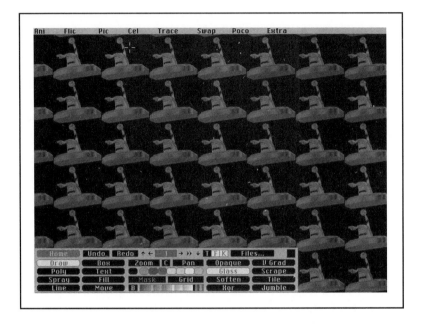

Figure 9.61. *A revised tiled-image background pattern.*

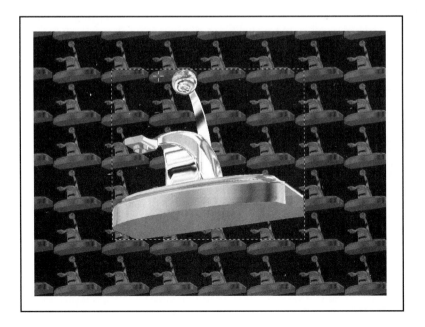

Figure 9.62. *The faucet as the current selection.*

Now you can click on the selection, move it, and then click again to drop it into place (see Figure 9.63).

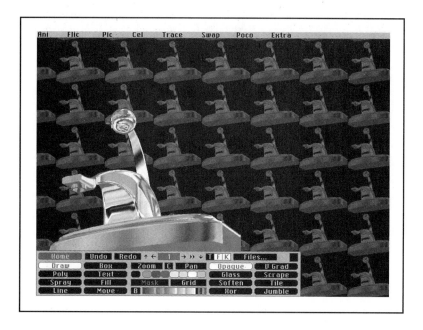

Figure 9.63. *An example of a placed selection.*

The animation consists of text that "flies" in from the left side of the screen. You can create 60 frames easily using Animate|Frame to display the Frame panel (see Figure 9.64).

In this example, all 60 frames contain the background image because the current image is always copied into new frames. Now you can use Swap|Trade to display the Swap screen. Because the working screen is still there (just hidden from view), you can clear the swap screen and enter the text on it (see Figure 9.65).

To animate the text, use Cell|Clip to copy it to the cel buffer (making the text the current cel) and Cell|Move to move it off-screen. This is the starting point for the motion.

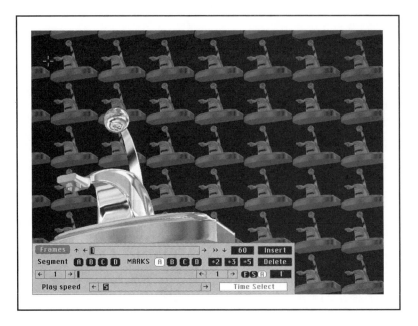

Figure 9.64. *The Animator Frame panel.*

Figure 9.65. *The Swap screen.*

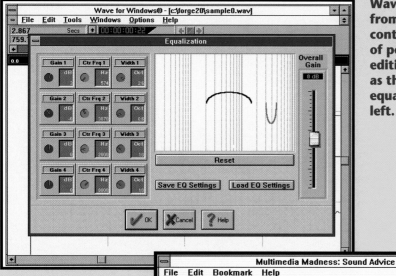

Wave for Windows from Turtle Beach contains a number of powerful sound editing tools, such as the parametric equalizer shown at left.

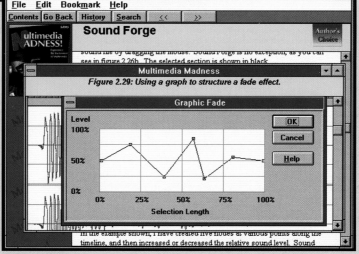

Sound Forge has a great interface and some nifty ways of working with sounds. Graphic editing of a fade effect is shown at right.

This is an example of a new breed of user interface—it looks just like a CD player, not like a computer program. This is the CD player in MCS Stereo from Animation.

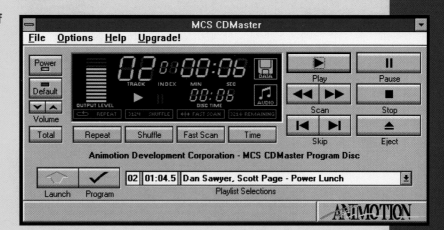

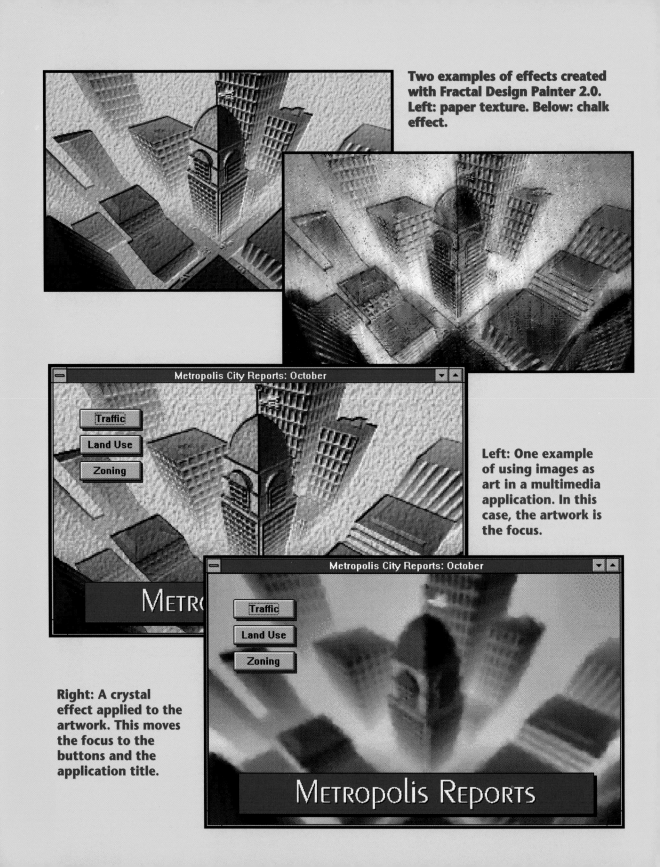

Two examples of effects created with Fractal Design Painter 2.0. Left: paper texture. Below: chalk effect.

Left: One example of using images as art in a multimedia application. In this case, the artwork is the focus.

Right: A crystal effect applied to the artwork. This moves the focus to the buttons and the application title.

I used PhotoStyler to change the photo at right with a watercolor filter from Aldus Gallery Effects (below).

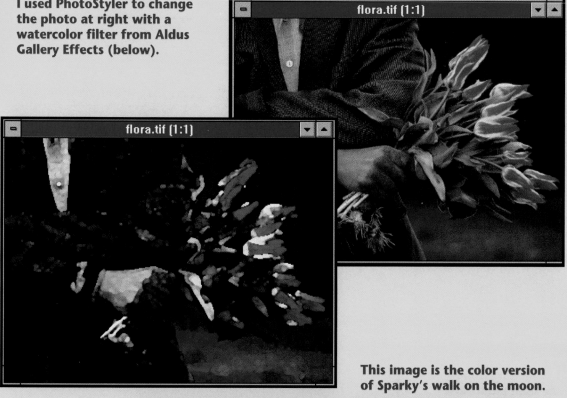

flora.tif (1:1)

This image is the color version of Sparky's walk on the moon.

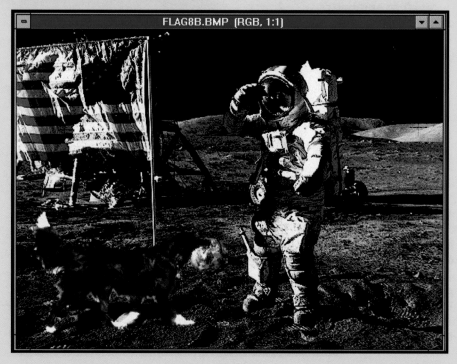

FLAG8B.BMP (RGB, 1:1)

The image at right has two components. The drawing itself is a freehand drawing of a rhubarb plant, done with a stylus and a drawing tablet in Fractal Design Painter 2.0. The background is a bit of clip art that came with Photoshop. I used Photoshop to combine the two elements into the graphic you see here.

Above: A detail showing how I used darkening (rather than painting a new color) to emphasize the leaves.

An example of a multimedia presentation in Action! This slide shows a title, some text, and a bitmap. A few sparkles also are visible—one of numerous special effects built into Action!

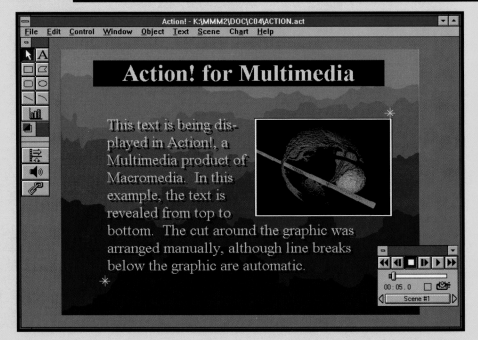

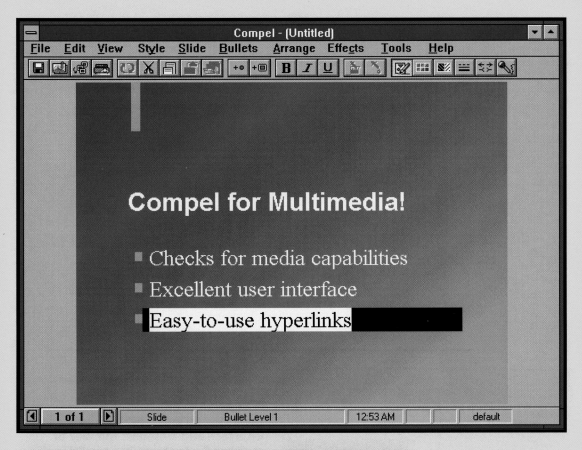

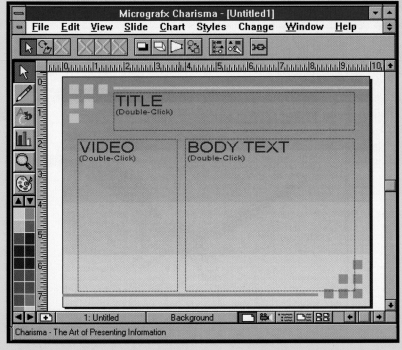

Above: The Compel interface. Note the toolbar below the menu; it contains icons for most of the things you'll do on a regular basis. Compel has excellent multimedia support.

Left: A sample screen of Charisma 4.0 (taken from a pre-release version; some features are not active). Note that Charisma makes it very easy to add multimedia elements to a slide.

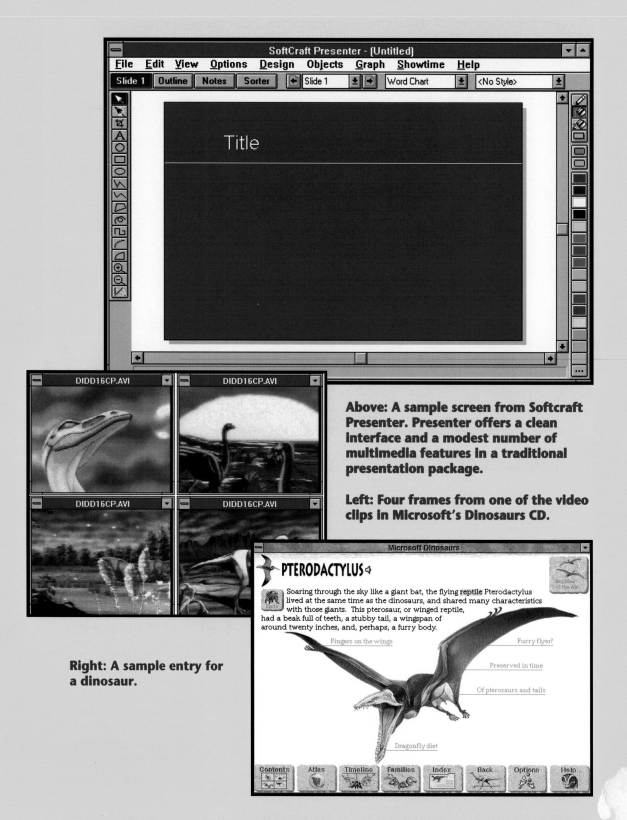

Above: A sample screen from Softcraft Presenter. Presenter offers a clean interface and a modest number of multimedia features in a traditional presentation package.

Left: Four frames from one of the video clips in Microsoft's Dinosaurs CD.

Right: A sample entry for a dinosaur.

PTERODACTYLUS

Soaring through the sky like a giant bat, the flying reptile Pterodactylus lived at the same time as the dinosaurs, and shared many characteristics with those giants. This pterosaur, or winged reptile, had a beak full of teeth, a stubby tail, a wingspan of around twenty inches, and, perhaps, a furry body.

Fingers on the wings

Furry flyer?

Preserved in time

Of pterosaurs and tails

Dragonfly diet

Contents   Atlas   Timeline   Families   Index   Back   Options   Help

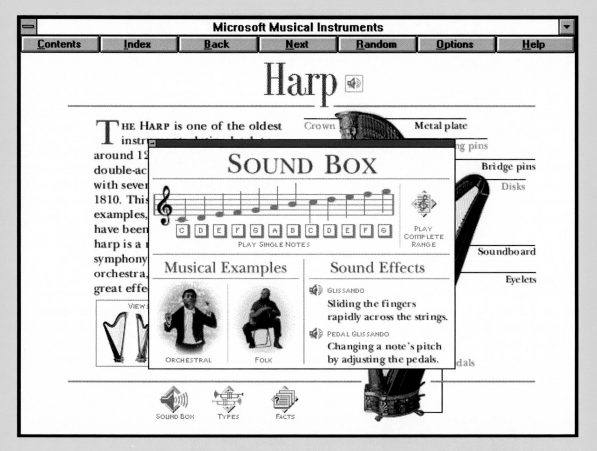

Above: A sample page from Microsoft's Musical Instruments. Also shown is the Sound Box, which lets you play specific notes, as well as sound effects and musical pieces, using the instrument.

Right: A scene from Arthur's Teacher Trouble. This interactive reading/play program for kids got a high rating from our family.

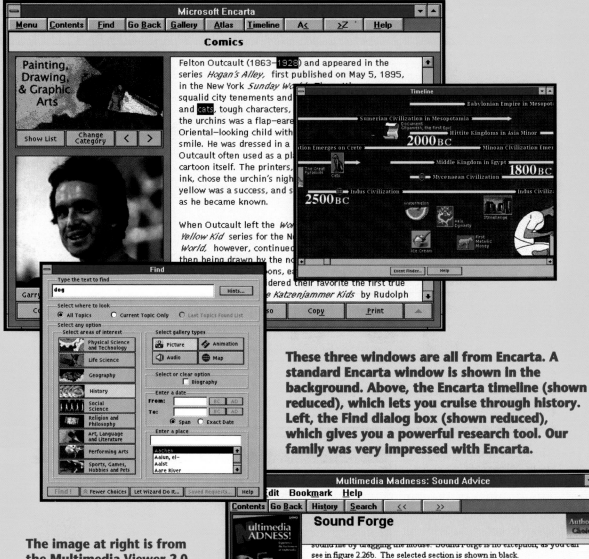

These three windows are all from Encarta. A standard Encarta window is shown in the background. Above, the Encarta timeline (shown reduced), which lets you cruise through history. Left, the Find dialog box (shown reduced), which gives you a powerful research tool. Our family was very impressed with Encarta.

The image at right is from the Multimedia Viewer 2.0 application I developed using Chapter 2 of this book. You can find the complete application on the Nautilus CD. The image of the book at upper left is in a separate pane, and the text is in the master pane. The green underlined text indicates hot spots. Clicking on a hot spot displays a bitmap.

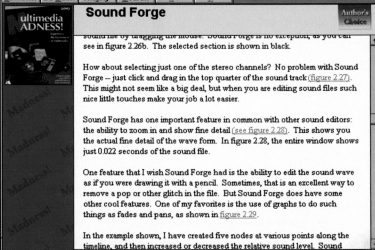

Above: This sample Toolbook application plays video files. It shows you how to program with video using Multimedia Toolbook. It also make a great video playback application.

Below: Example of using artwork in a multimedia title. The underlying image was lightened in Photoshop to make it fade into the background.

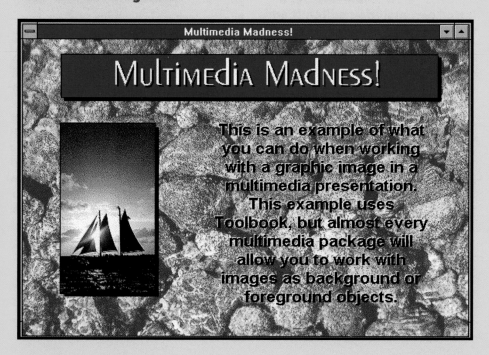

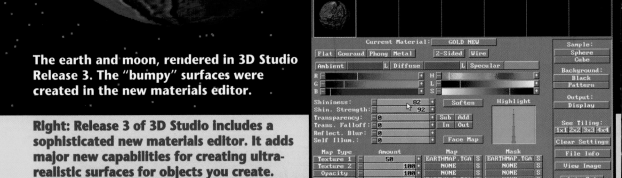

The earth and moon, rendered in 3D Studio Release 3. The "bumpy" surfaces were created in the new materials editor.

Right: Release 3 of 3D Studio includes a sophisticated new materials editor. It adds major new capabilities for creating ultra-realistic surfaces for objects you create.

Left: The Animation Works Interactive interface. The toolbar at left contains a number of tools for working with object and actor paths. An actor is shown in a window at top right, and the playback controller is at lower right.

A scene from the Newt animation created with Playmation.

Left: An image rendered with Pixar's Typestry.

Left: Typestry gives you an amazing number of extremely realistic textures to apply to the letters, walls, and floor of the workspace.

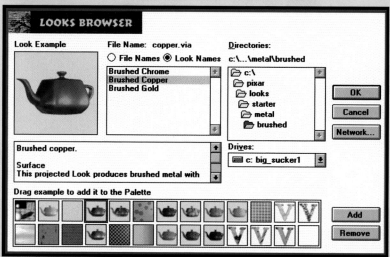

LOOKS BROWSER

Look Example

File Name: copper.via

○ File Names ● Look Names

Brushed Chrome
Brushed Copper
Brushed Gold

Directories:

c:\...\metal\brushed

c:\
pixar
looks
starter
metal
brushed

Brushed copper.

Surface
This projected Look produces brushed metal with

Drives:

c: big_sucker1

OK

Cancel

Network...

Drag example to add it to the Palette

Add

Remove

These eight frames are from an animation created with Pixar's Typestry.

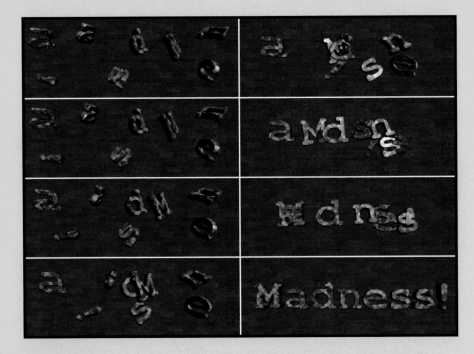

Below: Adding control points to a pair of images in PhotoMorph.

The project editor in PhotoMorph. It is your control center, and it gives you access to all morphing, warping, and special effects.

Above: A sample frame from a video created with the Media Merge Scene Editor.

Right: A frame at the midpoint of the morph of Arafat into Rabin.

From left to right, the three images above show how not to light a scene: too much light, light from only one side, and too little light. The large image at left shows my wife, Donna, in her best light.

This image, rendered in 3D Studio, shows how I set up lights for the shot of Donna.

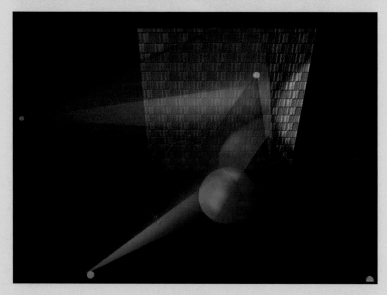

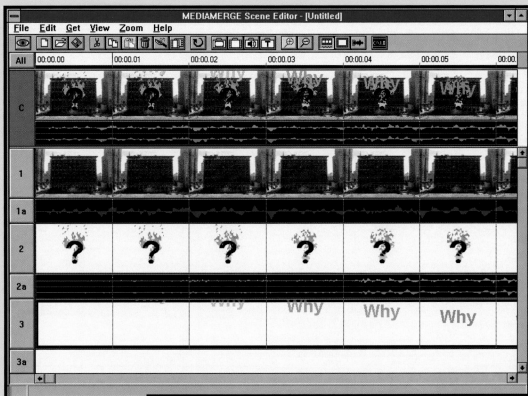

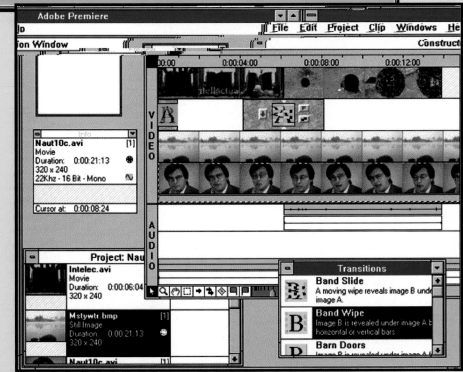

Above: The Scene Editor in Media Merge from ATI. The top line shows the composite result, and the other three lines show various video clips.

Right: The Premiere interface, with its own time-line arrangement. Note the Transitions window; this is one of Premiere's strongest features.

Above: Three sample still-frame captures. From left to right: Intel Smart Video Recorder, S-Video in; Captivator, composite in; Captivator, S-Video in.

Left: VidCap from Video for Windows.

Right: VidEdit from Video for Windows, showing a number of the editing features on the Video menu.

Below: The Audio Visual Recorder, an alternative video capture interface from in:sync.

Creating Motion

So far, you have been working with one frame at a time. Even though you created new frames, the preceding actions had no effect on the other 59 frames. There is a small box with the letter *T* in it at the top-center of the home panel. Clicking the T box puts you into Time Drawing mode. In this mode, drawing, pasting, or otherwise altering the image affects multiple frames. You can apply Time Drawing to a range of frames or to all frames.

Now that you are in Time mode, select Cell|Paste to put a copy of the current cel on the screen. Click to grab the cel, drag it to the right side of the screen (the end point for the animation), and click to drop it in place. Animator Pro doesn't have enough information to handle the Time Drawing yet, so the dialog box shown in Figure 9.66 appears.

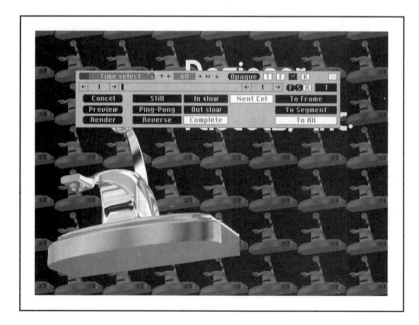

Figure 9.66. *The dropped-in Time Select dialog box.*

This box is called the Time Select panel, and it is the key to controlling Time Drawing. For example, the boxes at the right side of the panel enable you to choose over what range of frames the animation will take place. In this case, I selected

To All. This means that the text appears in the start position (off the left side of the screen) in frame 1, and in the final position in frame 60. In intermediate frames, the text is in an intermediate position.

Several options for special effects are located on the left-center portion of the panel (these options include such things as Ping-Ponging and Reverse animation). I chose Complete for this example.

The boxes on the left side of the dialog box enable you to preview the effect or render it. Normally, I choose Preview first to see what I've done, and, if I like it, I select Render.

Once you click Render, you can watch Animator Pro put the text into the 59 additional frames. The original location of the cel (on the left side of the frame) becomes the position for cel 1. For frame 2, Animator Pro puts a copy of the cel exactly one-sixtieth of the distance from the original position to the final position (where it was dropped). This process continues for each frame until all 60 frames have been rendered.

That's all there is to Cel-based animation. If the steps seem complex or confusing, don't be discouraged. After a few animations, you'll get the hang of it. Animator Pro has its own way of doing things, and animation itself is a complex process. Animator Pro does a good job of giving you the tools to create animations that are impressive and entertaining. You can export 3D animations created with 3D Studio and add to them in Animator Pro. You can also join or fade animations together.

Animation Works Interactive

Animation Works Interactive (AWI) provides a lot of animation muscle in a very accessible package. It is (mostly) not a drawing package. It uses path animation, which enables you to point to a starting and ending position for an object. The software then takes care of moving the object from frame to frame. This might seem limiting, but it's not—there are many kinds of objects, including ones called *actors*. An actor is itself an animation (usually a traditional cel-based animation), and the actor will act as it moves along the path. For example, you could have a bird flying, a man walking, and so on.

This is what gives Animation Works Interactive its power and flexibility. AWI comes with a large collection of actors to get you started. It also includes a variety of backgrounds and other resources that you can rely on to put a presentation together quickly. You can also create your own resources or use third-party clip art. Figure 9.67 shows the opening screen of AWI.

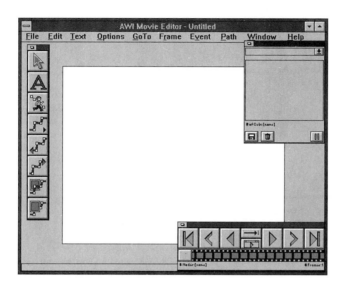

Figure 9.67. *Animation Works Interactive opening screen.*

The toolbar at the left of the AWI screen is used for entering text (the "A" tool) and paths. You'll learn more about paths shortly. The control at bottom right is a play controller; you can rewind, step forward and backward, play forward and reverse, and so on. The small window at upper right is a holding bin for actors. To load an actor, click the small disk icon at the lower left of the actor window. This displays the dialog box shown in Figure 9.68.

This is a modified file-open dialog; it displays a preview of the actor at bottom right (in this case, a cloud).

Now for some bad news: AWI operates only in 256-color mode. This means you are going to have to deal with palettes. You should, if at all possible, establish a palette for all objects in your animation—videos, bitmaps, actors, and so on. AWI offers some tools for reconciling palettes, but the best approach is to minimize palette differences between objects.

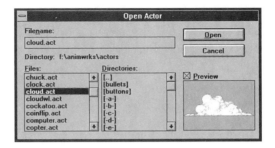

Figure 9.68. *Opening an actor.*

Figure 9.69 shows a dialog that will appear frequently if you don't take steps to control palettes. It enables you to remap the palette of an incoming object, select from a list of available palettes, or keep the palette of an object.

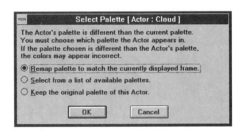

Figure 9.69. *Working with palettes.*

Figure 9.70 shows the AWI screen with an actor loaded into the Actor window. In fact, there are a number of actors loaded into this window as you can see in Figure 9.71. In general, you should load the actors you need for an animation to have them available in the Actor window.

To place the current actor (I chose the cockatoo) and its path, select one of the path tools, then click to establish the start point, drag the mouse to the end point, and release. This displays the Adjust Path dialog box (see Figure 9.72).

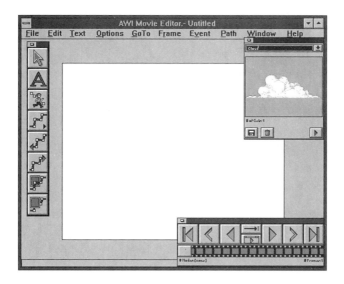

Figure 9.70. *An actor in the Actor window.*

Figure 9.71. *Multiple actors loaded into the Actor window.*

Figure 9.72. *The Adjust Path dialog box.*

You specify the number of frames for the path. In the example, I have specified 20 frames. That means the object will travel from the beginning to the end of the path over the course of 20 frames. You can also specify acceleration and deceleration parameters, which enables you to simulate more realistic motion. For example, you might have a car accelerate over the first 15 percent of the frames rather than just jump into motion.

Figure 9.73 shows the result of placing an actor along a path. In this example, I used a straight path, but you can use curved, angled, or many other kinds of paths—including closed loops. You can move any of the nodes of a path, one at a time; there is one node for each frame. This enables you to adjust or fine-tune the path.

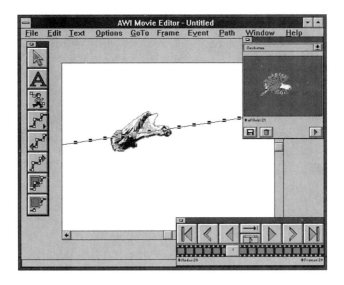

Figure 9.73. *An actor and its path.*

You can also use backgrounds for your animation. You can import any 256-color bitmap, but unless you are willing to be bound by its palette, I would suggest using a simpler background with fewer colors.[23] Figure 9.74 shows the

---

[23]One way to live with 256-color palettes is to use only some of the colors in each part of the animation.

Background Editor—it's a basic image editor, like Paintbrush but with a few more tools. If you require other capabilities to create the backgrounds you need, you can use an image editor as long as it saves .BMP files.

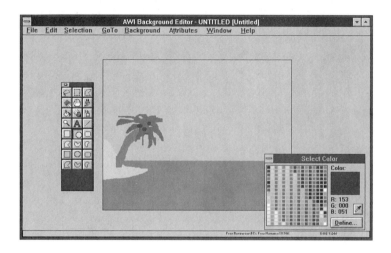

Figure 9.74. *Creating a background in the Background Editor.*

Figure 9.75 shows the background loaded into the animation as well as a few additional actors (a cloud and a cute little fish).

This is just a simple example of an animation. You can also add all kinds of multimedia elements to your animation. In this sense, AWI is a kind of presentation program with lots and lots of animation tools. Figure 9.76 shows the dialog box for adding a video event. You can specify the video name and the size and position of the playback window.[24]

The video will start to play at the frame where you add the video event. You need to make sure that there are sufficient remaining frames to allow the video (or any other multimedia event) to complete. Figure 9.77 shows the appearance of a frame with a video event. This makes it easy to size and position the frame.[25]

---

[24]You can also play the video full screen.

[25]You can't just grab it and resize it. However, you can use the Set Rect button in the Video Event dialog to do so.

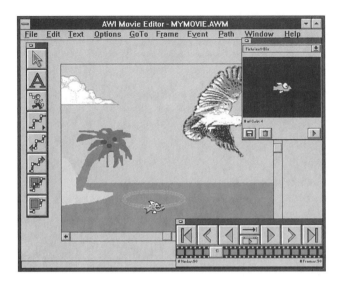

Figure 9.75. *A completed basic animation.*

Figure 9.76. *Adding a video event.*

Figure 9.78 shows the video file playing. Note that actors that move in front of a video take some of their background color with them; make sure no actors cross a video unless this effect is acceptable to you.

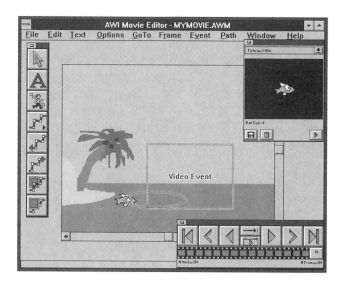

Figure 9.77. *A video frame in an event.*

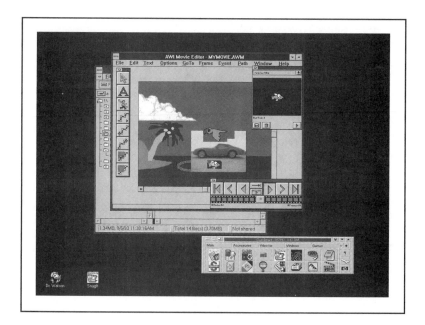

Figure 9.78. *Playing a video.*

Video files have their own palettes. Some video files use an embedded palette, whereas others will dither to the current palette. You can also use MCI commands to force the video to realize its palette in the background.[26] Alternatively, you can use the palette of an .AVI file as the palette for the animation. You can use PalEdit (it comes with Video for Windows) to extract palettes, but AWI will add the palette of a video file to the list of available palettes when you add a video event. Figure 9.79 shows the Select Palette dialog box. Note the entry for CARS2; this is the .AVI file that was added as an event.

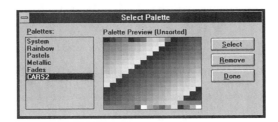

Figure 9.79. *Video files have their palette added to the list of available palettes.*

Working with palettes requires thought on your part. AWI makes it about as easy as it can, but the nature of 256-color palettes is complicated. The more visual elements you use in your animation and the more variety in types of elements (bitmaps, video, and so on), the more complex the palette issues.

Similarly, you can add .WAV or .MID file sounds to your animation. Just pick the frame where the sound is to start, and use the Event|Sound dialog to select the sound file.

Animation Works Interactive has many other powerful features—too numerous to mention here, so I'll just hit the high spots. You can fade using palettes, scroll backgrounds, enter MCI commands directly, execute other applications, link events to path animations, and so on. Figure 9.80 shows the dialog for Path Interaction. As you can see, just about any interaction with an actor can result in almost any kind of multimedia event.

I found AWI easy to work with and very feature rich. It has a very good combination of features for both animation and presentation. It's very flexible, and the interface is well organized. I recommend it.

---

[26]The syntax is `realize <alias> background`.

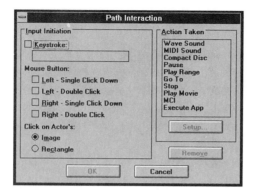

Figure 9.80. *Path Interaction dialog box.*

PhotoMorph

And now for something completely different: morphing. Since the first edition of this book, several good morphing programs have come out. However, one of them is head and shoulders above the rest—PhotoMorph from North Coast Software.

Morphing is cool stuff, and it's been great to see it on PCs. You've seen it at the movies (Terminator 2 is an excellent example) and on TV (that car that turns into a tiger, for example), and now you can do it yourself.

Different programs give you different tools for creating morphs. In this section, you learn how PhotoMorph manages its magic tricks. The program itself is deceptively simple looking, as shown in Figure 9.81.

At the time I was writing this chapter, the historic peace treaty between Israel and the PLO was being signed, so I had a little fun and dug up images of two of the principle players as you can see in Figure 9.81—Yitzak Rabin and Yassir Arafat. Naturally, it occurred to me to morph one into the other in honor of the historic occasion.[27]

---

[27]Morphing does seem to lend itself to a certain irreverence; for my book *PC Video Madness*, I tried morphing myself into Bill Gates.

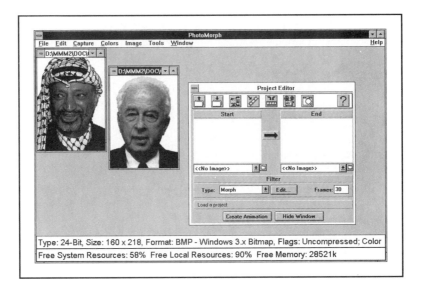

Figure 9.81. PhotoMorph, with two bitmaps loaded.

You can load a variety of images into PhotoMorph; it is also a good general-purpose image editor—nothing fancy like Photoshop, but it does have good tools for working with things like colors, borders, resizing, and so on.

The Project Editor

The actual morphing is done in the Project Editor shown in Figure 9.82.

The Project Editor has two slots for images. You can load any of the images currently loaded into PhotoMorph by clicking on the drop-down list boxes below the image slots, or you can load images directly from disk by clicking on the tiny little file folder button next to each list box. In Figure 9.82, I loaded an image into each slot. Note that the Type (bottom left) is set to Morph; PhotoMorph also includes other cool kinds of image transformations, such as image warps and fancy special effects like twists and rotations. Note also that the number of frames for the morph is set to 30. This is a good number for a smooth morph. If you have too few frames, the morph will be too jumpy. You can output the morph as a series of bitmaps, as an .AVI file, or as a flic file.

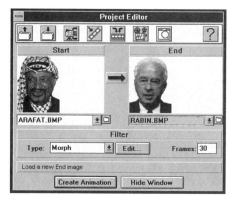

Figure 9.82. *The PhotoMorph Project Editor.*

Once you have loaded the images, it's time to get down to business. Click the Edit button to display the Morph|Warp Editor (see Figure 9.83).

Figure 9.83. *The Morph|Warp Editor window.*

This is where the action is. The two images appear side by side. There are four buttons for each image. From top to bottom they are:

Create new control point
Move control point
Delete control point
Adjust zoom factor

Yes, it's all about control points. What's a control point? It's a little square thing that you put all over the images as shown in Figure 9.84.

Figure 9.84. *Adding control points to the images.*

Control Points Explained

There is method to the madness. To place the control points, first click the Create control point button on one image, and the Adjust control point button on the other image. Add one control point to one image. PhotoMorph adds a corresponding control point to the other image. All you have to do is move that second control point to the right position. For example, if you click to place a control point on the left corner of Arafat's left eye, the corresponding point will appear on Rabin's forehead because the eyes in the two images aren't in the same place. All you have to do is drag that little control point to where it belongs at the left corner of Rabin's left eye, and you are ready for your next control point.

How many control points must you use? For many situations, you won't need as many as I used in Figure 9.84. I'm a bit of a perfectionist, and I wanted to have a really, really good morph for the CD, so I used lots of control points. For example, I used eight points for each eye; you might get by with just four for each. I also followed the outline very closely, and you could get by with just a few control points.

When you have enough control points, click the OK button in the Morph|Warp Editor to return to the Project Editor. Figure 9.85 shows an expanded version of the Project Editor revealing a few hidden features.[28]

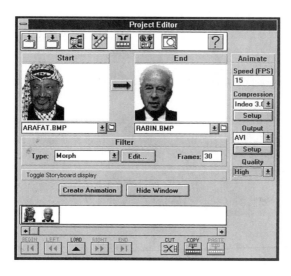

Figure 9.85. *Hidden features in the Project Editor.*

The new controls at the right are output functions. You can set the speed (frame rate), compression method, output format (.AVI, .FLC, .BMP), and the level of quality. The new controls at the bottom enable you to create multi-image morphs. For example, look at Figure 9.86. I have added in image of Captain Kirk (William Shatner) to the sequence.[29] Note that a second pair of images has been

---

[28]To expand the Project Editor, just click the two buttons at top center. One adds the controls at the right, and the other adds the controls at the bottom.

[29]It's a little bizarre, but I justify it by assuming that, in a lost Star Trek episode, The crew did a trip back in time and made the whole thing happen (the peace treaty, that is).

added at the bottom of the Project Editor window. Before you can generate output, however, you need to adjust the control points for the new image. Click the Edit button to display the Morph|Warp window again.

Figure 9.86. *Adding a second morph to the sequence.*

To change the control points, click the Adjust control point buttons for both images. Then click on any control point in the Kirk image—the corresponding point in the Rabin image turns red, and that tells you which control point you've got. Just move it to a point on the Kirk image that corresponds to the location in the Rabin image.

Note that the Kirk image is larger—this doesn't present any problems for PhotoMorph. As long as the control points are in the right place, everything will come out fine.

To create the morph animation, just click the Create Animation button. The time it will take depends on the size of the image, color depth (8-, 16-, or 24-bit color), image size, and so on. However, PhotoMorph is really fast compared to many other morph programs. The results definitely qualify as Really Cool. Figures 9.88 and 9.89 show what I mean.[30]

---

[30]The face in the latter example sort of reminds me of Biff in one of the *Back to the Future* flicks.

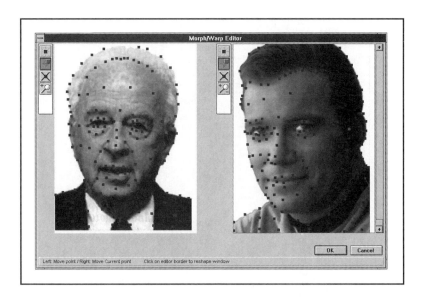

Figure 9.87. *Another set of control points.*

Figure 9.88. *The midpoint of the morph betwwen Arafat and Rabin.*

583

Figure 9.89. The midpoint of the morph between Rabin and Kirk.

Pixar Typestry

Typestry is an animation program for type. It's deceptively easy to use—simply enter some text, choose a font, and then render. However, the program has two features that make it an impressive product in its niche. You can control the position, rotation, size, and surface characteristics of the text, and the rendering quality is outstanding.

Pixar is known for its Renderman software, a high-end rendering package used to generate sophisticated animations. You've probably seen some of Pixar's work—they work with Disney on films. *Beauty and the Beast* was one of their recent efforts (remember that ballroom scene?).

Alas, Typestry won't make you the next Walt Disney; it's just for text. And it's easy to use. You create and modify the text objects in a wireframe mode and then render.[31] Figure 9.90 shows a very simple example of what you can

---

[31]Rendering takes time; there's no getting around that simple fact. All the programs in this chapter that render are slow—it takes an enormous amount of computing power to render realistically. Remember, it wasn't so long ago that you needed a mainframe computer to do this at all. Long rendering times aren't so painful when you realize that just a few years ago it cost millions of dollars to do this kind of stuff.

accomplish. The text uses a metallic surface, and there is a brick wall in the background. It is simply and tastefully lit from above and to the right. You can get this kind of result by accepting the default lighting and merely adding materials (called Looks) to the text and the wall.

Figure 9.90. *A simple text logo created with Typestry.*

However, Typestry comes with many more cool features. Figure 9.91 shows some of them in use. In this example, I have rotated the text, added a mask (called a *gel*) to the central spotlight, added shadows, and now there is both a floor and a wall, each with its own Look. The metallic look of the word "Madness!" has also been made shinier.

Figure 9.91. *An enhanced text logo.*

You can go just about as far as you care to with enhancements—too far, if you don't watch out. I noticed that there is a real temptation to keep adding features to your logos—it can lead to confusion in the rendered image. Figure 9.92 shows two further-enhanced images created with Typestry. The image at top left is a little out of control, but it's fun and I like it. The image at bottom right probably goes too far—the image is so confusing that it's hard to tell what is what.[32]

---

[32]Of course, if they were for an album cover for a punk band, they would probably be a little understated but acceptable.

Figure 9.92. *Two examples of Typestry rendering.*

Typestry uses a multiple-window interface as shown in Figure 9.93. You can show or hide any of the windows at any time using the Window menu. I usually just leave all the windows open, but if you create a very large image, you can easily shut a few windows.

When you run Typestry, the main window is blank; your first job is to add some text. Click the toolbar's "A" icon to change the cursor to an I-beam, and then click anywhere in the main window. This opens the dialog shown in Figure 9.94. You can type the text into the window at the bottom of the dialog box. Typestry supports all PostScript and True Type fonts. All currently installed fonts are available in the drop-down list box at the top of the dialog box. You can also set the size and style of the bevel that will be applied to the 3D object created from the text. A minimum bevel creates square, blocky text, whereas a larger bevel creates interesting angles at the edges of the letterforms.

Figure 9.93. *Typestry uses multiple windows.*

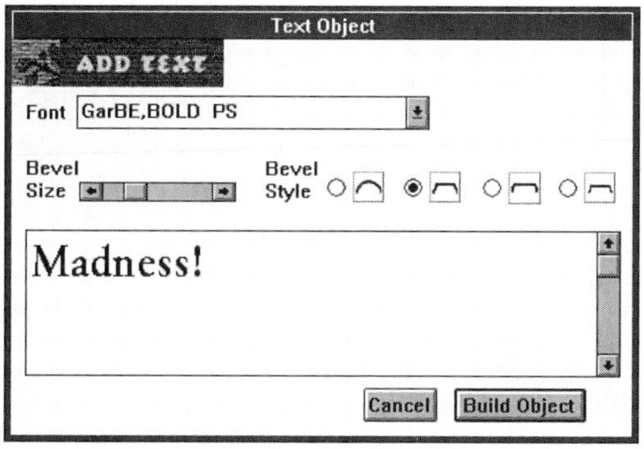

Figure 9.94. *Adding text.*

If you make no enhancements at all to the text or the background, the result is pretty plain (see Figure 9.95).

Figure 9.95. *No enhancements added to text or background.*

The key to cool renderings is the Looks Browser shown in Figure 9.96. You access the browser from the Looks window by clicking the New Look button. You can select looks by filename using the standard Open File controls in the dialog, or you can select from the palette at the bottom of the dialog.

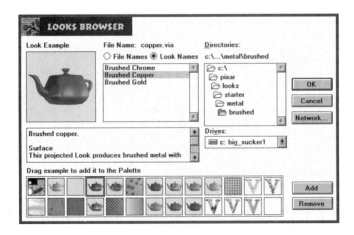

Figure 9.96. *Browsing for new Looks.*

When you select a look, it shows up in the Looks window (see Figure 9.97). The actual image that shows up will vary. It is part of the file that contains the look. Typestry comes with a variety of looks, including wood, stone, brick walls, shiny and brushed metals, dots, plastic, and so on. You can purchase additional looks, and you can also purchase Glimpse, a tool for editing looks, if you start getting serious.

Figure 9.97. *The Looks window.*

Many looks allow a modest amount of customization from the Looks window. The dialog box shown in Figure 9.98 results when you click the More Info button. It enables you to select a new base color, vary the opacity of the text object, scale the pattern used for the look, and rotate the pattern.

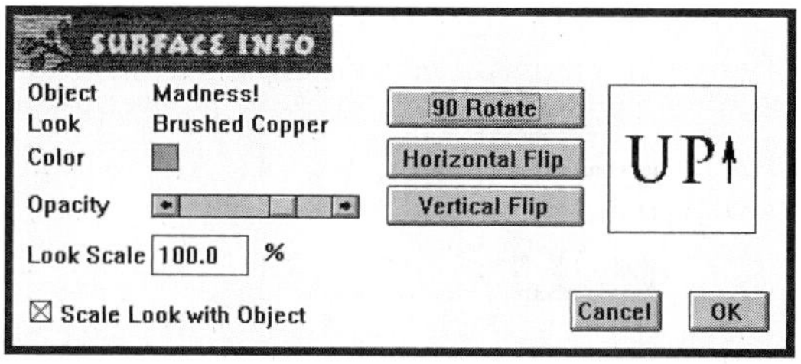

Figure 9.98. *Setting properties for a look.*

You can also control the lights in your scene. There are 18 lights available, plus an ambient (overall) lighting control. Figure 9.99 shows the Lights window. You can adjust the lights in the front or the back using the Intensity sliders. Move a slider to the right to make a light brighter. There are three check boxes for each light. The first one is for adjusting color, the second is for selecting a gel,[33] and the third determines if the light will cast a shadow.

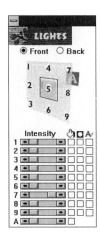

Figure 9.99. *Setting light parameters.*

There are six different gels you can use; each casts a certain kind of shadow. Figure 9.100 shows the dialog for selecting gels. It's very easy to tell which is which; the icon shows the kind of shadow that the gel will cast. Figure 9.101 shows a rendering that uses a gel.

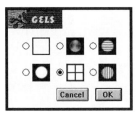

Figure 9.100. *Selecting a gel.*

---

[33]This terminology from the theater, where gels have a long history. Physically, a gel is a piece of plastic that is placed in front of a light to give it a color or to cast shadows in some pattern. Traditionally, gels were originally made of gelatin— hence the name.

Figure 9.101. *A rendering that uses a gel.*

Typestry also gives you simple control over the placement of floors and walls. Figure 9.102 shows the dialog box for setting up the floor. If you click Automatic, the floor will be below the lowest object in the scene. If you click Manual, you can adjust the height and angle of the floor. Walls are adjusted in a similar fashion.

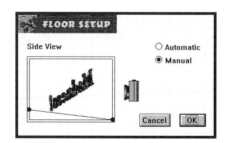

Figure 9.102. *Adjusting the position and angle of the floor.*

You are not limited to just letters and numbers with Typestry. Numerous fonts are available that use various kinds of images instead of text. Windows comes with the Widgets font, for example. Adobe has a number of fonts with interesting symbols in them, and most other font vendors also offer interesting, and sometimes amusing, fonts. You can also use a program like Fontographer to modify existing fonts or create your own. This is especially useful when you want to recreate a company logo—you can scan the logo and turn it into a font.

Typestry gives you access to multiple layers of objects, by the way. The highest level is a complete text object, consisting of all of the text (even multiple lines) that you entered when you created the object. However, you can also create your own groups of letters to create subsidiary objects, and you can apply all of the tools to any kind of object—text object, words, individual letters, even single faces of a letter. Thus, you can enter a string of characters and then move each letter independently.

Which neatly brings us to the animation capabilities of Typestry. You can use most of the tools and effects I have described in an animation. It's incredibly easy to create the animation. Pressing Control+= takes you to the next key frame, where you can enter the next step in the animation.[34] For example, you could create a simple logo scene in one key frame, rearrange it for the final appearance you want in another key frame, and then render. You can also create as many intermediate key frames as you need to control movement precisely. Figure 9.103 shows three key frames from an animation I created. The top image is from the first frame, the second image is frame 41, and the third image is the last frame, frame 61. At 15 frames per second, that will be a four-second animation. Typestry includes a simple animation manager that enables you to create new key frames, delete old ones, and so on.

When rendered, the animation is very effective. You can tell that best by playing the animation from the CD; the filename is PIXAR01.AVI.[35]

---

[34]You can easily move back and forth through the key frames using the Control+- and Control+= keys.

[35]I converted the .FLC to an .AVI file because it is so much easier to play. You need the Cinepak video codec installed to play it. If you installed the Video for Windows runtime that comes with this book, you have it for sure. Otherwise, if the video doesn't play, just install the runtime that comes with this book.

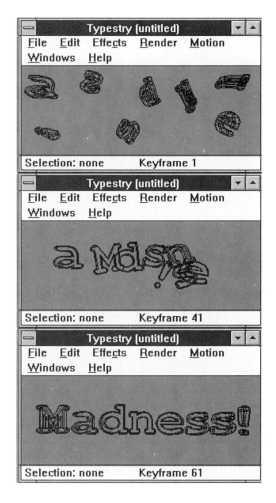

Figure 9.103. *Three key frames from an animation.*

Summary

It's bottom-line time, and the bottom line on animation is simple: Animation provides extensive bang for the buck. If you want animation with a lot of time, trouble, or money, packages like Interactive will do the job for you—especially in a business situation where you want a quick return on a budget.

If you want room to get creative, Animator Pro is an excellent choice—especially if you have the budget to couple it with 3D Studio. Even if you don't, the ability to move back and forth between Animator Pro and VidEdit gives you a lot of power.

Eenie-Meenie-MIDI: Keyboards

MIDI is, in many ways, the odd duck of multimedia. It's not like other methods of generating sounds—MIDI means music, sound effects, instruments, and, yes, those darn things called notes.

How many people are masters of the musical staff? How many people can sit down at a piano (or, more accurately, piano-like) keyboard and perform music that is good enough for others to enjoy? I took piano for eight years, but that was then, this is now, and I can't play a tune worth a darn. So the question is: why bother with MIDI at all?

When it comes to music, nothing works as well as MIDI—unless you have access to a digital recording studio (in which case, guess what: much of *that* is made with some MIDI involvement). Even though I can't *play* music anyone is going to listen to, I can still use MIDI in powerful ways. I can compose music with Power Chords, I can arrange and score music in Master Tracks Pro, and I can always play MIDI files using MCI commands in many programs. This chapter takes you on a grand tour of MIDI, including the software you need to make it work for you. I show you both the musical side of MIDI and how to integrate MIDI into multimedia.

Why Use MIDI?

The most important reason to use MIDI is that, with a good MIDI card, you can play some outrageous-sounding music and sound effects. Let's be honest here—if the only MIDI you have heard is from a Sound Blaster class of sound card, you ain't heard MIDI yet. With something like a Multisound, Maui, or Roland SCC-1 in your machine, you can create professional-sounding music with MIDI.

There are other good reasons for using MIDI. It gives you detailed, less-than-a-single-note-at-a-time access to the music as well as the ability to make changes to an entire piece of music. You can change everything from the velocity (loudness) of a single keypress to the timing of an entire song, or you can transpose a complete staff. There are plenty of other reasons to use MIDI as well; let's take a look.

Smaller File Sizes

MIDI files are much smaller than waveform files. Many games use MIDI to play sounds for just that reason. A waveform file must contain every nuance of the sound—using as much as 180K per *second*—to reproduce the sound. A MIDI file, on the other hand, stores material such as the note to play, how long to play it, and so on. MIDI files often are one percent or less of the size of equivalent Wave files.

Existing Music Can Be Modified

You can easily buy (or download from the MIDIFORUM on CompuServe) many MIDI music files. MIDI files are much easier to edit than they are to create from scratch, and you can even change instruments for a completely different sound.

A simple invention for piano, for example, becomes absolutely ethereal when played with synthetic, angelic voices for the right hand and soothing, deep base notes for the left—something like a celestial choir accompanied by Zeus. Alternatively, you could substitute a distorted rock guitar and a slap bass for a completely different effect. In my opinion, this ability to create your own orchestrations quickly and easily is the best thing about MIDI. I'm not a musician, but I know what I like when I hear it.

Access to a Multitude of Sounds

By investing in a (relatively) inexpensive synthesizer module, such as the Roland SCC-1 or the MultiSound from Turtle Beach, you can give your business presentations sounds I guarantee will impress any audience. You can tailor the sounds yourself by changing instruments or varying the tempo of the music. If you are musically talented, MIDI opens up even more possibilities than the other sound media.

What Is MIDI, Anyway?

If you are like most people getting involved with multimedia, MIDI is completely new. The kind of technical information I present in Chapter 2, "Sound Advice," doesn't give you a context for MIDI. I'd like to provide that information here.

In the first edition, here's what I had to say about MIDI: "MIDI has its own character and personality, but it's not a polished, smooth personality; MIDI still has the rough edge of a developing technology." The most recent versions of software for MIDI change that for the better. MIDI is easier than ever to use. The trick is that the software mostly let's you ignore the technical aspects of MIDI. Sure, experts need access to the guts of a MIDI file, but most of us just want to edit a MIDI file the same way we would edit a document with a word processor. Who cares what codes are used to indicate bold or italic? I just select some text, press the right keys, and—presto: I get **bold** or *italic.*

The same should apply to music. If I want a track to be a trumpet track, I should just be able to select the track, hit the right keys for trumpet, and—presto, trumpet sounds. The software now available for MIDI makes it that easy. However, for those who want the ultimate in control, many MIDI software packages let you work under the hood when you need to.

MIDI's "personality" reflects its origins in the music industry. MIDI began as a means for electronic instruments to communicate with one another. It enabled instruments from different manufacturers to describe to each other things such as note on, note off, pitch variations, and so on. This is actually a very simple task, and the MIDI standard is not all that complex when compared to, for example, the standards for modem communications.[1]

Anyone with an interest in MIDI can ultimately understand just about all its technical aspects. This is not true for many parts of the computer industry. For example, when was the last time you ran into someone who could tell you how modems communicate with one another? Then again, when would you ever have to know this? You can do anything you need to do with modems without knowing how they work. With MIDI, the more you learn about how it works, the more you can do with it. The key point, though, is that you don't *have* to know this stuff.

MIDI gives you a great deal of control over musical expression. Until someone invents a better way to represent and manipulate musical events, MIDI will endure. The good thing about MIDI is that it is an open specification. This enables various manufacturers to expand its possibilities. The bad thing about MIDI from the multimedia viewpoint is that it standardizes only the core issues involved (such as data transmission) and leaves other areas to the individual manufacturer's discretion.

I'm not going to make it easy for you to step lightly into MIDI; it comes with a sense of its own history, which shapes the ways it is used. Having grown up in

---

[1] The number of people who actually understand all those protocols has to be one of the smallest numbers in the universe.

the music industry, MIDI has been imbued with a certain capriciousness that is very uncomputer-like. It's a bit like family that way: if you love it, you've got to take the good with the bad. You might say that to succeed at MIDI, you have to have more of a tinkerer's approach than not: you have to play with it as well as work with it. If plug-and-play is what you want, you can do that, but you'd be missing most of what MIDI is about: power and control over the music.

I find MIDI frustrating at times—particularly when I have to explain it. MIDI is awkward, a mixture of computers and creativity. The best way to put it is this: If you want to get the most out of MIDI, you have to learn to think like MIDI. However, I wouldn't do without it. Even when I have no good reason to do so, I love to poke around with a MIDI file and create interesting—and sometimes beautiful—orchestrations. If you have a decent synthesizer, creating your own music can be very rewarding. I've met some other closet musicians out there lately. These are people who love music but don't play well enough to pursue it professionally. MIDI and synthesizers are liberating for us: we can create to our hearts' and ears' content without fussing over performance issues.

MIDI isn't for everyone because it involves the creative side of music. You'll know if you are the MIDI type if the rest of this chapter excites you about the possibilities of MIDI. On the other hand, if it sounds like MIDI is a bit obscure, MIDI might not be your cup of tea.

Power Chords

Before I get into the heavy stuff, let's have a little fun with MIDI. The program: Power Chords from Howling Dog software. With a company name like Howling Dog, you know this is going to be good, right? Right!

> This section uses some musical jargon. If you aren't familiar with terms like *beat* and *measure,* you might miss some of the meaning.

Power Chords does require some musical knowledge to use well, as you will see shortly. If you can handle concepts like chords, melody, and rhythm, Power Chords does exactly what its name implies: it puts a lot of power in your hands.

Figure 10.1 shows the opening screen of Power Chords.

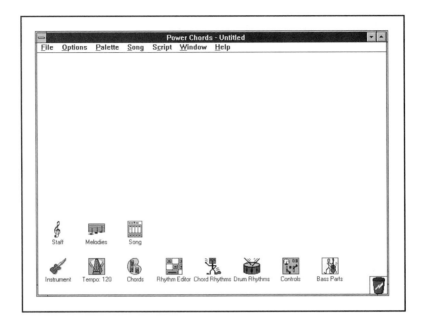

Figure 10.1. The Power Chords opening screen.

I was daunted by the large number of icons. Usually, I hate software that does that to me. However, it turns out that each icon has a simple job to do. I'll take you through the process of creating music with Power Chords. There is a demo version of the software on the CD, so you can play along at home if you have a MIDI card.[2]

There are different paths you can follow to create music with Power Chords; I'll show you the one I use.[3] To begin, double-click on two of the icons, and adjust the resulting windows, Instrument and Chords, to your own taste.

The Instrument window displays a stylized guitar. You can create chords on the strings manually, or you can use the Chord Requester by clicking the Rqst button. Figure 10.2 shows my usual setup for creating chords.

---

[2]It doesn't have to be anything fancy, but the better your MIDI card, the more fun you'll have.

[3]Power Chords comes with a great tutorial that will also help out quite a bit. The tutorial is extremely detailed and comprehensive, and I strongly recommend that you work through it if you buy the product.

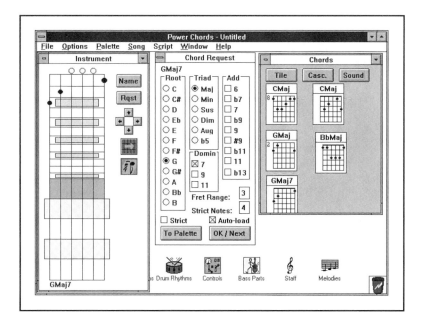

Figure 10.2. *Creating chords.*

The Chord Requester enables you to just point and click to create all the common—and many not-so-common—types of chords. Need an augmented ninth? No problem. Click on the Root of the chord, select Aug as the Triad, and select 9 in the Add list.

If you have ever played the guitar, you know that there are many different ways to play a given chord on it. To see each chord in turn, you can click the OK/ Next button. When you find the chord you want, you can paste it to the Chord palette using the To Palette button. You can put a whole bunch of chords on the palette. You'll use them later when you place chords in the song.

Chords are not just lumps of sound; they can be strummed, arpeggiated, or played in many other different ways. Chords form the rhythmic background for the melody. The Rhythm Editor enables you to specify how the chords will be played. For example, Figure 10.3 shows a simple chord rhythm. (The left window is the actual rhythm editor, even if it calls itself "Chord - Normal Chord." The smaller window, Chord Rhythms, is used as a holding bin for all of the rhythms you create.)

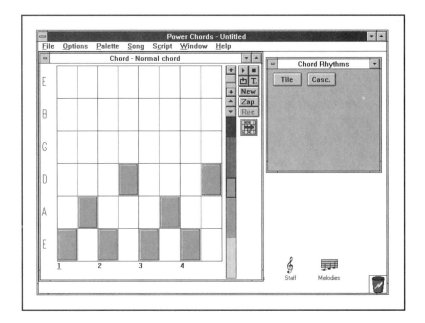

Figure 10.3. The Rhythm Editor being used to edit chords.

At the left of the larger window are the names of the six strings on a guitar. At the bottom are the beats. For each beat, you can specify which string will be played. In this example, there is a more or less 1-2 thing going with the two bass strings, but there are some variations for interest.[4]

Figure 10.4 shows a completely different kind of rhythm for a chord. This time, the high notes are used as well as the bass notes; this brings the rhythm somewhat into the foreground. You can use this effect to create complex and interesting complements to the melody. To paste a chord rhythm to its palette, drag the little box at the right side of the Rhythm Editor (it's right there under the greyed-out "Rec" button) over to the Chord Rhythms palette.

Next, I usually add the drum part. The Rhythm Editor is also used for drums. To convert the Rhythm Editor for different kinds of editing, use the Control menu in its upper-left corner. Figure 10.5 shows a drum-editing session in progress. The names of the various drums are on the left, and the beats are along the bottom.

---

[4]I thought that the guitar metaphor might be limiting, but it's actually quite flexible. Because this isn't a real guitar, you can do things rhythmically that you would never be able to do with a real guitar. Thus, when you want to play the music, you can use piano or flute or whatever instrument you want to play these notes.

The drum editor is cool to use—you can create very interesting and complex rhythms very easily. To place a drum beat, just click in a little square. You can make each sound louder or softer, and you can use the controls at far right to add quarter notes, eighth notes, or any other value all the way down to sixty-fourth notes.

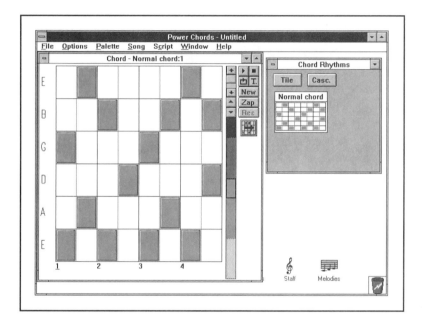

Figure 10.4. *A more complex chord rhythm.*

What makes drum editing so cool is that you can play the drum track over and over while you make changes to it. This makes it very easy to tailor the sound perfectly. It's also a lot of fun! As before, you can paste various drum rhythms to the Drum Rhythms palette by dragging the little box over to the palette.

Now that you have the various pieces on the various palettes, it's time to create a song. Figure 10.6 shows the Song Editor. I have placed chords in each measure (each measure has a number at its upper-left corner), as well as chord rhythms. You just drag chords and rhythms from their respective palettes to each measure.

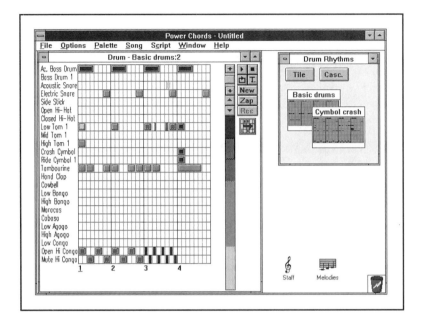

Figure 10.5. Editing drum rhythms.

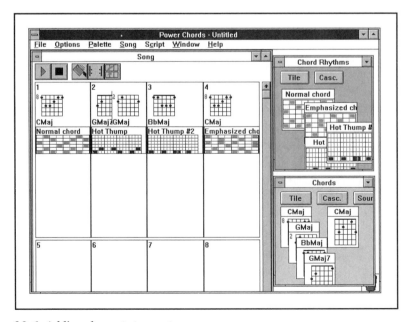

Figure 10.6. Adding elements to create a song.

To continue creating the song, open the other palettes and add elements that seem appropriate. In Figure 10.7, I have added the Basic drums rhythm to measure 1. Drum rhythms will continue to play until a new drum rhythm is encountered—in this case, in measure 4.

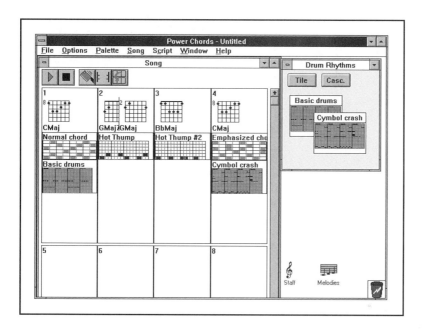

Figure 10.7. *Adding drum rhythms.*

You construct the melody in the same way. Figure 10.8 shows the Rhythm Editor being used to edit the melody. Notes are shown at the left, and beats are across the bottom. In the example, there are two little squares per beat, so all notes entered will be eighth notes.[5]

If you know a little about music and composing or arranging, you can see that the notes for each beat in each measure follow roughly the notes of the chords in the song. This is basic to writing music; the notes must stay somewhat close to the chords, or the music will sound too dissonant.

---

[5]You can enter notes of longer duration by holding down the Shift key and dragging across two or more little boxes. This is just one example of the finer points of the interface for Power Chords; it has lots of clever tricks that make it easy to use.

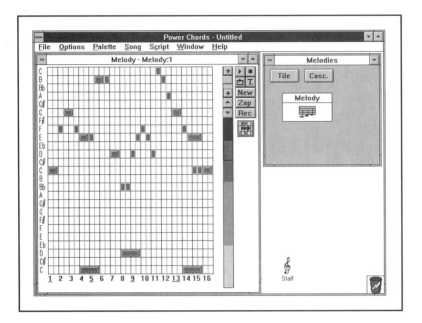

Figure 10.8. *Creating the melody.*

Whenever you create any element of the song—chord rhythms, drum rhythms, and so on—you can specify the number of measures for it. You can do one measure at a time, or groups of two or more. For example to create a melody, you might have several 2-beat introductory melodies, one basic melody for the core of each phrase of music, and several different ending variations. You could then arrange the pieces in different ways to create the overall song. Because most music relies on repetition, this works well.

You also can add a bass line to your song; I created a simple one as shown in Figure 10.9. This line simply uses two alternating notes from each of the chords in my 4-measure, 16-beat song.

Figure 10.10 shows the completed song. Naturally, I have included my handiwork on the Nautilus CD-ROM; the filename is RON.MID. You can play the file with Media Player if your sound card supports MIDI.

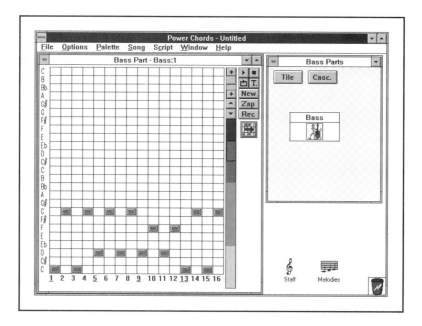

Figure 10.9. *Adding a bass line.*

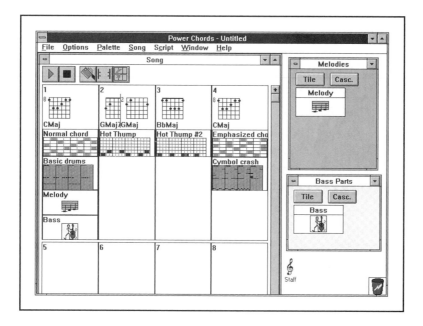

Figure 10.10. *A completed song.*

MIDI in Multimedia Presentations

Ultimately, MIDI is the best possible choice for business or other kinds of presentations. With MIDI and a good synthesizer, you can create presentations that are unique—even spectacular. You can buy a synthesizer that will reproduce the sounds of instruments and special effects with great fidelity; this makes quite an impression on the audience. More importantly, you can customize the sound no matter what the reason, such as your own taste, the preferences of a given audience, the need to add punch, and so on.

Good synthesizers start inexpensively, ranging from a few hundred dollars to a few thousand. Below that level, the sound quality is not good enough for presentations.

There are two basic approaches you can use to add support for MIDI: you can put a basic MIDI interface in your computer, or you can put a synthesizer (with its own MIDI support) in your computer. Each approach has advantages and disadvantages.

If you plan to take your multimedia presentation on the road or if you need to move from one machine to another, an external synthesizer (one without a keyboard) makes sense. These models are made for travel: they are small, they pack easily, and they do not have the static problems of a regular computer card. You can connect them to the computer either by a simple card (less than $100) or by the serial port (example: the Midiator). The serial port models are not supported by all software, but enough good packages support it to make it workable.

If your needs are closer to home, you can put a synthesizer in your computer. The two most popular are the MultiSound from Turtle Beach and the Roland SCC-1. The MultiSound is about twice as expensive, but it also has more realistic sound. The one you choose is a matter of budget and intended use.

The MultiSound includes the chips and memory of a Proteus/1 synthesizer, which is commercially sold by E-mu. The sounds are all digitally sampled, and they are superb. If you need top quality sounds, you need look no further than the MultiSound. The board also includes 16-bit Wave support, so you can record CD-quality sound onto your hard disk. For professional work, this is the unit of choice. I cannot overemphasize the fact that this is a fine unit. I've had it in my machine for months, and I still get goosebumps when I use it.

Not everyone can afford perfection, of course, so there is a place for the SCC-1. It does not include Wave support, but if you already have a sound card and want better synthesizer sounds, this is an excellent choice—I have found that it coexists well with both the Pro Audio Spectrum and the Sound Blaster, two of the most popular cards. You have to remove the MIDI and/or synthesizer drivers for the sound card if you do this; then the two cards will coexist peacefully.

I like the sound quality of the SCC-1 quite a bit. The card is a good value; it dramatically stretches what you can do with MIDI without hurting your checkbook. It is an excellent value and a neat way to upgrade your system. If you want to add a keyboard, Roland makes the PC-200, which is small and inexpensive.

You could purchase a complete synthesizer with a keyboard, but the bulk of most units doesn't make them easy to use next to your computer—plan on some extra space for the keyboard. In addition to the Roland unit, which is quite slim and convenient, look into the Yamaha Hello Music! setup—it includes an equally petite and useful keyboard, as well as speakers and a sound module. If you already have a keyboard, however, this can be the way to go. You can add a MIDI card (such as the Music Quest) and you can connect your MIDI keyboard to your computer. For business use, the keyboard/synthesizer combinations are usually too bulky—especially if you are taking your show on the road. The primary use for a keyboard is creating or modifying music during development.

I recommend three setups for business MIDI: one for a budget, one for traveling presentations, and one for advanced professional use.

Budget model: Any 16-bit sound card to handle wave files, and the Roland SCC-1 to generate MIDI sounds. If you are on a real budget, make sure you look for a sound card that uses wave-table lookup, not FM-synthesis. The next generation of the Yamaha OPL series of chips (the current version as I write is the OPL-3) is worth a look.

Traveling model: The ultimate approach is to use one of the Dolch lunchbox portables; see the Shopper's Guide for details. For the rest of you, use a MIDI card from Music Quest (if you have an ISA slot available) or the Midiator serial-port connector (if you don't). Neither contains a synthesizer, so you need an external synthesizer (such as the Roland Sound Canvas or Yamaha TG-100). Wave support is harder to come by if you don't have ISA slots; few of the portable sound devices (the ones that attach to your serial port) are worth using for professional presentations. DSP Solutions makes the Port-able Sound Plus, and it is one of the few portable sound devices that gets my Seal of Approval. If you do have an ISA slot or two, use any conventional sound card (16-bit is strongly preferred). If the sound card has MIDI support, you won't need a separate MIDI card, but I'd strongly recommend a sound module if you are not using the MultiSound—the synthesizer section is too low-quality.

Professional model: The Turtle Beach MultiSound. All by itself, this is a recording studio. I used it to record all the sound for the multimedia presentations I created for the CD-ROM. Don't let the sound quality of the material on the CD-ROM fool you—I had to use 8-bit sound to be compatible with the bulk of the available sound cards. At 16 bits and 44.1 KHz, the MultiSound is as clean as you will find. Many sound cards pick up subtle (and sometimes not so subtle!) electrical noises from the components around them; the MultiSound does not. If you need a more portable setup (no ISA slots), choose any MIDI hardware that will work with your machine and add a Roland Sound Canvass. With either the MultiSound or a Sound Canvass, quality speakers are a must—go with a subwoofer[6] if you can cart all three speakers around, or the Roland units if you can't (see Chapter 6 for details on speakers).

Combining Sound Sources

A good subtitle for this section might be "A Sound Is a Sound Is a Sound," with apologies to Ms. Stein. I've been ranting and raving about the differences between MIDI and Wave for so long, it's time to consider a basic fact: unless you know where a sound comes from, it's just a sound. Wouldn't it be nice if you could use a sound without wondering what kind it is? If not that, then wouldn't it be great to at least combine the two kinds of sound (MIDI and Wave) whenever you want to?

That latter goal is already achievable, thanks to your old friend MCI. Today's sequencer programs[7] are adding support for MCI. That means you can incorporate Wave files in your sequences. Isn't it great the way products support MCI? Pretty soon, you'll be able to pick your favorite interface and accomplish everything from there.

For example, Figure 10.11 shows the dialog box from Master Tracks Pro for adding MCI events during playback of a MIDI file. If you are familiar with MCI commands, you can see that most of the common command combinations are

---

[6]The Altec Lansing unit is my favorite.

[7]Master Tracks Pro makes it very easy.

available to you using just the mouse—you simply select the command and options you want, and the actual command string is constructed for you. You can also type your own command strings at the bottom of the dialog.

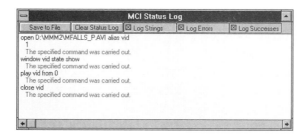

Figure 10.11. *Adding an MCI command to a sequence.*

It's easy to add MCI events this way—just click at the point in the song where you want the event, and the dialog box pops up. Master Tracks Pro adds some nice extra touches. Figure 10.12 shows the MCI Status Log; it logs the result of each MCI command for review. If there are any errors or problems, you will get a detailed report.

Figure 10.12. *The MCI Status Log.*

You can do anything MCI allows you to do with these events. You can play Wave files, animations, or even digital video (see Figure 10.13).

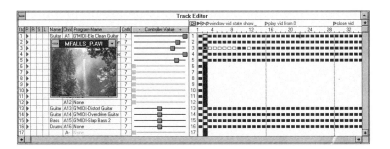

Figure 10.13. *Playing a video file during MIDI playback.*

The ability to execute MCI commands adds a new layer of possibilities to your multimedia world.

MIDI Software

The key to MIDI is the software you use to work with it. There are quite a few products out there ranging from inexpensive shareware sequencing packages to notation software that gives you total control over your music.

There are two completely different ways to work with MIDI: piano-roll notation and staff notation. Piano-roll notation does not use notes; it uses small marks of different lengths to indicate notes and durations. Programs that work with piano-roll notation are commonly called *sequencers.* Sequencers look and work much like a multitrack tape recorder. Normally, you put each instrument on a different "track." If you want to change note characteristics—duration, pitch, and so on—you use your mouse to erase or add to the piano-roll of notes. Programs that work with staff notation are variously referred to as *notation* or *scoring programs,* the latter because they often are used to create musical scores. Most MIDI software also enables you to work with an event list, a list of all MIDI events. Unlike notation or scoring programs, an event list enables you to edit information that relates solely to MIDI, such as instrument changes and pitch changes. You don't have to work with the event list or even be aware of its existence—it's just another layer of control you can access if you want to.

Figure 10.14, a screen from Cakewalk for Windows, shows multiple methods in use.[8]

---

[8]Not all MIDI software lets you work with both notes and piano-roll notation.

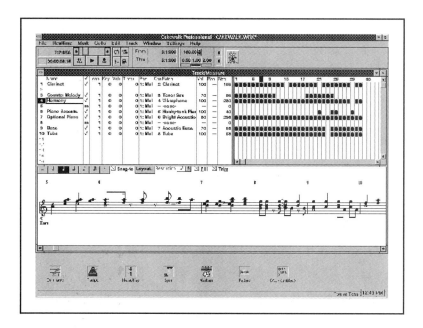

Figure 10.14. *A screen from Cakewalk for Windows.*

The upper portion of the screen shows a compressed form of musical representation; the box at the upper-right contains a box for measures that contain notes and a small dash for measures that have no notes. The upper-left box shows what instruments are on each track, and the lower window uses staff notation for one of the tracks (you can only put one track or instrument staff in a window, but you can have as many windows as you want). If all this seems confusing, you're in good company—I resisted sequencer software for years because it looked so foreign. However, it all fits together and works well—once you learn how to use it. I have included two detailed looks at sequencer software in this chapter that should give you a head start: Cakewalk and Master Tracks Pro.

If you really have no need for sequencing and are interested in the music, you can use specialized software to work directly with staff notation. Figure 10.15 shows a screen from Encore (from Passport Designs), which focuses on staff notation. You can click directly on notes, drag them around, add new ones, and so on.

You can also have a small window that shows you some of the information about MIDI tracks in non-note form, if you need or want that information.

Figure 10.15. *A screen from Encore, a program that uses staff notation.*

Product Overview

Each type of music software has its own strengths and weaknesses; you probably need more than one package if you are serious about music on your computer. Here is a breakdown of the packages that I liked (you learn about them in more detail shortly):

Cakewalk for Windows: I think of this as the technical sequencer. It has real depth when it comes to manipulating a MIDI file. It is heavily oriented toward MIDI; there are many menu choices for dealing with various aspects of MIDI. Recent improvements have made the interface easier to use.

Encore: This is notation software. It's easy to use, and you can record right from your MIDI instrument. Encore can create a rather good-looking score, but it's not the heavyweight player that Finale is. Of course, it costs much less. It may be the easiest entry into computerized music for those already familiar with reading notes on the staff.

Master Tracks Pro 4: This sequencer is my personal favorite. I find it easy to use. It doesn't have the technical nooks and crannies of Cakewalk, but I can always go right to what I want to do. It makes excellent use of the Windows interface—mouse clicks are intuitive, and everything seems natural in all kinds of different situations. Inevitably, when I click something, I get the result I expect.

WinJammer: This is a shareware sequencer program. It might be all you need to work with MIDI if you are a hobbyist, or just curious, or if you are exploring MIDI on a budget. It contains all the basic features you'll need to work with MIDI files. Access to those features, however, is not always intuitive or easy.

Finale: This is notation software. It is a powerful program capable of creating just about any score you can imagine. It's a fully professional product and is used by musicians at every level, from movie and television scores to arrangements for small bands. However, navigation of its many options and dialog boxes takes time to master. It isn't for the casual user.

Many of these products have related (but less expensive) packages that contain a subset of the more expensive software's features. Examples include Finale/Music Prose, Master Tracks Pro 4/Trax, and Encore/Music Time. In many cases, the less-expensive packages contain a surprising array of their parent's features and represent an outstanding value.

Because these software packages have such different personalities, this chapter is full of examples and screen captures to give you some sense of the flavors available in the market today.

Finale Notation Software

The most interesting MIDI software packages work directly with notes. I grew up on music for piano, so I like notes for reading music.[9] If you aren't familiar with musical notation, you might want to stick with the kinds of software that provide piano-roll styles of notation (see the "Sequencers for Mastering Multimedia" section later in this chapter).

---

[9]Power Chords, of course, are an important exception.

The Rolls Royce of notation packages is Finale from Coda. It is the AutoCAD of music software. If there is something that Finale doesn't do, I am willing to bet that if you called Coda and told them what it was, they'd probably try to put it in the next version. Even the documentation for the program is impressive. Coda has obviously spent a great deal of time creating the manuals for the program. There is a *Getting Started* guide, a *Learning Guide,* an *Encyclopedia of Finale,* and a *Finale Reference.* Each book serves its purpose well—the material is well organized, the explanations are clear and thorough, and the illustrations are well planned. And it's a good thing, too. Finale is so powerful, so all-inclusive, that you'd get lost rapidly without excellent documentation.

There is only one negative thing I could ever say about Finale: it is so powerful that it might intimidate you. It did me. It contains more than I've ever forgotten about music. On the other hand, if you understand the finer points of music, can be patient with a tool that is extremely powerful, and want absolute control over scores, Finale is the only possible choice—no question about it.

It is not possible for me to give you a complete tour of Finale. Every time I run the program or open one of the manuals, I learn about a new area of the program that has more functionality than some complete products. Suppose you want to put a symbol on your score and you can't find it in the music fonts that come with Finale. You can start up the Shape Designer, draw your symbol, and off you go, ready to use it wherever you like.

That's my idea of a complete program.

Finale meets the needs of professional musicians. Need to score a movie and don't have much time? Finale to the rescue.[10] Need to orchestrate a post-modern piece for a quartet of garbage can lids? No problem—you can invent the notation system on the fly.

With all the preamble and so much possible territory to cover, I thought I'd give you an idea of how complete Finale really is by examining one small part of the program in detail.

Creating a Basic Score

Finale is for creating scores. A score is a series of staffs that show the music to be played by each instrument in the band, orchestra, or ensemble. You can just as

---

[10]This is not mere hyperbole, either; the press kit that comes with Finale is full of examples of tough, tight-deadline, major projects that Finale handled with aplomb.

easily use Finale to prepare music for the Philharmonic as for playback on your computer. And the scores it can create are beautiful in every detail. You have complete control over the appearance of the score. Let's start with the opening screen shown in Figure 10.16.

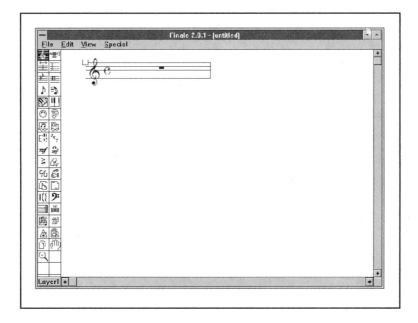

Figure 10.16. *Finale's opening screen.*

The only imposing part is that huge list of icons down the left side of the page. Each one has its purpose. There's no music yet, so there is just one bar showing. Figure 10.17 shows the first two bars of "Frere Jacques," with only the part played by the left hand added.

To enter the notes for the right hand, click the note entry icon. The contents of the tool palette change to icons related to note entry (Figure 10.18).

To enter notes, click the appropriate note tool—quarter note, eighth note, dotted half note, and so on—then click where you want the note to go. You can switch to any other note duration by clicking the appropriate tool. Finale automatically adjusts the position of each note based on its duration; you can click wherever you want to in the measure.

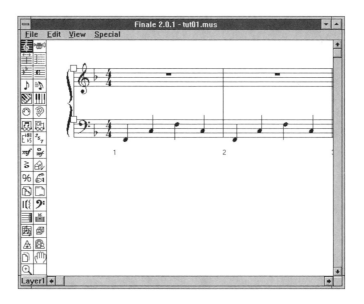

Figure 10.17. *The first two bars of "Frere Jacques."*

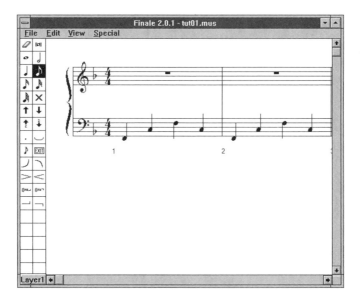

Figure 10.18. *Icons related to note entry in Finale.*

So far you have looked at only one line of music. The **V**iew menu enables you to switch to page view (Figure 10.19), which shows a more complete picture.

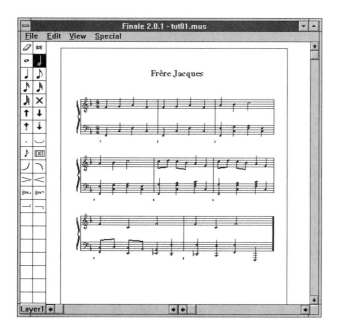

Figure 10.19. *The View menu enables you to switch to page view.*

Embellishing the Score

There is more to creating a score than just notes; you have to add some expression marks, such as crescendo, slur, and so on. Tools for creating these are located at the bottom of the tool palette for note entry. I added some (admittedly random) expression marks to give you some idea of the variety available. In real music, expression marks are used for such things as indicating that a passage should be played gradually more loudly or softly. If you return to standard mode, the score looks like Figure 10.20.

Notice that each measure has a small white box associated with it. This is a selection handle—clicking the handle selects the measure.

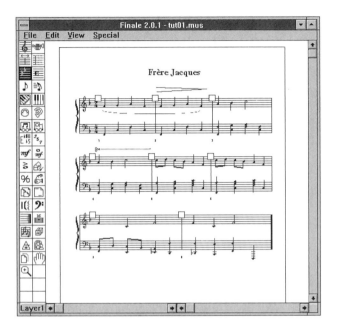

Figure 10.20. *The musical score, as it appears in standard mode.*

This brings up a sore point I have with Finale—yes, it is powerful, but what price power? I prefer to have selection based on notes rather than measures. You ultimately have to put a selected measure in an editing mode, and I would rather edit like I do in a word processor—anywhere I want. I don't like having to switch modes. It's awkward.

Changing Keys

Now for the fun part. Suppose you want to change to a different key (songs are played in a certain key, such as C major or A-flat minor). You see the dialog box in Figure 10.21.

Do you see the small check box at the bottom? It really does say "19th Century Western Tonality!" This is the point where I began to realize just how *deep* the power in Finale runs. Click the check box at the bottom of the dialog box and see what happens (Figure 10.22).

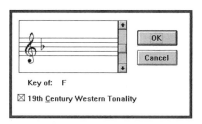

Figure 10.21. *The dialog box that enables you to change keys.*

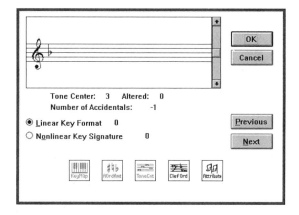

Figure 10.22. *The 19th Century Western Tonality dialog box.*

You get to define your own non-19th Century Western tonality. Or perhaps you would like to define the Accidental Octave Placement for Clefs? You can do it if you understand what it is. I strongly suspect that only serious musicians need this kind of feature.

The Appearance of the Score

Finale also gives you complete control over the appearance of every detail of the score with things like Page Boundaries, System Margins, Note Separations, and Tuplet Number Offset. If you're using a PostScript printer, you can exercise extremely detailed control over the appearance of the printed score.

Overall, Finale has an impressive level of detail and control. Unfortunately, access to Finale's features is awkward because of deeply nested levels of dialog boxes; finding all the features is a challenge to the newcomer. As you might expect, there are many system options (Figure 10.23). If you want the pure, raw power to do what you need to do with music, however, Finale has no equal.

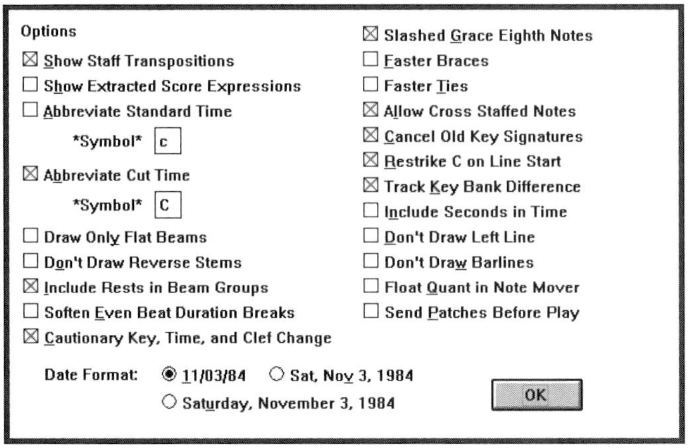

Figure 10.23. Finale's system options.

The Bottom Line

In the first edition of this book, I said, "But enough fun—I truly wish I had the time while writing this book to really learn Finale." Well, another year has gone by, and I still don't know as much as I would like about Finale. In fact, until I learn more about music, Finale will always offer more than I can handle.

Nonetheless, I always appreciate using a tool with real power. As with such real-world tools as the table saw or wood-carving tools, sharp, powerful tools can get you in trouble until you learn how to use them.

To verify my suspicions about Finale, I talked via electronic mail with a few musicians who use it.[11] It wasn't a scientific sample, but they all agreed that Finale is well worth the time and effort it takes to learn to use it well. Unlike lesser packages, Finale rewards you for your investment—in terms of both time and

---

[11]On CompuServe, of course.

money. For example, Figure 10.24 shows a printed score created with Finale. I'm not sure you would ever play it, but it is impressive. Finale also works well with more conventional scoring.

Figure 10.24. *A printed score created with Finale.*

Sequencers for Mastering Multimedia

You can use sequencing software to manipulate MIDI files without ever looking at standard musical notation. It's called sequencing software because the notes are shown sequentially, one after the next. Even if there is more than one staff[12] (as in an orchestral score), each staff is a sequence of notes. Chords are no problem: even though they are sent sequentially, the time difference between individual notes is too small to hear.

Sequencers are available as both hardware and software. For example, my first keyboard was a Korg M1. It includes a few hundred sound samples, but it also

---

[12]It's called a *track* in sequencing software lingo.

includes a sequencer with eight tracks. Tracks are essential for sequencing—you can put a different instrument on each track, and you can play back previously recorded tracks while you record a new one.

Although it's convenient to have a sequencer in a synthesizer keyboard, I never use mine. When compared to a computer, a hardware sequencer has one severe limitation: there is only a small LCD screen in a hardware sequencer. When compared to a high-resolution 1024×768 monitor, a built-in sequencer doesn't cut it. The primary use for hardware sequencers is on the road for traveling musicians. Sequencers are also handier than a computer during live performances, although many musicians are putting a computer right up on stage these days.

I have great fun using sequencer software. My personal favorite is Master Tracks Pro 4 from Passport Designs. Don't think the others aren't worthwhile— it's just that a sequencer is a highly personal choice. You don't have to buy a sequencer to test drive one, however. I included a shareware sequencer called WinJammer with this book. I'll give you a test drive of WinJammer, and then I'll show you some other products.

WinJammer

WinJammer is a shareware program located on the floppy disk. Even if you don't have a CD-ROM drive, you can load up WinJammer and play along with me. If you do have a CD-ROM drive, there is also a working model of Master Tracks Pro that you can examine. (See Appendix B for information about files and programs on the CD-ROM disk.)

The main screen is typical of a sequencer (Figure 10.25).

Each row (referred to as a *track*) contains information about one instrument. The sound or instrument is called a *patch* in MIDI terminology. (The jargon surrounding MIDI sometimes makes it hard to use and understand.)

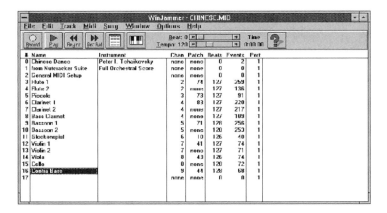

Figure 10.25. *WinJammer's main screen.*

The following list explains the screen's column headings for the information about each track:

#	The track number.
Name	A text description of the track. A nice feature of the MIDI file specification is that it enables you to store text descriptions; it makes the music file easier to work with (considering that everything else in MIDI is really just numbers).
Instrument	A text description commonly used for comments as well as instrument names. In Figure 10.12, there are no instrument names; they're all in the previous column. Go figure.
Chan	The MIDI channel number. Standard MIDI has 16 channels. Not all devices support all 16 channels, however. If you use a channel your device does not support, you won't hear the instrument on that channel. Even expensive keyboards might not support all 16 channels.
Patch	More MIDI terminology. This is the specific sound that is the default for the track (you can change it during the course of playback if you want). Unfortunately, WinJammer displays only the number of the patch. The patches have names in General MIDI, but they are not shown here.

Beats   The number of beats in the entire track.

Events   The number of MIDI events on the entire track. Events
               include more than notes—pitch wheel changes, patch
               changes, and other events also are counted.

Port   The number of the MIDI port currently in use. Unless
               you have more than one MIDI port, this setting is
               always 1.

At the top-left of the screen is a set of buttons similar to those on a tape re-corder. As ubiquitous as such controls have become, they serve a definite purpose here: a sequencer is a lot like a multitrack tape recorder. You can record on one or more tracks at a time, and you can play back tracks while you record a new track.

Configuring WinJammer

One of the most important considerations in choosing a sequencer is how easily you can configure it to work with your computer and your MIDI devices. A complex or confusing configuration process can make using your software painful instead of rewarding, especially if you change from one instrument or MIDI card to another with any frequency.

I had fun working with the various sequencers. I've orchestrated everything from a choral rendition of "Silent Night" to a pulsating blues number. Before I could do any of that, I first had to find a way to make all the hardware and software work together peacefully. WinJammer is easier than most sequencers when it comes to MIDI connections. The MIDI configuration dialog box looks like Figure 10.26.

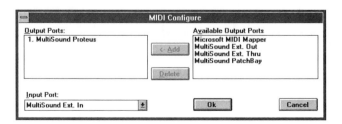

Figure 10.26. *The MIDI configuration dialog box.*

The box on the right of the dialog box lists available output ports, and all you have to do is select from the list. The ports are listed because WinJammer relies on Windows to tell it which MIDI drivers are installed. This prevents two serious problems:

➤ You won't be disappointed when it provides a list of MIDI drivers and none of them match your system.

➤ You won't have to hunt around for ways to make connections between WinJammer and your MIDI hardware.

WinJammer Features

The opening screen of WinJammer hides a number of other capabilities (Figure 10.27) that you can access with the Window menu.

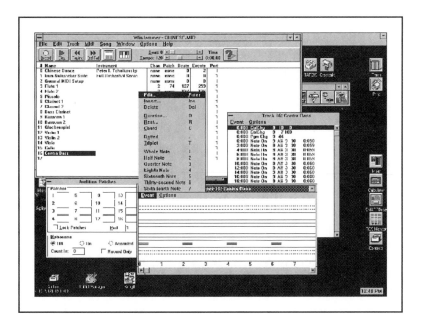

Figure 10.27. *Some of WinJammer's options.*

The two most interesting windows are the piano-roll window (bottom-right) and the event window (middle-right). The piano-roll window displays a menu.

From this menu, you can select the characteristics of notes you plan to enter, such as duration, chording, dotted notes, and so on. Although this is not the easiest way to enter music, it works.

The event window is hard-core MIDI. It's not as bad as pure binary data because it gives you some context for each event, such as note on and program change. If you examine the window carefully, you can see that it is telling you this instrument (the Contra Bass) plays a sequence of A# notes, one every two measures.

You can figure this out by looking at the first column. It consists of numbers of the form xx:yyy. The number to the left of the colon is the measure number; these numbers increase by two from line to line. The second column describes the kind of event (mostly note on). The third column is the channel number (each MIDI event is responsible for informing the user of its channel), followed by (in the case of a Note On) the pitch of the note—A#. The score for the Contra Bass is boring; Figure 10.28 shows the event window for track 11, the Glockenspiel.

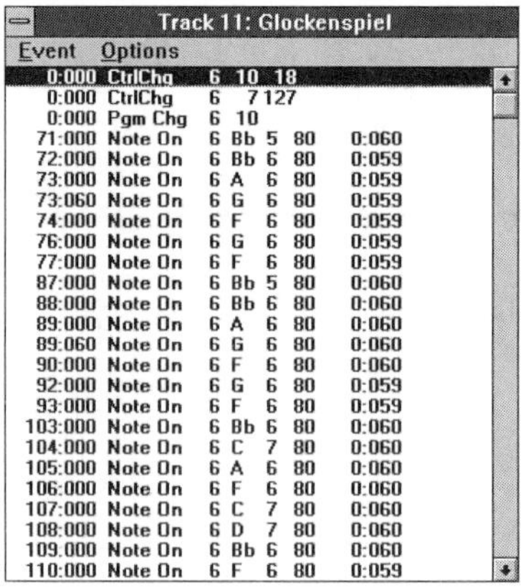

Figure 10.28. *The event window for the Glockenspiel.*

These notes differ from those for the Contra Bass in several ways. The timing of the Note On events varies more. For example, there is a note-on at 89:000, then another Note On at 89:060—two notes in the same measure. The notes that are played are also varied—A, G, F, even B flat. Speaking of sharps and flats, you can easily change the key the music is played in (Figure 10.29). This is one of the great strengths of MIDI.

Figure 10.29. *WinJammer's Song Key dialog box.*

The drop-down box contains a list of all keys; you can move from one key to the next until you find one suitable for accompaniment.

Another useful feature enables you to smooth out the rhythm in the song. For example, most live performances are full of little timing quirks. Most sequencers enable you to "straighten out" the performance by forcing it onto the beat (Figure 10.30). This is called *quantization*.

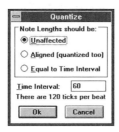

Figure 10.30. *WinJammer's performance quantization dialog box.*

Another strength of MIDI is that it enables you to adjust parameters along an entire track. For example, you can adjust note velocity either by adding a fixed value, or by multiplying or dividing it by a factor. Note velocity determines how loudly a note will play. MIDI stores the velocity with which the key was struck rather than the actual volume—you adjust volume on the instrument at playback time.

This concludes coverage of WinJammer—now I'll show you the personalities of the various sequencer packages that are on the market. Because they differ so much in style (more so than in terms of substance), I think it is important to take a look at how each sequencer functions. The examples won't cover the same features for each sequencer; they were designed to be good at different things.

Cakewalk for Windows

Cakewalk is the sequencer for anyone who enjoys the technical side of things. I have done (more than) my share of programming over the years, and I tend to like software that lets me get into the guts of things. I'm not happy unless the software allows me to really screw things up, should I desire to do so. Cakewalk comes fully armed for battle with MIDI. In the first edition of this book, I gave Cakewalk several demerits for having a non-intuitive interface. By all accounts, the new version of Cakewalk has improved things considerably.

Cakewalk still has an impressive array of technical features. You will probably use it for an extended period of time before you become familiar enough with the interface to use it effectively.

Cakewalk's strengths are a strong sense of the technical aspects of MIDI, simultaneous staff notation and piano-roll notation, and depth of detail in its features. Its weakness, like Finale's, is a consequence of its strength: a more complex than average interface. The screen in Figure 10.31 reveals Cakewalk's power.

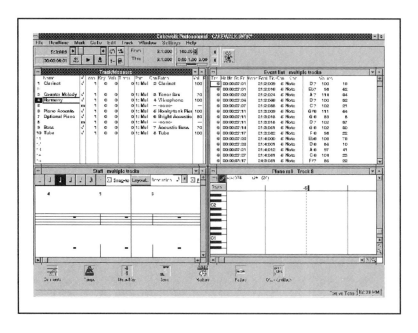

Figure 10.31. Cakewalk's powerful interface.

Four windows are shown, and Cakewalk has additional windows available for various features. The top-left window is the primary window; it contains a view of the tracks in the file. The top-right window lists the MIDI events. The lower-left window shows staff notation, and the bottom-right window contains piano-roll notation.

Instrument Patches

In Cakewalk, I found it was awkward to specify which patch (*patch* is a synonym for a sound or instrument) plays on which track. All the patches are displayed in a single drop-down list box as shown in Figure 10.32. This forces you to look for the patch you want in one giant list, making it hard to find the one you want. If you enjoy trying different arrangements of instruments, this is a hassle. Cakewalk comes with patch lists for many popular keyboards and synthesizers, as well as General MIDI.

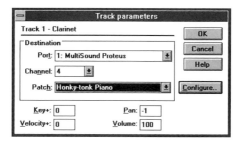

Figure 10.32. *Cakewalk's Track parameters dialog box.*

Methods of Recording

With sequencers, you can record music in two ways:

➤ In real-time while you play an instrument

➤ In step entry mode (one note at a time)

You can enter step entry mode either from your MIDI keyboard or using piano-roll notation. Step entry is awkward when you use a PC keyboard or a mouse because these devices are so different from a piano keyboard. For example, setting the step size and duration in Cakewalk takes you to the dialog box shown in Figure 10.33.

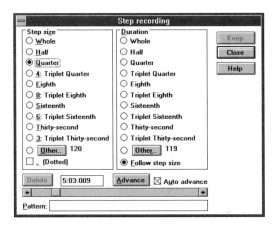

Figure 10.33. Cakewalk's Step recording dialog box.

Staff notation (Figure 10.34) makes the process much simpler. Not only are the notes and staffs a more familiar way for many of us to work with music, there is a toolbar with buttons for each note duration, and the note itself can be set easily on the staff with a mouse click.

Figure 10.34. Staff notation in Cakewalk.

Controls

To control the volume of each instrument,[13] Cakewalk provides a graphic fader control. This is different from the method used by Master Tracks Pro 4. In Pro 4, the volume controls are an expandable part of the Track window. Although this method is convenient, it takes up space needed for other features. Tradeoffs, tradeoffs—you can't do anything without tradeoffs.

---

[13]There is one instrument per track.

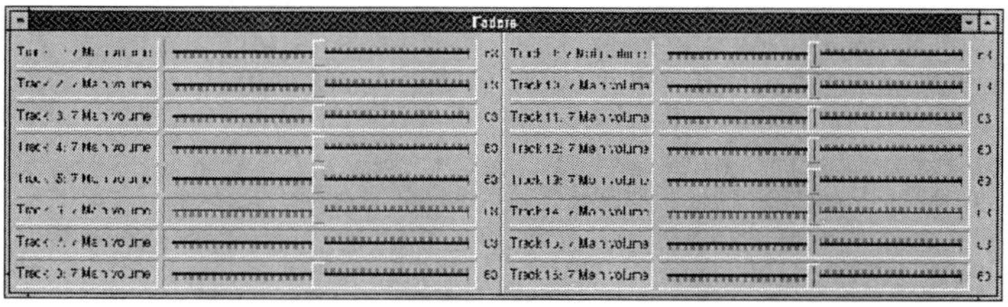

Figure 10.35. *Cakewalk's graphic fader control.*

That's why there are so many (and such different) sequencers available—there are many different ways to make the tradeoffs required to put MIDI support on a computer. Each product emphasizes a different aspect of the process. Some, such as Cakewalk, emphasize the details of MIDI control. Others, such as Master Tracks Pro 4, emphasize ease of use and accessibility at some cost in access to MIDI control. Which one you pick depends on what you intend to do. If you plan to push MIDI to the edge, you need a powerful program that gives you access to MIDI data. If you focus on the music, you need to pick a program that gives you tools for that. Remember, however, that you won't find everything in any one program.[14]

MIDI Events

MIDI is all about events: a note on, a note off, a patch change, aftertouch, and so on.[15] Most packages offer some way to filter out events you don't need to work with right now, and Cakewalk is no exception.

By selecting the events you want to work with, you can focus on your work. The need for such filtering points out a weak point with MIDI for new users: to really control what is going on, you need to get down and mess with the data itself.

Of course, you can accomplish quite a bit without touching the MIDI data. Most sequencers enable you to make changes to the music without ever seeing the MIDI data. But from the viewpoint of an accomplished electronic musician, the MIDI data is there to play with. Serious users need a way to access the actual

---

[14]This is so common, I'm inclined to think it must be a law of software—if you want real power, you often have to buy more than one program.

[15]This is why sequencers are so valuable—when you are working in traditional staff notation, the use of notes precludes easy access to the MIDI data about the preformance—how hard a key was pressed or how quickly it was released.

data. Cakewalk gives you that power. It even enables you to filter the events in sophisticated ways (Figure 10.36). You can look at note changes only, or program changes only, or mix and match the kinds of MIDI events you work with.

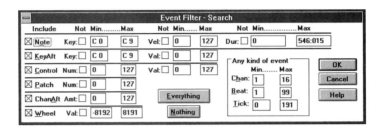

Figure 10.36. *Cakewalk enables you to filter events in sophisticated ways.*

This dialog box makes it as clear as possible: when it comes to messing with MIDI, Cakewalk is hard to beat.

Master Tracks Pro 4

This is my favorite sequencer. I find it friendly, and it's the best at what I like to do: orchestration. Last year I said, "However, I would like it more if it had built-in staff notation like Cakewalk." My wish has been granted; Version 4.9 of Master Tracks Pro adds staff notation (see Figure 10.37). It includes all the basic features you need for working with notes, but you may still want to have Master Tracks Pro's software sibling, Encore. Encore handles staff notation very well.

Figure 10.37. *Staff notation in Master Tracks Pro.*

Still, using a sequencer is one of the best ways to learn MIDI as well as music. With Master Tracks Pro 4, I could learn MIDI one step at a time. I never had to rely on MIDI for anything, but when I was ready to explore the next step, the menus made it easy to find the way. Figure 10.38 shows a typical Master Tracks Pro screen from Version 4.9.

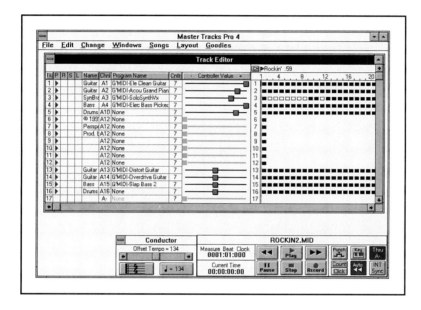

Figure 10.38. *A typical Master Tracks Pro screen.*

The bottom line is this: of all the sequencers I've worked with, Master Tracks Pro 4 is the easiest to learn.

The Track Editor Window

The most convenient window to work with is the Track Editor window (Figure 10.38).

The columns in the Track Editor window, from left to right, are:

Tk	The track number.
P	To play or not to play. Clicking the small triangle toggles playing of the track on and off. A filled triangle means play; an empty triangle means do not play.

635

R	Record toggle. A small red button indicates that recording is active for a given track; you toggle the setting by clicking the red button.
S	Track Solo toggle. A blue diamond indicates that a track plays solo.
L	Track Loop toggle. A curved arrow indicates the track loops back to the beginning when it completes.
Name	You can enter any text that you want.
Chnl	The MIDI channel the track data is sent to.
Program Name	This is the official name of the instrument rather than the number some other products use; it is the same as Patch in Cakewalk.
Cntlr	The controller number. Most of the time, this will be 7, the volume control.
Controller Value	The farther the slider is to the right, the higher the controller value.

Just visible in the right of the window are the music tracks—one small box for each measure. Empty measures show up as outlined boxes. To see more of the measures, you can shrink the wide columns by clicking the gray header box at the top of the column. A second click acts as a toggle, expanding the columns.

Editing Tracks

Although the Master Tracks screen resembles the Track window of other sequencer programs, there is a difference. Instead of editing the data in each box by entering new data, you can click many of the boxes to bring up just the right dialog box. Suppose you want to change to a different instrument. Clicking the Program Name (perhaps Overdrive Guitar) immediately brings up the well-organized dialog box in Figure 10.39.

In this dialog box, you can select the synthesizer (top-left), make it the default synthesizer (top-right), and assign the instrument (also known as patch or sound) of your choice. Very elegant, and it suits my hobby of orchestrating various instruments quite well.

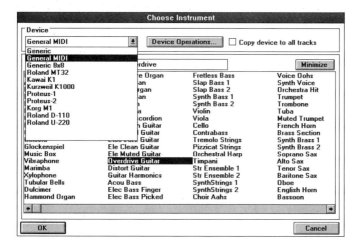

Figure 10.39. *The Master Tracks Pro 4 Choose Instrument dialog box.*

Working with the Music Score

Master Tracks Pro 4 offers several other ways of working with and viewing your music. The Step Editor (a piano-roll view) is well designed (Figure 10.40).

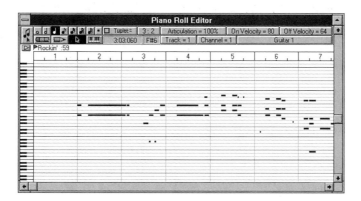

Figure 10.40. *The Step Editor in Master Tracks Pro 4.*

Notice the piano keys at the left; they make it easier to find the note you want. There are buttons at the top of the window to indicate the value of any notes you want to enter, and there are controls for changing tracks and channels. By

637

clicking the keyboard icon on the toolbar, you can enter notes directly from a keyboard. By clicking the pencil point, you can enter notes with the mouse; clicking the pencil eraser enables you to remove them just as easily. Master Tracks Pro 4 also includes an Event Editor (Figure 10.41); you can set a filter to select the kinds of events you want to see (Figure 10.42). Master Tracks uses the icons you see in Figure 10.42 to indicate the type of each event.

Figure 10.41. *The Event Editor.*

Figure 10.42. *The Master Tracks Pro 4 Event Editor icons.*

The editor itself is simple; there's not much you can do with an event except use it to directly edit the MIDI data.

The latest edition of Master Tracks Pro has added some additional tools. Figure 10.43 shows the Pitch Bend[16] window, which enables you to easily visualize the amount of pitch bend applied to a track.

---

[16]Pitch Bend is the amount by which a note's pitch is varied at any give time. Pitch bend is commonly used with guitars, for example, to simulate the effect of a tremolo arm.

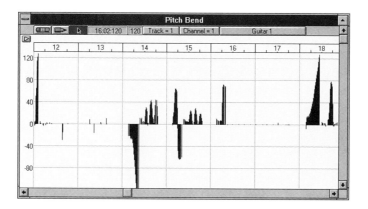

Figure 10.43. *Viewing pitch bend data graphically.*

Notation Software

When I first thought of putting music on a computer, I thought in terms of traditional musical notation. I always had thought of music in terms of notes, and it has always seemed to be the most natural way to work with music. Admittedly, sequencer software offers some important MIDI-specific capabilities, but sometimes the music itself is the most important thing. This is true when

➤ You want to work directly with music as notes on a staff.

➤ You need to print a musical score using traditional staff notation.

➤ You want to edit music you already have available in staff notation.

I've already shown you Finale, a high-end professional notation program; let's look at two other notation programs: Encore and Music Prose. Encore is a full-featured program that is used by many professionals, and Music Prose is the light version of Finale.

Encore

Although Encore is a powerful notation program—you can do all kinds of things to create a score—it falls short of Finale's power and depth of coverage. However, Encore makes up for this in ease of use. Here's my recommendation for notation software: if you can do it in Encore, use Encore. If Encore doesn't do what you need, buy Finale. It's that simple.

I like Encore's opening screen. Encore displays a sheet of music with staffs already on it, ready for you to work your musical will on it (Figure 10.44).

Figure 10.44. *Encore's opening screen.*

In the critically important area of MIDI configuration, Encore does a good job. Encore is designed by Passport Designs, the same company that designed Master Tracks Pro 4, and the MIDI configuration box is similar, as you can see in Figure 10.45.

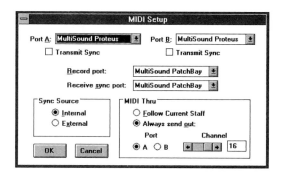

Figure 10.45. *Encore's MIDI Setup dialog box.*

Like Master Tracks Pro 4, Encore had no trouble using the Windows drivers I installed for the MultiSound.

Encore, like a sequencer, optionally outputs clicks on the beat.[17] You can use these clicks to keep correct time, just as you would use a metronome. You can select the channel, pitch, loudness, and duration of the bar and beat clicks. I found this helpful because different kinds of music required different kinds of click sounds for real-time playing. A high, bell-like click complements classical music, and a blues number needs something like a foghorn to get through the driving bass.[18]

Encore also supports quantizing, which enables you to correct beat irregularities when you record a live performance (Figure 10.46). I find this feature more useful in a notation program than in a standard sequencer. In notation, if you have too many minor variations in notes durations, the staff gets clogged up with complex note and rest placements. Even a simple tune looks like the Score from Hell if you don't quantize to some reasonable level, such as eighth or sixteenth notes.

Customizing the Display

You can customize the placement of text on the title page (Figure 10.47) to make it look like a professional score.

---

[17]To be fair, most computer music software has this capability.

[18]On the other hand, a driving bass line may be all the metronome you need; Encore lets you turn off the click.

Figure 10.46. *Setting transcription options in Encore.*

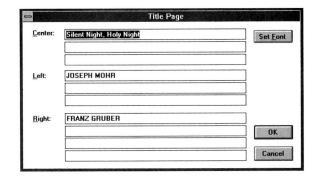

Figure 10.47. *Encore's Title Page dialog box.*

You can control the placement of musical details, and you can preview your score in a small window to see an entire page (Figure 10.48). I was quite pleased with Encore's ability to create a pleasing-looking score. You can add lyrics, for example, quite easily. Encore may lack the technical brilliance and custom capabilities of Finale, but it is very professional.

Note Controls

When placing or editing notes, you require access to a wide variety of note durations and qualifiers (sharps, flats, dots, and so on). Encore offers a huge variety of "note palettes" from which to pick (Figure 10.49). This use of palettes reflects a growing (and welcome) trend in Windows interface design. The palettes always "float" on top of other Encore windows for easy access.

With these palettes, you can change nearly everything about a score, from the appearance to the content. You can change pitch, tempo, and key signature of a note or group of notes, and you can also adjust the appearance of a measure to meet a variety of stylistic conventions. In addition, you can apply global changes using sophisticated techniques for selecting what notes the changes will affect (Figure 10.50).

Figure 10.48. *A full page of music displayed in Encore.*

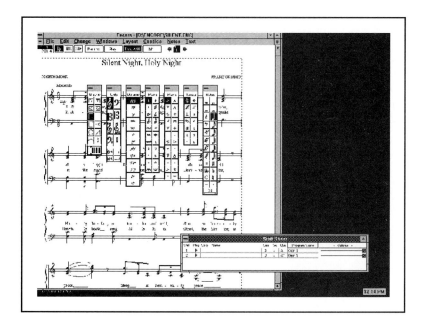

Figure 10.49. *Encore's many "note palettes."*

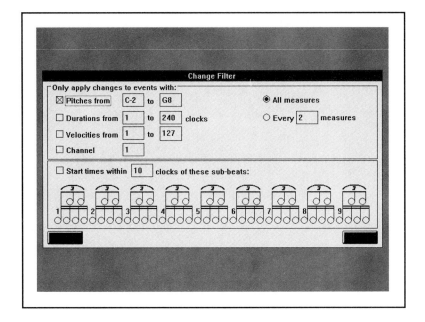

Figure 10.50. *Encore's note Change Filter.*

Encore supports a host of other features, and all of them are nicely integrated into the menus and dialog boxes—it's not hard to locate a needed feature. Admittedly, Encore is not as feature-rich as Finale. If you need full power to create complex or sophisticated scores, Finale is a must. If your needs are not as demanding, or you just want to have some fun with music, Encore is the best choice because it is easy to use.

Music Prose

This program is a little brother to Finale. It shows both its family origins and the ability to move in some new directions. It is intended to be a more accessible version of its bigger brother, a program for users who don't need Finale's awesome power or who simply need a more friendly interface. I preferred Encore myself, but if you are part of a team, and the final[19] result will be done with Finale, Music Prose is easier to use. The opening screen (Figure 10.51) is far simpler than Finale's.

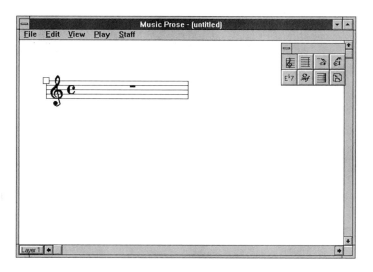

Figure 10.51. *The opening screen of Music Prose.*

The most noticeable difference is a small floating palette of icons rather than the potpourri of icons found in Finale. Otherwise, the interface is similar—a single measure of a single staff on the opening screen.

The Palette

Take a closer look at that floating palette in Figure 10.52. The following list describes the tools.

Figure 10.52. *The Music Prose tool palette.*

---

[19]Pun not intended, but there it is nonetheless.

Surprisingly, this small palette includes just about everything:

➤ Staff tool to add, delete, and control staves

➤ Measure tool to add, delete, and control measures

➤ Entry tool to enter music in step time or real time, from the computer or your MIDI keyboard

➤ Lyric tool to add or modify lyrics

➤ Chord tool to add or modify chord symbols

➤ Expression tool to add articulations, dynamics, shapes, and text expressions

➤ Repeat tool to add or modify repeats

➤ Page tool to control page layout

Making Changes

Music Prose effectively uses the graphical elements of Windows. The screen for changing keys, for example, is carefully laid out and communicates its function well (Figure 10.53).

Figure 10.53. The dialog box for changing keys in Music Prose.

As you change keys with the slider to the right of the staff, the appropriate sharps and flats appear. You have several choices to make the key change, and you can alter either a selected region or the rest of the song.

Changes in a song's meter—such as from 4/4 to 3/4—are also made in a graphical manner (Figure 10.54).

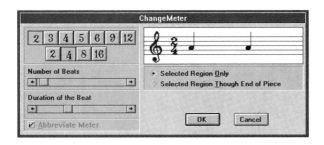

Figure 10.54. *The Music Prose ChangeMeter.*

As you select the meter, notes appear on the staff consistent with the meter you choose.

Entering Notes

When you enter notes, a small, floating palette keeps the various kinds of notes and symbols close at hand (Figure 10.55).

Figure 10.55. *The palette used to enter notes in Music Prose.*

Music entry occurs in a movable window; the window is drawn around the current measure. This is similar to how Finale handles this task; I prefer to edit directly the image on the screen rather than work in an edit window. To play back a score, press the space bar; the cursor turns into a speaker icon. Click the measure where you want to start playback.

MIDI Controls

In the area of MIDI configuration, Music Prose holds up well. It ties properly into Windows multimedia (Figure 10.56).

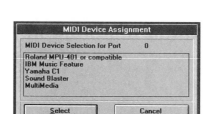

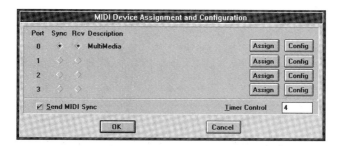

Figure 10.56. *The Music Prose MIDI Device Assignment dialog box.*

Music Prose directly supports the most common MIDI cards. It also checks to see what other card you have installed and lists it as "Multimedia," meaning anything you installed a Windows driver for. If you have more than one MIDI port, Music Prose can keep track (Figure 10.57).

Figure 10.57. *Keeping track of multiple MIDI ports in Music Prose.*

Big brother Finale also has Windows 3.1 MIDI support.

Music Prose is a good choice but not my first choice. If you also use Finale, or plan on moving up to its power, Music Prose becomes more attractive.

Lights, Camera, Action: Video for Windows

I n Chapter 6, "Pumping Iron: Hardware," I present some of the issues involved in digitizing video signals. This enables you to put video signals generated by a television, VCR, or camcorder onto your hard disk. However, video signals are different from VGA and Super VGA signals. The main point in Chapter 6 is that it takes well-engineered hardware to combine these two different types of signals.

Digitizing NTSC video signals can be a lot of fun, however, if you have the right hardware. There are all kinds of video files on the CDs, including some I have done and some that are part of the various demo programs on the CDs. Let's get started with video by demonstrating how it works.

To use video on your PC, you must install the Video for Windows drivers.[1] I provided the very latest version of Video for Windows runtime on the Nautilus CD-ROM. To install the Video for Windows runtime, put the Nautilus CD in your drive. The easiest shortcut is to use File Manager to open the directory \DRIVERS\VFWRUN, and double-click on the file SETUP.EXE. Setup walks you through the installation process.

Once you have installed Video for Windows, it's incredibly easy to play a video file. There are quite a few .AVI files on both CDs. You can either hunt around for files with an .AVI extension, or you can go to the \VIDEOFUN directory, where I have put a few fun .AVI files. Double-click on any one of these files. You should see the Media Player window, and the file should play all by itself. Files that start with a *c* use the Cinepak codec. Files that start with an *i* use Indeo, and files that start with an *m* use the Microsoft Video 1 codec.[2]

Figure 11.1 shows one of the fun video files I included playing in a default Media Player window. That's my neighbor's dog, Beauty (actually, she's a cousin of Sparky, the Moon Dog; see Chapter 3) hanging from a sock and spinning about.

If you want to get more control over playing a video file, run the Media Player application (it can usually be found in your Accessories group). Select Video for Windows from the Device menu, and then open any file you wish to play. The video will be displayed in a separate window (Figure 11.2).[3] To play the file, click

---

[1]Even if you have Video for Windows already installed (runtime or full retail package) you may want to install the version on the CD anyway. It includes the latest Indeo and Cinepak drivers.

[2]Lots of information about codecs is included later in this chapter, in the section "Video Codecs." A codec is basically a Windows driver that knows how to display the video files for you.

[3]The landscape in the background is a small portion of a much larger landscape I created with Vista Pro, one of those Really Cool software packages that people are always Recommending Highly. I highly recommend it.

the Play button at the lower left of the Media Player window. The rest of the buttons in Media Player work just like VCR controls.

Figure 11.1. *An example of how easy it is to play video files.*

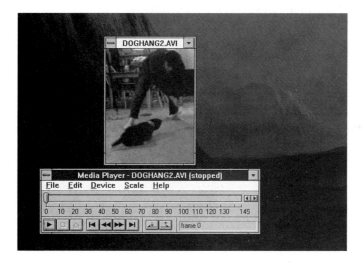

Figure 11.2. *Playing a video with Media Player.*

You can even use Media Player to place a video in an application using OLE.[4] While the video is open in Media Player, copy the video to the Windows clipboard using the Edit|Copy Object menu selection in Media Player. Then activate or run an application, and choose Edit|Paste from the application's Edit menu.

---

[4]Object Linking and Embedding.

As shown in Figure 11.3, an image of the video file appears in your application.[5] To play the video, just double-click anywhere on the video image. This displays a controller right in the application (see Figure 11.4). The controller is the same as the default Media Player window. You can play, pause, and stop the video— you can move the little slider with the mouse to position to any frame in the video.

Figure 11.3. *Adding a video with OLE.*

You can save a file that contains an OLE video, and when you reopen it, the video image will still be there. You can use this technique to play a video from any application that supports OLE—and most Windows applications do.

Of course, this is just the very beginning of what you can do with video. As Arsenio Hall would say, "Let's ... get ... busy!"

---

[5]In this example, that's Windows Write, with the README file for Encarta open. Note that the name of the file appears below the video. Using the Device|Configure menu in Media Player before you copy the media object, you can supply a default caption and set other attributes as well.

Figure 11.4. *Playing a video in an application using OLE.*

Using Digital Video

If you want reasons to use video, all you have to do is look at an application that incorporates video.[6] There are several key situations where video on a computer makes the most sense. I have seen digital video used in a variety of ways in various software packages. There are games that use video to create a sense of "you are there;" there are presentations that merely add a talking head. There are educational titles that extensively use videos and animation to make the subject matter come alive; there are encyclopedias that use video to show you things you would be hard-pressed to see on your own. I have distilled these various examples of video down to four basic situations where video can be used:

---

[6]Personally, I was hooked as soon as I saw a video on a computer screen.

➤ When you need the additional impact created by motion video.

➤ When you must show something to your audience that they haven't seen before.

➤ When you want to establish presence and immediacy in a message.

➤ When a video sequence needs words or still pictures beside it or behind it to help the audience make sense of it.

Before I move on to the "how-to" of digital video using Video for Windows, let's take a look at each of these situations.[7]

Video Impact

There is one overriding fact about video: it moves. Things that move catch your eye. Things that catch your eye are usually perfect for presentations, games, and "edutainment" software.

For example, if you were presenting a series of slides about a new product, wouldn't it be great if you could show the product in use? Or if you were showing a presentation about your company to prospective buyers, wouldn't it be great if you could show your company CEO or the head of marketing in a video? The customer would get a much clearer idea of who he is dealing with.

Video for New Stuff

There's a tired old phrase that I'm going to drag out here: "a picture is worth a thousand words." Have you ever asked yourself why that might be true? Probably not, so I'll go ahead and offer you my idea. If you have never seen something, it's really tough to get a clear idea of it through words. A picture, on the other hand, puts the thing right there in front of you.

Because video moves, it's even better at this process. For example, suppose you work for a robotics company that makes robots which clean used nuclear waste sites. And suppose further that one of your robots, out in the field

---

[7]When I wrote the first edition of this book, I had no plans to devote much space to real-time video capture. At that time, capturing video in real-time was still a big hassle. You had to invest in expensive ($2,000–$3,000) hardware compression boards to handle the enormous data rates involved. Then Microsoft introduced Video for Windows, the Author's Choice product for this chapter. Suddenly, video was all over the map.

somewhere, is acting a little strange. The customer calls you (you are on the technical support staff for the purposes of this example) and tells you the problem. You, being sharp, realize that the ramifroozis is busted. But the part has a weird shape, and it's hard to get in and out of the robot. So you click the "on" button for your desktop video camera and hold up a ramifroozis to show the customer.[8] You tell him that, to remove the part, he must first flip the little dohickey on the top side, "like this," you say, adding "and be sure to give the whole thing a little twist, like this" you say again. And of course because he can see you, that's it, you're done, on to the next call. Video has made a difficult support problem into a trivial one.

Video Power

Let's say you are the head of a sales department and that you have just received the sales reports for the last month. Let's further suppose that those reports don't look so good and that you think the field reps are lacking a little in the motivation department. You have three choices in today's world:

➤ You can draft a letter that they can use to line their parakeet cages.

➤ You can call each one on the phone and talk with him or her.

➤ You can pull out your trusty video camera and record a little motivational talk. If you have time, you can do it a few times to get it just right. You can even add some videos of key products and show them some clever techniques for selling specific products. You can then get a half-dozen CDs pressed on a CD-ROM recorder and send your motivational seminar out into the field.

With digital video, you can record the video, splice it together,[9] and have it out the door in a matter of hours. Try that sometime with video tape.

Video Plus

Sometimes, of course, a regular old video tape might be just right—when there isn't much editing, for example. But when you use video on a computer, you not

---

[8]You might also hold it up to the camera off-line and make a recording that you then send to the customer with the part.

[9]Including whatever special effects you might like to add, by the way.

only gain from the capabilities of the digital technology at your disposal, but you also gain from having the computer involved during playback.

You can play the video in a window and add text to support what the video is showing. You can easily add buttons in a product like Compel to let the user choose from several videos. You can add sound tracks. You can do whatever your imagination leads you to.

Video for Everyone?

I recently wrote a comprehensive book about digital video titled *PC Video Madness*. I found that people would come up to me and ask me why I had written a book about video on the PC. When I, in turn, asked them why they thought such a thing was strange, they told me that video was too complicated for PCs.

Nothing could be further from the truth. PC video will surely be easier a year or two down the road, but it's not very complicated at all. I have to admit, however, that if you try to push the envelope with video, you will find a few rough edges. That's true of any new cutting edge technology. Video production isn't for everyone, but neither does everyone know how to set the clock on their VCR. That doesn't mean VCRs aren't nice to have around.

Here are the commonly perceived obstacles and objections that I hear about video on PCs:

Objection	Ron's Reaction
Video hardware costs too much	That was last week; this week, the prices have come down so far you can buy the hardware just to play with it. Video capture used to cost $3,000 and up; now it costs less than $300.
You need a studio to do good video	You can actually create great-looking video using simple tools—a camera and one or two portable lights can give you super results. You can use your computer as the production studio for special effects.

Objection	Ron's Reaction
Digital video image quality isn't as good on the PC	This is true; I couldn't shoot down *every* objection! Video must be compressed to be used on a PC, and compressed further to put it on a CD-ROM disc. The good news is that the quality of compressed video is increasing rapidly, and this factor will fade over the next 6–12 months.
Video compression is confusing	There are a number of video compression schemes out there, but only a few need your serious attention. I'll point the way through the compression maze later in this chapter.
Desktop video is more complicated than desktop publishing	It isn't more complicated at all—today's computer users are simply more knowledgeable about desktop publishing because it's been around for so many years now. Give video a few years, and people will discover that the concepts behind video aren't any more complicated than those behind desktop publishing. By that time, lots of us will have experience with video, and it will seem commonplace. It's just new, that's all.
I don't know how to use a camera professionally	Well, I don't either, but I do know that if you use a tripod to steady the camera, make sure that there is adequate lighting, and avoid sudden camera changes, your video will look very good.
Video on a PC isn't full screen	So what? We already have full-screen video; it's called television. Video on a computer can take advantage of what the computer has to offer—interactivity, text to supplement the video content, on-screen video controls, digital special effects, video on CDs, and so on.

I think the only thing holding video back is its newness. Based on my experiences with a variety of new technologies over the years—including desktop publishing, music, and video—video isn't as complicated as some and is easier than most. The concepts behind video, like the concepts behind music or desktop publishing, are simply new and different.

Of course, if you don't want to simply take my word for it, the rest of this chapter should do the trick.

Video for Windows

Video for Windows has created a revolution on the PC, but it isn't actually very revolutionary in and of itself. It's just a standard, after all, not any terribly new technology. Video for Windows is more of a container that can be used to hold all kinds of new technology.

Video for Windows introduced a new file standard called *AVI*.[10] This new file standard doesn't define how the video will be captured, compressed, or played back. It merely defines how the video and audio will be stored on your hard disk—hence my earlier reference to Video for Windows as a container. All AVI does is tell us how to store video and audio data. The capturing, compression, and playback can do anything they want as long as they respect the storage requirements.

This means that as new technology for video is introduced, Video for Windows doesn't need to change. For example, international standards committees

---

[10]Audio Video Interleaved. This refers to the fact that audio and video data are interleaved on your disk. For example, the audio for frame 1 is followed by the video for frame 1, then comes the audio for frame 2, the frame 2 video, and so on. It's a simple idea, but it is a critical component in the operation of video on a computer. Without interleaving multiple data types, a program would have to jump from place to place on your hard disk to find the data. That slows things down. Because video makes such heavy demands on your computer, anything that reduces the demand is important. Before .AVI files came along, each type of media data lived in its own physical file on the disk.

have created several different generic compression techniques—JPEG[11] and MPEG are two of the most important. It is essential to compress video on the computer. Digital video requires vast amounts of storage space. A single minute of uncompressed video requires 1.5 gigabytes of storage! This is a phenomenally large number. A simple, two-hour movie would require 180 gigabytes—that's 193,273,528,320 bytes of data,[12] or nearly 2,000 100-megabyte hard drives.[13] Even Terminator 2 doesn't rate that kind of investment.

The good news is that you don't need special hardware to play most .AVI files—if you install a video driver (using the control panel), you can play .AVI files.[14] The easiest way to play a video file is to use the Media Player, as you saw at the beginning of this chapter. If you are interested in using video for programming, Chapter 8 contains several useful examples.

Video Data and Computer Hardware

As the last section was intended to make crystal clear, the most important characteristic of video data is its sheer size. Even with compression, a single minute of video can easily occupy from 5M to 25M of disk space. Capturing that much data, converting it to digital data, then writing it to the disk takes time—lots of it. Even playback requires a fair amount of computer power. The slowest part of the process usually involves the disk. If you are playing a video from a CD-ROM,

---

[11]Joint Photographic Experts Group. This standard comes in two flavors: standard JPEG and motion JPEG. Standard JPEG is a compression scheme that loses some of the data but does it in such a way that the eye hardly notices. This is called *lossy* compression. For example, the eye is less sensitive to color changes related to blue, so JPEG (and most other lossy compression schemes) sacrifice some blue tones to achieve high compression rations. Motion JPEG is a modified version of JPEG that calculates the differences between frames for some frames instead of storing every frame. Is that clear?

MPEG (Motion Picture Experts Group) is more advanced still. It takes the frame difference stuff to a higher level and also adds something called *predictive calculation*—it uses what's in the current frame to predict what will be in following frames. MPEG is where the future of video compression lies. You can expect the first hardware implementation of MPEG late in 1993, but it won't be mainstream technology until later in 1994.

[12]If bytes were inches, at one byte to the inch that would be 3,050,403 miles, or about 125 times around the earth at the equator. I am talking big here.

[13]If you prefer to calculate in terms of CD-ROM discs, that would be about 300 CDs. Even if CDs sell for, say, $10 each, that would take $3,000 worth of CDs for one movie. Ouch!

[14]Apple Quicktime for Windows is another video-plus-audio file format that can be used to play video on a PC, but as of the time I wrote this chapter, such video movies had to be created on a Mac, not a PC.

the disc is definitely the slowest part of the process—a CD-ROM disc is about 5–10 times slower than a hard disk.

The problem is not as severe during playback, however. To create .AVI files, you need a 486/33 or faster machine. However, you don't need that much hardware to play it back. For most users, of course, playback is the only thing to worry about. If you are interested in video capture, see the section on VidCap, "Video for Windows Capture," in this chapter.

Most videos will be played back from a CD-ROM. The maximum data transfer rate of most CD-ROMs is 150K per second—significantly less than a hard disk.[15] In addition to a slow transfer rate, CDs suffer from another bottleneck—the time it takes to seek to a new track.[16]

If a CD had to read video data from one track and audio data from another, and if those tracks were far apart, there would be no hope of playing video/audio files from a CD. Unlike a hard disk, which has a small head to move around, a CD-ROM drive has to move a comparatively clunky laser/mirror device.

Video for Windows deals with the slow speed of the CD-ROM by making the job as easy as possible. The .AVI file format stores a single frame of video, then a matching amount of audio data, then another frame of video, then more audio, and so on. The real strength of CD-ROMs lies in what is called *streaming* data. If they can continue to read data in the same track continuously, they can transfer data at the full transfer rate (at least 150K per second[17]). The .AVI file format lets the CD-ROM do just that.

Even though the average hard disk is faster than any CD-ROM drive, interleaving of audio and video data still helps out—even those short seek times are too much when you want to read data continuously.

Reducing the Hardware Strain

There is more to the .AVI file format than just interleaving. Interleaving doesn't change the amount of data; it only arranges it for efficient access. Compression

---

[15]A fast IDE hard disk should deliver 1M–1.5M of data per second, and some SCSI drives can deliver 5M–10M per second.

[16]A fast hard disk has an average seek time of 10–12 seconds, and even a slow hard disk can find data in an average of 25 ms. A CD-ROM is great if it has an average seek time of 250 ms or less. Big difference!

[17]So-called "double spin" CD-ROM drives are becoming much, much more common these days. This doubles the transfer rate and will change the use of video on CDs dramatically.

changes the actual amount of data that has to move on and off the disk. A standard CD-ROM's data rate of 150 k/sec translates into about 9M per minute. That is an achievable data rate, provided you are willing to make some compromises. Full-screen video would be 1.5 gigabytes per minute, and no form of compression is going to squeeze that down to 9M per minute. However, if you reduce the size of the video image to quarter-screen (160×120) or half-screen (320×240),[18] compression can deliver a workable solution for CD playback.

Here's what I had to say about this situation in the first edition of *Multimedia Madness:* "... you often find [that] you must play or record an .AVI file using less than a full screen. In fact, half-screen (320×240) is challenging on all but the fastest machine, which means you usually see video at only quarter-screen (160×120)." The good news: this has changed. Today, with the newest compression technology, 320×240 images can easily play from a CD-ROM. If you played the file at the beginning of this chapter, that was a 320×240 image, and it was played from a CD-ROM.

For more information on compression and what you can and cannot do with it, see the section "Video Codecs" at the end of this chapter.

But wait—there's still more you can do, and often have to do, to keep the data rate low enough. You can keep the number of colors you use to a minimum. In practical terms, 8-bit color (256 colors) works fairly well. That's enough color for a pleasing image but not so much that you clog up the data rate. However, you should have to go to 8-bit color rarely. Codec, like Indeo 3.0 and Cinepak which use 24-bit color, now dither quite well for 256-color systems. Even though they use 24-bit color, the compression is so efficient that they may be your best choice even when you plan to play the video only on 8-bit systems. See Tables 11.1 and 11.2 near the end of this chapter for comparisons of the effectiveness of various video codecs.

I need to mention one final compromise: frame rate. (I told you the compromises make or break digital video.) Capturing, or even playing back, 30 frames per second (the standard rate for NTSC video) is not easy on some hardware. Some capture cards use tricks to mimic 30 frames per second, but most are limited to 15 frames per second. For example, the Video Spigot captures 30 *fields* per second at 160×120—that is, every other scan line. Because the image isn't full size,

---

[18]Even though these terms are in common use, they are mistaken. A video window 160 pixels by 120 pixels is actually only 1/16 the screen area, whereas a 320×240 image is 1/4 the screen area. This is all for VGA, of course (640×480). Playing a 160×120 video window on a 1280×1024 monitor makes it pretty darn small.

MULTIMEDIA
M A D N E S S

you probably won't even notice. The Captivator from VideoLogic is another board that captures 30 frames per second without any hardware assistance. Many other cards, however, will not capture 160×120 at 30 frames per second.

If you are seriously into capturing, one of your best bets is the Intel Smart Video Recorder. It's affordable as video capture cards go, and it uses the Intel i750 chip to compress video in real time. You can capture 320×240 at 15 frames per second.

Real-Time Video for All of Us

Video capture is now within the financial reach of ordinary users (such as you and me). How does that translate into dollars? You need the following elements:

➤ Video for Windows from Microsoft. It has a retail price of $199, but almost every video capture card comes with a copy of Video for Windows. Cost: none.

➤ A video capture board ranging from non-compressing[19] products such as the Smart Video Recorder, Video Spigot, Captivator, and Super VideoWindows to the Bravado in the mid-range and Targa boards at the high-end. My recommendation: the Intel Smart Video Recorder.[20] Cost: about $300–$1,500 at street prices.

➤ A video source. Any camcorder, VCR, or laser disc player that outputs a composite (RCA-pin connector) or S-Video (such as Hi8) signal qualifies. You even can record from a TV monitor if you desire.[21] Cost: $300–$2,000.

➤ A sound card that has microphone or line inputs for the audio portion of the signal. Most video boards have an audio pass-through; this is not the same as a sound card! Cost: about $100–$500 depending on the audio quality you desire.

---

[19]Actually, several of these boards use clever techniques to simplify or reduce the data stream, but, technically speaking, these are not the same as codecs. Both the Video Spigot and the Captivator use such technology to advantage.

[20]One exception: if you plan to do a lot of still video capture, the Captivator from VideoLogic is probably your best choice—it does superb video stills.

[21]For that matter, you can get a video card that contains a TV tuner right on board. The Watch It! from New Media Graphics comes to mind as an example.

You can take this setup to the limit: expensive speakers, a big monitor, video and audio mixers, a professional video camera, and so on. Depending on the equipment you already have, you can turn your computer into a video studio for as little as $300 or as much as $5,000 and more.

Video for Windows Capture

Capturing is done with VidCap, a basic but complete program from Microsoft. Appropriately enough, it uses an icon representing a camcorder (Figure 11.5). When you install the AVI system, you also install a Media Control Interface (MCI) driver that all software uses to connect the video games.

Figure 11.5. *The VidCap icon.*

Video capture is straightforward. I positioned a video camera[22] and pointed it out the window, connected the camera video output to the video capture card,[23] connected the audio output to my audio card,[24] and started up VidCap. The result was a video image displayed in the VidCap window as shown in Figure 11.6. That's my front yard with the van at lower right and a portion of the house at upper left—all the rest is trees, bushes, and grass.

Notice which icon (third from the right) in the toolbar is depressed; this icon controls the display of the captured image. In this example, I am capturing using Indeo 3.0 with the Smart Video Recorder, so the button is not active. If you capture with an 8-bit codec, such as Microsoft Video 1, this button will be active. By default, 8-bit capture uses an all-gray palette so that when you start a session, the captured image is gray. If you use an 8-bit codec, you must use the Capture palette button to capture a palette while a video is playing. If you use a 24-bit codec, you can ignore palettes.[25]

---

[22]I got a great deal on a Canon A-1, which uses Hi8 (that's a hi-resolution video format) tape and has a great set of features.

[23]In this case, the Intel Smart Video Recorder—an excellent choice for most video capture.

[24]I use a Turtle Beach MultiSound—far and away the best performer in the sound card market today.

[25]This, in and of itself, is a very good reason to avoid an 8-bit codec if at all possible—palettes are a pain in the neck, as you are about to see.

Figure 11.6. *A sample video capture.*

The Color Palette

This section applies only if you are using an 8-bit codec. If you are using a 24-bit codec like Indeo 3.0 or Cinepak, skip to the next section, "Audio Format."

The first task in any 8-bit capture session is to analyze the incoming frames and create a custom palette. If you don't, the default gray palette is used. There is another reason to create a custom palette: because you are limited to 256 colors, you want them to be the colors that render the scene in the most realistic fashion. When VidCap creates a custom palette, it reduces the full set of colors in the image to those that are used most often and combines colors that are nearly the same into one color in the final palette.[26] The Capture Palette icon on the toolbar brings up the Capture Palette dialog box (Figure 11.7).

Notice that the default palette contains only 236 colors; VidCap reserves 20 of the 256 colors for its own use. To capture a palette, click the Start button while the video is playing, allow the program to capture palettes for a number of frames,

[26]Alas, if you try to play a video while a bitmap with a different 256-color palette is visible, the appearance of either the bitmap or the video must suffer. You can have only one palette active at one time. Video for Windows comes with a tool, PalEdit, that enables you to attach the same palette to several bitmaps and/or videos. You should do this if you will be using an 8-bit codec. Again, this is why it often is better to use one of the 24-bit codecs. However, certain images won't work well when dithered to 8-bit color; you're stuck using palettes in such a case.

and then close the dialog box. VidCap looks for the most common colors and creates a palette that, although not perfect for every frame, gives the best results when the frames are played in sequence.

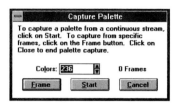

Figure 11.7. *The Capture Palette dialog box.*

The entire clip should use the same palette; palette changes are not recommended during playback. A palette change has far too much overhead, and it affects everything on-screen. Sometimes, the palette change isn't handled correctly by some software, and the video can look terrible in such situations.

Audio Format

Next, you must choose the format for the audio portion of the recording. In most cases, smaller audio files make for smoother capturing. I used the settings in Figure 11.8 for most of the .AVI files I included on the CD-ROM.

Figure 11.8. *Sample audio settings.*

An 8-bit, mono, 22-KHz audio signal doesn't put excessive demands on the hardware. I prefer 16-bit because it sounds better than 8-bit, but you can't use 16-bit for general distribution—there are too few 16-bit cards and too many 8-bit cards. If you have a 16-bit card and you create .AVI files for your personal use, don't settle for less than 16 bits unless you have no choice (in other words, if the data rate is too high for your hardware to handle).

Video Format

Next comes the video format. You have a different set of choices, as shown in Figure 11.9, depending on which video capture card you have installed. In this example, with the Smart Video Recorder installed, two possible compression modes are available: Indeo 3.0 (shown) or Indeo YVU9 Raw (that is, uncompressed). Different capture sizes are available depending on what capture card you use. Typical sizes include 160×120, 240×180, 320×240, and 640×480. Most cards that support 640×480 only support it for still-image capture or one-frame-at-a-time capture. Most hardware cannot play 640×480 video.

Figure 11.9. *A sample Video Format dialog box.*

If you choose a video compression method for capture, additional settings may be available by clicking the Details button. Figure 11.10 shows the additional settings for the Smart Video Recorder. In this example, you can elect to have the codec set an optimal quality level based on a desired data rate, or you can specify the exact quality level you wish to use.

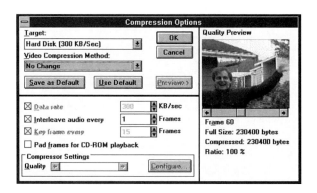

Figure 11.10. *Additional video format settings.*

Depending on the capture hardware you have installed, you may find a be-wildering array of capture choices. There are three basic kinds of video capture modes, and not all of them are supported by every card.[27]

Mode 1—RGB capture. This is the slowest method. It uses the color methods of the typical video display card to store images: RGB (red, green, blue).

Mode 2—YUV capture. This is a faster method. It uses the color methods of the television side of video: YUV (two channels of chrominance (color) and one of luminance (brightness)).

Mode 3a—Compressed capture, software. Some cards offer special enhanced YUV modes that compress the data somewhat. You must still use a compression codec like Indeo or Cinepak after capture. Such partial compression usually enables you to capture higher frame rates or larger image sizes. The Video Spigot and VideoLogic Captivator are two examples.

Mode 3b—Compressed capture, hardware. Some cards include the entire codec on a hardware chip, such as the i750 on the Intel Smart Video Recorder. These cards offer full real-time compression. The final file can often be played with software-only versions of the codec.

A Technical Note

Almost all computer video uses the RGB (red, green, blue) method for storing and displaying color information. However, this is not an efficient model for compression purposes. The reasons are complex—they deal with the mathematics of color representation—so I won't go into them here.

The bottom line is that compression methods used with video images must first convert the color information to a different mathematical model. Some boards work directly with another model, known as YUV.

These boards are slightly more efficient because they do not have to convert from RGB during recording.

---

[27]You may have to study the documentation that comes with your capture card to determine which modes it supports. It is not always obvious.

> Video compression uses lossy compression techniques; you see the effect of this when you view any .AVI file. One important advantage of lossy compression is that it can be done on the fly—it divides the image into small blocks, and the compression is done on a block-by-block basis. Conventional, non-lossy compression techniques usually work with the entire file at one time to achieve compression. If you look closely, you can see the results of blocking during playback; backgrounds sometimes look like they are made of square blocks. This is particularly pronounced if you try to compress too much.

Depending on your video source,[28] you might have to specify the source for VidCap (Figure 11.11).

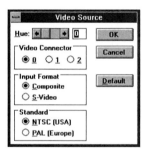

Figure 11.11. *A sample Video Source dialog box.*

The choices are basic, and they vary with different capture boards. Some enable you to connect several video sources even though only one is active at a time. Some enable you to set contrast, tint, saturation, and so on. If your capture card offers this capability, you can usually adjust these settings once and then forget about them (if you save them, of course).

---

[28]There are many variations. You can input composite (that's normal video cabling, such as from the average VCR to the average TV (not to be confused with cable TV, which uses a coaxial cable)) using RCA-pin jacks (the same as you would use on a home stereo system). You can input using S-Video (such as Hi8 or SVHS). You can input from a VCR, or from a live signal from a camcorder.

Setting Up a Video Capture

You can capture single frames, multiple frames in step fashion, or multiple frames in real time. Capturing individual frames is similar to screen-capture utilities. To capture in real-time, start with the dialog box shown in Figure 11.12.

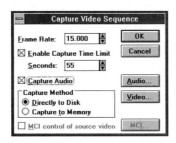

Figure 11.12. *The Capture Video Sequence dialog box.*

This dialog box is the heart of VidCap. At the top of the box, you choose a frame rate. Typically, it's about 15 frames per second. A rate less than 15 makes the sequence too jumpy, and rates over 15 might result in lost frames. Even at 15 frames per second, the image is jumpy. In particular, talking heads are hard to watch—the lip movements become too coarse to follow. In such cases, you might be better off increasing the frame rate to about 20 frames per second and reducing the size of the video format, if that compromise is acceptable.

If you click Capture Time Limit, you can limit the amount of hard disk space the capture uses. A Video for Windows capture rapidly eats hard disk space. Keep in mind you will be capturing uncompressed frames; in this case, megabytes are used quickly. Some of my captures used as many as 50M per minute!

You also can elect whether to capture the audio portion. The capture method you choose depends on available resources. Memory is faster, but there's less of it to use, so you might have to record to disk. If you have a video source that can be controlled by MCI, you can set options for it.

When you click OK, you see the dialog box in Figure 11.13.

At this point, VidCap has reserved sufficient hard disk space for the capture; it's ready to start capturing data. Start your video source and click OK. Sit back while the software does its work. During capture, you may or may not see live video in the VidCap window depending on what video capture card you have

669

installed.[29] A second click completes the capture. Figure 11.14 shows the results after a capture—the only difference is the status line, which tells you how many seconds of video you captured, how many frames that is, how many frames were dropped, the new frame rate, and the size of the captured data.

Figure 11.13. *Starting to capture a video sequence.*

Figure 11.14. *The results of the capture process.*

At this point, the capture file contains the data you captured; you do not need to save anything—it's already safe on your hard disk. With some codecs, in fact, you could mess things up by saving files an extra time. As far as capturing is concerned, you are done. You may want to edit the file, and that's covered in the next section, "Editing Video: Things to Watch For." First, a word about how to make your disk captures as efficient as possible.

---

[29]If the card is working hard to capture video—that is, you are using a high frame rate or a large image size—you may not see anything except whatever image was visible when you started capturing.

Because you are capturing to a hard disk at very high data rates, I strongly recommend that you create a default capture file on your fastest hard disk. This file must be unfragmented—that is, the file must be in one piece on your hard disk. Use a utility program such as Norton's Speed Disk to defragment your hard disk before you create the capture file.

Use VidCap to create a permanent capture file. From the File menu, select Set Capture File. This displays the dialog box shown in Figure 11.15. I use the filename CAPTURE.AVI because it is direct and to the point, but you are free to use any name you like.

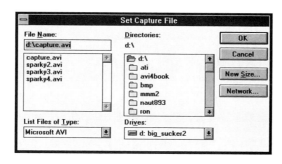

Figure 11.15. *Naming your video capture file.*

After you name your capture file, click the New Size button. This displays the dialog box shown in Figure 11.16. It tells you how much space is available, and you can then set the file size. As you can see, I keep a 100M capture file—that's a bit larger than you are likely to need. The actual file size you choose depends on many factors: the capture card you are using, the image size you plan to use, available hard disk space, the frame rate you desire, compression involved (if any), and so on. In general, video capture requires 5M–25M per minute of video. On average, reserve about 10M per minute, and you'll do OK. You'll find that most video clips are actually quite short, on the order of 10–20 seconds, so a 10M file will work for normal use. I have found myself needing to capture 15 minutes of video and more for CD-ROMs that come with my books, and if you will be distributing large files on CD-ROM, reserve enough space for your largest captures.

Figure 11.16. Setting the size of the capture file.

Other programs are available for video capture if VidCap isn't your cup of tea. For example, Figure 11.17 shows the Audio Visual Recorder, a capture program from In:Sync which features a VCR-like interface. It offers a completely different capture interface than VidCap.

Figure 11.17. The In:Sync Audio Visual Recorder.

Editing Video: Things to Watch for

Once you have captured the video and audio data, you can edit it in VidEdit or another video editor, such as Premiere or Media Merge. There are two classes of editing:

➤ Editing that preserves the file's internal structure

➤ Editing that does not

You should be very clear about which kind of editing you want to perform on each video clip you capture, for reasons that will become clear shortly.

When you captured the video, each frame was saved to disk as a lump of data in the .AVI file. Editing that removes entire frames doesn't mess with this scheme. Editing that removes parts of frames, or adds frames, does mess with this scheme.

Here are two simple rules about editing:

➤ Removing frames with the Edit|Cut or Edit|Delete menu selections in VidEdit preserves a file's internal structure.

➤ Almost anything else will not. This includes cropping, pasting, resizing, and changing the frame rate.

Here comes the clincher, the whole reason for this seemingly obscure and useless discussion:

> **If you change the file's structure, the file must be compressed all over again.**

There are three problems with recompression:

➤ It takes time away from more interesting activities.

➤ It can cause technical problems with playback for some codecs (that is, performance can suffer very, very badly).

➤ It results in a second round of lossy compression, which can result in bad-looking images.

Now that I have you all concerned about this, here's how to handle the situation:

*If you **will** be doing any editing that changes the file's internal structure,* capture without using any compression. That is, capture the video data in a raw, uncompressed format. Your capture card has its own name for raw format; consult the documentation. The occurrence of the word "raw" is a good sign, of course. In most cases, if no hardware compression is involved, you can *only* capture raw, uncompressed video. The Video Blaster, Video Spigot, Captivator, Bravado, Super VideoWindows and other similar boards all capture some version of raw data *only.* You should watch out for these boards: the Intel Smart Video Recorder, Media Space, and Super Motion Compression are all examples of boards that compress during capture. These boards require that you make a conscious choice about how to capture based on what you will do with the file.

*If you **will not** be doing any editing that changes the file's internal structure,* capture with any form of compression that meets your needs. The Intel Smart Video Recorder makes extra-special good sense if this describes your situation.

In general, you should only compress your video one time—it's lossy compression you will be applying, and the less you lose the better your video will look. The only kind of editing you can do to a file already compressed is to remove frames you don't want. Anything else will probably force you to recompress.

VidEdit

Let's take a look at VidEdit, the Video for Windows application you use to edit .AVI files. For this example, I used one of the .AVI files I recorded for the *Multimedia Madness* CD-ROM. The opening screen of VidEdit, with the file CAT16MON.AVI open, is shown in Figure 11.18. I labeled the most important buttons for easy reference. You can load any .AVI file into VidEdit, or you can edit the file you just captured by clicking on the VidEdit icon in the VidCap toolbar.

Figure 11.18. *The opening screen of VidEdit.*

The editor has more on-screen buttons and options than VidCap has. Even so, it is not so much a video editor as it is a video *file* editor. Notice the features of VidEdit. Starting from the top, you find a toolbar, the image area, and an area at the bottom that contains the bulk of the controls.

The long horizontal bar has a moving position indicator that shows the current frame relative to the entire file. The two small buttons to the right of this bar move you forward and backward one frame at a time. Below these buttons are two more buttons, labeled Mark In and Mark Out. Clicking the former marks the beginning of a selection area; clicking the latter marks the end of a selection area. You can cut, copy, and paste selections; a selection can be audio, video, or both.

The control panel, located below the Mark buttons, contains VCR-like buttons that you use to move around in the file. The following list identifies the buttons in the order they appear on-screen, from left to right:

Play	Plays the current sequence from the current position.
Stop	Halts playback.
Previous mark	If there is a mark in or mark out, this moves to the frame at the previous mark. Otherwise, it moves to the first frame.
Page left	Moves backward 10 percent of the total sequence.
Page right	Moves forward 10 percent of the total sequence.
Next mark	If there is a mark in or mark out, this moves to the frame at the next mark. Otherwise, it moves to the last frame.

To the right of the control buttons are three buttons you use to select what you are editing. From left to right, they are

➤ Combined audio and video

➤ Video

➤ Audio

These buttons are handy—you can use them to cut a portion of the audio without affecting the video, and vice versa.

At the bottom of the VidEdit window is a status bar that contains time information as well as other information about the current frame. The VidEdit toolbar, just under the menu bar, contains buttons for some of the most commonly used functions, such as File Open, File Save, Cut, Copy, Paste, and Undo. The other three buttons (Figure 11.19) control specific Video for Windows functions.

Figure 11.19. *The AVI function controls.*

Editing the Video File

Editing the video sequence is straightforward. It isn't all that different from editing, say, a word processing file. You can select any portion to cut or delete, you can paste from another file, and so on.

Remember, VidEdit is primarily a file editor, not a true video editor. Video editing involves fades, wipes, masks, and so on. There are currently two serious video editors: Premiere and Media Merge. Both are Author's Choices, and both are described later in this chapter.

Once you have the file where and how you want it, the key to effectively using AVI lies in balancing the various tradeoffs you have to make for later playback on the target machine. VidEdit comes preconfigured for a variety of targets ranging from fast hard disks to CD-ROM drives. A target is defined as a group of settings, including degree of compression, desired playback rate, and exact format for interleaving. If the predefined targets don't meet your needs, you can define your own settings. Table 11.3, near the end of this chapter, provides my suggestions for balancing the tradeoffs for the Indeo and Cinepak codecs.

Although you have to consider tradeoffs, such as frame rate, when you record, most of the tradeoffs are actually made in VidEdit. For example, before you save a file, you have to choose how you want to compress the file. The decisions you make are permanent ones—the data you lose when you save a file is lost permanently because of lossy compression.

You can save full frames if you so desire. This adds a step to the process, and the file sizes can be quite large. If you have the hard disk space, saving full frames is the safest way to go—if you goof up on compression, you can go back to the original and try again. Of course, if you have a 24M original, it quickly takes up your hard disk space.

The Video Menu

Most of the features of VidEdit are located on the Video menu. As I mentioned earlier, you won't find anything too exciting, but most of the features are essential for getting control of your video files.

There are 10 choices available:

Compression Options—Select a codec, and choose your target data playback medium.

Convert Frame Rate—Change the file's frame rate to a lower or higher one.

Synchronize—Adjust audio playback to resynchronize with the video, should they get out of whack.

Audio Format—Change audio characteristics, such as sample rate or bit depth.

Video Format—Change number of colors used.

Create Palette—Create a single 8-bit palette for the video or a portion of the video.

Crop—Select a portion of the video for viewing.

Resize—Change the size of the video image.

Statistics—Show important information about the file.

Load File into Memory—Load the entire video file into memory for quicker access (assuming there is room).

Video Compression Options

To choose among the compression options, select Compression Options from the Video menu, and the dialog box in Figure 11.20 opens.

Figure 11.20. Selecting compression options.

The Compression Options dialog box is an important tool. You will spend a lot of time here as you learn the finer points of video compression. The list of targets includes various hard disk and CD-ROM transfer rates. This indicates your maximum data rate to VidEdit. If you try to save a file with a set of options that are not possible for the chosen data rate, a message box alerts you and you can try new settings.

This section contains detailed information about selecting appropriate compression settings. If you want just a simple guide to the best settings for various video situations, consult Table 11.3 near the end of this chapter.

In addition to the transfer rate, you also have to choose a compression method. You can save full frames, or you can choose from several forms of compression.

If you compressed the video while you captured it and want to avoid recompression after deleting some frames, make sure you choose the "No Change" compression method (this is shown in Figure 11.21). If you cannot find a "No Change" method, then you did some editing that changed the file's internal structure, and you must recompress it.

It's hard to choose a compression method if you can't predict the consequences of your choice; Microsoft provides the Details>> button, which expands the dialog box (see Figure 11.21).

The choices in the lower-left portion of the expanded dialog box enable you to specify custom options, including transfer rate. You can also select the number of video frames that intervene between audio portions. I haven't yet described some of the other options, but they are worth a digression.

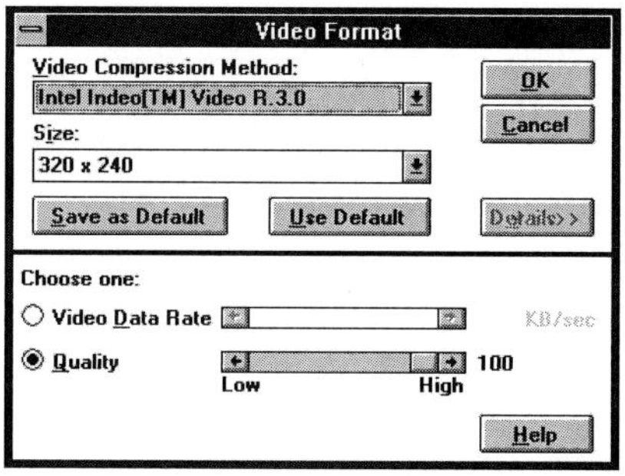

Figure 11.21. *The expanded Compression Options dialog box.*

A key frame is important when you consider compression options. Often a video sequence does not change much from frame to frame. For example, a talking head with a solid-color wall behind it changes only a little from one frame to the next. In these cases, it is economical to store just the data that changes from one frame to the next rather than the full frames. There is a limit to how many consecutive frames you can do this with, however. As you move further from the last key frame, there is a risk of accumulating too many small changes and losing the advantage gained. You can specify how often a key frame should be used. When a key frame is reached, the entire frame is saved, and the program begins the process of accumulating changes between frames all over again. You should generally have key frames no more than 15 frames apart. In some cases, you may want to make every frame a key frame to improve the appearance of the video clip.

When the video sequence is intended for play from a CD-ROM, you can specify that the frames be padded. Padding adds extra bytes to each frame to make every frame exactly the same size. This enables the CD-ROM to maintain a steady reading rate. Without padding, the CD-ROM must read a different number of bytes for each frame. The disk continues spinning, and the CD cannot read the next frame without completing at least one extra revolution. Under these conditions, the CD-ROM drive cannot use its streaming capabilities—it has to seek to find each frame, slowing things down and making playback jittery.

The right portion of the dialog box contains a *quality preview*—a sample of the current frame compressed using the Quality setting at the bottom of the dialog box. In Figure 11.21, the setting is 75, which leads to a compression ratio of 43 percent. Changing the Quality setting to 35 shows a significant loss of quality (see Figure 11.22).

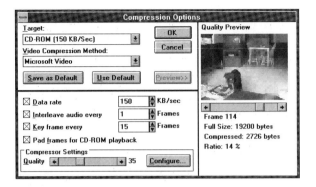

Figure 11.22. A frame with a Quality setting of 35.

Setting the best compression options is almost an art. There are some general principles, however, that you can use as a guide:

➤ If you intend to save sequences for playback on a CD-ROM, use Indeo for small image sizes and Cinepak for larger image sizes.

➤ Speed is critical. Use the fastest machine possible and make sure it has a fast hard disk too. Cinepak takes the longest to compress.

➤ Religiously defragment your hard disk.

➤ Use more frames between key frames when the source doesn't change radically every few frames. Fewer changes result in space savings on the disk.

➤ If you control the making of the original video, use plain backgrounds to decrease the changes from frame to frame.

➤ Reduce the audio fidelity if you have trouble saving at a given data rate. Stereo and high sample rates can put you over the limit.

➤ Experiment with different Quality settings (see Tables 11.1 and 11.2 near the end of this chapter). Because you can see the results before you save, try several settings to see how the image looks. Make sure you choose a representative image. Unfortunately, the image you have to use for evaluating quality cannot be resized; it can be deceptive until you get the hang of it.

Other VidEdit Features

Let's take a cook's tour of the other features of the Video menu. Figure 11.23 shows the dialog box for the Convert Frame Rate menu selection.

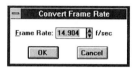

Figure 11.23. Converting a frame rate.

When you convert the frame rate using this dialog box, VidEdit adds or deletes frames to meet the new frame rate. For example, if you have a file that has a frame rate of 30 frames per second (30 fps), and convert the frame rate to 15 fps, VidEdit removes every other frame from the video.

Use this selection with discretion—the lost frames are gone forever.[30]

If you want to change the frame rate for special effects like slow motion or for speeding up playback, use the Synchronize menu selection instead (Figure 11.24). It converts the frame rate without changing the number of frames. For example, if you have a video with 30 frames per second, you can change the frame rate to 15 fps and it will play in slow motion. The main purpose of this dialog box, however, is to resynchronize the audio and video portions of the file should they happen to get misaligned. This doesn't happen often. Sometimes, after editing a file, it may seem that the video and audio are out of sync. Save the file, and see if the problem goes away. If it does, the problem simply resulted from VidEdit trying to keep track of the edited pieces. If it does not, you can fix it with the Synchronize dialog box.

To change audio format, use the Audio Format menu selection. This displays the dialog box where you can change the number of channels, the sample size, and the sample frequency.

---

[30]Except, of course, for the Edit|Undo option.

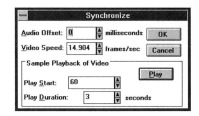

Figure 11.24. The Synchronize dialog box.

If you have trouble reaching a given data rate (especially 150 k/sec for CD-ROM), convert to an audio format that uses less disk space.

Changing the video format is limited to the color depth (Figure 11.25). If you are using Indeo or Cinepak for compression, don't bother changing the video format—these are 24-bit codecs. You only need to change the video format if you are working with the Microsoft Video 1 codec.

Figure 11.25. Changing the video format.

The Create Palette dialog (Figure 11.26) only applies to 8-bit video formats. You can create a palette from a single frame, all frames, or the selected frames. Once you create the palette, you are given the option to paste it into the current video.

Never use more than 236 colors in a palette; there are a total of 256 available, but 20 are reserved for Windows. If you will be using 8-bit videos and will be displaying more than one on the screen at a time, you should try to use the same palette for all videos and bitmaps shown at the same time. Use the PalEdit utility shipped with many Microsoft multimedia products to work with palettes.

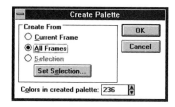

Figure 11.26. Creating a palette.

Cropping your video is very easy as shown in Figure 11.27. You only need to click and drag to mark the boundaries of the crop. You can drag the boundaries around or change them by dragging the handles at the corners. You can also type in coordinates for the crop operation. After a crop, the boundaries will be used for the video—you can't use different crop settings for different frames. Crop settings apply to the entire video file.

Figure 11.27. Cropping a video.

Resizing is easy, as shown in Figure 11.28. Just enter the new size, and VidEdit resizes every frame. If you don't want to distort the video, you need to take a moment to calculate the new width and height.

Figure 11.28. *Resizing a video.*

Figure 11.29 shows the File Statistics dialog box. It contains some important information about the video file.[31]

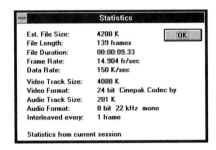

Figure 11.29. *The File Statistics dialog box.*

VidEdit Import and Export

VidEdit's File menu has two very powerful selections: Insert and Extract. These are more or less import and export capabilities. They enable you to do some interesting things with video files. You can easily save individual frames or series of frames as bitmaps, for example, or you can import an animation file for use in your video file.[32]

You can also work with the audio portion of the file. You can export just the waveform audio data and edit it with a program designed for that purpose, and then insert it back into the sequence.

---

[31]If you need additional information about video files, check out the VidTest application on the Nautilus CD.

[32]You can also export your video file as a series of bitmaps and then import them into Autodesk Animator Pro to add special effects of all kinds, from flying text to talking birds (see JBIRD.AVI on the Nautilus CD).

Video Hardware: Let the Buyer Beware

Here's a simple rule to follow when selecting hardware for video capture:

Ron's Rule The less you pay in money, the more you pay in lost time and decreased convenience.

For example, the least expensive video-capture board is the Video Blaster. I tried to install it in two computers, never getting it to run correctly—even with the help of the technical support staff at Creative Labs. In all fairness, these boards work well in some systems. For example, non-local bus machines and machines that aren't using the very latest video cards have had better success with the Video Blaster. Remember: If you are going to try less expensive equipment, make sure you can get your money back if it doesn't work properly. The amazing thing about the Video Blaster is that it does both video capture and video overlay in a very inexpensive board.

See Chapter 6 for detailed information about a number of video boards for both capture and overlay.

Video Capture and Video Overlay

There are two different ways to acquire video and use it on your computer. Video capture refers to the ability to convert a video signal into information on your hard disk. Video overlay refers to displaying a live video signal on your screen. These are very, very different activities. Some video cards do one or the other, and some do both.

The Video Spigot, Captivator, and Smart Video Recorder are all video capture cards. They work with Video for Windows to capture video to your hard disk. You can use them to view incoming video, but they may look pretty jittery because they are designed for capture, not display.

The Bravado, Super VideoWindows, and Video Blaster are all combination boards—they capture and do overlay.

All other boards that support overlay use a trick to put live video on a VGA screen. To explain, I first need to talk about video memory and how it is different from what shows up on your monitor.

What shows up on your monitor goes through a lot of different steps inside the computer. First, the software has to determine what it wants to put on the monitor—text, pictures, and so on. In Windows, this is then converted into graphical information—so many different windows, boxes, text, pictures, buttons, menus, and so on. Depending on the graphics display card you have, some of this graphical information may also get processed by an accelerator on your video card. Finally, a map of the video image is placed in video memory on your video card. This map is used to generate the physical electrical signals that your monitor understands.

To do video overlay, an additional layer is added to the process. The signals generated by your video card are intercepted before they go to the monitor. The software merely puts an empty window on the screen—there's nothing in that window, as you can see if you use a screen capture program to capture the screen. However, a very specific color is used for the window, and the coordinates of the window are also kept track of. (See Figure 11.30 for an example.)

The video overlay board looks for that window using some very clever techniques. It then converts the scan rate of the incoming video signal to match the VGA signal and adds it to the VGA signal. The combined signal is then sent to the monitor, where you see the video. The important point here is that at no time does the incoming video signal become digital—it is merely overlaid on the analog VGA signal.

Uses of Video Overlay

For better or for worse, overlay is a tricky business. If the overlay card and your video display card can't agree on the signal quality, you'll get wavy lines or complete garbage. That is why video overlay cards like the Video Blaster are picky about what video cards they will work with. I tend to prefer overlay cards that have their own VGA or SuperVGA capabilities included, such as the Bravado from Truevision. The Bravado is also great because you can purchase add-on modules that enable you to compress video in real time or send video out from your PC to a video tape machine.

Overlay is useful for the following activities:

➤ Watching TV while you work.

➤ Incorporating video tape into a presentation. With most VCRs, you will have to cue and play the tape yourself, not with your computer.

➤ Using laser disk video in a presentation or training package. Some laser disk players can be controlled from Windows.

If you buy a Bravado, get a Bravado 16—you can use a Bravado 16 at 1024×768 with 256 colors, a must for any editing operations.

When explaining how overlay works, I kept referring to VGA video. Some overlay cards only work at 640×480—they can't handle the higher scan frequencies involved with SuperVGA screen sizes such as 1024×768. Check your prospective purchase carefully to find out what Windows screen sizes it supports.

I also used the Bravado board at 800×600 and 1024×768 resolutions with overlaid video. It worked well at these specifications. The capability of the Bravado to work at higher resolutions is a testament to its solid engineering and design.

If you want to include live video in business presentations, the easiest way is to use a board that supports some kind of programming. There are two basic ways to do this:

➤ With a Dynamic Link Library (DLL) supplied by the board vendor (in which case you are limited to using products that enable you to access a DLL).

➤ With a vendor-supplied MCI driver that enables you to access video using any product that supports MCI command strings. This includes such products as Visual Basic, Toolbook, and HSC InterActive. For products that don't support direct MCI access, such as MediaBlitz, you have to wait for a version that supports AVI.

The latter approach is more flexible because many, if not most, multimedia authoring packages either support MCI or will support it soon (if they want to stay competitive). It is also more difficult to work with DLLs because you have to program with C, C++, Visual Basic, or similar languages in most cases. Toolbook has a decent interface for DLLs, but keep in mind that it's a programming-oriented environment, not a presentation program.

Capturing Video Stills

Video is not the highest resolution medium, but there are many situations where video is a simple and economical method for acquiring images. For example, you can use video stills for creating catalogs and image databases, putting employee photos on printed cards, and including stills in a multimedia presentation.

The process starts with a video image overlaid in a window (Figure 11.30). To capture this image, I set the camera on a shelf next to my computer, connected it to the input on a Bravado capture board, and double-clicked the Bravado icon.

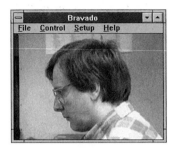

Figure 11.30. *A video image overlaid in a window.*

You have complete control over the appearance of the video overlay. As described in the previous section, the VGA image actually consists of nothing but an empty window (Figure 11.31).

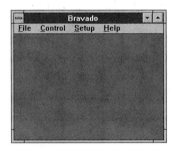

Figure 11.31. *The initial VGA image.*

You can control the appearance of the overlay with the controls pictured in Figure 11.32. You can adjust all the components of the image, including brightness, saturation, and the exact mix of colors. This is important because video sources vary in subtle ways. You can adjust the image and tune it for the best results.

You also can adjust the audio signal (Figure 11.33). There also is support for controlling an external video player (provided it's one that supports connection to your computer).

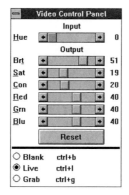

Figure 11.32. *The Video Control Panel.*

Figure 11.33. *The Audio Control Panel.*

The Bravado software gives you good control over the video setup (Figure 11.34). It goes beyond the controls available in the AVI driver.

Some of the additional functionality is directly related to overlays. For example, Variable Aspect Ratio and Optimized Window Size are useful when you position a live video-in-a-window.

Field Display is an important feature. Unlike a good computer monitor, NTSC video signals are always interlaced—half the scan lines are completed in each pass across the monitor. This means that every other line is completed on the first pass and the missing lines are filled in on the next pass. If an object is in motion, this can cause problems when you try to capture the image—the difference between the two images can be significant. If the software offers a choice between the two sets of scan lines, you can capture a clear image at a lower resolution. This choice can be useful. I have a camcorder that has a problem with matching the scan lines.

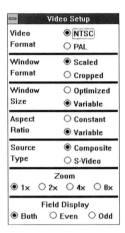

Figure 11.34. *A sample video setup.*

Because the resolution of video images is low compared even to standard VGA, you don't get great details. However, camcorders can be useful in applications that don't demand the highest quality images. Specialized equipment is available for applications that require high-quality, still-video capture. It costs thousands of dollars, however, and that puts it outside the scope of this book.

The Captivator

You do not need to have an overlay card to capture video stills. VidCap enables you to capture a single frame, and many capture cards come with applications that enable you to capture single frames. One capture card stands out when it comes to single-frame capture: the Captivator from VideoLogic.

The image quality of the Captivator is equal to that of boards costing two and three times as much money. This makes it an obvious Author's Choice. I was very impressed with the steadiness of the captures. However, unlike an overlay board such as the Bravado, the Captivator does not come with a set of MCI commands for capturing video stills. This feature, however, will be added in version 1.1 of Video for Windows. See the section "The Future of Video for Windows" at the end of this chapter for important information about MCI commands and video capture.

Figure 11.35 shows three single-frame images loaded into Adobe Photoshop. All three images are of the same frame from a video tape I made of the Badlands in South Dakota. The source is my Canon A-1, from a Hi8 tape. From left to right, these images are

> BADLAND3.PCX—Captured with the Intel Smart Video Recorder using an S-Video input.[33]
>
> BADLANDS.PCX—Captured with the Captivator using a composite input.
>
> BADLAND2.PCX—Captured with the Captivator using an S-Video input.

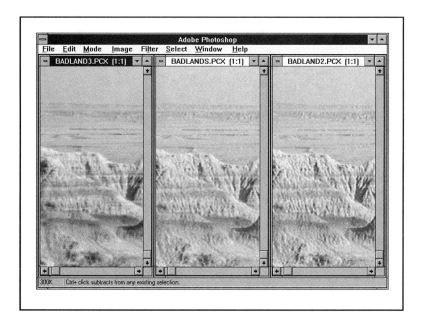

Figure 11.35. *Three still images captured with various capture cards.*

The differences between these images show up more clearly on a computer monitor than in black and white; you'll find the image in the color section of this book as well. The Smart Video Recorder (SVR) does a good job of maintaining image quality, but as you can see both of the images captured with the Captivator are better. The composite Captivator image (center) shows more crisp detail in the rocks at the center of the image, and the hills at the horizon show more detail than in the SVR image (left). The S-Video Captivator capture (right) is even better—the image has better contrast and slightly better detail.

---

[33]S-Video requires a special cable and has higher resolution than standard composite input. Most, but not all, capture and overlay cards support S-Video input.

You can improve image appearance still further if you use a live signal instead of tape for your capture. Figure 11.36 shows a pair of images of the kids' play room. The one on the top is from tape, and the one on the bottom is live.

Figure 11.36. *The top image was captured from tape, and the bottom image was captured live.*

Video and Animation

Video and animation both use frames played in sequence to simulate motion. Many users think video frames are based on a live video somewhere along the line, whereas animations are created from artwork. However, this is not necessarily true. For example, I can create an animation with my video camera. You can shoot one frame at a time with some cameras, and you can use time-lapse photography with others. You can create an animation by putting a series of images in front of the camera, recording each one as a single frame, and then playing them back at regular speed. I was tempted to take some modeling clay I have around the office (I bought it for a birthday party favor, but it was left over) and mold it, frame by frame, into something cool to create an animation, but I didn't have the time.

With Microsoft's VidEdit program, you can mix video and animation. You can easily insert an animation that is in either of the Autodesk animation formats (.FLI or .FLC); click File|Insert and enter the filename—VidEdit does the rest. Unfortunately, the program does not export animation files. There is a workaround, however. From VidEdit, you can export a video file as a series of Device-Independent bitmaps and then alter each bitmap in an animation program such as Animator.

As technology matures, the need to distinguish between video and animation probably will blur. When you can combine the two, who knows what you can create? Stay tuned!

MCI and Video

VidCap and VidEdit are great ways to create and manipulate .AVI files, but there is another way to work with AVI in your favorite authoring software, such as Toolbook or HSC InterActive.

You see, one of the neat things about AVI is that it includes the Digital Video command set for MCI.

These commands are accessible either through command strings (supported by most authoring packages) or command messages (for serious programmers). In Chapter 8, "Manning the Pump: Multimedia Programming," you learned about the command-string interface for other devices, such as wave audio and animations.

The command set is extensive, but it's worth a brief look to see how it can be used in conjunction with authoring software such as Toolbook or InterActive. For example, you can capture images, configure a device, cut or copy a sequence to the clipboard, cue a device, position windows for display of a sequence, select a compression/quality level, record a sequence, save it to a file, and much more. Here is a sequence of commands (from the sample application on the *Multimedia Madness* CD-ROM) that was developed with InterActive:

```
open e:\mania\monmulcd.AVI style popup alias AVI
query iconauthor window
window AVI handle @win
put AVI destination at 163 128 360 269
play AVI from 1 to 335 wait
play AVI from 335 wait
close AVI
```

Notice these commands will not work "as is." They contain variables specific to InterActive; you have to assign values to the variables.

The commands are shown exactly as you would enter them into content editors in InterActive. There are two commands that I should explain. The following command performs a query:

```
query iconauthor window
```

Something is missing: a place for the query response. You must specify a variable (using the content editor) to receive the reply. The command

```
window AVI handle @win
```

uses a variable to specify a window handle. If you try to perform the same action in a different authoring or programming environment, you use different methods for getting information from MCI, positioning windows, getting window handles, and so on.

These commands result in an .AVI file being displayed in a precise spot inside a specific window. Because InterActive includes full support for MCI, I could use these commands with a version of InterActive that was developed with no knowledge of AVI.

You also can use digital video in Toolbook. Like InterActive, Toolbook supports MCI. Although the format is different, it only reflects the differences between InterActive and Toolbook. InterActive is icon-based, whereas Toolbook relies on script programming. The following code plays an AVI video within the bounds of a bitmap if the bitmap (named `pix`) is clicked with the mouse:

```
to handle buttonDown
  system fileName

  if name of target is "pix"
    get tbkMCIchk("open" && fileName && "alias vidFile style popup",
"",1,1)

    — Place the video window within our rectangle.
    get tbkMCIPositionWindow("vidFile", bounds of self,"")

    — Display the video window.
    get tbkMCI("window vidFile state show","")

    —Play the file.
    get tbkMCIchk("play vidFile wait","",1)

    —Close the file
    get tbkMCI("close vidFile","")
  end if
end buttonDown
```

Of course, if you were content to let Windows determine where to put the playback window, you could use just one line of script:

```
get tbkMCI("play " && fileName && "wait","")
```

To see the full context for both these examples, check out the applications on the CD-ROM. You can do so only if you own Toolbook or InterActive, however; otherwise, you can't access the source code.

Video Recording Tips

There are two things you can do to make a dramatic improvement in the quality of your videos (if you haven't done them already):

➤ Use a tripod.

➤ Modify the lighting of your scene.

A tripod is easy to choose. You'll spend at least $50 for a video tripod, and it must have a fluid head and hold rock-steady when your camera is mounted on it. For a little more money, you can get a steadier tripod.

Lighting is a little more complicated, but not very. There is a basic lighting setup you can use that greatly improves the appearance of your videos. It involves three lights: main, fill, and key. You don't need to use all three, but if you are aware of how they work together, you'll have some idea of how to improve the lighting in every scene you shoot.

First, however, let's look at some lighting disasters.[34] Figure 11.37 shows Lighting Mistake #1: the light is coming straight at the subject from behind the camera. This provides illumination that is too even, and the result is a very flat-looking scene. This can occur when you use a light mounted on the video camera, when there is a bright window behind you, and so on.

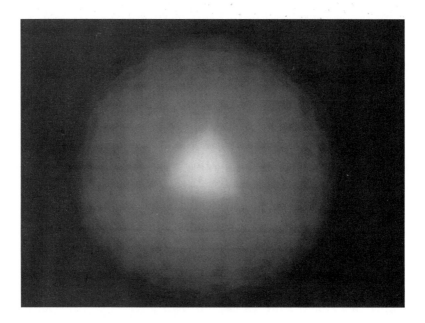

Figure 11.37. *Lighting from the front creates a flat look.*

In an office you often find lots of overhead lights. This provides a very unnatural form of light and can easily create Lighting Mistake #2: light from above. Figure 11.38 shows an extreme example—no light at all shows up on the sphere.

---

[34]I used 3D Studio, Release 2, to create these images. I created a simple sphere and then added lights at various positions to simulate the lighting conditions required. I then rendered the images as 640×480 bitmaps.

Figure 11.38. *Lighting from above.*

If you avoid these two situations, you can still find yourself facing Lighting Mistake #3: light from only one (and otherwise benign) direction. Figure 11.39 shows an example of a subject lit from only one side. This looks a little bit like a phase of the moon, but the deep shadows on the side away from the light leave you in the dark about the details on that side of the object.

Granted, you will seldom face such extremes of lighting. However, a video camera isn't as forgiving as the human eye. In technical terms, a camera increases the contrast of your scene—darks get darker, light areas get lighter. This tends to produce unnatural-looking images if you aren't careful about lighting.

I'll call the light in Figure 11.39 the *main* light and use it as a starting point. In most situations, there will be a dominant lighting source. Figure 11.40 shows a lighting setup similar to Figure 11.39. This time, a second light has been added on the right-hand side to illuminate the right side of the object. This second light is not nearly as bright as the first light; it is called a *fill* light.

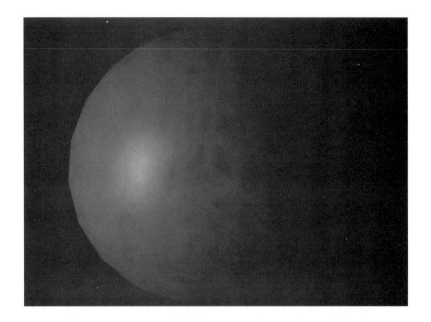

Figure 11.39. *Lighting from only one side.*

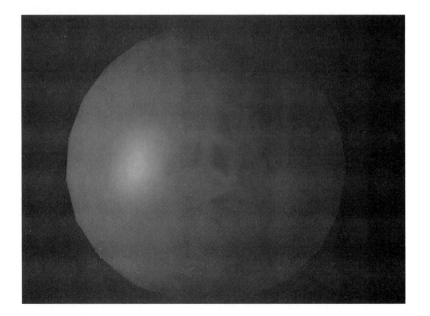

Figure 11.40. *Adding a fill light.*

As you can see, this reveals additional details about the object but still preserves a general 3D look—it doesn't flatten the appearance of the object because the fill light is dimmer than the main light. In many cases, just making sure you have adequate fill light for the main object in the scene goes a long way toward making your video clip look great. Fill light is easy to add. The obvious way is to add another light, but you can use low-cost creative approaches as well. You can move an existing light, open a curtain to let light in through a window, position the subject near a reflective wall, have someone wearing a white sweater stand in the right position to add some light, and so on.

To further define the 3D nature of objects in the scene, you can add a *key* light. This is a light above and slightly behind the subject. It adds a rim of light to the top of the subject enhancing the 3D appearance of the object or person. Figure 11.41 shows an example of using a key light.

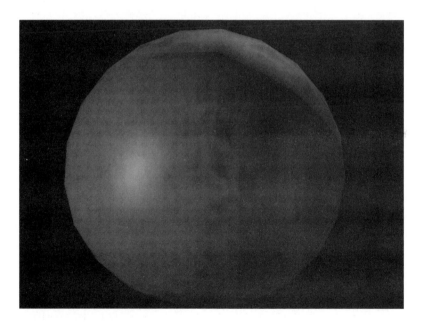

Figure 11.41. *Adding a key light.*

While I'm on the subject of lighting, don't forget to consider how the background is lit. Figure 11.42 shows a background behind the sphere. The main light spills over onto the background so that the left side is dark, and the right side is as bright as the main subject (that is, the sphere). Sometimes this works, and sometimes it doesn't—it depends on the nature of the subject. The more varied your background is, the more likely it will interfere with the clarity of the subject.

Figure 11.42. *An unevenly lit background.*

There are two easy methods you can use to force the background to be a background: darken it or lighten it. Figure 11.43 shows a dark background by way of example. Note how well the subject stands out. There are some tricks you can use to modify the background. To get a dark background, just move the subject and lights closer to the camera—none of the light will spill onto the background if it is farther away. In an outdoor shot, use the shady side of a row of trees for a background, and put the subject in sunlight. Or do the reverse—put the subject in shadow, use the manual exposure control to adjust for the subject's face, and then let the background go to white or nearly white.

The keys to good lighting are

➤ Make sure the subject stands out clearly against the background.

➤ Make sure the lighting is adequate—too little light results in grainy-looking images.

➤ Make sure the lighting doesn't change during the scene. Light changes combined with automatic exposure adjustments can ruin a shot by changing the brightness relationships in the scene.

➤ Use light to sculpt the subject: main, fill, and key.

Figure 11.43. A darker background.

You can also use light to illuminate the background, creating a four-light setup. Figure 11.44 shows a four-light setup. I have also included a video file, LIGHTS.AVI, on the Nautilus CD that "flies" you across this lighting arrangement to clarify the relationship of the various lights to the subject and background.

What happens when you apply these rules in real life? Figures 11.45 through 11.48 show some examples. Three of these images demonstrate bad lighting, whereas the fourth uses the three-light setup described previously. It's not hard to see the difference once you know what to look for. Let's start with Figure 11.45. This is a single frame of video captured with just the light in the room. Note that only the left side of the subject's face is exposed properly. The right side is dark and flat-looking. The hair more or less blends into the background.

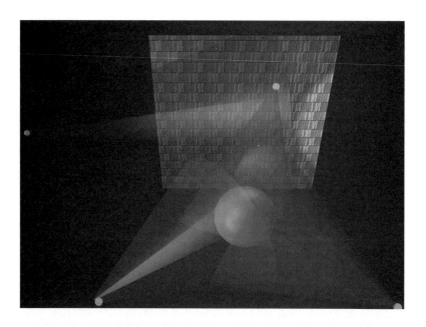

Figure 11.44. *A four-light setup.*

Figure 11.45. *The subject is lit with "normal" room light.*

In Figure 11.46, the background is too bright—the camera's automatic exposure control has compensated for the bright background leaving the figure too dark.

Figure 11.46. *The background is lit more brightly than the subject.*

Figure 11.47 shows an interesting problem. The subject's face is brightly lit, which pulls it out away from the background nicely. However, it is also evenly lit from the front, which loses detail and flattens the face.

Figure 11.48 shows how the classic three-light setup can be used to eliminate all of these problems. The background is subtly darker than the face. The hair highlight (from the key light) makes the head stand out clearly against the background and gives the head a solid, 3D appearance. A fill light adds some light to the shadowed side of the face (that's the left side). There are some nice highlights off of the facial bones to clearly delineate the shape of the face. Because there is good lighting throughout the scene, no part of the scene is too bright or too dark.

Figure 11.47. *The subject is lit evenly and brightly.*

Figure 11.48. *The three-light setup solves the problems.*

Just in case you think I used some fancy studio to do this, I'll fill you in. I did this in our living room. The key light was one of those halogen desk lights that clamps on; I attached it to the top of a door. The fill light was a second desk light turned to illuminate the subject's shadowed side. The main light was the light coming in through a large window. I hope this gets the idea into your head that you do not need expensive, high-tech solutions to tough lighting situations. It never hurts to have a bunch of lights and some stands to position them exactly where you want them (or a few reflectors and barn doors to adjust them exactly), but you can do a lot with a little imagination.

Hotshot Video Editing

VidEdit is useful software—it gives you a lot of control over the technical details of an .AVI file. However, it doesn't go much beyond cut and paste when it comes to artful revisions of your video clip. Fortunately, two recently released software packages provide a great deal of power for artful revisions; Premiere, from Adobe, and Media Merge, from ATI. In this section, you learn how to use both of these programs to edit your video clips.

Note my words. I said, "both of these programs." That's probably what you will want to do if you are at all serious about video editing. You might think that these two programs compete with one another, but mostly they don't—they complement one another. Where one is strong, the other is weak, and *vice versa*.

Premiere is strong in two areas: *filters* and *transitions*. The first Windows version is not as powerful as the current Mac version. However, Premiere has inherited the same interface as Version 2.0 of Premiere on the Mac. I found it a little complicated, but very workable.

Filters is image-speak for the ability to modify each frame of a video clip in some way. For example, Premiere has filters for blurring, sharpening, embossing, cropping, inverting, playing the video backwards, and many more.

Transitions are used to move from one video clip to the next. For example, you can have the second video push the first video out of the frame, or it can close over the first video like a door. Premiere comes with a large number of transitions, including Band Slide, Band Wipe, Barn Doors, Center Merge, Center Split, CheckerBoard, Cross Dissolve, and many more.

Media Merge also has strengths. It includes solid features for creating and moving text into and out of your video clips, enables you to overlay as many video clips as you want, and has an exceptionally easy-to-use interface. Media Merge has fewer transitions and does not have filters.

Thus, these two products are very complementary. One of them may come bundled with hardware that you purchase—if so, rush out and get the other one. It really takes both products to do real editing. However, if you can only afford one, which one you get depends on your needs. If text and Chroma key are your primary needs, Media Merge makes the most sense. If you expect to have to alter the appearance of the images in clever ways (filters), or want professional-level transitions, Premiere is your ticket. If you have lots of time to tinker with your video files or you want special effects, Premiere has more of these kinds of features. If you just want clean-looking video in a short time, Media Merge makes the most sense.

Thus, both products get my Author's Choice designation—you really do need both. You could even say that it's the combination of the two that really merits the Author's Choice.

Premiere

Adobe Premiere is based on a program which has been available on the Macintosh platform for more than a year. The Windows version doesn't have all the bells and whistles of Mac Version 2.0, but it does give you solid control over the image portion of the video clip. It also does a reasonable job of combining clips into video productions.

Figure 11.49 shows a typical Premiere window—there's a lot on screen at one time. I found this interface confusing at first, but it wasn't hard to learn my way around. There are five windows showing, each of which is labeled in Figure 11.49.

Each window has a specific purpose:

Preview window—You can get a "quick" look at how your produced video will look in this window. To see a preview, press the Enter key at any time—the current work area will be previewed. Caution: the preview can be rather crude sometimes, and it may not provide a useful clip to test your work. In such cases, you'll have to create a full .AVI file.

Construction window—This is where you arrange clips. There are seven tracks. Three are for video clips, one is for transitions, and three are for audio clips. Audio already in an .AVI file automatically appears on an audio track.

Information window—Information about the currently selected item is displayed here.

Project window—The clips (audio, video, and bitmaps) for your project are displayed here. You must load clips into the project window before you can use them. See Figure 11.50 for an example of a Project window with clips loaded.

Transitions window—A list of available transitions is displayed here. When this window is active, the icon for each transition animates to suggest the behavior of the transition. See Figure 11.51 for examples.

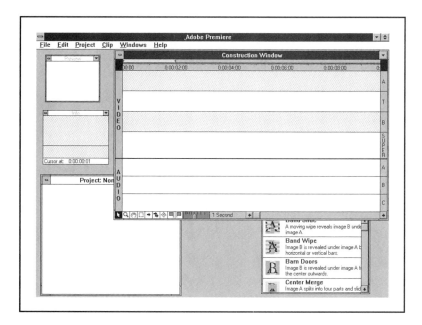

Figure 11.49. *The Premiere video editor.*

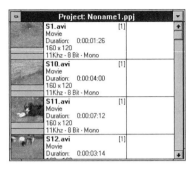

Figure 11.50. *The Project window.*

Figure 11.51. *The Transitions window.*

To create a video production, you first load clips into the project window. You can then simply grab a clip with the mouse and drag it into the Construction window. Figure 11.52 shows three video clips (and their associated audio tracks).

The video clips are shown with actual miniature frames from the video. The audio clips are in two parts. The top half, in gray, is the audio waveform.[35] The bottom half is a graphic volume control. Figure 11.53 shows an audio track whose volume level has been modified. You can create new control points merely by clicking on the volume line. If you don't want to use the audio that is already in the .AVI file, you can delete the track (Figure 11.54 shows only one of the audio tracks remaining). You can add tracks at any time by loading a .WAV file into the Project window and then dragging it to the Construction window.

---

[35]In these examples, there's not a whole lot of audio, so the waveform looks like a straight line.

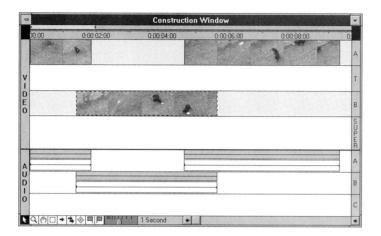

Figure 11.52. *The Construction window with clips loaded.*

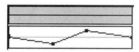

Figure 11.53. *Controlling volume on an audio track.*

When I work with Premiere, I usually drag all the video clips over to the Construction window, alternating between the "A" and "B" video tracks as shown earlier in Figure 11.52. You will normally overlap video clips and use some kind of transition during the overlap period. For example, you could dissolve one video into another or reveal the new clip by sliding the old clip out of the frame. Figure 11.54 shows two transitions added to the Construction window—these were simply dragged from the Transitions window.

If you are not sure of the contents of a clip, you can double-click it to open a Clip window (Figure 11.55). This enables you to view the contents of the clip, select a start point or end point, and so on.

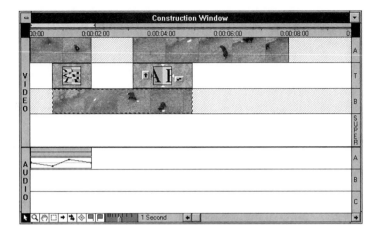

Figure 11.54. *Working in the Construction window.*

Figure 11.55. *Playing a video clip.*

Each transition involves settings that you can use to vary the characteristics of the transition. For example, Figure 11.56 shows the settings for the Band Slide transition. You can adjust anti-aliasing effects, create a colored border between the video clips, change the direction of the transition, and so forth.

By default, the letters "A" and "B" are used to refer to the incoming and outgoing video clips. You can adjust the starting point of a transition as shown in Figure 11.57. In the figure, the Band Slide will start with 30 percent of the transition already complete. You can also view a transition using actual frames from the video clips involved (see Figure 11.58).

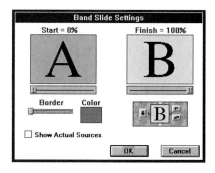

Figure 11.56. *Setting the characteristics of a transition.*

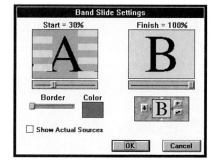

Figure 11.57. *Starting a transition at a non-zero point.*

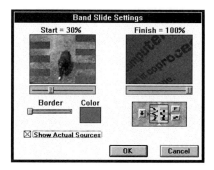

Figure 11.58. *Using actual frames to visualize the transition.*

In addition to working with the video portion of a clip, you can view the audio portion of a clip (see Figure 11.59). This is not a wave file editor; it is used primarily to select new beginning and ending points for an audio clip.

Figure 11.59. *Editing an audio clip.*

To use Premiere's filter, simply click on a video clip to select it and use the Clip|Filters menu selection to display a list of filters. Figure 11.60 shows a few of the many filters available. You can select multiple filters if you need them. For example, you could use the Brightness and Contrast filter to lighten all the frames at the same time that you use a Ripple filter for a special effect.

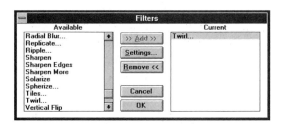

Figure 11.60. *Selecting filters.*

When you have all the clips, transitions, and filters ready, you can create an .AVI file. Premiere's Mac heritage shows in the Project|Make Movie menu selection—videos are called movies on the Mac. This opens the Project Output Options dialog box shown in Figure 11.61. This is similar to the "Video Compression" options you can set in VidEdit, but Premiere offers some interesting extra options.

The most important of these is tucked away at the bottom center of the window—Force Recompression. In some situations, Premiere simply copies already compressed frames from an existing file. This checkbox enables you to override this behavior and force Premiere to recompress all frames. In most situations, you will not check this box.

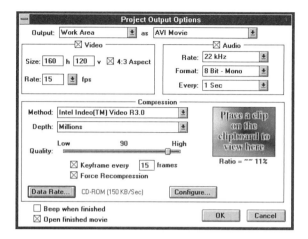

Figure 11.61. *Setting output options.*

That's it for Premier's basic features. If you were paying close attention, you may have noticed that I did not say anything about the video track labeled "Super." In Figure 11.62, I have loaded a video image into the Super track.

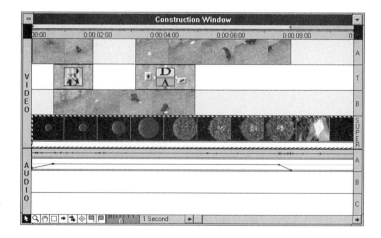

Figure 11.62. *Using the Superimpose video track.*

Any video you load into the Super track will be superimposed on the other video clips. In most cases, you will actually want the underlying videos to "show through" the superimposed track. This is called *keying,* and Premiere supports several different types of keying. Select a clip in the Super track and then use the menu selection Clip|Transparency to display the dialog box shown in Figure 11.63.

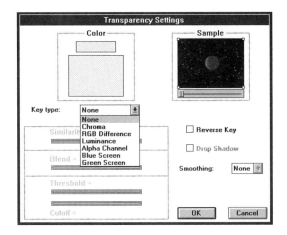

Figure 11.63. *Transparency settings.*

The most common keying method is called Chroma Key. This enables you to choose a color in the superimposed video that will disappear, allowing the underlying video clips to show through. In this example, the superimposed video has a nearly black background (well, there are a few stars behind the planet). To choose the Chroma Key color, just click in the sample image. This makes the color transparent as shown in Figure 11.64.

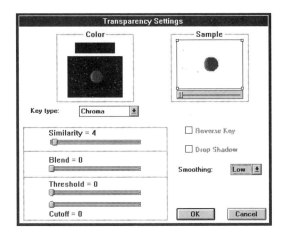

Figure 11.64. *Setting the Chroma Key color.*

It is unlikely that using a single color will give you satisfactory results. Adjust the Similarity slider so that the proper portions of the image become transparent. To avoid rough edges, try a Smoothing setting of Low. Figure 11.65 shows a series of frames from the resulting video. The planet explodes against a background of Sparky, our dog, chasing a flying disk.

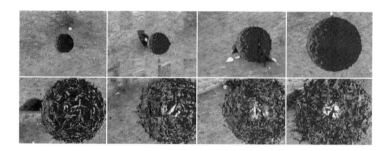

Figure 11.65. *An example of a superimposed video.*

Media Merge

I really like the front end of Media Merge. Working with video forces you to work with some completely new concepts, and I feel very comfortable with the way that ATI gives me access to video features.

Media Merge is a three-part program. I usually don't like programs that are split up, but I'm willing to make an exception in the case of Media Merge. The three programs you'll find in the program group are:

Storyboard Editor—Combines video clips and adds transitions.

Scene Editor—Adds text and enables you to layer (overlay) video clips.

Audio Editor—Edits—you guessed it—wave files.

You can use the Storyboard Editor to create basic video productions. If you require special effects, you can create them with the Scene Editor. The Audio Editor (Figure 11.66) rounds out the Media Merge package.[36]

---

[36]It's actually a great editor. It has lots of effects, and the interface is nicely done. For many situations, it's all the editor you'll need.

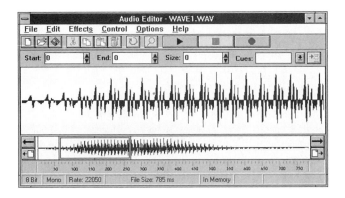

Figure 11.66. *The Media Merge Audio Editor.*

Figure 11.67 shows the opening window of the Storyboard Editor. It's very easy to use. The large boxes are used for video clips, and the small boxes are used for transitions between clips. For example, if you want to dissolve from one clip into another, just put a dissolve transition between the two clips.

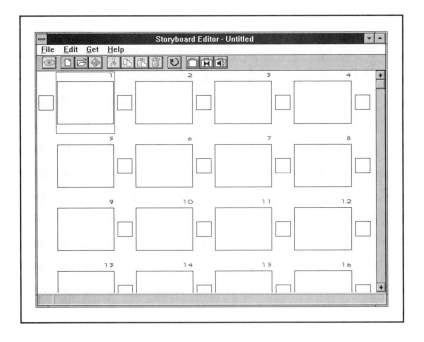

Figure 11.67. *The Media Merge Storyboard Editor.*

To load a video clip, use the Get menu. It enables you to load videos, bitmaps, animations, text, and so on. Figure 11.68 shows an .AVI file loaded into the Storyboard Editor.

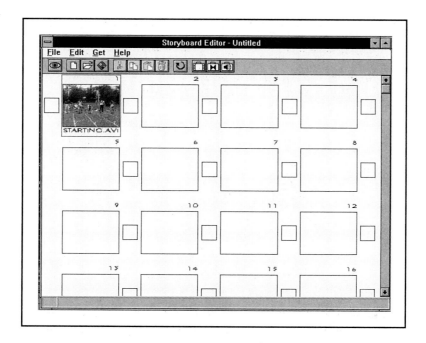

Figure 11.68. *An .AVI file loaded into the Storyboard Editor.*

To add a transition, you use the Get|Transition menu selection. This displays the Transition Browser (Figure 11.69). Just decide which transition you like, and click OK.[37]

Figure 11.70 shows a typical dialog for setting the characteristics of a transition. The starting video, bitmap, and animation—or, as in this case, a solid color—are shown at top left. The ending image is shown at top right. The box in the middle is used to control the duration of the transition. In this example, I start with two seconds of black followed by a 1.7-second transition. However, you won't actually get two seconds of black. The transition time comes out of those two

---

[37]Want some advice on which transitions to pick for common video situations? I just happen to have written a guest chapter for the Media Merge manual, so you can pick up all kinds of tips beyond what you find here.

seconds, so you actually get .3 seconds of black and 1.7 seconds of transition. The transition I have selected is the checkerboard.

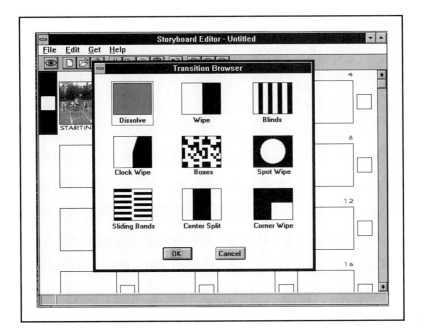

Figure 11.69. *The Transition Browser.*

You can continue to add clips and transitions to create a complete video production (see Figure 11.71). Most of the time, I load all the clips for a production into the Storyboard Editor and then select the transitions I'll use. I use File|Produce to create an .AVI file (see Figure 11.72) and check the effectiveness of the transitions.[38] After making any required changes, I create the final .AVI file at the level of compression I require.[39]

---

[38]Use a compression setting that will give you fast results—save serious compression for the final production.

[39]This is one weakness of Media Merge—you have no choice for determining the data rate of the file. You may need to use VidCap to compress the file if you are not satisfied with the default Media Merge data rate. If you do this, be sure to save the file as uncompressed in Media Merge.

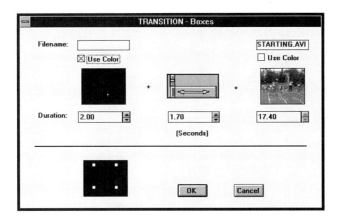

Figure 11.70. Setting transition characteristics.

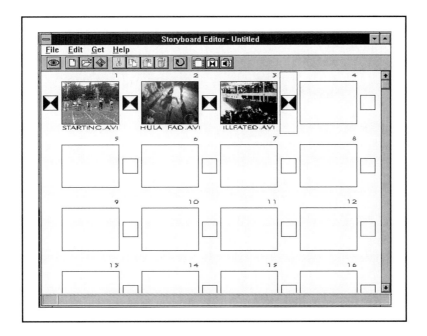

Figure 11.71. Several clips and transitions loaded.

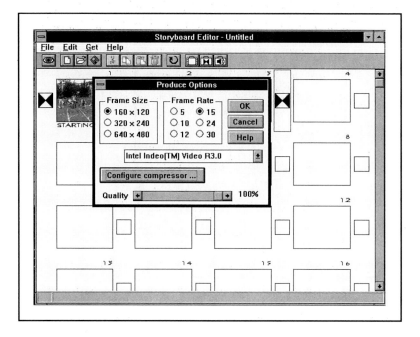

Figure 11.72. *Setting output options.*

The output files are nicely done. Figure 11.73 shows the checkerboard effect when the file is loaded into VidEdit, and Figure 11.74 shows a clock wipe in progress. The video clips are from the CD that comes with Media Merge. I found the selection of videos, bitmaps, wave files, animations, and other goodies to be more useful than most. You'll even find some animated borders—a nice touch that I haven't seen elsewhere.

The Scene Editor is a little bit more complicated to grasp, but it's extremely powerful. Figure 11.75 shows the opening window of the Scene Editor. The top line, labeled c, is the Composite track. Its role will be clear very shortly. The other lines, 1, 2, 3, and so on, are the tracks for video and audio clips. For example, you would place a video in track 1. If it has an audio file, the audio file shows up in track 1a automatically. If it doesn't, you can add audio to track 1a yourself.

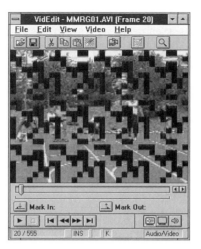

Figure 11.73. *The checkerboard transition.*

Figure 11.74. *A clock wipe.*

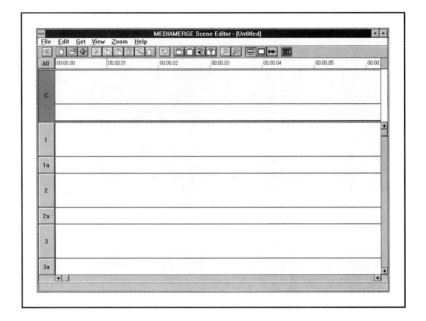

Figure 11.75. *The Scene Editor.*

Figure 11.76 shows two clips loaded into the Scene Editor. The clip in track 1 is a black-and-white video,[40] and the clip in track 2 is an animation file. However, look at the composite track—it shows the second clip overlaid on the first clip. Note also that the sound track in the Composite track is a combination of the sound for the two clips.

To edit the overlay settings, click the Edit|Set Overlay Options menu choice. This displays the dialog box shown in Figure 11.77.

The types of overlay are similar to those available for Premiere. However, there is an important difference between Premiere's overlay and Media Merge's. In Premiere, there is only one overlay track. In Media Merge, you have an endless series of overlay tracks.

In this example, the overlay is a Chroma key overlay—that is, it is based on color. To select the color that will drop out, click in the sample frame at upper right. To adjust the amount of drop out, adjust the Fall Off setting at lower right.

---

[40]Actually, it's a clip of that famous scene of a building being demolished by dynamite.

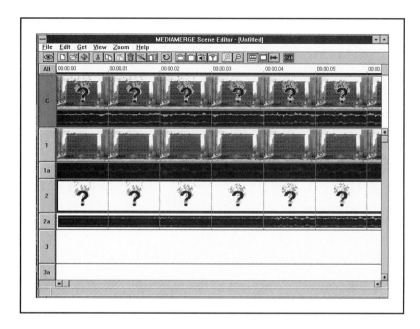

Figure 11.76. *Two clips loaded into the Scene Editor.*

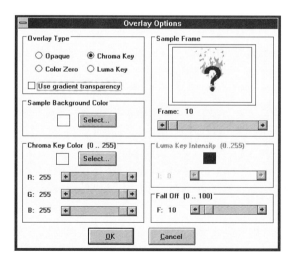

Figure 11.77. *Editing overlay characteristics.*

The Scene Editor also enables you to add text to your video production. Figure 11.78 shows the Text Editor dialog. Note that you can set an entry direction and duration, a hold duration, and an exit direction and duration. This gives you a lot of control over the behavior of text. You can do scrolling credits, dissolves, and more.

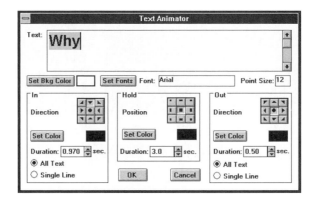

Figure 11.78. *Editing text.*

Figure 11.79 shows the effect of adding text—you can see the changes that will apply to the text both in track 3, where it was added, and in the composite track.

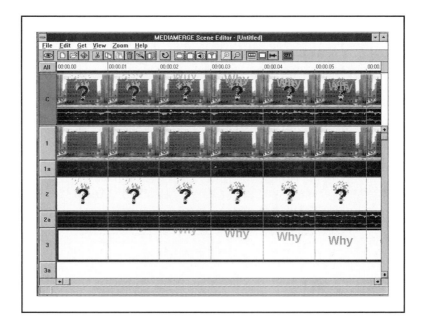

Figure 11.79. *Text added in track 3.*

Figure 11.80 shows a frame from the produced video clip.

Figure 11.80. *A frame from the final production.*

Video Codecs

The software driver that compresses and decompresses a video file is called a *codec*. As you might expect, this is a compound word that is short for compression/de-compression.[41] Each codec uses lossy compression to do its job. This means that each codec sacrifices more or less of the actual image to reduce the size of the file. As you might expect, some are better at it than others. To adjust the amount of loss, you typically set a number that represents the overall quality of the compression process. The highest quality is achieved with a setting of 100, and the greatest loss occurs with a quality setting of 0. However, most codecs are not useful with very low quality settings; a typical codec starts to look bad at a quality setting somewhere between 25 and 75.

In this section, you get a detailed look at the results you can expect from various software codecs. Since the first edition of this book, there have been some

---

[41]What *codec* stands for depends on your background. A strong case can also be made for it being a shortened form of "encoder/decoder."

major advances in video codecs. Probably the two biggest announcements were the introduction of Indeo 3.0 and the licensing of Cinepak by Microsoft.

Indeo 3.0 represents a substantial improvement over the version that shipped with Video for Windows 1.0. The original Indeo, 2.1, was actually designed for a previously developed technology, the Intel i750 chip. Special cards that used this chip, such as the Action Media II, are still in use because the i750 allows real-time compression and decompression of a video stream which provides very high-quality digital video. The original version of Indeo was written to make use of the logic on the i750 chip. When it was ported to the PC architecture, the CPU had to emulate the i750 chip—which slowed the process down quite a bit.

Indeo 3.0 is designed from the ground up to run on an x86 chip, such as the 386, 486, or Pentium. As a result, it runs much faster—there's no emulation to slow things down. This means that Indeo can now be used for playback of video files without the hardware assistance of the i750 chip.

The licensing of Cinepak is also an important advance because it makes this technology generally available. Before Microsoft licensed Cinepak, you would have had to license it yourself from SuperMac, the company that created it. That was a very expensive proposition. The license with Microsoft means that Cinepak is included in all versions of Video for Windows and can be distributed freely with your videos.

Cinepak is important because it is capable of the highest compression factors among commonly available codecs. It requires no hardware for compression or decompression, and it can achieve some remarkable data rates for video files.

To test the effectiveness of the various codecs available, I ran a series of tests based on a single video source. I used different amounts of compression with various codecs, and I include the full results here. These results include:

➤ Images that demonstrate the quality of the compression results on live, actual data

➤ Figures that show the actual compression achieved

➤ Results for various quality levels

Test Results

Before presenting the test results, I'd like to give you my overall impressions of each codec. This helps to put the results into some perspective.

Indeo 3.0—One of the most important advantages of Indeo is that it can be used for real-time compression with the Intel Smart Video Recorder. This enables you to save a lot of time when capturing a video. However, you shouldn't use real-time compression if you plan any serious editing of the video file. Overall, Indeo is an effective compression technology. It is especially useful on limited video displays (those with 8-bit video; that is, 256-color systems). At high compression rates or on slow systems, you can lose video/audio synchronization with Indeo. Indeo is a 24-bit codec and looks superb on 16-bit or 24-bit video displays.[42]

Cinepak—Cinepak, like Indeo, provides very good image quality. However, it is capable of higher compression ratios than Indeo, so when you need to compress a lot, such as for CD-ROM distribution, Cinepak is ideal. Cinepak also dithers well for 8-bit displays. The main disadvantage of Cinepak is that it has very long compression times—from 4 to 10 times slower than Indeo when you use Indeo as a software compression codec (that is, without an Intel Smart Video Recorder or when using Indeo after editing your video file). Also like Indeo, Cinepak is a 24-bit codec and provides superb color on 16- and 24-bit video displays.

Microsoft Video 1—This codec is useful, but it is not in the same league as Indeo and Cinepak. It cannot compress as much, and the image quality tends to be noticeably blocky. So why is it around? Indeo and Cinepak are both 24-bit codecs. Even if you reduce the colors to 256 with Indeo and Cinepak, the file will still be a 24-bit file. Video 1 can be used as a strict 8-bit codec, which can cut file sizes and allow playback on limited hardware. However, you should use Video 1 only when you have to.

RLE—This means run-length encoding, and it is a very primitive form of compression. Instead of storing every pixel of an image, RLE stores sequences of colors. If a color stays the same over 10 pixels, RLE stores the color and the length of its run—hence the name. This is useful for animation files you convert to .AVI files but not for regular video files. Regular video images just don't have much in the way of repeating colors.

---

[42]I highly recommend acquiring a 16- or 24-bit video display if you don't already have one—it makes video look so much better.

Table 11.1 includes additional information about working with Indeo and Cinepak. It shows the results of testing compression with various quality settings and various codecs. The results are arranged by codec, with each codec having a range of quality settings. In each case, the actual file size is shown as well as the reduction percentage for each codec at each quality setting.

Table 11.1. Video compression organized by codec.

Compression	Quality	File Size	Reduction	Image Quality
Cinepak	0	12520	95%	Poor
Cinepak	100	26852	89%	Excellent
Cinepak	45	16804	93%	Acceptable
Cinepak	75	20932	91%	Good
Indeo 3.0	0	15662	93%	Very bad
Indeo 3.0	100	30034	87%	Excellent
Indeo 3.0	45	18852	92%	Fair
Indeo 3.0	75	26600	89%	Good
Microsoft Video 1	100	85680	63%	Good
Microsoft Video 1	45	13848	94%	Horrible
Microsoft Video 1	75	28312	88%	Acceptable
RLE	0	78226	3%	Very good
RLE	100	78226	3%	Very good

Image appearance is judged as follows:

Horrible	Useless trash.
Poor	Pretty bad, but you can at least tell what it is.
Fair	Not good enough to use except in a pinch.
Acceptable	Acceptable for the average application.
Good	Better quality; decent contrast and colors.
Very Good	Image has only minor flaws from compression.
Excellent	You have to look closely to tell it was even compressed.

Video Gallery

Let's look at the images themselves to show what I mean. I hope you will excuse the fact that they are all of me.[43] A head shot shows loss of image clarity better than anything else, and it permits useful subjective judgments as well. I have included the original, uncompressed image followed by groups of images using the various codecs. For each codec, there are images using different quality settings as shown in Table 11.1.

Figure 11.81. *The uncompressed, original image.*

---

[43]No one else around the house—not even the kids—would volunteer for the project.

Figure 11.82. *Cinepak codec, quality setting of 100, 320×240.*

Figure 11.83. *Indeo 3.0 codec, quality setting of 100, 320×240.*

Figure 11.84. *Microsoft Video 1 codec, quality setting of 100, 320×240.*

Figure 11.85. *RLE codec, quality setting of 100, 320×240.*

Figure 11.86. *Cinepak codec, quality setting of 75, 320×240.*

Figure 11.87. *Indeo 3.0 codec, quality setting of 75, 320×240.*

Figure 11.88. *Microsoft Video 1 codec, quality setting of 75, 320×240.*

Modest Compression Levels

The three images on these pages all had a relatively modest level of compression. Most codecs give you a decent image with a quality setting of 75. You may just be able to make out some blockiness in the Microsoft Video 1 image (Figure 11.88); at a setting of 75, you can just begin to see the results of its algorithm for grouping of pixels. If you were to magnify the images, you would notice minor glitches in the Cinepak and Indeo images as well. For example, the lower lip in the Cinepak images (Figure 11.89) has a few bad pixels toward the left, and the Indeo image (Figure 11.90) has some patterning in the background that is barely noticeable when magnified 2X.

Figure 11.89. *Cinepak codec, quality setting of 45, 320×240.*

Figure 11.90. *Indeo 3.0 codec, quality setting of 45, 320×240.*

Figure 11.91. *Microsoft Video 1 codec, quality setting of 45, 320×240.*

High Compression Levels

The three images on these pages all had a high compression level applied. At a quality setting of 45, Microsoft Video 1 (Figure 11.91) has completely fallen apart—the blocking is so severe that the image is useless. Both the Indeo codec (Figure 11.90) and the Cinepak codec (Figure 11.89) are holding up surprisingly well. There is some additional background patterning in both images. The Indeo image has picked up a bit of contrast, and the Cinepak has picked up even a little more contrast. The Cinepak image is a bit sharper, however. Nonetheless, both images are quite usable.

Figure 11.92. *Cinepak codec, quality setting of 25, 320×240. Blockiness is beginning to be a problem, but the image is usable.*

Figure 11.93. *Indeo 3.0 codec, quality setting of 25, 320×240. Vertical streaking is quite pronounced; the image is of questionable usefulness.*

Figure 11.94. *Cinepak codec, quality setting of 0, 320×240. Blockiness is now severe; the image is useful only in extreme need.*

Figure 11.95. *Indeo 3.0 codec, quality setting of 0, 320×240. Vertical streaking is severe; the image is useless.*

Video Quality Revisited

Table 11.2 shows the same data as Table 11.1, but it's arranged by quality level to make it easy to compare the effectiveness of the various codecs in the tests. For example, look at the differences in the reduction percentage for all four codecs tested. RLE reduces the file size by only 3 percent, whereas Cinepak cuts the size by a whopping 89 percent. Microsoft Video 1 isn't quite as effective with a reduction of 63 percent, but Indeo is nearly as effective as Cinepak at 87 percent.

Table 11.2. Video compression organized by quality setting.

Quality	Compression	File Size	Reduction
100	RLE	78226	3%
100	Cinepak	26852	89%
100	Indeo 3.0	30034	87%
100	Microsoft Video 1	85680	63%
75	Cinepak	20932	91%
75	Indeo 3.0	26600	89%
75	Microsoft Video 1	28312	88%
45	Cinepak	16804	93%
45	Indeo 3.0	18852	92%
45	Microsoft Video 1	13848	94%
0	RLE	78226	3%
0	Cinepak	12520	95%
0	Indeo 3.0	15662	93%

At higher compression ratios, Cinepak consistently is a slightly better performer than Indeo. This shows what becomes obvious if you work with both codecs: if you need the greatest compression, Cinepak should be your choice.

The results of Table 11.2 are summarized in Figure 11.96.

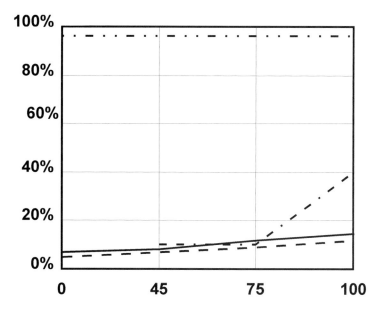

Figure 11.96. Video compression with different quality settings.

Indeo 3.0 and Cinepak

When compressing with Indeo 3.0, you set a data rate and a compression quality level. The codec will complain if the quality level is too high to achieve the desired data rate. However, you can only reduce the data rate so far. I conducted some tests to find out how far you could reduce the data rate with a 320×240 file.

The original file was 6,266,570 bytes—320×240, full frames (no compression) at 15 frames per second. When compressed with Indeo 3.0 at a quality level of 65 and a data rate of 300 k/sec, the file size was 543,500 bytes (9 percent of the original). It took 34 seconds to compress the file using Indeo software compression. (It could have been done in real time with the Intel Smart Video Recorder, however.)

When you compress with Cinepak and you set the quality level too high, the codec reduces the quality level on its own to reach the data rate you specified. Thus, to test Cinepak, I selected a range of data rates and then set the quality level to 100. This meant that Cinepak would use the highest possible quality setting at each data rate. I like this feature quite a bit; it takes the trial and error out of the process of deciding on a quality factor.

As with the Indeo tests, the original file was 6,266,570 bytes—320×240, full frames (no compression) at 15 frames per second. When compressed with Cinepak at a requested data rate of 300 k/sec, the file size was 407,414 bytes (7 percent of the original). It took just over four minutes to compress this file, or eight times longer than with Indeo software compression. Because the file had 27 video frames, that's an average of 9.3 seconds per 320×240 frame. At this compression rate, a minute of video would occupy 13.5M of disk space. However, Cinepak is capable of considerably higher compression.

When compressed with Cinepak at a target data rate of 150 k/sec, the file size was 282,622 (5 percent of the original). At this data rate, a minute of video would occupy 9.3M. The image quality was acceptable for most uses, so this is a realistic data rate for 320×240 images with Cinepak. The smallest achievable data rate was 80 k/sec, with a file size of 161,266 (2.5 percent of the original); that's 5.3M per minute. However, the image quality at such severe compression was poor.

The three sample files are included on the CD-ROM. The filenames are CINEPAK.AVI, CINEPAK2.AVI, and CINEPAK3.AVI, respectively.

Test Conclusions

From these tests, it is clear that Cinepak is the codec of choice when high levels of compression are required. Indeo excels when you are using the Smart Video Recorder, when moderate data rates are acceptable, and when you don't want to spend a lot of time compressing your file. Both codecs provide excellent image quality, although Cinepak maintains image quality down to lower data rates. Intel has announced that a "super compression" version of Indeo will be released, presumably later this year. This version of Indeo will be designed to compete directly with Cinepak's ability to achieve high compression while still maintaining acceptable image quality.

Based on my tests of Indeo 3.0 and Cinepak, I have come to the conclusion that it makes sense to use Indeo when you can and Cinepak when Indeo will not suffice. Both codecs currently deliver a similar quality of image at modest degrees of compression. Indeo is preferred for its speed of compression—especially if you are compressing in real time with the Intel Smart Video Recorder. However, if you require a high degree of compression or intend to play back on a slow machine, Cinepak is preferred for its image quality at high compression rates. Cinepak takes from four to eight times longer than Indeo to compress when you are using software compression. If you own an Intel Smart Video Recorder, the difference is much greater because the ISVR can compress with Indeo 3.0 in real time.

Of course, if you have a personal preference for one codec or the other, you can use either one at modest compression rates. This may seem a bit vague, so I constructed Table 11.3 to give you my specific recommendations for which codec to use in which situation. There are two compression methods you can use with Indeo: standard real-time compression, and CD-ROM rate compression. In the following table, "Indeo" refers to real-time capture capabilities. At press time, the Indeo CD-ROM rate compressor was not available for testing, and could not be included in this table. If it works as advertised, it will provide results similar to those for Cinepak.

Table 11.3. Ron's codec recommendations.

Image Size	Frame Rate	Data Rate	Recommended Codec
160×120	15 fps	150 k/sec	Indeo
160×120	30 fps	150 k/sec	Cinepak
160×120	30 fps	300 k/sec	Indeo
240×180	15 fps	150 k/sec	Cinepak/Indeo
240×180	24 fps	150 k/sec	Cinepak
240×180	30 fps	150 k/sec	Cinepak
240×180	15 fps	300 k/sec	Indeo
240×180	24 fps	300 k/sec	Cinepak/Indeo
240×180	30 fps	300 k/sec	Cinepak

continues

Table 11.3. continued

Image Size	Frame Rate	Data Rate	Recommended Codec
320×240	15 fps	150 k/sec	Cinepak
320×240	15 fps	300 k/sec	Cinepak/Indeo*
320×240	30 fps	300 k/sec	Cinepak**

*Some 320×240 files will not compress to 300 k/sec with Indeo 3.0; you'll need version 3.1.

**Common hardware cannot be used to capture this combination of size and frame rate in real time; you need to capture one frame at a time. Video for Windows version 1.1 adds automated step capture. See the section "The Future of Video for Windows" at the end of this chapter for details.

If you can make use of real-time compression, Indeo 3.0 and the ISVR make the most sense. You can still use the ISVR to capture raw data and then use Cinepak to compress that. If you plan any editing beyond removal of extraneous video, I strongly recommend capturing raw data and compressing after editing. Remember: compress only one time when using lossy compression.

Basically, Table 11.3 presumes that it is better to use Indeo when possible because of the shorter compression times. You can, if you wish, use Cinepak in any situation. Where both Indeo and Cinepak are listed, you should assume that Indeo will be able to compress only some of the files you will encounter at the given data rate. One final note: at the time these results were compiled, Intel had announced an intention to deliver an Indeo "super compressor" that would deliver results comparable to Cinepak. If you want to hear the latest comparisons between these two codecs, visit me on CompuServe in section 7 of the Multimedia forum, *Hands-on Multimedia*.[44]

---

[44]If you are not already a member of CompuServe, consider it seriously. I visit the Multimedia forum daily, and I regularly upload product reviews, new driver versions, cool videos, and other neat stuff to the forum libraries. You can keep up to date much more easily with weekly visits to the Multimedia forum. In addition to my own efforts, many, many professionals and new users visit regularly to exchange information and ideas. Given the fast rate of change in the world of multimedia, CompuServe seems to be the ideal way to get the word out.

The Future of Video for Windows

Just as we were going to press with the second edition of this book, Microsoft released a beta version of Video for Windows 1.1. The new version includes some exciting new features. Many of the features are intended for developers who will be using Video for Windows to add video to their software or CD-ROM titles. However, there are a few key goodies for users of Video for Windows, too. I've broken the new features into three categories:

Video Goodies for Users—These are changes and additions that will be useful to anyone who uses products that incorporate .AVI files, or who will be capturing video with a capture card.

Video Goodies for Developers—These are changes that will be of benefit to the average software developer. My definition of average includes anyone using Visual Basic, ToolBook, or other authoring/programming software at the same level.

Low-Level Goodies for Developers—These are changes that will be important to the serious programmer, especially those working in C/C++.

Although it may not look like a significant upgrade, Video for Windows 1.1 is actually a major step forward for video on the PC. By putting better tools into developers' hands, it makes it easier to put video into software products.

Video Goodies for Users

Several of the companies that make video compression tools will provide new versions of their video codecs in version 1.1. For example, the Cinepak codec will have improvements in compression times and image appearance. Intel will release a new version of Indeo (version 3.1) that adds higher compression rates.

It will now be much easier for software developers to add video support to an application. They will have several ways to provide video controls, and you will see improvements in performance in all applications.

If you own a camcorder that supports the Control-L or Sony VISCA protocols, you can greatly increase the quality of your video captures by having the computer control the camcorder during playback. These protocols allow two-way communication between the computer and your camcorder by way of the serial port. Support for the VISCA protocol is built right into VidEdit, while Control-L support can be provided either with a VBOX from Sony, or by third parties right from the serial port.

Why is this protocol support important? With the protocols, the computer can tell the camera to move one frame at a time, allowing you to capture without any form of compression at all. You can then edit or revise the video clips with programs like Media Merge and Premiere, and apply compression as the last step. This ensures the highest possible image quality. The base command set includes the commands show in table 11.4:

Table 11.4. MCI commands for controlling a VCR device.

Command	Description
capability	Determines the capabilities of the VISCA driver, or the hardware, depending on the parameters used.
cue	Prepare a device for the next play or record command.
freeze	Freezes the current frame for capture.
index	Turns on-screen display on or off.
info	Returns information about the VISCA driver.
list	Used to determine the number and type of video and audio inputs.
mark	Controls recording and erasing of marks on the tape. These are special signals written to tape that can be identified during a high-speed search; not all VCRs support marks.
pause	Puts the VCR in pause mode. A video frame is displayed.
play	Same as pressing the Play button on the VCR.
record	Same as pressing the Record button on the VCR.
resume	Resume a play, record, or seek mode that was interrupted by a pause command.
seek	Seeks a specific position on the tape.

Command	Description
set	Sets a variable for the driver. You can set time mode, the VCR clock, counter format, time format, and many other variables.
setaudio	Sets the audio track input, record, and monitor settings.
settimecode	Enables or disables timecode recording.
settuner	Gives you complete control over the tuner portion of a VCR—you can change channels, seek channels, etc.
setvideo	Sets the video track input, record, and monitor settings.
status	Obtains status information from the VCR — position, length, number of tracks, etc.
step	Steps forward or backward the specified number of frames.
stop	Stops playback; no image is displayed after a stop.
unfreeze	Return to displaying normal video

Video Goodies for Developers

Developers benefit the most from release 1.1 of Video for Windows. The product has been redesigned, and extended in powerful ways. Here's a list of some of the highlights:

➤ A new Visual Basic control, mciwnd.vbx, that expands on the capabilities of mic.vbx. The new control is designed specifically for multimedia data types, such as video, that require a window for playback. It gives you an easy way to add video to a Visual Basic application, while still providing full control over such things as window placement, window size, playback size, and so on.

➤ Also exciting is a video capture .vbx. This allows you to add video capture capabilities to any Visual Basic application. It's a full-featured capture control—it includes everything you'll need to capture video.

➤ A full set of AVIFile services is now included in Video for Windows. If you need to add detailed support for .AVI file input and output, you now have the resources you need to accomplish the task. This means that you can read and write .AVI files without needing an intimate knowledge of the file format. You can also use AVIFile services to cut, copy, and paste video sequences.

➤ An audio compression manager (ACM) is included with Version 1.1. This allows you to create and access compressed audio files using standardized techniques, without worrying about which compression technique is used.

Low-Level Goodies for Developers

There is a new window class, MCIWnd, which includes capabilities for playing back any MCI media (including video) by sending messages to the window. This window class is used as the foundation for a Visual Basic control as well, giving you expanded abilities to control an MCI device. Other important new changes include:

➤ The DrawDIB library has been expanded to include custom drawing procedures, support for 32-bit DIBs, and direct video access on many video display adapters.

➤ The installable compressor functions have been expanded. It is now easier to compress individual frames and sequences of frames. Installable compressor support now also includes hardware stretching, cropping, and color conversion.

➤ The internal AVI file structure has been expanded. It now supports multiple video streams, timecode chunks, and text strings describing the file and streams.

Summary

When all is said and done, video is my favorite thing about computers. I really enjoy the ability to add motion video to a presentation or a software title, or even using video as a screen saver. My main goal in this chapter has been to provide the kind of information you need to get started with video on your own computer. If you find that you still have questions, my book *PC Video Madness* includes a wide variety of information about video. I included an outline of the book in the appendix.[45]

---

[45]For those of you who feel that I am shamelessly attempting to get you to buy another of my books, I can only say: you bet! *PC Video Madness* contains information about everything pertaining to video on a PC—from how to hold a camera or light a scene to programming with video with a wide variety of languages and authoring systems.

IV R T
P A R T

Shopper's
Guide

Hardware Shopper's Guide

T he key to creating a useful multimedia PC is hardware—you can't do multimedia without it. The first items that usually come to mind are sound cards and CD-ROM drives, but there's much more to it than that. Multimedia hardware falls into two major categories:

➤ Hardware that is specific to multimedia. (Sound cards and video capture cards are good examples.)

➤ Hardware that enhances a computer's multimedia capabilities. (Memory upgrades and high-resolution video cards are good examples.)

Depending on the equipment you have, you might need hardware in one or in both categories. The choices depend on what you want to do. If you only want to have fun, of course, you can start anywhere.

If you want to use multimedia for business presentations, however, sound adds the most punch, and high-resolution video is a close second. A CD-ROM is not essential if presentations are your goal, unless the software you want provides sample clips you need on CDs. This is becoming increasingly common, and it's getting harder and harder to do multimedia without a CD-ROM drive.

If you need portable multimedia (for sales presentations, for example), your choices are more limited but not as limited as they were when I wrote the first edition of this book. At that time I said, "Most truly portable equipment barely qualifies as consumer grade, certainly not business grade." That has changed. You can now put high-quality sound on a portable (the Port-able Sound Plus is my personal choice because it supports 16-bit sound). Several manufacturers now have portable CD-ROMs with desktop-level performance. Most importantly, many portable computers now have high-resolution video drivers built right in—just connect a Super VGA multi-sync monitor, and you are ready to go.

If you want multimedia for the reason I like it—to make your computer more pleasant to work with—I recommend some careful research. Adding a sound card, for example, won't make life more pleasant if you are hounded by miscellaneous pops and clicks or if installation is a nightmare. Whatever hardware you purchase, keep one eye on the future because the field is constantly evolving.

Multimedia PCs

The list of companies that either ship or plan to ship fully multimedia PCs continues to grow. Most multimedia PCs are of conventional design (a sound card and a CD-ROM drive simply is added to a standard computer). A few also include accessories such as a microphone or a speaker.

Many mail-order computer sellers offer multimedia PCs as well. Not all of these units have the official blessing of the Multimedia PC Marketing Council. I haven't tested these units, so let the buyer beware. However, many of these computers use standard audio and CD-ROM components; ask questions to find out whether the components have familiar names and model numbers.

Since the first edition of this book, there has been an explosion in the number of companies that offer multimedia PCs. In fact, you can probably expect to find one or more multimedia offerings wherever you might look—mail-order house, discount store, computer store, and so on. Here's a sampling of companies offering specific multimedia computer models as of September 1993—and this is far from a complete list:

Advanced Logic Research (ALR)
9401 Jeronimo
Irvine, CA 92718
800-444-4257
FAX: 714-581-9240

Brysis Data, Inc.
17431 E. Gale Ave.
City of Industry, CA 91748
818-810-0355

Compaq Computer Corporation
ProLinea CDS
800-345-1518

CompuAdd Corporation
12301 Technology Blvd.
Austin, TX 78727
800-925-3000

Dell Computer Corp.
9505 Arboretum Blvd.
Austin, TX 78759
800-289-3355

Fujitsu America, Inc.
Support Center
101 California St., Suite 1775
San Francisco, CA 94111
415-616-9700

Gateway 2000
610 Gateway Dr.
North Sioux City, SD 57049
800-846-2000

IBM PS/2 Ultimedia
IBM United States
Department NCM
4111 Northside Parkway
H04l1
Atlanta, GA 30327
800-426-9402

Insight Distribution Network
1912 West Fourth St.
Tempe, AZ 85281
800-998-8046

MegaMedia Comp. Corp.
1701 D Fortune Dr.
San Jose, CA 95131
800-MEGAMEDIA

Mind Computer Products
892 Portage Ave.
Winnipeg, Manitoba, Canada
R3GOPA
204-786-7747

NEC Technologies, Inc.
Optical Media SBU
1255 Michael Dr.
Wood Dale, IL 60191
800-NEC-INFO

Olivetti Advanced Technology Center
20300 Stevens Creek Blvd.
Cupertino, California 95014
408-366-3000

Philips Consumer Electronics
PC Marketing Dept.
1 Philips Dr.
Knoxville, TN 37914
615-521-4316
(Canada and Europe)

Siemens Nixdorf
Research & Dev. Division
4 Cambridge Center
Cambridge, MA 02142
617-273-0480

Tandy Corporation
Customer Service
One Tandy Center
Fort Worth, TX 76102
817-390-3700

Technology Integrated Products
3064 Scott Blvd.
Santa Clara, CA 95054
408-980-5191

TC Computers
2725 Lexington Ave.
Kenner, LA 70062
800-723-8282

Tri-Star Computer Corp.
120 South Weber Dr.
Chandler, AZ 85226
800-800-7668

Zenith Data Systems
Multimedia Marketing Group
2150 East Lake Cook Rd.
Buffalo Grove, IL 60089
708-808-5000

Dolch: Portability at a Price

Dolch Computer Systems
372 Turquoise Street
Milpitas, CA 95035
408-957-6575

Dolch has staked out the high ground in multimedia portable computers. They offer an expandable line of lunch-box portables that enable you to take the very highest quality of multimedia hardware on the road. If you are in a no-compromise situation, the Dolch systems are at or near the top of the list.

The Dolch Mach line of computers is scalable. That is, you can add physical modules to expand capabilities. Need another ISA slot? Add an expansion module. Need a CD-ROM drive? Add a model with a CD. Add to this active matrix LCD technology, and you have the general idea.

You should expect to pay for this level of quality and flexibility; system prices are $7,000 and up. However, you can have all the power you need, up to 486/66.

Tandy Sensation

At least one multimedia PC is being targeted specifically to the home consumer market: the Tandy Sensation, as shown in Figure 12.1.

Like other Tandy products, it has an easy-to-use front end, this time featuring multimedia. It includes a full range of multimedia features in a 486SX box:

➤ Multimedia software (MS-DOS, Windows 3.1, Multimedia Microsoft Works, 1992 Microsoft Bookshelf, Tandy WinMate, America Online, Prodigy, and the Sierra Network)

➤ Voice mail

➤ Text to speech

➤ Digital stereo sound

➤ FM synthesis

➤ FAX capability

➤ Microphone

➤ Speakers

➤ Headphones

➤ Clip art, including digitized photos

➤ Front-mounted jacks for sound connections

➤ CD-ROM drive (no-caddy design)

➤ Optional TV display capability (122-channel, cable-ready)

The best part of this machine is its suggested list price: less than $2,000. Tandy was beginning to ship these units as this book was going to press, so I haven't had a chance to take one for a test drive. The Sensation is available from your local Radio Shack dealer.

Figure 12.1. *The Tandy Sensation.*

IBM Multimedia

IBM also is targeting a variety of audiences for its multimedia offerings. In addition to the professional Ultimedia PS/2 line, IBM offers the PS/ValuePoint line of PCs—a low-cost, high-feature line of computers well worth a look. This is a pure marketing decision on IBM's part—they have put together very attractive packages. IBM has joined with Creative Labs and other multimedia vendors to offer complete multimedia packages ranging from 486/25 to 486/66 VESA local bus machines.

There are two ways to look at the systems from IBM: from least power to most and from entertainment to business.

At the low end, you'll find a 486SX/25 with a 120M hard disk and 4M of memory. Even at the low end, you get 16-bit audio (Sound Blaster), a double-spin (300K/sec) CD-ROM drive, 16-bit color, and multi-session Photo CD support.

This is an interesting offering in all respects. I regret that I did not get a chance to personally review one of these units prior to completing work on this book. I will try to make arrangements to get a system in for testing, and I'll post results to Section 7 of the Multimedia forum on CompuServe. So far, there have been a few scattered problems with the included sound cards; I've seen messages to that effect posted to CompuServe but nothing else to indicate problems.

At the high end, you'll find a 486/66 DX with a 340M hard drive and up to 64M of memory, plus up to 2M of video memory on a VESA local bus video card, and a 256K L2 cache. And all of these machines are ISA bus—that's right; no MCA bus in these IBM machines. In addition, IBM is offering just about every product that has anything to do with multimedia, both hardware and software, in catalogs you can easily obtain. Just call IBM's multimedia hotline at 800-IBM-9402.

There are three types of PS/ValuePoint products:

Entertainment—Includes a range of games, reference software, and basic applications: Microsoft Works for Windows, Bookshelf, Software Tool Works Encyclopedia, HSC Interactive, LucasArts Loom, The Secret of Monkey Island, Secrets of the Luftwaffe, Broderbund's Grandma and Me, and Where in the World is Carmen Sandiego?—to name just a few.
Reference—Intended for small businesses and those who don't want games. Includes the same basic applications and reference software as the Entertainment offering but none of the games.
Office—Includes a "blank slate" for multimedia—just the multimedia hardware and operating system. You then add whatever software you require.

All machines feature four slots, ISA architecture with VESA local bus, integrated CD-ROM (multi-session XA compatible), Pentium upgradable, 16-bit sound, and full compliance with MPC level 2 specification.

At the time this was written, the PS/ValuePoint line was priced very aggressively and was supported with several comprehensive catalogs of additional multimedia hardware and software. IBM is clearly making the effort to join the multimedia mainstream.

Portable Multimedia

Aquiline offers a medium-format portable with a built-in CD-ROM drive. In addition, you'll find 16-bit sound support, 256 colors, voice recognition, and all of it on battery power. You can buy one of these units for as little as $3,000, but you might be tempted to hold out for the 486/66 version.

Hard disk sizes are generous, up to 540M. Also nice is the ability to add a single 16-bit ISA card to the unit. For more information, call Aquiline at (518) 785-6517. I haven't tried one of these units, so I can't speak to issues of performance or quality personally.

Scenario, Inc., also offers portable multimedia computing. The Dynavision series of laptops includes built-in CD-ROM drives and 256-color Active Matrix color. The standard system, the D4C-200-DA, comes with a 200M hard drive, 4M of RAM, 50-MHz 486 CPU, and an internal 200-ms (that's fast!) CD-ROM drive.

Unfortunately, the system does not include sound support, but the Port-able Sound Plus from DSP Solutions would solve that.

The lunchbox format offers more room for multimedia hardware. Micro Express offers the Regal Multimedia Portable PC for $4,995. It includes a 486/33 CPU, a 10-inch Active Matrix color display, a CD-ROM drive, a 200M hard drive, a Sound Blaster Pro sound card (that's 8-bit, unfortunately), external speakers, and a microphone. Call 800-989-9900 for more information.

Making the Upgrade

One way to go multimedia is to get the whole package in the form of a multimedia upgrade kit. The exact content of these kits varies—some include only a CD-ROM drive and a sound card, others add multiple software titles, speakers, a microphone, and so on.

Two kinds of units are available. One is the all-in-one external unit (including speakers, CD-ROM, and sound support) that connects by cable. The other kind is the component kit, consisting of a sound card that you mount inside your machine and an internal or external CD-ROM drive. The latter kit may or may not include such things as speakers and a microphone.

Many upgrade kits include components that are also available separately (check the individual listings for details).

Creative Labs Multimedia Upgrade Kits

Creative Labs, Inc.
1901 McCarthy Blvd.
Milpitas, CA 95035
800-998-LABS
408-428-6600
FAX: 408-428-6611

Creative Labs offers four upgrade kits, ranging from low-end to mid-level technology. Let's start at the top end of Creative's offerings.

The *Sound Blaster Digital Edge CD* upgrade kit comes with impressive statistics. The sound card is Creative Labs' best, the Sound Blaster 16 ASP. The kit includes a mid-level CD-ROM drive with double-spin technology, 350-ms access time, and multi-session Photo CD support. It also includes a joystick port, stereo speakers, microphone, and a variety of software packages. The software includes a special edition of Aldus PhotoStyler for image editing, Microsoft Bookshelf, Microsoft Works for Windows, Macromedia Action!, and Authorware Star as well as Creative Labs' own Voice Assist, a speech recognition system.

The Edutainment CD 16 upgrade kit includes a 16-bit version of the Sound Blaster (not the ASP version), a single-spin CD-ROM drive, MIDI interface and joystick port, stereo speakers, and a wide selection of software. The software is really the ace in this package (the slow CD-ROM is the weak spot). The software list includes The Animals, Secret Weapons of the Luftwaffe, Loom, Carmen Sandiego Deluxe Edition, Software Tool Works Multimedia Encyclopedia, Grandma and Me, Secret of Monkey Island, and Sherlock Holmes, Consulting Detective.

The Discovery CD 16 upgrade kit is similar to the Edutainment CD 16; it includes the same hardware but fewer software packages.

The Discovery CD 8 upgrade kit includes the 8-bit Sound Blaster Pro Deluxe; otherwise, it is the same as the 16-bit package.

Media Vision Upgrade Kit

Media Vision offers both varieties of upgrade kits: you can go with an all-in-one box, or you can go with components. At press time, the official name of the all-in-one upgrade kit had not been announced, but you will recognize it by its sleek, swept-back, high-tech design.

Upgrade Kit
Media Vision, Inc.
47300 Bayside Parkway
Fremont, CA 94538
FAX: 510-770-9592
BBS: 510-770-9522
CompuServe: GO MEDIAVISION

This PC-multimedia system comes with a double-speed CD-ROM drive that is Photo CD multi-session ready, a Yamaha 20-voice synthesizer, a multi-channel mixer, and support for several operating systems including DOS, Windows 3.1, Windows NT, OS/2 2.1, and NextStep. The upgrade kit is a fully integrated, MPC- and MPC2-compliant multimedia system for your PC, and it supports an IBM standard joystick as well as a full-duplex MIDI interface. It is backward compatible for Sound Blaster and AdLib. The upgrade kit includes detachable speakers that can be placed upright in customized stands.

Media Vision's upgrade kit features two software packages on CD-ROM:

Compton's Interactive Encyclopedia for Windows—This is Compton's 26-volume printed encyclopedia on CD. It contains over 9 million words; 38,000 articles; 13,000 images, maps, and graphs; 50 minutes of sound, music, and speech; 94 videos, slide shows, and animated sequences; over 800 color maps; 5,000 maps, charts, and diagrams; as well as the complete Merriam-Webster's OnLine Dictionary.

Arthur's Teacher Trouble from Broderbund's Living Books— This electronic book encourages your child to become actively involved in the story. You can have the book read to you, click on the printed words, or click on the pictures for surprising results! The book was written by renowned children's author Marc Brown and follows Arthur the Aardvark's third-grade adventures with his new teacher, Mr. Ratburn.

The upgrade kit offers the following features:

➤ 16-bit stereo recording and playback (16-bit linear CODEC)

➤ Sample frequency from 4 to 44.1 kHz

➤ Microphone, external line-in, and CD-ROM audio inputs

➤ 100 percent compatible with Sound Blaster, AdLib, Pro AudioSpectrum 16, MPC and MPC2, Windows 3.1, Windows NT, OS/2 2.1, NextStep

➤ Yamaha YMF262 (OPL-3) voice synthesizer

➤ Four-operator FM synthesis

➤ General MIDI compatible

➤ 16-bit DMA

➤ Selectable IRQs (2–7, 10–15) and DMAs (0–3, 5–7)

➤ Software-selectable DMA and IRQ settings with auto configuration

➤ MIDI interface

➤ Full duplex, for simultaneous record/playback

➤ MPU-401 compatible in DOS

➤ IBM standard joystick port

➤ 10-watt speaker amplification

Media Vision Fusion Double CD 16

Fusion Double CD 16
Media Vision
47221 Fremont Blvd.
Fremont, CA 94538
FAX: 510-770-9592
BBS: 510-770-9522
CompuServe: GO MEDIAVISION

Vision was kind enough to send me one of these systems for review, and I like it quite a bit. I'm not wild about the FM synthesis MIDI support, but on all other counts this is an outstanding system. In particular, there were two things I just loved about it. One, it installed quickly and easily. No fuss, no muss. Two, it has performed flawlessly; it's been compatible with every software package I've thrown at it.

The price/performance ratio is great too. You get an NEC 55 CD-ROM drive, which is a double-spin drive with average-but-respectable performance—350-ms average access time (as compared to 280 ms in Media Vision's top-end drives from NEC).

This package includes 16-bit sound support, speakers, and a good collection of CD-ROM software. The software includes the 7th Guest, Arthur's Teacher Trouble from Broderbund (a very cool title for kids of all ages), Battle Chess Enhanced, and Compton's Interactive Encyclopedia. The retail price for this kit is $899, but it sells for hundreds less on the street.

Media vision also offers a low-end version of this package, the Fusion CD 16, which includes a 150K/sec CD-ROM drive and a similar set of CDs. Its retail price is $699.

Media Vision Pro 16 Multimedia System II

Pro 16 Multimedia System II
Media Vision
47221 Fremont Blvd.
Fremont, CA 94538
FAX: 510-770-9592
BBS: 510-770-9522
CompuServe: GO MEDIAVISION

This is a high-performance system that includes

➤ Pro AudioSpectrum 16 sound card

➤ NEC SCSI Multimedia CD-ROM drive (double spin)

➤ Windows 3.1 drivers

➤ Mayo Clinic Family Health Book

➤ Compton's Multimedia Encyclopedia

➤ Carmen Sandiego Deluxe

➤ Microprose's Mantis and Civilization

➤ MacroMind Action! on CD-ROM

The Pro AudioSpectrum 16 plays and records true 16-bit, 44-kHz stereo sound and has a 16-bit PC bus interface. The kit includes the MVD101 Digital Audio Controller chip to provide compatibility with a broad range of hardware, including Sound Blaster, AdLib, and Thunderboard. It has a full-duplex MIDI port that enables you to record and play at the same time.

The kit includes an IBM standard joystick port and a 4-watt/channel stereo amplifier. Sample street prices: $998 from The PC Zone, 800-258-8088, and $949 from Insight Software, 800-326-2007.

Sigma Designs WinSound 16 CD-ROM Kit

WinSound 16 CD-ROM Kit
Sigma Designs, Inc.
Fremont, CA
510-770-0100

This is a 16-bit upgrade kit that includes the Sigma Designs sound card and a Sony CD-ROM drive as well as a variety of software packages.

The Sony CD is the Light Internal drive, which is somewhat slow—150K/sec transfer and 550 ms access time. The upgrade kit includes speakers, Multimedia Make Your Point, Compton's Multimedia Encyclopedia, Midisoft's Multimedia Music Library, and the Pocket series of sound applications.

Turtle Beach MultiSound MPC Upgrade Kit

MultiSound MPC Upgrade Kit
Turtle Beach Systems
Cyber Center #33
1600 Pennsylvania Avenue
York, PA 17404
717-843-6916
FAX: 717-854-8319

The MultiSound MPC Upgrade Kit includes a MultiSound sound board, a fast double-spin CD-ROM drive, and a SCSI controller card. The CD-ROM was selected to match the speed and quality of MultiSound; at press time, this was the Texel 3024. The upgrade kit is also available with an external drive, the Texel 5024. This kit is one of the best in its class; any kit with the MultiSound would be.

CD-ROM Drives

Often viewed as multimedia devices, CD-ROM drives are simply vehicles for multimedia—big, cheap data containers. Well, some of them are not so cheap, but you get the idea. The cost per megabyte for data distributed on a CD is much lower than data distributed on floppy or hard disks.

The basic issue to consider when buying a CD-ROM drive is money. The cheaper drives move data more slowly—some might not even meet the 150K transfer rate required for multimedia performance. Cheap drives also have slow access times (you have to wait longer for data to be found).

Even the fastest CD-ROM drives, however, fall far short of hard disk performance. For example, the NEC 83J (the drive I have in my machine) is fast for a CD-ROM at 280 ms, and Toshiba has a CD-ROM that goes all the way to 200 ms. My Fujitsu hard drive clocks in at 12 ms—a huge difference.

It may seem like everyone is offering CD-ROM drives these days; that's because it's true. The market is undergoing a fundamental shift right now, from 150K/sec transfer rates to 300K/sec (so-called *double-spin*) drives. You can get some really good deals on the older *single-spin* drives, but don't bother if you are looking toward the future. When the double-spin drives become common currency, more CDs will require double-spin to play, and you'll be left in the dust. That may take a few years, however. Nonetheless, there are good deals on double-spin drives. The cheap double-spin drives hit the 300K/sec transfer rate but have slower access times, on the order of 350–500 ms. You should be able to find a drive at 350 ms or better at affordable prices.

CD-ROM drives come in two flavors: those that use standard SCSI connections and those that don't. I prefer drives that use standard SCSI, but this can drive up the price; you might need a real SCSI card instead of the inexpensive, just-for-CDs cards that come with the non-standard drives. If you choose a real SCSI card, you need good drivers. Corel sells a standard set of drivers that work with most cards, although most vendors offer their own. Find out whether the vendor has more recent drivers than the ones in the package. CD-ROM technology is moving ahead so fast that you may need them.

Corel SCSI Kit

The Corel SCSI Kit includes a CD-ROM drive with CorelDRAW! and Corel-ARTSHOW on CD and more than 10,000 clip-art images. The kit is available from

Insight Software (800-326-2007). Corel's SCSI drivers are also available for most SCSI cards and are well regarded in the industry.

CD Technology

> CD Technology
> 766 San Aleso Ave.
> Sunnyvale, CA 94086

This company offers one drive that uses a SCSI interface. You can mount it internally or externally. It operates at 150K/sec and can read single-session Photo CD discs.

Chinon America

> Chinon America
> 615 Hawaii Ave.
> Torrance, CA 90503
> 800-441-0222

Chinon offers SCSI drives, with models at 150K/sec and 300K/sec transfer rates. The more expensive drives are multisession Photo CD capable.

Creative Labs

> Omni CD
> Creative Labs, Inc.
> 1901 McCarthy Blvd.
> Milpitas, CA 95035
> 800-998-LABS
> 408-428-6600
> FAX: 408-428-6611

This recently introduced, aggressively priced CD-ROM upgrade kit includes a double-spin CD-ROM drive, an adapter card, and bundled software.

The drive has great specs for the price (a modest $299 on the street). Access time is 320 ms, transfer rate is 300K/sec. It does multi-session Photo CD and is

XA ready. It comes with a special edition of Aldus PhotoStyler and a CD music player for both DOS and Windows.

Hitachi

> Multimedia Division
> Hitachi
> 401 West Artesia Boulevard
> Compton, CA 90220
> 310-537-8383

Hitachi offers several drives that deliver 150K/sec transfer times. These drives are not Photo CD capable. Some work with SCSI; some use a proprietary interface.

Magnavox

The Magnavox external CD-ROM drive is a combination external CD-ROM and CD audio player. It comes with a stereo audio cable, MS-DOS extensions/driver software, a power cord, an interface card, and a cable. It features CD audio playback with front panel control. It has a relatively slow access time of less than 700 ms. This unit costs $299 and is available from USA FLEX (800-800-4395).

The Magnavox internal CD-ROM drive meets MPC standards. It achieves an access time of less than 375 ms and includes an AT interface. It features CD audio playback with front panel and is made in the United States. This unit costs $319 and is also available from USA FLEX (800-800-4395).

MicroNet Technology

> MicroNet Technology
> 20 Mason Ave.
> Irvine, CA 92718

Micronet offers a 150K/sec SCSI drive that is single-session Photo CD capable.

NEC Internal and External Drives

Int/Ext
NEC Corp.
800-NEC-INFO
415-960-6000

NEC distributes internal and external CD-ROM drives that have access times as low as 280 ms and can transfer data at up to 300K/second. These are excellent figures for CD-ROM drives (these figures are the result of NEC's MultiSpin technology—basically, the drives spin twice as fast as standard drives). The drives (some of the best in their class) are MPC-compliant and CD-ROM XA-ready, and they include a two-year warranty. AT interface cards are available, and the drives have a 64K cache. I use the internal 84J model in my PC, and I've been happy with it.

NEC recently released a lightweight portable CD-ROM that accesses data at 400 ms and transfers data at 300K/sec. This portable CD-ROM can be connected to portable computers with NEC's Parallel-to-SCSI Interface Kit and comes with an optional battery pack.

New NEC CD-ROM readers can read Kodak Multisession Photo CD format, which enables you to use your PC to view and manipulate 35-mm images that have been transferred to a Photo CD. The new readers also have SCSI 1 and 2 switchable settings.

The estimated selling price (ESP) for the internal drive is $550; the ESP for the external drive is $615; and the ESP for the portable drive is $465.

NEC CDR-74 and CDR-84

CDR-74/84
NEC Corp.
800-NEC-INFO
415-960-6000

The Intersect CDR-74 and CDR-84 use MultiSpin technology that achieves access speeds of 280 ms and data transfer rates of 300K/sec. Video data can be played back without any pauses or lapses in motion.

Audio data also uses the MultiSpin technology to transfer data at twice the speed of standard CD-ROM drives (300K) while maintaining a 150K/sec transfer rate for audio tracks.

The CD-ROM drives come with an XT/AT interface kit with cable and card. Street prices were around $600 at the time this book went to press, but expect those to drop as NEC introduces triple spin (3X speed) drives early in 1994.

Optical Access

Suite 2050
800 West Cummings Park
Woburn, MA 01801

Optical Access offers a 150K/sec SCSI-2 drive that is multi-session Photo CD capable.

Orchid CDS-3110

This unit offers mid-level capabilities. It comes complete with all the cards and cables you need to install it in your machine; it does not require any separate cards or cables. Everything comes in the box. Average access time is 380 ms, a bit higher than average. Data transfer, at 307K/sec, qualifies it as a legitimate double-spin drive.

This unit also supports XA and multi-session Photo CD. It comes in both internal and external versions as well as in a package deal with the Orchid SoundWave 32 sound card. The Orchid CD uses a tray loading system, so there are no CD caddies to mess with.

Panasonic DRM-604X

Ads bill this unit as "the world's fastest CD-ROM." Fortunately, this is true. However, it's also a bit more. Unlike most CD-ROM drives you've seen, this unit is actually a changer—it holds up to six CDs in a magazine. It takes about five seconds to change from one CD to the next. You can daisy-chain up to seven of these units to put up to 42 CDs online at one time.

Performance is outstanding—it uses quadruple spin to achieve a data rate of 600K/sec. This unit is a bit pricey (over $1,000), but it's ideal for situations involving networking of CDs. For more information, call Panasonic at 800-LASER ON.

769

Philips

Philips
1 Philips Drive
Knoxville, TN 37914
800-722-6224

Philips offers both 150K/sec and 300K/sec drives. The faster drives are multi-session Photo CD capable and use a SCSI interface; the standard drives use a proprietary Philips interface. The faster drives are the CM405ABK (internal) and the CM435ABK (external). These drives use a 64K buffer and are SCSI-2 compliant.

In addition to standard CD-ROM drives and double-spin drives (Philips calls them RapidReaders), Philips now offers a CD recorder that records to blank 5 1/4-inch disks available from Philips. Recorders are not cheap—figure anywhere from $6,000–$8,000 depending on what configuration you buy. Expect these prices to come down during 1994, when several new companies (such as Yamaha) enter the market with aggressively priced CD-ROM recorders.[1]

Philips is also spearheading CD-I (Compact Disk Interactive), and they offer a series of players that support it. CD-I disks cannot be played in a CD-ROM machine—they require a CD-I player. The CD-I player is designed for connection to a TV screen; it is not normally connected to a computer except for development of new titles.

Procom Technology

Procom Technology
2181 Dupont Ave.
Irvine, CA 92715
800-800-8600

Procom offers a number of CD-ROM drives with both proprietary and SCSI interfaces. All are 150K/sec drives; only one model supports single-session Photo CD.

---

[1]They are also known as "CD-ROM burners," and those in the know call the recording process "burning a CD-ROM." I suppose this refers to the fact that a laser is doing the recording.

Sony

Sony Corporation of America
Computer Peripherals Products Company
655 River Oaks Parkway
San Jose, CA 95134
(408) 432-0190

Sony offers a wide variety of CD-ROM drive products, including drives, systems, and a CD-ROM recorder. The following products are the key Sony products worth a closer look:

CDU-7811 Double-Speed CD-ROM Drive—This unit features a 300k/ sec data transfer rate and a very good average access time—290ms. Both an internal and external version are available.

Figure 12.2. *The internal version of Sony's high-performance CD-ROM drive.*

Desktop Library Multimedia CD-ROM Systems—These are one-stop packages for getting started in multimedia. There are several different configurations, and each includes a multisession CD-ROM drive, a 16-bit sound card, speakers, and several CD-ROM titles.

Figure 12.3. *These personal computer speakers from Sony include a subwoofer.*

CDU-31A—A very inexpensive drive, intended for entry-level use. It is MPC level 1 compliant, and uses a caddyless tray loading system. The list price is a very affordable $189.95.

CDU-535/541—Internal drives that come with either the Sony or a SCSI bus connection. They are older technolgoy—150k/sec data transfer, with average access times of 340-380ms.

CDW-900E—A double-speed CD write-once subsystem. It allows direct recording of CD-ROM, CD-ROMXA, CD-I, and Redbook audio CDs.

Talon

The Talon CD-ROM is a half-height 5 1/4-inch internal drive that plays both CD-ROM and audio discs. The drive meets multimedia specifications and comes as a complete kit with an interface card, sound board connector, and all mounting hardware. The Talon CD-ROM player includes Compton's 26-volume encyclopedia on a CD, with more than 10 million words, 32,000 articles, 15,000 images, charts and graphs, and a rotating world atlas. It includes a United States history time line and Webster's Dictionary. The unit costs $795. Hard Drives International carries several Talon drives (800-998-8041).

Texel

Texel
1605 Wyatt Ave.,
Santa Clara, CA 95054
800-886-3935

Texel offers 150K/sec and 300K/sec drives that use the SCSI interface, but their 300K/sec drive is catching the most attention because it combines high performance, multi-session Photo CD support, and competitive pricing in one package. It comes in two models: an internal (the 3024) and an external (the 5024).

Also worth a look is a hot new drive introduced late in 1993, the 3028/5028 (internal and external code numbers). It features sustained throughput of 335K/sec, and an average access time of 240ms. These are excellent numbers, and the units are priced aggressively. The list price of the internal unit is $499; the external unit is $599. Expect significant discounts from dealers. They are designed specifically to compete with the hot Toshiba units introduced in the summer of '93.

The 3028 and 5028 are full-featured. They support Photo-CD multisession discs, CD-XA, SCSI-2, and the MPC Level 2 specification.

Toshiba America

Toshiba
P.O. Box 19724
Irvine, CA 92713
714-583-3000

A press kit covering the various Toshiba CD-ROM drives was not available by press time, but from everything I've heard from satisfied users on CompuServe, these units are high-performance and reliable. This is one of the rare times I am willing to grant an Author's Choice to a unit I have not used personally. The exclamations of satisfaction were too numerous and consistent to ignore. If you are in the market for a high-performance CD-ROM, make sure that Toshiba is on your list of drives to check. At press time, the 3401 was the first choice of many professionals. Its average access time of 200 ms probably accounts for most of the interest, but by early 1994 other manufacturers will also offer such high-speed drives.

Yamaha CDR100

Yamaha Corporation of America
Systems Technology Division
981 Ridder Park Drive
San Jose, CA 95131
(408) 437-3133

Yamaha has announced, but was not shipping at press time, a high-speed CD-ROM recorder that will be priced aggressively. The unit will record CDs at various speeds, from 1X to 4X normal. This can cut the recording time by up to 75%.

The unit supports all standard CD-ROM formats, including CD-ROM, CD-ROMXA, CD-I, and Redbook audio. It supports the SCSI II interface, and will be available in internal and external versions. It will come with several mastering software options, including QuickTopix from Optical Media International, disComposer from Trace Mountain, Easy-CD Pro from IncatSystems, or Personal SCRIBE from Meridian Data.

At 4X speed, the unit will have a throughput of 40M per minute, cutting the time to record a 680M CD from more than an hour to about 17 minutes. Another key feature is multiple-mode support (disc-at-once, track-at-once, and multisession).

Kodak Photo CD

Photo CD
Eastman Kodak Company
343 State Street
Rochester, NY 14650-0519
716-724-6404
FAX: 716-724-9829

The Photo CD from Kodak is a new way to work with photographs. It enables you to store your images on a CD-ROM disc instead of conventional negatives, prints, and slides. Once the images are on the CD-ROM, you can view them using a special player connected to your TV, or you can use them in desktop publishing and multimedia applications. To put your photos on a Photo CD, you take the film or negatives to any photo outlet that offers the service; Kodak expects most outlets with on-site processing to eventually support Photo CDs.

Kodak has big plans for Photo CD, as you'll see in a moment.

There are four formats for Photo CDs:

➤ Kodak Photo CD Master discs, which store standard consumer-format images such as 35-mm film.

➤ Kodak Pro Photo CD Master discs, which store larger film formats, like those used by professional photographers (120 and 4-inch by 5-inch).

➤ Kodak Photo CD Catalog discs, which allow easy distribution of disc catalogs containing hundreds of pictures of vacation destinations, art works, and retail products.

➤ Kodak Photo CD Medical discs, which can store computed tomography (CT) scans and magnetic resonance images (MR) in addition to film-based images.

Kodak has introduced an additional format, Photo CD Portfolio. Like Kodak's Photo CD master format, the Photo CD Portfolio discs combine sound, text, graphics, and interactive branching with photographs. The new Photo CD format extends your ability to use the Photo CD discs in the following three ways:

➤ The Photo CD Portfolio discs can hold up to 800 images at TV-resolution, or one hour of audio CD-quality stereo sound, or a combination of images and sound (for example, 400 images and 30 minutes of sound).

➤ The Portfolio discs must be created from Kodak Photo CD Master discs or other Photo CD Portfolio discs.

➤ The Photo CD Master discs are created from consumers' original 35-mm slides or negatives or are reproduced from other Photo CD Master discs. Because the Photo CD Master discs contain images of full photographic quality, they are limited to approximately 100 images.

You can use Photo CD Portfolio discs for personal pictures, business presentations, and premastered prerecorded discs that will be sold through retail channels.

Personal Pictures

This category includes family pictures that are displayed on either a Photo CD player or a computer's Photo CD-compatible (XA) CD-ROM drive. It is possible to select a group of photos (for example, relatives, holidays, and birthdays) from an on-screen menu. When the picture is displayed, any sound or graphics linked to the image will play.

It is possible to include on-screen text for each of the photographs to note the year and location as well as a voice recording to go along with it. (You can have Grandma or Grandpa record a description of an old photograph, for example.)

You need to use special authoring software to create the Photo CD Portfolio discs, which are available at minilabs and other locations; check with your local photofinisher for locations. You bring in your Kodak Photo CD Master or Portfolio discs and audio selections and then follow the directions in the authoring software to assemble a program uniquely your own.

There are easy-to-use templates for the most popular applications, such as family trees, weddings, and birthdays. Once you assemble your program, you turn it over to the photo finisher who creates a Photo CD Master or Portfolio disc at a Kodak Photo CD Imaging Workstation.

Business Presentations

These applications include anything produced in quantity, either large or small, that will be distributed to others. This includes business presentations, real estate listings, travelogs, and so on. The same branching, audio, and visual options as those mentioned for personal pictures are available.

The difference between this category and personal pictures is based on the way discs are created. In addition to Photo CD Imaging Workstations with authoring software, desktop computers with appropriate configurations can combine text, graphics, and images on either a Photo CD Master or Portfolio disc. These computers need to be set up with Photo CD-compatible CD-ROM XA drives, Kodak authoring software, and Kodak Photo CD 200 writers (these drives may be shipping by the time you read this). Using the authoring software, you can select images from existing Photo CD discs and add graphics, text, and sound to create a program script.

Using the program script, you can produce finished discs in moderate quantities at the photo finisher or on your own compact disc writer.

Pre-Mastered Discs

Kodak expects software publishers to use Kodak Photo CD Master or Portfolio discs for creating multimedia-style titles that can be stamped for mass production under the disc publisher's brand. This is based on the assumption that the widespread use of Photo CD-compatible playback devices, including Photo CD and CD-I players, will make this technology feasible for software publishers. So far, this hasn't happened to any great degree.

Kodak has initiated discussions with organizations interested in publishing guided tours of major museums, narrated summaries of fine art collections (accompanied by mood-setting music), a series of children's books, and so on. For example, Rick Smolan, the author of the photographic *A Day in the Life of ...* book series, included a Kodak Photo CD Portfolio disc in his book *From Alice to Ocean*. The book documents the story of a woman's journey across the Australian Outback, and contains photos, narration, and ambient sound that could not be included in the book itself.

These pre-mastered discs are produced the same way as Personal Kodak Photo CD Portfolio discs: at a desktop computer or workstation. Final production of large quantities of discs will take place at a compact disc mastering house, similar to those that stamp thousands of audio CDs.

Scanners and Image Acquisition

Multimedia certainly has a lot to do with fancy stuff like video and animation, but it also is full of still images. Chapter 13 contains many different sources for images, but you might also want to create your own. Drawing pictures is one way to create images; scanning, video, and electronic photography are other ways you might want to try.

Scanning is very easy these days; the main issue involves the kind of scanner you use. There are hand scanners, flat-bed scanners, and sheet-feed scanners.

Hand scanner—In the first edition of this book, I wasn't very positive about using hand-held scanners. However, several key problems have been addressed since then. Logitech sent me a ScanMan, which uses software to align images and control scanning speed and has improved rollers to help you scan in a steady, straight line. My recommendation has changed, but only somewhat. It is easier to do a good job with a hand scanner, so if you need to scan, and you are on a budget, a hand scanner is an inconvenient but workable alternative.

Flat-bed scanner—This is the ideal choice for graphic scanning. You need a unit that scans at least 400 dpi, although high-end units at 600 dpi and 1200 dpi are now available at a moderate cost. I use the Hewlett Packard Scanjet IIc, and it's been great for my needs. It has excellent color, the images are sharp, and the scanning software is very convenient to use. Best of all, a flat-bed scanner gives you the best control over aligning the image—if it's angled, you just fix it and re-scan.

Sheet-feed scanner—Sheet feeding works best for OCR (optical character recognition), where high volume is more important than perfect alignment. I find it is very difficult to align an image correctly on most sheet feeders; it's easier to hand scan correctly (mostly because the unit probably comes with software that corrects small misalignments).

Electronic photography is a technology that is still in its infancy. That means that, if you want excellent results, you'd better plan on spending at least $5,000–$10,000 to acquire professional-level equipment. At the low end (under $1,000), you will be limited to either black and white, modest image resolution, or both.

Still video is available at a modest cost (the VideoLogic Captivator, for example, retails for $349), but you can't count on it for professional results. Video is inherently a low-resolution medium, and video stills cannot have anywhere near the same clarity as a scanned image. In a pinch, I've even taken a Polaroid shot and scanned that in.

With that in mind, let's look at some of the image acquisition hardware available now.

Scanjet IIc

Hewlett Packard
1030 NE Circle Blvd.
Corvalis, OR 97330
(208) 323-2551

This is the model of scanner that I use, and I've been extremely happy with it. It's been a steady performer for me. The good points include:

➤ It's the industry standard; it's compatible with just about everything.

➤ Image quality is excellent.

➤ It's fast.

➤ It's versatile—you can add a sheet feeder for OCR work.

➤ It supports TWAIN, which enables you to scan from many major image editing applications.

There just hasn't been a situation where I have not been satisfied with the Scanjet. It has always done the job, and it gets an unqualified recommendation.

FotoMan Plus

Logitech Inc.
6505 Kaiser Drive
Fremont, CA 94555
800-231-7717
510-795-8500
FaxBack: 800-245-0000

FotoMan Plus is a digital camera that enables you to take pictures and add them to your computer. It includes image editing software that basically puts a dark-room in your computer. Because FotoMan Plus comes with a built-in flash, you can snap shots inside or outside. The camera saves images in gray scale that you can use in desktop publishing, multimedia, database, and other applications.

The Plus version is an improved version of FotoMan. It takes higher-resolution snapshots (32 images at 496×460 pixels and 256 gray levels). Other key new features include the following:

➤ A flash that is effective from 16 inches to 6 feet.

➤ Faster serial communication with your computer; it now takes about 12 seconds to transfer one image.

➤ Support for JPEG format as well as TIFF, PCX, BMP, and EPS.

➤ More accurate gray shades.

➤ Optional wide-angle and close-up lenses.

I used the FotoMan, and I found it to be a useful addition. However, it's not cheap and is a rather specialized tool. It is most useful for desktop publishing in situations where you'll be doing final output on your printer. It is useful for 300-, 600-, and 800-dpi printers. High-resolution image setters (1200 dpi and up) really require higher resolution images for best results.

ScanMan

> Logitech Inc.
> 6505 Kaiser Drive
> Fremont, CA 94555
> 800-231-7717
> 510-795-8500
> FaxBack: 800-245-0000

Logitech offers two models of ScanMan for Windows:

> **ScanMan Model 256** scans images in 256 shades of gray. It features Logitech AutoStitch, which automatically joins scanned images up to a total size of 15 by 22 inches. The FotoTouch image editing software offers darkroom features and enhancement techniques. The ScanMan Model 256 scans images or text that you can use in word processing applications. ScanMan Model 256 also comes bundled with Logitech CatchWord Pro Optical Character Reader (OCR) software.
> **ScanMan Color** is a 24-bit scanner for Windows in 16.8 million colors and true 256 gray scale. FotoTouch Color software enables you to edit in full color or gray scale, or to mix them into one image. You can scan large images by automatically merging scanned strips with the Logitech AutoStitch feature. You can also use the scanner to scan text for OCR applications.

Sound Cards

A sound card is the one piece of multimedia hardware that makes the biggest difference—often for the least money. The street price of a 16-bit card (8-bit is only good for voice, not music) is less than $200.

The buyer, however, should beware. Most cards sold today are manufactured by companies experiencing rapid growth. Their ability to provide technical support, bug fixes, and technical innovation is constantly stretched to the limit. This is one of the prices you pay for moving exotic technology down to the consumer level.

I suggest you follow the following guidelines when purchasing a sound card:

➤ Be sure you obtain a money-back guarantee. There is some risk that even the popular boards will not work properly in your computer. Make sure you can take it back and either get a refund or exchange it for a different brand. The problem might not be with the card—the card and the computer simply might not work well together.

➤ Be prepared to work with the board when you get it. If you don't know hardware or Windows very well, find someone who does. This is useful if the company that makes your card cannot provide complete or timely technical support. I have seen this time after time—an otherwise perfectly functioning card is neglected because there is no one available to resolve a simple problem.

➤ Be prepared to shift your existing hardware around. You might have to try the new board in different slots or you might have to do without some of your existing goodies to use a consumer-grade sound card.

➤ Focus on the areas where solvable problems occur: hardware interrupts (does more than one card use an interrupt?), memory access (does more than one device use a DMA channel?), and high-memory conflicts (does the card map to RAM that other hardware or software needs or is using?).

Remember: If you experience any hassles, you only have to install the card one time. Once you get it figured out, you're on your way.

The big news in sound cards is the introduction of the new Yamaha OPL-4 synthesis chip. At press time, the chip design was complete, and the drivers were under development. You should see sound cards with the OPL-4 before the end of 1993. This new chip is well worth a close look. I listened to some pre-production samples, and I was very impressed. The sounds were much better than you are used to with FM synthesis. I could clearly make out the specific instruments being used. My big complaint about FM synthesis is that it has been nearly impossible to tell which instrument is supposed to be playing—it all sounds like beeps and boops. The OPL-4 changes that, giving us more realistic sound at the low end of the sound card market. Of course, there are still limitations; don't expect sound quality at the level of the Turtle Beach MultiSound, for example. However, the difference is very noticeable, and I definitely recommend that you look for a card with the new Yamaha chipset when you buy.

AdLib Gold 1000

Ad Lib Multimedia
350 Frankquet St.
Suite 80
Ste. Foy, PQ G1P4P3
418-656-8742
FAX: 418-656-1646

Ad Lib got the sound card revolution started, before Creative Labs stepped in and took over. Ad Lib is back with the Ad Lib Gold, a mid-level Wave and MIDI card that includes a variety of software packages, including a sample editor, a music box, and a play-along program. The retail price is $299.

Advanced Graphics Computer Technology UltraSound

UltraSound
Advanced Graphics Computer Technology
Vancouver, British Columbia, Canada
(604) 431-5020

This board supports Windows' Multimedia Extensions and is capable of performing on-card mixing of external CD audio, digital audio, synthesizers, a microphone, and line input. The cost is $199.

ASL Cyber Audio

Alpha Systems Labs
2361 McGaw Ave.
Irvine, CA 92714
800-998-3883
FAX: 714-252-0887

This card uses the Aria chipset to provide wavetable sound synthesis—a step up from the conventional FM synthesis found in the Sound Blaster.

It supports 16 MIDI channels, has 1M of sound samples on the card, 16-bit digital audio, and 44-kHz sampling. The card is bundled with speakers, headset microphone, and audio software.

ATI Stereo-F/X Multimedia Series

Stereo F/X
ATI Technologies, Inc.
3761 Victoria Park Avenue
Scarborough, Ontario, Canada M1W 3S2
416-756-0718
FAX: 416-756-0720
BBS 416-756-4591

Stereo-F/X is part of ATI's multimedia series. It includes an 11-voice FM synthesizer with stereo-generation technology that enhances existing mono applications as well as supporting full stereo sound.

The sound board provides CD-quality (16-bit) sound, at sampling rates up to 44 kHz, with a dynamic range of 48 dB. The onboard eight-watt power amplifier has twice the built-in power of many other cards for speakers or headphones.

Stereo-F/X comes with Windows and DOS applications for recording, playback, and editing of digital audio samples; it also includes full driver support for DOS and Windows, MIDI sound files for playback, and other sound utilities. The Stereo-F/X is compatible with Sound Blaster and AdLib.

It has the following features:

➤ Adjustable joystick speed setting

➤ Support for single or dual joysticks

➤ Optional MIDI expansion box with full MIDI In, MIDI Out, and MIDI Thru interfacing and the Sequencer Plus Jr. MIDI software

➤ Separate in and out stereo jacks

➤ Easy installation

Stereo-F/X runs on IBM PCs and compatibles, and it requires DOS 3.0 or higher. It supports IBM PC or AT buses, with an 8- or 16-bit slot.

ATI VGAStereo-F/X

VGAStereo-F/X
ATI Technologies, Inc.
3761 Victoria Park Avenue
Scarborough, Ontario, Canada M1W 3S2
416-756-0718
FAX: 416-756-0720
BBS 416-756-4591

ATI's Stereo-F/X is a multimedia sound card that combines multiple graphics and sound options, including Super-VGA graphics, audio in/out ports, a joystick port, a MIDI breakout box, and a Microsoft-compatible inport mouse (400 dpi).

It includes the same features as the Stereo-F/X 11-voice FM synthesizer and digital sound support, but this board is based on ATI's VGAWonder technology and is capable of displaying up to 32,768 high-resolution colors. ATI's Color Depth Enhancement increases the color depth by eight times, which displays up to 252,144 colors. It supports standard 1024 × 768 high-resolution graphics, with vertical refresh rates up to 76 Hz. Video memory can be expanded to 1M for full color support.

The board comes bundled with software drivers for sound and graphics. It includes Windows and DOS applications for recording, playback, and editing of digital audio samples, plus full software driver support for DOS and Windows, AutoCAD, and Lotus 1-2-3 Plus. The board is compatible with VGAWonder XL, Sound Blaster, and AdLib.

The board runs on IBM PCs and compatibles using DOS 3.0 or higher. The product is available in both 512K or 1M versions. It supports IBM PS/2 85xx analog monitors and multisync monitors compatible with their system requirements.

Covox Sound Master

Sound Master II Covox

This sound card is compatible with AdLib, MIDI, and most other internal PC sound systems. It includes Voice Master speech recognition software, which you can use to add voice commands to existing programs. It provides high-speed digital sampling and direct-to-RAM or direct-to-disk digital recording and playback software, and it includes MIDI cables and twin mini-speakers. The price is $149.

Creative Labs Sound Blaster Pro

> Sound Blaster Pro
> Creative Labs
> 1901 McCarthy Blvd.
> Milpitas, CA 95035
> 408-428-6600
> BBS: 408-428-6660

The Sound Blaster Pro is a descendent of the Sound Blaster, a PC standard. The Sound Blaster Pro is an 8-bit sound card that rates high on compatibility—other cards brag if they are compatible with it, not the other way around. Many DOS software packages support the Sound Blaster specifically, and most work fine with the Pro model.

The Sound Blaster Pro provides a mostly clear sound when playing waveform (.WAV) files. It includes a MIDI port, but MIDI sounds are created using FM synthesis. This is fine for games but is not capable of realistic instrument sounds. On some hardware, the Sound Blaster might pick up stray signals and make odd noises (it is difficult to eliminate them in the modest but significant number of cases where they occur). I tried the Sound Blaster in two different computers and had this problem in one of them, a Gateway 2000 386/33.

The Sound Blaster is the largest-selling sound card (thanks to a low price and software compatibility). The problems experienced by Sound Blaster are not unique to it; they apply to the entire class of consumer-level sound cards. However, I have had slightly more problems with Sound Blasters than with other brands. Broad appeal and high sales are, unfortunately, not a guarantee of performance.

This latest enhancement of the Sound Blaster board uses a proprietary SCSI interface to one of two CD-ROM drives made by Matsushita. This interface limits you to using the two drives that conform to Sound Blaster. Although neither drive is cutting edge stuff, performance meets MPC standards.

Creative Labs Sound Blaster 16

Sound Blaster 16
Creative Labs
1901 McCarthy Blvd.
Milpitas, CA 95035
408-428-6600
BBS: 408-428-6660

This card is the next step up from the Sound Blaster Pro. Its primary claim to fame is that it offers 16-bit sound capability. It also comes with an outstanding collection of software, including HSC Interactive, Software Toolworks Multimedia Encyclopedia, PC Animate Plus, Monologue for Windows, Voice Assist, and several sound utilities.

Creative Labs Sound Blaster 16 ASP

Sound Blaster 16 ASP
Creative Labs
1901 McCarthy Blvd.
Milpitas, CA 95035
408-428-6600
BBS: 408-428-6660

This card is the top of the Creative Labs sound card line. It includes the same software packages as the Sound Blaster 16. This card can be upgraded with the Wave Blaster for better MIDI sound capabilities. The ASP stands for Advanced Signal Processing and refers to a programmable chip on the card that is used to enhance performance and sound quality.

Creative Labs Wave Blaster

Wave Blaster
Creative Labs
1901 McCarthy Blvd.
Milpitas, CA 95035
408-428-6600
BBS: 408-428-6660

The Wave Blaster is a daughter card for the Sound Blaster 16 series of cards. It adds wavetable sound, a better-sounding method for providing MIDI sound support. It supports 32-note polyphony for multiple instruments, and contains 4M of sample sounds.

Digital Audio Labs CardD

CardD
Digital Audio Labs
14505 21st Avenue North
Plymouth, MN 55447
612-473-7626
FAX: 612-473-7915

The CardD is part of a complete hard disk-based recording system. It is designed as a high-quality system (note the sample rates it supports: 48 kHz, 44.1 kHz, and 32 kHz). The specs are excellent: adjustable input levels via jumper; dual 16-bit delta-sigma A/D converter with 64x oversampling; 20 Hz to 20 kHz response, plus or minus .25 dB; 92 dB dynamic range, and a total harmonic distortion of .003 percent at 1 kHz. Crosstalk is a minuscule –95dB at 1 kHz.

SCSI controllers that use bus mastering techniques, however, do not work with the CardD.

Included with the card is a sound editing program, the EdDitor. This non-destructive editor gives you complete control over the editing process. Some sound file editors edit the sound file right on the disk just as though it were a tape recorder. That is called *destructive editing* because it immediately overwrites the data. A non-destructive editor doesn't modify the original file until you save the changes.

You can add an optional accessory card, the I/O CardD, for digital input and output in the S/PDIF(IEC) format.

The CardD sells for $795; the EdDitor sells for $250; and the I/O CardD sells for $295.

Logitech Soundman 16

Logitech Inc.
6505 Kaiser Drive
Fremont, CA 94555
800-231-7717
510-795-8500
FaxBack: 800-245-0000

The Soundman 16 is basically the same physical unit as a Pro AudioSpectrum 16 from Media Vision.

Media Vision Pro Audio Studio 16

Pro AudioSpectrum 16
Media Vision
47221 Fremont Blvd.
Fremont, CA 94538
800-845-5870
FAX: 510-770-9592
BBS: 510-770-9522
CompuServe: GO MEDIAVISION

This unit is similar to the Pro AudioSpectrum 16, but it includes some additional software: voice recognition (Execuvoice), simplified installation, a waveform editor, and MIDI software.

Media Vision Pro AudioSpectrum 16

Pro AudioSpectrum 16
Media Vision
47221 Fremont Blvd.
Fremont, CA 94538
800-845-5870
FAX: 510-770-9592
BBS: 510-770-9522
CompuServe: GO MEDIAVISION

The Pro AudioSpectrum 16 (PAS16) sound card provides 16-bit and 44-kHz playback and recording capability. It delivers somewhat better sound than the Sound Blaster Pro (an 8-bit card) and is more flexible.

The PAS16 is actually two cards in one—it has its own 16-bit card and the capability to emulate Sound Blaster (not the Pro, however). With this feature you can play two MIDI and two waveform sounds at the same time. The card includes a 20-voice stereo FM synthesizer and a standard SCSI controller that can be used to add a CD-ROM to your system. Compared to other CD-ROM drives, the dual-speed SCSI NEC CD-ROM drive provides twice the throughput (300K/sec) and faster access (280 ms).

One good point about the Pro Audio Spectrum 16 is that it's tolerant of other boards in your system. I have used one with a MultiSound, a Roland SCC-1, and various video cards with no problems.

This card, however, can be difficult to install (unless you have the Version 1.2 software upgrade), and the procedures for adjusting microphone levels are complicated. The cost is $349.

Media Vision Pro AudioSpectrum Plus

Pro AudioSpectrum Plus
Media Vision
47221 Fremont Blvd.
Fremont, CA 94538
800-845-5870
FAX: 510-770-9592
BBS: 510-770-9522
CompuServe: GO MEDIAVISION

The Pro AudioSpectrum Plus is an 8-bit version of the Pro AudioSpectrum 16. It has many of the same features, except the CD-ROM is less expensive and has lower performance ratings.

Media Vision Pro AudioSpectrum Basic

> Pro AudioSpectrum Basic
> Media Vision
> 47221 Fremont Blvd.
> Fremont, CA 94538
> 800-845-5870
> FAX: 510-770-9592
> BBS: 510-770-9522
> CompuServe: GO MEDIAVISION

The Pro AudioSpectrum Basic is a low-cost (street price under $130) 16-bit audio card from Media Vision. It offers 16-bit sound at modest price and quality and is a good choice when budget is a primary concern.

Media Vision ThunderBoard

> ThunderBoard
> Media Vision
> 800-845-5870
> FAX: 510-770-9592

This is an inexpensive, entry-level 8-bit audio board for Windows that also contains an FM synthesizer. It is 100 percent compatible with Sound Blaster and AdLib applications, according to Media Vision.

The board has digitized audio playback (DAC) as much as 22 kHz, and audio recording (Digital Sampling). The ThunderBoard has a sampling rate of 2-22 kHz. The board supports real-time hardware compression and decompression of digitized audio. It includes the following features:

➤ DMA transfer

➤ Dynamic filtering for low noise sampling and playback

➤ 8-bit linear PCM

➤ Microphone input with automatic gain control (AGC)

➤ 11-voice FM music synthesizer

➤ Standard IBM joystick port

➤ 2-watt power amplifier (with built-in volume control)

ThunderBoard for Windows supports Sound Blaster, AdLib, and Windows 3.1 standards. It comes bundled with several Windows applications, including Lotus Sound, Sound Forge for Windows, At Your Service, Monologue for Windows, Master Tracks Pro Demo, and Pocket Recorder.

The ThunderBoard includes a Yamaha 3812 11-voice synthesizer with 8-bit FM DAC. It has a 2-watt (4 ohms) power amplifier, and a mini jack output connector.

The ThunderBoard runs on PC compatibles, including 486 machines, and requires a minimum of 1M of RAM, although 2M is recommended for best performance. The board requires DOS 3.0 or higher and Windows 3.1. It uses EGA, VGA, or SVGA graphics cards.

Microsoft Windows Sound System

Microsoft Corporation
One Microsoft Way
Redmond, WA 98052-6399
800-426-9400
206-882-8080
FAX: 206-93-MSFAX

This is a 16-bit add-in sound card (with a sampling rate up to 44 kHz) that comes with an innovative set of software applications. The Sound System includes a microphone and headphones. It also includes voice-recognition software that enables you to use voice commands to trigger macros in Windows programs.

The Windows Sound System works with the audio capabilities of the Windows 3.1 operating system to create audio applications, such as voice annotation, proofreading, and voice recognition. It uses Object Linking and Embedding (OLE) to integrate audio into mainstream business applications.

The Windows Sound System consists of the following three productivity applications:

Quick Recorder generates and adds voice annotations to documents and files. With it, you can
  ➤ Annotate figures in a spreadsheet to qualify underlying assump tions.

  ➤ Record comments when reviewing a wordprocessing document or spreadsheet.

➤ Attach explanatory comments to a file or e-mail message.

➤ Provide online instructions, such as in training.

➤ Combine messages from different sources, in each person's voice, to preserve the speaker's original tone and intent.

ProofReader provides audible proofing of numbers and common spreadsheet terms with a high-quality human voice. This feature eliminates the need to involve two people in the proofing process, saves time, and improves accuracy.

It is intended to check the accuracy of numerical data, and it comes with a standard dictionary of more than 170 financial terms. ProofReader works with Microsoft Excel 3.0 and 4.0, and Lotus 1-2-3 for Windows 3.1.

Voice Pilot enables you to execute commands by voice using the microphone that comes with the Windows Sound System. It enables you to navigate through the Windows operating system (and 15 Windows-based applications) via limited voice recognition. You can execute menu commands (Next Window), or commands in a word processing document (Cut and Paste).

The Voice Pilot also controls customizable commands, such as "Closing" or "Boilerplate," that enable you to insert standard text into a document upon command. Although the Voice Pilot can understand most people's speech, it has a training mode that enables you to customize words using different accents or pronunciations. This enables you to create individual profiles for several users.

The Windows Sound System includes a Setup utility as well as several utilities that simplify working with audio, including an excellent Guided Tour, which is an interactive tutorial for the Windows Sound System.

The Sound System requires at least a 386SX with a 16-MHz processor, a minimum of 2M of RAM, a VGA display, and Windows 3.1.

The add-in sound board is not Sound Blaster compatible but is being promoted as a "business audio" card. The software enables you to associate icons with sounds and comes with a library of both sounds and icons. The cost is $289; with Windows 3.1, $349.

Omni Labs AudioMaster

AudioMaster
Omni Labs, Inc.
Irwindale, CA
818-813-2630

This sound board offers Windows and DOS interfaces and utilities for recording, playing, and editing digitized audio files. The AudioMaster also includes an interface for playing audio CDs. The board can be upgraded to offer compatibility with Creative Labs' Sound Blaster sound card with an add-on module that sells for $69.95. Other upgrades include a $99.95 RAM expansion module and a CD-ROM interface module that starts at $69.95. The board is available through distributors and retailers. This unit costs $299.

Orchid SoundWave 32

Orchid Technology
45365 Northport Loop West
Fremont, CA 94538
800-7-ORCHID
FAX: 510-490-9312

The SoundWave 32 adds to the growing list of high-end audio cards, a territory formerly held alone by the Turtle Beach MultiSound. It offers 8- and 16-bit sampling, an 85 dB signal-to-noise ratio, and 8 megabits of wavetable sound samples. It offers outstanding compatibility, including Sound Blaster, AdLib, Windows Sound System, Roland MPU-401 MIDI interface, General MIDI, Roland MT-32, and MPC level 1 and 2 support.

It also includes some nice touches, such as automatic gain control on the microphone input, a joystick/MIDI port, CD-ROM interface, and combination compatibility modes. The combo modes offered include Sound Blaster/MT-32 for game support, Sound Blaster/General MIDI for Windows support, and MPU-401/General MIDI for musical applications.

The card includes speakers and a microphone.

Roland RAP-10/AT Audio Producer

RAP-10/AT Audio Producer
Roland Corporation US
7200 Dominion Circle
Los Angeles, CA 90040-3647
213-685-5141
FAX: 213-722-0911

Roland has joined the mainstream of PC multimedia sound cards by combining the SCC-1, a very good MIDI card, with 16-bit 44kHz digital audio capability. I have used the SCC-1 card and really like it (see the next section). The addition of .WAV file support makes this card well worth a look. I haven't had the chance to try one, so I cannot speak for its actual performance, but based on the quality of other Roland products I would expect high quality.

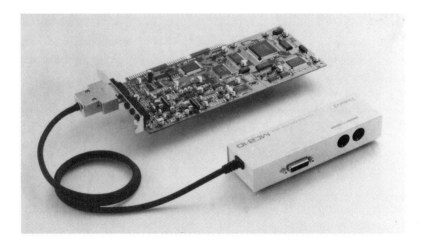

Figure 12.4. *The combination of the Roland RAP-10 and MCB-10 provides solid MIDI support, including excellent sound and mulimedia flexibility.*

This card is a good choice if you are at all serious about MIDI in your work, because it comes with the Audio Producer software package, which enables you to combine up to 16 MIDI tracks with up to two tracks of digital audio. The list price is $599, with an optional MIDI connector, the MCB-10, which lists at $120.

Roland SCC-1 GS Sound Card

SCC-1 GS
Roland Corporation US
7200 Dominion Circle
Los Angeles, CA 90040-3647
213-685-5141
FAX: 213-722-0911

The SCC-1 GS sound card (a good value) is a sound synthesizer and MIDI interface for IBM-compatible personal computers. The SCC-1 supports Roland's GS format, which is a superset of the General MIDI standard endorsed by Microsoft for Windows and MPC applications. These standards enable the SCC-1 to consistently and accurately play back music created on any General MIDI system. I used this card in two different machines, and I was very happy with the realistic sounds it created.

The SCC-1 offers the following features:

➤ 317 acoustic and electronic instrument sounds, plus nine separate drum sets.

➤ On-board digital reverb/delay and chorus.

➤ The capability to simultaneously produce sounds from as many as 16 different individual and ensemble instruments.

➤ 24-voice polyphony.

➤ 128 Tones that simulate factory presets of the MT-32, CM-32L, LAPC-1, and LA section of the CM-64. Using MT-32 Emulation utility software (included with the sound card), you can play back most song data created for the Roland MT-32, LAPC-1, or CM-32L with no modification.

The SCC-1 includes an MPU-401-compatible MIDI interface, which means you can immediately use all available MPU-401-compatible software. Windows 3.1 comes with a driver for the MPU-401 interface; you can use the SCC-1 in Windows just by installing the driver. The cost is $499.

Sigma WinStorm

WinStorm
Sigma Designs, Inc.
Fremont, CA
510-770-0100

The WinStorm sound card combines 16-bit stereo sound with Windows video-acceleration technology. The board includes a Yamaha Corp. YMF262 synthesizer chip for MIDI (FM synthesis), a SCSI port for a CD-ROM drive, joystick support, and dynamic filtering capability up to 60 kHz. It also includes an AVGA 3/5422 graphics accelerator chip from Cirrus Logic that provides accelerated 24-bit color video. The board is available through various distributors. This unit costs $429.

MultiSound

MultiSound
Turtle Beach Systems
Cyber Center, Unit 33
1600 Pennsylvania Ave.
York, PA 17404
714-843-6916
FAX: 717-854-8319
CompuServe: GO MULTIVEN

MultiSound, one of the best sound cards available, is a high-resolution, 16-bit multimedia sound card. It probably provides the cleanest sounds of any sound card available today. Unlike other MPC sound output cards that use FM Synthesis, MultiSound uses 126 CD-quality, 16-bit, digital samples of real instruments (these samples are stored in ROM chips on MultiSound). MIDI inputs and outputs are also on-board, so MultiSound can trigger, or have its internal sounds triggered by, an external MIDI device. These are the card's features and product specifications:

1. Digital Audio:

   ➤ Sample rates of 44.1 kHz, 22.05 kHz, and 11.025 kHz

   ➤ 16- and 8-bit resolution

   ➤ Stereo or mono audio channels

➤ Audio converters:

A/D: 64x oversampled sigma-delta 16-bit

D/A: 8x interpolating filter

64x oversampled sigma-delta, 18-bit

2. Stereo Mixer:

➤ Inputs—digital audio, MIDI synthesizer line in, Auxiliary line in (CD-ROM audio)

➤ Auxiliary in can be connected internally for internal CD-ROM drives

3. MIDI Synthesizer:

➤ Wavetable playback synthesis method

➤ Wavetable digital audio (4M of 16-bit audio)

➤ 126 Wavetable instruments

➤ 384 preset storage

➤ MIDI channels (16 channels, individual volume and stereo pan by channel)

➤ 32 simultaneous voices

➤ 100 percent compatibility with E-mu Proteus 1/XR synthesizer and with General MIDI MPC standard

4. MIDI Interface (requires optional connector):

➤ Connections are MIDI In, MIDI Out, and MIDI Thru

5. Digital Signal Processor:

➤ Speed: 20 million instructions per second (MIPS)

➤ Type: Motorola DSP-56001

➤ Internal data width: 24 bits

6. Joystick port that is compatible with all PC joysticks

7. 16-bit bus interface

8. Full-size AT style card

9. Audio Performance:

➤ Signal-to-noise
–91 dB (A weighted)
–87 dB (unweighted)

➤ Total harmonic distortion
<.01 percent (A weighted)
<.02 percent (unweighted)

➤ Phase response
+0.5°

➤ Stereo Crosstalk
100 Hz –75 dBV
1 kHz –73 dBV
10 kHz –58 dBV

➤ IM Distortion < .01 percent

➤ Frequency Response
DC-19 kHz +0.5 dB
DC-20 kHz +0/–3 dB

One disadvantage of the board is that it only plays back .WAV files at the standard 11-kHz, 22-kHz, or 44-kHz rates. The list price is now $599, making this an exceptional value.

MultiSound Tahiti

Turtle Beach Systems
1600 Pennsylvania Avenue
York, PA 17404
717-843-6916
FAX: 717-854-8319

MultiSound Tahiti is a digital audio recording card; basically, it is a MultiSound card without a MIDI synthesizer. There is a connector for an optional MIDI synthesizer, like Creative Labs' Wave Blaster or other compatibles. The card supports 44.1-kHz, 22.05-kHz, and 11.025-kHz sample rates. The Tahiti features the Motorola 56001 DSP chip, which provides 20 MIPS of processing power.

Turtle Beach Maui

Turtle Beach Systems
52 Grumbacher Road
York, PA 17402
717-767-0200
FAX: 717-767-6033

Turtle Beach Maui is a wavetable synthesizer upgrade. Maui adds 24 voices using digital recordings of real instruments. Turtle Beach's SampleStore technology offers 256K of sample RAM, which is upgradable to 8M. The synthesizer upgrade gives you 128 General MIDI instruments, and you can use the extra memory to create your own instruments. Maui is compatible with Roland's MPU-401, General MIDI, and with Creative Labs' Wave Blaster Connector.

Portable Sound

The search for a portable sound device has been very frustrating. In the first edition, I made no recommendation—there just wasn't anything I was happy with. Every unit involved too many compromises to be acceptable for real-life, day-in-day-out, on-the-road use.

This time, there is a unit that I feel is ready to hit the road: the Port-able Sound Plus from DSP Solutions. It's the first item in this section, so let's get right to it.

DSP Port-able Sound Plus

Port-able Sound Plus
DSP Solutions
2464 Embarcadero Way
Palo Alto, CA 94303
415-494-8086
FAX: 415-494-8114

This is my personal choice for portable sound. It is the only unit that really performs at a professional level via the parallel port of your computer. It supports 16-bit sound, has a sleek design, and delivers solid, reliable performance. You can set this unit up with confidence for presentations.

The package includes two pieces of hardware. One is a hinged device that connects to your parallel port, and the other is a speaker unit that has decent volume and sound quality. It also includes a microphone that was surprisingly good. I would be comfortable using the built-in microphone for general-purpose tasks, but if I were creating a major presentation, I would probably rely on a separate, quality microphone.

I have tried numerous portable sound devices, and this is the best I've seen. And I'm not alone in that opinion; I've heard from plenty of happy customers on CompuServe. If you are serious about portable multimedia, this is worth a close look.

InterActive SoundXchange Model A

InterActive, Inc.
204 N. Main
Humboldt, SD 57035
800-292-2112

The SoundXchange is an external sound device that connects to an internal sound card. It provides sound input and output through a built-in amplified speaker, microphone, handset, headset jack, and volume control. It mounts on the side of the computer monitor for easy access. The cost is $149.

Logitech AudioMan

Logitech Inc.
6505 Kaiser Drive
Fremont, CA 94555
800-231-7717
510-795-8500
FaxBack: 800-245-0000

AudioMan is a compact portable digital audio tool for Windows that enables you to add spoken messages, sound effects, and music to your presentations, spreadsheets, e-mail and other work. AudioMan has an internal speaker and microphone so you can do sound recording and playback in the field. Logitech was kind enough to send me a unit for review. It was easy to set up, and is probably the only acceptable low-cost portable sound device. The sound quality is not 16-bit, however, so it might not meet your needs in demanding situations. However, if you need a general-purpose portable audio solution, the AudioMan can handle the job. If you need top quality, look into the Port-able Sound Plus from DSP Solutions. However, quality does cost more; the AudioMan is the affordable solution.

Media Vision Audio Port

Audio Port
Media Vision
47221 Fremont Blvd.
Fremont, CA 94538
800-845-5870
FAX: 510-770-9592
BBS: 510-770-9522
CompuServe: GO MEDIAVISION

The Audio Port is a peripheral sound device that connects to your parallel port. Although it is a convenient means of producing sound, it does not produce comparable sound quality to that found in internal audio boards. If you need to produce sound on a portable computer without any internal slots, however, such an external unit is your only choice.

Audio Port takes advantage of Media Vision's proprietary Transportable Sound technology that provides a fully integrated audio module small enough to fit in your shirt pocket. You can connect this mobile sound module to any IBM PC/AT, PS/2, or Notebook machine with a parallel port. It is flexible enough to run on batteries (four AAA), a +6V battery eliminator for extended use, or the AC power adapter (included). Overall, I found the AudioPort to be somewhat problematic. Performance wasn't bad, but I had problems with the drivers spontaneously deinstalling themselves when I ran Windows without the Audio Port connected to the computer.

The Audio Port has been specifically engineered and optimized for Windows 3.1. One of its deficits is that Audio Port does not include pass-through printer support—you have to remove it to use your printer. The cost is $199.

Video Associates MicroKey/AudioPort

MicroKey/AudioPort
Video Associates Labs
4926 Spicewood Springs Road
Austin, TX 78759
800-331-0547
512-346-5781
FAX: 512-346-9407

The MicroKey/AudioPort plugs into the parallel printer port of your PC desktop, IBM PS/2, laptop, or notebook. You can add a microphone, a powered speaker, or headphones to add audio support for DOS and Windows presentations. This package offers solid quality, but if you will be using video files in your presentations, you'll find that it does not support them properly—the sound has a pronounced tendency to skip. Otherwise, this is a solid unit.

By the way—note that it has the same name as the unit from Media Vision. These are completely different products.

Monitors for Multimedia

Without a good monitor, multimedia images aren't crisp, colors aren't true, and edges aren't well-defined. For presentations, a large monitor and high resolution are a must.

MAG MX17F

MAG Innovision
4392 Corporate Center Drive
Los Alamitos, CA 90720
800-827-3998
714-827-3998
FAX: 714-827-5522

This 17-inch monitor is a flat, square tube featuring Invar Shadow Mask technology. The MX17F dynamic focus circuitry maintains the focus across the screen. It provides up to 1280×1024 non-interlaced high resolution.

Nanao F550i

Nanao F550i
Nanao USA Corporation
23535 Telo Ave.
Torrance, CA 90505
800-800-5202
310-325-5202
FAX: 310-530-1679

The Nanao FLEXSCAN F550i, my choice as one of the best in its class, is a 17-inch monitor that has a 0.28-mm dot-pitch and a non-glare screen. The unit weighs 47 pounds and comes with a tile-and-swivel base, a one-year parts-and-labor warranty, and toll-free technical support. The horizontal scanning frequency for the F550i ranges from 30 to 65 kHz, with a vertical frequency of 55 to 90 Hz, which complies with VESA standards. It has nine factory preset selections and 23 user-definable selections. The F550i is compatible with several modes: VGA, Super-VGA, 8514/A. It has flicker-free, high-resolution, 1024×768 non-interlaced mode, and Macintosh 640×480, up to 1280×1024 non-interlaced mode. This is the model of monitor I use, and I am extremely happy with it. This unit costs $1,749.

Also available are the 17-inch FLEXSCAN T560i (with flicker-free 1280×1024 ultra-high resolution, and 0.26-mm trio pitch) and the T660i FLEXSCAN 20-inch screen. These T-series monitors conform to Swedish MPR II and TCO guidelines as well as VLF and ELF emission standards. Nanao monitors have an intelligent front control panel that can memorize settings for later recall.

NEC 4FG Monitor

NEC MultiSync 4FG Monitor
NEC Corp.
415-960-6000
800-NEC-INFO

This 15-inch monitor has a flat, square, high-contrast, anti-static screen. The 4FG has a 0.28-mm trio dot pitch and provides 36 percent more active display area than 14-inch monitors. It includes a tilt-and-swivel base that enables you to adjust the monitor. Although the anti-static screen coating is designed to eliminate dust attraction, it causes glare on the tube (you can resolve this problem by purchasing a NEC lens). The unit costs $949. It is available at Computer Discount Warehouse, a mail-order company, for $739.

NEC 5FG Monitor

NEC MultiSync 5FG Monitor
NEC Corp.
415-960-6000
800-NEC-INFO

This 17-inch monitor has a flat, square, high-contrast, anti-static screen. Another of my best-in-its-class choices, the 5FG is 20 percent brighter than most conventional monitors, and it provides 19 percent more active display area than 16-inch monitors. It includes a tilt-and-swivel base and is available at Computer Discount Warehouse, a mail-order company, for $1,329.50.

NEC 6FG Monitor

NEC MultiSync 6FG Monitor
NEC Corp.
415-960-6000
800-NEC-INFO

This 21-inch monitor has a flat, square, high-contrast, anti-static screen. The 6FG is 20 percent brighter than most conventional monitors and provides 24 percent more active display area than 20-inch monitors. It includes a tilt-and-swivel base and is available at Computer Discount Warehouse, a mail-order company, for $2,369.50.

Proxima Corp ColorWorks sx

ColorWorks sx
Proxima Corp.
6610 Nancy Ridge Dr.
San Diego, CA 92121
(619) 457-5500

The ColorWorks sx is a six-pound LCD overhead projection panel. The 9-inch display can produce up to 24,389 colors. The ColorWorks sx is compatible with Proxima's Cyclops interactive pointer system, which enables you to use either a Cyclops wand or a laser pointer when you use this panel to display presentation graphics software. This unit costs $3,995.

Samsung

Samsung CSA7571

Samsung offers a 17-inch multiscan color monitor with a non-glare screen. It supports 1024 × 768 maximum resolution with 0.31mm dot pitch and provides VGA/Super and VGA compatibility. It accepts Analog/TTL signal input and comes with a one-year warranty. This unit costs $789.92.

Sony CPD-1604S

Sony Corporation of America
Computer Peripherals Products Company
655 River Oaks Parkway
San Jose, CA 95134
(408) 432-0190

This 17-inch multiscan monitor has a 0.25-mm dot pitch that displays 1024 × 768 resolution. It supports Super VGA, VGA, and 8514/A modes. The Multiscan monitor supports a variable scan frequency of 30 to 57 kHz. It includes a VGA cable and a tilt-swivel stand. This unit costs $995.42.

Super VGA Video Boards

As I have stated many times elsewhere, multimedia works best at higher resolutions. The cost of high-resolution cards has fallen to the point where you can buy a decent card for less than $200. The more expensive cards add speed and clarity that might well be worth the cost for critical applications.

#9GXi

#9GXi
Number Nine Computer Corporation
18 Hartwell Ave.
Lexington, MA 02173
800-GET-NINE
617-674-0009
FAX: 617-674-2919
BBS: 617-862-7502 (1200-9600 bps, N,8,1)

Designed to drive large monitors, the #9GXi displays effectively at high magnifications. The graphics coprocessor enables you to display 16.7 million colors at 1024×768 resolution and 65,000 colors at 1280×1024 and 1152×870 at a 72-Hz refresh rate.

A Lite version is also available, as well as the #9GXe, which uses the S3 chipset.

#9GXiTC

#9GXiTC
Number Nine Computer Corporation
18 Hartwell Ave.
Lexington, MA 02173
800-GET-NINE
617-674-0009
FAX: 617-674-2919
BBS: 617-862-7502 (1200–9600 bps, N,8,1)

The #9GXiTC is a true-color board with two video ports that are selectable by a dip switch. One port directs both high-resolution and standard VGA signals through a single port. The other port supports a dual-monitor environment. The board is designed to work with a standard VGA board or VGA display built into a motherboard.

The #9GXiTC is based on a 40-MHz TMS34020 coprocessor, and it has 4M of VRAM and 1M of DRAM. It also includes a socket for a TI floating-point unit. This unit costs $2,295.

ATI Graphics Ultra

Graphics Ultra
ATI Technologies, Inc.
3761 Victoria Park Avenue
Scarborough, Ontario, Canada M1W 3S2
416-756-0718
FAX: 416-746-0720

The Ultra's VRAM capabilities put it among the fastest standard Windows accelerator cards. This card uses the 8514 proprietary technology but provides the capability of switching between 8514/A and VGA modes.

The Graphics Ultra displays 1024 × 768 graphics non-interlaced and 1280 × 1024 interlaced resolution. It comes with a bus mouse port, Crystal Fonts that deliver WYSIWIG, and an easy-to-use installation program. Its one weakness is that it does not support more than 256 colors. With 1024K of video memory, the cost is $699.

ATI Graphics Ultra Pro

This card creates a new price/performance standard for Windows accelerator cards. With a score of 25 million WINMARKs, it is easily the fastest windows video card on the market—at least for now.

I use this card in my main machine, a 486/66 DX2 from Gateway. I have tried other cards in the same computer, and I can attest to the performance of the Ultra Pro. Windows snap onto the screen (there are almost no visible signs of being painted piece by piece). This card features

➤ Mach32 graphics accelerator, which includes hardware support for BitBlt, line draw, polygon fill, clipping, a hardware cursor, and linear memory addressing

➤ VRAM memory for maximum performance gain

➤ Non-interlaced 1280 × 1024 (with 2M of VRAM)

➤ Up to 65,000 colors at 1024 × 768

➤ 76-Hz vertical refresh rate at high resolutions

➤ Built-in acceleration for AVI

➤ Zero wait-state VGA

➤ Bundled with AutoCAD display-list driver from UltraCAD

➤ Support for dual-monitor operation

➤ Integrated mouse port

ATI Graphics Ultra+

Another card in the mach32 series, this one focuses on providing 24-bit color support. Although not quite as fast as the ATI Graphics Ultra Pro, it has a WINMARK score of 21 million—still an outstanding score. This board is a good choice if the Ultra Pro is beyond your budget.

The 24-bit color is supported for both 640×480 and 800×600 modes, although the higher resolution support is only available on the 2M version. See the ATI Graphics Ultra Pro for more information.

ATI Vantage

Graphics Vantage
ATI Technologies, Inc.
3761 Victoria Park Ave.
Scarborough, Ontario, Canada M1W 3S2
416-756-0718
FAX: 416-756-0720
BBS: 416-756-4591

This card uses the same accelerator chip as the Graphics Ultra (which is ATI's proprietary mach8 accelerator chip), but because it is based on the slower (and less expensive) DRAM, it is not as fast. It includes a three-button 400-dpi (dots per inch) mouse that uses the bus port on the adapter. The 1M version supports $1280 \times 1024 \times 16$ color interlaced and 1024×768 non-interlaced resolution. It has a 76-Hz refresh rate, but it shares the same flaw as the Ultra: no support for high-color modes (Hi-Color RAMDAC). Its performance was good in Corel tests but poor in word processing tests. With 1024K, the cost is $349; with 512K, the cost is $299.

Diamond SpeedStar 24X

SpeedStar 24X
Diamond Computer Systems, Inc.
532 Mercury Dr.
Sunnyvale, CA 94086
408-736-2000
FAX: 408-730-5750
BBS: 408-730-1100

This graphics card replaces its predecessor, the SpeedStar. It offers 16.7 million colors in 640×480 mode and monitor resolution up to 1280×1024. Using Diamond's specially tuned drivers, the card provides increased performance over the SpeedStar. Video memory limits 24-bit true-color support to 640×480-mode. Running Windows, the board supports resolutions from 640×480 to 1280×1024. Based on the Western Digital WD90C31 graphics accelerator chip, the slot-length card uses 1M of 70-nanosecond DRAM video memory. Street prices are currently less than $200, making this a good value.

Diamond recently introduced a Pro version of the SpeedStar; review copies were not available at press time.

Diamond Stealth VRAM

Stealth VRAM
Diamond Computer Systems, Inc.
532 Mercury Dr.
Sunnyvale, CA 94086
408-736-2000
FAX: 408-730-5750
BBS: 408-730-1100

This video acceleration board uses an S3-based 86C911 chip and 15-bit Sierra Hi-Color RAMDAC. It is a half-slot card with 1M of VRAM that speeds up Windows applications. It generally ranks fastest in overall performance speed tests and offers a large selection of video modes. With 1024K, the cost is $445.

Use caution with this and other cards from Diamond—make sure you have the very latest video drivers if you plan to work with Video for Windows.

Focus GUI-6000

GUI-6000
Focus Information Systems, Inc.
4046 Clipper Ct.
Fremont, CA 94538
510-657-2845
FAX: 410 657-2158
BBS: 510-657-9451

The GUI-6000 video board is based on the S3 accelerator chip. This board provides good speed performance. It is a half-slot 1M card with a Sierra 16-bit Hi-Color RAMDAC that supports 640 × 480 resolution. It provides above-average support for 16-bit color, displays more than 64,000 colors, and includes the newest 86C924 acceleration chip. With 1024K, the cost is $309.

Hercules Chrome

Chrome
Hercules Computer Technology
3839 Spinnaker Ct.
Fremont, CA 94538
800-532-0600
510-623-6030
FAX: 520-540-6621

This 8-bit video card offers 24-bit graphics with 16.7 million colors. The Chrome is a true-color board that comes in three models based on a TMS34020 coprocessor. All of the Chrome models support 1024 × 768 display, but the maximum resolution for each board is 1152 × 900. The refresh rate is 90 Hz. The cost is from $1,695 to $2,695 (based on model and on-board RAM).

Hercules Gold 16+1

Graphics Station Gold 16+1
Hercules Computer Technology
3839 Spinnaker Ct.
Fremont, CA 94538
800-767-2443
FAX: 520-540-6621

This 15-bit video card supports 32,768 colors and displays at up to 75 MHz and 16.7 million colors within 3-D Studio and 2,546 colors in AutoCAD. The card is based on a 60-MHz TI TMS34010 graphics coprocessor. The Graphics Station Gold card is optimized to increase performance on vector-based graphics packages such as CorelDRAW! or other programs that heavily utilize images. Unfortunately, performance enhancement is much less on Windows applications that are more text-intensive.

Hercules Graphite, Graphite VL

Hercules Graphite, Graphite VL
Hercules Computer Technology
3839 Spinnaker Ct.
Fremont, CA 94538
800-767-2443
FAX: (520) 540-6621

These are Windows accelerator cards that provide up to 1280 × 1024 Windows resolution (with 2M of VRAM). 24-bit True color is available at up to 800 × 600. The product includes menu-driven installation, Windows drivers, and display tuning capabilities.

The VL version is a VESA local bus card, for additional graphics speed.

Matrox Impression/Impression Pro

Matrox Electronic Systems, Inc.
1055 St. Regis Blvd.
Dorval, Quebec, Canada, H9P 2T4
514-685-2630
FAX: 514-685-2853
BBS: 514-685-6008 (300–9600 bps, N,8,1)

The Impression series includes some of the first 64-bit graphics cards. The series offers outstanding 24-bit graphics performance in Windows. It uses the MGA graphics card architecture, which effectively doubles the bandwidth for PC video.

The Impression is one hot card, and you should expect to pay a higher-than-average price for the heat. For example, the VL version comes with up to 4.5M of video RAM and supports 24-bit video at resolutions up to 1280 × 1024. Even at this large screen size, you can expect 60-Hz to 74-Hz refresh rates and 25 million WINMARKs (Version 3.11). If you work with CAD software, you can add an additional 4M of DRAM to provide high-resolution CAD scaling and display.

The drivers for the card support mode-switching without rebooting, a 1600 × 1200 virtual desktop, hotkey driven pan and zoom as well as anti-aliased font technology.

This is a family of cards, with several levels of price and performance, memory ranges from 3M to 4M of VRAM, and 24-bit support at various resolutions. For less demanding needs, Matrox offers the MGA Ultima line, with 1M to 2M of memory. The Pro line supports only 24-bit color (no falling back to 8-bit or 16-bit modes for games or any other software that might require it). The Pro units are ideal for anyone who works regularly in true color (24-bit) and requires maximum image size (up to 1280x1024 in 24-bit mode) and fast performance.

Multimedia support includes live video input with the optional Mavel Broadcast Quality Video Input and Windowing Controller, and the Quality Video Encoder for output to tape.

Matrox also offers a full line of professional video products for broadcast work, including Matrox Studio, the Illuminator Pro, and the Personal Producer.

Orchid Celsius

Orchid Celsius
Orchid Technology
45365 Northport Loop West
Fremont, CA 94538
510-683-0300
FAX: 510-490-9312

This is a new high-end video card from Orchid. It offers up to 90-Hz refresh rates, giving you a rock steady image. It also supports 24-bit color at a number of resolutions, and a local bus version is available. Performance is about 15 percent faster than Orchid Technology's Fahrenheit board.

Orchid Fahrenheit VA

Fahrenheit VA
Orchid Technology
45365 Northport Loop West
Fremont, CA 94538
510-683-0300
FAX: 510-490-9312

The Fahrenheit VA is a Windows accelerator board that provides 24-bit color at up to 1024 × 768 resolution. The board uses Orchid Technology's proprietary software drivers. The *VA* stands for *voice annotation*. The board comes with software that will work with any sound card. A 1M version of the board sells for $299. A local bus version is available.

Quickpath Cyclone XGi

Cyclone XGi
Quickpath Systems, Inc.
46723 Fremont Blvd.
Fremont, CA 94538
800-995-8828

This is a Windows accelerator board that has excellent performance, sharp color resolution, and an affordable price of $279.

Radius MultiView 24

MultiView 24
Radius, Inc.
1710 Fortune Dr.
San Jose, CA 95131
408-434-1010
FAX: 408-434-6437
BBS: 408-954-1689 (1200/2400 bps, N,8,1)

The MultiView 24 is a true-color board that works with (rather than replaces) a VGA card. It is based on three Western Digital 8514/A coprocessors and a custom ASIC. Because the MultiView supports the 8514/A standard, it is incompatible with VGA boards based on the same standard (for example, ATI 8514/Ultra or Paradise 8514/A Plus). It supports a Windows high-resolution display of 1024 × 768. This unit, another hot performer, costs $1,499.

VidTech WinMax

WinMax
VidTech Micro Systems, Inc.
1701-93rd Lane Northeast
Minneapolis, MN 55434
800-752-8033
FAX: 612-785-7963
BBS: 612-780-3577

The WinMax board uses the Weitek 5186 acceleration chip, and it is optimized for basic business applications such as WinWord and Excel. It supports 256 colors at 1024 × 768 × 8-bit resolution in both interlaced and non-interlaced modes. The board includes a Sierra 15-bit Hi-Color RAMDAC that supports 32,768 colors at 800 × 600 resolution. Although performance on text-intensive applications is excellent, it performs poorly on image-intensive tasks. With 1024K, the cost is $249; with 512K, the cost is $199.

Western Digital Paradise

Paradise
Western Digital Corporation
8105 Irvine Center Dr.
Irvine, CA 92718
800-832-4778
FAX: 714-932-6324
BBS: 714-753-1234

This unit runs under Windows in 15-bit color, offers above-average performance with products like Corel, and uses Western Digital's WD90C31 accelerator chip (with a 15-bit Hi-Color RAMDAC that supports 32,768 colors at 800 × 600 resolution). The board is capable of supporting 1280 × 1024 resolution in 16 colors, and it provides extremely crisp displays in 1024 × 768 mode. Unfortunately, this board has poor performance ratings for word processing packages.

NTSC and Video Capture Boards

These boards enable you to work with the NTSC video signals associated with VCRs, camcorders, and televisions. There are several different kinds of boards:

➤ NTSC input (NTSC to VGA)

➤ NTSC output (VGA to NTSC)

➤ Internal cards

➤ External converters

NTSC input is used for everything from watching television in a window on your monitor to recording digital video. NTSC output is used for recording animations to videotape, for presentations, and for creative video production.

Like sound boards, NTSC video boards have a fairly strict price/performance curve: the more you pay, the more likely you are to get good results.

ADDA AVer VGA Producer

> ADDA VGA-AVer
> ADDA Technologies, Inc.
> 4801 Warm Springs Blvd., #105
> Fremont, CA 94539
> 510-770-9899
> FAX: 510-623-1803

This is a high-end video production board that allows you to do multi-source video, video effects, and titling on your PC. It features:

➤ 4 source video input with S-Video and composite in and out

➤ Hardware fade and mix

➤ Genlocking

➤ Anti-flicker filter

➤ DVE moves, including shuffle, ping-pong, and sling shot.

➤ Gradient screens, boxes, and titles

➤ Scalable video windows

➤ Multiple file format support, including .pcx, .bmp, and .tga.

➤ Special effects include posterizing, colorizing, and strobe.

➤ Titling features include timed pages, sprite object movement, gradients, image import, shadowing, and transparency.

Cost is $1,900.

ADDA AVer 1000-V

ADDA AVer 1000-V
ADDA Technologies, Inc.
4801 Warm Springs Blvd., #105
Fremont, CA 94539
510-770-9899
FAX: 510-623-1803

This is a VGA to video converter card (also known as an encoder), with a built-in VGA chip (the Tseng Labs ET-4000). It is used to output computer graphics to videotape. The board offers the following features:

➤ All standard video formats are supported, including S-Video, composite, RGB and SCART RGB.

➤ Supports VGA (640x480) for NTSC output, and up to 800x600 for PAL output.

➤ Built-in flicker reduction circuitry.

➤ Overscan and underscan control.

➤ Interlaced and non-interlaced capabilities.

➤ You can put up to 16 cards in one machine for multi-channel support.

➤ Works in conjunction with the AVer 2000 series for complete video solution.

ADDA AVer 2000

ADDA AVer 1000-V
ADDA Technologies, Inc.
4801 Warm Springs Blvd., #105
Fremont, CA 94539
510-770-9899
FAX: 510-623-1803

This is an overlay video board—it puts live video onto your PC monitor. It supports up to 3 source inputs, and will capture images in real time (single frames). It supports most popular file formats, including .bmp, .pcx, .tga, etc.

The board can be controlled via a DOS software driver to give you programmatic control over capture. It can be combined with the AVer 1000 for a complete video input, output, and frame grabber solution.

ADDA AVer 2000 Pro

ADDA AVer 1000-V
ADDA Technologies, Inc.
4801 Warm Springs Blvd., #105
Fremont, CA 94539
510-770-9899
FAX: 510-623-1803

This is an upgraded version of the AVer 2000 card. It adds support for SuperVGA resolutions up to 800x600 for NTSC video. It also adds audio input and output, with volume and stereo balance controlled in software. It comes with Windows utilties and developer software for custom applications.

ADDA AVerKey

ADDA AVerKey
ADDA Technologies, Inc.
4801 Warm Springs Blvd., #105
Fremont, CA 94539
510-770-9899
FAX: 510-623-1803

This is a portable VGA to video converter—a small black box that can be connected to the VGA output of any computer, including laptops, to convert the VGA signal for use on NTSC or PAL video monitors. The unit includes the following features:

➤ Anti-flicker filter

➤ Windows support

➤ Supports 640x480 at any color resolution

➤ Simultaneous display on both the video monitor and the computer monitor

➤ Brightness control

➤ Unsupported video modes are automatically blanked on the video monitor.

The AVerKey outputs S-Video, composite video, and Video RGB.

ADDA VGA-AVer

ADDA VGA-AVer
ADDA Technologies, Inc.
4801 Warm Springs Blvd., #105
Fremont, CA 94539
510-770-9899
FAX: 510-623-1803

The ADDA VGA-AVer is an 8-bit ISA board with a VGA pass-through cable, a speaker connector cable, DOS control utilities, and a Video Titler. This relatively inexpensive card works with your PC's VGA card to perform VGA-to-NTSC conversion functions. It has average performance but does not include an anti-flicker filter. The board includes the capability to overlay a computer display onto video input.

The board fits into an 8-bit slot and works with any standard VGA adapter. It comes with video input and output jacks for composition video, but you can purchase an add-on for S-video and RGB for $75. The board requires a standard VGA or multiscanning monitor, an NTSC video monitor, and a VGA or Super VGA board. This unit costs $645.

Aitech ProPC/TV

> ProPC/TV
> Aitech International Corp
> 830 Hillview Ct., #145
> Milpitas, CA 95035
> 800-882-8184
> 408-946-3291
> FAX: 408-946-3597

This pocket-size external unit can be attached to a VGA port (it uses software to convert the VGA signal). ProPC/TV attaches to a television with an S-video connector and to a PC with a VGA connector. This unit costs $299.

Aitech ProVGA/TV Plus

> ProVGA/TV Plus
> Aitech International Corp
> 830 Hillview Ct., #145
> Milpitas, CA 95035
> 800-882-8184
> 408-946-3291
> FAX: 408-946-3597

This is a 16-bit ISA board that includes a single BNC-to-RCA adapter, VGA pass-through cable, and a Video Titler. It includes a flicker-reduction circuit and is a generator-locking (more commonly called *genlocking,* a signal synchronization technique that controls rolling or tearing of a picture) and overlay board.

This product comes with DOS and Microsoft Windows control utilities software and requires a standard VGA or multiscanning monitor, an NTSC video monitor, and a VGA or Super VGA board. This unit costs $995 (composite, S-video, and RGB cables: $59 each).

Cardinal SNAPplus

SNAPplus
Cardinal Technologies, Inc.
1827 Freedom Rd.
Lancaster, PA 17601
800-233-0187
717-293-3000
FAX: 717-293-3055

The Cardinal SNAPplus is a video-in-a-window board you can use to overlay NTSC video on a VGA computer monitor and perform operations such as panning, zooming, and cropping with your PC. This 16-bit ISA board includes 1M of VRAM and 1M of DRAM. The board supports a maximum non-interlaced graphics resolution of 1024×768 and a palette of 65,000 possible colors and offers the following features:

➤ PAL video sources

➤ On-board VGA and genlocking

➤ Live video image capture

➤ Graphics animation

I received a SnapPLUS from Cardinal for testing, and things did not go very well. The documentation did not match either the hardware or the software that I received, so I was unable to install the unit. Comments from other users on CompuServe reflect similar experiences, so this unit is Not Recommended. The feature list might make you think it's a good deal, but until the package is cleaned up I recommend against purchasing it.

Communications Coconut

Coconut
Communications Specialties
Hauppauge, NY
516-273-0404

This external unit uses hardware to convert the VGA signal and costs $1,595.

Creative Labs Video Blaster

Video Blaster
Creative Labs, Inc.
1901 McCarthy Blvd.
Milpitas, CA 95035
408-428-6600
FAX: 408-428-6611

The Creative Labs Video Blaster is a video overlay card that brings full-motion video to VGA screens. It enables you to combine full-motion video from NTSC or PAL with computer-generated graphics and animations. Resulting images can be captured in a "freeze-frame"; saved in file formats such as .BMP, .TGA, .MMP, .TIF, or Encapsulated PostScript (EPS); manipulated by adding titles or changing colors; and exported to other applications.

Video Blaster is based on the PCVIDEO chip and requires a full-length, 16-bit slot in an AT compatible, MS-DOS 3.1 or higher, and a VGA or multisync monitor. You cannot have more than 14M of memory in the system because the Video Blaster maps a frame buffer into the lower 16M of memory. The unit offers a large number of features, including both video overlay and video capture, but its low-cost design includes many compromises. It is useful for fun or hobby-level video work but not for professional efforts. It sometimes has trouble with very fast motherboards, and will only work with a limited set of SuperVGA cards. Check with Creative when you buy to verify that your video display card is supported.

It is compatible with Microsoft Windows 3.1 and contains the following features:

➤ Switches between video sources (video cassette recorders, videodisc players, video cameras, and camcorders)

➤ Uses four audio inputs with external sources and Creative Labs' CD-ROM drive: Sound Blaster, Sound Blaster Pro Basic, or Sound Blaster Pro audio systems

➤ Crops or scales input

➤ Pans images horizontally or vertically

➤ Supports .PCX, .TIF, .BMP, .MMP, .GIF, .TGA, and .JPG (JPEG compression) file formats

821

➤ Software selectable port address

➤ Software selectable IRQ

➤ A memory-mapped video buffer above system memory

➤ A digital and analog audio mixer with programmable individual and master volume controls and pass-through

Video Blaster is useful as a presentation or teaching tool and also can be used for video training, presentations, and security monitoring. It is capable of displaying two million true colors on an interlaced screen and has the following capabilities:

➤ Overlay computer text and graphics on video

➤ Capture, freeze, store, manipulate, and import images from VCRs, videodisks, cameras, and broadcasts

➤ Scale images from full-screen to an icon

➤ Video control of an image's hue, saturation, brightness, contrast, and RGB

Video Blaster comes bundled with the following software:

➤ Windows 3.1-compatible Video Kit utilities with JPEG compression

➤ Macromind Action! presentation package

➤ Mathematica's Tempra

➤ MMPlay presentation software

➤ VBDEMO (demo of Video Blaster capabilities)

Creative Labs Video Spigot

Video Blaster
Creative Labs, Inc.
1901 McCarthy Blvd.
Milpitas, CA 95035
408-428-6600
FAX: 408-428-6611

The Video Spigot is intended solely for video capture with Video for Windows, and it does the job very well. The unit provides very good image quality, fast capture rates, and is a reliable performer. I used one of these and was very happy with it. It is well ahead of the pack in terms of quality, ease of use, and reliability. It can manage real-time capture at 160 × 120 at 30 frames per second and can capture single frames at up to 640 × 480.

At press time, this card was bundled with Toolbook, making it an outstanding deal. Even if Creative Labs cuts the software bundles, this card still does a great job and is worth consideration.

DigiTV

Videomail, Inc.
568-4 Weddell Drive
Sunnyvale, CA 94089
408-747-0223
800-FON-PCTV
FAX: 408-747-0225

The DigiTV board displays TV in a window, even while you work on other applications. It is easy to install and plugs into any 386, or 486 PC. DigiTV displays live TV in real-time at 30 frames per second with more than 2 million colors. You can reposition the DigiTV window on the screen, resize between 1/9 or 1/16 window, or maximize to full screen. Software for operation in DOS and Windows is included, which enables you to change channels, adjust audio and video settings, and switch between TV tuner or external audio/video source, including VCRs, video cameras, camcorders, and laser-disk players. The board contains a 122-channel, cable-ready TV tuner, four-watt stereo amplifier, and external audio/video inputs and video output. DigiTV comes with stereo speakers. The price is $495. A developer tool kit (SDK) is available.

Digital Vision TelevEyes

TelevEyes
Digital Vision
Dedham, MA
617-329-5400

This pocket-size external unit uses software to convert the VGA signal. TelevEyes attaches to a television with an S-video connector and to a PC with a VGA connector. The cost is $300.

Everex Vision VGA with Overlay

Vision VGA with Overlay
Everex Systems, Inc.
48431 Milmont Dr.
Fremont, CA 94538
510-683-2100
FAX: 510-651-0728

This product offers overlay, and an anti-jitter filter designed to produce a low-flicker NTSC image from VGA graphics. This 16-bit ISA board comes with 1M of DRAM and requires a standard VGA or multiscanning monitor, and an NTSC video monitor. This unit costs $895.

Everex Vision VGA HC

Vision VGA HC
Everex Systems, Inc.
48431 Milmont Dr.
Fremont, CA 94538
510-683-2100
FAX: 510-651-0728

Vision VGA HC is an internal board you can use to display computer output on a television monitor or videotape. However, it does not have the capability to overlay. This board has on-board VGA and Super VGA, and it is especially designed for setting up a VGA-to-NTSC system from scratch. This unit costs $615.

Genoa VGA2TV

VGA2TV
Genoa Systems Corp.
75 E. Trimble Rd.
San Jose, CA 95131
408-423-9123
FAX: 408-434-0997

VGA2TV performs genlocking of VGA and NTSC signals and includes a VGA pass-through connector cable. It includes the capability to overlay a computer display onto video input. The VGA2TV is an internal 16-bit ISA board that accepts NTSC and S-video inputs and outputs using RCA jacks and standard S-video connections.

The board requires a standard VGA or multiscanning monitor, an NTSC video monitor, and a VGA or Super VGA board. This unit costs $499.

High Res VGA Video Gala

VGA Video Gala
High Res Technologies
Lewiston, NY
416-497-6493

The VGA Video Gala is an internal board that performs VGA conversion. It is capable of displaying full-motion video in a window on a VGA monitor. This unit costs $595.

IEV ProMotion

ProMotion Multimedia Engine
IEV International, Inc.
3030 South Main St., Suite 300
Salt Lake City, UT 84115
800-IEV-6161
801-466-9093
FAX: 801-466-5921

ProMotion is a digital video overlay board that supports high-resolution video windows, overlay, capture, and audio control.

With ProMotion, you can input full-motion video from any VCR, video camera, television tuner, or laserdisc—put it in a window; integrate it with graphics at resolutions up to 1024 × 768 interlaced; and display it flicker-free on a VGA monitor with audio accompaniment. It also can capture still images or motion clips from the video and save, manipulate, compress, or replay the video.

ProMotion has video windowing capabilities you can use to zoom in and out of a video picture and place the full-color, real-time video window anywhere on the screen. ProMotion can run in the background while other applications are running without affecting their performance.

You can capture and save, restore, or manipulate motion or still-frame images in 1/30 second in a $512 \times 512 \times 16$-bits-per-pixel frame buffer.

ProMotion uses an NTSC and S-Video decoder, comb filters, color transient improvement circuitry, and other features to improve picture quality. This package includes the following:

➤ ProMotion board

➤ VGA feature connector and VGA loop-through cables

➤ Image capture and display utilities for Windows and DOS

➤ Multimedia MCI driver and AVI driver for Windows 3.1

➤ DLL for Windows 3.0 or 3.1

➤ Pascal and C software libraries with source code

➤ UNIX System V device driver with source code

➤ Operation manual

The system runs on an IBM PC AT with a 16-bit interface or on a VGA or Super VGA card with a feature connector. It requires a standard VGA or Super VGA mode monitor. The board needs one full-length IBM-AT slot. This unit costs $995.

IEV SimulScan

SimulScan
IEV International, Inc.
3030 South Main St., Suite 300
Salt Lake City, UT 84115
800-438-6161
801-466-9093
FAX: 801-466-5921

This external unit uses hardware to convert a VGA signal for output to an NTSC TV or videocassette recorder. This unit costs $495.

Intel Smart Video Recorder

Intel Corporation
FaxBack: 800-525-3019

The Smart Video Recorder offers something that no other card in its price range can boast: real-time compression of the incoming video signal. This enables it to outperform the other cards. You can capture up to 320×240 frames at 15 fps, whereas other cards are limited to, at best, 240×180 at 15 fps or even less—some cards can handle no more than 160×120 at 15 fps.

There are two advantages to real-time compression. One, it saves time—you compress at the same time you capture. Two, it increases the size of the video images you can capture. Both of these are substantial advantages, and I highly recommend the Smart Video Recorder.

I have used more than a dozen video capture cards, and the Smart Video Recorder is the one that lives in my personal machine for video capture.

Jovian Genie

Genie
Jovian Logic Corp.
Fremont, CA
510-651-4823

This external unit uses hardware to perform VGA signal conversion and has genlocking capability. However, it requires a video overlay board or a video editing system to overlay VGA on video. This unit costs $1,695.

Macro Data 123A

123A
Macro Data
Tempe, AZ
602-966-2221

This external unit uses software to convert the VGA signal. It costs $625.

Magni VGA Producer Pro

VGA Producer Pro
Magni Systems, Inc.
9500 SW Gemini Dr.
Beaverton, OR 97005
800-624-6465
503-626-8400
FAX: 503-626-6225

The VGA Producer Pro is an 8-bit, ISA board with 1M of field RAM and an external control box. It includes anti-jitter and anti-flicker filters that effectively reduce this side effect of scan conversion software. It also includes the capability to overlay a computer display onto video input.

The Producer Pro produces 768×480 graphics with 256 colors and supports genlocking. It comes bundled with DOS control utilities, Pro Video VGA-16, VGA Director, and animation software. The board requires a standard VGA or multiscanning monitor, an NTSC video monitor, and a VGA or Super VGA board. This unit costs $1,995.

Media Vision Pro MovieStudio

Pro MovieStudio
Media Vision
47221 Fremont Blvd.
Fremont, CA 94538
800-845-5870
FAX: 510-770-9592
BBS: 510-770-9522
CompuServe: GO MEDIAVISION

This high-performance video capture card offers 160×120 (30 fps) and 320×240 (15 fps) capture rates. It also captures single frames at up to 640×480. It supports NTSC, PAL, and SECAM video standards. The high performance rates result from hardware compression using the Microsoft Video 1 codec. I don't like this codec as well as Indeo, the codec used by the Smart Video Recorder. However, the MS Video 1 codec does offer some speed advantages for playback, and if your needs are for playback on slower hardware, you should check into this card.

New Media Graphics Super Motion Compression

Super Motion Compression
New Media Graphics
780 Boston Rd.
Billerica, MA 01821
800-228-2207
508-663-0666
FAX: 508-663-6678

Super Motion Compression works with Super VideoWindows-CM to capture clips of high-quality video and stereo audio, compress them, store them on a hard disk, and do instant playback. This product does real-time compression and decompression, and it provides frame-accurate addressing of the compressed video.

Super Motion Compression connects directly to the Super VideoWindows-CM board via the high-speed, bi-directional NMG-Video Bus. It supports Microsoft MME and MCI, and it runs under New Media Graphics' Common Interface Library (CIL). CIL enables developers to integrate hard disk-based motion video and audio into existing applications running under Windows or DOS.

New Media Graphics supplies an easy-to-use Windows application with Super Motion Compression that enables you to record and play back clips of video and audio to and from a hard disk or mass-storage device. They also distribute a standard Developers' kit that provides hooks into New Media Graphics' libraries. The libraries are available in Microsoft C 6.0- and Borland C 2.0-compatible versions.

New Media Graphics Super VideoWindows

Super VideoWindows
New Media Graphics
780 Boston Rd.
Billerica, MA 01821
800-228-2207
508-663-0666
FAX: 508-663-6678

Super VideoWindows receives and displays television in a window on an ISA-bus PC. With the pop-up menus, you can select from 122 channels of USA cable and broadcast television and adjust the controls for audio (volume, bass, treble, and balance) and video (contrast, hue, saturation, brightness, and sharpness).

Video can be scaled into a window of any size, anywhere on the screen. This feature enables you to run other applications concurrently in other windows. Super VideoWindows accepts input from a camera, VCR, and videodisc. This board has the following features:

➤ Computer-controlled, 122-channel selection

➤ USA broadcast (antenna) or USA cable TV input

➤ Full-motion digital video in any size window

➤ The capability to freeze, store, manipulate, and export images

➤ Graphics and text overlay

➤ Audio control

➤ MS Windows 3.0 or DOS compatibility

The video board requires a PC-AT with a 16-bit slot. It runs on a VGA or multisync monitor at 50–70 Hz with a horizontal scan rate of 31.5 kHz, and it requires either a Super VGA daughter board from New Media or a third-party VGA board with a feature connector.

This board receives good reactions from the folks I know who use it. I ran into some problems with the sample I had when I tried to run it on a 486/66 local bus machine, but New Media tells me the problem will be solved in a revised design due out early in 1994. If you have a local bus motherboard, be sure to confirm that you are getting the correct version for your computer before you buy.

Super VideoWindows digitizes and scan converts NTSC video for display on a VGA or multisync monitor. At any time, you can grab the video frame in 1/30 second, edit (cut, copy, and paste), and store it to disk in YUV, TARGA, Windows bitmap, or PCX file formats.

The Super VideoWindows board comes with VDev, a program you can use to view and capture video images, a configuration program (it's very detailed—you can get a good image under adverse conditions), Windows drivers, and examples of how to access the board from Windows programming languages.

Additional software available for the board includes:

➤ End User Kit, which includes VEditor, an application that accesses all Super VideoWindows functionality, and ImagePrep, a file conversion program.

➤ Developer Kit, which includes VDev with annotated source code; VDemo with annotated source code; third-party demos with annotated source code (Visual Basic, Toolbook, and so on); Microsoft C libraries for Windows and DOS use; and VEditor, a sample application.

The following software programs can access the Super VideoWindows board directly:

> MS Windows via MCI driver
> Toolbook and Multimedia Toolbook
> Knowledge Pro
> IconAuthor
> Authorware Professional
> Wicat System's Sage
> Spinnaker Plus
> Owl Guide
> SuperBase 4
> Animation Works
> Video Titler
> MetaWindows
> MM Studio
> Quest

The Super VideoWindows card comes in several configurations and is priced from $795 to $1,195.

New Media Graphics also sells a hardware compression board, the Super Motions Compression Board. It sells for $2,000–$3,000, depending on the options you choose. If you want to create sophisticated video presentations, hardware compression offers much better speed and fidelity than software-based solutions like AVI.

New Media Graphics WatchIT!

WatchIT!
New Media Graphics
780 Boston Rd.
Billerica, MA 01821
800-228-2207
508-663-0666
FAX: 508-663-6678

WatchIT! is a multimedia add-on board that enables you to watch TV on your PC—you can work in another application while watching TV. A pop-up remote control enables you to make television adjustments, such as channel changes, channel scans at set time intervals, volume control, screen size changes, picture freezes, and picture snaps and shows. You can connect WatchIT! to cable, a TV antenna, or any other 75–300 ohm source. You cannot connect a composite output without some kind of RF converter.

WatchIT! runs under DOS or Windows. It has 640 × 480 graphics resolution and an internal 8-bit ISA board, and it requires VGA with a feature connector and a PC with an 8-bit slot.

PC2TV

Redlake Corporation IPG
718 University Ave., Ste. 100
Los Gatos, CA 95030
800-543-6563

The PC2TV board is an XT or AT Bus-compatible card that converts analog VGA video to NTSC or PAL video. The PC2TV board does not require any software. It continuously converts VGA signals with resolutions up to 640 × 480 and 16.8 million colors.

Presenter and Presenter Plus/2

Presenter and Presenter Plus/2
Consumer Technology Northwest
4900 SW Griffith Drive
Suite 249
Beaverton, OR 97005
800-356-3983
FAX: 503-671-9066

These external units enable you to play your computer screen's VGA images on a TV monitor or output them to tape. The Presenter is a DOS product and supports 16-color VGA. The Presenter Plus/2 supports up to 15-bit color (32,000 colors) in Windows.

Redlake Tape Caster

Tape Caster
Redlake Corp.
Morgan Hill, CA
408-399-5000

The Tape Caster is an internal board that performs VGA conversion in hardware. This board uses an external cable to connect to an existing VGA card and costs $750.

STB Channel 4

Channel 4
STB Systems
Richardson, TX
214-234-8750

This internal board uses software to convert the VGA signal and is useful for setting up a VGA-to-NTSC system from scratch.

The Channel 4 board has four S-video output jacks and holds four VGA chips with 512K each. The board produces 640×480 resolution with 256 colors. It costs $1,799.

Telebyte Pocket Video-Verter

Model 701 Pocket Video-Verter
Telebyte Technology
Greenlawn, NY
516-423-3232

This portable external unit uses software to convert the VGA signal. The Pocket Video-Verter is well suited for on-the-road presentations, sales calls, or for using a TV as a display device. This unit costs $399.

Truevision Bravado

Truevision, Inc.
7340 Shadeland Station
Indianapolis, IN 46256
800-344-TRUE

I used this board extensively during the writing of this book. I found it to be the most consistently reliable NTSC overlay video board I tested.

The Bravado features two new add-ons from Truevision that make it an all-in-one solution for many different kinds of video work. There is an encoder module for outputting to tape, and a hardware compression module for real-time capture and compression. See the end of the Bravado listing for information about these two add-ons.

The Bravado board and software contain the following features:

➤ Video in a window in full color from up to three (non-simultaneous) sources

➤ Support for composite and S-Video input

➤ Ability to cascade several Bravado boards for multiple video windows simultaneously

➤ On-board VGA (make sure you get the 16-bit version if you want 256 colors at 1024×768)

➤ Non-interlaced display

➤ VGA overlay

➤ Audio pass-through

➤ VGA drivers for Windows and most popular DOS programs

➤ NTSC and PAL compatibility

This is supported by several third-party products:

Avocado—a video editing and device control system with digital effects and time base correction. (Contact Vivid Visions at 313-453-7770.)

Electronic Pass and Security System—(Contact Data Link Information Solutions, Inc., at 703-318-7300.)

Interactive Information System—a system for developing kiosk interactive video systems. (Contact KAMDON Interactive Information Systems, Inc., at 317-286-0650.)

PC-VCR—an RS-232 controllable S-VHS tape deck with a built-in time-code generator offering frame-accurate control of any VHS or S-VHS tape. It is used for education, computer-based training, presentations, and kiosk/point of sale. (Contact NEC Technologies at 800-788-6268.)

MPG-1000—a full-motion MPEG video compression and expansion card designed specifically for the Bravado. (Contact Optibase, Inc., at 818-719-6566.)

Visionary—a real-time JPEG video compression board also designed specifically to work with the Bravado. (Contact Rapid Technology Corporation at 716-833-8533.)

Bravado16 Video Compressor

The compressor unit attaches to the Bravado using a bus built onto the card. It pulls the video data from the Bravado in real time, captures it, scales it, compresses it, and then stores it to the hard disk. During playback, it decompresses the video data and passes it to the Bravado for display.

The board supports both the NTSC and PAL video standards, and will handle composite or S-Video signals. It receives video from the Bravado at 704x486 pixels (NTSC) or 704x576 (PAL). In order to write the video data to disk, this is scaled down to 352x240 (NTSC) or 352x288 (PAL) before compression. This is necessary to fit the throughput limitations of the ISA bus. On a typical high-end ISA machine, video throughput is limited to about 350k/sec.

The frame rate can be from 1 to 30 frames per second. Three compression schemes are available; you can tailor compression to balance quality and size of the resulting file.

During playback, the signal is fed to the Bravado unscaled—that is, at the resolution it was scaled down to. The Bravado's on-board scaling capabilities can be used to scale the image up to full VGA size.

Bravado Encoder

The encoder allows you to output anything you can display on your computer screen to tape. For example, you can create a Windows or DOS presentation, and then record it out to tape while you play it back on the comptuer. The Bravado encoder allows you to output the entire VGA display, including any live video windows, in composite or S-Video modes. It operates in both NTSC or PAL. You can encode from 2 to 16 bits per pixel for lifelike color.

The best news, however, is that you can accomplish this in any video resolution up to and including 1024x768. You can control underscan and overscan in software, as well as the degree of flicker reduction. The board comes with MCI drivers for Windows, making it very easy to integrate into your programs.

Truevision Targa+

Truevision, Inc.
7340 Shadeland Station
Indianapolis, IN 46256
800-344-TRUE

In one form or another, Targa boards have been around longer than most other video boards. It was, in fact, a Targa+ board on which Microsoft developed the original version of Video for Windows back in 1992. However, the Targa+ board is a much more capable board that just another video capture card. The Targa series of boards are primarily designed for video output, and are used by folks who, for example, need to output computer images to a frame-accurate VCR. The Targa+ series supports S-video, composite video, and RGB input. Genlocking is a standard feature, as are 1x, 2x, 4x, and 8x zoom and panning. It supports multiple sync methods, including interlaced, non-interlaced, horizontal and vertical scan rate, horizontal and vertical sync width, horizontal and vertical blanking, vertical serration and equalization, and others.

There are a total of five Targa+ models:

Targa+ 16	512k memory, and supporting up to: 8-bits/pixel at 1024x512, and 16 bits/pixel at 512x512.
Targa+ 16/32	1M memory, and supporting up to: 8-bits/pixel at 1024x512 (double buffered), 16 bits/pixel at 1024x512, 24 bits/pixel at 512x512, and 32 bits/pixel at 512x512.
Targa+ 64	2M memory, and supporting up to: 8-bits/pixel at 1024x1024 (double buffered), 16 bits/pixel at 1024x1024, 24 bits/pixel at 512x1024, and 32 bits/pixel at 512x1024.
Targa+ 16P	1M memory, and supporting up to: 8-bits/pixel at 1024x1024, and 16 bits/pixel at 512x1024. Supports PAL standard.
Targa+ 16/32P	2M memory, and supporting up to: 8-bits/pixel at 1024x1024 (double buffered), 16 bits/pixel at 1024x1024, 24 bits/pixel at 512x1024, and 32 bits/pixel at 512x1024. Supports PAL standard.

The latest versions of the Targa+ cards add VGA pass-through and overlay capabilities. However, you will need a multisync monitor that supports NTSC scan rates to get full use of this feature. Otherwise, you'll need two monitors—one for your comptuer, and one for the NTSC output.

Truevision VideoVGA

VideoVGA
Truevision, Inc.
7340 Shadeland Station
Indianapolis, IN 46456
800-344-8783
317-841-0332
FAX: 317-576-7700

This card has good color fidelity and supports NTSC genlocking and on-board VGA. It includes the capability to overlay a computer display onto video input. The internal VGA-to-NTSC adapter comes with 512K of DRAM (8-bit version) or 1024K of DRAM (16-bit version) and a Tseng ET4000 VGA controller that supports 640 × 480, 800 × 600, and 1024 × 768 resolution. Non-interlaced, 256-color high resolution is only available on the 16-bit card.

Video VGA requires a standard VGA or multiscanning monitor, and an NTSC video monitor or VCR to receive the NTSC output. The board lacks controls for horizontal and vertical positioning, but the automatic adjustments are reasonably accurate. The anti-jitter/anti-flicker module is an optional add-on. This unit costs $1,195.

VideoLogic Captivator

Captivator
VideoLogic
Cambridge, MA
617-494-0530

The Captivator is an excellent video capture card. It does an outstanding job at capturing single video frames—the image quality is as good as that of boards costing five times as much. The only board even close (and it costs more) is the Super VideoWindows card from New Media Graphics.

The Captivator also is a very good choice for motion video capture. However, the Intel Smart Video Recorder is probably a better choice unless you have a lot of single-image captures to do. For example, if you plan to use video to acquire images for desktop publishing, the Captivator is hard to beat. I keep one in one of our machines for exactly that reason.

Perhaps the best reason to try the Captivator is its price. It lists for only $349.

VideoLogic MediaSpace and DVA-4000

MediaSpace
VideoLogic
Cambridge, MA
617-494-0530

The combination of the MediaSpace and the DVA-4000 gives you professional-level video overlay and capture capabilities. The MediaSpace uses the C-Cubed video compression chips—a high-end real-time compression codec in hardware—to provide full-screen, full-motion video. It uses the overlay display capabilities of the DVA-4000 to provide stunningly sharp video images on the desktop.

Because the MediaSpace uses hardware compression techniques, you need the same hardware in the playback computer to handle decompression. This is expensive but ideal for high-end kiosks or boardroom presentations, where quality is critical.

At press time, VideoLogic was beta-testing a Video for Windows driver for this product that would make it much easier to use. The quality of this unit is outstanding. The combined price for the two units is $2,995.

VideoLogic Mediator

Mediator
VideoLogic
Cambridge, MA
617-494-0530

This external unit uses hardware to perform VGA signal conversion. It also does genlocking, but it requires a video overlay board or video editing system (for example, NewTek's Video Toaster) to overlay VGA on video. It supports output to a wide variety of tape formats and is a thoroughly professional product. This unit costs $2,395.

VideoLogic also offers a low-cost version, the Mediator LC. It is a consumer-level product at the much lower price of $599.

Visionetics VIGA-VGA

VIGA-VGA
Visionetics International
Torrance, CA
310-316-7940

This internal board uses software to convert the VGA signal, and it's useful for setting up a VGA-to-NTSC system from scratch.

The VIGA-VGA board comes with on-board Super VGA and produces 1024 × 768 resolution with 256 colors. It can support up to 16 VIGA-VGA boards in a single PC. This unit costs $495.

Visionex Desktop TV

Desktop TV
Visionex

The Desktop TV is an add-on board that turns PCs into full-screen, enhanced-definition television monitors. It uses an ITT chip set that provides double scanning with advanced interpolation technology and comb filters. This product is cable-ready and capable of receiving 119 channels. It includes an external speaker and is well suited for computer-based training, security, and closed-circuit monitoring. This unit costs $249.

Willow LaptopTV

LaptopTV
Willow Peripherals
190 Willow Ave.
Bronx, NY 10454
800-444-1585
718-402-9500
FAX: 718-402-9603

This external unit uses hardware to convert the VGA signal for output to a NTSC TV or videocassette recorder. It costs $1,195.

Willow VGA-TV GE/O

VGA-TV GE/O
Willow Peripherals
190 Willow Ave.
Bronx, NY 10454
800-444-1585
718-402-9500
FAX: 718-402-9603

This 16-bit board uses the Tseng ET3000 video chip. It was one of the first cards to use genlocking VGA-to-NTSC board technology and includes the capability to overlay a computer display onto video input.

The VGA-TV GE/O displays VGA graphics on an NTSC monitor in 640 × 480 resolution with 256 colors. It does not include an anti-flicker filter and requires a standard VGA or multiscanning monitor, and an NTSC video monitor or VCR for output. This unit costs $695; for the PAL version, the cost is $795.

Win/TV

Hauppauge Computer Works
91 Cabot Court
Hauppauge, NY 11788
516-434-1600
FAX: 516-434-3198

This is one of the more interesting video capture/overlay boards. It adds a 122-channel, cable-ready tuner to the traditional capabilities of this class of video card. It gives you a little bit of everything, including Video for Windows support.

I have not used the unit myself (it's one of the few video capture tools I didn't get around to testing), but I've heard generally positive comments on CompuServe. It is interesting mainly for its tuner, which enables you to watch TV on your PC as well as capture. If you don't need the TV feature, other cards are a better choice.

WorldWide Video TVGA

TVGA Card
WorldWide Video

This TVGA card is a 16-bit, VGA display card that supports IBM's VGA modes and Super VGA modes up to 1024 × 768 resolution. It outputs a National Television Standards Committee (NTSC) signal you can display on a TV monitor, record on a VCR, or output to video equipment that accepts video input. This unit costs $389.

XingIt!

XingIt!
Xing Technology
1540 West Branch St.
Arroyo Grande, CA 93420

This is the first of a new generation of video capture cards: it produces MPEG file. MPEG (Motion Picture Expert Group) is a very sophisticated video compression standard that will eventually play a larger role in digital video on the desktop. Since the XingIt! card is the first such card to appear in the under $1,000 range (it lists for $795), you might expect a few kinks. There are, but nothing terribly serious if Xing follows through on some promised revisions and additions.

The XingIt! features real-time compression during capture, filtering of the incoming video image, and MPEG. It comes with a software-only MPEG playback codec for Windows, but the results are not as good as hardware-assisted playback.

There is a catch to the real-time compression. MPEG is a very computationally intensive compression algorithm. In order to compress it in real time, the XingIt! board has to make a few compromises. For example, MPEG compression is clever enough to use previous and following frames to calculate the contents of the current frame—that can't be done in real time. Thus, the MPEG files created in real time are not true MPEG files. Xing has announced a post-capture utility that will convert the capture file into a true MPEG file, but it was not available at press time.

The specs on the XingIt! board are impressive. It will do 320x240 playback at 30 frames per second. That's double what many boards can deliver.

Video Editing Systems

At the high end of what is possible with video on a PC, you'll find complete video editing systems. These systems allow you to use the power of the PC to edit video. There are two kinds of systems—those that use the PC just to handle the current frame during an edit session betwen two or more VCRs, and those that capture the video to a hard disk, edit it, and send it back out to tape.

The entry level for this kind of video production equipment is quite steep. Expect to pay at least $3,000 just for the board that goes in the computer to handle the video and/or VCRs, with software and the VCRs themselves extra. You'll need top-of-the-line VCRs for this kind of editing—the computer must be able to tell the VCR exactly which frame to go to. Such VCRs sell at prices ranging from about $1,500 to $5,000.

FAST Video Machine

FAST Electronics
5 Commonwealth Road
Natick, MA 01760
(508) 655-FAST

The Video Machine combines many of the funcitons of a video studio on a single computer board:

➤ Edit control unit for A/B roll operation

➤ Video mixer with 6 inputs

➤ Video printer driver as character and graphics generator

➤ Two frame synchronizers

➤ 4-channel audio rerecording in stereo

Also included is VM-Studio video editing software. Because it runs under Windows, you can use the tools you normally use in Windows to create or enhance video productions.

For professional work, you can expand the Video Machine's capabilities with the Studio Control Box. It adds a wealth of additional inputs and features.

FAST now has a section in the MULTIBVEN forum on CompuServe. You can get more information about the Video Machine there, or talk to folks who are already using it. For serious video work on the PC, the Video Machine is relatively low cost (around $3,000 for a starter system) and reasonably full featured.

Video Toaster 4000 (Amiga)

NewTek, Inc.
215 SE 8th Street
Topeka, KS 66603
800-847-6111
913-231-0100
FAX: 913-231-0101

The Video Toaster 4000 is a video system designed to take advantage of the increased capabilities of the Commodore Amiga 4000 computer. The Video Toaster

4000 includes a switcher with four video inputs and three internal digital sources. It also includes an integrated graphics loader, which enables you to load and display video frames, still stores, and animations. The system includes a 24-bit, 35-ns resolution character generator. The Toaster also comes with integrated paint, 3-D, video effects, and transition tools, and cost $2,395.

LightWave 3D is Toaster's 3-D modeling, rendering, and animation software system. LightWave has been used extensively in 3-D software for Hollywood on shows such as *Babylon 5* and *Unsolved Mysteries*. The Toaster 4000 is also used to create the 3-D graphic effects for Steven Spielberg's new series, *SeaQuest DSV*.

MIDI Interface Cards

These cards provide the connection between your computer and the various MIDI devices that are available. Generally speaking, these cards focus on the MIDI connection and do not include any sounds or sound-generating capabilities.

Key Electronics MIDIATOR

MIDIATOR
Key Electronics, Inc.
7515 Chapel Ave.
Fort Worth, TX 76116
800-533-MIDI
817-560-1912
FAX: 817-560-9745

The MIDIATOR MS-124 is a MIDI interface that connects to a serial port. It offers 64 channels and is specifically targeted for notebooks, laptops, and IBM PC-compatible interfaces for portable and live performances. This innovative product provides compatibility with all MIDIATOR models and more than 45 popular programs. The interface supports one MIDI In port, four MIDI Out ports, IBM PC serial ports, and full speed data transfer. It is self-powered, with an optional AC supply. This unit costs $179.95.

Music Quest PC MIDI Card

PC MIDI Card
Music Quest
1700 Alma Dr., Suite 300
Plano, TX 75075
800-876-1376
214-881-7408
FAX: 214-422-7094

This card, a good value, is targeted as a low-cost MIDI interface for the IBM PC or compatible computer. It is MPU-401 compatible and runs more than 100 of the popular programs.

Music Quest MQX-32M

MQX-32M
Music Quest
1700 Alma Dr., Suite 300
Plano, TX 75075
800-876-1376
214-881-7408
FAX: 214-422-7094

The MQX-32M provides a multi-port MIDI interface for an IBM PC or compatible computer. It has a dual-port interface with professional-level tape sources. It is supported by all professional sequencers for IBM, such as Cakewalk Professional, 64-Track PC, Cadenza, Master Tracks Pro, Forte II, Musicator, Sequencer Plus Gold, and Texture. The MQX-32M is MPU-401 compatible.

Roland Super MPU/AT MIDI Card

Super MPU/AT
Roland Corporation US
7200 Dominion Circle
Los Angeles, CA 90040-3647
213-685-5141
FAX: 213-722-0911

The Super MPU/AT is a professional-level MIDI interface for IBM PCs and compatible computers. The Super MPU/AT interface includes independent CPUs for MIDI and SMPTE data processing. This enables you to use software applications that let the Super MPU handle most of the MIDI and SMPTE signal processing, whereas the host computer focuses on graphics and other user interface issues. Not all sequencing software supports this capability.

The S-MPU/AT offers the following features:

➤ SMPTE synchronization

➤ 32-channel MIDI output

➤ Programmable data processing capabilities

➤ Compatibility with MPU-401

➤ Five levels of resolution from 24 to 960 pulses per quarter note

➤ Advanced MIDI features:

   MIDI message re-channelize

   MIDI message modify

   MIDI In merge

   MIDI Out message monitor

   MIDI chase

   MIDI overdubbing and tempo recording

The S-MPU/AT comes with two independent MIDI Ins, two MIDI Outs, and a SMPTE time-code input and output, which is optimized for applications integrating MIDI and SMPTE synchronization. The interface's advanced processing capability enables you to develop applications software for PC control over peripheral equipment. This makes it well suited for post-production and sound recording facilities. The cost is $295.

PC Speakers

You always can go to the local audio store and buy a pair of self-amplified speakers for $20, but the sound quality is usually poor. If you are looking for good sound, it's going to cost you several hundred dollars. All of the speaker systems listed in the following sections provide good results.

Things to look and listen for in PC speakers:

➤ Will they fit into your setup? Some speakers are smaller than others or have a more convenient shape.

➤ How many inputs does each speaker have? Can you connect everything you have to connect (audio board outputs, CD outputs, or non-computer outputs)?

➤ Are the speakers shielded to prevent magnetic interference with your video monitor? Speakers use magnets, and magnets can distort the video image—they can even permanently magnetize and therefore permanently distort the image. Some monitors have the ability to degauss (demagnetize), but even if you have that capability, you should still make sure you get shielded speakers. Most speakers designed for use with PCs use this technology.

➤ Does the speaker provide enough controls to suit your tastes (volume, separate treble and bass, and so on)?

➤ If you will be traveling with the speakers, how portable (and how heavy) are they? Better speakers have heavier magnets, so you'll probably have to compromise.

Altec Lansing ACS300

Altec Lansing Consumer Products
Routes 6 and 209
P.O. Box 277
Milford, PA 18337
800-548-0620
FAX: 717-296-2213

This speaker system was designed specifically for use with PCs. The unique clamshell design of the satellite speakers enables you to aim the sound right where you want it, and the detached subwoofer provides the bass boost required for good fidelity.

The clamshells are small, and you can set them on your desk or mount them on a wall. The subwoofer can go anywhere, even under or behind your desk. You can connect two audio sources. Controls include volume, treble, bass, balance, and digital effects (stereo separation enhancement). For all three components, the cost is $400.

Roland CS-10

CS-10
Roland
7200 Dominion Circle
Los Angeles, CA 90040
213-685-5141
FAX: 213-722-0911

This integrated amplifier and speaker unit can be placed under your computer monitor to conserve desktop space.

The CS-10 has line-level audio inputs for both an audio card and a CD player or other audio component. Volume and tone controls are located on the front of the unit along with a headphone jack. This unit costs $150.

Roland MA-12C Monitors

MA-12C Monitors
Roland
7200 Dominion Circle
Los Angeles, CA 90040
213-685-5141
FAX: 213-722-0911

The Roland speakers are built to last. They are heavy but extremely sturdy. They have been built in the best "traveling musician" tradition, and they should stand up well to rough use. The speaker case is thick, tough plastic, and the cord is heavy-duty. The speaker grill is a sturdy, open-mesh design that protects the speaker cone effectively.

The sound is good, too. These speakers are not at the top of the class in fidelity, but they come with both bass and treble controls that you can use to tailor the sound to your liking. I used a pair for several weeks and was very satisfied with them. These would be great speakers to put in the kids' room or to use for a traveling sales presentation (if you can handle the weight).

One especially nice feature is the range of inputs each speaker can take—two line-level inputs and a microphone input. You can attach a CD or audio card to one line input, the output of a MIDI keyboard to another input, and still have a place to plug in a microphone. The cost is $290 per pair.

Persona PC/Persona Subwoofer

Persona Speakers
Persona Technologies
274 Wattis Way
South San Francisco, CA 94080
415-871-6000

This is a great-sounding combination in terms of both sound and convenience. The Persona speakers are slim, upright units that don't take up much space, and with the optional subwoofer, they sound great.

Each speaker has controls for volume, stereo separation, and bass. You can connect one audio source, and there is a jack for headphones.

The satellite speakers cost $230 per pair. The subwoofer costs $200.

Yamaha CBX-S3

Yamaha CBX-S3
Yamaha Corporation of America
Digital Musical Instruments
P.O. Box 6600
Buena Park, CA 90622

This is a four-inch, shielded speaker designed specifically for use with computers. It is marketed with the Hello Music! system from Yamaha listed near the end of this chapter.

The unit includes a 10-watt power amplifier, three inputs, and bass and treble controls.

Bose Roommate Computer Monitor

Bose Corp.
The Mountain
Framingham, MA 01701
800-444-2673

These speakers, mounted in a heavy-duty case, are about as easy to use as speakers can be. They are well suited to life on the road.

There is one volume control for both speakers; all other adjustments are made automatically by the internal electronics. The lack of tone controls is a problem, however. In general, these speakers do not have the level of fidelity found in the other units listed here. The cost is $339 per pair.

MIDI Instruments

The real fun of MIDI comes from two activities: creating your own music and playing with various sounds. Not everybody can create or perform music, but most people know the sounds they enjoy.

Most MIDI keyboards come with a built-in synthesizer. The range of prices is large—from a few hundred to a few thousand dollars. The quality of both the keyboard and the sound usually goes up with cost, but not always.

You also can buy a synthesizer without a keyboard. If you already have a keyboard or if you don't plan to play any music on a keyboard, this makes sense. These synthesizers are commonly referred to as *sound modules* because what you are buying in such cases are the sounds the unit can make.

All MIDI instruments fall into two classes from the standpoint of a Windows multimedia user: those that support General MIDI and those that don't. General MIDI specifies the order of instruments in a synthesizer. If a synthesizer supports General MIDI, you can assume it will play back General MIDI files properly. If a synthesizer does not support General MIDI—and there are many good synthesizers that do not—you have several methods available for playing General MIDI files properly. The two best are the Windows MIDI Mapper (see Chapter 2, "Sound Advice") and a software sequencer (see Chapter 10, "Eenie-Meenie-MIDI: Keyboards").

Because most sound cards come with simple, FM-synthesis sounds, you usually have to upgrade your MIDI capabilities if the MIDI format appeals to you. Exceptions are the MultiSound from Turtle Beach and the SCC-1 from Roland.

Keyboards

I don't know how you feel about playing the piano, but piano-like keyboards are the best thing in the world for working with MIDI files. You do, of course, have to read music to use one.

Another advantage of keyboards is that they often come with a synthesizer inside. Connecting such a keyboard to your computer via the MIDI In port can add a whole new range of sounds to your setup.

High-end (translation: expensive) keyboards often have weighted keys to simulate the touch of a piano as closely as possible. Such keyboards, when used by someone who plays well, can add a great deal of subtle expression to music that you record. Less expensive keyboards have very little in common with real pianos, but are great for entering notes, or editing a passage of music.

E-mu Proteus Master Performance System

Proteus Master Performance System
E-mu Systems, Inc.
P.O. Box 660015
Scotts Valley, CA 95067-0015
408-438-1921

The Master Performance System (MPS) offers 16-bit, sampled sounds from the Emulator III library. The instrument features a five-octave velocity and pressure-sensitive keyboard as well as controller capabilities such as Quick Keys and Performance Maps. The MPS contains 200 internal presets with an additional 100 on the RAM card. It also includes 32-voice polyphony and 16-channel multitimbral operation.

ELKA MK Series

MK 76 and MK 88II
ELKA

ELKA produces professional MIDI keyboard controllers with polyphonic aftertouch and six split zones. Each has 128 presets, high-resolution dynamics, weighted keys, and more.

➤ MK 76, costs $2,395 (76-note MIDI keyboard)

➤ MK 88II, costs $2,595 (88-note MIDI keyboard)

For more information and the name of an authorized ELKA dealer, contact the following:

Music Industries Corp
Dept. KC
99 Tulip Avenue
Floral Park, NY 11001
800-431-6699

FATAR Studio 88 Series

Studio 88 Plus, Studio 88c, and Studio 88
FATAR

FATAR sells three MIDI keyboard controllers with professionally weighted keys and user-friendly programming.

➤ Studio 88 Plus; the cost is $1,750 (includes on-board programs)

➤ Studio 88c; the cost is $1,150 (comes with standard case)

➤ Studio 88; the cost is $1,250 (includes road case)

For more information and the name of an authorized FATAR dealer, contact the following:

Music Industries Corp.
Dept. KC
99 Tulip Avenue
Floral Park, NY 11001
800-431-6699

Generalmusic MusicProcessor

MusicProcessor
Generalmusic
800-323-0280

The S-2 and S-3 versions of the MusicProcessor have advanced editing features over other synthesizers. With the MusicProcessor, you can create new sounds with the keyboard still operative and without going into an edit mode. It offers the following features:

Sound Generation:

➤ PCM, wavetable, multiloop, crossfade multiwave, and subtractive synthesis

➤ 6M of ROM, 2M of RAM

➤ Up to 32-note polyphony with dynamic voice allocation

➤ 16 multitimbres, 16 layers, 16 splits

➤ 32 fully programmable digital filters (two filters with resonance for each voice)

➤ Dynamic stereo panning

Controllers:

➤ 61-note (S-2) and 76-note (S-3) keyboards

➤ Polyphonic after-touch

➤ 7 buttons and 7 sliders, all programmable

➤ 2 programmable foot controllers

➤ 1 volume pedal

Memory:

➤ Motorola MC68302 processor

➤ Sounds library (over 300 programs)

➤ Up to 100 performances

➤ Up to 10 songs

➤ Sound patch matrix for drum kits, and special sound configurations

➤ General MIDI configuration

Editor:

➤ User-friendly desktop editing

➤ Undo, compare, and clipboard features

➤ 240 × 64-pixel florescent backlit graphic display

➤ 14 function keys

MIDI:

➤ Full function master keyboard

➤ 32 independent MIDI channels

➤ 2 MIDI In, 2 MIDI Out, 2 MIDI Thru

➤ MIDI merge, clock in/out, MIDI dump

Sequencer:

➤ 16 tracks

➤ 1/192 quarter-note resolution

➤ 250,000-event storage

➤ Background song loading

➤ Real-time, overdub, quantize, and microscope editing

Floppy Drive:

➤ 3 1/2 inch

➤ 1.78M formatted (also Atari and IBM compatible formats)

➤ Loads and saves PCM data, sounds, songs, performances, and DSP effects

➤ Software upgrades, user programs, and software options loaded from floppy disk

➤ Full background operation

Audio Outputs:

➤ 6 polyphonic outputs (stereo master and 4 individual outs)

Gulbransen KS Series MIDI Controllers

KS5, KS10, and KS20
Gulbransen
800-677-7374

This series of controllers is unique—you use them to retrofit almost any piano as a MIDI controller. These are high-quality units, with prices to match, of course. They are used by many big-name musicians, including Chick Corea, Ronnie Milsap, and Bruce Hornsby.

The units consist of two major parts. A strip of sensors is installed beneath the keys in an electronic unit mounted under the piano case. The sensor strip does not interfere with the keyboard characteristics, which gives the player the advantages of MIDI without the hassles of a plastic keyboard.

Korg 01/W

Korg 01/W
Korg U.S.A.
89 Frost Street
Westbury, NY 11590

This keyboard has 32 voices, 200 programs, and 200 combinations. You can access up to 800 sounds using Korg's SRC-512 RAM card. The 01/W keyboard provides wave shaping you can use to modify waveforms. It includes a 7,000-note, 16-track sequencer.

Korg 01/WFD

Korg 01/WFD
Korg U.S.A.
89 Frost Street
Westbury, NY 11590

This keyboard includes the capabilities of the Korg 01/W as well as a built-in disk drive for storing programs, combinations, sequences, and sysex data. The 01/WFD includes two Stereo Dynamic Digital Multi-Effect processors with 47 effects and real-time control. It includes a 48,000-note, 16-track sequencer.

Korg 01/W Pro

Korg 01/W Pro
Korg U.S.A.
89 Frost Street
Westbury, NY 11590

This keyboard includes the capabilities of the Korg01/WFD. The 01/W Pro has been extended to 76 notes and 10M of PCM memory with 256 multisounds and

129 drum and percussion sounds. Like the 01/WFD keyboard, the Pro can be used as a MIDI data filer. It includes a 48,000-note, 16-track sequencer, but it also includes advanced editing functions. It features import and export sequences in the Standard MIDI file format.

Korg 01/W ProX

Korg 01/W ProX
Korg U.S.A.
89 Frost Street
Westbury, NY 11590

This keyboard is the most sophisticated of the Korg 01/W series. It includes an 88-note weighted-action keyboard, which makes the ProX a Master MIDI Controller. Like the 01/W Pro version, the ProX provides sequencing power and storage capability.

Roland JV-30

JV-30
Roland Corporation US
7200 Dominion Circle
Los Angeles, CA 90040-3696
213-685-5141

This synthesizer offers 16-part, multitimbral capabilities with 24-voice polyphony. It has three sliders for editing and four key modes for performing.

Roland PC-200 Mark II

PC-200 Mark II
Roland Corporation US
7200 Dominion Circle
Los Angeles, CA 90040-3647
213-685-5141
FAX: 213-722-0911

The PC-200 Mark II is a MIDI keyboard controller that features a 49-note, velocity-sensitive keyboard and full MIDI capabilities. The 49-key note range can be shifted up or down one octave by pushing the Octave Up or Octave Down buttons located on the front panel.

The keyboard has a slim design that makes it particularly suitable for use with a PC—it won't crowd your workspace. The keyboard action is unusually good for a controller in this price range.

The PC-200 MIDI/Select button located on the front panel enables you to transmit MIDI commands from the keyboard. This is not as convenient as the Yamaha CBX-K3, but it works. The front panel indicates how each note on the keyboard transmits specific MIDI information. You can send MIDI messages such as Volume and Pan to external sound sources by using the Data Entry slider. This simplifies recording MIDI information, such as volume, in real time.

The PC-200 uses either six AA batteries or an optional AC adapter. The cost for the unit is $350.

Yamaha CBX-K3

Yamaha CBX-K3
Yamaha Corporation of America
Digital Musical Instruments
P.O. Box 6600
Buena Park, CA 90622

This unit is similar to the Roland PC-200 Mark II, but it adds some interesting additional functionality. It has the basic features—49 keys, narrow for use near the computer (but not as narrow as the Roland), modulation, and pitch bend. It adds two rows of buttons for access to MIDI control, which is easier to use than the Roland keyboards use of the piano keys. It is these buttons that add the extra 3 inches in front-to-back size.

This unit makes a nice adjunct to your computer keyboard for working with MIDI. It may well replace my Roland, if I can make a little extra space for it. I like the feel a little better, and I can control more easily such things as velocity and touch sensitivity. Recommended.

Yamaha PSR410 and PSR510

Yamaha PSR410 and PSR510
Yamaha Corporation of America
Digital Musical Instruments
P.O. Box 6600
Buena Park, CA 90622

This is a complete line of keyboards, not all of which are suitable for use with your computer—the low end does not support MIDI, for example. The two units that make sense as music workstations, the 410 and 510, contain a combination of features, including general MIDI, at a very affordable price.

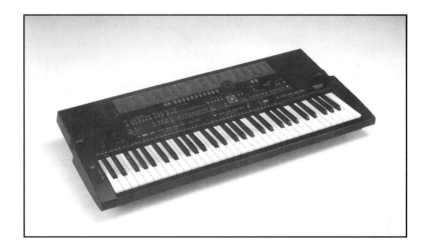

Figure 12.5. *The 510 is a low-cost General MIDI keyboard with excellent sound.*

Price/performance is the key here. Yamaha was kind enough to send me a 410 for evaluation, and I am very happy with the sound and performance of the unit. The sound quality is extremely noise-free and clear. The sounds are not always exactly like the instrument they were sampled from, but the sounds are always attractive, clean, and easy to listen to. When you choose a low-cost keyboard, the most important elements to consider are the quality of the sound and low noise. The 410 is outstanding in both respects. This unit definitely breaks new ground at the low end. Highly recommended.

If you are interested in creating music for use on your computer, you can route the sound output of the unit into your sound card and record—the sounds are well worth recording and will enhance any presentation or title. This is about the cheapest music studio you are going to find right now.

Key features shared by the 410 and 510 include:

➤ 61 keys

➤ General MIDI supported

➤ Stereo bass boost speaker system

➤ 28-note polyphony

➤ Touch sensitivity

➤ MIDI In/Out

➤ Four multi-pads with chord matching function

➤ Keyboard splits

➤ 10 types of auto harmony

➤ Orchestration control

➤ Pitch bend wheel

➤ Registration memory

➤ Page memory

The 510 adds the following features:

➤ Eight types of DSP (digital signal processing) reverb

➤ 102 (instead of 80) AWM rhythms/styles

➤ Sound shaper dial

➤ 12 types of echo/effects

➤ Custom accompaniment

If you are looking for budget keyboard/synth, these units deserve a close look.

Yamaha PSR-SQ-16

Yamaha PSR-SQ-16
Yamaha Corporation of America
Digital Musical Instruments
P.O. Box 6600
Buena Park, CA 90622

This is an impressive-looking keyboard with 200 sounds, good built-in speakers, a 16-channel, 20,000-note sequencer, and digital effects processing. It also includes a 3 1/2-inch disk drive for storing sequences and custom styles, 68 rhythm patterns, and a 61-note touch-sensitive keyboard. There are also 276 built-in musical styles, each with individual introductions, fill, and endings.

Digital signal processing includes reverb, delay, echo, early reflection, reverse gate, and distortion.

The keyboard also includes something called ABC-Auto Bass and Chord. This can be used by non-keyboard players to provide accompaniment. The list price of the keyboard is more than $2,000; a specific figure was not available at press time.

Yamaha was kind enough to ship one of these units to my home where I had a chance to work and play with it. There were things I liked and things I didn't.

The unit has one of the most impressive arrays of buttons and controls you are likely to see on one electronic device. They are logically arranged, but the sheer number of them is intimidating. By the time I learned how to work a new set of buttons, I forgot how to handle a previous set. I suppose this is the price of power—and make no mistake, this unit provides many powerful ways to control and create music.

The sequencer is particularly easy to use for a hardware sequencer. Just about every sequencer control has a dedicated button on the face of the unit—copy, paste, insert, note change, value+, value, and so on. This means you don't have to spend time learning how to access obscure menu selections; you can get right to work. The downside is that there are many buttons to deal with; it can be hard to find the one you want first. Fortunately, the logical grouping of the buttons helps out.

I was not impressed with the sounds programmed into the unit. They had a digital edge to them that I did not care for. This type of sound might appeal to you, however, if the punch of a sound is more important to you than the fidelity to the original instrument. Keyboard touch is probably my biggest disappointment—I had a great deal of difficulty getting the exact loudness I wanted because the key travel resistance was not uniform from top to bottom, nor from key to key.

Yamaha QY20

Yamaha QY20
Yamaha Corporation of America
Digital Musical Instruments
P.O. Box 6600
Buena Park, CA 90622

This is a very small, portable music tool. It's not another keyboard; it doesn't even *have* a piano-style keyboard. It has complete MIDI capabilities (warning: it's not general MIDI) and the ability to do such things as accompaniment and voicing.

Figure 12.6. *A tiny, portable, and feature-filled music workstation.*

You can use the QY20 as a portable music-design tool. It is for folks who know music, and you should check to see if the small size and simplified interface suits your style. It's really a miniature workstation/sequencer that enables you to work electronically with music anywhere.

Piano Teaching Systems

This is a relatively new idea in electronic instruments: a MIDI keyboard and software that teaches you how to play it. It's not for everyone, but the better programs can be a lot of fun.

Keep in mind that although such programs might be capable teachers of musical theory, they can't correct for improper physical technique.

Software Toolworks Miracle Piano

Miracle Piano
The Software Toolworks
60 Leveroni Ct.
Novato, CA 94949-9913
800-234-3088
FAX: 415-883-3303

Software Toolworks' Miracle Piano is a piano-teaching system that works on a Nintendo Entertainment System (NES), Super NES, IBM PC, Amiga, and Macintosh computers. Miracle has the following features:

➤ Interactive educational software.

➤ 36 sections, each with multiple lessons that offer standard and video game-based keyboard/music exercises.

➤ Lesson activities that include sight-reading, pitch practice, rhythm practice, and multiple-choice questions. The video game exercises include Roboman (rhythm), Shooting Gallery (note recognition), and Ripchord (note and chord recognition).

➤ Performance analysis and feedback with customized exercises.

➤ Eight-way multitimbral operation.

➤ 16-note polyphony.

➤ Keyboard split.

➤ Built-in performances with accompaniment.

The keyboard interface has MIDI In and MIDI Out ports, left and right audio out (RCA), stereo headphone out (minijack), 12-V power input, damper pedal input (custom two-pin configuration), and a 25-pin keyboard/computer communication port. If you add a MIDI interface board, you can use the keyboard with any MIDI software.

The system comes with a Synthesizer-action, 49-note, velocity-sensing keyboard that is 12 keys short of most MIDI units. It includes built-in speakers, headphones, a sustain pedal, and amplifier jacks. The synthesizer has 128 preset instrument sounds and sound effects.

The Nintendo version comes with a game cartridge in super or regular NES format. The PC version comes with floppy disks containing lesson software, and it requires 640K of RAM, DOS 3.1 or higher, and a serial port; a mouse is optional.

The dimensions of the keyboard are 31 1/2 inches × 13 inches × 3 3/4 inches; the unit weighs 11 pounds. For the regular NES version, the cost is $379.95; IBM PC and Amiga versions, $479.95 ($339 from Insight Software, 800-326-2007); Macintosh version, $499.95; conversion kits for Super NES, IBM PC, Amiga, and Macintosh, $129.95 each.

TAP PianoWorks

PianoWorks
Temporal Acuity Products, Inc.
300-120th N.E., Bldg. 1
Bellevue, WA 98005
800-426-2673
206-462-1007

PianoWorks is a self-paced, MIDI-interactive instructional software package for beginning piano. It is produced by the publishers of MusicPrinter Plus. PianoWorks includes the following features:

➤ Software for IBM and compatible PCs

➤ PianoWorks Level 1 software course

➤ Alfred Basic Piano Library complete level-1 lesson book

➤ MIDI Interface card and cables

It is recommended for ages 9 through adult; younger children should be supervised. The cost is $195 with MIDI card, $129 without MIDI card.

Sound Modules

Sound modules are synthesizers without keyboards—little black boxes that connect by MIDI to either a sequencer or a keyboard, and they generate sounds. They are a good upgrade path from the typical FM-synthesis sound card. Make sure that your sound card supports MIDI before you invest in a sound module.

ART DRX 2100

DR-X 2100
Applied Research and Technology, Inc.
215 Tremont Street
Rochester, NY 14608
716-436-2720
FAX: 716-436-3942

The DR-X 2100 is a rack-mount, multi-effects/dynamics processor. It includes all the effects and same 24-bit VLSI engine as the ART Multiverb Alpha 2.0 plus a full-function dynamics processor. The DR-X also features a compressor, limiter, exciter, expander, noise gate, and digital frequency routine. It can perform 12 simultaneous audio functions at 20-kHz bandwidth.

The following is a list of its features:

➤ Up to nine effects elements per preset, depending on the complexity of effects

➤ Digital effects that include a seven-band EQ, an acoustic environment simulator, lowpass filter, pitch transposer, dual-pitch transposer, phaser, flanger, chorus, panning, tremolo, reverb, gated reverb, and delay

➤ Analog effects that include a compressor, expander, harmonic exciter, and noise gate algorithms

➤ Utility algorithms that include programmable level, effects crossover, and guitar/bass tuner

➤ Programmable output levels for dry, digital, and analog busses

➤ Real-time control of up to eight effects parameters via MIDI

The DR-X comes with 200 programs and has a sampling time (mono) of 1.58 seconds. The dimensions are 19 inches × 9 3/8 inches × 1 3/4 inches, and the unit weighs 11 pounds. The interfacing includes left and right inputs, left and right outputs, two programmable foot-switch inputs (all 1/4 inch), and one MIDI In, MIDI Out, and MIDI Thru. It also has a DC power Out. The cost is $619.

ART Multiverb Alpha 2.0

Multiverb Alpha 2.0
Applied Research and Technology, Inc.
215 Tremont Street
Rochester, NY 14608
716-436-2720
FAX: 716-436-3942

The Multiverb Alpha 2.0 has a 24-bit processing system that is a digital engine capable of producing reverbs and effects with accuracy and precision. It has the following feature list:

➤ Seven simultaneous, full-bandwidth effects in stereo.

➤ New chorus, flange, and reverbs through a 24-bit VLSI processing system.

➤ 7-band programmable equalizer that can be used with all effects.

➤ Acoustic environment simulator.

➤ Multi-interval pitch shifter with over 2.5 octaves.

➤ Remote-triggerable sampler.

➤ Digital instrument tuner and tone/pitch generator. It tunes the guitar and 4-, 5-, and 6-string bass and is useful for frequency tones to test P.A. system set-up.

➤ Space phaser.

➤ Programmable bypass level.

➤ Independent programmable mixing system you use to vary the Dry level, the EQ'd level, and the Wet level.

➤ Comprehensive performance MIDI that is also easy to use.

➤ X-15 foot pedal for individually turning on and off effects and for controlling up to eight parameters in real-time.

➤ MIDI data monitor that monitors any MIDI data that goes through the system.

➤ Over 50 effects from which to select sound combinations.

ART Multiverb LTX

Multiverb LTX
Applied Research and Technology, Inc.
215 Tremont Street
Rochester, NY 14608
716-436-2720
FAX: 716-436-3942

The Multiverb LTX offers the same rich sounds as the Alpha and DR-X models, but the LTX requires no programming knowledge. It includes 250 studio-designed, multiple effects combinations and is MIDI switchable.

E-mu Proteus/3

Proteus/3 Sound Module
E-mu Systems, Inc.
P.O. Box 660015
Scotts Valley, CA 95067-0015

The Proteus/3 contains 192 sounds that you can use to emulate traditional world instruments or to create your own synthesized sounds. It supports 16-bit sound quality, with MIDI capabilities of up to 16 channels, and 32-voice polyphony.

Korg 01R/W

Korg 01R/W
Korg U.S.A.
89 Frost Street
Westbury, NY 11590

The Korg 01R/W is a two-rack MIDI module that includes all the sounds and features of the Korg 01/W. It also includes a 7,000-note, 16-track sequencer that has editing control. The 01R/W receives on 16 independent MIDI channels, and it has MIDI overflow and four polyphonic outputs.

Korg 03R/W

Korg 03R/W
Korg U.S.A.
89 Frost Street
Westbury, NY 11590

The Korg 03R/W single-rack MIDI module provides 32 voices, 128 General MIDI ROM programs, and 100 user-programmable programs and combinations. The program and PCM card slots use a 2M PCM card. The 03R/W is compatible with Korg's RE-1 Remote Editor, and it receives on 16 individual MIDI channels.

Peavey DPM SP/SX

DPM SP/SX
Peavey Electronics Corporation
711 A Street
Meridian, MS 39301
601-483-5365
FAX: 601-484-4278

The DPM SP/SX is a 16-bit sampling system: the DPM SP rack-mount sample playback module offers 16-bit resolution and a 44.1h kHz stereo sample playback rate. The SP can handle up to 32M of internal sample memory, and the sample RAM is expandable with industry-standard SIMMs expansion boards.

The DPM SX Sampling Xpander module enables you to digitally record 16-bit samples and send them over SCSI to the DPM SP, or in standard SDS format to your DPM 3 or another compatible instrument.

Roland SC-55 Sound Brush

SC-55 Sound Brush
Roland
7200 Dominion Circle
Los Angeles, CA 90040
213-685-5141
FAX: 213-722-0911

The Roland Sound Brush is a disk-based sequencer/MIDI file player. It was designed as a playback device for sequences created on other machines. It can read MIDI files from a floppy disk formatted on MS-DOS; you can transfer Macintosh MIDI files to DOS disks using the Apple File Exchange. The Sound Brush can accept both 0 and 1 types of MIDI files, but type 1 multi-track files can only be 17 tracks wide.

You also can send MIDI files in real-time by connecting the MIDI Out on an external sequencer to Brush's MIDI In, putting Brush into record mode, and starting the sequence. You can align the timing of both units with clock resolution.

Sound Brush accesses MIDI data directly from floppy disk in real-time, which is a useful feature for live performance applications. You can control Brush remotely with a footswitch that connects the unit allowing hands-off start and stop; or you can use the wireless remote controller that comes with the unit. It has the following features:

➤ 3 1/2-inch disk drive

➤ Reads and writes MIDI files

➤ Accepts files directly from IBM, Atari ST, and Roland MC-series disks

➤ Selectable clock resolution of 96, 120, 192, or 240 ppq

➤ Tape recorder-type shuttle controls

➤ Wireless remote control card

➤ Performance mode for playback of customized set lists

The MIDI interfacing consists of two mergeable MIDI Ins, one MIDI Out, and one MIDI Thru. The dimensions of the unit are 8 9/16 inches wide by 1 3/4 inches high by 9 3/16 inches deep; it weighs 3.7 pounds. Because of the small size of the Sound Brush and Sound Canvas, you can use a rack-mount adapter, which is available as an option from Roland, and anchor the units side-by-side into a single-rack space. The cost is $695.

Roland SC-55 Sound Canvas

SC-55 Sound Canvas
Roland
7200 Dominion Circle
Los Angeles, CA 90040
213-685-5141
FAX: 213-722-0911

The Roland Sound Canvas is a 16-part multitimbral sample playback module with a built-in effects processor. One of the best performers in its class and a great value, it comes with 3M of sampled waveforms in ROM banks.

The effects processor offers eight types of reverb and chorus, although only one reverb and chorus combination can be active at a time. Unfortunately, this means every active instrument, regardless of its MIDI channel assignment, shares the same effects. However, the Sound Canvas enables you to set the amount of reverb and chorus for each of the 16 parts (from 0 to 127).

The interfacing has stereo outputs, stereo inputs (all RCA jacks), a mini-jack headphone out, two mergeable MIDI Ins, one MIDI Out, and one MIDI Thru. It has the following features:

➤ 3M sampled ROM wave memory

➤ 24-note polyphony

➤ 16-part multitimbral

➤ Dynamic voice allocation

➤ Channel and polyphonic after-touch response

➤ General MIDI and GS-format compatible

➤ MT-32 emulation mode

➤ Wireless remote control card

➤ Audio input for chaining sound modules

The dimensions of the unit are 8 9/16 inches wide by 1 3/4 inches high by 9 3/16 inches deep; it weighs 3.1 pounds. Because of the small size of the Sound Brush and Sound Canvas, you can use a rack-mount adapter, which is available as an option from Roland, and anchor the units side-by-side into a single-rack space. The cost is $795.

Waldorf MicroWave

MicroWave
Waldorf

The MicroWave sound module is the only synthesizer that has Real-Time Harmonic Just-Intonation that enables you to fine-tune chords. It is the descendant of the PPG Wave synthesizer and combines the best analog filters with unique digital sound-generation. For the 76-note controller, the cost is $625.

The MicroWave is distributed in the United States by:

Steinberg/Jones
17700 Raymer Street, Ste. 1001
Northridge, CA 91325
818-993-4091
FAX: 818-701-7452

In Canada, contact:

The Russ Heinl Group,
a division of Gould Marketing
3003 Etingin
Montreal, P.Q., Canada H4S 1Y7
514-333-4446
FAX: 514-333-6211

Yamaha SPX900 and SPX1000

SPX900 and SPX1000
Yamaha
800-937-7171, Ext. 300

The Yamaha SPX900 and SPX1000 are digital effects processors that provide reverb, early reflection delay, echo, modulation and pitch change. These units have a high degree of reliability and audio clarity.

Yamaha Hello Music!

Yamaha CBX-T3
Yamaha Corporation of America
Digital Musical Instruments
P.O. Box 6600
Buena Park, CA 90622

Wow! I like this product. It's a thin, vertical unit that connects to either your serial port (if you don't have a sound card with MIDI Out connections) or to the MIDI Out port of your sound card. I connected it to the PC I have that uses a MultiSound so I could compare the two units directly for sound quality. It was trivially easy to do—I connected the supplied cable to the MIDI Out cable of the MultiSound and used the MultiSound patch bay application to switch to External output. Bingo—in less than a minute I had the unit connected and was playing with it in Master Tracks Pro 4.

Figure 12.7. *The "Hello Music!" tone generator from Yamaha provides great MIDI sounds; it's the tall, thin vertical unit between the computer and speaker.*

The real name of the Hello Music! system is the CBX-T3. It is a combination of a tone generator and computer software, all in a format that is ideal for use with PCs. The unit stands vertically next to your PC, where you can see the little lights and access the volume and input controls (yes, it adds an audio In port— a nice touch).

The sounds are great; they are on a par with, and are often better than, the General MIDI sounds in the MultiSound. Most of the "better" comes in the form of digital echo/reverb/sound shaping effects that subtly "widen" the sounds—you may or may not like this; I loved it because it gave the music the feel of being played in a real, physical space. The Proteus unit of the MultiSound is a little better for some instruments, but either the Yamaha or the MultiSound is good for professional work. Yamaha did a great job with selecting and implementing the sampled sounds. They are spacious and clear, the highs are crisp and well defined, and the lows are solid and undistorted. The sounds of specific instruments are, in almost all cases, very realistic and sharp. In other words, this is a unit you can use with confidence. My evaluation unit arrived very late—just as we were going to press—but many of the video sound tracks on the Nautilus CD (such as vase4.avi and light.avi) were created with the Hello Music! unit. They illustrate the sound quality of the unit.

If you currently own a low- to mid-level sound card (Sound Blaster 16 and Pro Audio Spectrum 16 are what I would call mid-level cards), you can add superb MIDI sounds with this unit. When combined with a keyboard like the Yamaha CBX-K3, you'll have a professional music workstation. The best news is that you can route the audio outputs of the Hello Music! unit into the inputs of your sound card and record it to .WAV files for playback on machines that don't have a quality MIDI synthesizer.

This system is fully general-MIDI compatible, so it will fit right in with any Windows multimedia products you buy or develop. It incorporates 202 16-bit samples for CD-quality sounds. It also includes digital signal processing that enables you to shape and color the sounds.

Here's a list of key features of Hello Music!:

➤ 192 instrument voices and 10 drum kits

➤ 64 user voices

➤ 28-note polyphony

➤ 16 simultaneous voices

➤ Sampled sounds (wave tables)

➤ Supports MIDI In, Out, and Through

➤ Supports MIDI and serial connection to your PC—you don't have to have a MIDI card to use Hello Music!

➤ Includes Passport's Trax software, a MIDI Player, and Quick Tunes

Yamaha TG-100 and TG-500

Yamaha TG-100/500
Yamaha Corporation of America
Digital Musical Instruments
P.O. Box 6600
Buena Park, CA 90622

The TG-100 is a compact half-rack unit (8.5 inches × 1/4 inches × 1 1/4 inches). The small size makes it ideally suited for travel. It supports General MIDI, which makes it a true plug-and-play unit. It has all the voices, drum sounds, sound effects, and multi-note polyphony you need. (Polyphony refers to the number of simultaneous notes you can play.)

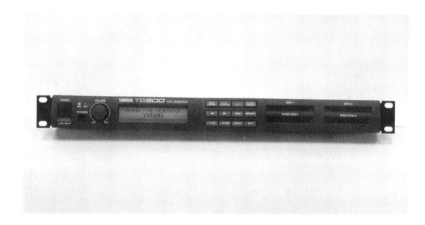

Figure 12.8. *A rack-mount tone generator with high-quality sound.*

The sounds are not the cleanest that I heard in testing, but they are good sounds for the price point. The sounds have a slight digital cast, a kind of minor ringing sound that is only noticeable when compared with a higher-cost card. It does not have the full complement of sound adjustments that the Roland Sound Canvas does, but it lists for $50 less than the Sound Canvas.

The key features of the TG-100 include:

➤ Support for General MIDI

➤ 28-note polyphony

➤ 200 voices (192 instrument voices and 8 drum kits)

873

➤ Built-in computer and MIDI interfaces, including In, Out, and Thru

➤ Audio In as well as audio Out

The unit has the basic controls you need, including master volume, input level, LCD screen contrast, play, part selection, edit button, cursor movement, and two buttons for +1/–1 or yes/no responses. The LCD screen is very small: one 16-character line. The unit can be run by battery or AC adapter. The list price is $449.

The TG-500, which Yamaha calls a second-generation advanced wave memory device (whew!), offers substantially more power and features than the TG-100. The key features are:

➤ 64-note polyphony

➤ 8M of waveform ROM

➤ 384 presets

➤ 252 voices

➤ Four multi-instrument drum voices

➤ Advanced programmable digital filters

➤ The same effects processing as on the SY99 synthesizer

The TG-500 is an ideal setup for creating professional-level MIDI arrangements for recording as .WAV files.

Software Shopper's Guide

I t seems as though there is a new multimedia software title coming out daily. The competition to get out a new product, or a new category of product, has become intense.

That made the job of putting together a Shopper's Guide difficult. I couldn't always get a current phone number or the exact list price, but I have tried to include the widest possible variety of products. The products are grouped into the following categories:

- ➤ Authoring and presentation software
- ➤ Mainstream software gone multimedia
- ➤ CD-ROM magazines
- ➤ Sequencers
- ➤ Wave-file editing
- ➤ Notation software
- ➤ Clip notes
- ➤ Miscellaneous music
- ➤ Image software
- ➤ Screen and video capture
- ➤ Animation software
- ➤ Materials for everything multimedia
- ➤ Multimedia reference, learning tools, and more
- ➤ Fun and games
- ➤ Kids' stuff

Authoring and Presentation Software

Authoring software is used to create multimedia presentations or programs. Common uses for authoring include kiosks at trade shows, sales presentations, corporate boardroom presentations, software demonstrations, and even animated entertainment. Presentation programs usually offer significantly less detailed control over the multimedia contents, and the best programs include tools for organizing and arranging the presentation.

Here's a last-minute tip. If you are converting an existing non-computerized presentation to multimedia (or creating a computerized presentation), you will sometimes be faced with a large quantity of printed text that must be part of the presentation. I was recently faced with such a task, and I wasn't sure how to get all the text into the multimedia/hypertext presentation. I have a scanner, but I hadn't done much OCR (optical character recognition) with it. I tried several OCR programs and found one that I want to recommend enthusiastically: OmniPage Direct, from Caere Corporation.

OmniPage Direct is inexpensive as OCR software goes. List price is $595, but I have seen it sold mail order for less than $400; Caere has offered it for as little as $300 as part of an introductory offer. (Contact Caere at 408-395-7000.)

Unlike stand-alone OCR software, OmniPage Direct links directly to your Windows applications. It adds a menu choice, "Scan text..." to your application's File menu making scanning very convenient. It works with most Windows programs, excluding, of course, paint and image-editing programs.

OmniPage Direct made the process of transferring a transparency-based presentation to multimedia seamless and easy, and it is a useful tool for the multimedia author's toolbox.

Now, back to our regularly-scheduled coverage of authoring packages.

Authorware Professional (Authoring)

Authorware, Inc.
275 Shoreline Drive, Suite 535
Redwood City, CA 94065
800-288-4797
FAX 415-595-3077

Authorware Professional is an icon-based development application for Windows. With Authorware Professional, non-programmers can create interactive multimedia applications without scripting. Applications are arranged in a "flow line" using icons that represent program events or multimedia objects (sounds, animations, calculations, and so on). Authorware provides an engine to package your program into a stand-alone application.

Authorware is pricey, but I've spoken with several developers on CompuServe who have used it. All the reviews have been positive. However, the high cost of Authorware insures that it will be used only in a small percentage of the total multimedia programs being developed. Its main advantage is that you can develop for both the Mac and Windows platforms.

$4,995.00 ($4,745.00 through IBM Ultimedia Tools Series, 800-887-7771).

Compel (Presentation)

Asymetrix Corporation
110-110th Ave. N.E., Suite 717
Bellevue, WA 98004
800-624-8999
206-462-0501
FAX 206-455-3071

Compel is a presentation graphics program for Windows 3.1 or higher that enables you to create and deliver a multimedia slide show. Use Compel's templates to make it easy to get started, then add bullets to format your topics, draw and import graphics for illustrations, create charts for numeric information, and add special effects for added emphasis of key ideas. You can easily take advantage of multimedia devices to add sound effects, animations, or video to the presentation. Of all the recent multimedia presentation tools, Compel has done the most to integrate multimedia into presentations. The only competition for such multimedia power is the forthcoming version 4.0 of Charisma due out by the end of 1993.

With Compel, you can create the usual slide-show trickery—fade previous bullets to focus on a current one, animate bullets, create slide transitions (fades and dissolves), and so on. The real power of Compel lies in its media links. Any object or slide can trigger a multimedia event—playing files, playing sections of files, stopping playback, and so on. Compel also offers useful hyperlinks to define connections between two slides in the same or in different presentations or to trigger a link to another DOS or Windows application. The cost is $295.00.

HSC InterActive (Authoring/Presentation)

> HSC Software
> 1661 Lincoln Blvd., Suite 101
> Santa Monica, CA 90404
> 310-392-8441
> FAX 310-392-6015

With HSC InterActive, non-programmers can create interactive multimedia applications for presentations, demonstrations, training, and more. The icon-based interactive development method is easy to learn and use. It includes a path-based animation module, a paint and editing module, a Windows screen capture, sizing, color conversion utility, and a license-free, runtime module.

I used this package to create one of the multimedia demos on the CD-ROM. It is based on another package listed here, Icon Author, but is much less expensive. It does not include the sophisticated database tools of Icon Author. InterActive is a bit awkard to use and is better at presentations than true interactive authoring efforts. The cost is $495.00.

HSC QuickShow! (Presentation)

> HSC Software
> 1661 Lincoln Blvd., Suite 101
> Santa Monica, CA 90404
> 310-392-8441
> FAX 310-392-6015

QuickShow! offers 640×480 or 800×600 charts, graphs, or photo-realistic imaging. It supports 8-, 16-, 24-, or 32-bit color graphics on high color or standard SVGA cards.

Hyperties (Authoring)

> Cognetics Corporation
> 55 Princeton Heightstown Road
> Princeton Junction, NJ 08550
> 609-799-5005
> FAX: 609-799-8555

Cognetics advertises Hyperties as "Industrial Strength Hypertext Plus Multimedia," and it is an accurate description. Hyperties is a DOS program that comes in three flavors:

Hyperties Standard Edition—Contains several sets of predefined visual designs that you can use to set up hypertext presentations (multimedia is not supported). Each set contains colors, buttons, graphic backgrounds, and fonts that are designed to present a unified visual appearance.

Hyperties Professional Version—Adds a set of tools that enable you to create your own visual designs for presentations. It also adds tools for including multimedia elements in a presentation or hypertext document. The Professional version includes the predefined visual designs of the Standard Edition.

Hyperties for DVI Technology—An extension of the Professional Version that enables you to use Hyperties with Intel's DVI (Digital Video InterActive) technology. (DVI is not the same as AVI, the technology behind Video for Windows.)

Hyperties is best suited for situations where the information, and the relationships within the information (hypertext connections), are the primary concerns. Examples include computer-based education, catalogs, and interactive sales aids that don't need the razzle-dazzle offered by some of the Windows packages.

Icon Author for Windows (Authoring)

AimTech Corporation
20 Trafalgar Square
Nashua, NH 03063
603-883-0220
800-289-2884
FAX 603-883-5582

With Icon Author for Windows, non-programmers can develop interactive multimedia applications that include text, graphics, animations, full-motion video, and enhanced audio. Using Icon Author's visual programming you can produce your own business presentations, computer-based training, self-service kiosks, performance support systems, simulations, and interactive product presentations—all without scripting.

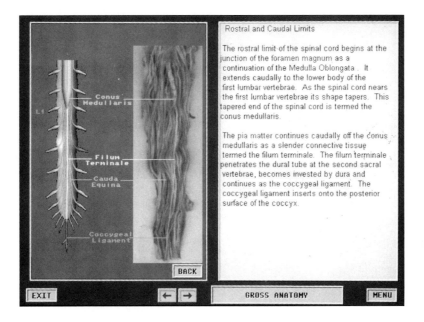

Figure 13.1. *Icon Author allows you to create professional-looking multimedia titles.*

You build the application using the icons provided and then add contents through dialog boxes. Icon Author separates the application content from its structure, which enables you to reuse the original structure and only modify its content to create new applications. Icon Author features built-in WYSIWYG editors, database support, and unlimited user-defined variables. The product provides support for both analog and digital full-motion video. Icon Author is extremely powerful, and the icon interface makes it accessible to someone without a lot of programming experience. It also supports a wide variety of sophisticated (translation: expensive) video storage and display devices, so it is ideal for ultra-high-end presentations or interactive applications. Its biggest weakness is that it requires you to accomplish everything using the icon interface; sometimes, I would have preferred to just write a little code. The cost is $4,995.00 ($4,745.00 through IBM Ultimedia Tools Series, 800-887-7771). This price includes four days of training at Aimtech and one year of technical support. There is a runtime fee, ranging from $50 per unit to 1% of revenue generated by a title. Additional training is available from Aimtech.

Image Q (Presentation)

Image North Technologies
180 King Street South, Suite 360
Waterloo, Ontario, Canada N2J 1P8
(800) 570-9111
BBS: 519-570-9353

Image Q allows you to create presentations that include sound, images, and digital video. A demonstration version is included on the Sampler CD-ROM disc. Further information was not available at press time.

Kodak CD Authoring Software (Authoring, sort of)

Eastman Kodak Company
343 State Street
Rochester, NY 14650
800-242-2424, Ext. 52 (Customer Assistance)
716-724-5034
FAX 716-724-9829

Eastman Kodak recently developed a number of CD authoring products that enable desktop computer users to output their computer files or to create multimedia presentations on recordable compact discs. The following is a list of new products, summarized from Kodak press releases. I have (unfortunately!) not had the opportunity to try these myself.

➤ Kodak has developed new software for authoring Kodak Photo CD Portfolio discs at the desktop. The Portfolio discs can contain combinations of photographic images, audio, graphics and text screens, and programmed access. Applications include consumer "picture stories" (like weddings or family trees), business presentations, and commercial titles. The Portfolio discs can be played on television using a Photo CD or CD-I player. Computers can play the discs using a Photo CD-compatible CD-ROM XA drive and appropriate software.

➤ Kodak writable CD publishing software enables individual users to format digital information stored on personal computers in conformance with the ISO 9660 file and volume structure standard. This standard ensures that data written to a write-once compact disc (CD) is interchangeable across the major computer platforms, including Windows, DOS, Macintosh, and UNIX. Kodak writable CDs can store 550–650M of data, text, images, and digital audio, depending on the format.

Kodak CD publishing software also can drive the Kodak PCD Writer 200 from a customer's host computer. Currently, the writer transfers data to a writable CD in a single session, although Kodak will offer multi-session formatting software for major operating systems in the latter part of 1993. The cost is $2,495.00.

➤ Kodak has developed a writable CD system that enables you to write your own CD-ROM discs for about four cents per megabyte. The writable CD media with InfoGuard data protection system store 550–650M of data, text, images and/or digital audio, which is the equivalent of 240,000 pages of ASCII text, 550 floppy discs, or 3 reels of 9-track tape. The discs are compatible with the ISO 9660 file and volume structure and, if properly authored, can be read in all standard hardware devices, such as CD-ROM, CD-ROM XA, CD-I, and CD audio players.

➤ Kodak also markets a new high-capacity disc that stores 74 minutes of sound capacity; the original disc offers 63 minutes. The new media can store 680M of data, text, images (CD-ROM mode 1), and/or digital audio on a single disc. The original Writable CD media store 580M. Like the original discs, the new disc uses the InfoGuard Protection System. The new higher capacity disc is targeted for users with large-volume storage requirements, such as multimedia publishing or data-intensive archiving.

➤ The Kodak PCD LAN writer 200 is a CD-Recordable (CD-R) production system that bundles Kodak media and hardware with Netscribe Access Client software from Meridian Data, Inc. This system enables users on a PC network to output data to writable CDs as easily as you choose a printer. The PCD LAN Writer 200 offers CD-ROM data retrieval from any node on the network, which enables all network users to access data stored on CD-ROM discs. It supports DOS, Windows 3.*x*, and Windows for Workgroups environments, and it is compatible with all Novell networks, including NetWare Lite and NetWare versions 2.*x*, 3.*x*, and 4.*x*. The cost is $13,995.00 (includes the disc writer and software for up to five users).

LinkWay Live! (Authoring)

IBM Corporation
Multimedia Division
4111 Northside Parkway
Atlanta, GA 30327
(800) 426-9402

This product is a new version of IBM's LinkWay. LinkWay Live! is a DOS-based multimedia authoring and delivery tool that now includes motion-video windows, digital audio buttons, and animated movies. The cost is $308.00 ($245.00 through IBM Ultimedia Tools Series, 800-887-7771).

Make Your Point (Presentation)

Asymetrix Corporation
110-110th Ave. N.E., Suite 717
Bellevue, WA 98004
800-624-8999
206-462-0501
FAX 206-455-3071

Make Your Point for Windows is a low-end tool that simplifies the creation of multimedia presentations. It uses a single dialog box to combine sound, animation, and graphics. The cost is $93.00 ($89.00 through IBM Ultimedia Tools Series, 800-887-7771).

MediaBlitz! (Presentation)

Asymetrix Corporation
110-110th Ave. N.E., Suite 717
Bellevue, WA 98004
800-624-8999
206-462-0501
FAX 206-455-3071

MediaBlitz! enables you to create multimedia shows that can be included in Windows 3.1 applications. With the Clipmaker, you can create a library of clips from media files. With the Scoremaker, you can select media files and bitmap graphics and then play or display them, or you can use the timeline to create a score. With the Scoreplayer, you can play and distribute your multimedia shows, scores, clips, and files. You can easily use MediaBlitz! to arrange the elements of a score and then use OLE to add it to just about any Windows application. It's very easy to use. For example, I was recently on the road, and we needed to quickly add some music and images to a part of our presentation. It was only minutes before the presentation was to start, and we were able to select several bitmaps, add a MIDI selection, and set up the display times and sequence of presentation in just a couple of minutes. Version 3.0, released just as we went to press, adds a .vbx file that allows you to use scores in Visual Basic programs, as well as a DLL for adding scores to any program that can call a Windows DLL. It also adds a number of useful refinements to the user interface, and the ability to create screen-saver scripts.

Micrographx Charisma

Micrografx, Inc.
1303 Arapaho Road
Richardson, TX 75081-2444
800-733-3729

Charisma was undergoing a major rewrite as I was preparing this guide. The early pre-release version I saw included an excellent collection of multimedia features in a well-thought-out interface. It should be worth investigating if you are looking for a solid multimedia presentation package. Contact Micrographx for more information.

Motion Works Multimedia Enabler

Motion Works International
130-1020 Mainland St.
Vancouver, BC V6B 2T4
(604) 685-6105

This is an add-on product for Visual Basic. It adds a number of useful multimedia tools to your programming arsenal. It includes controls for interactive operation of video, audio, and image files. There are a total of five .vbx-based controls: interactive animation, interactive digital video, picture button, sound annotation, and interactive picture.

I am pleased to have a Lite version of Multimedia Enabler on the Sampler CD-ROM disc. You can install it to your hard disk, and use it with Visual Basic. The Lite versions of the controls omit some of the features found in the full version. The differences are documented in the readme.wri file in the setup directory.

Here's a closer look at the features you'll find in the full version of the product:

Interactive Animation control—This is a .vbx front-end to the complete PROmotion animation engine. It allows you to manipulate animation elements as objects with paths. It includes an animation editor, a path editor, support for .wav sounds, a timeline display, a cel-sequencer for controlling actors (animation objects), and a cue editor for adding basic scripts to animations.

Interactive Digital Video control—Includes an editor for defining hot spots in each frame of an .avi file, as well as a .vbx for detecting run-time events (such as clicks on the hot spots). This allows you to create video files that can be played back in an interactive fashion. For example, clicking on an object in the video (even one that moves) creates an event that you can detect and handle in your Visual Basic program. This is the first such program of its kind, and is very useful for anyone working with video. The Lite version on the CD-ROM is completely functional, but it is missing some convenience features.

Picture Button control—This allows you to create buttons that can take on different appearances based on a sequence of images.

Sound Annotation control—This control combines text and .wav files to allow you to highlight specific words as the wave file plays.

Interactive Picture control—This control allows you to define hot spots on a bitmap. Each hotspot causes an event to occur; you can respond to it in your Visual Basic program.

I was very impressed with the design, utility, and capability of this product, and recommend it highly to anyone developing multimedia projects with Visual Basic.

Multimedia ToolBook (Authoring)

Asymetrix Corporation
110-110th Ave. N.E., Suite 717
Bellevue, WA 98004
800-624-8999
206-462-0501
FAX 206-455-3071

ToolBook is a high-level, object-oriented application construction kit for Windows-based applications. You place objects into a window using graphic tools and then add code to the objects using Toolbook's English-like OpenScript language. The latest version includes context-sensitive help. The included Multimedia Resource Kit (MMRK) enables you to link to and control multimedia hardware and software using Windows' built-in multimedia support, the Media Control Interface (MCI). The MMRK supports CD-ROM, laser disc players, animation software, wave-form audio cards, overlay video boards, digital video, and MIDI sequencers. The package includes two sample applications, printed and online documentation, and a function encyclopedia. Take some advice from someone who has been there: you should definitely supplement your study of the documentation with the excellent, well-thought-out sample code. When in doubt, look for an example. The cost is $695.00.

Presenter

16 North Carroll St.
Madison, WI 53703
608-257-3300

Presenter is a traditional presentation program with a number of multimedia features added. It provides a bridge between a gung-ho, multimedia-first program like Compel and more traditional presentation packages.

Quest Multimedia Authoring System

Allen Communication, Inc.

This product enables you to create interactive multimedia courses and presentations using 2-D animation, graphics and audio software, digital and analog video, as well as clip art, clip animation, and clip video. The cost is $3,995.00 (through IBM Ultimedia Tools Series, 800-887-7771).

Storyboard Live! (Presentation)

IBM Corporation
Multimedia Division
4111 Northside Parkway
Atlanta, GA 30327
800-426-9402

Storyboard Live!, Version 2.0, for DOS is a new version of the multimedia authoring tool from IBM. One of the product's key features is that it can play presentations and demonstrations that have sound and video on computers that have limited memory and do not have audio or video cards. The cost is $395.00.

TEMPRA Media Author (Authoring)

Mathematica, Inc.
402 S. Kentucky Ave.
Lakeland, FL 33801
800-852-MATH

TEMPRA Media Author is a high-end desktop/multimedia authoring tool with the following features: time-out; multiple deck, videodisk, and serial device control; tilting; text overlay; freeze frame; animation; and database functions. The cost is $995.00. (Note: Tempra, or various pieces of it, is often bundled with multimedia hardware products.)

Mainstream Software Gone Multimedia

Many mainstream software packages now offer some form of multimedia support. The support varies from such things as multimedia help files to direct support for sound. Among the titles leading the way to multimedia are

Microsoft Word for Windows, Multimedia Edition—The multimedia edition adds support for sound annotations (microphone and sound card required) and integrated support for direct access to Microsoft Bookshelf (described here under the heading "Multimedia Reference, Learning Tools, and More").

Microsoft Works for Windows, Multimedia Edition—The multimedia edition adds digital sound, animation, and pictures to the online tutorial and reference sections. I've seen the animation, and it's entertaining as well as instructive.

Lotus 1-2-3 for Windows, CD-ROM Version—This version includes Multimedia Smarthelp, a help facility that uses a narrated, animated tutorial.

Several other software packages support multimedia (in less dramatic fashion). For example, Harvard Graphics for Windows supports sounds in presentations, and you can use OLE (Object Linking and Embedding) with almost all Windows 3.1 programs to add sound and animation to your programs.

CD-ROM Magazines

Although there will be more CD-ROM magazines in the future, only one has begun distribution that I know of.

Nautilus CD

Metatec Corporation
7001 Discovery Blvd.
Dublin, OH 43017
614-761-2000

Nautilus CD is the first subscription-based multimedia information service available on CD-ROM, and was first published in August 1990. Subscribers receive a new disc every 28 days. Contributions from all over the world include software demos and applications, games, news, multimedia presentations, DTP resources, and so on. Contact Metatec for information about sample issues and subscriptions. However, you shouldn't need a sample issue; one of the CDs included with this book is a special issue of Nautilus and should give you the general idea.

Sequencers

With sequencing software, you can create or modify musical data stored in the MIDI format. There are many ways to get or create MIDI music files, ranging from commercially purchased music to music you play on your own MIDI keyboard. Playback is supported for different numbers of tracks (instruments, sounds, or voices). Some sequencer packages include notation capabilities.

MIDI is the Most Misunderstood Resource in the multimedia universe. With the right hardware and software, you can create absolutely stunning music for presentations. My favorite setup includes a Yamaha Hello Music! tone module connected to whatever sound card you have handy, and the Master Tracks Pro synthesizer. With such a setup, you can design new music or modify existing music (usually via re-orchestration) and then record it via the input port on your sound card.

Ballade

Dynaware USA, Inc.
950 Tower Lane, Suite 1150
Foster City, CA 94404
415-349-5700
FAX 415-349-5879

Ballade GS provides sequencing for Roland GS products (SCC-1 card, SC-55 module), the JV-30 synthesizer, and more.

Ballade 2.51 provides general sequencing for MIDI hardware. You can sequence and score as many as 10 tracks, and print your score on HP Laserjets, HP Deskjets, and dot-matrix printers.

Cadenza for Windows and Cadenza for DOS

Big Noise Software, Inc.
P.O. Box 23740
Jacksonville, FL 32241
904-730-0754

Cadenza provides a 64-track sequencer with a broad range of editing functions, real-time or step recording, MIDI file import (Types 1 and 0) and export (Type 1 only) capabilities, and a good graphical interface. A track sheet displays information for 16 tracks at a time, including solo and play status, number of events, MIDI channel, mode (linear, loop, or link), volume, and so on. Editing screens are provided for velocity mix, pitch bend, tempo, aftertouch, and others. These click-and-drag mouse screens enable you to finesse a recording to sustain vocal notes, tweak the tempo, and view and change sections of data. It includes a help feature. The cost is $299.95 (Windows) and $199.95 (DOS).

Requires: PC AT or better, 512K RAM or more, a mouse, DOS and Windows 3.*x*, Roland MPU-401 or compatible, and Music Quest MQX series. Recommended: 640K RAM and a hard disk.

Cakewalk for Windows and Cakewalk for DOS

Twelve Tone Systems, Inc.
P.O. Box 760
Watertown, MA 02272
800-234-1171
617-273-4437

Cakewalk Professional for Windows 3.1 uses the Windows standard point-and-click graphical interface. Cakewalk for DOS uses a text-based, pseudo-graphical user interface that provides mouse support, pull-down menus, hot keys, dialog boxes, and other features designed to make it easy to use. The benefits of this interface are speed and accuracy on many timing and event synchronizations. Cakewalk has 256 available tracks and provides editing views of tracks, measures, and notes. The program includes SMPTE and MIDI Time code synchronization, channel-to-track translation, filters for selecting ranges of music and events to edit, and the ever-needed undo-edit function (you can even undo your undo!). Cakewalk Professional adds the ability to address multiple MIDI boards, includes SMPTE with MTC sync, and the Cakewalk Application Language (CAL). CAL is a script language you can use to create macros to make repetitive tasks easier. The cost is $349.00.

Requires: 286 PC or better, 2M of RAM, hard disk, mouse, Windows 3.1. It supports as many as 16 MIDI devices with Multimedia Extensions drivers.

Master Tracks Pro 4

Author's Choice

Passport Designs, Inc.
100 Stone Pine Road
Half Moon Bay, CA 94019
415-726-0280
FAX 415-726-2254

Master Tracks Pro features 64-track recording and playback, and it accepts MIDI or keyboard control. Using the standard Windows graphical editing methods or an Event List Editor, you can edit individual notes, pitch, duration, location, tempo, and so on. You also can edit continuous controller data, and Master Tracks Pro includes support for sysex, SMPTE, and Windows Media Control Interface (MCI). It prints notation through MusicTime or Encore. The cost is $395.00 ($279.00 through IBM Ultimedia Tools Series, 800-887-7771).

Requires: PC AT, PS2, or 100 percent compatible (286 or greater), or MPC; Windows 3.0 or higher; DOS 3.1 or higher; mouse; Passport MIDI Interface, MPU-401 MIDI interface or compatible. Recommended: 386 PC, 2M RAM.

Midisoft Studio for Windows

Midisoft Corporation
P.O. Box 1000
Bellevue, WA 98009
800-PRO-MIDI
206-881-7176
FAX 206-883-1368

Midisoft Studio for Windows is a full-featured sequencer that also displays standard music notation as it is being recorded, edited, and overdubbed. The program includes read and write support for standard MIDI file formats as well as comprehensive online documentation.

MusicCad

Alla Breve Music Software, Inc.
1105 Chicago Avenue, Suite 111
Oak Park, IL 60302
708-524-9441

MusicCad is an integrated scoring and sequencing package. The cost is $295.00.

Power Chords

> Howling Dog Systems, Inc.
> Kanata North Postal Outlet
> Box 72071
> Kanata, ON, Canada K2K2P4
> 613-599-7927
> FAX 613-599-7926

Power Chords is unique and a lot of fun (I had a hard time leaving it alone). It uses an original system of notation, based on guitar chording, to give you instant access to music writing. If you don't know notes but walk around humming original tunes in your head, this program may well give you the tools you need to write your own music.

Prism

> Dr. T's Music Software, Inc.
> 100 Crescent Road
> Needham, MA 02194
> 617-455-1454
> FAX 617-455-1460

Prism's interface is window-based (but not Windows compatible) and utilizes most of the user-interface capabilities that make Microsoft Windows popular. This is a pattern-oriented sequencer; you program patterns (parts of a song) and link them to make a complete song. Prism provides an event list editor as well as a track sheet to tweak notes and merge tracks. Graphical representation of music data enables you to edit data such as velocities and pitch bend. Also, a conversion routine enables you to translate files to Texture format, and you can import and export MIDI files. This is a good, versatile program for novices and experienced users alike; it contains good documentation and instruction.

Requires: PC AT or XT, non-MCGA PS/2, or Yamaha C1; 384K RAM; mouse; DOS; Roland MPU-401 or compatible; IBM Music feature (Note: Yamaha C1 tape synchronization is not supported).

Sequencer Plus

Voyetra Technologies
333 Fifth Avenue
Pelham, NY 10803
800-233-9377
914-738-4500
FAX 914-738-6946

Voyetra's Sequencer Plus series offers three related products: the entry-level Sequencer Plus Jr., the intermediate Sequencer Plus Classic, and the professional do-it-all sequencer, Sequencer Plus Gold. These programs offer from 64 to more than 2,000 independent polyphonic tracks, multiple MIDI port support, various playback options, complete MIDI note and controller data editing, and, in Sequencer Plus Gold, MIDI network organizer and data analyzer, universal patch librarian, and so on. No matter what level of sophistication you need, Voyetra has a sequencer solution for you. The cost is $299.95 ($249.00 through IBM Ultimedia Tools Series, 800-887-7771).

Requires: PC AT or XT, or Yamaha C1; 512K RAM; hard drive; DOS 2.01 or higher; Roland MPU-401 or compatible; Voyetra VAPI series; Music Quest MQX series; SAPI-compatible multimedia cards; IBM Music Feature. Recommended: 640K RAM, mouse.

Texture

Magnetic Music

Texture is a pattern-based sequencer. It has a variety of options that enable you to sync to tape recorders. It supports FSK, MIDI clock, SPP, and SMPTE methods. The user interface is a text-based, pseudo-windows environment. Editing functions include quantization, humanization, shifts, MIDI event editing, the usual cut-and-paste functions, and more.

Requires: PC XT or AT, or Yamaha C1; 384K RAM; DOS; Roland MPU-401 or compatible; Music Quest MQX series. Recommended: 512K RAM.

Trax

> Passport Designs, Inc.
> 100 Stone Pine Road
> Half Moon Bay, CA 94019
> 415-726-0280
> FAX 415-726-2254

Trax is a 64-track, 16-channel basic sequencer offering graphic step, measure view, song editing, and (of course) compatibility with Master Tracks Pro files. Easy to learn and use, Trax uses a tape-recorder-style format, and you can record your music live or step-by-step. For those who don't need fancy editing capabilities, this could be your answer. The cost is $99.00 ($69.00 through IBM Ultimedia Tools Series, 800-887-7771).

Wave-File Editing

Just as sequencers enable you to edit and create music files, wave-file editors enable you to modify sound files. These editors range from the simple, such as the Sound Recorder that comes with Windows, to the sophisticated, such as Wave for Windows from Turtle Beach. Some have fun capabilities like echo, and some address the needs of professional recording.

AudioView

> Voyetra Technologies
> 333 Fifth Avenue
> Pelham, NY 10803
> 800-233-9377
> 914-738-4500
> FAX 914-738-6946

With this full-featured graphical audio editor you can record, edit, and play files in .VOC and .WAV file format. It supports echo and other effects, data compression, sample rate and bit resolution conversion, and so on. It also includes a CD Audio Controller program. The cost is $129.95 ($109.00 through IBM Ultimedia Tools Series, 800-887-7771).

Sound Forge 2.0

Sonic Foundry
1110 East Gorham
Madison, WI 53703
608-256-1432
FAX 608-256-7300

Sound Forge was one of the more pleasant surprises of the last year. I included a demo version of the software on the CD-ROM, so you can check it out and see if I'm right. I love the interface of this program. Everything is right where I want it, and mouse clicks always seem to do just what you'd expect them to do. I never once had to refer to the manual, or even the help system, to figure out how to work with sounds.

The current version of this program, 2.0, is missing a few key features, so you won't be able to use it for all of your sound work. Wave for Windows, which has a less-likable interface, does have a more complete feature set. However, with any luck, the next version of Sound Forge will close the gap and give you the best of both worlds (interface and features) in one package. For the time being, you'll need both packages for serious sound work. The cost is $179.00 list.

Wave for Windows

Turtle Beach Systems
P.O. Box 5074
York, PA 17405
717-843-6916

With Wave, you can record and edit professional quality music. This editor uses any digital audio hardware to record professional quality music in stereo, with the file size limited only by available hard-disk space. Edit functions include the standard cut, copy, and paste. The software also includes gain adjustment; a programmable, parametric equalizer; digital mixing of as many as three sound files into one; programmable cross-fading tool; import/export function, and so on.

Wave 2.0 has added online context-sensitive help and a speed controller, which changes the speed of a recorded file as much as 200 percent faster, and 50 percent slower. Wave now supports ADPCM compression. The cost is $99.00, but substantial discounts are available.

Requires: MPC with CD-ROM.

Notation Software

With notation software, you can compose music and print it to paper. Usually, you can enter the notes with your PC or a MIDI instrument, edit the displayed score to various extremes, and print the song to supported printers.

As with most multimedia software, there are entry-level and professional packages out there with prices to match. The following packages are a few of those available.

Encore

> Passport Designs, Inc.
> 100 Stone Pine Road
> Half Moon Bay, CA 94019
> 415-726-0280
> FAX 415-726-2254

Encore transcribes as many as 64 staves of music from live performances, or from MIDI files or a Passport sequencer. Using a mouse, you can enter music or record in step-time from a MIDI instrument. Editing functions are fairly straightforward using standard Windows graphics. You can choose from six palettes of notes, clefs, graphics, marks, and dynamics to enter or edit your score. Encore can play your score, or individual parts, on MIDI instruments. It produces acceptable output from PostScript printers. The cost is $595.00.

Requires: PC AT, PS2, 100 percent compatible (286 or better), or MPC; 2M RAM; Windows 3.*x*; DOS 3.1 or higher; mouse; Windows-compatible printer; MPU-401-compatible or Windows-Multimedia-Extensions-compliant MIDI interface. Recommended: 386 PC or better.

Finale

> CODA Music Technology
> 6210 Bury Dr.
> Eden Prairie, MN 55346-1718
> 800-843-2066
> 612-937-9611
> FAX 612-937-9760

Finale is a complex, comprehensive, and flexible music-printing package. Any part of a score that you might need to change can be changed; if you need mixed staff sizes and character scaling, unusual symbols, personally designed shapes, or other custom elements, you can do it with Finale. The time required to learn Finale might be somewhat higher than for other output packages, but for serious users, it's worth the extra effort. Documentation is voluminous and well-indexed. Instead of clicking on and moving the actual object, Finale attaches "handles" to the object that enable you to manipulate it as you would in a drawing package. You can manually enter and place each note, record music live, or use an option to edit measure by measure. For those operations that take time, adding a math coprocessor can improve performance significantly. Finale produces acceptable quality from PostScript and 24-pin dot matrix printers. The cost is $749.00 retail; $250.00 academic.

Requires: 286 PC; 1M RAM; hard disk; mouse; Epson-compatible dot matrix, LaserJet, or PostScript printer; DOS and Windows 3.0 or higher; Roland MPU-401 or compatible. Recommended: 386 PC, 2M RAM or more.

MIDIScan

> Musitek Music Recognition Tech.
> 800-676-8055
> 805-646-8051

MIDIScan is a musical OCR, or rather optical music-recognition software (MRS), program that converts sheet music into multi-track MIDI files. You'll need a scanner to capture TIFF images of a musical score. After processing the score image, MIDIScan displays both the original and reconstructed scores in a window for easy graphic editing. A toolbar makes it easy to add frequently used musical symbols. MIDI conversion produces a multi-track MIDI file of the music that you can port to sequencers for playback. The cost is $379.00.

MOSAIC

> Mark of the Unicorn, Inc.
> 222 Third Street
> Cambridge, MA 02142
> 617-576-2760
> FAX 617-576-3609

MOSAIC contains all the standard score editing in a click-and-drag interface. It enables you to do real- and step-time MIDI input and playback.

MusicPrinter Plus

Temporal Acuity Products, Inc.
300-120th Ave. NE
Bldg. 1, Suite 200
Bellevue, WA 98005
800-426-2673
206-462-1007
FAX 206-462-1057

MusicPrinter Plus (MPP) is a good, all-around, music-scoring system. MPP is easy to use and fast, and you can use it to sync with external devices using FSK and SMPTE. You can add data by placing notes, playing notes, incorporating real-time input, or importing MIDI files (Type 1). You can have MPP play your score on a MIDI instrument and hear a mechanically correct rendition including dynamics, articulations, and tempo changes. Text capabilities are adequate but not extravagant. MPP contains an extraction utility for printing a single part from the full score and can also do simultaneous extractions. The cost is $495.00.

Requires: PC AT or greater, or Yamaha C1; SVGA, VGA, EGA, CGA, Hercules, or Yamaha C1 High Resolution; 640K RAM; Epson-compatible, Canon BubbleJet, or LaserJet printers; DOS 2.01 or higher; Roland MPU-401 or compatible, Music Quest MQX series, IBM Music Feature, Voyetra VAPI series. Recommended: hard disk, mouse.

MusicProse

CODA Music Software
1401 E. 79th Street
Bloomington, MN 55425
612-854-1288
FAX 612-854-4631

MusicProse is from the makers of Finale. It is a simpler version of the program that enables less-experienced folks to work on files that will later be completed in Finale. The cost is $249.00.

MusicTime

Passport Designs, Inc.
100 Stone Pine Road
Half Moon Bay, CA 94019
415-726-0280
FAX 415-726-2254

MusicTime, low-end notation software based on Encore, transcribes as many as six staves of music from music you play, from MIDI files, or from a Passport sequencer. Editing functions are easy to follow because the interface uses standard Windows graphics, enabling you to cut, copy, paste, and so on. MusicTime can play your score on MIDI-equipped musical instruments or through sound cards. It ships with Adobe Sonata Music Font and Adobe Type Manager. The cost is $249.00 ($199.00 through IBM Ultimedia Tools Series, 800-887-7771).

Requires: PC AT, PS2, 100 percent compatible (286 or better), or MPC; Windows 3.*x*; DOS 3.1 or higher; mouse; Windows-compatible printer. Optional: Passport MIDI interface, MPU-401 MIDI interface, or compatible. Recommended: 386 PC, 2M RAM.

QuickScore Deluxe

Dr. T's Music Software, Inc.
124 Crescent Road
Needham, MA 02194
800-989-MIDI
617-455-1454
FAX 617-455-1460

With QuickScore Deluxe, you can play your music in, or import, MIDI files. Your music is scored, and you can play it back using MIDI or other popular sound cards. Scores as many as 16 tracks. The cost is $149.00.

SongWright

SongWright Software
7 Loudoun St. S.E.
Leesburg, VA 22075
800-877-8070
703-777-7232

SongWright is a PC music processor that enables you to compose, record, edit, and score your music. It supports dot-matrix and laser-printer output. The cost is $119.95.

Clip Notes

Clip notes are the audio equivalent of clip art. The titles listed here include audio-only clips. Titles that include video, animation, art, or other clip and paste objects are listed in the section "Materials for Everything Multimedia."

Audio Tracks

> HSC Software
> 1661 Lincoln Blvd., Suite 101
> Santa Monica, CA 90404
> 310-392-8441
> FAX 310-392-6015

Audio Tracks provides you with digitally mastered special effects and music for use with presentations, games, and educational applications. It was developed to fully support Sound Blaster/Pro, Media Vision, and ATI sound cards. The cost is $79.95.

Audio Tracks Libraries 1 and 2

> HSC Software
> 1661 Lincoln Blvd., Suite 101
> Santa Monica, CA 90404
> 310-392-8441
> FAX 310-392-6015

Audio Tracks also distributes collections of digitally mastered special effects and music in .WAV file format that you can use in presentations, games, educational, and multimedia applications. No licensing fees are required. The cost is $49.00 per library.

DigiSound Audio Library

Presentation Graphics Group
270 N. Canon Dr., Suite 103
Beverly Hills, CA 90210
213-277-3050

Each volume in this library includes a minimum of 120 audio clips compatible with any MPC application. Volumes include MIDI Music Volumes 1 and 2, Sound Effects Volumes 1–4, and the Starter Disc (containing 400 sound effects and voice clips and more than two hours of MIDI music).

The Hollywood Sound Library

New Eden Multimedia
7652 Hampshire Ave.
Minneapolis, MN 55428
800-735-EDEN
612-561-2557
FAX 612-566-2148

The Hollywood Sound Library is the high-end of sound files. This service offers thousands and thousands of sound files that are the same ones used by the movie industry. New Eden Multimedia acquired the computer distribution rights to the complete digital sound libraries of Sound Ideas (North America's oldest sound studio), and The Hollywood Edge (Hollywood's motion picture sound studio). You can purchase individual sound clips from over 12,000 sounds and distribute them royalty-free. The sound files are in Microsoft's ADPCM wave format. Sound clips are sold individually based on length (in seconds): 1–15 seconds, $3.00; 15–45 seconds, $6.00; 45+ seconds, $9.00; add $7.95 shipping and handling charge per order. Send $4.95 for a Hollywood Sound Library catalog and sample disk.

I received some samples from New Eden that I included on the CD-ROM. In addition, you'll find a text file with the complete catalog of clips offered in the collection. You can judge for yourself if these clips are worth the cost. The quality and variety are ideal for serious sound work.

Media Music

Passport Designs, Inc.
100 Stone Pine Road
Half Moon Bay, CA 94019
800-443-3210
415-726-0280
FAX 415-726-2254

Media Music is a collection of original music in digital audio (8- and 16-bit) and MIDI formats. All styles of music are included. You can import and export the music to sequencers for customization.

Mr. Sound FX

Prosonus
11126 Weddington St.
North Hollywood, CA 91601
800-999-6191
818-766-5221
FAX 818-766-6098

Mr. Sound FX contains more than 150 sound effects from Michael Winslow (from the Police Academy movies) that you can add to your Windows applications. Sounds include explosions, sirens, planes, trains, automobiles, electronic effects, and so on. Mr. Sound FX also includes the Mr. Sound FX Player and Windows Sound Driver that can add sounds to various Windows events, as well as a speaker driver in case you do not own a sound card. No audio card is necessary. The cost is $29.95.

Requires: Windows 3.1. Recommended: 4.5M of hard disk space. Available on 5 1/4- or 3 1/2-inch high-density diskettes.

MusicBytes

Prosonus
11126 Weddington St.
North Hollywood, CA 91601
800-999-6191
818-766-5221
FAX 818-766-6098

The MusicBytes CD-ROM contains more than 634M of clip music, comprising 108 sound effects and 28 songs. The songs are recorded in several styles and arrangements, including 60-, 30-, 15-, and 5-second versions in Red Book audio (16-bit, 44.1-KHz stereo), and 22- and 11-KHz digital audio (Wave format), with General-MIDI-compatible files transcribed from the original recordings. Musical groups including Toto, Pink Floyd, and the Doobie Brothers recorded these songs. The Media Librarian, an applet included with MusicBytes, enables you to catalog, audition, and copy files. The selections provided are indexed, and all are proprietary to Prosonus. You can use the music license-free in your presentations, however. I included several of these sounds and musical beds in my own multimedia presentations for the Multimedia Madness CD-ROM.

MusicBytes includes Media Librarian, which is a cataloging database that enables you to audition, catalog, modify, and search for any file on MusicBytes. If you copy the Media Librarian to your hard disk, you can catalog and access files from any CD-ROM in your Prosonus collection.

The musical styles represented include Rock, Classical, Jazz, Industrial, Novelty, Pop, Bluegrass, Fusion, New Age, Reggae, Island, Bebop, Romantic, Corporate, Funk, Dramatic, Urban, International, Orchestra, News, and Fanfare, among others.

Noise for Windows

Erudite Software
2408 Glenmary Avenue
Louisville, KY 40204-2108
502-451-7712
800-78-NOISE
FAX 502-451-7681

With Noise for Windows, you can add sound effects to your actions in Windows. The software includes prerecorded sounds (thermonuclear explosion, dragging boulder, and so on) and MIDI notes. It also enables you to record your own sounds.

Prosonus Sample Library

> Prosonus
> 11126 Weddington St.
> North Hollywood, CA 91601
> 818-766-5221
> FAX 818-766-6098

Sixteen volumes provide more than four gigabytes of instrument samples. If your MIDI instrument supports this capability, you can use the samples to "teach" your MIDI instrument new sounds. Instruments from pianos to percussion, and sounds from Foley effects to speech are covered in these volumes. The cost is $69.95 for each volume.

Miscellaneous Music

This section presents any products that didn't fit into another musical category.

Band-in-a-Box

> PG Music Inc.
> 111-266 Elmwood Avenue
> Buffalo, NY 14222
> 800-268-6272
> 416-528-2368

After you enter the chords to any song and choose the style you want for your song, Band-in-a-Box creates your five-instrument accompaniment: base, drums, piano, guitar, and strings. Play any of 24 styles from Band-in-a-Box Standard Edition, or 75 styles from the Professional Edition. Standard Edition (24 styles), $59.00; Professional Edition (75 styles), $88.00; upgrade or crossgrade, $29.00.

The Jammer

Soundtrek
3384 Hill Dr.
Duluth, GA 30136
404-623-0879

The Jammer is a MIDI music program that runs on PCs with 401 cards or Sound Blasters. It includes 256 built-in musicians that play drums, drum fills, drum solos, bass parts, rhythm guitars and keys, melodies, lead breaks, and chord progressions. You control the style of these musicians on each track and decide which tracks and measures to keep or redo. The Jammer includes 125 band styles files, including rock, pop, blues, funk, jazz, ballads, classical, bluegrass, Latin, reggae, and more. You can enter your own chords on any eighth note boundary or let the Jammer create new chord progressions for you.

The mixing console includes digital track faders, panning, reverb, chorus, relative velocity, mute-solo-play switches, and GS-compatible automatic patching. Standard Jammer, $88.00; Jammer Professional, $175.00; Jammer Standard Plus the Roland SCC-1 Sound Card for PCs, $449.00; Jammer Pro 2.0 update, $39.00; Demo disk, $5.00. Call 404-623-5887 for a recorded demo.

The Jazz Guitarist

PG Music
266 Elmwood Ave., Suite 111
Buffalo, NY 14222
800-268-6272
416-528-2368

The Jazz Guitarist is a music program containing over 60 jazz standards, played on MIDI Guitar by top Jazz/Studio Guitarist Oliver Gannon. The on-screen fretboard shows you what guitar notes are being played. Play in real time, or step through the piece chord by chord.

General MIDI modules, such as the Roland Sound Canvas and SCC-1, can use the built-in mixer to change volumes, patches, panning, reverb, chorus, and tuning. The Jazz Guitarist also supports non-General MIDI interfaces with drum kits for over 40 synths built in. Since the pieces are saved as Standard MIDI files, you can use them in other music programs or as background music for presentations. Use your existing sound card, digital piano, sound module or MIDI synthesizer to play the music back. Windows users can play back through their sound card (Roland, Sound Blaster, and so on).

The software includes a jazz trivia game, "Guess the Song" game, jazz guitarist biographies, and more. The cost is $49.00.

MIDI Toolkit

> Voyetra Technologies
> 333 Fifth Avenue
> Pelham, NY 10803
> 800-233-9377
> 914-738-4500
> FAX 914-738-6946

MIDI Toolkit is a set of three applications that help you use and manage your Windows-based MIDI setup. The MIDI Data Analyzer enables you to view the incoming MIDI data stream. The MIDI Mapper is a replacement for Microsoft's MIDI Mapper. A third utility re-orchestrates standard MIDI files. The cost is $99.95.

MusiClips

> Voyetra Technologies
> 333 Fifth Avenue
> Pelham, NY 10803
> 800-233-9377
> 914-738-4500
> FAX 914-738-6946

MusiClips is a comprehensive library of over 400 selections in MIDI file format. The clips play correctly right out of the box with a sound card or General MIDI synth. The cost is $69.95.

PC Karaoke

Sirius Publishing, Inc.
7320 E. Butherus Dr., Ste. 100
Scottsdale, AZ 85260
800-247-0307
602-951-3288

PC Karaoke offers a CD-ROM with 10 musical tracks featuring digitized audio versions of favorite music selections, such as The Muppet Movie theme, "Pretty Woman," "Twist and Shout," and many more. Sirius also offers CD-ROMs for $15.95 per title with music from artists like Garth Brooks and Elvis Presley, or musical themes like Christmas carols, rock hits, and country favorites.

You can sing along to these favorites using your PC. When you play a musical track on your CD-ROM drive, the words to the song appear on your computer screen. Each of the words is highlighted in 36-point type when you're supposed to sing it. Or, if you prefer, use the KJ, which plays AVI video clips to introduce each of the songs. The cost is $99.95.

Requires: 386SX; 2M of RAM; CD-ROM drive; 2.5M of hard disk space; 8- or 16-bit sound card with microphone input; VGA graphics.

PatchView FM

Voyetra Technologies
333 Fifth Avenue
Pelham, NY 10803
800-233-9377
914-738-4500
FAX 914-738-6946

PatchView is a patch editor/sound palette arranger for all sound cards and multimedia PCs, and it is based on Yamaha's FM synthesis technology. It enables you to access every FM sound parameter and create custom palettes so you don't have to use the standard one in Windows. The cost is $99.95.

The Pianist

PG Music
266 Elmwood Ave., Ste. 111
Buffalo, NY 14222
800-268-6272
416-528-2368

The Pianist is a music program for Windows and the Mac containing a collection of over 200 of the world's most popular classical piano pieces performed by world-class concert pianists. All the pieces have been recorded in "real time" by concert pianists on an 88-note weighted MIDI piano keyboard. You can sort and play music by composer name, type of piece, historic period, mood, difficulty, title, or create your own "favorite files." You can play single selections or sets of your favorite pieces or composers. The Pianist includes a Music Trivia Game with over 400 questions about the music, piano, and composers. You can also play the "Guess That Song" game, which selects and plays a piece at random.

Learn how to play the music using an on-screen piano keyboard that enables you to see the music as it is played. You can also learn the music by watching the on-screen keyboard or by slowing down the performance. You can stop, pause, rewind, go in slow motion, change tempo, transpose, or alter the volume and velocity.

The music pieces have been saved as Standard MIDI files so you can use them in other music programs or as background music for presentations, telephone on-hold, and so on. Play the music back through your existing MIDI synthesizer, digital piano, or sound module. Windows users can play back through their sound card (Roland, Sound Blaster, and so on). The cost is $49.00.

Stereo

Animotion Development Corporation
3720 Fourth Avenue South
Suite 205
Birmingham, AL 35222
205-591-5715
FAX 205-591-5716

Stereo emulates a component stereo system on your PC. In addition, it provides a tool for storing and maintaining all your CDs, cassette tapes, records, and .WAV and MIDI files.

X-oR

Dr. T's Music Software, Inc.
100 Crescent Road
Needham, MA 02194
617-455-1454
FAX 617-455-1460

X-oR is a MIDI system organizer that enables you to get, send, load, and save individual patches or entire songs from any MIDI system instrument.

Image Software

Many programs are available for creating or editing images. The images fall into two major categories: vector and raster.

Vector images are made up of objects. If you put a circle in your drawing, for example, you can go back later and change its size, orientation, color, line thickness, and so on. Because the object has defined properties, the program can always access the object.

Raster images are made up of pixels. If you put a circle in a drawing, you might not be able to modify it—the circle is just a bunch of pixels in the image.

Which format you work with is up to you. In general, you should use a raster package for working with photo-realistic images and a vector package to create illustrations. This is not a hard-and-fast rule, however. I recommend at least one software package in each category.

Aldus PhotoStyler (Raster)

Aldus Corporation
Consumer Division
5120 Shoreham Place
San Diego, CA 92122-5926
800-888-6293, Ext. 2
619-558-6000
FAX 691-558-8774

Aldus PhotoStyler is a color-photo design and production program that enables you to acquire images from a wide range of sources and in industry-standard file formats, and then to enhance or modify them for use in publications or presentations. You can also use PhotoStyler's painting and effects tools to create original images in color or gray scale. PhotoStyler enables you to exchange files with the Mac and other computers, do minor or extensive retouching and color correction, or produce color separations on any image setter supported by Windows or PostScript. The cost is $795.00.

CA-Cricket Image (Raster)

> Computer Associates International, Inc.
> One Computer Associates Plaza
> Islandia, NY 11788-7000
> 800-CALL-CAI
> 516-342-5225
> FAX 516-342-5734

CA-Cricket Image is a professional image processing system for raster-based PC graphics. You can import or export using several Windows file formats or scan pictures directly from TWAIN-compliant scanners, and then you can process them with filters and special effects. You can do image conditioning by adjusting brightness and contrast, color reduction and dithering, edge sharpening and noise removal. You also can perform transformation functions, including creating negatives, cropping, scaling and rotating any amount, and generating color separations. CA-Cricket Image includes several compression systems to help keep file sizes manageable. The cost is $92.00.

CA-Cricket Paint (Raster)

> Computer Associates International, Inc.
> One Computer Associates Plaza
> Islandia, NY 11788-7000
> 800-CALL CAI
> 516-342-5225
> FAX 516-342-5734

CA-Cricket Paint is excellent for retouching images, painting pictures, and composing multiple images into single works of art. You can start with a scanned image and duplicate or remove parts of the image, sharpen or soften edges, overlay another image into the background, add text, or create special effects like pastel, charcoal, watercolor, oil, acrylic, tinting, glazing, and more. CA-Cricket Paint's tool set includes paintbrush, airbrush, smearing, line drawing tools, filled shapes, anti-aliased text, lasso, stamp, fill, rotate and scale, perspective, distort, and automatic gleam. You also can combine photos and backgrounds seamlessly or do photo retouching using Ca-Cricket Paint's 24-bit color and full anti-aliasing. It comes with floating tool palettes that you can toggle on and off to view images full-screen. The cost is $92.00.

Color Wheel (Raster)

North Coast Software, Inc.
P.O. Box 343
Barrington, NH 03825
603-332-9363

Color Wheel is an object-based painting and imaging program for Windows. It enables you to create pictures for presentations, advertising, compositions, animation, and much more. All objects can be stacked in layers and manipulated freely and independently. You use the Color and Palette Management Color Wheel to create numerous color palettes as well as specially blended fountain palettes to simulate real paintbrush effects. You can edit and save your palettes. Color Wheel supports 256 to 16.8 million (24-bit) True Color. The cost is $395.00.

Conversion Artist (Raster)

North Coast Software, Inc.
P.O. Box 343
Barrington, NH 03825
603-332-9363

Conversion Artist imports and converts more than 25 popular image formats from the IBM PC, Macintosh, Amiga, Sun, and Silicon Graphics platforms. It previews Edsun CEG and true-color images with up to 16.6 million colors under Windows, and it supports six 24-bit image formats.

CorelDRAW! (Vector)

Corel Systems Corporation
1600 Carling Avenue
Ottawa, ON K1Z 8R7
Canada
613-728-8200
800-836-DRAW
FAX 613-728-9790

CorelDRAW!, a flexible and comprehensive image-creation package, offers you editable preview, unlimited layers, live blends, and many more features, all with on-line help. CorelDRAW! includes CorelCHART!, a data-driven chart program; CorelPAINT!, a paint and photo editor program; CorelSHOW!, a slide show and animation program; and CorelTRACE! and CorelMOSAIC!. In Version 4.0, CorelDRAW! added CorelMOVE.

CorelDRAW! Version 4.0 contains toolbars and roll-up palettes that provide access to features like fractal fill patterns, defined paragraph styles, paintbrush stroke effects, and dimensioning tools. Version 4.0 also contains several desktop publishing functions, and it supports documents up to 999 pages, displays spreads onscreen, and links text frames so that copy flows from page to page. The cost is $595.00.

CorelDRAW! Version 3.0 is offering a bonus CD-ROM disc that contains 10,000 pieces of vector-based clip art and over 200 additional TrueType or PostScript typefaces. The cost is $199.00.

Freehand 3.1 (Vector)

Aldus Corporation
411 First Avenue South
Seattle, WA 98104-2871
800-333-2538
206-622-5500
FAX 206-343-4240

Freehand is a complete design and illustration software package. It enables you to work in full-color, full-screen preview mode. Freehand supports pressure-sensitive drawing tablets, and exports designs, colors and/or separations to various hardware and software environments. The cost is $595.00.

Gallery Effects (Raster)

Aldus Corporation
Consumer Division
5120 Shoreham Place
San Diego, CA 92122-5926
800-888-6293, Ext. 2
619-558-6000
FAX 691-558-8774

Gallery Effects is a family of products that offer automatic image-enhancement tools to add visual impact to electronic and printed documents. Gallery Effects: Classic Art, Volume 1 provides 16 special effects you can apply to scanned photographs and bitmapped images. The effects are Graphic Pen, Dry Brush, Poster Edges, Dark Strokes, Charcoal, Fresco, Film Grain, Spatter, Chalk & Charcoal, Emboss, Ripple, Smudge Stick, Chrome, Mosaic, Craquelure, and Watercolor. Volume 1, $99.00.

Gallery Effects: Classic Art, Volume 2 is an extension of Volume 1 and offers additional photographic effects and painterly effects in bold painting and drawing styles. Its 16 new filters are Accented Edges, Angled Strokes, Bas Relief, Colored Pencil, Diffuse Glow, Glowing Edges, Grain, Note Paper, Palette Knife, Patchwork, Photocopy, Rough Pastels, Sprayed Strokes, Stamp, Texturizer, and Underpainting. Volume 2, $99.00.

All effects are available as plug-in filters that you can apply from within the Gallery Effects application or from other Mac or Windows programs that support this plug-in technology. Each effect in a Gallery Effects library can be applied alone or with others.

Illustrator (Vector)

Adobe Systems Incorporated
1585 Charleston Road
Mountain View, CA 94039-7900
415-961-4400
800-83-FONTS (800-833-6687)
FAX 415-961-3769

Illustrator is a complete illustration and single-page design package. Supports 8-, 16-, and 24-bit color onscreen. It supports file exchange between Macintosh, NeXT, other versions of Adobe Illustrator, and other graphics programs. It includes Adobe Type Manager, Adobe TypeAlign, and so on. The cost is $695.00 ($459.00 through IBM Ultimedia Tools Series, 800-887-7771).

ImageFast (Raster)

ImageFast
7926 Jones Branch Drive
McLean, VA 22102
703-442-4545
FAX 703-893-7499

ImageFast is an electronic-document management system that scans, stores, and retrieves images. You can define your own electronic folder structure, data forms, and indexed fields, and you can scan documents, transmit images as faxes, and so on. ImageFast contains many options for text and fields as well as text/image search and retrieval. A demo is available for $25.00. The cost of the system ranges from $995.00 to $9,500.00.

ImagePals (Raster)

U-Lead Systems, Inc.
970 West 190th Street
Suite 520
Torrance, CA 90502
800-858-5323
310-523-9393
FAX 310-523-9399

This integrated image-management, image-enhancement, and screen-capture package does it all. Use Capture to capture screen shots from any Windows program. In Album, you can organize and find your images easily. And for real artistic license, take an image to Enhancer where you can paint, color correct, filter, add special effects, resize, rotate, and more. You can even import scanned images, or use captured images from digital cameras or video frame grabbers. The cost is $249.00.

IntelliDraw 2.0 (Vector)

Aldus Corporation
Consumer Division
5120 Shoreham Place
San Diego, CA 92122-5926
800-888-6293, Ext. 2
619-558-6000
FAX 691-558-8774

Aldus IntelliDraw is a drawing program that offers standard drawing tools but speeds up the drawing process with a number of "intelligent" tools. For example, with the Symmetrigon you can produce symmetric shapes by drawing just one side. The Connectigon draws a shape whose sides remain attached when moved or reshaped. The Number tool creates numeric labels that update as you change your graphics. You can create Symbols with clones of any graphic. Also, you can edit one master clone, and all clones change automatically (even clip art and bitmaps). IntelliDraw comes with intelligent templates and clip art that you can use intact or as a starting point.

IntelliDraw 2.0 has added several new features: new drag-and-drop Smart Templates that enable you to create artwork without drawing. The images have built-in smart features with changeable attributes such as duplicating, stretching, and specifying distances or sizes numerically. Version 2.0 offers expanded file support and connectivity; it now supports cross-platform file sharing between Macintosh and Windows. IntelliDraw 2.0 offers several new special effects for objects and text, such as warping envelopes and polymorphing. The cost is $199.00 (Upgrade: $49.95).

Fractal Design Painter (Raster)

Fractal Design Corporation
335 Spreckels Drive, Suite F
P.O. Box 2380
Aptos, CA 95001
408-688-8800
FAX 408 688-8836

Fractal Design Painter 2.0 is a natural-media paint and photo-design software program that enables you to create original artwork from scratch or base your design on scanned images or EPS artwork. Like its predecessor, Version 2.0 duplicates traditional media and textures in 24-bit color.

Painter 2.0 has added tear-off tools, snap-to and adjustable grid paper, quick-access window controls, Brush Designer, and straight-line tools. Version 2.0 now enables you to preview effects before applying them to an image. And you can select from more than 80 individual art tools, such as pencils, crayons, chalks, charcoals, water-color brushes, airbrushes, bristle brushes, and artist's brushes (like Van Gogh), and so on.

To use Painter 2.0, simply choose your media (charcoal, felt pens, crayons, and so on), choose your surface (canvas, cotton bond, and more), and paint! Choose an existing brush or design your own.

Painter supports Wacom, Kurta, and CalComp pressure-sensitive styluses. As of August 3, 1993, Painter 2.0 was being bundled with Wacom's digitizing tablets and pressure-sensitive pens. It's one of my choices for best in the class. The cost is $399.00 ($299.00 through IBM Ultimedia Tools Series, 800-887-7771).

Fractal Design PainterX2 (Raster)

Fractal Design Corporation
335 Spreckels Drive, Suite F
P.O. Box 2380
Aptos, CA 95001
408-688-8800
FAX 408 688-8836

Fractal Design PainterX2 is an add-on to Fractal Design Painter 2.0. It provides an environment where an artist can cut out any part of a Painter 2.0 image and retain it as a separate visual item. You can paint into, around, or under these floating items as well as scale, rotate, and distort them. You also can apply visual effects to each floating selection using either Painter's own effects menu or third-party plug-ins.

Each floating item has independent feathering and frisket (masking) controls. You can generate drop shadows for any selection using these friskets. Because each floating selection has its own frisket, you can feather the frisket's edge to any degree. For example, you can airbrush a highlight and shadow on the edges of an item without altering the surrounding image area.

917

PainterX2 contains tools that enable you to build your own palettes of colors called Color Sets. You can assign each color a name, and you can control the organization of the palette.

Fractal Design Sketcher (Raster)

Fractal Design Corporation
335 Spreckels Drive, Ste. F
P.O. Box 2380
Aptos, CA 95001
408-688-8800
FAX 408 688-8836

Fractal Design Sketcher offers natural-media and imaging technology for gray-scale graphics. It is ideal for artists and designers working in gray scale. The cost is $149.00 ($109.00 through IBM Ultimedia Tools Series, 800-887-7771).

Micrografx Designer (Vector)

Micrografx, Inc.
1303 Arapaho
Richardson, TX 75081-2444
800-733-3729

Micrografx Designer 3.1 plus OLE is a precision illustration program for Windows. It includes Adobe Type Manager, Adobe TypeAlign, and more than 175 Type 1 fonts.

PhotoShop 2.5 (Raster)

Adobe Systems Incorporated
1585 Charleston Road
Mountain View, CA 94039-7900
415-961-4400
800-83-FONTS (800-833-6687)
FAX 415-961-3769

Adobe PhotoShop 2.5 is a photo design and production tool that enables you to create original artwork, correct and retouch color or black-and-white scanned images, and generate high-quality output and prepare high-quality color separations in CMYK mode. You can start with a blank screen or scan images directly into PhotoShop. Use photographic techniques to correct color, retouch, dodge, burn, mask, and montage. The cost is $895.00 ($589.00 through IBM Ultimedia Tools Series, 800-887-7771).

Professional Draw (Vector)

> Gold Disk, Inc
> P.O. Box 789, Streetsville
> Mississauga, ON
> Canada L5M 2C2
> 416-602-4000

Professional Draw is a full-featured freehand and precision illustration program with an extensive array of tools. It features full-color editing, layers, multiple pages, text-handling capabilities, and 150 Type 1 fonts. The cost is $495.00 ($319.00 through IBM Ultimedia Tools Series, 800-887-7771).

An upgrade that provides True Type, Adobe, and Corel fonts and reads all major file formats is available for owners of CorelDRAW!, Micrografx Designer, Harvard Draw, Arts and Letters, Ventura Publisher, and PageMaker. The cost is $129.00.

Rightpaint (Raster)

> ICOM Simulations, Inc.
> 648 South Wheeling Road
> Wheeling, IL 60090
> 800-877-4266

With Rightpaint, you can use a wide selection of painting tools and palettes to create your artwork. It features 256-color bitmap editing, a tool box, multiple zoom levels, a pattern palette (and editor), dithering support, and multiple file formats.

Streamline (Vector)

Adobe Systems Incorporated
1585 Charleston Road
Mountain View, CA 94039-7900
415-961-4400
800-83-FONTS (800-833-6687)
FAX 415-961-3769

Streamline enables you to produce graphical effects on the PC; convert black-and-white, gray scale, and color images into PostScript line art. You can scan a photograph, technical drawing, form, sketch, or other image into your PC and then bring the image into Adobe Streamline and add effects. You can convert the image using outline, centerline, or line recognition and produce up to 256 colors or 16 levels of gray. Use Streamline's tools to select and alter bitmaps and enhance converted images. You also can export an image to a page-layout program or modify it in Adobe Illustrator, which enables you to scale, skew, rotate, or add type or other effects to the image. The cost is $195.00.

Visio Shapes (Vector)

Shapeware Corp.
800-446-3335
206-467-6723

Visio Shapes is an add-on for Visio, Shapeware Corp.'s drawing program. Visio enables you to drag and drop shapes from a stencil to a work area; the shapes remain proportionally correct when you size them. Diagram shapes are available for the office or home, including the kitchen, bathroom, and landscape planning. Stencils are also available for many specific professions, such as marketing, network administration, chemistry, medicine, insurance, and electrical, mechanical, chemical, and petroleum engineering. The cost ranges from $39.00 to $79.00.

Screen and Video Capture

This section describes a few of the screen- and video-capture applications you might want to use to illustrate your presentations. Some packages also include conversion between different file formats.

AppART

Application Arts
1932 First Avenue, Suite 308
Seattle, WA 98101
206-441-2518
FAX 206-441-6759

With AppART, you can capture screen images and convert them to TIFF, BMP, PCX, and GIF formats. AppART is easy to use, and it works in Windows and DOS. The cost is $59.00.

Clip'nSave

Dynalink Technologies, Inc.
P.O. Box 593
Beaconsfield, PQ H9W 5V3
Canada
514-489-3007
FAX 514-489-3007

Clip'nSave provides comprehensive capturing, storing, editing, and viewing functions to capture screen images to the Windows clipboard as bitmaps. It supports 1- to 24-bit color, compression, and many file formats, and its images import easily into Windows desktop publishing, graphics, or word processing applications.

Collage Complete

Inner Media, Inc.
60 Plain Road
Hollis, NH 03049
800-962-2949
603-465-3216
FAX 603-465-7195

Collage Complete provides screen-capture and image-handling capabilities for Windows and DOS. You can capture all or part of any Windows screen—including the cursor, drop-down menus, and so on—to a file, the clipboard, or a printer.

It supports many standard image formats and all image types from black and white and gray scale to 24-bit color. You can print, scan, convert, crop, annotate, size, flip, rotate, invert, and combine images as well as build custom catalogs of images for "thumbnail" browsing and selection of multiple images for batch operation. The cost is $199.00.

HiJaak

Inset Systems
71 Commerce Drive
Brookfield, CT 06804-3405
203-740-2400
203-775-5866
FAX 203-775-5634

With HiJaak, you can capture screen images and convert them to one of more than 60 different formats. The program supports 15 vector formats and many more raster graphics formats. You can customize images by specifying options such as dithering, color reduction, halftoning, and more. You also can print your image or document to a LaserJet printer file and HiJaak then converts it to one of 24 fax card formats. The cost is $249.00.

Paint Shop Pro

JASC, Inc.
10901 Red Circle Drive, Ste. 340
Minnetonka, MN 55343
612-930-9171
FAX 612-930-9172

With Paint Shop Pro, you can display, convert, alter, and print images. It supports the following file formats: TIFF, GIF, TGA, WPG, BMP, PCX, PIC, MAC, MSP, IMG, RAS, RLE, DIB, and JAS. You can zoom images and alter images by rotating, resizing, resampling, trimming, applying filters, adjusting color and brightness/contrast, changing color depth, gamma correcting, gray scaling, dithering, and manipulating the palette. You also can capture screens. The cost is $49.00.

SnapPro!

Window Painters, Ltd.
7275 Bush Lake Road
Minneapolis, MN 55439
612-897-1305
FAX 612-897-3648

Use SnapPro! to capture the full screen, an active window, or custom-defined areas of your screen. Use Image Builder (included) to combine several image files even if they were saved in different formats. SnapPro! is easy to learn and use. The cost is $69.95.

Video Editing Software

Sophisticated editing software has been the most important missing ingredient in video. The first edition of this book had a huge gap in this area, and I am pleased to be able to include several excellent video editing packages this time.

However, none of the packages currently out there can be called complete. To give yourself real power, you will need to buy two packages: Premiere and MEDIA MERGE. Between them, they give you the tools you need for serious digital video editing. The results, by the way, are intended for playing on your PC; low-end tools aren't yet available for capturing video to the PC, editing it, and putting it back out to tape with broadcast quality.

Adobe Premiere 1.0

Adobe Systems Incorporated
1585 Charleston Road
P.O. Box 7900
Mountain View, CA 94039-7900
800-833-6687
408-986-6555
Fax Request Line 408-986-6587

Premiere Version 1.0 gives you some basic but important tools for working with video. It has several important strengths:

➤ A timeline-based editing window for arranging clips in a sequence and for adding transitions

➤ A long list of visual effects. These range from the basic—sharpening, brightness changes, and so on—to the fancy—crystallizing, faceting, and so on

➤ A wide variety of scene transitions, including wipes, fades, folding door effects, and so on

Premiere also has some weaknesses. There is no direct support for adding text to video clips (you must do text as bitmaps and then use overlay or transitions to add it to video clips), and you can only overlay one video at a time.

Audio/Visual Recorder

In:Sync Corporation
301-983-9623
FAX 301-983-9674

Audio/Visual Recorder provides an alternate interface for recording incoming video with video capture hardware such as the Smart Video Recorder or Video Spigot. Instead of a simple window, the Recorder interface looks just like a VCR.

An important feature for serious users of video is Recorder's capability to save a video as a .FLC file. This enables you to easily use video clips in products like Animator Pro or 3D Studio.

CameraMan

Vision Software
3160 De La Cruz Blvd.
Santa Clara, CA 95054
408-748-8411

CameraMan is more than the average screen saver, so it gets mentioned here instead. With CameraMan, you can save a windows session as an .AVI file or as a series of bitmaps. For example, you could set a capture window the same size as an application's window and then capture a sequence of screen shots and save them as a movie that you can play back.

Jasmine Clipper

Jasmine Multimedia Publishing
6746 Valjean Ave., Ste. 100
Van Nuys, CA 91406
800-798-7535, Ext. 3108

Clipper is an OS/2 tool that enables you to splice DVI video and audio files together into a master Real Time Video (RTV) file. Use Jasmine Viewer if you want the opportunity to view DVI video files before and after editing. The cost is $199.00 ($135.00 through IBM Ultimedia Tools Series, 800-887-7771).

MEDIAMERGE

ATI Technologies Inc.
33 Commerce Valley Drive East
Thornhill, Ontario
Canada L3T 7N6
416-882-2600
FAX 416-882-2620

MEDIAMERGE is one of the "big two" in the video editing field. It offers fewer transitions and effects than Premiere, but it provides virtually unlimited overlay capabilities and excellent animated text creation for videos. I also like the interface quite a bit—it's easy to learn and use. I ought to know; I wrote the tutorial for the manual.

PhotoMotion Developers Kit

IBM Corporation
Multimedia Division
4111 Northside Parkway
Atlanta, GA 30327
(800) 426-9402

The PhotoMotion Developers Kit is a supplement to IBM's DOS-based PhotoMotion product. PhotoMotion is a videotape editing tool that enables you to edit and compress video and/or audio clips. You can use the PhotoMotion Runtime Modules to integrate PhotoMotion clips into authoring environments that allow DOS command-line calls. The cost is $695.00.

SPLICE for Windows

Digital Media International
352 Arch St., Suite B
Sunbury, PA 17801
717-286-6068
FAX 717-286-3011

SPLICE for Windows enables you to view and edit Video for Windows files. You can edit movies from original audio and video clips and capture source video using ActionMedia II hardware. SPLICE supports the following digital video formats: Indeo, Microsoft Video Compression (MSVC), and Full Frames, as well as the AVS formats (PLV1.0 and 2.0, RTV 1.5, 2.0 and 2.1). The cost is $395.00. SPLICE is also available for OS/2. The OS/2 version is $495.00. A new version with expanded features was in the works at press time. The original version, which is little more than a simple file stitcher, is no longer viable due to the introduction of powerful editors like Premiere and Media Merge, so be sure to wait for the new version which adds transition effects and image filters.

VideoDirector 1.0

Gold Disk, Inc.
5155 Spectrum Way, Unit 5
Mississauga, Ontario
Canada L4W 5A1
800-465-3374
416-602-4000

VideoDirector is a videotape editing system that enables you to use your PC to transfer scenes—in any order you specify—from one videotape to another. The software comes with a "smart cable" that enables you to connect a computer to a VCR and a camcorder. You can log scenes from the source videotape to tell the computer where scenes start and stop and which tape they are on. If your camcorder and VCR have time-coding features, you can use these features for more precise control of where to start and stop. The software keeps track of this information by creating a tape log file that is stored in VideoDirector's tape library.

When you are ready to create a new tape, you can use this log to re-order scenes from a single tape or by combining scenes from several tapes. The computer controls the camcorder and the VCR, and it fast forwards or reverses the source tape to play the specified scenes. You can use VideoDirector to edit video-tapes. but you can't digitize the video images or store them on your computer. If you want to add graphics or special effects such as dissolves, fades, or wipes, you need a VGA-to-NTSC video card. The cost is $199.95 ($149.00 through IBM Ultimedia Tools Series, 800-887-7771).

Animation Software

Animation software can be used both for fun and to create sophisticated presentations. Some software, such as Animator Pro, is intended for the creative animator, but you can also use it to create powerful business presentations (if you can take the time to learn all the ins and outs). Other software, such as Animation Works Interactive, is intended for business use, and is easier to use but not as powerful.

I have also included a new sub-category here in this edition: morphing. Morphing packages enable you to transform one image into another more or less smoothly. You can create some amazing animations using this technology.

3D Studio, Release 3

Autodesk Inc.
2320 Marinship Way
Sausalito, CA 94965
800-525-2763
FAX 415-491-8308

Author's Choice

3D Studio is the top of the line when it comes to 3D imaging—its latest version offers stunning realism. It also enables you to animate the objects in a 3D scene in complex ways using a wide variety of tools. 3D Studio is a professional product in every respect (including price). However, if you are serious about animation, there aren't too many programs that compete. In many ways, 3D Studio is about as much fun as you can have with a computer. The interface is complex and therefore complete, but count on taking some serious time to learn your way around. The cost is $2,995.00.

3D Studio's strength is in what I'll call architectural realism—if you can do it as an engineering drawing, 3D Studio is ideal. If you are interested more in organic objects and animation, you can probably force 3D Studio to do what you want, but a product like Playmation might be better for your needs.

Action! 2.5

MacroMind, Inc.
600 Townsend Street, Suite 310 West
San Francisco, CA 94103
415-442-0200
415-626-0585

Action! is a vector-based, object-oriented animation program that uses the slide metaphor. In Action! the slide is called a scene, and each scene has a duration and can contain animation. Similar to authoring software, Action! enables you to turn an object into a button. It supports scalable fonts via True Type and Adobe Type Manager and enables you to attach sounds (.WAV files or CD-audio) to your animation. Version 2.5 adds support for digital video (Video for Windows files), data-driven charting functions, and MIDI support. The cost is $495.00 ($359.00 through IBM Ultimedia Tools Series, 800-887-7771).

Requires: 386-based PC or better, 2M RAM, 1M hard disk space, VGA display, DOS 3.3 or higher, Microsoft Windows 3.*x*. Recommended: 4M RAM, 9M hard disk space, 256-color graphics adapter, Microsoft Windows with Multimedia Extensions and compatible sound board.

Animation Works Interactive

Gold Disk Inc.
5155 Spectrum Way
Mississauga, Ontario
Canada L4W 5A1
416-602-4000
800-465-3375
FAX 416-602-4001

Animation Works Interactive uses three modules, Background Editor, Cel Editor, and Movie Editor, to break down the animation task. The Background and Cel Editors enable you to import images (.BMP, .PCX, .RLE, .FLI) to use for the background and to use in the cels. This program is not designed for creating full background images, so the painting capabilities are limited. The Movie Editor is vector-based and object-oriented, and it enables you to create, edit, and enhance paths to control actors (multi-frame cels). You can include sounds and digitized video in your presentations. Version 1.1 can compile your animations for distribution and playback, which speeds up the somewhat unimpressive Version 1.0 playback. The cost is $495.00 ($309.00 through IBM Ultimedia Tools Series, 800-887-7771).

Requires: 286-based PC or better, 2M RAM, 2M hard disk space, VGA display, DOS 3.3 or higher, Microsoft Windows 3.*x*. Recommended: 386-based PC or better, 5M hard disk space, Microsoft Windows with Multimedia Extensions and compatible sound board.

Animator Pro

> Autodesk Inc.
> 2320 Marinship Way
> Sausalito, CA 94965
> 800-525-2763
> FAX 415-491-8308

Autodesk Animator Pro includes extensive paint capabilities for creating the elements you want to animate. All standard 2-D animation tools are represented in eight modules, and special effects are available. Overall, Animator Pro is a comprehensive animation tool. Animator Pro has an awkward interface, but the painting tools and animation functions make up for the steep learning curve. Animator Pro runs in protected mode and includes the POCO utility, a C-language-based interpreter that you can use to extend Animator Pro's functions. The cost is $795.00 ($659.00 through IBM Ultimedia Tools Series, 800-887-7771).

Requires: 386SX-based PC or better, 4M RAM, 11M hard disk space, VGA display or better, DOS 3.3 or higher, mouse. If you are working with Windows, make sure you get version 1.3 of Animator Pro. It adds support for .BMP files and Postscript fonts.

Autodesk Multimedia Explorer

> Autodesk Inc.
> 2320 Marinship Way
> Sausalito, CA 94965
> 800-525-2763
> FAX 415-491-8308

Autodesk Multimedia Explorer contains Autodesk Animator, Version 1.0, Autodesk Animation Player for Windows, and more than 150 clip-flics. As the precursor to Animator Pro, Autodesk Animator has similar but limited capabilities, such as single-frame cel functions rather than multi-frame cel functions. Using Animation Player for Windows, you can create playback scripts with loops, fades, and pauses. You also can access many sound formats, including .WAV files, MIDI files, and CD-audio. The cost is $199.00 ($135.00 through IBM Ultimedia Tools Series, 800-887-7771).

Requires: (for Animator) 286-based PC or better, 640K RAM, 6M hard disk space, DOS 3.1 or higher, VGA display, mouse or SummaSketch tablet; (for Animation Player for Windows) 2M RAM, Microsoft Windows 3.*x*. Recommended: 386-based PC, 2M RAM, Microsoft Windows with Multimedia Extensions, compatible sound board.

Caligari for Windows

Caligari Corporation
(415) 390-9600
FAX: (415) 390-9755

This is a 3D modeling, rendering, and animation program. It was not yet released as this book went to press, but I have compiled a list of features that will be included in the program:

➤ You work in a perspective-based interface, not in the 3-view interface of products like 3D Workshop

➤ You can move objects in real time

➤ You can glue primitives to create more complex objects

➤ You can draw freehand and then sweep shapes into objects

➤ You can create hierarchical objects in two modes: structured (plane, bicycle) and jointed (robot, animal)

➤ You can animate single or hierarchical objects

➤ You can stretch and squeeze objects during animation

➤ You assign materials interactively

➤ You can manipulate local and direction lights

➤ You can use textures and bump maps for realistic effects

Caligari supports output of animations to video tape. You will need a video output card (an encoder) to perform the actual output, and an appropriate VCR for recording. Both real-time and timecode output are supported. The package includes a videotape tutorial.

Deluxe Paint Animation

Electronic Arts Inc.
1450 Fashion Island Blvd
San Mateo, CA 94404
415-572-2787
800-245-4525
FAX 415-571-7993

Deluxe Paint Animation includes thorough painting tools and animation tools in a raster-based program. Animation is often as simple as clipping an object to a brush and defining the object's path. Although the program is limited to 320 × 200 resolution, it's easy to learn and to use and includes a playback utility. The cost is $134.95.

Requires: 640K RAM, 3M hard disk space, VGA display, DOS 2.11 or higher, mouse.

Imagine 2.0

Impulse, Inc.
6870 Shingle Creek Parkway
Minneapolis, MN 55430
617-566-0221

Imagine, originally an Amiga program, is a bit of an odd duck. It is an extremely powerful 3D animation program, but the interface is difficult to learn and even harder to master. However, if you take the necessary time to learn this program, you can produce some amazing 3D animations. I have used it myself and am impressed with both the difficulty of learning how to use it and the power of its unique interface. If you tend toward the artistic rather than the scientific, you'll do better with this package. However, I think you should also look at Playmation, which offers even better tools for designing 3D animations.

Morph for Windows

Gryphon Software Corp.
3298 Governor Drive
P.O. Box 221075
San Diego, CA 92122
619-536-8815

Morph for Windows enables you to transform one image into another on any 386 PC with 5M of RAM. You begin the morphing process by displaying the beginning and ending images in windows that are positioned side-by-side on the screen. Then you match and adjust key points in the images and specify the number of intervening frames needed. Morph creates the animation, which you can then save as a Video for Windows movie, or an FLI or FLC animation. Single images or a series can be saved in TIFF, GIF or Targa formats. The cost is $149.00.

MOVIE

LANTERN Corporation
63 Ridgemoor Drive
Clayton, MO 63105
314-725-6125

With MOVIE, a general-purpose, screen-image animator, you can capture images from Windows applications and put them in motion. You can write scripts to play, loop, show, save, and pause images for slide shows or continuous demonstrations. The cost is $49.00.

PC Animate Plus

Presidio Software Inc.
2215 Chestnut Street
San Francisco, CA 94123
415-474-6437
FAX 415-474-6349

PC Animate Plus provides the Frame F/X function for adding sophisticated action to imported images (TIFF, PCX, and GIF files). With these actions, you can cause images to loop, spin, and move across the screen. Special effects such as wipes and ripples are available. Paint capabilities are limited, but you can import images more sophisticated than PC Animate can create. A playback utility is included as well as built-in support for Sound Blaster files. The cost is $199.95.

Requires: 640K RAM, EGA display, DOS 3.2 or higher. Recommended: 386-based PC or better, 2M RAM, hard disk, VGA display.

PhotoMorph

North Coast Software, Inc.
P.O. Box 459
265 Scruton Pond Road
Barrington, NH 03825
603-664-6999
FAX 603-664-7872

PhotoMorph is an extremely well-designed and well-thought-out product. It has a great, easy-to-use interface that will have you morphing quickly, and it also delivers smooth, realistic morph files. You can generate .AVI, .FLC, or bitmap sequences.

In addition to morphing, PhotoMorph gives you warps, transitions, and storyboards, and it also chains multiple clips. It includes sample 24-bit movies and still images. A runtime version of Video for Windows is supplied so you can distribute your files. PhotoMorph supports the following formats: GIF, TIFF, Targa, PCX, BMP, JPEG, PICT and IFF. The cost is $149.95.

Playmation

Hash Enterprises
2800 E Evergreen Blvd
Vancouver, WA 98661(206) 699-5360

I received a review copy of Playmation too late to include it in the chapter on animation, so this is the only place you will see it in this book. If I had received it earlier, I definitely would have included it! It's a wonderful program quite unlike anything else out there.

Playmation bears some similarity to products like 3D Studio and Imagine but only because all these programs enable you to model 3D objects in wire-frame and then render them. Playmation adds some clever and useful twists to the process—sometimes quite literally! For example, Playmation enables you to create spines and muscles for your objects, and you can control them much more easily than with other products. Playmation is thus more of a character animation program—it gives life to whatever you create, from pitchers and airplanes to cartoon characters. Unlike many other 3D rendering/animation products, Playmation uses *patches* and *splines* in place of *polygons*.

> **Patch**—A surface (curved or flat) defined by three or four splines. A patch can have an infinite number of shapes and curves.
> **Spline**—A curved line defined mathematically and infinitely editable to any degree of curvature.
> **Polygon**—A three-sided flat object. When polygons are combined, they form complex 3D shapes. Rendering capabilities are limited because each polygon is flat, and curved surfaces require tricks to render correctly.

Using patches and splines enables Playmation to generate more realistic shapes more quickly. They also enable you to define complex animated behaviors with minimal effort. The addition of spines and skeletal hierarchies gives you even more modeling power.

As with any 3D modeling program, you should expect to spend some time learning how to apply Playmation's techniques—3D modeling is a complex art. The hardest part of 3D animation, in fact, is creating good-looking characters/objects. However, once you have applied your artistic talents to creating them, you will find that animating them is remarkably easy.

Playmation consists of six modules, all of which can work together simultaneously via background processing:

> **Sculpture**—In this module you design the form of an object. It is excellent for creating organic, curved shapes. You can create individual segments, such as arms, legs, handles, and so on.
> **Character**—In this module you can combine segments in hierarchical relationships. For example, you can define how the arms attach to the body and how they move together. You also can specify the surface characteristics of the objects.
> **Action**—In this module you define the movements that an object makes, such as walking, waddling, rolling, bending, and so on. You can build a library of actions and apply them to similar classes of objects and characters.

Director—In this module you choreograph your animation. For example, you might have a pitcher dancing around and popping its lid occasionally, while in the foreground a salamander wanders around snuffling for food, and overhead a butterfly wanders by. The possibilities are literally endless. It is much like working on a stage with actors.

Render—Once you have defined all other aspects of your animation, you can render it to a .FLC file in this module. It uses the ray-tracing rendering method, which provides a stunning degree of 3D realism. The rendering is definitely first rate. You also can render to .TGA files for output to tape. The Renderer works well in the background while you do other work (it doesn't hog CPU cycles), but it locked up the machine once, and that made me leery of using it as a background application.

Display—You play animations in this module. You also can convert them to .AVI files and add sound effects.

About the only negative aspect of Playmation was that it occasionally crashed. This is not a minor consideration, and others who have used the product have reported similar problems. I still use Playmation—it is simply too clever and too much fun to ignore. However, use caution if you decide to work with it, and save your work often. This problem is the only reason I did not give Playmation an Author's Choice designation—in every other respect, it's a top-notch program.

A professional version of the product containing even more cool features is expected in the last quarter of 1993 or early 1994. It will be called Promation, and I urge you to keep an eye out for it.

Vistapro

Virtual Reality Laboratories, Inc.
2341 Ganador Court
San Luis Obispo, CA 93401
805-545-8515

Vistapro is one of those programs that is simultaneously extremely different from anything else you've seen, and perfectly done. Vistapro enables you to create lush, detailed landscapes that literally take your breath away. I made a special effort to put some sample landscapes on the CD-ROM. You also can purchase some add-on products, such as Flight Director, to create animations that simulate flying or driving through a landscape.

This is absolutely addictive, must-have software. You can get a simplified version of the software by purchasing another of my books, *Virtual Reality Madness*. That book includes a coupon for obtaining the current full version at a substantial discount—the book pays for itself, as they say.

WinImages:morph

Black Belt Systems
398 Johnson Road
Glasgow, MT 59230
406-367-5513
800-TK-AMIGA

WinImages:morph transforms one image into another on Windows-based systems. WinImages:morph can perform three types of morphing: distortion morphing, which enables you to manipulate the features of a single image; transition morphing, which enables you to merge the characteristics of two images; and motion morphing, which shows in-between frames of a transition morph as it occurs. The default screen displays a Start, End, Result, and Filmstrip window for images so you can monitor the morphing process. The Filmstrip window enables you to display an animated version either of your morph or of a motion morph.

Creating your own morphs involves a step-by-step approach. Begin the process by loading the first and last images, as well as any intermediate images you want to use, into a sequence. Assign control points to the first image; these control points are automatically added to the final image. Manually move the final image's control points to indicate the position/shape of the morphed image. When you are satisfied with the result, render the complete sequence into a filmstrip. You can play the animation within WinImages or any compatible player, or you can store it as an FLI or FLC file. You also can save morphs as projects so you can reload them from your hard drive. WinImages:morph supports most graphic file formats, ranging from BMP, GIF, PCX and TIFF to Amiga IFF and Animator FLIC files. The cost is $199.95.

Requires: 386 PC or higher; 4M RAM; accelerated 256-color or higher graphics display; Windows 3.1.

Materials for Everything Multimedia

This section describes libraries of images, animations, video clips, and audio clips (when included with any of the images). If a title contains audio clips exclusively, it is listed in the Clip Notes section. Also listed in this section are applications designed to work with others to add voice, special objects, or motion to your presentations.

AddImpact!

> Gold Disk, Inc.
> 5155 Spectrum Way, Unit 5
> Mississauga, ON
> Canada L4W 5A1
> 416-602-4000

AddImpact! brings multimedia capability to many popular Windows spreadsheets, word processors, or presentation programs. It offers a simple-to-use toolbar that pops up in your current application so you can add sound, animation, and voice annotation using OLE. The cost is $149.95.

Aris CD-ROMs

> Aris Entertainment
> 310 Washington Blvd., Suite 100
> Marina del Ray, CA
> (310) 821-0234

Aris Entertainment distributes the following three image CD-ROMS:

> **Deep Voyage** features 100 color photographic images of exotic ocean creatures and plants, shipwrecks, hidden caves, and underwater scenes along with 100 audio clips and 25 underwater action videos. The cost is $39.95.
> **Full Bloom** features 100 color photo images of bright, beautiful flowers from all over the world and taken from a variety of angles. It includes 100 audio clips of classical piano and 25 live-action videos of flowers blooming in time-lapse photography. The cost is $39.95.

Tropical Rainforest features 100 color photo images of life in a tropical rain forest along with 100 audio clips of Andean Pan Flute music and 25 live-action videos. All the sounds, videos, and color images used in this CD were produced by Bolivian artists living in the rain forest. The artists will receive royalties for their works, and a portion of the proceeds from the title will be donated to help preserve the world's rain forests. The cost is $39.95.

All three CDs include Windows/MPC, MS-DOS, and Macintosh support on the same disk, as well as self-running slide shows. All three formats use a built-in "search engine" to locate specific images and sounds. You may use images, sounds, and videos royalty-free in any presentation as long as you give credit to Aris Entertainment and the artist.

CatchWord Pro

Logitech Inc.
6505 Kaiser Drive
Fremont, CA 94555
800-231-7717
510-795-8500
FaxBack 800-245-0000

CatchWord Pro enables you to use scanned text in documents so you don't have to waste time retyping text. CatchWord Pro recognizes all common typefaces in 11 languages and automatically merges multiple scans into one file. You can use CatchWord Pro in Windows and Macintosh environments; CatchWord is available for DOS.

ClickArt EPS Illustrations

T/Maker Company
1390 Vukka Street
Mountain View, CA 94041
415-962-0195

ClickArt EPS Illustrations is a collection of high-quality PostScript art for the Macintosh or PC. These images were created by professional artists using Adobe Illustrator. The Macintosh disks are distributed on four 3 1/2-inch 800K diskettes; the PC version is distributed on eight 5 1/4-inch 360K diskettes.

Clip-Art Windows Shopper

Adonis Corporation
12310 N.E. 8th Street, Suite 150
Bellevue, WA 98005
800-234-9497

Clip-Art Windows Shopper is an electronic catalog of clip-art combined with an online ordering service. Browse through 16 publishers' libraries to find the image you want.

Clipper

Dynamic Graphics
6000 N. Forest Park Dr.
P.O. Box 1901
Peoria, IL 61656-9941
800-255-8800
FAX 309-688-5873

Clipper contains clip art that is available in traditional (paper) or electronic (floppy diskette or CD-ROM) formats. The traditional version of Clipper offers camera-ready art in loose-leaf binders and entitles you to receive Clip Bits, which is a monthly magazine of layout and design ideas. The electronic version of Clipper features digitized clip art (60 percent TIFF, 40 percent EPS) images, plus a subscription to Options, a monthly supplement of electronic how-to tips and ideas. Traditional Clipper (alone) costs $32.50/month plus postage and handling; electronic Clipper (alone) costs $67.50/month plus postage and handling; both electronic Clipper and traditional Clipper costs $85.00/month plus postage and handling.

ConvertIt!

Heizer Software
P.O. Box 232019
Pleasant Hill, CA 94523
800-888-7667

ConvertIt! converts HyperCard stacks into ToolBook books. It translates hypermedia documents from one environment to a form that works in a different environment: buttons, fields, text, scripts, and graphics are translated. Requires: HyperCard 2.0 and ToolBook 1.5.

Crystal Desktop Animator

CrystalGraphics, Inc.

Crystal Desktop is an integrated DOS program that enables you to create presentations using modeling, rendering, and animation capabilities. The cost is $1,995.00 through IBM Ultimedia Tools Series, 800-887-7771.

Crystal Flying Fonts!

CrystalGraphics, Inc.

Crystal Flying Fonts is a DOS program that enables you to create 3D title and logo animations for use in presentations or videos. The cost is $295.00 through IBM Ultimedia Tools Series, 800-887-7771.

DIGITAL ZONE Inc.

DIGITAL ZONE Inc.
P.O. Box 5562
Bellevue, WA 98006
800-538-3113
206-623-3456

DIGITAL ZONE Inc., is a Seattle-based computer special effects company that offers ultra-high-resolution, magazine-quality images on Kodak's Photo CD platform. The stock photography was taken by professional photographers: Cliff Hollenbeck, Wolfgang Kaehler, Kevin Morris, and Christopher Roberts. These photographers currently provide Digital Sampler disks, and will later distribute specialty title disks. Each sampler disk contains 50 images that were originally scanned using the KODAK Photo CD System. The disks are compatible with all KODAK Photo CD players as well as many third-party CD-ROM XA Mode, single- or multi-session players.

DIGITAL ZONE will develop customized Photo CDs in categories of your choice or take existing images and photographs and convert them to CD-ROM. DIGITAL ZONE currently owns the rights to 1.3 million images from approximately 150 countries worldwide. It offers unlimited usage and manipulation of images, and reproduction to four-color separations for multimedia or broadcast. You can create in-house libraries of images for resale. The cost is $599.00 per each sampler disk.

The Font Company

The Font Company
7850 E. Evans Road, Suite 111
Scottsdale, AZ 85260
800-442-3668

The Font Company is a library of PostScript fonts available for the Macintosh or the PC with over 2,000 typefaces and including over 400 kerning pairs. These PostScript fonts are created using the IKARUS point-on-curve digital rendering method on a 15,000-unit square grid. The fonts are published in standard PostScript Type 1 format, which includes advanced hinting for ATM 2.0. You can select fonts from a CD-ROM package or a 400-page catalog. If you want to purchase a font from the CD-ROM, use your modem or send a fax to obtain an access code that enables you to download the printer fonts to your hard drive.

FontMinder 2.0

Ares Software Corp.
565 Pilgrim Drive, Suite A
Foster City, CA 94404
415-578-9090
FAX 415-378-8999

FontMinder 2.0 is a font management utility for Windows 3.1. It enables you to organize PostScript and TrueType fonts into user-defined groups called font packs. Font packs can contain any number of fonts in TrueType or PostScript Type 1 format. If you have more than 15 fonts installed in Windows, FontMinder improves Windows and application start-up time.

FontMinder enables you to preview TrueType or PostScript Type 1 fonts as well as print type samples from a floppy disk or CD-ROM without installing the fonts. If you are using Adobe Type Manager Version 2.5 or TrueType, FontMinder will automatically install your fonts without leaving your application program or restarting Windows. As with the original version of FontMinder, system configuration files (WIN.INI and ATM.INI) are automatically managed. The cost is $79.95 (Upgrade: $29.95).

FontMonger Windows

Ares Software Corp.
565 Pilgrim Drive, Suite A
Foster City, CA 94404
415-578-9090
FAX 415-378-8999

FontMonger Windows enables you to convert your type library in any direction between PostScript Type 1, PostScript Type 3, TrueType, and Nimbus Q. You can modify your existing fonts by generating a new font composed of small caps, obliques, and subscript or superscript characters using FontMonger's preset modifications. You also can design your own modifications and change the height, width, degree of slant, and rotation of a character either visually or by typing directly into a read-outs panel. You can build fractions, composite characters, and logos directly into a font.

FontMonger also has a set of drawing tools that enable you to create and modify existing font outlines and to draw new fonts from scratch. The cost is $149.95.

Ares also distributes the following products:

FontChameleon enables you to build a font library from one master font outline. It includes over 200 preset text fonts, but you can blend between any two fonts to produce intermediate font weights and new font designs. The FontChameleon descriptor files support both Macintosh and PC platforms. The cost is $295.95.

FontHopper offers font conversion software for converting format-specific fonts between Macintosh and Windows computers. The cost is $65.00.

FontFiddler is three font utilities in one: (1) You can rename and change the properties of your fonts; (2) You can output print samples without having the font installed; and (3) You can set kerning pair information to improve the quality of output. FontFiddler works with TrueType or PostScript Type 1 fonts. The cost is $99.95.

HyperClips

The HyperMedia Group
5900 Hollis Street, Suite O
Emeryville, CA 94608
415-601-0900
FAX 415-601-0933

The HyperClips CD-ROM contains hundreds of animation and audio clips designed for use in your presentations. All clips are indexed in a graphical storage-and-retrieval system, so you easily can find and play the stand-alone .MMM and .WAV files.

Jasmine CD-ROMs

Jasmine Multimedia Publishing
6746 Valjean Ave., Ste. 100
Van Nuys, CA 91406
800-798-7535, Ext. 3108

Jasmine distributes royalty-free CD-ROMs that feature videos with music, videos with text, and stills with music.

Videos with Music features four CD-ROMs of professionally shot videos and orchestrated music. All the clips come bundled with Aldus Fetch, which is multimedia cataloging, browsing, and retrieval software. The AMERICA IN MOTION CD-ROM contains videos of the American Dream, including events, holidays, places, and landmarks with music ranging from Ragtime to Rock 'n Roll. BUSINESS IN MOTION contains videos of workers of every kind in manufacturing, agriculture, aerospace, and construction. This CD also includes popular business themes. NATURE IN MOTION contains videos of the plant and animal kingdoms combined with classical orchestrated music. SPACE IN MOTION has U.S. videos, Soviet videos, and NASA animations, along with music. The cost is $99.95 for each CD-ROM.

Videos with Text features two CD-ROMs. The FAMOUS FACES CD-ROMs include the 100 most prominent people of the twentieth century. These include inventors, politicians, celebrities, artists, and business and religious leaders who made history. Educational biographies and famous quotes are combined with the historic footage. The interactive CD-ROMs include Churchill, Sadat, Ghandi, Disney, Ford, Edison, Einstein, Thorpe, Hirohito, De Gaulle, Wright Brothers, Ruth, Houdini, King, Chaplin, and many more. The cost is $99.95 for each CD-ROM.

Stills with Music features three CD-ROMs. The WILDERNESS STILLS CD-ROM includes extraordinary photos of nature and animals. SCENIC STILLS includes striking photographic backgrounds, textures, and famous locations. WORKING STILLS has exceptional photos of business and industry. For each CD, there are over 300 color photos, music, and Conversion Artist Software for changing TIFFs into other formats. Also included is Aldus Fetch. The cost is $59.95 for each CD-ROM.

LIPS

First Choice Computers, Inc.
600-C Walt Whitman Road
Melville, NY 11747
516-673-2255
FAX 516-673-4820

With LIPS you can record a message and post it to any file or program without doing any programming. You can add voice annotations to help files, tutorials, word processing applications, and any other program that runs in Windows.

Mannequin

HumanCad
1800 Walt Whitman Road
Melville, NY 11747
800-437-4441

Mannequin is a library of 2-D and 3D human figures that you can incorporate into multimedia presentations and CAD designs. The figures are wire-frame and can be moved to the limits of human motion, which allows true human simulation. The Mannequin figures have vision range and ergonomic simulation, and they can be exported to a wide variety of programs. The cost is $499.00 ($329.00 through IBM Ultimedia Tools Series, 800-887-7771).

Mannequin Designer

HumanCad
1800 Walt Whitman Road
Melville, NY 11747
800-437-4441

Mannequin Designer enables you to add people of any size and shape to your drawings. It works with your design, publishing, or presentation application. The cost is $99.00 ($75.00 through IBM Ultimedia Tools Series, 800-887-7771).

Masterclips

Masterclips, Inc
5201 Ravenswood Road, Suite 111
Fort Lauderdale, FL 33312-6004
800-292-CLIP(2547)
305-983-7440
FAX 305-967-9452

Masterclips contains over 6,000 artist-drawn clip-art graphics in CGM format. Each image is hand-drawn, not scanned in, in vector format so the image retains its high quality even if you enlarge it. The clip art is certified by Microsoft for use in Windows or DOS. Masterclips includes an on-line browser with key-word search for locating and viewing images. The cost is $299.00.

MediaRights

Sense Interactive Corporation
1412 West Alabama
Houston, TX 77006
800-75-SENSE (sales)
713-523-5757
FAX 713-523-3057

Sense Interactive produces interactive multimedia compact discs that focus on environmental education about the earth and its ecological systems. MediaRights is a series of CD-ROM-based electronic catalogs that features nature and life science imagery from award-winning photographers. It provides royalty-free, professional-quality imagery for use in presentations, multimedia, television, kiosks, newsletters, comps, and desktop displays. Earth Air Fire Water is the first disc in the MediaRights stock photography series and includes 304 color photographs that have been selected from the works of professional photographers. You can use the photographs for everything except for advertising and resale or for reuse as stock. There are no limits on frequency, nor are any credit lines required. The cost is $99.95.

The second disc in the stock photography series is AMERICA, which features 150 color photographs of the country and its culture. The photographs show familiar places, celebrations, and people at work and play.

MediaRights includes a Kudo Image Browser that quickly finds, previews, and opens photos. Large thumbnails of the photos are displayed in a resizable grid that can be enlarged up to full-screen. Or, you can use the RIFFLE tool to scroll through the images at variable speeds—up to 10 photographs per second. The CD-ROM also includes a try-out copy of Adobe Photoshop 2.5. It is available in Macintosh or Windows formats.

Mediasource

Applied Optical Media Corporation
1450 Boot Road, Bldg. 400
West Chester, PA 19380
800-321-7259
215-429-3701
FAX 215-429-3810

Mediasource produces a series of image and audio libraries providing royalty-free reuse of materials for presentation development. The collection contains 1,500 digitized photos from one of the top stock agencies in New York City along with 60 minutes of music and 30 minutes of sound effects. Mediasource comes with an easy-to-use search engine to help you find and use the proper material.

Libraries include: General Topics (Volume 1 and 2), Historical, Military/Aerospace, Natural Sciences, Corporate & Industrial, Sound FX, Medicine & Health Care, International, and Presentation Backgrounds/Graphics. The cost is $395.00.

Monologue

> First Byte
> P.O. Box 2961
> Torrance, CA 90309
> 800-545-7677 (sales)
> 800-556-6141 (customer service)

Monologue enables you to add speech to virtually all Windows applications. Any pronounceable combination of letters and numbers can be spoken clearly by the software. Speech parameters enable you to control the volume, pitch, and speed, and an Exception Dictionary enables you to save your own preferred pronunciations if needed.

Monotype

> Monotype Typographic Inc.
> 53 West Jackson Blvd., Suite 504
> Chicago, IL 60604
> 800-MONOTYP (800-666-6897)
> 312-855-1440
> FAX 312-939-0378

Monotype Typography has created a new typeface designed by Patricia Saunders that captures the history of Spain during the time of Columbus' voyage. The Columbus typeface family, with the Expert Set and Ornaments, is available for either the Macintosh or PC (3 1/2-inch or 5 1/4-inch diskettes). The fonts come in PostScript format on CD-ROM or floppy disk (Monotype Classic Fonts, volumes 1492 and 1196) for electronic publishing systems, and in Qubic format for Monotype image setters. The cost of Columbus Volume 1492 is $240.00, and the cost of Columbus Expert Volume 1196 is $105.00.

Multimedia Animals Encyclopedia

> Applied Optical Media Corp.
> 1450 Boot Road, Bldg. 400
> West Chester, PA 19380
> 800-321-7259
> 215-429-3701
> FAX 215-429-3810

Multimedia Animals Encyclopedia offers detailed color illustrations of 2,000 vertebrates with animal sounds, correct pronunciations of all names, and descriptions of diet, habitat, range, size, and behavior. The unique visual interface enables you to browse or search for a specific species. The cost is $79.95.

Multimedia Audubon's Mammals

> Creative Multimedia Corporation
> 514 NW 11th Ave., Ste. 203
> Portland, OR 97209
> 800-776-9277
> 503-241-4351
> FAX 503-241-4370

Multimedia Audubon's Mammals is a CD-ROM version of Audubon's Quadrupeds of North America that features 150 full-color mammal lithographs and sounds for 47 animals. The cost is $49.99.

Requires: DOS 3.1 or higher, 500K available memory, MSCDEX 2.0 or higher, 450K hard disk space, and a CD-ROM drive with audio output, standard VGA. Recommended: For optimum display of images, use SuperVGA with 512K, 256 colors, 640 × 480 display,

Newsweek on CD-ROM

Newsweek Magazine offers a subscription to Newsweek Interactive, which is a general-interest multimedia quarterly on CD-ROM. The first issue is available for the MMCD player from Sony and is free when you purchase an MMCD. It will also be available in MS-DOS and CD-ROM XA formats. This issue was a collaborative effort between Mammoth Micro Productions and The Software Toolworks. Future issues will be available for MPC and other platforms and will be developed by The Software Toolworks.

The theme of the first issue is global threats to the environment and potential solutions. Subsequent issues will cover topics such as science and technology, sports, the arts, and politics.

PANORAMIC! for Windows

Cimmetry Systems, Inc.
1430 Mass Ave., Ste. 306
Cambridge, MA 02138-3810
514-735-3219
800-361-1904
FAX 514-735-6440

PANORAMIC! is a powerful utility that automatically links to the Windows File Manager thereby enabling you to view, convert, and print files. It supports over 100 different file formats including word processors, spreadsheets, databases, graphics (CAD, raster, vector, bitmap), faxes, and archive (Zip, Arc, LZH). You can view files by highlighting the appropriate file from the File Manager. PANORAMIC! enables you to view multiple windows, Cut and Paste to the Windows Clipboard, Zoom and Pan, perform text searches, scroll pages, and launch an application directly from within PANORAMIC! You also can perform single file conversions or batch conversions to various graphic formats. PANORAMIC! enables you to choose multiple files to print , regardless of the format of each file. The cost is $129.00.

Remark! for Windows

Simpact Associates, Inc.
9210 Sky Park Court
San Diego, CA 92123
619-565-1865

With Remark! you can record, play, and manage voice information in any Windows OLE- or DDE-compatible application. Use Remark! to annotate documents, spreadsheets, databases, and more.

Roger Ebert's Movie Home Companion (1992 Cumulative Edition)

Quanta Press, Inc.
1313 Fifth St. SE, Ste. 208C
Minneapolis, MN 55414
612-379-3956
FAX 612-623-4570

Roger Ebert's book, Roger Ebert's Movie Home Companion, is available in the 1992 cumulative edition on CD-ROM. This CD includes reviews of 1,300 full-length movies, over 80 reviews of stars and directors, and 20 essays on various subjects.

You can use Folio Views, which is a database menu, to search by actor, title, and director as well as to globally search the reviews for specific words or phrases. The cost is $79.95.

Scan-N-Clean

Artistic Visions, Inc.
2075 Winchester Blvd., Ste. 105
Campbell, CA 95008
408-378-1444
FAX 408-378-1444

Scan-N-Clean automatically removes unwanted speckles and lint lines from faxed or scanned images. These "extras" can inhibit the efficient OCR interpretation, transmittal, and storage of an image. Accuracy and speed of OCR is improved by removing elements that may cause incorrect identification. Cleaned, compressed images take 10–60 percent less storage. Scan-N-Clean has fully-automatic, semi-automatic, and manual images. The cost is $99.00.

Scrapbook+

Central Point Software
15220 N.W. Greenbrier Parkway, #200
Beaverton, OR 97006
800-445-4208
503-690-8090
FAX 503-690-8083

Cut an image into the Windows Clipboard, then bring up Scrapbook+ to store as many as 4,500 items in each Scrapbook+ file. Many file formats are accepted.

SmartPics

Lotus Development Corp.
55 Cambridge Pkwy.
Cambridge, MA 02142
800-635-6887
617-577-8500

SmartPics contains more than 2,000 images arranged in groups of 50 to 60 for flexible installation. Clip the image you want, then import it into a Windows application and scale and size it as needed. The cost is $199.00.

StrataVision 3d/PC

Strata Incorporated

StrataVision 3d/PC is a DOS program that enables you to perform three-dimensional modeling, scene layout, animation scripting, and photo-realistic rendering. The cost is $995.00 ($795.00 through IBM Ultimedia Tools Series, 800-887-7771).

TEMPRA Turbo Animator

Mathematica, Inc.
402 S. Kentucky Ave.
Lakeland, FL 33801
800-852-MATH

TEMPRA Turbo Animator has two major features: the animation (aka Movie Maker) feature enables you to edit existing 8-bit FLC and FLI files, or create original 8-bit FLC and 16-bit FLX files. You can capture "time-lapse video" files that can be stored on your hard disk for playback in programs such as Mathematica's TEMPRA Show and TEMPRA Media Author, which is a multimedia/desktop video authoring software. The Turbo Charger feature of TEMPRA Turbo Animator enables you to take advantage of 386/486 microprocessors with 32-bit model operation and advanced memory. The cost is $495.00 ($299 through IBM Ultimedia Tools Series, 800-887-7771).

Video Movie Guide 1993

Advanced Multimedia Solutions, Inc.
300 Fairview Avenue North
Seattle, WA 98109
800-626-4105

Advanced Multimedia Solutions' Video Movie Guide is a useful reference tool for selecting movies. The CD-ROM, which is based on Mike Martin's and Marsha Potter's Video Movie Guide 1993, offers brief reviews of over 12,000 movies. You can search for movies by title, genre, cast member, director, and Academy Award winners. The CD plays on Windows 3.1/MPC-compatible machines and Tandy's Video Information System (VIS). The cost is $34.95.

Voice Type Control for Windows

IBM Corporation
Multimedia Division
4111 Northside Parkway
Atlanta, GA 30327
(800) 426-9402

Voice Type Control for Windows is an entry-level navigation and command program that supports the Sound Blaster standard. It is a voice-command software package that provides built-in support for 10 Windows applets and 11 business applications. The cost is $129.00.

TypeAlign

Adobe Systems Incorporated
1585 Charleston Road
Mountain View, CA 94039-7900
415-961-4400
800-83-FONTS (800-833-6687)
FAX 415-961-3769

TypeAlign enables you to enhance your type, particularly headlines, logos, and graphic effects. You can instantly set type on a curve, conform it to shapes, manipulate it in a variety of ways, and instantly see the results onscreen. You can also rotate your type in any amount and around any point, and you can add control handles to the text envelope to create new shapes or perspectives. Typographic controls are also included. A camera tool enables you to see the window behind Adobe TypeAlign for use as a template. After you complete the artwork, use the clipboard to transfer it to a page-layout or drawing program, or save it in EPS format for subsequent printing on a PostScript printer. Adobe TypeAlign supports all PostScript Type 1 fonts. The cost is $99.00.

Typestry for Windows

Pixar
1001 W. Cutting Blvd.
Richmond, CA 94804
510-215-3457

With Typestry for Windows, you can create dimensional text from Type 1 and TrueType fonts. Use Typestry to transform simple words into works of art. It's an excellent tool for publishing, presentations, and multimedia. You can create 3D text that has texture, marbling, special effects, and so on. The cost is $299.00.

VOICE BLASTER

Covox, Inc.
675 Conger St.
Eugene, OR 97402
503-342-1271
800-733-0420

The developers of the U.S. Air Force's "Bionic Ear" created VOICE BLASTER, voice-recognition software for popular sound cards. With VOICE BLASTER, you can add voice commands to educational, business, and entertainment programs such as WordPerfect, F117A, Lotus 1-2-3, Secret Weapons of the Luftwaffe, DAC Easy, and more.

VOICE BLASTER comes with a high-fidelity headset/microphone that connects to your PC via the parallel port. The software includes recording, editing, and playback programs. The cost is $120.00.

Wired for Sound Pro 2.0

Aristosoft
7041 Koll Center Parkway, Ste. 160
Pleasanton, CA 94566
800-338-2629
800-426-8288
FAX 510-426-6703

Wired for Sound Pro 2.0 is a utility for your sound card that contains 200 realistic sounds. It includes the Talking Alarm Clock, Talking Calendar, Talking System Monitor, 400 Icons that can talk, 100 cursors, Talking Solitaire, Minesweeper, 10 video screen savers, and four other programs. Wired for Sound is compatible with Norton Desktop for Windows. To hear a live demo, call 800-551-4547. The cost is $79.00.

Multimedia Reference, Learning Tools, and More

This section contains a variety of titles from the expected to the surprising. Some titles are geared toward children, and some only adults can appreciate. All are educational, and some are great reference tools.

American Vista Multimedia Atlas

Applied Optical Media Corporation
1450 Boot Road, Bldg. 400
West Chester, PA 19380
800-321-7259
215-429-3701
FAX 215-429-3810

American Vista is a multimedia atlas of the United States. The atlas includes more than 1,000 photographs, high-definition maps from Hammond, Inc., and cross-referenced facts and text from many sources. Region-specific folk music and speech patterns from the Smithsonian comprise the audio selections. Historical maps and documents, flags, symbols, and statistics, such as data from the U.S. 1990 Census, round out this reference tool. The cost is $79.95.

Berlitz Think and Talk Series

The HyperGlot Software Company
5108-D Kingston Pike
Knoxville, TN 37919
615-558-8270
FAX 615-588-6569

Available for French, German, Italian, and Spanish, the Berlitz Think and Talk Series helps you learn to think in the language. You practice listening, speaking, reading, understanding, and writing by using the 50 scenes included on the CD-ROM. Sound effects, graphics, animation, and intonation help you understand without English translations. Dictations test your skill, and a recording feature enables you to compare your pronunciation with native speakers.

Birds of North America

Applied Optical Media Corporation
1450 Boot Road, Bldg. 400
West Chester, PA 19380
215-429-3701
FAX 215-429-3810

This bird watcher's multimedia reference tool not only provides Roger Tory Peterson's Field Guide to Birds of North America but includes calls for each bird as well. Instructions on identifying birds, illustrations of characteristic features, nests, statistical data, maps of birding ranges for all seasons, and descriptions of habits and habitats are included.

The Book of MIDI

Opcode Systems, Inc.
3641 Haven Drive, Suite A
Menlo Park, CA 94025-1010
415-369-8131
FAX 415-369-1747

The Book of MIDI is an interactive ToolBook application that teaches you about MIDI and electronic music principles. Animation and digitized sounds enable you to learn about synthesis methods, MIDI protocol, and the history of electronic instruments. Topics range from basic (such as setting up a studio) to advanced (such as system-exclusive information).

The CD-ROM Developer's Lab, Second Edition

Software Mart, Inc.
3933 Steck Avenue, Suite B-115
Austin, TX 78759
512-346-7887

The CD-ROM Developer's Lab is a comprehensive reference guide to CD-ROM development that takes users step-by-step through the entire development process. The process is illustrated using indexed and keyword-searchable technical articles, demonstrations, and working model applications. The cost is $395.00.

Cinemania

Microsoft Corporation
One Microsoft Way
Redmond, WA 98052-6399
800-323-3577
206-882-8080
FAX 206-93MSFAX

Cinemania is an interactive movie guide for the multimedia PC. You can call up 19,000 movie reviews, capsule summaries, biographies of actors, directors, and producers, and listings of Academy Awards, dialog, and stills. Cinemania includes a glossary of movie industry language. The cost is $79.95.

Requires: MPC or equivalent PC with MPC upgrade kit, DOS 3.1 or higher, Windows 3.1 or 3.0 with Multimedia Extensions and CD-ROM.

Composer Quest

Dr. T's Music Software, Inc.
100 Crescent Road
Needham, MA 02194
617-455-1454
FAX 617-455-1460

With Composer Quest you can learn music history from 1600 to the present by listening to great musical performances and investigating the great composers and important events and developments in art and history. You also can play an adventure game that tests your knowledge as you use Composer Quest.

Compton's Multimedia Encyclopedia

Compton's NewMedia
2320 Camino Vida Roble
Carlsbad, CA 92009
619-929-2500
800-533-0130

Compton's Multimedia Encyclopedia, geared more toward children than adults, includes 32,000 articles, 15,000 illustrations, 60 minutes of audio, 45 animations, and 5,000 charts and diagrams. Point-and-click access and definable searches make this reference tool easy to use. The Encyclopedia includes the Merriam-Webster Intermediate Dictionary so you can look up words as needed to understand the information.

Desert Storm: The War in the Persian Gulf

Warner New Media
3500 W. Olive Avenue
Burbank, CA 91505
818-955-9999

This journalistic record includes hundreds of reports, photos, and tape-recorded interviews from Time Magazine correspondents. Features include personal profiles of key people, maps of the area, a glossary of weapons, audio reports, interviews, original story reports (before integrated by Time editors), and more than 400 photographs.

Distant Suns

Virtual Reality Laboratories, Inc.
2341 Ganador Court
San Luis Obispo, CA 93401
805-545-8515
FAX 805-545-8515

You can explore the universe with Distant Suns. This planetarium for your PC enables you to display any night sky from 4,173 B.C. to 10,000 A.D., produce star charts, reproduce eclipses and lunar phases, and more. The cost is $129.95.

Electronic Library of Art

EBook, Inc.
1009 Pecten Court
Milpitas, CA 95035
408-262-0502
FAX 408-262-0502

The volumes of the Electronic Library of Art assemble a large variety of art images, artists, historical, and explanatory text for the art enthusiast or the student. Painting, sculpture, architecture, photography, and theater are all covered, and collections of text essays, museum and artist listings, databases, dictionaries, and more are included.

Encarta

Microsoft Corporation
One Microsoft Way
Redmond, WA 98052-6399
206-882-8080
FAX 206-93MSFAX

Encarta is a comprehensive reference tool that includes the complete text of the 29-volume 1992 *Funk & Wagnalls New Encyclopedia* plus more than 1,000 new articles written for Encarta. Thousands of photographs, animations, illustrations, and hours of music, speech, and other sounds enhance this multimedia title. Encarta includes an easy-to-use search utility, a history timeline, and an adventure game, as well as a dictionary and thesaurus.

Global Explorer

DeLorme Mapping
Lower Main Street
Freeport, ME 04032
800-452-5931, Ext. 8164
FAX 207-865-9291

The Global Explorer CD-ROM gives you full-color maps of the world with indexed references to more than 120,000 places. It offers street maps of major world cities and descriptions of 20,000 historical, cultural, and geographical features. It contains detailed topographic maps of our planet as well as country profiles with up-to-date economic, social, and cultural statistics. Global Explorer also includes a network of world air routes. DeLorme Mapping also distributes a CD-ROM of the United States called Street Atlas USA.

Great Poetry Classics

World Library, Inc.
12914 Haster St.
Garden Grove, CA 92640
(714) 748-7197

This CD contains a huge treasury of poetry. Poets such as Shakespeare, Keats, Byron, Blake, Coleridge, Wilde, Browning, and Dickinson are represented. The CD includes both DOS and Windows access software. The cost is $49.95.

Guinness MultiMedia Disc of Records 1991

Compton's NewMedia
2320 Camino Vida Roble
Carlsbad, CA 92009
619-929-2500

The Disc of Records features the full text of the well-known *Guinness Book of Records*. Included are more than 70,000 world records, 300 color pictures, and many audio clips such as an earthquake, the world's fastest talker, and so on.

Image Workshop

Optibase, Inc.
7800 Deering Avenue
Canoga Park, CA 91304
800-451-5101

Image Workshop 2.2 for Windows and DOS provides JPEG image compression, file format conversion, a viewer, file batch mode process, and thumbnails. The cost is $149.00.

Learn to Speak Spanish

The HyperGlot Software Company
5108-D Kingston Pike
Knoxville, TN 37919
615-558-8270
FAX 615-588-6569

Through 30 interactive lessons with native Spanish speakers, you can learn to speak this language. This course equals a full first-year college-level course or two years of high school Spanish. It contains complete grammar explanations and listening-comprehension and sentence-writing exercises. A recording function enables you to compare your voice to native speakers' words.

Macmillan Dictionary for Children— Multimedia Edition

> Maxwell Electronic Publishing
> 124 Mt. Auburn St., Suite 324S
> Cambridge, MA 02138
> 617-661-2955
> 617-868-7738

This electronic version of America's best selling children's dictionary contains more than 13,000 word definitions and more than 1,000 photographs, illustrations, and other images. Audio and animation examples enhance many definitions, and every word includes an audio pronunciation. Word games such as a spelling bee and Hangman make this an entertaining learning tool for children in grades four through seven.

MediaDeveloper

> Lenel Systems International, Inc.
> 19 Tobey Village Office Park
> Pittsford, NY 14534-1763
> 716-248-9720
> FAX 716-248-9185

MediaDeveloper simplifies multimedia application development in Windows. You can integrate full-motion video, audio, animation, graphic, and document data into a new or existing application using any development environment that supports DLL calls (Visual Basic, Object Vision, C, C++, and so on). A built-in MCI engine controls peripheral devices, including video decks, laser disc players, CD-ROM and hard disk drives, and audio and video compression boards. An integrated multimedia database helps manage data used in your applications. MediaDeveloper includes support for over 30 graphic, animation, document, and digital video and audio file formats, including Microsoft's Video for Windows and Intel DVI. Free runtime distribution for most applications. The cost is $395.00.

MediaOrganizer

Lenel Systems International, Inc.
19 Tobey Village Office Park
Pittsford, NY 14534-1763
716-248-9720
FAX 716-248-9185

MediaOrganizer is multimedia object-management software that organizes, searches, retrieves, and displays multimedia in analog or digital formats. You can catalog video, audio, animation, graphic, and document data using free-text names and descriptions. You can create multimedia "shows" with audio synchronized to video, animation, and graphics. You also can embed multimedia in other Windows applications with OLE. MediaOrganizer provides support for major peripheral devices and file formats, including .WAV, MIDI, Microsoft, and Intel digital video. It is compatible with network/workgroups. The cost is $295.00 ($239.00 through IBM Ultimedia Tools Series, 800-887-7771).

Mega Movie Guide

INFO Business
887 S. Orem Blvd.
Orem, Utah 84058
(800) 657-5300

The 1993-1994 version of this title includes two hours of film clips, bibliographies, and nearly 60,000 movie reviews. It includes movies from *Birth of a Nation* to *Jurassic Park*.

You can search for movies in a variety of ways—even by the length of the film, MPAA rating, place of origin, and availability on video. The film clips range in length from two to four minutes, and include scenes with such stars as Cary Grant, John Wayne, Elizabth Taylor, and others.

Microsoft Bookshelf for Windows

> Microsoft Corporation
> One Microsoft Way
> Redmond, WA 98052-6399
> 800-541-1261
> 206-882-8080
> FAX 206-93MSFAX

Microsoft Bookshelf for Windows contains the *Concise Columbia Encyclopedia, Bartlett's Familiar Quotations, Hammond Atlas, The Concise Columbia Dictionary of Quotations, The World Almanac and Book of Facts 1992, Roget's II Electronic Thesaurus,* and *The American Heritage Dictionary.* Bookshelf includes audio effects, animations, pronunciations, and graphics. The cost is $195.00.

Microsoft Word for Windows & Bookshelf, Multimedia Edition

> Microsoft Corporation
> One Microsoft Way
> Redmond, WA 98052-6399
> 800-426-9400
> 206-882-8080
> FAX 206-93MSFAX

Microsoft Word For Windows & Bookshelf, Multimedia Edition, enables you to add audio and video to the latest version of Microsoft Word 2.0. You can access eight reference volumes off the CD-ROM: *The Concise Columbia Encyclopedia, The American Heritage Dictionary, Roget's II Electronic Thesaurus, The World Almanac and Book of Facts 1992, Bartlett's Familiar Quotations, The Concise Columbia Dictionary of Quotations, Hammond Atlas,* and *Microsoft Word for Windows User's Guide.* Check out more than 1000 images and maps, dozens of animations, and more than 65,000 audio pronunciations in the dictionary and encyclopedia.

Embed, edit, and play video clips in Word documents using a runtime version of Microsoft Video. The CD-ROM disc has a sample video library with historic footage, as well as 50 .WAV files that you can embed in documents or attach to events in Windows. You can access Bookshelf's reference library directly from the Word toolbar and integrate text and graphics from Bookshelf into your Word document with a click of the mouse. The cost is $595.00.

Microsoft Works, Multimedia Edition

Microsoft Corporation
One Microsoft Way
Redmond, WA 98052-6399
800-426-9400
206-882-8080
FAX 206-93MSFAX

Microsoft Works, Multimedia Edition, combines integrated productivity tools—
a word processor, spreadsheet, charting, drawing, and database with reporting—
with the sights and sounds of multimedia. To get you started, an entertaining
tutorial features music, speech, "movies," and more than 40 interactive lessons.
Learn as you go using an online reference that displays steps for specific procedures, or learn from "movies" that show and tell you how things work.
WorksWizards speed up the process of creating custom documents; you can use
these automated templates to create address books, mailing labels, and form letters. The online documentation comes on CD-ROM, but an order form is included
if you want to purchase a hard copy.

Monarch Notes

Bureau Development
141 New Road
Parsippany, NJ 07054
201-808-2700
FAX 201-808-2676

This CD-ROM version of Simon & Schuster's *Monarch Notes* contains the full text
of the entire collection—more than 200 notes. Monarch Notes includes author
biographies, story synopses, critical commentary, essay questions, spoken excerpts
with selected period music, pictures and drawings of authors and characters, and
more. The menu choices make searches easy.

MPC Wizard

Aris Entertainment
310 Washington Blvd. Suite 100
Marina Del Rey, CA 90292
(310) 821-0234

Aris is now shipping version 2.0 of the MPC Wizard. It includes 100M of Windows sound and video drivers, as well as a large collection of media clips. The CD also includes Video for Windows runtime, 60 color photos, and 60 audio tracks. It also includes a diagnostic utility to asses the performance and operation of your CD-ROM drive. The price is $14.95.

MpcOrganizer

> Lenel Systems International, Inc.
> 19 Tobey Village Office Park
> Pittsford, NY 14534-1763
> 716-248-9720
> FAX 716-248-9185

MpcOrganizer enables you to quickly locate and display desired multimedia files, including digital video and audio, animation, graphic, and document data. The software is fully MCI compatible. It offers multimedia database software that enables you to create multimedia shows with synchronized audio. You can use OLE server capabilities to embed multimedia objects and shows in other Windows applications. It supports networks, including Windows for Workgroups, and many peripheral devices. The cost is $149.00 ($119.00 through IBM Ultimedia Tools Series, 800-887-7771).

Multimedia Beethoven: The Ninth Symphony

> Microsoft Corporation
> One Microsoft Way
> Redmond, WA 98052-6399
> 206-882-8080
> FAX 206-93MSFAX

A multimedia extravaganza, Multimedia Beethoven plays the music and displays an onscreen analysis of each passage. You can detour to explore any part of the symphony, have a lesson on sonata form, learn about Beethoven's life, and take a course on the art of listening. The cost is $79.95.

Multimedia Works

Lenel Systems International, Inc.
19 Tobey Village Office Park
Pittsford, NY 14534-1763
716-248-9720
FAX 716-248-9185

Multimedia Works is an integrated multimedia player that plays both analog and digital video and audio as well as animation, graphic, and document data. You can create multimedia shows with audio synchronized to video, animation, and graphics. Multimedia Works offers support for OLE, DDE, and API calls so you can embed multimedia data or shows in other Windows applications. It supports networks, including Windows for Workgroups. The cost is $99.00 ($69.00 through IBM Ultimedia Tools Series, 800-887-7771).

Multimedia World Fact Book

Bureau Development
141 New Road
Parsippany, NJ 07054
201-808-2700
FAX 201-808-2676

The Multimedia World Fact Book includes 248 comprehensive country profiles giving you details on geography, the people, government, economy, and more—all compliments of the CIA. This CD-ROM also gives you color flags, national anthems, sound clips, and maps. This fact book contains all the information you need to launch your own coup. (Disclaimer: Neither the author, Prentice Hall, nor Bureau Development accept any responsibility for your coup, successful or otherwise.)

Music Mentor

Midisoft Corporation
P.O. Box 1000
Bellevue, WA 98009
800-PRO-MIDI
206-881-7176
FAX 206-883-1368

Music Mentor combines text and graphics with animation and MIDI-generated sound to teach you about music attributes and history. It includes Recording Session, which is a MIDI program that records, edits, and displays music notation.

New Grollier's Multimedia Encyclopedia

Grollier Electronic Publishing
Sherman Turnpike
Danbury, CT 06816
203-797-3803

This is an excellent multimedia encyclopedia. It comes in both Windows and DOS versions. The underlying information is the same in both cases. However, the Windows version uses a more cluttered interface, and I personally prefer the DOS version. My kids did, too. Before Encarta came along, they seemed to have the best success with their research projects using the DOS version of Grollier's. Other encyclopedias were not as easy for them to use, nor was the information always as complete and accessible. Some of the features of the New Grollier's Multimedia Encyclopedia are

➤ Digitized video (the Windows version will use Video for Windows, also known as AVI)

➤ Animations

➤ Timeline, useful for historic overviews and access to specific historic information

➤ Knowledge Tree, useful for starting with a broad idea and moving to detailed information

➤ Audio, including excerpts from famous speeches and musical compositions, animal sounds, bird calls, and musical instruments

➤ More than 250 maps

➤ Mouse support

➤ Search-and-retrieval software (Grollier's has the best search-and-retrieval interface; in my opinion it's very easy to use)

➤ Electronic bookmarks and electronic notepads for copying portions of articles

➤ A teacher's guide for classroom use

The cost of the encyclopedia is $395.00. If you do not need the latest and greatest version, you can often find steep discounts on a prior year's edition.

Playing with Language

Syracuse Language Systems
719 E. Genesee Street
Syracuse, NY 13210
315-478-6729
FAX 315-478-6902

The Playing with Language series, Introductory Games in Spanish and Introductory Games in French, involves children in games and stories that teach a new language in context (the same way you learn your first language). Playing these games teaches children to understand more than 200 words and phrases that are taught in typical first-year elementary foreign language class. For children four years or older.

Q/Media for Windows

Q/Media Software Corporation
312 East 5th Avenue
Vancouver, BC
Canada V5T 1H4
604-879-1190

Q/Media enables non-technical users to create presentations or add video, animation, and audio to presentations already created in programs such as Powerpoint or Harvard Graphics. Q/Media supports Microsoft Video for Windows. The cost is $99.00.

Shakespeare Study Guide

World Library, Inc.
12914 Haster St.
Garden Grove, CA 92640
(714) 748-7197

This CD contains the complete works of William Shakespeare, as well as 14 Baron's Notes for various plays. The cost is $24.95.

SimCity for Windows

> Maxis
> Two Theater Square, Suite 230
> Orinda, CA 94563-3041
> 510-254-9700

With SimCity, you can govern your own city, determine zoning, road construction, and build houses and parks. This, and SimEarth, could have gone into the Fun and Games category, but you can learn so much playing with it that I decided to put it here.

SimEarth for Windows

> Maxis
> Two Theater Square, Suite 230
> Orinda, CA 94563-3041
> 510-254-9700

With SimEarth, you can experiment with a planet's ecosystem and see the effects of the events you create, such as cooler climates or natural disasters. There is another Windows game from Maxis, SimLife, which also makes use of multimedia.

StatMap III for Windows

> GEOVISION, INC.
> 5680 Peachtree Parkway
> Norcross, GA 30092
> 404-448-8224
> FAX 404-447-4525

StatMap III is a statistical mapping program that can match demographic census or user-supplied data to geographic coordinate files to create maps for analysis or presentation. You can access the Census Bureau's TIGER map files and statistical databases and then link your new maps to many popular applications. StatMap includes state boundary files and a data starter kit, and it supports DDE linking with Excel or dBase files. The cost is $595.00.

Survival Manual Series

The HyperGlot Software Company
5108-D Kingston Pike
Knoxville, TN 37919
615-558-8270
FAX 615-588-6569

Available for French, German, and Spanish, the Survival Manual is an electronic phrase book arranged by topic for travelers. Approximately 500 recorded phrases covering greetings, transportation, hotels, dining and food, and other travel necessities, and hundreds of other phrases and words. Using a microphone, you can record your own voice and compare pronunciation with a native speaker's pronunciation.

Take-1

Pacific Gold Coast, Corp.
15 Glen Street, Ste. 201
Glen Cove, NY 11542
516-759-3011
800-732-3002
FAX 516-759-3014

Take-1 is an interactive authoring tool that supports OLE. It enables you to combine graphics, text, voice, and music to produce instant interactive animation. You can make text scroll across the screen simultaneously with voice and music. The management functions and interactive scenario-driven presentations make it suitable for use in a business or home environment. The cost is $395.00.

Time Almanac

Compact Publishing, Inc.
5141 MacArthur Blvd.
Washington, DC 20016
800-964-1518

Time Almanac is a compendium of events, trends, and trivia from Time's 69-year publishing history. The almanac contains 20,000 articles from *Time Magazine,* including complete text from 1989 through January 4, 1993, and selected articles from 1923–1988.

Tropical Rainforest

Aris Entertainment
310 Washington Blvd. Suite 100
Marina Del Rey, CA 90292
(310) 821-0234

This CD includes 100 color photos of life in the tropical rain forest, as well as 100 audio clips of Andean pan flute music and 25 live-action videos. All of the materials were created by Bolivian artists living in various areas of the rain forest. The cost is $39.95.

U.S. History on CD-ROM

Bureau Development
141 New Road
Parsippany, NJ 07054
201-808-2700
FAX 201-808-2676

U.S. History makes learning about history entertaining. Included are photographs of Civil War battlefields, the historic speeches of JFK and FDR, and topical information spanning from Lewis and Clark to the evolution of NASA. The information you need is only a Boolean search away.

VideoBase Multimedia Database

Videomail, Inc.
568-4 Weddell Drive
Sunnyvale, CA 94089
408-747-0223

VideoBase is a full-featured database with integrated audio/video capture and playback capabilities. Each record in the database is linked with audio/video files that are automatically sorted and searched on alphanumeric fields. It also offers direct printing and fax support. The cost is $295.00.

Walkthrough

Virtus Corporation
117 Edinburgh S., Ste. 204
Cary, NC 27511
800-847-8871

Walkthrough is a 3D drawing and visualization package the enables you to create real-time 3D models you can move through, around, and in. You can create interactive presentations that enable you to visually explore ideas. The cost is $595.00 ($395.00 through IBM Ultimedia Tools Series, 800-887-7771).

WinGRASP

Paul Mace Software, Inc.
400 Williamson Way
Ashland, OR 97520
503-488-2322, Ext. 100

WinGRASP is a Windows interface for GRASP multimedia development software. It enables you to develop and run animations with sound without having to end the Windows session. It comes with a user-modifiable PIF for end-user control of playback. The cost is $129.00.

World Atlas

> The Software Toolworks
> 60 Leveroni Court
> Novato, CA 94949-9913
> 800-234-3088
> 415-883-3000
> FAX 415-883-3303

World Atlas is a combination of an atlas, fact book, and almanac in one title. The full-color maps, created by professional cartographers, include topographical details for every country, region, and body of water. Information on nearly 300 topics is arranged in 10 categories.

World Vista Multimedia Atlas

> Applied Optical Media
> 1450 Boot Road, Bldg. 400
> West Chester, PA 19380
> 800-321-7259
> 215-429-3701
> FAX 215-429-3810

World Vista is a multimedia world atlas based on Rand McNally's maps and includes the new Russian republics. It features more than 1,000 images, audio examples of representative music from the Smithsonian Folkways collection, standard phrases spoken in the native language, and more. A visual interface gives you easy access to this information. The cost is $79.95.

Fun and Games

Many games are also learning tools. If you are serious about multimedia games, you should also look through the listings in the category "Multimedia Reference, Learning Tools, and More."

Airwave Adventure: Murder Makes Strange Deadfellows

Tiger Media
5801 E. Slauson Ave., Suite 200
Los Angeles, CA 90040
213-721-8282
FAX 213-721-8336

This Airwave Adventure is an interactive mystery. At Steere Manor, the ancestral home of industrialist Randolph Steere, something strange stalks the halls where Mr. Steere died and was buried. Solve the mystery of Steere's will, and find who his friends really are (and if ghosts really haunt the Manor).

Airwave Adventure: The Case of the Cautious Condor

Tiger Media
5801 E. Slauson Ave., Suite 200
Los Angeles, CA 90040
213-721-8282
FAX 213-721-8336

This Airwave Adventure is an interactive mystery. Solve the murder by exploring hundreds of images, hours of audio, and thousands of possibilities. This mystery is set in 1937 aboard a luxury flying ship—the Condor—where wealthy industrialist Bronson Barnard is trying to expose the killer of a U.S. Customs official, Gerald Weltner. Plot twists are common, so try your hand at sleuthing with Barnard.

Battle Chess

Interplay Productions
3710 S. Susan, #100
Santa Ana, CA 92704
714-549-2411
800-969-GAME

Battle Chess is animated chess complete with CD audio. You can direct your pieces across a 3D chess board, watch them battle the opponent, and listen to their cries of victory. Battle Chess contains a tutorial, so the pieces can even teach you to play if needed.

Critical Path

Media Vision
47300 Bayside Parkway
Fremont, CA 94538
(510) 770-8600

This game details the adventures of Kat, a 24-year-old renegade helicopter pilot who must be guided to safety through a gritty, post-apocalyptic factory setting, where she is being pursued by a gang of thugs and an insane dictator with a hankering for high explosives. Players interact with live-action human actors. The title combines motion video, video game effects, and computer-generated animations in a single interface. The CD includes original music and extensive sound and visual effects. The cost is $79.95.

Jones in the Fast Lane

Sierra On-line
P.O. Box 485
Coarsegold, CA 93614
800-326-6654
209-683-4468
FAX 209-683-3633

As many as four players can compete for their goals using digitized live characters in a hand-painted, board-game environment. The interaction of player decisions and the social and environmental responses made by the computer make this parlor game unpredictable and funny. Jones in the Fast Lane uses digitized graphics and stereo sound.

King's Quest V

Sierra On-line
P.O. Box 485
Coarsegold, CA 93614
800-326-6654
209-683-4468
FAX 209-683-3633

An animated adventure in the Daventry saga, King's Quest V uses studio-quality stereophonics. More than 50 voice actors give each character a distinct voice, personality, and life of its own.

LINKS

Access Software, Inc.
4910 W. Amelia Earhart Drive
Salt Lake City, UT 84116
801-359-2900

LINKS for Multimedia PC re-creates the golfing experience on your MPC. This golf simulator tees up golf courses from around the world.

Microsoft Golf

Microsoft Corporation
One Microsoft Way
Redmond, WA 98052-6399
800-426-9400
206-882-8080
FAX 206-93MSFAX

Microsoft Golf is a great implementation of the game of golf. I should warn you: I personally agree with Mark Twain—I think golf is merely a way to spoil a pleasant walk in the country. However, this game does such a clever job of using the mouse for simulating a golf stroke that it quickly gets you involved. Of course, I did set it up for a beginning player; you can increase the challenge level substantially. The game includes a variety of both realistic and amusing sounds as well as video fly-throughs of the golf course (Pebble Beach).

This game uses video, graphics, and sound to simulate golf on the computer intelligently and with real panache. I recommend it.

Peak Performance

Media Vision
47300 Bayside Parkway
Fremont, CA 94538
(510) 770-8600

This is a tongue-in-cheek interactive adventure that includes video, trivia questions, and a race against the record books. It is aimed at ages 12-16, and is billed as a non-violent adventure game. The players race against an on-screen chronometer to break the record for climbing the highest points in all 48 continental states. The cost is $59.95.

Personal Daily PlanIt

Media Vision
47300 Bayside Parkway
Fremont, CA 94538
(510) 770-8600

Created by Iguana Productions, each CD in this series of three personal information managers includes thematically related photographs, full motion video, and stereo sound. The three editions are

PlanIt Earth—a nature calendar, featuring images and videos selected in conjunction with the National Wildlife Federation

PlanIt Paradise—the equivalent of a swimsuit calendar (it features models from *Swimwear Illustrated*)

PlanIt Adrenaline—features high-drama images and videos, such as extreme skiing, surfing, and rock climbing.

The cost for each CD is $49.95.

Quantum Gate

Media Vision
47300 Bayside Parkway
Fremont, CA 94538
(510) 770-8600

This is a science-fiction adventure saga. It was developed by HyperBole Studios of Bellevue, Washington. It is the first chapter in a multi-CD epic. The title includes 1,000 pages of text, two hours of video (including 45 minutes of full-motion video), extensive music, a 3D landscape, and the VirtualCinema™ interface. The cost is $79.95.

Quick Flicks

Aldia Systems, Inc.
P.O. Box 37634
Phoenix, AZ 85069
602-866-1786

Quick Flicks is a video screen saver for Windows containing over 50 clips on sports, comedy, cartoons, nature, and space. It works on 386-and-up PCs with CD-ROM. It includes Video for Windows runtime, video clips, video effects tools, and password protection. It plays any VFW-compatible clip, and it works with After Dark. The cost is $49.95.

Secret Weapons of the Luftwaffe

LucasFilm Games
P.O. Box 10307
San Rafael, CA 94912
415-721-3300
FAX 415-721-3344

LucasFilm has created a flight simulator that puts you in the pilot's cockpit of an historical combat plane. You can enlist in the Luftwaffe or U.S. Air Force and select your mission and aircraft. The missions include aerial dogfights, bombing runs, and defensive maneuvers. The cost is $99.95.

Requires: 12-MHz 286 PC or better, CD-ROM drive, MSCDEX 2.1 or better, EGA Tandy or VGA graphics. Recommended: Adlib or Sound Blaster-compatible sound board, joystick or mouse.

WayForward Fun Pack

WayForward Technologies, Inc.
119 E. Alton Ave., Suite. D
Santa Ana, CA 92707-4444
800-959-GAME
714-668-1025
FAX 714-668-0441

Fun Pack includes seven games, all variations on popular arcade games. You can play Blitzer, Jewel Thief, Warhead, Chomp, Emlith, Hyperoid, and Block Breaker on your PC.

Where in the World is Carmen Sandiego? (Deluxe Edition)

Broderbund Software
500 Redwood Blvd.
Novato, CA 94948-6121
800-521-6263
415-382-4700

This CD-ROM challenges adults and children to use their knowledge of world events and geography to track down members of an international crime ring. Each program comes with an atlas, almanac, and reference book. The deluxe CD version makes good use of digitized photographs, speech, and authentic folk music recordings. Several of the maps and photographs were provided by the National Geographic Society, and additional photography was provided by The Image Bank and Magnum Photos, Inc. The cost is $89.95.

Kids' Stuff

This section covers several packages that are geared for the youngsters among us. But don't be fooled; this sort of entertainment is great for children of all ages. Look in the "Multimedia Reference, Learning, and More" section for additional items of interest.

AmandaStories: Interactive Stories for Children

The Voyager Company
1351 Pacific Coast Highway
Santa Monica, CA 90401
800-446-2001

AmandaStories contains animated adventures starring Inigo the Cat and Your Faithful Camel. Kids simply point and click to send Inigo and the camel through various interactive adventures. Graphics and audio effects add to your child's fun. The cost is $59.95.

Forever Growing Garden

Media Vision
47300 Bayside Parkway
Fremont, CA 94538
(510) 770-8600

This is an animated, interactive children's title created by C-Wave, a San Francisco multimedia company. It is aimed at ages 4-8. Players shop for seeds at an old-fashioned hardware store, then plant them at one of three garden sites. The players then must watch the calendar, prepare the soil, deal with pests, etc. in order to grow a successful garden. The garden grows in "real time." For example, if you leave the program alone for a week, when you resume a week later, the garden will be a week older. At the end of the growing season, players can pick flowers and arrange them, weigh vegetables, and so on. The game also includes a number of fantasy plants. The cost is $49.95.

Living Books

Broderbund Software
500 Redwood Blvd.
Novato, CA 94948-6121
800-521-6263
415-382-4700

Living Books are animated storybooks for 3- to 10-year-olds. Animations, sound effects, narration, and original music inspire children to read and to learn storytelling skills.

One of my family's favorites is *Arthur's Teacher Trouble,* which is an electronic book that encourages your child to become actively involved in the story. The story is presented in either English or Spanish and can be played as a narration or as an interaction adventure. The interaction portion enables you to select the printed words and have them read to you, or you can click the characters and scenery for surprising results! The entire package includes the CD-ROM disc and the original book. The book was written by renowned children's author Marc Brown and follows Arthur the Aardvark's third-grade adventures with his new teacher, Mr. Ratburn. The cost is $49.95.

The Madness of Roland

Sense Interactive Corporation
1412 West Alabama
Houston, TX 77006
800-75-SENSE (sales)
713-523-5757
FAX 713-523-3057

Sense Interactive was founded in June 1992 with the goal of developing innovative education products for school, home, and business markets. In 1992, the company collaborated with Greg Roach and HyperBole Studios to create The *Madness of Roland*, which is an interactive novel. Sense Interactive focuses on producing educational materials that have an environmental theme, and they are in the process of creating prototypes of three additional CDs for families and schools. First is *Rads Ergs and Cheeseburgers*, an interactive multimedia adventure about science, energy, and the environment. Although targeted for kids ages 8–12, the CD-ROM will be fun for families, schools, and children of all ages. It features video, animations, graphics, words, and music and is scheduled for release in the Fall of 1994.

Rads Ergs and Cheeseburgers is a story about the magical energy blob Ergon who takes a fantastic journey through Earth and outer space. Ergon introduces you to our planet and how all our energy systems work together and then zooms to outer space to visit three planets (Noxious, Barren and Dead End) where life has been squelched by poor energy planning. *Rads* was adapted from the book by Bill Yanda published by John Muir Publications.

The second prototype is *Treasure Hunt: The Search for Endangered Species,* which is an amusing interactive field trip through the lives of some very special plants and animals. *First People: The Great Journey,* the third prototype, is an exploration of the wisdom and myths of native cultures as sources of inspiration for contemporary life.

Mixed-Up Mother Goose

Sierra On-line
P.O. Box 485
Coarsegold, CA 93614
800-326-6654
209-683-4468
FAX 209-683-3633

Your children can help Mother Goose find the missing pieces to her nursery rhymes. Requiring no reading skills, this game and learning tool uses 256-color graphics and digitized speaking and singing voices for the characters. The characters can speak and sing in five languages: English, Spanish, French, German, and Japanese. This is a good introduction to multimedia computers and a second language for children and adults alike.

Mr. Drumstix' Music Studio

Howling Dog Systems, Inc.
Kanata North Postal Outlet
Box 72071
Kanata, ON, Canada K2K2P4
613-599-7927
FAX 613-599-7926

Mr. Drumstix' Music Studio provides an introduction to music that is entertaining and educational. It is recommended for children ages 3–9 and provides music, games, and activities. It includes 20 kids' tunes, such as Pop Goes the Weasel, Mary Had a Little Lamb, This Old Man, Here We Go 'Round the Mulberry Bush, and Three Blind Mice. The song lyrics are shown karaoke-style so children can sing along.

Mr. Drumstix is the star of the karaoke song player and plays along with his drums. If you click the drums, the names of each of the drums are displayed. Guitar George shows how to make chords, and kids can play the strings with the mouse. Ms. Florida Keys plays melodies from songs and says the names of the notes when your child clicks the keys with the mouse.

The product includes educational music games as well as creative activities. For instance, the rhythm editor gives your children the opportunity to try their skills at creating melodies and drum parts. Or, kids can use the musical instrument picture index to create their own arrangements of songs.

Our House

Context Systems, Inc.
333 Byberry Road
Hatboro, PA 19040
215-675-5000

Our House is a discovery program designed to answer two of youngsters' most-asked questions, "How does it work?" and "What was it like when you were young?" The animated characters from the comic strip The Family Circus host this CD-ROM tour of a typical American home. Kids can explore how objects in each room are actually used and discover what life was like in past generations.

Sing-A-Long

Dr. T's Music Software, Inc.
100 Crescent Road
Needham, MA 02194
617-455-1454
FAX 617-455-1460

Dr. T's Sing-A-Long combines music, animation, song lyrics, and musical notation to encourage children and adults to sing along. Each song has a cast of characters and an animated story. Some of the characters are Itsy Bitsy Spider, Old
McDonald, Mary and her Little Lamb, and Yankee Doodle.

A Guide to NautilusCD

There are two CD-ROM discs accompanying this book. CD-ROM One contains a special edition of NautilusCD©, the multimedia magazine on CD-ROM. CD-ROM Two contains demo versions of dozens of commercial multimedia programs and hundreds of sample multimedia clips. This appendix tells you how to install and get started with the NautilusCD disc. See Appendix B for information about the sampler disc.

Each CD-ROM holds more than 680 megabytes of data. That's a total of more than 1.3 gigabytes of stuff. If those discs were a collection of books, that would be 1,395,864,371 characters, or 199,409,195 words, or about 498,523 pages. If you were aggressive about it, and read at least 100 pages every day, it would take you almost 5,000 days or about 13.7 years to read it all. This book and the accompanying CDs should keep you busy for a while.

NautilusCD is a CD-ROM magazine. It has the usual features of a magazine, with two important differences: hyperlinking and multimedia. NautilusCD is a monthly compilation of a wide variety of subjects, ranging from traditional magazine articles (with multimedia additions, of course) to music to images to free software to shareware to editorial opinions and more.

If you've ever seen Nautilus before, you're in for a treat with NautilusCD. The magazine has been redesigned and rebuilt from the ground up.

There is so much material on the CD-ROM that I can't possibly point it all out to you. The best way to find out what is on the CD-ROM is to go exploring. In this appendix, I'll give you an overview of the CD-ROM, and tell you how to install it and navigate around in it; the rest is up to you!

To find out more about NautilusCD, look in the back of this book—you'll find a special advertisement from NautilusCD. Be sure to check it out; it offers a special deal for the readers of this book.

You'll also find a special NautilusCD Close Up booklet that is packaged behind the CD-ROMs. It's a quick-reference guide to using NautilusCD.

Installing NautilusCD

The Nautilus installation program is easy to use. To begin, run the program SETUP.EXE from the root directory of the NautilusCD CD-ROM. You can do this by selecting File + Run in Program Manager, or by double-clicking the filename in File Manager. It will take the setup program a moment or two to load from the disc.

You will see the dialog box shown in Figure A.1. You use it to determine which NautilusCD options will be installed for you. The setup program will automatically detect what you need to install, so it's best leave these options as you find them.

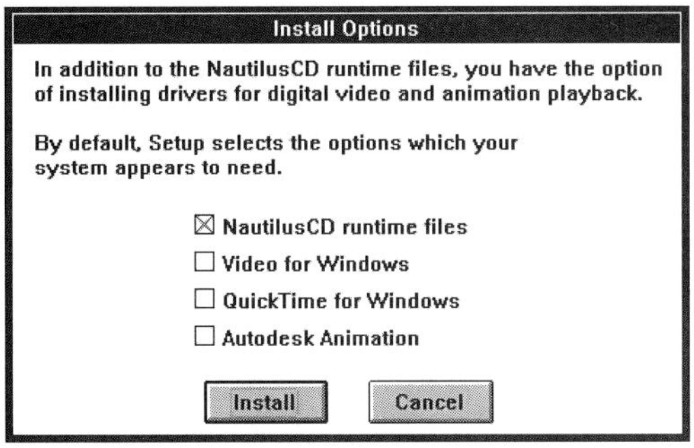

Install Options

In addition to the NautilusCD runtime files, you have the option of installing drivers for digital video and animation playback.

By default, Setup selects the options which your system appears to need.

☒ NautilusCD runtime files
☐ Video for Windows
☐ QuickTime for Windows
☐ Autodesk Animation

[Install]   [Cancel]

Figure A.1. *Setting NautilusCD installation options.*

The four options are:

NautilusCD runtime files—This will copy various files needed to access the CD to your hard disk.

Video for Windows—This installs the latest version of the Video for Windows runtime files. Even if you already have Video for Windows or the runtime installed, it may be worthwhile to install again. The drivers included on the CD are the very latest available at press time—Version 3.0 of Indeo, and version 1.5 of Cinepak. In any case, the Video for Windows installation program will not replace newer drivers with older ones.

QuickTime for Windows—This will install the QuickTime for Windows drivers.

Autodesk Animation—This will install the Autodesk Animation drivers.

It's important that you install all the options that SETUP determines you need. Some of these drivers will also be used by programs on CD-ROM Two.

Once you're satisfied with the options that are checked, click the Install button to continue. This displays the Installation Location dialog box (Figure A.2). This will determine where the NautilusCD runtime files will be installed. Other drivers will be installed to your Windows directory.

Figure A.2. *The Installation Location dialog box.*

Click on OK and the files will be installed to your hard drive. If Video for Windows drivers are being installed, a separate setup program will be run to install them.

The setup program will display a message to inform you when the installation is complete. A NautilusCD group will be created in Program Manager.

Starting NautilusCD

Once you've installed the NautilusCD shell software, you can access the CD-ROM by clicking the NautilusCD Startup icon (at the left in Figure A.3). You can ignore the NautilusCD Disc Index icon for now; I'll provide details later in this section.

Figure A.3. *The icons in the NautilusCD program group.*

The NautilusCD screens shown in this section are taken from a regular issue of Nautilus. The screens you will see in the *Multimedia Madness!* Special Edition will be slightly different.

The first thing you see is the NautilusCD startup window, shown in Figure A.4.

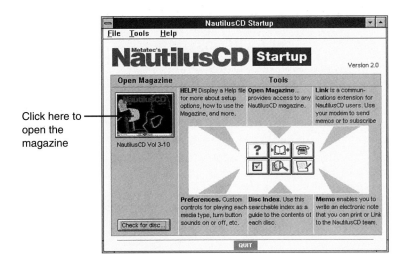

Click here to open the magazine

Figure A.4. *The NautilusCD startup window.*

If Nautilus does not detect your CD-ROM drive, click the button marked Check for disc... in the bottom-left corner of the page. If you want help, click the Question-mark button near the center of the window. This will display an on-line Help window, as shown in Figure A.5.

You open the magazine by clicking the image of the magazine at upper left. Since Nautilus is a true electronic magazine, it has pages and a "cover." The cover of a recent NautilusCD issue is shown in Figure A.6.

To see a movie with information about the contents of the magazine, click the "In This Issue..." button at lower right. To move to the contents page, click the red arrow at bottom right. The contents page of a recent NautilusCD issue is shown in Figure A.7.

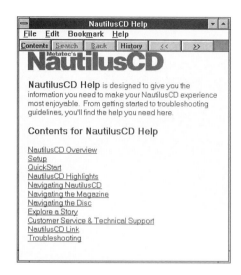

Figure A.5. *Online help for the NautilusCD.*

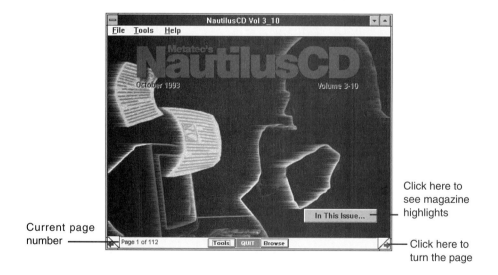

Figure A.6. *The NautilusCD magazine "cover."*

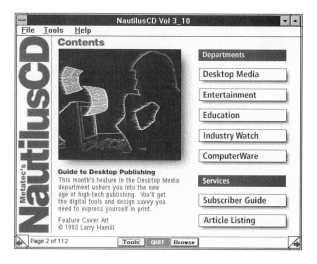

Figure A.7. *The contents page.*

You can access any of the departments or services by clicking the title of that section or feature. Each title takes you to that section; once you are in a section, you can page backward or forward using the little red arrows at the bottom corners.

Figure A.8 shows a sample page from an article I wrote about debunking the myths of digital video. You can return to a higher level by clicking the desired level's icon in the bar at left, or you can access hyperlinks or multimedia goodies by clicking on the various icons on a page.

If you click and hold down the mouse button on one of the icons at the left of a page, a summary of what's in that section will appear. You can click on any item in the list, and you'll be taken to that area.

Sometimes, you will see a little folder icon (Figure A.10). Clicking on this icon will open the NautilusCD Disc Index. From the index, you can access special articles, programs, and other features. You can install, view, and copy files from the Disc Index.

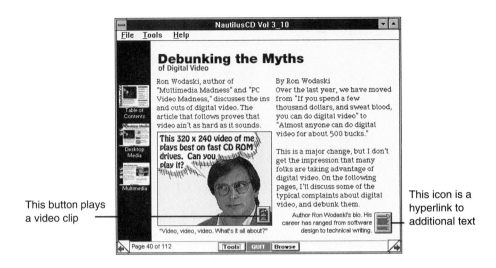

Figure A.8. *A typical NautilusCD page.*

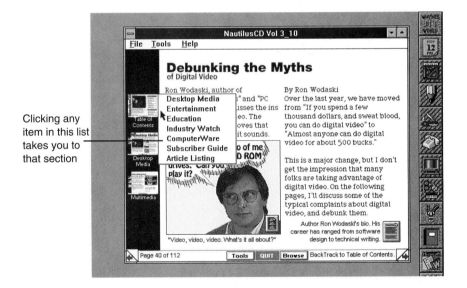

Figure A.9. *A list of what's in the Table of Contents section.*

Figure A.10. *The folder icon takes you to the NautilusCD Disc Index.*

Figure A.11 shows the Disc Index open, ready to install the shareware program PaintShop Pro.

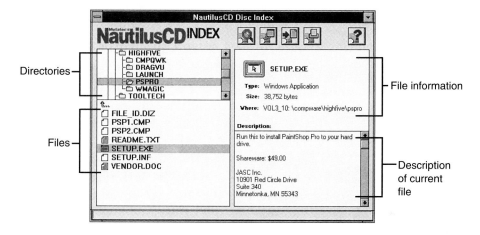

Figure A.11. *The NautilusCD Disc Index.*

You are now well-versed in the use of the NautilusCD disc. If you haven't already, go explore! I think you'll really enjoy what you find.

 Look in the Services section and you'll find an article titled "For New Users." This article takes you on an interactive tour through NautilusCD, letting you experiment and learn all the features.

The following section illustrates some highlights you can expect to find on the disc.

An Overview of NautilusCD

Here is a brief overview of the material you will find on the *Multimedia Madness!* NautilusCD disc. This overview is arranged in the same order of the disc's table of contents.

Departments

Desktop Media—*Multimedia Madness* articles, applications and utilities; Music and Sound; Photos and Images.

Entertainment—Performing Arts, including special performance video and CD tracks; Games and Diversions.

Education—Reference Library demos; Self-Help; Kid's Corner

Industry Watch—Product News, including sample media clips; Press Room information; online CD-ROM directory; MPC Marketing Council guides and information.

ComputerWare—Software Demos; High Five shareware programs; Tools and Technical section, including video drivers; Anti-Virus programs.

Services

Subscriber Guide—Special "For New Users" article; Customer Service information; Nautilus Product Catalog and subscription information.

Article Listing—A complete index to all articles on the CD.

The Demo
Treasure Chest
CD-ROM

You'll find a wealth of multimedia software on this CD-ROM, including demos of commercial programs, sample stock photos and graphics, music and sound effects clips, video and animation clips, shareware programs and much more. More than 650M of multimedia software is packed on this CD-ROM.

In addition, you'll find a special offer from the CompuServe Information Service, including a free copy of Windows CompuServe Information Manager software.

You'll also find some software demos, music clips, sound clips, graphics, and photos on the NautilusCD disk.

The Multimedia Madness! Menu

To use the demos, clips, and other software on this CD-ROM, all you have to do is install and launch the Multimedia Madness! Menu application. This menu was written using Asymetrix Multimedia ToolBook, and it makes navigating and exploring the CD-ROM easy. You can view graphics, install demos, run software, listen to sound clips, and much more from this menu.

Before installing and using CD-ROM Two, you need to install CD-ROM One—the special edition of NautilusCD. It contains software drivers that you'll need for some of the programs and clips on this CD-ROM. NautilusCD will install drivers for Video for Windows (including the latest Indeo and Cinepak drivers), QuickTime for Windows, and Autodesk animations.

Installing the Software

Insert the Demo Treasure Chest CD-ROM in your drive and follow these steps to install the menu software on your hard drive. You'll need at least 2M of free space on your hard drive.

1. From File Manager or Program Manager, select **F**ile + **R**un from the menu.

2. Type *<drive>*:\INSTALL and press Enter. *<drive>* is the drive letter of your CD-ROM drive. For example, if your CD-ROM drive is drive D, you would type D:\INSTALL.

3. The installation program will start. At the opening screen, you are given the option of where to install the software. To accept the default location of C:\MULTIMAD, click on the **C**ontinue button.

4. The installation program will begin copying files to your hard drive. When everything has been installed, the program will attempt to set up a Program Manager group for the menu. Click on the **C**reate button to create a group named "Multimedia Madness!".

5. The file MULTIMAD.TXT will be displayed for you to read. It contains important information about configuring and running the menu. Click on the **C**ontinue button when you're finished.

The files were installed to the C:\MULTIMAD directory of your hard drive, unless you changed this name during the installation program. A configuration file, MADNESS.INI, was copied to your Windows directory.

Configuring the Software

Before you run the menu application, you need to tell it what your CD-ROM drive letter is. Click on the Configure Icon in the "Multimedia Madness!" Program Manager group. This will run Notepad and load the MADNESS.INI file.

Follow the instructions in the text — you need to enter the letter of your CD-ROM drive immediately after the word CDROMDrive=. Here's an example of what a correct setting for drive F would look like:

CDROMDrive=F:

When you have finished editing this INI file, save the file and exit Notepad. You're now ready to run the menu application and explore the CD-ROM!

Running the Menu

To start the Multimedia Madness! Menu, double-click on its icon in the Multi-media Madness group. For best performance, close other applications while you're running the menu and exploring the CD-ROM.

The opening screen of the menu application looks like Figure B.1. Click anywhere on the screen background to continue.

Figure B.1. *The opening screen of the Multimedia Madness! Menu.*

The next screen you see is the main menu (Figure B.2). From here, you can click on any of the buttons to jump to other pages in the menu. You can also navigate by selecting categories from the **I**ndex menu on the menu bar.

To view a help screen, click on the HELP button, press the F1 key or select **H**elp from the menu bar.

When you click on one of the category buttons at the main menu page, a new page will be displayed. Figure B.3 shows a typical page, this one for the Authoring Programs and Tools category. On pages like this one, you can install or run programs by clicking on one of the red buttons. When you are at certain pages of the menu, these red buttons will display graphics, play sound clips, or play videos.

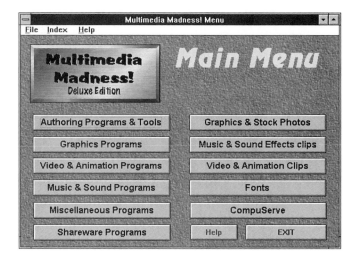

Figure B.2. *The main menu screen.*

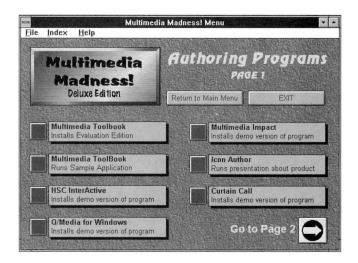

Figure B.3. *A typical page of the menu.*

There are also INFO buttons for certain items. When you press one of these buttons, a file will be displayed that contains information about the product.

Some categories take up more than one page of the menu. For these categories, an arrow will appear in the lower right or lower left of the page. These arrows take you forward or back one page within that category.

To exit from the menu, click on the EXIT button or choose the E**x**it Menu item on the menu bar.

Types of Software

Most of the software on this CD-ROM can be broken down into these categories:

➤ Commercial software demos

➤ Samplers of commercial products

➤ Shareware programs

Many retail software publishers produce demonstration disks that contain limited versions of their programs. These demo programs are normally limited by the publisher in some manner. For example, the software publisher may disable the save and print functions within the demo version. This allows you to try out the features and see how the software actually works. Software that fits into this category is referred to as a *working demo*.

Some of the software publishers represented here do not have special demo versions. They have contributed multimedia presentations that show how their product works. Software that fits into this category is referred to as a *demo presentation*.

A wide variety of *sample clips*—graphics, photos, music, sounds and videos—are included on the CD-ROM. These files have been provided by software publishers to expose you to their collections. You'll find everything from samples of stock photos and backgrounds to video clips and music beds.

The working demos, demo presentations, and sample clips on this CD-ROM are intended to provide a glimpse of the full program's capabilities. Obviously, the software publishers who created these demonstrations hope you will be impressed enough with what you experience to purchase their full product. If you would like to order any of these products, you can either visit your local computer store or contact the software publisher directly.

In addition to the commercial demos and clips, we've included a selection of *shareware* programs on the CD-ROM. Shareware is a software distribution method that provides users a chance to try software before buying it. If you try a shareware program and continue to use it, you need to register the program with the author.

Shareware products are not free. They are marketed by companies (usually small ones) that cannot afford the time and frustration of packaging and distributing a software product through other means. This gives users the chance to try out different programs before paying for them. The key factor to keep shareware developers working is that you *do* pay for the software you continue to use after a reasonable trial period.

If you decide to use one or more of the shareware programs distributed with this book, you should write, call, or send electronic mail to the appropriate shareware author. Each of the shareware programs included with this book is accompanied by a text file that describes how to register the software.

Copyright laws apply to both shareware and retail software, and the copyright holder retains all rights, except as already noted.

Software Listings

For each piece of software on this CD-ROM, you'll find a listing in the following pages. The listing has the following information:

➤ Contact information for the company or author

➤ Location on CD-ROM

➤ Command to install or run a program (not needed when you run the menu application)

➤ Name of the documentation file (when there is one)

Your best bet is to use the menu application to navigate through the CD-ROM and try out the software. If you don't use the menu, you might find yourself lost among the dozens of programs and hundreds of clips. You'll also lose out on the features of the menu that allow you to easily install software or browse through the clips on the CD-ROM.

If a software product does not have a documentation file listed, there will often be a file by the name of README.TXT, or a similar name, that explains about the product.

Authoring Programs and Tools

The demos in this section are multimedia authoring programs, presentation programs, and multimedia tools.

Multimedia Toolbook

Asymetrix Corporation
110-110th Avenue NE, Suite 700
Bellevue, WA 98004
(800) 448-6543
(206) 637-1500

Location on CD-ROM: \DEMOS\MMTBOOK

Command to install demo: SETUP

This special evaluation version of Multimedia ToolBook allows you to experiment with the full power of ToolBook, with just a few restrictions:

➤ You are restricted to six hours of work at the authoring level for each project

➤ Some of the more advanced controls and multimedia widgets are not included

For details about Author level and Reader level in ToolBook, look up these terms by choosing the Index command from Toolbook's Help menu.

You'll find a special coupon in the back of the book that allows you to purchase the complete version of Multimedia Toolbook for a reduced price. There is also a page which lists the licensing agreement for this evaluation version of Toolbook.

HSC InterActive

HSC Software
1661 Lincoln Blvd.
Suite 101
Santa Monica, CA 90404
(310) 392-8441

Location on CD-ROM: \DEMOS\HSCIA

Command to install demo: SETUP

HSC InterActive is an authoring system that allows non-programmers to create their own interactive multimedia applications under Windows. It uses an icon-based visual development method, with no script language to learn. You can combine graphics, animation, video, text, voice, and music in presentations and applications. This demo version of InterActive does not allow you to save presentations.

Q/Media for Windows

Q/Media Software Corp.
312 East 5th Ave.
Vancouver, BC
Canada V5T 1H4
(800) 444-9356
(604) 879-1190

Location on CD-ROM: \DEMOS\QMEDIA

Command to install demo: INSTALL

Q/Media includes everything you need to develop multimedia presentations. Using the tools it provides, you can combine text, audio, animation, image, and video files into presentations that educate, sell, or entertain.

If you are already comfortable with the charting functions in your spreadsheet, or the slide-making capabilities of your other presentation programs, you can easily bring these static files together into a dynamic Q/Media multimedia presentation.

Multimedia Impact

Syncro Development Corp.
580 Middletown Blvd.
Suite D-203
Langhorne, PA 19047
(215) 741-0300

Location on CD-ROM: \DEMOS\MIMPACT

Command to install demo: SETUP

Multimedia Impact lets you quickly create complete multimedia presentations with its intuitive icon-based user interface. Choosing and positioning presentation elements is fast and easy.

Multimedia Impact lets you combine standard still images, full-motion video animation, and CD-quality audio, as well as moving text, push buttons, and "hot spots." Add sound and motion to your existing spreadsheets, PowerPoint files, graphs, and pictures.

Motion Works Multimedia Enabler

Motion Works
#130—1020 Mainland St.
Vancouver, B.C.
Canada V6B 2T4
(604) 685-9975

Location on CD-ROM: \DEMOS\MMENABLE

Command to run demo: MWMEDEMO (DEMO subdirectory)

Command to install "Lite" tools: SETUP (INSTALL subdirectory)

Documentation: README.WRI

Motion Works Multimedia Enabler is the premier multimedia development add-on for Microsoft Visual Basic. The Multimedia Enabler facilitates the creation of titles, demos, and presentations by providing powerful features such as Interactive Animation, Digital Videos, and Pictures, without the complexity of doing custom programming.

The CD-ROM contains both a demo presentation, which shows off some of the features of the product, plus a "Lite" version of the actual tools than can be installed to your hard drive.

Curtain Call

Zuma Group
6733 N. Black Canyon Hwy.
Phoenix, AZ 85015
(800) 332-3492
(602) 246-4238

Location on CD-ROM: `\DEMOS\CURTCAL`

Command to run program: `CC`

Curtain Call is a program which assists in creating presentations and videos incorporating graphics, digital sound, and MIDI music. It Includes drawing tools for creating lines, boxes, ellipses, polygons and spline curves. The Paintbox module loads Windows DIB or PCX format images for manipulation and enhancement. You can even create 3-D special effects with text by rendering any font available in Windows.

ImageQ

Image North Technologies, Inc.
180 King Street S., Suite 360
Waterloo, Ontario
Canada N2J 1P8
(800) 363-3400
(519) 570-9111

Location on CD-ROM: `\DEMOS\IMAGEQ`

Command to install demo: `INSTALL`

ImageQ is an application builder which creates a copyright free portable show which requires no runtime version. It includes attention-grabbing transitions between images, image loading, panning and zoom commands for images, optional color dithering, control over size and position of each image, speaker notes, file conversion, and more. Uses a Hyperscript-like programming language for presentation control.

Graphics Programs

The demos in this section are for graphics editing programs and graphics creation tools.

Fractal Design Painter

Fractal Design Inc.
P.O. Box 2380
335 Spreckels Drive
Aptos, CA 95003

Location on CD-ROM: \DEMOS\FDPAINT

Command to install demo: SETUP

Fractal Design Painter allows you to transform photos and graphics into artistic masterpieces, or you can create your works of art. It includes drawing tools for colored pencils, crayons, calligraphy pens, airbrushes, and a variety of paint brushes for oils and water color. Painter features special-effects tools such as Artists, which emulate brush strokes of masters such as Van Gogh and Seurat.

This working demo of Fractal Design Painter 2.0 allows you to experiment with the full program, but you cannot save or print images. After you've started the install program from the menu application, follow these steps:

1. At the opening screen, click on the Continue button.

2. At the next screen, you will see "Install from Drive\Directory:". Type in the path where the install program is stored: *<drive>*\DEMOS\FDPAINT.

3. After you finish selecting any other options, click on Continue. If you have the "Mouse smoothing" option set, a special mouse driver will be installed.

4. When the install program asks you to insert disk number two or number three, press Enter, and the installation will continue from the CD-ROM.

Adobe Photoshop

Adobe Systems, Inc.
PO Box 7900
1585 Charleston Rd.
Mountain View, CA 94039-7900
(800) 833-6687
(415) 961-4400

Location on CD-ROM: \DEMOS\PSHOP

Command to install demo: SETUP

This working demo of Adobe Photoshop allows you to experiment with all the image processing features of the software, but you cannot print or save images. Photoshop offers photo-realistic image enhancement for processing color, gray scale, and B&W images.

Photoshop offers a number of professional features, including color correction, prepress, and darkroom systems. Created files are binary-compatible with the same version for the Macintosh, enabling users to freely exchange files between platforms.

Picture Publisher

1303 E. Arapaho Rd.
Richardson, TX 75081
(800) 487-2116
(214) 234-1769

Location on CD-ROM: \DEMOS\PICTPUB

Command to install demo: INSTALL

Picture Publisher 4.0 is one of the world's best-selling image editors for Microsoft Windows. The winner of 11 awards in 1992, it sets a number of standards for ease of use and productivity.

Unique features include Object Layers, where images remain moveable and editable; FastBits, for quickly editing sections of large images; and an ImageBrowser for opening, searching, and cataloging images.

Matisse

Fauve Software
875 Walnut Street
Suite 320
Cary, NC 27511
(800) 898-ARTS (Orders only)
(919) 380-9933 (Outside US)

Location on CD-ROM: \DEMOS\MATISSE

Command to install demo: INSTALL

Matisse is a paint and image-processing program that is built around objects. Objects can sit on top of other objects, blend into them, and be resized, rotated, or distorted. The result is that you can produce—in minutes—photo-paint compositions that would take hours in other packages, if you could do them at all.

Matisse's brushes perform like their natural counterparts. Aspects such as paper texture, grain control, blackness, smoothing, and scatter are incorporated into the design. On the other hand, the number of brush controls is limited to avoid the feeling of overload.

Kai's Power Tools

HSC Software
1661 Lincoln Blvd.
Suite 101
Santa Monica, CA 90404
(310) 392-8441

Location on CD-ROM: \DEMOS\KAITOOLS

Documentation: KAITOOLS.WRI

These sample graphics were created with Kai's Power Tools for Windows, the new add-in software that works with CorelDRAW!, Fractal Design Painter, PhotoShop, and PhotoStyler. Kai's Power Tools provides 33 tools and plug-in filters, which can create a nearly infinite variety of gradients, textures, fractal textures, and fills.

Kai's Power Tools also includes fractal creation tools, a glass lens feature to create spherical sections of objects, sharpen and intensity tools, and a cyclone filter to capture 24-bit color animation of images.

Typestry

>Pixar
>1001 W. Cutting Blvd.
>Point Richmond, CA 94804
>(510) 236-4000
>
>*Location on CD-ROM:* \DEMOS\TYPESTRY
>
>*Command to start the demo:* PIXAR
>
>*Documentation:* TYPESTRY.WRI

The sample graphics in this interactive presentation were created with Typestry, Pixar's software that turns your Type 1 and TrueType fonts into three-dimensional text. Typestry includes Pixar's RenderMan, so the images will have the same professional quality you've seen in many movies. There are also samples of other Pixar products in this demo.

Music and Sound Programs

The demos in this section are for music composition and sound editing programs.

Master Trax Pro 4

>Passport Designs
>100 Stone Pine Road
>Half Moon Bay, CA 94019
>
>*Location on CD-ROM:* \DEMOS\TRAX
>
>*Command to install demo:* SETUP

This is a fully featured demo of Passport Design's Master Trax Pro 4 MIDI sequencer for Windows. The demo has the same functionality as the full version, although the saving to disk function is disabled. Read the file README.TXT for more information on installing the demo.

CakeWalk Professional

Twelve Tone Systems
44 Pleasant Street
P.O. Box 760
Watertown, MA 02272
(800) 234-1171
(617) 926-2480

Location on CD-ROM: \DEMOS\CAKEWALK

Command to install demo: SETUP

CakeWalk Professional for Windows is a MIDI sequencer with 256 MIDI tracks that includes professional music recording, editing, performance, and synchronization capabilities. It also has a music notation display and a built-in programming language.

Encore

Passport Designs
100 Stone Pine Road
Half Moon Bay, CA 94019

Location on CD-ROM: \DEMOS\ENCORE

Documentation: README2.TXT

Command to install demo: SETUP

This is a demo of Encore, the MIDI/music notation program from Passport Designs. It has the same functionality as the full version, although the saving to disk and printing functions are disabled. Read the file README.TXT for more information on installing the demo.

Music Time

Passport Designs
100 Stone Pine Road
Half Moon Bay, CA 94019

Location on CD-ROM: \DEMOS\MUSICTIM

Command to install demo: SETUP

This is a demo of Passport Designs' music notation editor, MusicTime for Windows. It has the same functionality as the full version, although the saving to disk and printing functions are disabled. Read the file README.TXT for more information on installing the demo.

Sound Forge

Sonic Foundry
1110 East Gorham
Madison, WI 53703
(608) 256 3133

Location on CD-ROM: \DEMOS\SFORGE

Command to install demo: SETUP

Sound Forge is a sound file editor which enables you to easily play, record, and edit digitized (sampled) sound files. The Sound Forge 2.0 Demo contains all the features of the Sound Forge 2.0 package except you can't save files and you can't paste to other applications using Windows Clipboard.

WinJammer Pro demo

WinJammer Software Limited
69 Rancliffe Road
Oakville, Ontario
Canada L6H 1B1

Location on CD-ROM: \DEMOS\WJPRO

Command to install demo: SETUP

WinJammer Professional is a MIDI sequencer for Windows 3.1. It uses standard MIDI files, giving you access to a huge number of songs. This is a demonstration version of the software—it will not save files.

> The help file for this software has been downsized by removing the pictures that would appear in the normal help file. Throughout this help file you will see boxes that say "unable to display picture" whenever a picture has been removed.

Cubase for Windows

Steinberg/Jones
17700 Raymer St.
Suite 1001
Northridge, CA 91325
(818) 993-4091

Location on CD-ROM: \DEMOS\CUBASE

Command to install demo: INSTALL

Cubase LITE (the version of Cubase included with this book) is the entry-level MIDI sequencer program in the Cubase line of products. Cubase LITE gives you the same graphical user interface and the same intuitive concepts as its big brother Cubase: you can record your music on up to 16 tracks, edit your music in the Score Editor, and print your composition.

Everything works in *real-time.* You'll find the functions you need right on the Arrange Window: Quantize settings, Song Position, and a graphical overview of your song. By double-clicking on a part, you open the Score Editor. Here, your music is automatically displayed in a musical score format.

Power Chords

Howling Dog Systems
Kanata North Postal Outlet
Box 72071
Kanata, Ontario
Canada K2K 2P4
(613) 599-7927

Location on CD-ROM: \DEMOS\PCHORDS

Command to install demo: INSTALL

Power Chords is designed to let you work with music using the skills that you already have, and provides tools that make it easy for you to do the things that you don't have the skills for. The basic input "metaphor" in Power Chords is that of a guitar or other stringed instrument. However, you do not have to be a stringed instrument player to use Power Chords.

Mr. Drumstix

Howling Dog Systems
Kanata North Postal Outlet
Box 72071
Kanata, Ontario
Canada K2K 2P4
(613) 599-7927

Location on CD-ROM: \DEMOS\DRUMSTIC

Command to run demo: CPLSHOW DRUMSTIX.CPL

Mr. Drumstix is a music software package for kids that lets them explore and create music using MIDI. This demo was created using Asymetrix Compel.

Video and Animation Programs

The demos in this section are for video/animation programs and morphing software.

MediaMerge

ATI Technologies, Inc.
33 Commerce Valley Drive
East Thornhill, Ontario
Canada L3T 7N6
(416) 882-2600

Location on CD-ROM: \DEMOS\MEDMERGE

Command to run demo presentation: MMSNEAK

MediaMerge is a digital video editing system. You can cut, copy, and paste source material, as well as create, edit, and record audio to customize the finished product. Special transition effects can be added between scenes in the Storyboard Editor. This demo starts with a brief introduction to the product, then it allows you to interactively explore different features and functions of MediaMerge.

PhotoMorph

North Coast Software
P.O. Box 459
265 Scruton Pond Road
Barrington, NH 03825
(603) 664-6000 (Sales)

Location on CD-ROM: \DEMOS\PMORPH

Command to install demo: INSTALL

PhotoMorph is the easy-to-use Windows-based morphing software from North Coast Software. PhotoMorph can easily create morphs of various types and in different formats, including Video for Windows .AVI format. The quality of morphs created with this software can rival what you see in movies and on television.

This demo has much of the functionality of the retail version, with some restrictions. Read the README.TXT file for more details.

Digital Morph

HSC Software
1661 Lincoln Blvd.
Suite 101
Santa Monica, CA 90404
(310) 392-8441

Location on CD-ROM: \DEMOS\DMSHOW

Command to run demo presentation: HSCRT DMSHOW33.IW

Digital Morph allows the user to work with still images, animation, and video sequences to create morphing and warping effects. Animation or video sequences can be integrated into productions in file formats such as AVI, FLC, or sequential image files. This presentation shows how the product is used to create morphing and warping effects.

Win:Images Morph

Black Belt Systems
398 Johnson Road
Glasgow, Montana 59230
(800) 852-6442
(406) 367-5513

Location on CD-ROM: `\DEMOS\WINMORPH`

Command to install demo: `INSTALL`

Morph allows you to create morphing effects in a variety of formats, including FLC animations and individual file frames. The program supports a wide variety of graphics file formats for input. Read the README.TXT file for more information.

Miscellaneous Programs

These programs are demos that don't easily fit into any of the other categories.

Vistapro 3.0

Virtual Reality Laboratories, Inc.
2341 Ganador Court
San Luis Obispo, CA 93401
(800) 829-VRLI
(805) 545-8515

Location on disk: `\DEMOS\VP3`

Command to install demo: `INSTALL`

Vistapro is a DOS three dimensional landscape simulation program. Using U.S. Geological Survey data, Vistapro can accurately re-create real world landscapes in vivid detail. The demo begins with a self-running tutorial, which you can stop by pressing the Escape key. Then, you can explore the features of Vistapro and render your own landscape.

Distant Suns

Virtual Reality Laboratories, Inc.
2341 Ganador Court
San Luis Obispo, CA 93401
(800) 829-VRLI
(805) 545-8515

Location on disk: \DEMOS\DSUNS

Command to install demo: INSTALL

Distant Suns is the Windows-based desktop planetarium that displays the night sky from anywhere on the planet from 4173 BC to AD 10000. One of the new features in Distant Suns 2.0 is the off-earth mode that can display the heavens from anywhere in the solar system. The full product includes photos of astronomical objects; a few samples are included with this demo.

Graphics Clips

The graphics in this section are samples from different graphics collections. They are mostly graphics that would be used for backgrounds. Actual photos are represented in the "Stock Photos" section.

Artbeats

Artbeats
Box 1287
Myrtle Beach, OR 97457
(503) 863-4429

Location on CD-ROM: \GRAPHICS\ARTBEATS

Artbeats offers a number of unusual graphics collections, including:

Full Page Images Library—EPS background images of marble and wood textures, landscapes, paint splatters, 3-D textures and more.
Backgrounds for Multimedia, volumes I and II—8-bit and 24-bit high quality images designed with video, animation, and texture mapping applications in mind.

Marble & Granite—An extensive and varied library of high-resolution digitized images of marble and granite textures.
Marbled Paper Textures—Dramatic and unusual digitized images of marbled paper, such as that found inside antique book covers.

You'll find samples of all of these products in this directory. The full collections of these products are available on CD-ROMs.

Mountain High Maps

Digital Wisdom
Box 2070
Tappahannock, VA 22560
(800) 800-8560

Location on CD-ROM: \GRAPHICS\MAPS

Mountain High Maps is a CD-ROM collection of relief images of the world's continents, countries, and ocean floors. Each dimension and contour of our planet is portrayed in a detailed and accurate topographical view.

In addition to the sample image in this directory, you'll find the complete Mountain High Maps catalog, which shows thumbnail images of the complete collection.

Hot Clips backgrounds

Eagle Software
P.O. Box 2706
Peachtree City, GA 30269

Location on CD-ROM: \GRAPHICS\HOTCLIPS

Documentation: PATTERNS.TXT

Hot Clips is a collection of Windows resources and multimedia clips. These graphics are samples of background patterns. For more information on the complete collection and licensing, read the .TXT files in this directory.

Textures and Gradients

Sams Publishing

Location on CD-ROM: `\GRAPHICS\TEXTURES`

Documentation: `TEXTURES.WRI`

These graphics were created by Sams Publishing for your use in multimedia projects. Read the documentation file for information on usage rights.

Stock Photos

These sample stock photos will give you an idea of the wide range of photos that are available electronically. Most of these stock companies offer their photos for sale on a limited use basis—once you've purchased their disk of photos, you can use the photo in several projects without additional fees, but subject to certain restrictions. Check with each individual company for more details.

Digital Zone

Digital Zone, Inc.
PO Box 5562
Bellevue, WA 98006
(800) 538-3113

Location on CD-ROM: `\PHOTOS\DIGIZONE`

Documentation: `DIGIZONE.WRI`

The Digital Zone offers CD-ROMs of dramatic and colorful photography from some of the world's top professional photographers. The pictures on the CD-ROMs are in Kodak PhotoCD format.

The samples on this disk are from the International Photographers CD-ROM, and they are in TIFF format. In addition, there are images that show the complete range of photographs in each of the CD-ROM collections. These mosaic images are named DISK1.TIF, DISK2.TIF, and so on.

For more information on the complete collection, see the file DIGIZONE.WRI. Also, be sure to see the Digital Zone ad in the back of this book.

FotoBank

Wayzata Technology
Post Office Box 807
Grand Rapids, Minnesota 55744
(800) 735-7321
(218) 326-0597

Location on CD-ROM: `\PHOTOS\FOTOBANK`

Documentation: `FOTOBANK.WRI`

These high-res TIFF images are a sample of what you'll find in the FotoBank Photo Pro (Vol 3) collection. The full collection contains more than 125 24 bit TIFF color images on a CD-ROM. Also included on the FotoBank CD are 9 QuickTime slide shows for each category.

Photos on Disk

Cantrall's Photos on Disk
7070 Fisherman Lane
Pilot Hill, CA 95664
(916) 933-1260

Location on CD-ROM: `\PHOTOS\CANTRALL`

Documentation: `CANTRALL.WRI`

Cantrall's Photos on Disc is a set of CD-ROMs, each containing more than 100 digitized photographs. Subject areas include Western United States, Flowers and Trees, Wild and Domestic Animals, Coastal and Ocean Themes and Patterns, Textures, and Cloud Formations.

MediaRights

Sense Interactive
1412 West Alabama
Houston, TX 77006
(800) 75-SENSE (757-3673)
(713) 523-5757

Location on CD-ROM: \PHOTOS\MRIGHTS

Command to start demo: SENSE

This presentation demonstrates the power of using MediaRights stock photography in your multimedia projects. MediaRights is a professional stock photography series on CD-ROM. Images can be used for everything except advertising and resale or reuse as stock.

Birds of New Zealand

Sunbreak Technology
14118 168th Ave NE
Woodinville, Washington 98072
(206) 485-3222

Location on CD-ROM: \PHOTOS\BIRDS

Documentation: INTRO.WRI

New Zealand Birds is a multimedia title which documents the incredible range of birds found in that country. New Zealand has always been synonymous with interesting and unusual species of birds, many of which are found only on these islands. There are more than 600 megabytes of gorgeous high-res photographs, sound, video, and text, providing details on all living bird species in that country.

Hot Clips Photos

Eagle Software
P.O. Box 2706
Peachtree City, GA 30269

Location on CD-ROM: \PHOTOS\HOTCLIPS

Documentation: PHOTOS.TXT

Hot Clips is a collection of Windows resources and multimedia clips. These stock photos are 256 color images. For more information on the complete collection and licensing, read the .TXT files in this directory.

Music Clips

The sample clips in this section are music clips, in Wave and MIDI formats. In some cases, 8-bit and 16-bit formats are both included.

Sound Choice

Cambium Development
28 Vanderbilt Road
Scarsdale, NY 10583
Location on CD-ROM: \MUSIC\SOUNDCH

Command to install/run program: SETUP

Sound Choice is a collection of high-quality production music on CD-ROM. WaveRider, the software music assistant for Sound Choice, is designed to allow the user to quickly and effectively choose a set of music from the database to audition, audition the music in its various versions and formats, and copy the music you select to hard drive.

Sound Choice includes music across a broad range of styles, including classical, jazz, rock, contemporary, new age, country, and several others. Each volume contains approximately 30 main selections. Each main selection has several short subsets of the music ("bumpers").

MIDI Collection

Voyetra Technologies
333 Fifth Ave.
Pelham, NY 10803
(800) 233-9377

Location on CD-ROM: \SOUNDS\VOYETRA

These samples are from Voyetra's complete collection of multitrack MIDI sequences. The collection contains more than 150 songs and drum patterns. The MIDI format allows users to modify songs to make them shorter, change key, reassign instruments, and tailor to individual needs. Contains full performances including drums, bass, piano, and solos.

Hot Clips Music Clips

Eagle Software
P.O. Box 2706
Peachtree City, GA 30269

Location on CD-ROM: \MUSIC\HOTCLIPS

Documentation: MUSIC.TXT

Hot Clips is a collection of Windows resources and multimedia clips. These music clips are in a variety of styles, and there are clips of various lengths for each style. For more information on the complete collection and licensing, read the .TXT files in this directory.

Sound Effects Clips

The sample clips represented in this section are sound effects, which are in Wave format. In some cases, 8-bit and 16-bit formats are both included.

Hollywood Sound Library

New Eden Multimedia
7652 Hampshire Avenue
Minneapolis, MN 55248
(800) 735-EDEN
(612) 561-2557

Location on CD-ROM: \SOUND\HSLIB

Documentation: HSLINFO.WRI

Command to install the program: SETUP

The Hollywood Sound Library is the world's largest library of digital computer sound files. Unlike other suppliers, which sell CD-ROM based collections of only a few hundred sound clips, the Hollywood Sound Library sells individual sound files from its library of more than 10,000 sounds. Because this massive collection requires more than 50 Gigabytes of storage, it will never be sold at your local computer store (at least not in this century).

The sound effects are all high-quality, 16-bit, 44K stereo wave files licensed from some of the world's leading sound studios, including The Hollywood Edge and Sound Ideas. These sounds have been used in everything from radio and TV commercials to Academy Award-winning movies. See the ad in the back of this book for more information.

Also included is New Eden's WAVEVIEW sound browser application, which allows you to play sounds from the library and view descriptions for each of them. Run the INSTALL.EXE program in this directory to install it to your hard drive. The file HSLCAT.WRI is a catalog of the complete sound effects library.

The 16-bit versions of the WAV files are located in the \SOUND\HSLIB\DEMO16 directory. If you have an 8-bit sound card, you'll find 8-bit versions of the sounds in the \SOUND\HSLIB\DEMO8 directory.

Hot Clips Sound Effects

Eagle Software
P.O. Box 2706
Peachtree City, GA 30269

Location on CD-ROM: \SOUND\HOTCLIPS

Documentation: SOUNDS.TXT0

Hot Clips is a collection of Windows resources and multimedia clips. These sound effects are recorded at 8-bit resolution. For more information on the complete collection and licensing, read the .TXT files in this directory.

Wave Library

Graphica Software
CIS Address 100026,2317

Location on CD-ROM: \SOUND\WAVELIB

Documentation: SOUNDS.TXT

This is a small collection of 8-bit sounds, created by John Hartley of England.

Video and Animation Clips

The samples in this section are Video for Windows and QuickTime for Windows video clips and Autodesk format animation clips

Jasmine Multimedia

Jasmine Multimedia Publishing
6746 Valjean Ave.
Suite 100
Van Nuys, CA 91406
(800) 798-7535

Location on CD-ROM: \VIDEO\JASMINE

Jasmine Multimedia offers a wide range of video clips in more than 15 CD-ROM collections. Sixteen of these collections are represented by clips on this CD-ROM, and they are all viewable from the Jasmine Catalog program. These clips are in Video for Windows format.

The catalog can be run from the Multimedia Madness Menu, or it can be run by changing to the \VIDEO\JASMINE\TBKRUN directory and entering TBOOK.EXE JASCAT.TBK.

Canyon Clipz

The San Francisco Canyon Company
150 Post Street
Suite 620
San Francisco, CA 94108

Location on CD-ROM: `\VIDEO\CANYON`

Canyon Clipz and Canyon Action are CD-ROM collections of video clips. Clipz is in Video for Windows format, and Action is in QuickTime for Windows format. The sample clips on this CD-ROM are in QuickTime format.

See Canyon's ad in the back of this book for a special offer on these CD-ROM video collections. The ad is for Canyon Action, but you can also order the Canyon Clipz collection.

CUCUMBER.MOV—"Everything Goes," by *The Cucumbers.* © 1985 Fake Doom Records, Publisher (ASCAP). Jon Fried and Deena Shoshkes, Composers.
ARCANUM3.MOV—© 1992 N.C. Gorski.
VEGETABL.MOV—© 1992 Lamb & Company, courtesy Doug Pfeifer.
SRL1.MOV—© 1992 N.C. Gorski. Additional footage courtesy Survival Research Laboratories, circa 1982.

Madness Videos

Location on CD-ROM: `\VIDEO\MADVID`

The video clips in this directory live up to their name. You'll find a variety of unusual, cool, and otherwise wacky videos that were created by the author— everything from space animations to morphing effects. They are Video for Windows clips, and you can browse through them from within the menu application.

Madness FLCs

Location on CD-ROM: `\VIDEO\MADFLC`

The clips in this directory were also created by the author. They are in Autodesk FLC and FLI formats. You can browse through them in the menu application. You'll find a wide range of subjects represented here.

1025

Fonts

The sample fonts on this CD-ROM are in TrueType format. Some of these fonts are samples from commercial companies, while others are shareware and freeware offerings.

The Font Company

The Font Company
7850 E. Evans Rd., Suite 111
Scottsdale, AZ 85260
(800) 442-3668
(602) 998-9711
(602) 998-7964 Fax

Location on CD-ROM: \FONTS\FONTCO

Documentation: FONTCO.WRI

Twenty TrueType fonts from The Font Company's collection of over 2,000 faces are included on this CD-ROM. A coupon for ordering 100 more typefaces at a special price is included in the back of this book.

TypeTreats Sampler

Raynbow Software Inc.
P.O. Box 1541
Rapid City, SD 57709
(800) 456-5269

Location on CD-ROM: \FONTS\RAYNBOW

Documentation: RAYNBOW.TXT

TypeTreats is a CD-ROM collection of more than 500 public domain and shareware fonts. The fonts in the full collection are stored in a wide variety of formats.

The TypeTreats font finder program is included on this disk to give you a peek at all the fonts that are included in the complete collection. To start the font finder, run the WFONTFIN.EXE program found in this directory.

The FONTS subdirectory contains 10 sample fonts from the collection in TrueType, Type 1, and WFN formats. The file AUTHORS.TXT contains information on the creators of these fonts.

35Fonts Collection

Thomas E. Harvey
420 N. Bayshore Blvd., #206
Clearwater, FL 34619

Location on CD-ROM: \FONTS\SAMPLER

Documentation: 35README.TXT

Five TrueType fonts are included here from the 35 Heads font collection. To view the fonts in the full collection, run Windows Cardfile, found in the Accessories group of Program Manager. Open up the file SEE35HDS.CRD, which contains cards showing each font in the collection, as well as additional technical information.

Publisher's Paradise Sampler

Publisher's Paradise BBS
(205) 882-6886 (modem)

Location on CD-ROM: \FONTS\PUBPARA

Documentation: PUBPARA.WRI

These sample fonts were created by the Publisher's Paradise bulletin board system (BBS). This BBS is created for people with interests in desktop publishing and graphics. See the file PUBPARA.WRI for more information on how to contact this bulletin board.

Safari Sampler

Computer Safari
353 West Main Street
Suite K
Woodland, CA 95695
(916) 666-1813

Location on CD-ROM: \FONTS\SAFARI

Documentation: SAFARI.WRI

Computer Safari offers a collection of fun, weird, wacky, and unique typefaces in the Safari Big Deal Collection. The full collection includes Alien and Egyptian Heiroglyphics fonts.

Shareware Programs

The programs in this section are distributed as shareware. Please read the "Types of Software" section at the beginning of this appendix for more information on shareware.

Graphic Workshop for Windows

Alchemy Mindworks Inc.
P.O. Box 500
Beeton, Ontario
Canada L0G 1A0
(800) 263-1138
(905) 729-4969

Location on CD-ROM: \PROGRAMS\GWSWIN

Command to install program: SETUP

Documentation: GWS.WRI

Graphic Workshop for Windows allows you to work with bitmapped graphics files. You can view, convert, print, add special effects, change color depth, change brightness and contrast, crop, and much more. Photo CD files are supported, as are a wide variety of graphics formats.

Paint Shop Pro

> JASC, Inc.
> 10901 Red Circle Drive
> Suite 340
> Minnetonka, MN 55343
> (612) 930-9171
>
> *Location on CD-ROM:* \PROGRAMS\PSPRO
>
> *Command to install program:* SETUP

Paint Shop Pro is a Windows program that will display, convert, alter, and print graphics images. It works with files in a wide range of graphics formats. Altering includes resizing, trimming, applying filters, dithering, palette manipulation, and much more. Paint Shop Pro also does screen capturing.

Picture Man

> Igor Plotnikov, Mike Kuznetsov, Alex Bobkov
> c/o Igor Plotnikov
> 519 Barry Court,
> Mechanicsburg, PA 17055
>
> *Location on CD-ROM:* \UTILS\PICTMAN
>
> *Documentation:* PMAN.WRI
>
> *Command to install program:* INSTALL

Picture Man is a powerful true color image processing tool. It offers a large variety of 46 different bitmap operations, including geometrical transforms, halftone/color correction, filtering, and color fills. Seven types of selected areas are available, including rectangle, ellipse, polygon, text, freehand, pen, and magic wand.

Mandel

Phillip Crewes
cerious software
5424 Chedworth Drive
Charlotte, NC 28210

Location on CD-ROM: \PROGRAMS\MANDEL

Command to install the program: INSTALL

This program produces displays of the Mandelbrot fractal set. It has a wide variety of options and features, including the ability to apply 3-D special effects and easily save fractal images.

LView

Location on CD-ROM: \PROGRAMS\LVIEW

Command to install program: INSTALL

LView is an image file editor for Microsoft Windows 3.1. It can load and save image files in these formats: JPEG, JFIF, GIF 87a/89a, Truevision Targa, and Windows and OS/2 BMP.

Wave Editor

Keith W. Boone
c/o ASG Inc.
11900 Grant Place
Des Peres, MO 63131

Location on CD-ROM: \UTILS\WAVEEDIT

Documentation: WAVEEDIT.WRI

Command to install program: INSTALL

Wave Editor is an application that allows you to input, create, modify, and analyze wave files. You can also add special effects to the sounds.

Whoop It Up!

Starlite Software
c/o ASG Inc.
11900 Grant Place
Des Peres, MO 63131
(800) 767-9611

Location on CD-ROM: `\PROGRAMS\WHOOP`

Command to install program: `INSTALL`

Whoop It Up allows you to attach sounds, music, and video to Windows system events, applications events, icons, and more.

WinJammer

WinJammer Software Limited
69 Rancliffe Road
Oakville, Ontario
Canada L6H 1B1

Location on CD-ROM: `\UTILS\WINJAMM`

Command to install program: `SETUP`

WinJammer is a fully featured MIDI sequencer for Windows 3.1. It uses standard MIDI files, giving you access to a huge number of songs. WinJammer also contains a companion program called WinJammer Player, which is used to play MIDI song files in the background.

Windows Music Sculptor

Aleph Omega Software
Box 61085
Kensington Postal Outlet
Calgary, Alberta
Canada T2N 4S6

Location on CD-ROM: `\PROGRAMS\WINMUSIC`

Command to install program: `SETUP`

Music Sculptor is a user friendly MIDI sequencer that allows you to record, edit, and play music. It also works with an external MIDI keyboard and includes an on-screen music keyboard.

Makin' Waves

Geoff Faulkner
11664 Silvergate Drive
Dublin, CA 94568-2208

Location on CD-ROM: \UTILS\MAKEWAVES

Documentation: MAKEWAVE.WRI

Command to install program: INSTALL

Makin' Waves is a sound file converter and wave file player. It can convert .VOC, .SOU, and .SND to .WAV format.

Font Monster

Leaping Lizards
7F, No. 8, Lane 197
Chuang Ching Road
Taipei 110
Taiwan, R.O.C.

Location on CD-ROM: \UTILS\FMONSTER

Command to install program: INSTALL

Font Monster is a powerful utility that allows you to view, edit, and examine TrueType and Type1 fonts. You can rename any font, edit internal font data, preview TrueType fonts before installing, create font groups which you install by clicking on a Program Manager icon, and much more.

When you register Font Monster, be sure to send only cash to the author—no checks or money orders. See the help information in the program for more information.

Printer's Apprentice

Bryan T. Kinkel
Lose Your Mind Development
506 Wilder Square
Norristown, PA 19401

Location on CD-ROM: \UTILS\PRINTAPP

Command to install program: INSTALL

Printer's Apprentice is a font management utility that helps you manage all your TrueType and Adobe Type 1 fonts by printing three different types of inventory sheets, ANSI charts, keyboard layouts, and specimen sheets.

Movie Time Screen Saver

Starlite Software
c/o ASG Inc.
11900 Grant Place
Des Peres, MO 63131
(800) 767-9611

Location on CD-ROM: \WINPROGS\MOVIETIM

Documentation: MVTIME.TXT

The Movie Time Screen Saver plays .AVI videos or displays still graphics in .GIF, .PCX, and .BMP formats. You can customize Movie Time with passwords and turn the sound on and off. The movies play in full-screen .AVI mode.

The .AVI file included in this directory is a low-resolution sample of what is contained on the Classic Clips CD-ROM from Starlite. See the file NEATSTUF.TXT for more information.

Drag and View

Dan Baumbach
Canyon Software
1537 Fourth Street Suite 131
San Rafael, CA 94901

Location on CD-ROM: \UTILS\DRAGVIEW

Command to install the program: DVSETUP

Drag and View allows you to drag files from File Manager to an icon, and view files in a variety of formats. You can view most popular graphics, word processor, spreadsheet, and database formats, plus also ASCII and HEX. Has search and goto functions. You can also open multiple windows and compare files.

WinZip 5

Nico Mak
P.O. Box 919
Bristol, CT 06011
CompuServe 70056,241

Location on CD-ROM: \UTILS\WINZIP

Documentation: WINZIP.DOC

Command to install program: INSTALL

WinZip brings the convenience of Windows to the use of ZIP, LZH, ARJ, and ARC files. It features an intuitive point and click interface for viewing, running, extracting, adding, deleting, and testing files in archives. Optional virus scanning support is included.

Sonarc

Speech Compression
P.O. Box 2481
Laguna Hills, CA 92654-2481

Location on CD-ROM: \PROGRAMS\SONARC

Documentation: SONARC.DOC

Command to install program: INSTALL

Sonarc is a new compression technology specifically optimized for digital audio. Sonarc features variable-rate compression that can be reversed to precisely reconstruct the original, uncompressed signal.

CompuServe Information Service

More than 1 million computer users are a part of CompuServe Information Service, and for good reason. CompuServe has special interest areas for nearly any subject you're interested in. And you'll find users from across the United States and around the world.

Joining and using CompuServe is now a lot easier, because CompuServe is offering readers of this book a free membership and $15 of free connect time. Plus, a free copy of Windows CompuServe Information Manager software is included on the CD-ROM.

Another good reason for joining CompuServe is the multimedia-related forums. In these forums, you'll find product updates, technical information, useful utilities, hints and tips, and more.

The PHCP forum is the Prentice Hall Computer Publishing forum. Sams Publishing is a part of PHCP, and you'll find Sams Publishing areas in the files libraries and message areas. This forum contains information on our books, tips and information, programs and utilities, and technical support information.

Behind the CD-ROM, you'll find a special registration card for CompuServe with your temporary user number and password. This number and password is unique for every copy of this book.

To learn how to sign up and receive your free connect time, read the file SIGNUP.WRI in the \WINCIM directory of the CD-ROM. You'll dial a special 800 number with your modem and the Windows CIM software, and you'll be on-line immediately. Then, you can find your local CompuServe numbers for your area. It's that easy.

Windows CIM

CompuServe International
P.O Box 20212
Columbus, OH 43220

Location on CD-ROM: \WINCIM

Documentation: SIGNUP.WRI

Command to install the program: SETUP

Windows CompuServe Information Manager (WINCIM) is the communications software that makes being on-line easy. Instead of typing commands, you can click on icons or choose from menu items to explore forums, download files, read and create messages, send and receive electronic mail, and much more.

Full instructions on how to install and configure WINCIM are contained in the SIGNUP.WRI file in this directory. After installing the software, you'll need to configure WINCIM for your modem. Then, you'll need to enter your special user number and password, which are on the CompuServe coupon behind the CD-ROM.

WINCIM contains extensive on-line help, which is always available by pressing the F1 key. You can even browse through a list of the forums on CompuServe without being on-line.

Index

H

Q

X-Z

The
Multimedia Madness!
Special Coupon

Now that Ron Wodaski has introduced you to multimedia and you've experimented with the evaluation edition packaged with this book, you'll want to go all the way with Multimedia ToolBook!

Now you're ready to construct your own multimedia worlds with a full development copy of Multimedia ToolBook from Asymetrix.

Receive a 25% discount off the suggested list price by sending the coupon below. You must send this entire original page; no copies will be accepted. Call (800) 448-6543 for price and further details.

Mail To: Multimedia ToolBook Sales Offer
Asymetrix Corporation
110-110th Avenue NE, Suite 700
Bellevue, WA 98004

Phone: (800) 448-6543 or (206) 637-1500

Intl'l Fax: 001-206-637-1504

Ship To:

Name _____   Phone # (   ) _____
Street _____   Fax # (   ) _____

City/State _____   ZIP _____
Country _____

Payment Method:

❏ Check enclosed (payable to Asymetrix Corp.)

❏ MC/VISA Card # _____   Exp. Date _____

❏ AMEX # _____   Exp. Date _____

Authorized Signature _____

Offer Expires December 1994

Asymetrix Multimedia Toolbook Evaluation Edition License Agreement

Top Ten Reasons to buy
the *Canyon Action!* CD-ROM

for your multimedia equipped computer

1. Comes with *QuickTime for Windows*, Apple Computer's digital video standard now available for Microsoft Windows (so you can play any QuickTime for Windows movie).

2. Playable on both the Macintosh and IBM-compatible PC.

3. Contains a wide variety of exciting QuickTime movies (see below).

4. Also available in Video for Windows format (AVI) as *Canyon Clipz*.

5. Easy to install—playable right out of the box.

6. Tested on all major brands of video and audio hardware.

7. Featured in *PC Magazine*, *Variety*, *PC Week*, *Publish!*, *PC World*, etc.

8. Includes high-level browser program for easy movie watching.

9. Demonstrates the power of cross-platform technology.

10. Software-only operation—no special hardware required.

Retail Price: *$29.95*. Call 415-398-9957 to order.

Visa/Mastercard accepted. Also available for bundles.

Description of Product: *Canyon Action!* is a cross-platform CD-ROM designed to showcase QuickTime for Windows. Along with a movie player and associated DLLs, the user gets a wide selection of QuickTime movies to enjoy, including full length MTV-style music videos (nationally known performers), vintage Hollywood animation and old movie clips, high quality computer graphics shorts, and segments from contemporary documentaries.

Canyon Action! is a production of The San Francisco Canyon Company, a Bay Area Multimedia corporation specializing in CD-ROM publishing and contract software development.

Hollywood Sound Library

New Eden Multimedia's *Hollywood Sound Library* is the world's largest library of digital computer sound files. The Hollywood Sound Library provides a unique and valuable service to anyone looking for royalty free, high quality sound effects.

Unlike other suppliers who sell CD-ROM based collections of only a few hundred sound clips, the Hollywood Sound Library sells *individual* sound files from their library of over 10,000 sounds. Because this massive collection requires more than 50 Gigabytes of storage, it will *never* be sold at your local computer store (at least not in this century!).

Just how complete is our collection? Here's an example... if you need the sound of footsteps, we have:

> footsteps, concrete, cowboy boots, jumping
> footsteps, concrete, gritty, combat boots
> footsteps, sand, wet, female, barefoot
> footsteps, snow, male, scuff
> footsteps, wood, solid, boots, up stairs
> footsteps, wood, male, leather sole, down stairs
> *and several hundred additional assorted footsteps!*

The sound effects are all high quality 16 bit 44k stereo wave files licensed from some of the world's leading sound studios, including *The Hollywood Edge* and *Sound Ideas*. These sounds have been used in everything from radio and TV commercials to Academy Award winning movies.

"The Hollywood Edge—the best sound effects library, without a doubt!"
Oliver Stone, Director
"Excellent! I recommend The Hollywood Edge."
Martin Scorsese, Director

New Eden Multimedia
7652 Hampshire Ave.
Minneapolis, MN 55428

Voice
(612)561-2557

Fax
(612)566-2148

A sound proposal from

Voyetra®

If you use a PC to create music or sound —for multimedia presentations, corporate identity programs, commercial film or video productions, or simply for your own enjoyment —Voyetra has a part to play. Since 1975, Voyetra has been a leader in the evolution of PC music software technology, providing MIDI, Digital Audio and CD-ROM software to the "Who's Who" of the computer sound industry, including Corel® Corporation.

Voyetra's full range of software and hardware products can turn your PC into a complete sound workstation. Voyetra products include:

Sequencer Plus™ – Manipulate MIDI data to create custom synthesized music.

AudioView™ – Record and edit digital audio sound as easily as you would text.

PatchView FM™ – Take charge of the synthesis technology in PC sound cards.

Multimedia Toolkit™ for Windows™ – An integrated set of Windows applications for most major PC sound cards.

V-Series MIDI Interfaces – Connect your PC to your synthesizers, with upgrade options for everyone from beginner to pro.

MusiClips™ song files – Inexpensive, convenient, and free of royalty headaches.

In fact, the MIDI files included with this book are a sample of Voyetra's extensive MusiClips library. MusiClips can enhance your multimedia projects with a wide selection of musical styles, from classical favorites to professional drum tracks.

To encourage you to learn more about Voyetra products, we're offering to readers of the *Multimedia Madness*, Deluxe Edition our MusiClips Collectors Edition, Group 1, containing more than 50 MIDI song files, for just $29.95 —a 25% savings!

Take advantage of this offer today. Fill out the coupon below and Mail or FAX it to Voyetra —The Multimedia Sound Specialists™!

GO AHEAD. PLUG YOURSELF INTO PRENTICE HALL COMPUTER PUBLISHING.

Introducing the PHCP Forum on CompuServe®

Yes, it's true. Now, you can have CompuServe access to the same professional, friendly folks who have made computers easier for years. On the PHCP Forum, you'll find additional information on the topics covered by every PHCP imprint—including Que, Sams Publishing, New Riders Publishing, Alpha Books, Brady Books, Hayden Books, and Adobe Press. In addition, you'll be able to receive technical support and disk updates for the software produced by Que Software and Paramount Interactive, a division of the Paramount Technology Group. It's a great way to supplement the best information in the business.

WHAT CAN YOU DO ON THE PHCP FORUM?

Play an important role in the publishing process—and make our books better while you make your work easier:

- Leave messages and ask questions about PHCP books and software—you're guaranteed a response within 24 hours
- Download helpful tips and software to help you get the most out of your computer
- Contact authors of your favorite PHCP books through electronic mail
- Present your own book ideas
- Keep up to date on all the latest books available from each of PHCP's exciting imprints

JOIN NOW AND GET A FREE COMPUSERVE STARTER KIT!

To receive your free CompuServe Introductory Membership, call toll-free, **1-800-848-8199** and ask for representative **#K597**. The Starter Kit Includes:

- Personal ID number and password
- $15 credit on the system
- Subscription to CompuServe Magazine

HERE'S HOW TO PLUG INTO PHCP:

Once on the CompuServe System, type any of these phrases to access the PHCP Forum:

GO PHCP	**GO BRADY**
GO QUEBOOKS	**GO HAYDEN**
GO SAMS	**GO QUESOFT**
GO NEWRIDERS	**GO PARAMOUNTINTER**
GO ALPHA	

Once you're on the CompuServe Information Service, be sure to take advantage of all of CompuServe's resources. CompuServe is home to more than 1,700 products and services—plus it has over 1.5 million members worldwide. You'll find valuable online reference materials, travel and investor services, electronic mail, weather updates, leisure-time games and hassle-free shopping (no jam-packed parking lots or crowded stores).

Seek out the hundreds of other forums that populate CompuServe. Covering diverse topics such as pet care, rock music, cooking, and political issues, you're sure to find others with the same concerns as you—and expand your knowledge at the same time.

Add to Your Sams Library Today with the Best Books for Programming, Operating Systems, and New Technologies

The easiest way to order is to pick up the phone and call

1-800-428-5331

between 9:00 a.m. and 5:00 p.m. EST.
For faster service please have your credit card available.

ISBN	Quantity	Description of Item	Unit Cost	Total Cost
0-672-30248-9		FractalVision: Put Fractals to Work for You (book/disk)	$39.95	
0-672-30322-1		PC Video Madness! (book/CD)	$39.95	
0-672-30391-4		Virtual Reality Madness! (book/CD)	$39.95	
0-672-30373-6		On the Cutting Edge of Technology	$22.95	
0-672-30301-9		Artificial Life Explorer's Kit (book/disk)	$24.95	
0-672-30320-5		Morphing Magic (book/disk)	$29.95	
0-672-30362-0		Navigating the Internet	$24.95	
0-672-30315-9		The Magic of Image Processing (book/disk)	$39.95	
0-672-30308-6		Tricks of the Graphics Gurus (book/disk)	$49.95	
0-672-30376-0		Imaging and Animation forWindows (book/disk)	$34.95	
0-672-30270-5		Garage Virtual Reality (book/disk)	$29.95	
0-672-30282-9		Absolute Beginner's Guide to Memory Management	$16.95	
0-672-30352-3		Blaster Mastery (book/CD)	$34.95	
❏ 3 ½" Disk		Shipping and Handling: See information below.		
❏ 5 ¼" Disk		TOTAL		

Shipping and Handling: $4.00 for the first book, and $1.75 for each additional book. Floppy disk: add $1.75 for shipping and handling. If you need to have it NOW, we can ship product to you in 24 hours for an additional charge of approximately $18.00, and you will receive your item overnight or in two days. Overseas shipping and handling: add $2.00 per book and $8.00 for up to three disks. Prices subject to change. Call for availability and pricing information on latest editions.

201 W. 103rd Street, Indianapolis, Indiana 46290

1-800-428-5331 — Orders   1-800-835-3202 — FAX   1-800-858-7674 — Customer Service

The
Multimedia Madness!
CD-ROMs

You'll find more than 1.3 gigabytes of incredible multimedia software on our two CD-ROMs! The appendix describes what's on the CD-ROMs, how to install them, how to navigate through them, and much more.

CD-ROM One: NautilusCD

In addition to the information in the appendixes, you'll find a special NautiusCD booklet behind the CD-ROMs. This booklet explains how to install the disk and how to use the exciting, new NautilusCD interface. Plus, you'll discover how you can win $500 of software in a special contest for *Multimedia Madness!* readers.

CD-ROM Two: Demo Treasure Chest

Before you use this disk, you need to follow a simple setup procedure. The CD-ROM appendix explains how to do this. The appendix also contains details about the various demos, sample clips, and other files on the disk.

Free CompuServe Membership

As a bonus for *Multimedia Madness!* readers, you'll find a special signup card behind the CD-ROMs. This card entitles you to a free membership in the CompuServe™ Information Service, the premiere on-line service. You'll get $15 in free connect time when you join.

Plus, the latest version of Windows CompuServe Information Manager (WinCIM™) software is included on this CD-ROM!

Note: To run most of the software and use the files on these CDs, you need to have an MPC- or MPC2-compatible computer with the following:

➤ Windows 3.1

➤ 386 or 486 processor

➤ CD-ROM drive

➤ 4 megabytes of RAM

➤ Windows-compatible sound card and speakers